Praise for
WARMONGER

"Who first set us on this disastrous road of endless war and imperial overreach? Who won over liberals by saying that military interventions were for humanitarian purposes? Who first raised false fears of WMD in Iraq and set in motion the U.S. invasion? Who first carried out the odious practices of extraordinary rendition and drone attacks in the War on Terror? Who first violated the U.S. pledge [not to extend] the borders of NATO and triggered the new Cold War with Russia? Jeremy Kuzmarov brilliantly answers these questions in his stunning new book, *Warmonger: How Clinton's Malign Foreign Policy Launched the U.S. Trajectory From Bush II to Biden.*"

JAMES BRADLEY, author, *Flags of Our Fathers: The China Mirage*

"Bill Clinton's jolly amorality personified the superficial self-confidence of an American elite intoxicated with the notion it had "won the Cold War" and so from now on, anything goes. Thus the Clinton administration forged ahead with policies based on blatant lies and unlimited confidence in the ability of U.S. power to get its way forever. Jeremy Kuzmarov's new book records how Clinton's short-sighted opportunism contributed to long-term disasters all over the world."

DIANA JOHNSTONE, author of
Queen of Chaos: The Misadventures of Hillary Clinton

"Prolific and faultless researcher-writer, in addition to being *CovertAction Magazine's* managing editor who brought [the magazine] back to the fore as a leading leftwing and investigative reporting website, Jeremy Kuzmarov found spare time to write this unique tome about one of the U.S.'s greatest warmongering presidents. With Jeremy's fifth book on U.S. foreign policy (perpetual war-making) he has unclothed egregious, jingoist Bill Clinton's presidency—albeit not so recognized by the general public, mainly due to 'liberal,' 'progressive' negation of this indisputable truth. These apologists are significantly Democrats and European Social Democrats whose hyperbole—'Democrats are better than Republicans'—seeks to obscure complicity with U.S. 'color revolutions'/'human rights' wars. Bring 'democracy' to the world, they contend, with untold millions murdered and/or tortured, or left starving by crippling sanctions."

RON RIDENOUR, author, *The Russian Peace Threat: Pentagon on Alert*

Praise continued…

"Before Obama's drones, there were Clinton's cruise missiles. For those curious about how liberals became today's most fervent cheerleaders of the national security state and the intelligence community, look no further than this devastating revisionist account of the foreign policies of William Jefferson Clinton, who authorized more military interventions in his first term than during all eight years of Ronald Reagan. More than just a catalog of Clintonian interventionism, *Warmonger* draws on primary sources to construct a convincing origins narrative for how the seemingly progressive Clinton became one of the most dedicated American imperialists of the post– Cold War era."

THOMAS C. FIELD, JR., Associate Professor and Department Chair of Global Security and Intelligence Studies at the Embry-Riddle College of Security and Intelligence; author, *From Development to Dictatorship: Bolivia and the Alliance for Progress in the Kennedy Era*

WARMONGER

How Clinton's Malign Foreign Policy Launched the U.S. Trajectory from Bush II to Biden

Jeremy Kuzmarov

Clarity Press, Inc.

ISBN: 978-1-949762-76-1
EBOOK ISBN: 978-1-949762-77-8

In-house editor: Diana G. Collier
Book design: Becky Luening

Library of Congress Control Number: 2023933982

Clarity Press, Inc.
2625 Piedmont Rd. NE, Ste. 56
Atlanta, GA 30324, USA
https://www.claritypress.com

To Chanda and Olivia Kuzmarov,
Donna and Irwin Kuzmarov, and
the late Ann and Oscar Weinstein, and
the late Harry and Rose Kuzmarov.

Contents

Introduction

In early April 1999, as American war planes bombed Yugoslavia in what Clinton aide Sidney Blumenthal considered "the first war ever fought to reverse an act of genocide," Elie Wiesel, author of the Pulitzer-prize winning Holocaust survival story *Night* (1956), gave a lecture in the East Room of the White House Executive residence entitled "The Perils of Indifference." Wiesel asked the audience "why the railroads to the concentration camps had not been bombed in 1944 and why the St. Louis ship loaded with Jewish refugees had been turned away from American shores?" Now in Kosovo, Wiesel said, crimes against humanity were being inflicted against the Albanian population in Yugoslavia's province of Serbia, but this time, "the world was not silent. This time we do take responsibility. This time we intervene." Sitting in the audience, President Clinton rose from his seat in response to Wiesel's remarks and gave an impromptu speech in which he said that the peace of the world was "threatened by the oldest demon of human society—our vulnerability to the hatred of the other. In the face of that, we cannot be indifferent at home or abroad. That is why we are in Kosovo."[1]

These remarks captured Clinton's adaptation of the Wilsonian liberal internationalist tradition to reinforce his own policies at the end of the 20th century by dramatically invoking government inaction during the Nazi Holocaust in support of U.S./NATO bombing of a sovereign country. In the wake of the Vietnam War, many Americans had become weary of traditional military intervention, but at the same time were looking to reaffirm American exceptionalism and to attach themselves to a new moral crusade. Tapping into a growing public awareness of human rights introduced earlier as a foreign policy lever by the Carter administration and increasing aversion towards racism and ethnic exclusion, Clinton framed the bombing of Kosovo as part of a moralistic undertaking that could avenge past historical wrongs, such as the abandonment of the Jews in the Holocaust and end inhumane acts.

In reality, the conflict in Kosovo was not black and white or one of good versus evil—as that of the Nazis versus the Jews. While the Serbs had behaved in a heavy-handed manner towards the Albanian majority in Kosovo, the Albanians had in the past discriminated against the Serbs and had now gone on to form a guerrilla army (the Kosovo Liberation Army), which murdered moderate Albanians and incited the Serbs through acts of terrorism. The Clinton administration exaggerated by ten times the number of Kosovo Albanians who had been the victim of Serbian ethnic cleansing operations. The U.S.-NATO bombing significantly intensified the humanitarian crisis in Kosovo and resulted in an increase in Serb ethnic cleansing operations directed against the Kosovo Albanians, who responded with vicious counter-reprisals against the Serbs and Roma Gypsy minority in Kosovo.[2]

Coming on the heels of the Monica Lewinsky impeachment debacle, Clinton's performance in selling the air war over Kosovo was one of the high points of his presidency. A CNN/USA Today poll found that fifty four percent of Americans approved his handling of it. Polling by Dick Morris found that while the American people mostly opposed foreign intervention, the numbers changed when the words "humanitarian" and "moral imperative" were invoked, combined with the demonization of America's foe.[3]

Clinton had been gearing up for this moment for many years, honing his skills as a public speaker and master of political double-speak during his twelve years as Governor of Arkansas (1978–1980; 1982–1992). Senator Bob Kerrey once said that Clinton was an "uncommonly good liar."[4] He was able to project a good image for America in part because of his unparalleled people skills and ability to convey empathy for oppressed groups and victims of natural disasters. His promotion of micro-financing loans for small businesses—which Hillary Clinton advertised as a mechanism of female empowerment—lent weight to his positive humanitarian image. Clinton's diplomatic triumphs—Clinton helped broker the 1998 Good Friday agreement ending the conflict between the Irish Republican Army (IRA) and British government, and the Oslo accords between the Israelis and Palestinians—further enhanced his image as a peacemaker.[5]

When Clinton traveled abroad, he was swarmed by children and other admirers as if he was a rock star—even in places where the policies he helped advance were harmful. A statue of him today stands in the middle of the Kosovar capital of Pristina, though Clinton's policies resulted in widespread killing and displacement there, and transformed the city into a mecca of organized crime.[6]

Clinton perfectly embodies the cooptation and betrayal of the 1960s' antiwar movement by America's political establishment. During the so-called "Age of Aquarius," young Bill had served as an intern for the antiwar Senator J. William Fulbright. He dressed in hippie garb, benefited from the libertine mores of the sexual revolution, and helped coordinate a protest against the Vietnam War in London's Trafalgar square.[7] Unbeknownst to many of his colleagues, Clinton, according to CIA agent Cord Meyer Jr., was recruited by the CIA as an informant on the antiwar movement and undertook a successful clandestine mission into Soviet Russia to smuggle out Nikita Khrushchev's diary. Later as Arkansas Governor, Clinton enabled the use of his state as a base for clandestine operations into Central America.[8]

By that time, Clinton had shed his hippie garb for a bankers' suit and had courted Arkansas' financial elite. He succeeded in securing the aging hippie vote nevertheless through such marketing coups as his playing a saxophone rendition of "Heartbreak Hotel" on the Arsenio Hall show and admitting that he had smoked marijuana—the counter-culture symbol—albeit without inhaling.[9] Lance Morrow wrote in *TIME* magazine that the 1992 election was a referendum on the 1960s generation and that Clinton's success would "carry the baby boomers to the power and responsibility that they clamored to overthrow in the streets a quarter century ago."[10]

The real Clinton, however, had more in common with Hubert Humphrey, "Tricky Dick" Nixon, Lyndon B. Johnson, and other establishment figures from the 1960s then the kids marching in the streets against them. On the campaign trail, Clinton tellingly distanced himself from counter-cultural icon Hunter S. Thompson, treating him, according to Thompson, "like a roach" when Thompson went to interview him in Little Rock.[11] Clinton's 1996 campaign brochure *Between Hope and History* asserted a string of successes (Bosnia, Haiti) in saving America from the "dire fate of isolationism," which the youthful protesters had advocated during the Vietnam era.[12] Clinton also referred to earlier American military interventions during the Cold War in Berlin, Korea, the Congo, Cuba, Vietnam, Nicaragua, Angola, and Afghanistan as "noble," and supported the 1991 Operation Desert Storm against Iraq.[13]

Clinton's strategy of "democratic enlargement" sought to use the capital from America's "Cold War victory" to work now to "enlarge the world's free community of market democracies." The reduction of trade barriers was designed to "tilt the playing field for U.S. businesses," as Treasury Secretary Lloyd Bentsen put it, and "help Toys 'R' Us and Nike flourish in Central Europe and Asia," in Clinton's words.[14]

Because of his gregarious personality, Clinton proved to be an even more effective front man for U.S. capitalist interests than any 1960s-era politician—save perhaps John F. Kennedy. His persona as a child of the sixties made him seem authentic when he spoke about the need to protect human rights and promote multiculturalism—even if through bombing and military interventions. Had a "square" from the 1950s tried to advance these same positions, the middle-aged hippie set may well have dragged out the old protest signs from the attic. Instead, here was Jan Wenner, editor of *Rolling Stone Magazine,* a onetime counter-cultural mouthpiece, publishing a full-page appeal to readers urging them to "vote for the first presidential candidate of their generation [Clinton]," now that "the rare possibility of real change has arrived."[15]

Clinton had come to power at a time many were calling for cutbacks in overseas military commitments with the end of the Cold War and a transfer of military funds to domestic programs such as health care and education. The idea of a "peace dividend" was encouraged by former Secretary of Defense Robert McNamara who testified before Congress on December 13, 1989, that the $300 billion annual Pentagon budget could be safely cut in half over the next decade. "By such a shift," said McNamara, "we should be able to enhance global stability, strengthen our own security and, at the same time, produce the resources to support a much-needed restructuring of the economy."[16]

McNamara's vision, unfortunately, was never implemented. After the Republican Party gained control of the House of Representatives in January 1995, in an effort to appease opposition on his political Right, Clinton increased military spending more than the Pentagon had requested, and in the fiscal year 2000, he sought an increase of $4 billion and then $100 billion over the next six years.[17] By the end of Clinton's first term, he had already ordered U.S. troops into 25 separate military operations, compared to 17 in Reagan's two terms.[18] A top National Security Council official bragged at the end of Clinton's presidency that U.S. military expenditures were now "larger than [those of] all other countries combined."[19]

The U.S. zone of military hegemony was expanded into Eastern Europe through the North Atlantic Treaty Organization (NATO) and into the formerly neutral Yugoslavia with the disintegration of the Soviet Union. Clinton also deepened U.S. involvement in the Middle East and Africa,[20] with 73,000 U.S. troops acting in support of various United Nations (UN) peacekeeping missions—including in Cambodia, the Middle East, Western Sahara, Macedonia, Somalia, Liberia, Sierra Leone, the Democratic Republic of Congo, Korea, Iraq, and Kuwait.[21]

The UN cover helped sustain the illusion of a disinterested and humanitarian intervention while winning over liberal opinion. As Peter Krogh, the Dean of Georgetown University's School of Foreign Service, put it in 1999, the Clinton administration promoted a "foreign policy of sermons and sanctimony accompanied by the brandishing of tomahawks."[22]

The Clinton administration was particularly aggressive in using international criminal tribunals as "a battering ram in the execution of U.S. and NATO policy," in the words of David Scheffer, U.S. ambassador at large for war crimes issues (1997–2001).[23] The U.S. meanwhile evolved under Clinton's presidency into the world's leading arms trading nation, holding a 70 percent share of the world market. In 1993, Clinton loosened export controls of military related technologies and blocked an arms sales code of conduct that would prevent weapons transfers to nations with poor human rights records.[24] Clinton also bowed to Pentagon pressure by refusing to sign UN treaties banning anti-personnel landmines and the use of child soldiers, and failed to effectively challenge the Pentagon's opposition to the Comprehensive Test Ban Treaty banning nuclear weapons tests.[25]

Whereas Clinton's first appointment as Secretary of State, Warren Christopher, had been on the Board of Lockheed Martin, Clinton's appointment of William Perry as Defense Secretary in 1994 signaled Clinton's support for the Revolution in Military Affairs—i.e., development of exotic weapons such as smart bombs, drones and satellite based surveillance, which Perry had championed as head of military research in the Carter administration.[26] Senator Tom Harkin (D-IA) complained that Clinton "had seemed to have forgotten that the Cold War was over, and the Pentagon does not need new expensive toys."[27] Pierre Sprey, a former Pentagon weapons specialist, added that "the amount of money being spent in proportion to 'the threat' involved" had "never been so out of balance."[28]

Clinton had jumped on the bandwagon of Cold War triumphalism at the beginning of his presidency in 1993 when he signed legislation establishing the Victims of Communism Memorial Foundation, whose purpose was to publicize Communist atrocities—both real and imagined—and to demonize communism.[29] Clinton tried to burnish his progressive bonafides by apologizing for selected CIA misdeeds—such as orchestrating the 1954 coup in Guatemala most notably—though continued to cover up for the Mena drug smuggling operation to the Nicaraguan Contras that he oversaw as Governor of Arkansas and sanctioned a State Department report whitewashing U.S. atrocities in El Salvador. Clinton released some Kennedy assassination documents while saying on the campaign trail that Oswald was the lone assassin.[30]

Clinton's true fealty to the "deep state" was apparent in his appoiinting future CIA Director Leon Panetta, as his Chief of Staff (1994–1997); his Attorney General's blocking investigation into the CIA's theft of spyware software from a private entrepreneur and wider criminal activity associated with it; and in his expansion of America's covert empire of overseas surveillance outposts and spying. Clinton significantly increased the budget for intelligence spending and the National Endowment for Democracy (NED), a CIA offshoot which promoted regime change in foreign nations.[31] This established an imperial trajectory which would enable CIA Director, George Tenet (1996–2004), to win major budget increases and reopen its stations in Africa, and accordingly, "the CIA's old risk-taking spirit began to return."[32]

An imperial mindset was apparent in the May 1997 Quadrennial Defense Review (QDR), which laid the foundation for an era of endless war by announcing that the U.S. would no longer be bound by the UN Charter's prohibition against the threat or use of military force for purposes other than self-defense.[33] In 1999, Clinton enthused that "we have people on the seas, people in foreign countries, all over the world, on every continent, we are everywhere."[34] One hundred thousand U.S. troops were stationed in both Southeast Asia and Europe, and 23,000 in the Middle East.

When Clinton administration officials tried to develop a memorable phrase to describe America's post-Cold War role, Sidney Blumenthal came up with "the indispensable nation" and passed it on to Secretary of State Madeleine Albright (1997–2001), a protégé of former hawkish National Security Council adviser, Zbigniew Brzezinski, who used the term most prominently in February 1998 while defending the policy of coercive diplomacy against Iraq. During an interview on NBC's *The Today Show,* she said: "If we have to use force, it is because we are America; we are the indispensable nation. We stand tall and we see further than other countries into the future, and we see the danger here to all of us." In his memoir of the Clinton presidency, Blumenthal elaborated on what the phrase was intended to represent: "Only the United States had the power to guarantee global security: without our presence or support, multilateral endeavors would fail."[35]

Besides Blumenthal, the intellectual mood of the 1990s that sustained public support for the American empire was captured by Francis Fukuyama, a former State Department executive, in his influential book, *The End of History and the Last Man.* Its central thesis was that liberal capitalism had justly triumphed over Soviet totalitarianism and that everyone in the world was now poised to embrace the former over the latter. Americans, according to Fukuyama, had a responsibility to advance liberal capitalism and open markets in a newly globalized world that would pave the way for a new epoch of global prosperity.[36]

Russian philosopher Aleksandr Dugin pointed out that Fukuyama's outlook was ethno-centric in its belief that "the history and values of Western, and especially American society," were "equivalent to universal laws" that should be "imposed onto all humanity as something that is universal." Implict was the argument that "the values of other peoples and cultures are imperfect, underdeveloped, and should be subject to modernization and standardization in imitation of the Western model."[37]

New York Times columnist Thomas Friedman had the same underlying prejudice as Fukuyama. He wrote that: "the hidden hand of the market will never work without a hidden fist. McDonald's cannot flourish without McDonnell Douglas, the designer of the F-15. And the hidden fist that keeps the world safe for Silicon Valley's technologies to flourish is called the U.S. Army, Air Force, Navy and Marine Corps."[38] This echoed Clinton's celebration of U.S. help for Toys R' Us and Nike in Europe and Central Asia, albeit more bluntly put.

Clinton's foreign policy demonstrated the influence of and contributed to these dominant intellectual ideas, representing a greater continuity from the Reagan era than is often acknowledged. Clinton's first appointee as Defense Secretary, Les Aspin, one of Robert S. McNamara's original whiz kids, had supported President Reagan's decision to deploy MX missiles and to supply arms to the Nicaraguan Contras; another key Clinton foreign policy appointment, Anthony Lake, once told a reporter he thought "Mother Theresa and Ronald Reagan were both trying to do the same thing—one helping the helpless, one fighting the Evil Empire."[39]

During the 1992 election, more than three hundred high-tech companies provided significant financial contributions to Clinton's campaign, including businesses engaged in telecommunications, computers, and micro-electronics. They were attracted to Clinton's foreign policy of globalism that would open new markets and opportunities to extract raw materials and liberalize regulations in the U.S. and global economy.[40] Though embracing protectionism at times when it benefited his corporate donors, Clinton claimed to have negotiated 240 free trade agreements as part of a drive to open foreign markets—a drive that could often only be achieved through violence.[41]

President Clinton wound up dispatching an estimated 864 cruise missiles against the governments of Iraq and Serbia as well as against Afghanistan and Somalia while sponsoring covert military interventions in Latin America and Central Africa. A military commander warned that "the [Clinton] administration is enamored [with] with the cruise missile [which created a TV-spectacle without risking capture of a single American pilot], and wants to use it on everything."[42]

Warmonger makes use of documents in the William J. Clinton Presidential Library and other primary and secondary materials to present readers with the first major comprehensive overview and critical analysis of Clinton's foreign policies, discussing how they set the groundwork for the disastrous era that followed. Several critical accounts of Clinton, most notably Roger Morris' book, *Partners in Power: The Clintons and Their America,* present Clinton as an amoral political player who effectively courted large corporations and compromised any liberal-progressive principles in order to satisfy his large donors and win the presidency. In Morris' account, Clinton is the master of the pay-to-play political system that developed in America in which government policies are enacted to reward donors and the public interest is betrayed.[43]

This betrayal was seen in Eastern Europe, where the Clinton administration laid the groundwork for a new Cold War through the promotion of North Atlantic Treaty Organization (NATO) expansion at the urging of private military lobbies. The rapid privatization of state-led industry in Russia further tarnished Russian feelings of goodwill, as Russians suffered from rampant corruption and decline in quality-of-life indicators and indeed, longevity, with the cutback of public services. The triumph of corporate greed under Clinton was epitomized by the growth of the private military industry, whose annual budget during his term exploded to indeed become larger than the entire defense budgets of all other NATO countries combined.[44]

Despite all the violence and injustice associated with his policies, Clinton has rated as high as number two in one presidential ranking poll and in the top 15 or 20 in many others.[45] One biographer, Nigel Hamilton, alleges that Clinton "came close to greatness as president."[46] Another, Michael Tomasky, suggests that Clinton "left an enviable record of achievements."[47]

These assessments need to be reevaluated in light of many voters' repudiation of Hillary Clinton in the 2016 election owing in good part to misgivings over her husband's record (along with an emotional aversion to her character). A mostly progressive wing within the Democratic Party criticized the Clintons' support for a sweeping crime bill that resulted in mass incarceration, repeal of the Glass Steagall Act separating routine and investment banking functions, the downgrading of America's welfare system, and free trade agreements that led to the offshoring of many manufacturing jobs.

The existing scholarly literature on Clinton's foreign policy is generally behind the curve. Neo-McCarthyism in the U.S. academy has led to the rejection of the so-called "Wisconsin school" of critical politico-economic analysis—which has, sadly, impoverished historical scholarship. Many authors who are critical of Clinton tend to blame "lack of vision" for his disastrous foreign policy decisions, and his haphazard intervention or inaction in the face of major human rights crimes—as if this most intelligent of U.S. Presidents had been clueless and absent-minded for eight years, instead of very deliberately marching to the tune of his corporate donors.

Even more bewildering, those who praise Clinton called him a responsible "internationalist, multilateralist and free-trader," to quote international relations scholar Stephen M. Walt.[48] And Michael Tomasky, the editor of the *New Republic* and contributor to *The New York Review of Books,* wrote that Clinton came to command "respect as a global leader" while learning "that the world still requires American attention after all."[49]

According to Tomasky, Clinton's accomplishments in foreign policy included: a) his "brave and risky military intervention in Haiti," which "accomplished U.S. objectives with no loss of life," b) the signing of the Dayton agreements—which Tomasky claimed "stopped the bloodshed in

Bosnia; and c) Clinton's helping to broker peace in Northern Ireland and the Middle East to some extent.[50]

These claims—which largely echo Clinton's own talking points[51]—are almost entirely illusory. The peace Clinton helped broker in Northern Ireland served British interests, and the peace he helped broker in the Middle East, the Oslo accords, was a neocolonial arrangement that famed Palestinian writer Edward Said characterized as a "Palestinian Versailles."[52] The Dayton accords in Bosnia were also derided by peace groups as a neocolonial arrangement because they resulted in the occupation of Bosnia by 60,000 NATO troops, 20,000 of them American, and deprived the Bosnian people of any democratic say in their future, while laying the groundwork for war in Kosovo.[53] Clinton's "brave" and "risky" military intervention in Haiti, meanwhile, led to yet another neocolonial takeover in which U.S. military advisers were given a desk in most of Haiti's ministries, trained Haiti's notoriously brutal police, and blocked Haiti's restored leader, Jean Bertrand Aristide, from enacting a raise in the $1 minimum wage.[54]

The CATO Institute's Jonathan G. Clarke more aptly gave the Clinton-Gore administration a D Grade, citing its creation of colossal messes in the Balkans and in Colombia as a result of the administration's prosecution of the drug war; the devastation of Iraq from an economic embargo and bombing attacks which "barely bothered Saddam Hussein"; a sterile and cruel policy towards Cuba; retention of 100,000 troops in Southeast Asia and an ambivalent attitude towards a historic summit between North and South Korea; and damaging of relations with China and Russia, the latter because of support for NATO expansion.[55]

This work builds upon and advances Clarke's negative appraisal of the Clinton administration, which laid the groundwork for U.S. foreign policies in the 21st Century. Rather than being a time of tranquility when the U.S. failed to pay attention to the gathering storm of terrorism, as *New York Times* columnist David Brooks frames it, the Clinton presidency saw rising tensions among the U.S., China and Russia, and U.S. complicity in terrorist acts.[56]

Widely overlooked in the scholarly literature—books like Hal Brands' *From Berlin to Baghdad: America's Search for Purpose in the Post-Cold War World*[57]—was Clinton's championing a new style of techno-war that, alongside the privatization of military functions, was designed to lessen the political fallout of war by using paid mercenaries to fight and kill instead of U.S. soldiers, so that Americans would not rise up in angry mass protests, as they had during the Vietnam War when they saw their children coming home in body bags. The bombing of Kosovo deployed sophisticated satellite surveillance technologies and unmanned aerial vehicles (UAVs), or drones, along with record numbers of smart bombs. No U.S. soldiers were killed, and collateral damage was limited, at least compared to previous conflicts. Propaganda demonizing American foes, the invocation of a moral imperative to intervene, and the illusion of surgical precision and a "clean war"—however false—helped limit antiwar activism, while raising confidence that the U.S. could wage war in the future at a minimal political cost.

Besides the so-called revolution in military affairs, studies of Clinton's foreign policy evade his alliance with Islamic extremists in the Balkans, which built off a Cold War precedent and set the groundwork for similar alliances in the War on Terror.[58] They further fail to address the Clinton administration's support for an illegal arms pipeline through Croatia, which bore some resemblances to the Reagan administration's illegal violation of the Boland Amendment during the Iran-Contra affair.[59] When covering the bloodletting in Rwanda, most writers accept the official narrative that the U.S. government was negligent in failing to intervene to halt the purported genocide by Hutu Interhamwe militias targeting the Tutsi population living in Rwanda.[60] However, a wealth of evidence has come to light showing that the Clinton administration actually intervened militarily to support the conquest of Rwanda by the Tutsi-led Rwandan Patriotic Front (RPF) and then backed the RPF's invasion and plunder of the Congo.[61]

Warmonger starts with two chapters surveying Clinton's tenure as Governor of Arkansas and how it set the groundwork for his presidency. Rather than being progressive in any way, Clinton courted big money donors, most notably Tyson Chicken, Wal Mart and Stephens Inc. Investing House, and covered up clandestine operations into Central America that involved drug and gun running from Mena in Western Arkansas. The next chapters analyze Clinton's foreign policies in different parts of the world. Chapter three focuses on the Balkans War and the underlying illusions that guided it.

Chapters four and five cover the Clinton administration's policies towards Russia, Ukraine and the Baltics and Clinton's close friendship with Boris Yeltsin and support for NATO expansion. Chapter six looks at Clinton's policies towards Southeast Asia and the 1997 financial crisis and includes discussion of his close relationship with Indonesian dictator Mohamed Suharto and policies towards East Timor.

Chapter 7 focuses on Clinton's international War on Drugs and its double standards. Chapters 8 and 9 look at Clinton's War on Terror and the corruption underlying it and injustices to which it led to. Chapter ten provides an overview of Clinton's policies towards Israel and the Arab-Israeli conflict. The subsequent two chapters address Clinton's policies towards Africa and the Rwandan genocide, and the final chapter focuses on Latin America.

Bill Clinton possessed a magnetic personality and was an incredible political campaigner, public speaker, and fund raiser. However, these personal qualities did not translate into progressive or even sound public policies. Quite the contrary. Clinton displayed a lack of ethics throughout his political career and had no compunction about twisting the facts and misleading the American people—a skill that made him an effective crippler of the very policies the American people had elected him to support. More skillfully than Richard Nixon and Lyndon Johnson, Clinton was able to make it seem as if the use of military force was being carried out for a moral cause. His carefully crafted persona as an ex-1960s radical—alongside his wife, Hillary—only helped to advance the illusion.

A study of the Clinton years is not just a study of one man, it is ultimately the study—like my previous book on Obama[62]—of the structural forces that enabled a smart, charismatic, and ambitious young hustler with extraordinarily flexible moral convictions to cozy up to dictators, to launch bombing attacks around the globe, and to advance an economic vision that enabled corporate pillage.

In the end, Clinton was all too human. Like many kings and emperors, he used his power to satisfy his lust for financial, sexual, and ego gratification, with little evident remorse for the lies he told, the promises he broke, and the hundreds of thousands of innocent men, women and children whose deaths he caused or deliberately declined to prevent.

Lord Acton's observation that "power tends to corrupt and absolute power corrupts absolutely" has become part of the common wisdom. But the opposite may actually be true. Power tends to attract corrupt men, who then behave according to their nature. "[P]ower doesn't change people as much as it accentuates their preexisting traits," says organizational psychologist Adam Grant. "It is like an amplifier. Whoever we were before just gets louder."[63]

And with Bill Clinton, these became very loud indeed. Because the United States is so powerful, Bill Clinton was able to do much more damage to the world as president than if he had become, say, a used car salesman. The sad irony is that, as a used car salesman, had he committed even a fraction of the crimes he committed as President from 1993 to 2001 and before that as Arkansas Governor, he would now be serving a life sentence in the Jefferson County Maximum Security Unit at 2501 State Farm Road in Arkansas. (Although, given Arkansas's enthusiastic embrace of the death penalty, he might not.)

Endnotes

1 Sidney Blumenthal, *The Clinton Wars* (New York: Plume Books, 2003), 642.

2 See David Gibbs, *First Do No Harm: Humanitarian Intervention and the Destruction of Yugoslavia* (Nashville: Vanderbilt University Press, 2009).

3 Keating Holland, "Poll: Congress Should Have Authority Over U.S. Involvement in Kosovo," *CNN,* May 3, 1999, https://www.cnn.com/ALLPOLITICS/stories/1999/05/03/kosovo.poll/. Alexander Cockburn and Jeffrey St. Clair, *Al Gore: A User's Manual* (London: Verso, 2000), 222.

4 Quoted in Roger Stone and Robert Morrow, *The Clintons' War on Women* (New York: Skyhorse Press, 2016), 36.

5 On the Clintons and microfinance, see Thomas Frank, "Nor a Lender Be: Hillary Clinton, Liberal Virtue and the Cult of Microloan," *Harper's Magazine,* April 2016; On Clinton's policy towards Ireland, see Timothy J. Lynch, *Turf War: The Clinton Administration and Northern Ireland* (Aldershot, England: Ashgate, 2004).

6 On the latter, see for example Chuck Sudetic, "The Bullies Who Run Kosovo," *Politico,* July 21, 2015, https://www.politico.eu/article/kosovo-hashim-thaci-un-special-court-tribunal-organ-trafficking-kla-serbia-milosevic-serbia-ramush/

7 See Nigel Hamilton, *Bill Clinton: An American Journey* (New York: Random House, 2003).

8 See Roger Morris, *Partners in Power: The Clintons and Their America* (Washington, D.C.: Regnery, 1999).

9 William McKeen, *Outlaw Journalist: The Life and Times of Hunter S. Thompson* (New York: W.W. Norton, 2008), 316.

10 Bernard Von Bothmer, *Framing the Sixties: The Use and Abuse of a Decade from Ronald Reagan to George W. Bush* (Amherst, MA: University of Massachusetts Press, 2010), 134.

11 McKeen, *Outlaw Journalist,* 316.

12 William Jefferson Clinton, *Between Hope and History: Meeting America's Challenges for the 21st Century* (New York: Crown, 1996).

13 Von Bothmer, *Framing the Sixties,* 165; "Bill Clinton, New Covenant—Engagement for Democracy," Draft Speech Outline II, *Diane Blair Papers,* MC 1632, Series II, Subseries 4, Box 1, Folder Campaign Aid for Governor, 1979–1991, University of Arkansas Fayetville, Mullins Libraries, Special Collections.

14 Douglas Brinkley, "Democratic Enlargement: The Clinton Doctrine," *Foreign Policy,* Spring 1997, http://archive.wilsonquarterly.com/in-essence/clinton-doctrine. Bentsen quoted in Noam Chomsky, "The Clinton Vision," *Z Magazine,* December 1993, https://chomsky.info/199312__/ He had also said that he was "tired of a level playing field," and that "we should have done this [tilt the playing field for U.S. businesses] 20 years ago."

15 McKeen, *Outlaw Journalist,* 316.

16 David E. Rosenbaum, "Spending Can Be Cut in Half, Former Defense Officials Say," *New York Times,* December 13, 1989. Lawrence J. Korb, a former assistant Defense Secretary in the Reagan administration, agreed with McNamara, saying that transferring funds to the domestic sector "can have a dramatic impact on our economic well-being and our competitive position in the world."

17 Ann Devroy and Bradley Graham, "Clinton Seeks to Boost Defense by $25 Billion," *The Washington Post,* December 2, 1994, https://www.washingtonpost.com/archive/politics/1994/12/02/clinton-seeks-to-boost-defense-by-25-billion/185d79aa-f6e9-4d7b-bf3b-492dadc3f6a7/; Steven Lee Myers, "Clinton Proposes a Budget

Increase For the Military," *The New York Times,* January 2, 1999, https://www.nytimes.com/1999/01/02/us/clinton-proposes-a-budget-increase-for-the-military.html. At a ceremony announcing the 1994 budget request, Clinton pledged that "throughout the life of this administration our military will remain the best-trained, best equipped, the best-fighting force on earth." Kenneth M. Duberstein, Ronald Reagan's former chief of staff, told *The Washington Post* that "the only thing missing from the Rose Garden was Cap Weinberger," referring to Reagan's defense secretary who presided over a major increase in defense spending.

18 John Dumbrell, "Was There a Clinton Doctrine? President Clinton's Foreign Policy Reconsidered," *Diplomacy & Statecraft* (June 202), 52.

19 Sandy Berger quoted in Andrew Bacevich, *American Empire: The Realities and Consequences of U.S. Diplomacy* (Cambridge, MA: Harvard University Press, 2002). In actuality, it was only larger than the total of its nine closest competitors. Under Clinton, U.S. military spending actually decreased from $331.3 billion to $289 billion annually though Clinton requested an extra $12 billion in military outlays in his January 1999 State of the Union address and spoke about the need to fight back against defense cuts.

20 Jacob Heilbrunn and Michael Lind, "The Third American Empire," *The New York Times,* January 2, 1996, https://www.nytimes.com/1996/01/02/opinion/the-third-american-empire.html

21 David N. Bossie, *Intelligence Failure: How Clinton's National Security Policy Set the Stage for 9/11* (Nashville, Tennessee: WND Books, 2004), 79.

22 Walter Isaacson, "Madeleine's War," *TIME,* May 9, 1999, referring to Clinton's Secretary of State Madeline Albright, who egregiously stated in relation to the estimated 500,000 Iraqi children who died due to American sanctions that "We think the price is worth it." https://www.youtube.com/watch?v=RM0uvgHKZe8

23 David Scheffer, *All the Missing Souls: A Personal History of the War Crimes Tribunals* (New Jersey: Princeton University Press, 2012), 252. While he was willing to set up ad hoc war crimes tribunals through the Security Council that pursued U.S. objectives, Clinton shied away from having the U.S. sign on to the International Criminal Court (ICC), which would enhance the prospect of the U.S. itself being put on trial.

24 Bossie, *Intelligence Failure,* 117, 118; William Hartung, "Nixon's Children: Bill Clinton and the Permanent Arms Bazaar," *World Policy Journal, 12,* no. 2 (Summer 1995), 25; Alexander Cockburn and Ken Silverstein, *Washington Babylon* (London: Verso, 1996), 178, 179.

25 Melvin Goodman, "Clinton and the Origins of the Militarization of National Security Policy," in *Foreign Policy in the Clinton Administration,* ed. Rosanna Perotti (New York: Nova Science Publishers, 2019), 34, 45, 46, 47; Philip Shenon, "Clinton Still Firmly Against Land Mine Treaty," *The New York Times,* October 11, 1997. John F. Kennedy by contrast had stood up to the Pentagon and secured a limited test ban treaty after the Cuban missile crisis. Clinton signed the test ban treaty in 1996 but failed to secure Senate approval where it was voted down in 1999. To his credit, Clinton did help engineer an expansion of the 1968 Nuclear Non-Proliferation Treaty (NPT), though this treaty was largely meaningless, inter alia, in that it stipulated that nuclear armed powers would eliminate their nuclear weapons stockpiles, an undertaking with which these powers never complied.

26 Alexander Cockburn and Ken Silverstein, *Washington Babylon* (London: Verso, 1996), 162; Sam Smith, *Shadows of Hope: A Freethinkers Guide to Politics in the Time of Clinton* (Bloomington: Indiana University Press, 1994), 109; Jeremy

Kuzmarov, "The Improbable Militarist: Jimmy Carter, the Revolution in Military Affairs, and Limits of the American Two Party System," *Class, Race and Corporate Power,* 6, 2 (2018), https://digitalcommons.fiu.edu/classracecorporatepower/vol6/iss2/7/ Clinton's appointment of Harold Brown as Chairman of the president's foreign intelligence advisory board after the death of Defense Secretary Les Aspin was also significant. One of Robert S. McNamara's "whiz kids" at the Pentagon who oversaw bombing operations in Vietnam, Brown spearheaded the revolution in military affairs as Defense Secretary in the Carter administration. Neoconservative Michael O'Hanlon credits Clinton with championing GPS-guided weaponry as part of what he considers a "strong defense legacy." Michael O'Hanlon, "Clinton's Strong Defense Legacy," *Foreign Affairs,* November/December 2003, https://www.brookings.edu/wp-content/uploads/2016/06/20031101.pdf

27 Emily O. Goldman and Larry Berman, "Engaging the World: First Impressions of the Clinton Foreign Policy Legacy," in *The Clinton Legacy,* ed. Colin Campbell and Berl A. Rockman (New York: Chatham House Publishers, 2000), 249.

28 Cockburn and Silverstein, *Washington Babylon,* 185.

29 Justin Moyer, "A New Anti-communism museum in D.C. Tallies 100 Million Victims of Marx's Ideology," *The Spokesman-Review,* September 28, 2022, https://www.spokesman.com/stories/2022/sep/28/a-new-anti-communism-museum-in-dc-tallies-100-mill/

30 Richard Bartholomew, *The Deep State in Texas* (Say Something Real Press, 2018), 418, 419. Clinton also characteristically declined to act on a congressional resolution to exonerate General Walter Short and Admiral Husband Kimmel for the intelligence failure at Pearl Harbor who had been scapegoated by the Roosevelt administration for having failed to adequately warn them after having foreknowledge of the attack. He was thus covering up again for executive branch criminality and deceit. Donald Jeffries, *Crimes and Cover Ups in American Politics, 1776–1963: The History They Didn't Teach You in School* (New York: Skyhorse Publishing, 2019), 247.

31 *Dime's Worth of Difference: Beyond the Lesser of Two Evils,* ed. Alexander Cockburn and Jeffrey St. Clair (Oakland: AK Press/Counterpunch, 2004), 12; James Ciment and Immanuel Ness, "NED and the Empire's New Clothes," https://thirdworldtraveler.com/NED/NED-EmpiresNewClothes.html; Susan B. Epstein, "National Endowment for Democracy: Policy and Funding Issues," https://www.everycrsreport.com/files/19990816_96-222_c4d603ed41513187b32654f9aacd3050636c9712.pdf; Anthony Frank, *Destroying America: The CIA's Quest to Control the Government* (2022), 150, 151. On Clinton's AG, Janet Reno's role in blocking investigation into the theft of spyware software by the CIA, see Richard L. Fricker, "Brooke vs. the Justice Department: The Texas Delegation's Dean Seeks INSLAW's Answers," *The Texas Observer,* November 11, 1994, 6–9. When Reno offered to pay a financial settlement to INSLAW, it was rejected by White House staff on "national security" grounds.

32 James Risen, "The Nation; the Clinton Administration's See No Evil CIA," *The New York Times,* September 10, 2000. In the mid-1990s, according to official figures, U.S. Special Forces conducted between 2,000 and 3,000 deployments, including secret operations in more than 130 countries each year.

33 William S. Cohen, *Report of the Quadrennial Defense Review,* May 1997, https://history.defense.gov/Portals/70/Documents/quadrennial/QDR1997.pdf?ver=2014-06-25-110930-527

34 Bacevich, *American Empire,* 127, 128.

35 See Sidney Blumenthal, *The Clinton Wars* (New York: Farrar, Strauss and Giroux, 2002). A Czech émigré whose father served as chief of staff to Czechoslovakia's anti-communist foreign minister, Jan Masaryk, who died under suspicious circumstances after the communists took over Czechoslovakia in 1948 and then went on to teach Condolezza Rice at the University of Denver, Albright had studied under Brzezinski when he was a professor at Colombia University. Like her mentor, she was a fervent cold warrior who had supported the arming of the mujahadin in Afghanistan to induce a Soviet invasion and bring down the Soviet empire. See Jeremy Kuzmarov, "Albright Was a Key Figure Sparking New Cold War by Championing NATO Expansion as Secretary of State in 1990s," *CovertAction Magazine,* March 29, 2002, https://covertactionmagazine.com/2022/03/29/albright-was-a-key-figure-sparking-new-cold-war-by-championing-nato-expansion-as-secretary-of-state-in-1990s/

36 See Frances Fukuyama, *The End of History and the Last Man,* reissue (New York: The Free Press, 2006)

37 See Aleeksandr Dugin, *The Fourth Political Theory,* translated by Mark Sleboda (Budapest: Arktos Media, 2012). Fukuyama recycled some ideas from Walt W. Rostow's modernization theory, as advanced in his influential book, *Stages of Economic Growth: A Non-Communist Manifesto* published in 1960.

38 Thomas L. Friedman, "A Manifesto for the Fast World," *New York Times Magazine,* March 28, 1999, 65. For a critique of Friedman, see Belen Fernandez, The Imperial Messenger: Thomas L. Friedman at Work (London: Verso, 2011).

39 Patrick J. Maney, *Bill Clinton New Gilded Age President* (Lawrence: University Press of Kansas, 2016), 117, 118.

40 Bossie, *Intelligence Failure,* 113, 114. Lauri Fitz-Pegado, who ran a Commerce Department Agency, stated that "the United States prior to this administration [Clinton] had never aggressively advocated for the private sector." In Steven A. Holmes, *Ron Brown: An Uncommon Life* (New York: John Wiley & Sons, 2000), 250.

41 Goldman and Berman, "Engaging the World," in *The Clinton Legacy,* ed. Campbell and Rockman, 233. On the contradictions of Clinton's trade policy, see James Bovard, *"Feeling Your Pain": The Explosion and Abuse of Government Power in the Clinton-Gore Years* (New York: St. Martin's Press, 2000).

42 Michael R. Rip and James M. Hasik, *The Precision Revolution: GPS and the Future of Aerial Warfare* (Annapolis, MD: Naval Institute Press, 2002), 362, 367.

43 Morris, *Partners in Power.*

44 Andrew Thomson, *Outsourced Empire: How Militias, Mercenaries, and Contractors Support U.S. Statecraft* (London: Pluto Press, 2018), 125, 126.

45 "Historical Ranking of Presidents of the United States," https://en.wikipedia.org/wiki/Historical_rankings_of_presidents_of_the_United_States; David Vine, Base Nation: How U.S. Military Bases Abroad Harm America and the World (New York: Metropolitan Books, 2015), 175.

46 Nigel Hamilton, *Bill Clinton: Mastering the Presidency* (New York: Public Affairs, 2007), xiv.

47 Michael Tomasky, Bill Clinton (New York: Times Books, 2017), 2.

48 John Dumbrell, *Clinton's Foreign Policy Between the Bushes, 1992–2000* (London: Routeledge, 2010), 3, 4; Stephen M. Walt, "Two Cheers for Clinton's Foreign Policy," March/April 2000. Fifteen years later, Walt said he had changed his views about Clinton and was now more critical of many of his policies, including his Middle East policies and support for NATO expansion, which he said, "helped sow

the seeds of much future trouble." Stephen Walt, "I Changed My Mind," *Foreign Policy,* March 13, 2015. Even as astute an analyst as Andrew Bacevich in *American Empire* criticizes Clinton for his inaction and approves certain military interventions like in Bosnia, Sierra Leone, and East Timor which he suggests were belated.

49 Tomasky, Bill Clinton, 87.

50 Tomasky, Bill Clinton, 45, 87.

51 At a 2005 conference at Hofstra University on his presidency, Clinton characterized as his great foreign policy successes: a) Haiti—where he said military intervention had helped oust a dictator; b) Bosnia, where he was proud that he had gotten NATO allies to agree to use military force; c) peace accords in Ireland and the Middle East; d) support for NATO expansion; and e) getting serious about the fight against terrorism. *Foreign Policy in the Clinton Administration,* ed. Perotti, xiv, xv.

52 Edward Said, "The Morning After," *London Review of Books,* October 21, 1993, https://www.lrb.co.uk/the-paper/v15/n20/edward-said/the-morning-after.

53 Michael Chossudovsky, "Dismantling Yugoslavia, Colonizing Bosnia," *CovertAction Quarterly,* Spring 1996.

54 See Peter Hallward, *Damming the Flood: Haiti and the Politics of Containment* (London: Verso, 2007), 61.

55 Jonathan G. Clarke, "A Foreign Policy Report Card on the Clinton-Gore Administration," CATO Institute, Policy Analysis, October 3, 2000. Clarke acknowledges some positives like helping to broker peace agreements in Northern Ireland and between Israel and the Palestinians and normalization of relations with Vietnam, though this work provides a more critical take on the latter.

56 Tarpley, *9/11 Synthetic Terror,* 113.

57 Hal Brands, *From Berlin to Baghdad: America's Search for Purpose in the Post-Cold War World* (Lexington: University Press of Kentucky, 2008). The author is the Henry A. Kissinger Distinguished Professor of Global Affairs at the Johns Hopkins University School of Advanced International Studies (SAIS) and a Resident Scholar at the American Enterprise Institute.

58 Examples where these alliances are omitted include: Dumbrell, *Clinton's Foreign Policy;* and Brands, *From Berlin to Baghdad.* See John R. Schindler, *Unholy Terror: Bosnia, Al Qaida and the Rise of Global Jihad* (London: Zenith Press, 2007) for the neglected story.

59 See Gibbs, *First Do No Harm* for the precise story omitted in many other works.

60 See faulty accounts in Dumbrell, *Clinton's Foreign Policy* and Brands, *From Berlin to Baghdad,* 137, 138. Even critical books like Nathan J. Robinson's, *Superpredator: Bill Clinton's Use and Abuse of Black America* (Sommerville, MA: CA Press, 2016) embrace the dominant narrative about Rwanda and present a lot of misinformation.

61 See Wayne Madsen, *Genocide and Covert Operations in Africa, 1993–1999* (New York: Edwin Mellen, 1999); Edward S. Herman and David Peterson, Enduring Lies: The Rwandan Genocide in the Propaganda System, 20 Years Later (Create Space Independent Publishing, 2014).

62 Jeremy Kuzmarov, *Obama's Unending Wars: Fronting the Foreign Policy of the Permanent Warfare State* (Atlanta; Clarity Press, 2019).

63 Adam Grant, "Power Doesn't Corrupt: It Just Exposes Who Leaders Really Are," *The Washington Post,* February 22, 2019, https://www.washingtonpost.com/business/economy/power-doesnt-corrupt-it-just-exposes-who-leaders-really-are/2019/02/22/f5680116-3600-11e9-854a-7a14d7fec96a_story.html

CHAPTER 1

The Education of a Governor

"Clinton's first impression knocks you out. You think this is the most impressive son of a bitch you've ever seen, gregarious, with a sense of humor. What a Governor! It's a slick veneer. Some of us were talking about Slick Willie the other day, and we decided, well we know what he's really like and what he's done as governor, but hey he might make a good president."

—John Brummett, columnist *Arkansas Times*, 1992[1]

In October 1978, Bill Clinton was elected as the youngest Governor in the history of the state of Arkansas at the age of 32. After two years out of office from 1980–1982, he was reelected and maintained that position for another ten years. Clinton was a genius at interpersonal chemistry with a magical presence on the campaign trail, who came across as empathetic and admirable in overcoming his personal demons. George Jernigan, an Arkansas politician, said that when Clinton showed up as a candidate for Congress in 1974 and opened his mouth at the Pope County picnic, Arkansas' traditional political kickoff, "everyone just knew [that he would be a political star]."[2]

Clinton proved effective in tapping into the dominant cultural impulses of the time, most notably the infatuation with self-help and improvement in an era of political demobilization and prosperity. Journalist David Halberstam noted that Clinton was a "political extension of the new popular culture, the age of empathy television, symbolized by Oprah Winfrey," which valorized "the need to feel better about yourself in a difficult, emotionally volatile world. Indeed, Clinton himself was good at telling different audiences that when he was young, he was overweight and unhappy and had not been popular."[3]

The New Narcissist: Background and Student Days

Originally known as Billy Blythe, Clinton was born in Hope, Arkansas in 1945 to Virginia Dwire, a nurse and William Jefferson Blythe III, a hard-drinking World War II veteran and womanizer who was killed in a car wreck before Bill was born. Author John D. Gartner believes that Dr. George Wright may have been Clinton's father. He found eerie resemblances between Bill and Wright's son, Larry. One of Dr. Wright's best friends said Wright told him: "I'm Billy Blythe's father." Others in Hope, Arkansas, said that it was an open secret in town that Wright was the father.[4] Bill may have inherited various traits from Wright, including his intelligence.

After her first husband died, Clinton's mother Virginia moved to Hot Springs and married Roger Clinton, a hard drinking car salesman who had an ill temper and was abusive towards her.[5] In children who grow up in abusive homes, there is always a part of them that identifies with the aggressor, as Anna Freud wrote in *The Ego and the Mechanism of Defense.* Consistent with this assessment, Clinton would become known for eruptions of aggression behind closed doors and has been accused of acts of violence and sexual assault towards women.[6] His adviser Dick Morris would write that "his is a primitive anger manifested by red-faced screaming, a wildly pointing accusatory finger, and utterly self-righteous tirades ... For those on the receiving end, it is a frightening and unforgettable encounter."[7]

Hot Springs was a resort town known as the "bible belt Gomorrah" which was dominated by casinos, bordellos, night clubs, and the infamous Dixie mafia. Clinton's mother, who abandoned herself to the tawdry scene, wrote that Hot Springs was "one of the premier playgrounds in America. It had been a place where gangsters were cool, and rules were made to be bent, and money and power, however you got them, were the total measure of man." In that town, furthermore, the "con job was considered an art form."[8] Inevitably, young Clinton would have been very much shaped by the town he grew up in and its ethos, whose tendencies he would carry with him throughout his career.

In November 1971, when the Young Democrats of America Convention was held in Hot Springs, several attendees would aid in Clinton's political rise[9]—it was right near Bill's uncle Raymond's Vapors nightclub, which allegedly offered up party girls. (Raymond was tied with the Dixie mafia).[10] Al Gore Jr.'s mother, Pauline, who had been around politicians all her life, warned her son about Clinton's character in the mid-1980s when she was first introduced to Bill. "She thought he had bad moral character [Clinton that is]," said James Fleming, a Nashville physician and longtime family friend. Fleming remembers standing in the senior Gore's living room one day in the mid-1980s with Gore Jr. and his brother-in-law, Frank Hunger, discussing the Arkansas Governor, who had just finished a visit to Nashville. Fleming said that Pauline "looked at [her son] and said, 'Bill Clinton is not a nice person. Don't associate too closely with him.'"[11]

Clinton's political ambitions emerged in high school when he was photographed shaking hands with John F. Kennedy on a visit to the White House. A born leader with an inquisitive mind, Clinton was elected to the school council in the tenth grade, was a national merit semifinalist, president of an academic honor society and played saxophone in the school band. A journalist wrote that no one in Hot Springs could then imagine that thirty years later the *Arkansas Democrat-Gazette* editor would ever label clean cut Bill Clinton "that lying son of a bitch."[12]

After Clinton's high school graduation, he attended Georgetown University where he was influenced by Professor Carroll Quigley, author of *Tragedy and Hope: A History of the World in Our Time* (1966), which traced the power of a small Anglo-Saxon banking elite and how they effectively ruled the world.[13] From that time forward, Clinton strove to become part of that elite. His ascension to power began with his winning a Rhodes scholarship which enabled him to attend Oxford University. A student there who knew Clinton, Cliff Jackson, said Clinton was "fun to be around but obsessed with power."[14]

Clinton never actually graduated from Oxford, allegedly because he was accused by another student, Eileen Wellstone, of sexual assault. The State Department official who investigated the incident said Clinton's interests appeared to be drinking, drugs and sex, not studies. "I came away from the incident with the clear impression that this was a young man who was there to party, not study," he said.[15]

Clinton's views on the military were shaped by the conservative political culture of the 1950s. He stated that he grew up "on John Wayne movies."[16] When he was a student at Georgetown University, he initially supported the Vietnam War. Though moving to an antiwar position, he was not involved with the small campus antiwar movement. Clinton's antiwar position solidified when he served as an aide to Arkansas' Senator William J. Fulbright, the head of the Senate Foreign Relations Committee who opposed the war. While at Oxford he attended an antiwar protest in Trafalgar Square and served, according to an FBI report, as a quasi-ambassador with the Washington, D.C.–based antiwar Vietnam Moratorium Committee. Still, Clinton biographer Robert E. Levin wrote that "by the standards of the counterculture of 1968, Clinton was a pro-establishment moderate."[17]

White House correspondent Todd Purdum characterized Clinton as the "classic good boy, never anti-establishment or even close to it. He might have affected hippie dress but he always wanted to preserve his viability. There was nothing at any time radical about him."[18] Journalist Christopher Hitchens noted: "who else in the 1960s was asking: 'how will this play in New Hampshire around 1992?'"[19]

When Clinton heard a lecture from Communist Party leader Le Kha Phieu in February 2000 condemning American imperialism in Vietnam, Clinton told Phieu that while he had disagreed with America's Vietnam policy, those who had pursued it were "not imperialists or colonialists, but good people who believed they were fighting communism." One day walking back from gym, Clinton told Oxford classmate Jackson how he was awestruck about a story he heard about LBJ having sex with a woman with a peace medallion dangling from her breasts in the Oval Office—after he had just ordered a massive expansion of the Vietnam War. "Bill thought it was so neat—that he had audacity to do it and wanted to do the same."[20]

When Clinton ran for president, right wingers would attack him for being a draft dodger, invoking a letter that he had written to Colonel Eugene J. Holmes, an ROTC officer at the University of Arkansas. Clinton had misled Holmes by asking to be admitted to ROTC as a way of getting out of the draft when he had no intention ever of going there. Colonel Holmes later stated that Clinton "purposely deceived me, using the possibility of joining the ROTC as a ploy to work with the draft board to delay his induction."[21] This episode was significant because it embodies Clinton's ability to effectively "game the system" and employ deceit to manipulate it, as he would effectively do throughout his career.

Laying the Ground for the Presidency: Governor of Arkansas

The groundwork for Clinton's presidency was established during his years as Governor of Arkansas (1979–1981; 1983–1992), when according to journalist Roger Morris, he "presided over the prospering of the political-corporate nexus as no other politician in the state's history had ever had."[22]

Arkansas had long been one of the most corrupt and violent states in the Union (the capital, Little Rock, had one of the highest murder rates in the country). It was dominated by the Democratic Party whose popularity was rooted in the white supremacist backlash against Reconstruction and the Republicans (the party of Lincoln). Arkansas' economy was dominated by a small financial elite that included bankers, speculators, owners of tenant farms, the great extractive industries in timber, oil and minerals, the big utilities and poultry operations. The major powers also included the Baptist Church, Arkansas Power & Light Company, and associations of sheriffs and county judges.[23]

Over the decades there had developed an important symbiosis of politics and commerce. Aversion to government ran so deep that any tax increase required a three fourths majority. According to one analyst, the rural population were "the nearest approach to medieval serfdom ever achieved on the North American continent." So little changed over the years that the *Arkansas Times* wrote in 1992: "Nowhere in America is the range so great as in Arkansas from the multi-billionaire status of the Wal-Mart Waltons to the abject poverty of the Delta region."[24]

Bill Clinton entered Arkansas' political scene in the post-Watergate era espousing at times a populist rhetoric which drew on a rich heritage in the state dating back to Governor Jeff Davis (1901–1907). He had denounced the banking interests in Little Rock as "high collared roosters" who dressed in "collars so high they can't see the sun except at high noon."[25] In 1932, Arkansan Hattie Carraway became the first woman elected to the U.S. Senate vowing to cap individual incomes at $1 million per year.[26]

Despite Clinton's Oxford education, he was able to cultivate the image of a local boy. He had the political skills to, on the one hand, win over a roomful of business executives and, on the other, a crowd at a state fair in rural Arkansas where he would change his language in order to speak their vernacular. [27] As a fundraiser, Clinton was unparalleled. His friend, Paul Fray, stated: "There's [no one] alive in this country that can raise money like he can. Nobody can."[28]

Like most successful politicians, Clinton would tell one group one thing, and another something else, leaving many feeling betrayed. Clinton allegedly told Larry Patterson on his security detail, that he didn't care that he was lying so long as he got the man's vote and political contribution. Patterson said that Clinton would "tell them anything they wanted to hear [regardless of whether he meant it]."[29]

Clinton had become connected to Arkansas' Old Boy network through a) Senator J. William Fulbright, b) two senior partners at the Rose Law Firm, Gaston Williamson and William Nash, whom he met during his Rhodes scholarship interviews through Governor Winthrop Rockefeller (1967–1971) who invited Clinton to his mansion while he was still in college, and c) through his Uncle Raymond Clinton, a successful Buick dealer in Hot Springs whose showroom, according to Virginia Dwire, "was a gathering place for powerful, politically savvy men in Hot Springs."[30]

These men included associates of New Orleans crime boss Carlos Marcello, to whom Raymond is alleged to have given kickbacks from slot machines that he ran. An FBI agent said he thought Raymond's car dealership was a façade for illegal gambling, drug money laundering and other illicit ventures that were part of the Marcello franchise.[31]

During Clinton's first campaign for Congress in 1974 against Republican John Paul Hammerschmidt—a close friend of George H.W. Bush who would run his 1988 presidential campaign in Arkansas—Uncle Raymond and an associate, Gabe Crawford, gave him $10,000 in seed money, provided houses around the district to serve as campaign headquarters, the use of Crawford's private plane and helped him secure a loan from the First National Bank of Hot Springs. Crawford presided over a backroom bookie operation that was one of Hot Springs' most lucrative criminal enterprises. Clinton's political career by implication was bankrolled from the beginning with mob money.[32]

During his governorship, Clinton found a powerful benefactor in the Stephens investment house in Little Rock, the largest bond firm outside of Wall Street, which had financed Orval Faubus' political machine. In the 1990 Gubernatorial race, a dozen different Stephens-owned companies wrote checks for the maximum amount allowed—$1,000—and chipped in $5,000 for television ads which helped Clinton defeat Republican challenger Sheffield Nelson, with whom the Stephens' had a bitter business feud.[33]

Stephens was Clinton's second biggest contributor over his political career. He rescued Clinton after his unexpected defeat in the 1992 New Hampshire Democratic Primary, providing him with a $3.5 million dollar line of credit through Worthen Bank, which Stephens owned.[34] A redacted FBI report from 1998 describes Stephens as having "lengthy and continuing ties to the Clinton administration and associates" and also discusses allegations that Stephens had been involved in the "illegal handling of campaign contributions to the Democratic National Party."[35]

The Stephens' got a lot in return for their investment in Clinton—the firm was involved with 61 percent of the $7 billion worth of bonds issued by the state of Arkansas during the 1980s, more than any other underwriter.[36] Jackson Stephens' billlion dollar data mining company, Acxiom, whose board of directors reflected Stephens' close ties to the Democratic Party, continued rolling in sensitive government contracts after Clinton became president.[37]

In 1988, Stephens Inc. provided a $100 million equity investment to facilitate the acquisition of Holly Farms by Tyson Chicken, which marked the beginning of the large-scale consolidation of the chicken-processing industry. Tyson's CEO Don Tyson, had been a big-time Clinton donor since the late 1970s who would deliver cash-filled envelopes to the Governor's mansion.[38] The investment paid off as Tysons's profits shot up from $18.1 million in 1984 to over $200 million by 1994.[39] When Clinton became president, the agricultural department bypassed Tyson's 66 chicken processing plants when it tightened environmental regulations. Millions were also authorized by the federal aviation administration for a Northwest Arkansas regional airport, whose prime purpose was to help Tyson ferry its chickens to Japan.[40]

In 1970, Stephens Inc. raised $4.95 million in an initial public offering (IPO) for a small Arkansas-based discount retailer, Walmart Stores Inc. which by the 1980s became one of the largest retailers in the world.[41] Walmart's founder, Sam Walton, was a life-long Republican but felt compelled to write a letter to Walmart corporate managers in November 1991 asking them to support Clinton for President, saying that Bill was a "good friend and supporter." In spring 1984, Walton had been an honored guest at a luncheon at the Governor's mansion, where Clinton encouraged his purchase of a local garment maker's clothes and helped lay the groundwork for Walmart's "Buy America" program, which aimed to pressure American manufacturers to lower their prices to better compete with foreign competition.

Through this program, Walmart converted around $1 billion of purchases from imported goods to products made in the USA from 1984–1988 alone. In fall 1985, Walton appointed Hillary Clinton to Walmart's Board after working with her on an educational reform initiative establishing teacher competency standards, which he felt would spur investment and economic growth in the state. Walmart at the time was a client of Hillary's Rose Law Firm. According to *The New York Times,* Hillary promoted female advancement and more eco-friendly stores, though stood silent about Walmart's low wage and anti-union policies, which benefitted from Arkansas' status as a "right to work" state—something Bill had supported from the beginning of his political career in 1976. In 1988, Arkansas State Senator Jay Bradford criticized Walmart for paying its employees so little that they had to turn to the state for welfare.[42]

Turning on McGovern

In the fall of 1970, Clinton says that he "missed about half of my law school" campaigning for Joe Duffey for a Senate seat in Connecticut against incumbent Thomas J. Dodd, a Vietnam war hawk. Clinton stated that "there were so many of us who were drawn to [Duffey's] deep commitment to peace, economic fairness, and civil rights."[43] Two years later, Clinton served as regional coordinator in Waco, Texas for the presidential campaign of George S. McGovern—one of the most liberal men to ever contend for the presidency, who ran on a "come home America" platform. *Rolling Stone* correspondent Hunter S. Thompson recalled twenty years after the election that "some dingbat named Clinton" had been "almost single-handedly [held] responsible for losing 222 counties in Texas," including Waco, and was "terminated without pay, with prejudice, and sent back to Arkansas with his tail between his legs," as an aide put it.[44]

Afterwards, Clinton publicly disassociated himself from McGovern and the liberal wing of the Democratic Party. He stated that "the average person watching [the elections] on TV in some small town in Arkansas, the kind of person who is the backbone of my support there, had the unsettling feeling that this campaign and this man did not have a core, a center that was common to the great majority of the country."[45] Bill's classmate Nancy Bekavac said that deep in his bones, Clinton had learned from the McGovern campaign that "the age of the [New Deal] titans" had passed.[46]

Claiming that the 1960s movements had been "unstable" and "irrational," Clinton advocated for economic austerity in his first run for Congress, even though his opponent John Hammerschmidt attacked him for his supposedly "radical left wing philosophy."[47] Clinton said that "we need a congressman who's not afraid to say no to the unnecessary government spending that has hurt the economy of the country."[48] After being sworn in as Arkansas' fortieth governor on January 9, 1979, Clinton repeated the same conservative theme, pledging to "diminish" the "waste in government operations" and also speaking about the "limits of what government can do."[49]

Roger Morris wrote that in Clinton's first two years as Governor:

> there were many promised changes and little true change, new budgets that ended with old priorities, heralded policy innovations never quite sustained, seemingly ambitious legislation yet no authentic challenge of the established regime, record numbers of women and minorities appointed to offices, boards and commissions, but much the same resulting governance. There were alliances abandoned or betrayed, enemies accommodated. There were seemingly constant Clinton appearances and consultations with national organizations yet scant impact on the life of ordinary people in the state.[50]

Clinton's conservatism was evident in his backing a constitutional amendment to give tax breaks to utilities. He also came out against exemption of food and prescription medicine from the sales tax, opposed gun control, and buckled to the pressure of the logging industry that got away with clear-cutting forests, and trucking industry lobbyists and its allies like Tyson Chicken which pushed motorists to pay for highway improvements by increasing the price of car tags.[51]

When Cuban boat refugees held in an emergency holding pen at Ft. Chaffee protested against their confinement and rioted in May 1980, the boyish Governor activated the National Guard and beefed-up security at the base to "protect" local citizens, giving orders that "if somebody has to die, it'd better be a Cuban." Fearing the reaction of armed nativist locals in the small town of Barling, Clinton also vowed to prevent any more Cubans from landing on Arkansas soil, declaring loudly that he would defy the federal government "even if they bring the whole United States army down here." Paul Green of the *Arkansas Democrat-Gazette* described his actions as a "credible imitation of Orval Faubus," the infamous pro-segregation Governor and anti-hero of the civil rights movement.[52]

Clinton's Deal with the Devil

When he ran for reelection in 1982, Clinton went to business leaders and apologized to them for overtaxing them and persuaded them he would never again obstruct their economic schemes.[53] He then raised $1.6 million—a fortune in Arkansas at that time.[54] A colleague marked the period from 1980–1982 as a turning point in which Clinton lost any idealism and guts he might have possessed and decided he'd "do whatever necessary to get elected and stay elected. He made his deal with the devil."[55]

The devil included Tyson—who had boasted about shifting his campaign contributions in 1980 after Clinton failed to follow through on a promise to raise the ceiling on the weight that a poultry truck may bear over state roads—and Dan Lasater, a bond trader and owner of a chain of steakhouses, thoroughbreds and a ski lodge thought to be drug smuggling front whose ties with Clinton enabled him to become a multi-millionaire.[56]

Mastering how the game of politics is played, Clinton's political machine secured the loyalty of most local media, judges, prosecutors, and law enforcement personnel.[57] Journalist Ian Tyrrell wrote that

> assisted by the innovative commissions and agencies that his brand of progressive politics government prescribes, Clinton soon had as much power as an urban machine boss. What is more, he had the sweet reputation of being progressive in the tradition of, say, Woodrow Wilson. No Mayor Daley or Boss Tweed could have imagined such a dispensation.[58]

Nor did Mayor Daley and Boss Tweed have a counterpart to Hillary Rodham Clinton, a master at public relations who effectively managed her husband's every move and used her position as a partner at the prestigious Rose Law Firm to cultivate support for him among Arkansas' economic elite. As part of the quid pro quo, Hillary appointed many of the regulators and judges that wound up favoring the clients of her employer, who donated money to her husband's campaign.[59]

By the mid-1980s, the Clintons together had compiled the most impressive list of corporate donors in Arkansas' political history. They included Union Pacific, Pepsi-Cola, Coca-Cola, Weyerhauser (timber company), Walmart, TCBY Yogurt, Worthen Bank (the state's largest), Arkansas Power & Light, Acxiom, one of the world's largest collector of consumer data, American Express, Merrill Lynch, Drexel Burnham, Reynolds Metals, and Solomon Brothers. Clinton furthermore secured the support of the Democratic Party's top fundraiser, Pamela Harriman, the husband of Averell Harriman, a son of one of the original "robber barons" and leading architect of U.S. foreign policy during the Cold War.[60]

A former U.S. Attorney who watched the FBI's tracking of organized crime figures, stated that the 1984 election was "the election when the mob really came into Arkansas politics, the dog-track and race-track boys, the payoff people who saw a good thing.... It wasn't just Bill Clinton and it went beyond our old Dixie mafia, which was penny-ante by comparison. This was eastern and West Coast crime money that noticed the possibilities just like the legitimate corporations did." Local money passed under the table as never before. "If you wanted to sit on the Highway Commission or the Fish and Game Commission or another commission, well it would cost, and that's how they laundered money," former state party official and Clinton fund-raiser Bert Dickey admitted.[61]

Liking the Good Ol' Boys Best

Clinton's rating as the nation's most effective governor was based largely on the fact that the state's economy expanded by 29 percent during Clinton's term, five times ahead of the national rate. Between 1985 and 1989, while the percentage of manufacturing jobs in the nation grew by only 0.3%, Clinton claimed that Arkansas experienced an increase of 10.2%. From 1979 to 1987, there was also a 77% increase in the number of Arkansas companies which exported products.[62]

Clinton was a natural salesman who promoted Arkansas businesses abroad—he set up Arkansas development offices in Brussels and Tokyo and led the state's first trade mission to Taiwan, which led to the purchase of over $30 million of Arkansas soybeans. When the Sanyo Company planned to close its television-assembly plant in the Arkansas Delta, where unemployment was above 10%, Clinton flew to Japan and got the president of Sanyo to agree to keep the plant open in exchange for Wal-Mart selling Sanyo's televisions.[63]

While Clinton embraced many innovative programs, including an Israeli one that taught parents of 4,500 low income families how to read and teach their pre-school children, on too many issues Clinton caved to the special interests.[64] One of Clinton's signature policies was a welfare to work program that led to 6,000 Arkansans being denied food stamps and another 500 seeing reductions in their already meager welfare benefits, just in Clinton's first term.[65] As part of the program, the Arkansas welfare office gave its women clients a questionnaire that asked about their sexual partners.[66]

Despite its reputation as an educational reformer, Arkansas continued to rank near the bottom in teachers' pay and spending per pupil in the nation at the end of Clinton's governorship.[67] During his 1992 presidential campaign, Clinton bragged that Arkansas had the second lowest tax rate in the country—above only Mississippi; the tax burden (Arkansans paid $1,191 per capita yearly in state and local taxes compared to the national average of $1,888) was the same in 1992 as it was when Clinton first became governor in 1979.[68] There was a heavy reliance on sales and food taxes that were designed to offset a huge tax break for industrial corporations Clinton passed in 1985. Families earning less than $9,000 a year paid nearly four times more in state tax proportionately than families making over $600,000.[69]

In the wake of the 1970s energy crisis, Clinton created a new state department of energy to be endowed with broad powers of conservation, development and inspection, but then watched timorously as the authority of the new office was crippled by the utility lobby of the giant Arkansas Power & Light (AP &L), some of whose major shareholders and partners were among his wealthiest backers. A journalist familiar with the Grand Gulf episode, in which Clinton at first endorsed censure of AP&L for gouging Arkansas rate payers to build a nuclear power plant in Mississippi but then backed off, wrote that "Clinton did like to be seen fighting the utilities. He just liked the good ole boys of AP&L, and their contributions a lot better."[70]

Offering Up the Public Commons

During his fourth term, Clinton faced a lawsuit from the Sierra Club and Arkansas Wildlife Federation by signing legislation authorizing testing and exploratory drilling for diamonds in Crater of Diamonds State Park in the Ouachita Mountains. His decision followed lobbying by mining magnate Jean Raymond Boulle, who located his new company, Diamond Fields, in Hope, Clinton's hometown. The area Clinton allowed to be mined—the nation's only public diamond mine—had been designated one of the world's most significant natural areas by the International Union for the Conservation of Nature.

Stephens Inc. happened to be a stakeholder in Boulle's company, while another major investor, Sanford Robertson, gave hundreds of thousands of dollars to Democratic Party causes and hosted fundraisers for Clinton. Hillary wore a ring bearing a 3.5 carat diamond mined by Diamond Fields at the Crater of Diamonds State Park at the first presidential inaugural ball.[71] Journalist Jeffrey St. Clair wrote that the sleazy backroom deal with Boulle, who had been introduced to Clinton by Tyson Attorney James Blair, "set a pattern that Clinton would mercilessly pursue as president where the public commons was quietly offered up for exploitation by private enterprises with financial ties to the administration."[72]

For a time, Governor Clinton had tried to promote small businesses in Arkansas, but dropped this in favor of industrial concessions and bond promotion for brokerage houses, developers and corporations who donated generously to his campaigns.[73] Minimum wage increases were paltry and workers compensation benefits—$226.11 per week—remained below poverty levels for a family of four.[74] Though keeping some businesses in the state, heavy tax breaks prevented the collection of millions of dollars in potential taxes and forced the legislature to enact budgetary cuts to state services.[75]

Slick Willie—Liberal Counterpart to Tricky Dick

When Clinton passed an ethics bill—which he termed "a big step forward in the quality of government in Arkansas"—the governor's office characteristically was excluded.[76] Clinton's corruption was apparent in his protection of Witt Stephens after his Worthen Bank lost $52 million in state tax receipts by investing it in an unscrupulous churning operation in New Jersey (in Arkansas, only the governor had the authority to convene a Grand Jury).[77] Clinton also repeatedly reappointed a corrupt state medical examiner, Fahmy Malak, who had helped cover up for his mother in June 1981 after she botched the transfer of oxygen tubes on a 17 year-old patient, Susan Deer, while working as a nurse at Ouachita Medical hospital, resulting in Deer's death. Malak thereafter repeatedly protected Arkansas' old boy network by filing false reports.[78]

To win votes in the black community, Clinton's machine paid off black ministers charged with making sure black voters reached the polling booths. A reporter caught Clinton's brother, Roger, on camera asking "big brother" to do a favor for a friend of his by fixing a county commissioner's board to ensure that he got a sewer permit for condominiums that he was building after Roger was paid a $30,000 bribe and offered a well-paying job.[79]

Thousands of Canadians were infected with hepatitis and HIV during Clinton's governorship after Arkansas prisoners had been allowed to sell them their blood, which had not been properly screened.[80] Inmates who paid bribes for the right to sell blood were paid by corrupt prison authorities—not with cash but with drugs. Despite media attention and subsequent investigations, the program for selling Arkansas' inmates' blood was allowed to continue for the last three years of Clinton's governorship.[81] The president of the company that brokered the tainted blood, Leonard Dunn of Health Management Associates, was close to Clinton and worked on Clinton's 1990 gubernatorial campaign.[82] Whistleblowers and journalists who tried to expose the truth about this case were threatened, fitting a wider pattern.[83]

Clinton's adoption of Nixonian tactics was guided often by Hillary, "a cool and hardened political operative," according to contemporaries, who was "the take-charge alpha of the Clintons," according to Roger Stone and Robert Morrow.[84] A domineering woman with a history of domestic violence towards Bill, Hillary had worked as a young lawyer on the Watergate prosecutions and learned from the master at political dirty tricks.[85] According to Barbara Olson, chief counsel for the House Oversight Committee that investigated an assortment of Clinton scandals, Hillary inverted Nixon's charge of a vast left-wing conspiracy (those exposing Clinton's crimes were said to be part of a "vast right-wing conspiracy"), and skillfully used an arsenal of "opposition researchers and private detectives," that her mentor Dick Morris identified as "secret police," in a systematic campaign to "intimidate, frighten, threaten, discredit and punish" any perceived opponents of the Clintons. According to Morris, these were mostly "innocent Americans whose only misdeed is their desire to tell the truth."[86]

A Law and Order Man

With Hillary by his side, Governor Clinton combined neoliberal austerity measures with tough law and order policies fueling mass incarceration. Arkansas's incarceration rate increased by 100 percent between 1982 and 1992, though the operating cost of Arkansas' prisons was kept the lowest in the nation.[87] In an April 1990 letter to J. Bill Becker, the head of Arkansas' AFL-CIO branch, Clinton bragged about doubling the number of prison beds during his governorship and increasing sentencing, stating that people "go to jail in Arkansas for an average time far above the national average."[88]

The state's juvenile justice and adult corrections systems were described as "nightmarish."[89] *The Arkansas Gazette* reported in April 1987 that the Department of Corrections needed $3.5 million more than the state legislature had given them that year, causing jail overcrowding and a backlog in the ability to serve arrest warrants—since there was nowhere to take people that were arrested. Sherriff Dale Madden of Prairie County said, "we've worked ourselves into a situation where we're making a mockery of our system of justice."[90]

Jessica Mitford, author of an exposé of the American prison system and an old friend of Hillary Clinton, stated after visiting Little Rock in the early 1980s, that Governor Clinton was "too preoccupied with his own ambitions to care about prison reform."[91] Arkansas State trooper L.D. Brown wrote that as governor, Clinton "never lifted a finger to reform the prison system," and that "when he left office, the same prison officials were in power [as when Clinton started]."[92] Among them was Art Lockhart, head of the Arkansas

Department of Corrections from 1981–1992, who used a disciplinary measure known as "Texas TV," that involved an inmate standing two feet from a wall or fence and leaning his forehead or nose against the wall or fence for extended periods, sometimes for hours.[93]

Clinton's support for harsh measures was apparent in his championing military style boot camps for first time drug offenders and support for a state tradition in which all new inmates at the state penitentiary were assigned to the "hoe squad," in which they had to manually hoe the state prison farm. As Arkansas attorney general, Clinton helped in the adoption of a habitual offender law that required mandatory minimum sentences for individuals previously convicted of a felony, and in 1983 as governor he signed legislation strengthening that law.[94]

In 1998, the state of Arkansas was sued over a police program Clinton had defended that used racial profiling against Hispanics.[95] When Clinton had to make a call on the death penalty, he allowed it to go forward three times, and then on the eve of his presidential election, traveled back to the state to sign off on the execution of a mentally ill cop killer, Rickey Ray Rector, who was so dysfunctional that he was given to howling and asked guards at his last meal to save his pie for later.[96] Less then two years later, Clinton signed into law one of the harshest crime laws in the history of the country, which allocated nearly $10 billion for the construction of new prisons, expanded death penalty eligible federal crimes, introduced a "three strikes law" that gave mandatory life sentences for third offenses, and allowed children as young as thirteen to be tried as adults.[97]

Despite his hippie veneer, Governor Clinton was a strong supporter of the War on Drugs. Penalties for drug trafficking offenses were strengthened during his governorship, and Clinton doubled the number of personnel involved in efforts to stop illegal drug use in Arkansas. Clinton further enacted a program with the Arkansas state police in which random stops were made of suspicious vehicles on state highways in an effort to seize drugs.

In November 1989, Clinton bragged to a civil servant, Mary Lingo, that Arkansas was ranked in the top five states in the country in the value of drugs seized, and said that he was working diligently to challenge a Supreme Court ruling that restricted his anti-drug policies. Clinton also told Lingo that he had requested and received permission to use the Arkansas National Guard in an effort to wipe out drugs in Arkansas and that Arkansas National Guard helicopters flew thousands of hours of missions to spot marijuana crops and destroy them.[98] The marijuana eradication campaign resulted in the destruction of 75,000 marijuana plants in 1990 and one million plants overall valued at around $1 billion.[99]

In May 1991, Clinton requested from the Pentagon the donation of C-26 aircraft for his drug interdiction program, which was popular among Arkansans.[100] Mary Lingo, in an exchange with Clinton, blamed politicians for "appeasing the criminal element in society," and said that Clinton's new drug czar should hire special forces veterans to go after pushers. Claiming that the American Civil Liberties Union (ACLU) and Supreme Court had sold the country out, Lingo asked: "What is wrong with using some flamethrowers on the grass plants located." She added: "if we can't use the military to wage war against an enemy within, then something is very wrong."[101]

Clinton's Governorship Bested by Bumpers

Though hampered by federal budget cuts, Clinton's record as governor did not ultimately match that of Dale Bumpers (1971–1975), who has been judged Arkansas' best 20th century governor.[102] Bumpers effectively reorganized the government and, while known as a deficit hawk, convinced the legislature to raise the income tax for the first time since 1957. This enabled him to finance education reforms and accelerate funding of higher education and rural health care, including in the impoverished Delta region bordering Mississippi, resulting in the reduction of the death rate of black infants by 50 percent between 1970 and 1975. Bumpers further tapped into a growing environmental consciousness by awarding the state parks system a record $22.5 million to finance improvements and expansion.

Under Clinton, Arkansas' economy remained mired in a "low wage, low skill trap," ranking near the bottom of the country in annual pay, income distribution, joblessness, health care and poverty, with infant mortality reaching third world levels. Arkansas further ranked last in worker safety, and was one of only two states without a civil rights law.[103] Journalist Meredith Oakley wrote that by the end of Clinton's governorship, "the state's median income was still near the bottom, with a full 20 percent of the population living below the national poverty line, yet the state was financing the governor and his family to the tune of almost $800,000 per year."[104]

The proliferation of corruption was evident in the area of bond trading, where securities fraud in Arkansas was estimated to be the highest in the nation.[105] An IRS audit of 11 Arkansas businesses found only 1 to have followed laws on reporting cash sales involving $10,000 or more; one business had $123,000 in unreported cash sales.[106]

Despite Clinton's reputation as the first "black president," the black unemployment rate during his governorship peaked at 17.5%.—higher than in most southern states.[107] The number of black farm-owners also fell by nearly forty percent.[108] The state's Medicaid program went bankrupt under

Clinton and required a financial bail-out.[109] Clinton did little to reform a scandalous child welfare system, which was subject to a class action lawsuit in 1991 for abuses in foster homes and constituted what a witness called a "silence and stench one can't forget."[110]

"Reminiscent of What Reagan Is Doing"

Many of the state's labor leaders felt that Clinton had betrayed them by supporting the right to work law and by siding with management in strikes such as at a minority owned auto-parts plant in Conway County, Morrilton Plastics, where his administration gave out a $300,000 loan guarantee to build up inventory against an expected strike. Arkansas' AFL-CIO president J. Bill Becker said that "almost any [Clinton] activity, in so far as our folks are concerned, is reminiscent of what Reagan is doing to us," the main difference being that Clinton would first "pat you on the back and then piss on your leg."[111] Becker recalled an incident in 1983 when Clinton had promised him that he would provide a tax rebate for poor and working class people after proposing a one percent increase in the food tax to pay for educational reforms. However, when the bill went to the state senate, Clinton reneged and dropped the exemption, something Becker said he "would never forget, as long as he lived."[112]

In April 1992, Becker wrote to Clinton to tell him how much he resented his administration's continued marketing of Arkansas as a non-union environment and low-wage "right to work" state in order to lure industry to Arkansas—something Clinton had claimed in his 1990 gubernatorial campaign that he had stopped doing.[113] In April 1990, a group of AFL-CIO convention members drew up a resolution condemning Clinton for "deceiving us with broken promises of support for worker's compensation, right to know and other beneficial legislation. (He has) tricked us on taxes and has further rigged the tax system against workers with more special interest exemptions and loopholes."[114]

The poultry industry during Clinton's tenure kept its workers in near indentured servitude, journalist Norman Solomon wrote, "working its underpaid, frequently injured workers at an extraordinary pace," while "discharging half a million tons of chicken shit into Arkansas rivers every year." The latter resulted in an abundance of sick wildlife and dead fish and the spread of blood disorders in Arkansan children and increased risk of cancer. Tyson's cash donations got him $12 million in state tax breaks—contingent in part on his creation of over 4,000 new jobs—and what Charles Lewis of the Center for Public Integrity called "laggard and unaggressive enforcement of environmental regulations," with even the state inspection laboratory falling under the control of poultry producers.[115]

The Arkansas Department of Pollution and Ecology found in 1990 that 94 percent of Arkansas waterways were unusable for swimming and fishing because they were filled with chicken waste. One town was even declared a disaster area.[116] While Clinton initiated solid-waste recycling and reduction,[117] the state ranked near last in environmental indicators during his governorship.

Beginning in his first term, Clinton worked to revitalize the development of coal in Western Arkansas. Jacksonville—the site of Hercules Inc., which produced the two components of Agent Orange—was listed by the EPA as one of the worst sites of dioxin contamination in the country.[118] Chuck Creeman, the Director of the Arkansas Sierra Club, told *The Washington Post* that Clinton "constantly sided with industry, either through appointments to the pollution and ecology commission or his decisions on toxic waste burn sites and the rights of poultry processors versus the rights of residents whose drinking water was polluted."[119]

Clinton continued to side with industry as president where he did more damage to the envirnoment than either Reagan or Bush, according to former Sierra Club Director David Bowers.[120] Blatant cronyism was evident in President Clinton's championing natural gas when his chief of staff, Thomas F. "Mack" McLarty III, had been head of the Arkansas-Louisiana Natural Gas Company formerly owned by Witt and Jack Stephens.[121] The main beneficiary of the privatization of a California oil field that was the source of the 1920s Teapot Dome Scandal, Occidental Petroleum, gave $50,000 in 1996 for Clinton's reelection. Vice president Al Gore Jr. owned $1 million of stock in the company, whose founder Armand Hammer had bankrolled Al Gore Sr.'s political career.[122]

A Pro-Military Orientation

Clinton's pro-military disposition was evident in his deployment of the Arkansas National Guard to assist the U.S. Southern Command during the December 1989–January 1990 Operation Just Cause—the invasion of Panama to oust Manuel Noriega, a dictator accused of drug trafficking who had close ties in the past to U.S. intelligence.[123] Clinton also supported the Contra War (see next chapter) and hosted a major welcome home celebration for veterans of Operation Desert Storm in Iraq, a war that Clinton supported.[124] Clinton further spoke at a dedication ceremony of a General Dynamics plant in Camden, Arkansas, which produced Sparrow missiles for the U.S. Navy.[125]

Military Loans, "Pinstripe Patronage" and Money Laundering

Clinton's chief economic development agency, the Arkansas Development Finance Authority (ADFA), issued bonds of more than $700 million and claimed to have created twenty-seven hundred jobs in Arkansas. However, most of the new wages were well below the national standard (the average salary was only $15,000 per year) and the number of jobs (averaging less than 400 per year) was well below the ninety thousand produced by Orval Faubus' Arkansas Industrial Development Commission (AIDC) over nine years with no bonding power.

The real beneficiaries were Clinton's campaign donors and Arkansas' financial elite. ADFA records show investments in Tyson Foods totaling $6,900,000 in Berryville and over $45 million in 1990 and 1991 in Arkansas Power & Light.[126] Roger Morris writes that ADFA was a "bonanza for Lasater and company as well as for Stephens, Goldman, Sachs and other large financial houses" while providing what *U.S. News* would call "pinstripe patronage" and "insider lending for a number of smaller, lesser known Arkansas companies whose chief distinction was often a tie to partners in the Rose firm, the owners' contributions to Clinton, or both."[127]

In the 1990 Gubernatorial race, the *L.A. Times* reported that beneficiaries of ADFA business contributed $400,300 to the Clinton campaign—nearly 20 percent of the total amount Clinton raised to fend off Republican Sheffield Nelson.[128] The ADFA's 10-person board was appointed by Clinton himself, which made it possible for corrupt or insider deals to go forward. At least two appointees were from Stephens Inc., which made three to five million in bond underwriting fees between 1985 and 1991 and received ADFA loans for companies that it had invested in. Stephens was part owner of Beverly Enterprises, the country's largest operator of nursing homes, which received an $83 million ADFA loan at a time its stock was being hammered by the company's persistent losses.[129]

Dan Lasater had written at least eight letters to Clinton recommending people for the ADFA's board, most of whom were appointed. His company underwrote fourteen of the agency's bond issues entirely or in part, earning $649 million from the transactions.[130] Documents made public during the Whitewater hearings showed that Llama, an Arkansas investment bank set up by Alice Walton, the heir of the Walmart fortune, was another key firm tapped by the ADFA to underwrite the bonds it issued.[131]

The legislation creating the ADFA significantly prohibited it from using the state's public auditors. On four occasions, the ADFA board approved loans in spite of its own staff's recommendations against them. In three of the four cases, the companies were owned by people who were friends of board members. Many of the ADFA contracts were deals worked through the Rose Law Firm, which made at least $175,000 in the arrangement. Park-O-Meter (POM), which established the world's first parking meters, received a $2.75 million ADFA bond issue in 1985: Webb Hubbell, the son-in-law of POM president Seth Ward and its lawyer, was a Rose Law Firm partner and ADFA board member whom Governor Clinton subsequently named to the Arkansas Supreme Court; in 1993, he became associate attorney general of the U.S.[132]

According to whistleblower Michael Riconoscuito, in 1981 POM began producing external fuel canisters designed to fuel long range transport missions on C-130s, and used an ADFA loan to build 500 M-16 bolt and carrier assemblies in conjunction with the Iver Johnson arms company for transport to the Nicaraguan Contras, counterrevolutionaries funded by the CIA seeking the overthrow of the socialist Sandinista government.[133] Seth Ward Jr. told *The Nation* magazine that POM instead made re-entry nose cones for the nuclear warheads on the M-X missile and nozzles for rocket engines, and had contracts with McDonnel Douglas to make aircraft parts.[134] Either way, it was involved in military contracting.

ADFA loans went to additional military contractors like Missouri Research Labs Inc. (MRL) in the northeast corner of Arkansas, which produced untraceable circuit boards and critical electronic components used in Stinger-missile guidance systems being made for the CIA. Another loan recippient, Arkansas Systems, which exported encrypted computer software and hardware to foreign banks, may have enabled U.S. intelligence or other parties to spy on financial transactions and been used to facilitate financial crimes and money laundering.[135]

In December 1988, the ADFA raised $50 million ostensibly for the purpose of building and laying houses for the needy of Arkansas, but instead invested the money with Fuji Bank in Grand Cayman Islands and made a profit of $1 million, which it may or may not have spent.[136] Other bonds were sold to shell companies and out of state banks based in money laundering havens like Barbados or that were affiliated with the Bank of Credit and Commerce International (BCCI), a money laundering haven used for CIA operations brought into the U.S. by Witt Stephens through his firm, Systematics. In at least one case, the shell companies' stocks were not registered under U.S. securities law or approved by the U.S. Securities and exchange commission. The company, Coral Reinsurance, was a subsidiary of American International Group (AIG), a $30 billion multinational company based in New York.[137]

It was never properly explained where the money for ADFA loans came from, as the state budget had little to no money set aside for ADFA and many of the loans were never paid back. A 1988 audit by the Deloitte and Touche accounting firm found funds of unknown origins. It also found that records from the Coral Reinsurance case were lost and that money for that investment was borrowed from the Chicago branch of Sanwa Bank headquartered in Japan.[138]

Former ADFA marketing director Larry Nichols said he discovered two sets of accounting books, a classic sign of fraud.[139] Nichols told author Rodney Stich that "tthere was virtually no accounting of the money received by the ADFA, or the repayments of the loans. He said that money would appear in a particular account and suddenly disappear, a technique that IRS investigator William Duncan said was "a zero-balance tactic commonly used in drug-money laundering."[140]

Neophyte Investor Hillary's Cattle Trading Bonanza

During Clinton's first term as Governor, Hillary appears to have been involved in an illicit pay to play scheme involving cattle futures trading that enabled the Tyson Chicken Dynasty to give the Clintons in excess of $100,000 in campaign donations. The scheme was orchestrated by Tyson's principal outside council, James Blair, a Clinton friend, who set Hillary up with a $1,000 investment that yielded a dividend of over $100,000. The original investment was recorded as $12,000 from the records of the Chicago Mercantile Exchange, but Clinton only had $1,000 in her account at the time. Despite her claims of actively managing her own account, on the three days when the trading was most active, she was involved in an all-day meeting out of town. Blair's partner in the operation, Robert L. "Red" Bone was at the time under investigation for fraud in manipulation of the cattle trading market.

Roger Morris notes that Clinton's "spectacular 10,000 percent return on her investment" had all the trappings of being part of "prearranged trades." An expert wrote that there is "no way a commodities trader or broker would permit a novice speculator to control $280,000 worth of cattle with $1,000, unless a friend or partner guaranteed her investment. If they did, that would amount to a payoff." Another Dow Jones analyst said that the odds of a neophyte like Hillary winning that kind of money fairly would "have been about the same as those finding the Dead Sea Scrolls on the steps of the State House in Little Rock." Hillary's $100,000 hit was "a money transfer disguised as commodity profits." If "she had allowed Blair and Red Bone to allocate other customers winnings to her accounts and to park her losses in those others, then she had committed the ultimate fraud."[141]

The Whitewater Affair: "Screwing People Left and Right"

In 1978, Bill invested with James McDougal in 200 acres of land in the Ozarks of Northwestern Arkansas known as Whitewater. Originally owned by International Paper, the land was supposed to be used to develop vacation homes and as a "Camp David" retreat for Arkansas politicians.[142] Describing him as a "country boy charmer with a sharp mind," McDougal had taken Clinton under his wing when both worked for Senator William F. Fulbright and served as his political fundraiser, banker, and senior aide during his first Gubernatorial term.

In 1979, the young Governor Clinton had eased restrictions on clear cutting of forests and granted permission to International Paper to do wholesale clear cutting on the Whitewater land, enabling the building of the vacation homes. Clinton also gave International Paper a multi-million dollar tax break.[143] In addition, he used the governor's office to secure taxpayer funds for the construction of a miles long access road from highway 101 (dubbed by critics the "road to nowhere") to a remote mountain retreat on Whitewater lands, which helped increase the potential return on his investment.[144] In return for their support in building the road, the Game and Fish Commission received a quiet donation of a riverfront lot near Whitewater estates for a boat ramp. Clinton fired the fishing and highway commissioners and put two loyal servants in place of the "old fogies" running those agencies who opposed Clinton's scheme.[145]

Numerous Whitewater investors lost their life savings because of trickery by the Whitewater Corporation; the company refused to extend the mortgage and then seized the property of grain elevator operator Clyde Soapes Jr., for example, who fell ill with diabetes and was only $2,500 away from full ownership. A local businessman said that "they screwed people left and right ... taking advantage of a bunch of poor old folks on a land deal.... The future President and First Lady."[146]

The Whitewater Company and Clintons were accused of misreporting their revenue—over $100,000–$150,000—and defrauding the IRS. Clinton was also accused of pressuring the Arkansas small loans administration office to make small business loans to help get bad loans off Whitewater's books, and appointed Beverly Basset Schaffer to head the Arkansas Security Commission, which granted McDougal special favors.[147]

Nicknamed "Diamond Jim" because of his flamboyance, McDougal alleges in his memoirs that he channeled money to Clinton's campaign by having an intermediary contractor pad his monthly bill for maintenance repairs, and that Clinton did him favors like transferring an inspector who refused to grant septic tank permits on his properties and appointing the president of Madison Guaranty, a Savings and Loan (S&L) bank in which he gained a controlling interest in 1982—to the state's S&L board.[148]

As part of the quid pro quo, "Diamond Jim" and his wife, "hot-pants Susan"—with whom, typically, Clinton had an affair—hosted a fundraiser at the Art Deco headquarters of Madison to help pay off Clinton's 1984 campaign debt. Roger Morris noted that some of the donations were attributed to "phantom contributors" and that "an examination of Madison's books would show suspicious movements of cash—inflated closing costs, commissions, and transfers—coinciding with the final free-spending weeks of the Clinton's 1984 run."[149]

A federal investigation found evidence of at least $60,500 siphoned from Madison Guaranty to Clinton's 1984 reelection campaign. The governor's official campaign committee was named in Justice Department criminal investigative documents as an alleged co-conspirator in the diversion of depositors' funds. It was believed that Madison amounted to a "veritable slush fund" for the Clintons' land business as well as an alleged kitty and counting-house for their reelection campaigns.[150] Government regulators noticed that Whitewater was making loan payments to Clinton when its accounts at Madison were overdrawn and the overdrafts were covered by a Madison subsidiary—a classic sign of S&L fraud.[151]

McDougal also recounted episodes where Clinton came to him begging for loans and said that he bought land from a Democratic Party municipal judge in Little Rock, David Hale, for hundreds of thousands of dollars more than the land was worth, enabling Hale to provide a $300,000 loan to Susan McDougal. The loan—which was never repaid and cost taxpayers $672,000—appears to have been in part an illegal campaign contribution or bribe.[152] Clinton passed an ethics law in Arkansas that protected he and Hillary from having to publicly disclose their Ozark Mountain and Madison Guaranty deals. McDougal was eventually indicted on eighteen counts of fraud in U.S. District Court after federal regulators seized Madison Guaranty; Bill and Hillary then committed perjury at the trial and McDougal was convicted, subsequently dying in jail in 1997 of a heart attack at the age of 57.

Calling himself "Bill Clinton's Brutus," McDougal wrote that the pain of his association with the Clintons would "never go away."[153] During the 1992 campaign, he said he was "damn near nauseated" by the "show of sanctimony" of the Clintons. "They were like a tornado who came into people's lives" and "destroyed them"; they "took without giving back in return." Bill was immensely likeable but never took principled stands politically and "milked [his friends] for what they were worth . . . when their usefulness wore out, he disposed of them."[154]

Arkansas—A Prelude to Clinton's Presidency

In his classic 1968 book *The Drugstore Liberal,* journalist Robert Sherrill details the betrayal of liberal ideals by Hubert Humphrey, LBJ's Vice President and the 1968 Democratic Party nominee for president. While Mayor of Minneapolis in the 1940s, Humphrey led the purge of leftists in the Farmer-Labor Party after it merged with the Democratic Party and went on to support the anticommunist witch-hunts of the era—through the legal system. As a U.S. Senator and Vice-President, Humphrey sustained his ties with corrupt union bosses who sold out labors' rank and file and supported an aggressive anticommunist foreign policy and the war in Vietnam.[155]

By Clinton's standards, Humphrey, whom Hunter S. Thompson called "treacherous" and a "shallow, contemptible and hopelessly dishonest old hack,"[156] was actually progressive. After all, Humphrey supported organized labor, the New Deal, and a full employment bill (the Humphrey-Hawkins Act). Clinton by contrast worked to roll back core New Deal programs, adopted right-wing rhetoric valorizing personal responsibility and attacking welfare mothers, and betrayed the unions, while promoting draconian crime control measures.

Clinton's trademark policies were first rolled out during his tenure as governor of Arkansas, which should be seen as a bellweather of U.S. politics in the second Gilded Age. This period saw the triumph of money and politics and the restoration of unfettered capitalism as the political left withered and declined, and the idealism of the 1960s receded. Cronyism, corruption and elite deviance further became the norm. The White House under Clinton became "like a subway: you have to put in coins to open the gate," to quote Taiwanese-born lobbyist Johnny Chung.[157] Journalist Gleen Greenwald wrote that Clinton helped turn "the Democratic Party from one of the working class to one of Wall Street, Silicon Valley, banks, credit card companies, and the military industrial complex."[158] This transformation was very much in evidence during the 1980s when Governor Clinton made sure that Arkansas' wealthiest elite was well taken care of. Clinton also in this time perfected the art of political double speak, betrayal and lying, which would prepare him well for his tenure as commander in-chief.

Endnotes

1 David Maraniss, "Clinton's Record in Arkansas: Mixed Reviews," *The Washington Post,* February 3, 1992.

2 Michael Tomasky, *Bill Clinton* (New York: Times Books, 2017), 7. Jernigan lost to Clinton two years later in the race for state Attorney General.

3 David Halberstam, War in a Time *of Peace: Bush, Clinton and the Generals* (New York: Scribner, 2001), 108.

4 John Gartner, *In Search of Bill Clinton: A Psychological Biography* (New York: St. Martin's Press, 2008), 78.

5 Bill Clinton, *My Life* (New York: Alfred A. Knopf, 2004), 19, 20.

6 See Roger Stone and Robert Morrow, *The Clintons' War on Women* (New York: Skyhorse Publishing, 2015).

7 Gartner, *In Search of Bill Clinton,* 118. David Gergen stated that "once on Air Force One, Clinton erupted so violently that I wished I had a parachute." In another incident, Morris claims that Clinton "tackled me and knelt over my prone body, ready to punch me, before Hillary pulled him off, shrieking at him to control himself." Hillary then told Morris: "he only does that to people he loves." (p. 118).

8 In Ian Tyrrell, *Boy Clinton: The Political Biography* (Washington, D.C. Regnery, 1996), 148. Al Capone was said to have had permanent rights to suite 443 of the Arlington Hotel in Hot Springs.

9 Stone and Morrow cite: Betsey Wright, Spencer Oliver (former YDA President), Steny Hoyer, and Jim McDougal.

10 Stone and Morrow, *The Clintons' War on Women,* 205.

11 Bill Turque, *Inventing Al Gore: A Biography* (Boston: Houghton Mifflin, 2000), 21.

12 Martin Gross, *The Great Whitewater Fiasco: An American Tale of Money, Power and Politics* (New York: Ballantine Books, 1994), 40. For positive recollections about Clinton from his classmates in high school, see Robert E. Levin, *Bill Clinton: The Inside Story,* with introduction by David Pryor (New York: SPI Books, 1992). There had, though, been allegations of vote rigging on behalf of Clinton even in high school elections.

13 Dave Maraniss, *First in His Class: A Biography of Bill Clinton* (New York: Simon & Schuster, 1996); Carroll Quigley, *Tragedy and Hope: A History of the World in Our Time* (New York: McMillan, 1966). Clinton got only one of two As in Quigley's course. In a speech given on the 75th anniversary of the Edmund J. Walsh School of Foreign Service, Clinton said that Quigley had "left a lasting impression I think on every one of us who ever entered his class. . . . He drummed into us that western civilization was the greatest of all, and America was the best expression of western civilization because of its commitment . . . to the belief that the future could be better than the present." "Remarks by the president to the 75th Anniversary of the Edmund J. Walsh School of Foreign Service," Gaston Hall, Georgetown, Washington, D.C., November 10, 1994, in Clinton's Presidential Records, Press Office, box 7, William J. Clinton Presidential Library, Little Rock, Arkansas. Quigley believed that both the Democrats and Republicans were dominated by big business and that "the argument that the two parties should represent opposite ideals and policies was foolish. Instead, the two parties should be almost identical so that the American people can throw the rascals out at any election without leading to any profound or extensive shifts in policy."

14 Cliff Jackson quoted in Gross, *The Great Whitewater Fiasco,* 43. Clinton was smart but not considered by his peers as an outstanding student. Rather he was thought to be absent-minded. According to some sources, he only did respectfully at Yale law school because of Hillary's tutoring.

15 Stone and Morrow, *The Clintons' War on Women,* 42. See also Gary Aldrich, *Unlimited Access: An FBI Agent Inside the Clinton White House* (Washington, D.C.: Regnery, 1998), 221. Clinton admitted having sex with Wellstone but claimed it was consensual.

16 Alessandra Stanley, "Most Likely to Succeed," *New York Times Magazine,* November 22, 1992.

17 Meredith Oakley, *On the Make: The Rise of Bill Clinton* (Washington, D.C. Regnery, 1994), 64; FBI report in Aldrich, Unlimited Access, 221.

18 Bernard Von Bothmer, *Framing the Sixties: The Use and Abuse of a Decade From Ronald Reagan to George W. Bush* (Amherst, MA: University of Massachusetts Press, 2010), 170.

19 Christopher Hitchens, *No One Left to Lie To: The Triangulations of William Jefferson Clinton* (London: Verso, 2000), 22.

20 Oakley, *On the Make,* 66, 67.

21 See William C. Rempel, "Ex-ROTC Leader Says Clinton Deceived Him, Cheated Military," *Los Angeles Times,* September 17, 1992. Rather than attending the University of Arkansas, Clinton went back to Oxford before applying to Yale law school as he made his climb to political power. He reentered the draft knowing he would pull a high number and not be at risk of going.

22 Roger Morris, *Partners in Power: The Clinton's and Their America* (Washington, D.C.: Regnery, 1998), 199.

23 See Jim McDougal, with Curtis Wilkie, *Arkansas Mischief: The Birth of a National Scandal* (New York: Henry Holt, 1998); Ben Johnson III, *Arkansas in Modern America Since 1930* (Fayetteville: University of Arkansas Press, 2019).

24 Morris, *Partners in Power,* 194, 195; R. Emmett Tyrell Jr., *Boy Clinton: The Political Biography* (Washington, D.C.: Regnery Publishing, 1996), 100.

25 In McDougal, *Arkansas Mischief.* Orval Faubus, who won a record six straight terms as Governor, was part of this tradition. He was a populist critic of the Arkansas Power & Light Company and moderate liberal whose father gave him the middle name Eugene after Socialist party leader Eugene V. Debs. Faubus had attended Commonwealth College which advanced socialist doctrines and was shut down by the authorities in 1940 because it allegedly was subversive. Faubus was best known for opposing the integration of Little Rock High School, prompting the Eisenhower administration to send in federal troops. He was moderate on race by Arkansas standards and was attacked by a political opponent for being a "nigger lover" and supporter of the NAACP.

26 Carraway's sponsor was Huey Long. James M. Perry, "State of Contrasts: Home to Bill Clinton, Arkansas is Foreign to a Lot of Americans," *The Wall Street Journal,* June 4, 1992, A1.

27 John Brummett, *Highwire: From the Backwoods to the Beltway—The Education of Bill Clinton* (New York: Hyperion, 1994), 73, 74.

28 Nigel Hamilton, *Bill Clinton: An American Journey* (New York: Random House, 2003); Stone and Morrow, The Clinton's War on Women.

29 David N. Bresnahan, *The Larry Nichols Story: Damage Control – How to Get Caught with Your Pants Down and Still Get Elected President* (New Jersey: Camden Court, 1998), 43.

30 Tyrell, *Boy Clinton,* 112; Victor Thorn, *Hillary (and Bill) l: The Sex Volume* (Washington, D.C. The Free Press, 2008), 40. Raymond had been a generous supporter of Arkansas' Senior Senator John McLelland and of segregationist George C. Wallace of Alabama, whom he would personally drive whenever he visited Arkansas. Clinton's relationship with Winthrop Rockefeller may have come through a cousin of his mother, Frank Newell, Rockefeller's best friend from the military in World War II who had encouraged Rockefeller to buy land in the 1950s and move to Arkansas.

31 Thorn, *Hillary (and Bill) l,* 28–32; Sam Smith, "Arkansas Connections," *The Progressive Review,* 1998, http://ontology.buffalo.edu/smith/clinton/arkansas.htm; Roger Morris, "Don't Pardon Corruption," *The Globe and Mail,* March 7, 2001, https://www.theglobeandmail.com/opinion/dont-pardon-corruption/article1337751/. Roger Morris characterized Uncle Raymond as the "mob proconsul of Hot Springs." He says that Raymond helped Clinton gain admission to Georgetown University's School of Foreign Service, where he was allegedly recruited by the CIA.

32 Morris, "Don't Pardon Corruption"; Thorn, *Hillary (and Bill),* 28–32. Crawford and by implication Clinton's ties to organized crime are left out of most mainstream accounts of Clinton's political rise and presidency—an example is William H. Chafe's study, *Bill and Hillary: The Politics of the Personal* (Durham, NC: Duke University Press, 2014).

33 Barbara Demick, "Meet the Family That Bankrolled Clinton," *Seattle Times,* January 31, 1993.

34 L. J. Davis, "In the Name of Rose: An Arkansas Thriller," *The New Republic,* April 4, 1994; Jeff Gerth, "The 1992 Campaign: Personal Finances, Wealthy Investment Family a Big Help to Clinton," *The New York Times,* February 5, 1992; Gene Tatum, *The Tatum Chronicles: Oliver North, William Barr, Robert J. Mueller, George H.W. Bush. They Have This Dark Secret in Common* (D.G "Chip" Tatum, 1996). Jack Stephens supported Clinton's career at the beginning, became a Reagan Democrat, and supported Clinton in his 1990 run for Governor in Arkansas and 1992 presidential campaign. Hillary represented the Stephens in litigation during the 1980s, and her Rose Law Firm represented many of its entities. Larry Nichols, an anti-Clinton activist and former marketing director with the state economic development agency, claimed that he was enlisted by the Stephens to install Clinton as Governor. In 1985, Worthen Bank was indicted for extending million dollars' worth of illegal, preferential loans to companies owned by Stephens and the Riadys (Indonesian tycoons who helped promote warm U.S. relations with Indonesian dictator Mohammed Suharto during Clinton's presidency), though a fire of unknown causes broke out in the bank at 3 AM, destroying all the records sought by prosecutors.

35 Whitney Webb, "From 'Spook Air' to the 'Lolita Express': The genesis of the Jeffrey Epstein–Bill Clinton Relationship," *Mint Press,* August 23, 2019, https://www.mintpressnews.com/genesis-jeffrey-epstein-bill-clinton-relationship/261455/

36 Demick, "Meet the Family That Bankrolled Clinton."

37 Tatum, *The Tatum Chronicles.* Stephens appointed Mack McLarty, Clinton's boyhood friend and former chief of staff, to the board of Acxiom along with former NATO commander and onetime Democratic Party candidate, Wesley Clark, and former Lippo senior executive Stephen Patterson. For more on Acxiom, see Richard Behar, "Never Heard of Acxiom? Chances Are It's Heard of You. How a little-known Little Rock company—the world's largest processor of consumer data—found itself at the center of a very big national security debate," *CNN Money,* February 23, 2004, https://money.cnn.com/magazines/fortune/fortune_archive/2004/02/23/362182/index.htm

38 Morris, *Partners in Power,* 171, 172, 173; George Carpozi Jr., *Clinton Confidential: The Climb to Power: The Unauthorized Biography of Bill and Hillary Clinton* (Del Mar, CA: Emery Dalton Communications, 1995), 215; "Tyson's Corner," *The Wall Street Journal,* April 14, 1995 in *Whitewater, Vol. II: From the Editorial Pages of the Wall Street Journal,* ed. Robert L. Bartley et al. (New York: Dow Jones & Co., 1997), 61. After receiving the cash envelopes from Tyson, Clinton told Arkansas state trooper Larry Patterson that "if Don Tyson gives you something, it's because he wants something back. You'll never shake him off." In Carpozi Jr., *Clinton Confidential,* 285. Tyson gave at least $22,000 to Clinton's 1992 presidential campaign and $12,000 more to the Democratic Party.

39 Douglas Frantz, "How Tyson Became the Chicken King," *The New York Times,* August 28, 1994.

40 Bruce Ingersoll, "Tyson Foods, with a Friend in the White House, Gets Gentle Treatment from Agricultural Agency," *The Wall Street Journal,* March 17, 1994, A18; Alexander Cockburn and Ken Silverstein, *Washington Babylon* (London: Verso, 1996), 263, 264. Pressure from the White House and Arkansas' congressional delegation prompted agricultural secretary Mike Espy to abandon a reorganization plan that would have given Ellen Haas, a strong-willed consumer advocate, control of meat and poultry inspection. The Arkansas Northwest Regional airport also offered a hub for Wal Mart's vast commercial operations. Equipped with a 12,500-foot runway nearly as big as Chicago's O'Hare, the airport was located in Highfill, Arkansas near the headquarters of Tyson Foods and Walmart.

41 Demick, "Meet the Family That Bankrolled Clinton."

42 Laurence H. Shoup, "The Clinton Dynasty and the Shadow Government," *Z Magazine,* February 26, 2016; David Maraniss, "How Clinton Moved to Handle State's Economy," *The Washington Post,* October 18, 1992; David Maraniss, "Clinton's Record in Arkansas"; Bob Ortega, *In Sam We Trust: The Untold Story of Sam Walton and Wal-Mart, the World's Most Powerful Retailer* (New York: Times Books, 2000), 203, 207; Matea Gold, Tom Hamburger and Anu Narayaswamy, "Two Clintons, 41 Years, $3 Billion: Inside the Clinton Donor Network," *The Washington Post,* November 19, 2015; Michael Barbaro, "As a Director, Clinton Moved Walmart Board, but Only So Far," *The New York Times,* May 20, 2007; Dave Harrington to Bob Nash, September 22, 1988, Bill Clinton Gubernatorial Group, Natural and Cultural Resources, Economic Development Series, Bob Nash, box 7, Butler Center for Arkansas Studies, Bobby L. Roberts Library of Arkansas, Central Arkansas Library System, Little Rock, Arkansas. Clinton's close ties to Walmart remained evident after his presidency when he spoke frequently to one of Walton's successors as Walmart CEO, H. Lee Scott Jr., about issues like health care and played host to Mr. Scott at the Clintons' home in Chappaqua, New York in July 2006 for a private dinner.

43 Sam Roberts, "Joseph D. Duffey, Apostle of Liberalism and Humanities, is Dead at 88," *The New York Times,* March 4, 2021, B11.

44 Hunter S. Thompson, *Better Than Sex: Confessions of a Political Junkie* (New York: Ballantine Books, 1994), 12.

45 David Osborne, *Laboratories of Democracy: A New Breed of Governor Creates Models for National Growth* (Boston: Harvard Business School Press, 1988), 87.

46 Chafe, *Bill and Hillary,* 79.

47 Charles F. Allen and Jonathan Portis, *The Comeback Kid: The Life and Career of Bill Clinton* (Washington, D.C.: Carroll Publishing, 1992), 43. The attacks by Hammerschmidt would be followed up by similar ones from figures like Newt Gingrich (R-GA) who referred to Bill and Hillary as "countercultural McGovernicks."

48 Levin, Bill Clinton, 109.

49 Levin, *Bill Clinton,* 126.

50 Morris, *Partners in Power,* 218.

51 Morris, *Partners in Power,* 221; Maraniss, "Clinton's Record in Arkansas"; Webb Hubbell, *Friends in High Places: Webb Hubbell and the Clintons' Journey From Little Rock to Washington, D.C.* (Beaufort Books, 2015), 66; Jim Moore, *Clinton: Young Man in a Hurry* (The Summit Publishing Group, 1997), 57; Cockburn and Silverstein, *Washington Babylon,* 253, 258.

52 Christopher Hitchens, *No One Left to Lie To: The Triangulations of William Jefferson Clinton* (New York: Twelve, 1999), 22; Levin, *Bill Clinton,* 138; Nathan J. Robinson, *Superpredator: Bill Clinton's Use and Abuse of Black America* (Sommerville, MA: CA Press, 2016), 240. A few days later, Hillary insisted on accompanying Bill as he went to confront Fort Chaffee's commander, General James "Bulldog" Drummond, to demand federal help in containing the prisoners, though none was forthcoming. Chrsitopher Anderson, *American Evita: Hillary Clinton's Path to Power* (New York: Avon Books, 2004), 83. Five of the rioters were shot and 62 people suffered injuries. For Clinton's account, see *Clinton, My Life,* 274–277. Clinton made sure to highlight that the Cubans had been fleeing a "Communist dictatorship."

53 Hamilton, *Bill Clinton.*

54 Gross, *The Great Whitewater Fiasco,* 124.

55 Morris, *Partners in Power,* 276.

56 Ambrose Evans-Pritchard, *The Secret Life of Bill Clinton: The Unreported Stories* (Washington, D.C.: Regnery Publishing, 1997); Tyrell, *Boy Clinton,* 101. Larry Nichols who worked with Clinton wrote that Clinton "went to Tyson and Stephens with his hat in his hand and told them that he would do absolutely anything they wanted. Absolutely anything." In Bresnahan, *The Larry Nichols Story,* 42.

57 Bresnahan, *The Larry Nichols Story,* 49.

58 Tyrrell, *Boy Clinton,* 115.

59 Christopher Andersen, *American Evita: Hillary Clinton's Path to Power* (New York: HarperCollins, 2009); Davis, "In the Name of Rose." Rose's clients included Walmart, Stephens Inc., Dan Lasater, and Tyson Chicken.

60 Morris, *Partners in Power,* 331; Gross, *The Great Whitewater Fiasco,* 127.

61 Morris, *Partners in Power,* 331; Gross, *The Great Whitewater Fiasco,* 127.

62 "Governor Bill Clinton's Record in Arkansas: Jobs and Economic Growth," Bill Clinton for President Committee, *Dianne Blair Papers,* MC 1632, Series II, Subseries 4, Box 1, Folder Campaign Aid for Governor, 1979–1991, University of Arkansas Fayetteville, Mullins Libraries, Special Collections.

63 Maraniss, "How Clinton Moved to Handle State's Economy"; "Bill Clinton is Fighting for Arkansas—Its Paying Off for You," campaign brochure, June 2, 1980, *Dianne Blair Papers,* MC 1632, Series II, Subseries 4, Box 1, Folder Campaign Aid for Governor, 1979–1991, University of Arkansas Fayetville, Mullins Libraries, Special Collections.

64 Osborne, *Laboratories of Democracy,* 108; Allen & Portis, *The Comeback Kid,* 147; Clinton, *My Life,* 307, 362; Bill Clinton is Fighting for Arkansas—Its Paying Off For You," campaign brochure, June 2, 1980; "Governor Bill Clinton's Record in Arkansas: Reinventing Government," "Governor Bill Clinton's Record in Arkansas: Farmers and Agriculture," Bill Clinton for President Committee, *Dianne Blair Papers,* MC 1632, Series II, Subseries 4, Box 1, Folder Campaign Aid for Governor, 1979–1991, University of Arkansas, Mullins Libraries, Special Collections.

65 "Bill Clinton is Fighting for Arkansas—Its Paying Off for You," campaign brochure, June 2, 1980; "Governor Bill Clinton's Record in Arkansas: Welfare Reform"; *Dianne Blair Papers,* MC 1632, Series II, Subseries 4, Box 1, Folder Campaign Aid for Governor, 1979–1991, University of Arkansas, Mullins Libraries, Special Collections. Clinton claimed to have saved the state $2.8 million through welfare cutting initiatives in his first term as governor. This previewed his role in passing the 1996 Personal Responsibility and Work Opportunity Reconciliation Act (PRWORA), which instituted a work requirement and imposed a five-year lifetime cap on welfare benefits, mandating that nobody could receive benefits for more than two years at a time. Welfare benefits under the new system were delivered as a series of block grants to state governments, with federal funds significantly cut back.

66 Sam Smith, *Shadows of Hope: A Freethinkers Guide to Politics in the Time of Clinton* (Bloomington: Indiana University Press, 1994), 84.

67 B. Drummond Ayres, Jr., "The 1992 Campaign: Candidate's Record; Despite Improvements, the Schools in Arkansas Are Still Among the Worst," *The New York Times,* April 1, 1992, https://www.nytimes.com/1992/04/01/us/1992-campaign-candidate-s-record-despite-improvements-schools-arkansas-are-still.html. Clinton supported "school choice," a policy endorsed by George H. W. Bush, who said that all American students should have this "free enterprise" type of education system.

68 "Governor Bill Clinton's Record in Arkansas: Tax Fairness," Bill Clinton for President Committee, *Dianne Blair Papers,* MC 1632, Series II, Subseries 4, Box 1, Folder Campaign Aid for Governor, 1979–1991, University of Arkansas, Mullins Libraries, Special Collections.

69 Morris, *Partners in Power.*

70 Morris, *Partners in Power,* 219. As examples of Clinton's waffling, Roger Morris emphasized Clinton's championing educational reform, but his withdrawal of support for school district consolidation and reorganization, which would have made his education bill meaningful in the face of legislative opposition. Clinton also stood by in silence when the interest-dominated Public Service Commission slashed the big utilities' already underassessed property taxes by several million, dooming his second-year education budget increase.

71 "Arkansas Allowing Four Companies to Explore Public Diamond Mine," *The New York Times,* November 20, 1989; "Only U.S. Diamond Mine Sparks a Conflict in Arkansas State," *Chicago Tribune,* May 5, 1992; "Friends in High Places," *Forbes Magazine,* August 9, 1998; Jeffrey St. Clair, "Diamond Dogs: Clinton Family Jewels," *Counterpunch,* June 3, 2016, https://www.counterpunch.org/2016/06/03/diamond-dogs-clinton-family-jewels/. Diamond Fields executive Mike McMurrough had worked as a land surveyor in Hope. James Stanley, a Little Rock lawyer and member of the Sierra Club and of the Friends of Crater of Diamonds State Park Coalition, which was also supporting the lawsuit, told *The New York Times:* "If we allow commercial diamond mining here it may lead to further exploitation, such as timber cutting or gravel removal elsewhere. State parks are off limits . . . and the companies have no business going in there and even doing exploratory drilling.'"

72 St. Clair, "Diamond Dogs."

73 Morris, *Partners in Power,* 229. Clinton early in his second term dismantled the Governor's Task Force on small business, favoring big business instead. The Chairman of the Commission, Benjamin Talbot Sr., subsequently lost his life in a highway accident after having gone out on the campaign trail to speak out against Clinton's neglect of small businessmen. His son suspected malfeasance, stating that "somebody up there in that ol' statehouse sure as hell didn't want my ol' man buzzing

about a subject [the best interests of the small businessman] that Clinton and his mafia wanted kept at arms-length from his administration." He added: "ya know, they say that Lyndon B. Johnson left a lot of bodies lying on the Texas countryside in his march to the presidency. But I ask you to look at the road Bill Clinton traveled to the White House. Clinton's journey makes Johnson's look like that of a piker." Carpozi Jr., *Clinton Confidential,* 474.

74 Gloria to Governor, "Meeting with AFL/CIO," January 19, 1990, Bill Clinton Gubernatorial Group, Natural and Cultural Resources, Economic Development Series, Bob Nash, box 23, Butler Center for Arkansas Studies, Bobby L. Roberts Library of Arkansas, Central Arkansas Library System, Little Rock, Arkansas.

75 David Maraniss, "How Clinton Moved to Handle State's Economy," *The Washington Post,* October 18, 1992. Statistics later compiled by the Arkansas Fairness Council, a non-profit progressive-tax research organization, indicated a potential state revenue loss of $166 million between 1985 and 1990 for tax credits issued during that period.

76 Moore, *Clinton,* 145; Oakley, *On the Make,* 364.

77 Richmond Odom, *Circle of Death: Clinton's Climb to the Presidency* (Lafayette, LO: Huntington House Publishers, 1995), 131. Clinton gave state jobs to women with whom he had affairs while asking his security detail to solicit women for him. Gary Aldrich, *Unlimited Access: An FBI Agent Inside the Clinton White House* (Washington, D.C.: Regnery Publishing, 1998). .

78 Oakley, *On the Make,* 436; Carpozi Jr., *Clinton Confidential,* 240; James Risen and Edwin Chen, "Clinton's Ties to Controversial Medical Examiner Questioned," *Los Angeles Times,* May 19, 1992, https://idfiles.com/wp-content/uploads/2022/05/Clintons-Ties-to-Controversial-Medical-Examiner-Questioned.html.

79 Ibid., 95.

80 Thorn, *Hillary (and Bill): The Sex Volume,* 166.

81 Mara Leveritt, *All Quiet at Mena* (Little Rock: Bird Call Press, 2021), 247, 248. A class-action lawsuit resulted in a 1998 decision by the Canadian government to set aside $1.2 billion to compensate those infected. One thousand people had been infected with AIDS and 20,000 with Hepatitis-C. Canada added another $875 million to the fund in 2006. But Arkansas never apologized for its role in the tragedy.

82 Stone and Morrow, *The Clintons' War on Women,* 269. Richard Mays, a black lawyer who received $25,000 as an ombudsman to the troubled program, also had a connection with Clinton.

83 Stone and Morrow, *The Clintons' War on Women,* 66, 67; On the wider pattern, see Victor Thorn, *Hillary (and Bill): The Murder Volume* (Washington, D.C.: The Free Press, 2008).

84 Stone and Morrow, *The Clintons' War on Women,* 198.

85 Arkansas state trooper Larry Patterson said that one time when he went into the governor's mansion, Hillary was screaming at Bill, calling him all kinds of bad names. When he went into the kitchen, the cook, Miss Emma, turned to him and said: "the devil's in that woman." Jerry Zeifman, the general counsel and chief of staff to the House Judiciary Investigative Committee during Watergate said that he fired Hillary because she had tried to deny Nixon counsel during the Watergate proceedings, which was illegal. Zeifman claimed that Clinton was "an unethical, dishonest lawyer. She conspired to violate the Constitution, the rules of the House, the rules of the committee, and the rules of confidentiality." In Stone and Morrow, *The Clintons' War on Women,* 10, 204.

86 Barbara Olsen, *Hell to Pay: The Unfolding Story of Hillary Rodham Clinton* (Washington, D.C.: Regnery, 2001), 4, 5. That the right-wing conspiracy theorist argument was as wrong as Nixon's notion of a "left-wing conspiracy" is exemplified by the fact that many of Clinton's detractors were Liberal Democrats: Terry Reed, for example was an admirer of Harry S. Truman, and Jim McDougal ran for Congress as a Democrat, while numerous authors who wrote books critical of Clinton identified with the New Deal tradition which they felt Clinton had betrayed. The Clintons' devious methods were seen most recently in the manufacturing of the Russia-Gate scandal involving the adoption of fake dossier and McCarthy-type smears in the attempt to malign Hillary's political rival, Donald Trump.

87 *Dianne Blair Papers,* MC 1632, Series II, Subseries 4, Box 1, Folder Campaign Aid for Governor, 1979–1991, University of Arkansas, Mullins Libraries, Special Collections.

88 Bill Clinton to J. Bill Becker, April 14, 1990, Bill Clinton Gubernatorial Group, Natural and Cultural Resources, Economic Development Series, Bob Nash, box 23, Butler Center for Arkansas Studies, Bobby L. Roberts Library of Arkansas, Central Arkansas Library System, Little Rock, Arkansas.

89 Morris, *Partners in Power,* 456; Oakley, *On the Make,* 429–431.

90 Bob Wells, "Solutions on Prisons Considered," *The Arkansas Gazette,* April 24, 1987, Bill Clinton Gubernatorial Group, Natural and Cultural Resources, Economic Development Series, Craig Smith, box 11, Butler Center for Arkansas Studies, Bobby L. Roberts Library of Arkansas, Central Arkansas Library System, Little Rock, Arkansas.

91 Mitford quoted in Thorn, *Hillary (and Bill),* 46.

92 L. D. Brown, *Crossfire: Witness in the Clinton Investigation* (San Diego, CA: Black Forrest Press, 1999), 13.

93 Art Lockhart (1940–), *Encyclopedia of Arkansas,* https://encyclopediaofarkansas.net/entries/art-lockhart-5269/. A Texan, Lockhart was accused in the early 1970s of verbally abusing and striking inmates. The state police had evidence that Lockhart was personally and illegally taking $200,000 per year from the blood program.

94 Bill Clinton to Mrs. Don Billingsley, Ft. Smith, Arkansas, April 22, 1988, Bill Clinton Gubernatorial Group, Natural and Cultural Resources, Economic Development Series, Craig Smith, box 8, Butler Center for Arkansas Studies, Bobby L. Roberts Library of Arkansas, Central Arkansas Library System, Little Rock, Arkansas. Bill Clinton to Mary Lingo, November 14, 1989, Bill Clinton Gubernatorial Group, Natural and Cultural Resources, Economic Development Series, Craig Smith, box 12, Butler Center for Arkansas Studies, Bobby L. Roberts Library of Arkansas, Central Arkansas Library System, Little Rock, Arkansas.

95 James Bovard, *"Feeling Your Pain:" The Explosion and Abuse of Government Power in the Clinton-Gore Years* (New York: St. Martin's Press, 2000).

96 Morris, *Partners in Power;* Maraniss, "Clinton's Record in Arkansas." In 1988, Clinton signed into law a bill mandating military boot camps instead of jail for first time offenders without considering alternatives. Levin, *Bill Clinton,* 178; Moore, *Clinton,* 157.

97 Nathan Robinson, *Super Predator: Bill Clinton's Use and Abuse of Black America* (New York: Current Affairs, 2016), 45.

98 "Bill Clinton to Mary Lingo, November 14, 1989, Bill Clinton Gubernatorial Group, Natural and Cultural Resources, Economic Development Series, Craig Smith,

box 12, Butler Center for Arkansas Studies, Bobby L. Roberts Library of Arkansas, Central Arkansas Library System, Little Rock, Arkansas; Peter Applebone, "Clinton's Record in Leading Arkansas: Success but Not Without Criticism," *The New York Times,* December 22, 1991; Johnson III, *Arkansas in Modern America, 1930–1999,* 206; Clinton, *My Life,* 271.

99 "Drug Eradication Operations," in Arkansas National Guard: Military Department of Arkansas, *Annual Report, FY 1990,* Bill Clinton Gubernatorial Group, Natural and Cultural Resources, Economic Development Series, Craig Smith, box 8, Butler Center for Arkansas Studies, Bobby L. Roberts Library of Arkansas, Central Arkansas Library System, Little Rock, Arkansas; "Governor Bill Clinton's Record in Arkansas: Drugs and Crime," Dianne Blair Papers, Mullins Library, Special Collections, University of Arkansas.

100 Bill Clinton to Lt. General John B. Conaway, Chief National Guard Bureau, Pentagon, May 17, 1991, Bill Clinton Gubernatorial Group, Natural and Cultural Resources, Economic Development Series, Craig Smith, box 12, Butler Center for Arkansas Studies, Bobby L. Roberts Library of Arkansas, Central Arkansas Library System, Little Rock, Arkansas.

101 Mary Lingo, letter to Bill Clinton, August 17, 1989, Bill Clinton Gubernatorial Group, Natural and Cultural Resources, Economic Development Series, Craig Smith, box 12, Butler Center for Arkansas Studies, Bobby L. Roberts Library of Arkansas, Central Arkansas Library System, Little Rock, Arkansas.

102 Johnson III, *Arkansas in Modern America, 1930–1999,* 169–172.

103 Carpozi Jr., *Clinton Confidential;* Morris, *Partners in Power,* 453, 454; Smith, *Shadows of Hope,* 10; Cockburn and Silverstein, *Washington Babylon,* 254. According to Meredith Oakley, a survey of 422 business executives released in January 1988 gave the governor an overall grade between B- and C+ in education and a C in economic development. At the end of Clinton's tenure, a group called Citizens for Tax Justice revealed that Arkansas was taxing its poor at a ratio of one-seventh times higher than its wealthiest residents and that the percentage of income an Arkansan paid in taxes dropped across the board as income increased. Oakley, *On the Make,* 428.

104 Oakley, *On the Make,* 364, 370. Taxpayer support for the Clintons went towards a 12-person security staff, food, utilities, maintenance and operation of the governor's mansion, plus a $35,000 per year salary. The extravagance prompted a Republican bill advocating for austerity in government.

105 Tyrrell, *Boy Clinton,* 122.

106 Larry Sullivan, "IRS Finding Cash Sale Violations," *Arkansas Gazette,* November 17, 1990, 2C, University of Arkansas Special Collections, Mullins Library, Arkansas Committee Records, Box 3.

107 Carpozi Jr., *Clinton Confidential.*

108 Johnson III, *Arkansas in Modern America, 1930–1999,* 204.

109 Tyrrell, *Boy Clinton,* 122.

110 Morris, *Partners in Power,* 456; Oakley, *On the Make,* 429–431; Applebone, "Clinton Record in Leading Arkansas." John Brummett wrote that "human services, welfare, I think these sort of things bore him [Clinton]. They're necessities of government but they're just sort of messy, there's not a lot of political capital in championing those things as there are in championing education."

111 Oakley, *On the Make;* Carpozi Jr., *Clinton Confidential,* 276; Moore, *Clinton,* 174; Cockburn and Silverstein, *Washington Babylon,* 258; Jack Anderson

and Michael Binstein, "Arkansas Unions Are No Fans of Clinton," *The Washington Post,* January 23, 1992. Clinton later appointed Morrilton Plastics' lead attorney to a state ethics commission. Ronald Reagan was strongly anti-union; one of his first measures as president was to fire the air traffic controllers after they went on strike.

112 Maraniss, "Clinton's Record in Arkansas"; Brummett, *Highwire,* 215, 216. Clinton had received more national labor money than any other Democratic challenger in the country during his 1974 congressional campaign and had long been supported by the AFL-CIO. Matea Gold and Tom Hamberger, "How Bill Clinton's Losing 1974 Race Helped Launch Clinton's Donor Network," *The Washington Post,* November 20, 2015. In a letter to J. Bill Becker written on April 14, 1990, Clinton claimed that he "had always been a friend of the working people of the state." Clinton said that in 1983 he had been asked by the Department of Labor to draft a collective bargaining agreement which he did—the first time it was ever done in the state, and that his labor department had filed and received an emergency injunction to enter a factory in Camden where two employees had been killed. Clinton also said he had supported conferences and petitions on workers compensation—which his predecessors, David Pryor and Dale Bumpers, never did—and that he had fought for a more progressive tax system with the AFL-CIO but had been defeated in the legislature, which was not his fault. In cases, where he had acted against labor like in the Morrilton plastics factory, Clinton said he was working to save jobs and prevent plant closure—which was often his number one priority. In the end, Clinton said that he had always fought for the jobs of the people of the state of Arkansas and took many trips and worked late into the night and early in the morning doing so. Bill Clinton to J. Bill Becker, April 14, 1990, Bill Clinton Gubernatorial Group, Natural and Cultural Resources, Economic Development Series, Bob Nash, box 23, Butler Center for Arkansas Studies, Bobby L. Roberts Library of Arkansas, Central Arkansas Library System, Little Rock, Arkansas. A main purpose of the letter was to try and sustain Becker's political support for the upcoming gubernatorial election—at the time Becker was threatening to withdraw AFL-CIO support for Clinton because of his repeated betrayals. Becker took flack for the latter position from the president of the United Steelworkers in Arkansas, Jim Brumley, who said that the Democrats were all the unions had as the Republicans were "never a workingman's friend." Brumley even accused Becker in his criticism of Clinton of being advised by Lee Atwater, the Republican campaign strategist.

113 Bill Clinton Gubernatorial Group, Natural and Cultural Resources, Economic Development Series, Bob Nash, box 23, Butler Center for Arkansas Studies, Bobby L. Roberts Library of Arkansas, Central Arkansas Library System, Little Rock, Arkansas.

114 Moore, *Clinton,* 173. When Becker sent a report on Clinton's abysmal labor record to national headquarters, AFL-CIO president Lane Kirkland ordered it to be kept in a desk drawer. On Clinton's betrayal of organized labor, see also Michael Pierce, "How Bill Clinton Remade the Democratic Party By Abandoning Unions," *The Labor and Working Class History Association,* November 23, 2016, https://www.lawcha.org/2016/11/23/bill-clinton-remade-democratic-party-abandoning-unions-working-class-whites/.

115 Morris, *Partners in Power,* 452; John T. Holleman, "In Arkansas Which Comes First, the Chicken or the Environment?" *Tulane Environmental Law Journal,* 6, 21 (1992), https://www.animallaw.info/article/arkansas-which-comes-first-chicken-or-environment. The House Speaker for a period, Leon L. "Doc" Bryan of Russellville, happened also to be the director of the state chicken industry's lobbying association. Brummett, *Highwire,* 240.

116 Patrick Matriscana, *The Clinton Chronicles Book* (Hemet California: Jeremiah Books, 1994), 43; Gross, *The Great Whitewater Fiasco,* 104; Holleman, "In Arkansas Which Comes First, the Chicken or the Environment?" For a defense of the tax breaks, see Archie R. Schaffer, "Tyson Foods Behaved Properly with Clintons," *The New York Times,* May 9, 1994.

117 Clinton, *My Life,* 362.

118 Morris, *Partners in Power;* Paul Derienzo, "Arkansas Governor Bill Clinton, President George Bush, CIA Drugs for Guns Connection," http://www.ncoic.com/clinton.htm?fbclid=IwAR0ZLyztXgHCkfxqXupSzSLLOOyoa1r8pHIxCXwn7NYT2z3paGHJ-L7z0Nc. Hercules produced 2,4-D, which was still used in agriculture in the 1980s and 2,4,5,T, which was banned by the federal government in 1983 as a carcinogen.

119 Maraniss, "Clinton's Record in Arkansas"; Cockburn and Silverstein, *Washington Babylon,* 253, 254. The same article quoted Steve Work, a resident of Green Forest Arkansas where locals had fought against water pollution for a decade, who said that Clinton never demonstrated any interest in the problem. Work added thar "Clinton was trying to balance industry interests against environmental interests, but he would never make it as a high wire performer."

120 Alexander Cockburn and Jeffrey St. Clair, *Al Gore: A User's Manual* (London: Verso, 2000), 246.

121 John N. Maclean, "Clinton Places Commitment to Natural Gas on Front Burner," *The Chicago Tribune,* January 5, 1993.

122 Alexander Cockburn, "Al Gore's Teapot Dome," *The Nation,* July 17, 2000; David Stratton, "Clinton's Oil Policy and Teapot Dome," *The Seattle Times,* November 17, 1998.

123 General George A. Joulwan to Bill Clinton, April 20, 1991, Bill Clinton Gubernatorial Group, Natural and Cultural Resources, Economic Development Series, Craig Smith, box 8, folder Arkansas National Guard, Butler Center for Arkansas Studies, Bobby L. Roberts Library of Arkansas, Central Arkansas Library System, Little Rock, Arkansas.

124 Ibid.

125 Bill Clinton Gubernatorial Group, Natural and Cultural Resources, Economic Development Series, Phil Price, box 3, Butler Center for Arkansas Studies, Bobby L. Roberts Library of Arkansas, Central Arkansas Library System, Little Rock, Arkansas.

126 State of Arkansas, Private Activity Bonds, January 1984–January 1992, ADFA, University of Arkansas Special Collections, Mullins Library, Arkansas Committee Records, Box 3.

127 Morris, *Partners in Power,* 453; Ambrose Evans Pritchard, *The Secret Life of Bill Clinton: The Unreported Stories* (Washington, D.C.: Regnery Publishing, 1997), 309; Davis, "The Name of Rose." Oakley in *The Rise of Bill Clinton,* 202, writes that "Faubus created the Arkansas Industrial Development Commission in 1953—a catalyst for economic growth for two decades which instigated and mitigated the state's transition from a state primarily dependent on agriculture to one with a burgeoning industry."

128 *Los Angeles Times,* June 28, 1992; Floyd G. Brown, *"Slick Willie:" Why America Cannot Trust Bill Clinton* (Annapolis, Maryland: Annapolis Publishing Co., 1992); Davis, "The Name of Rose."

129 Davis, "The Name of Rose"; Terry Reed, *Compromised: Clinton, Bush and the CIA* (New York: S.P.I. Books, 1994).

130 Mara Leveritt, *The Boys on the Tracks: Death, Denial, and a Mother's Crusade to Bring Her Son's Killers to Justice* (Little Rock: Bird Call Press, 1999); Evans-Pritchard, *The Secret Life of Bill Clinton,* 310.

131 Whitney Webb, *One Nation Under Blackmail, Vol. II: The sordid union between Intelligence and Organized Crime that gave rise to Jeffrey Epstein* (Walterville, OR: Trine Day, 2022), 211. Alice Walton was involved in numerous drunk driving crashes, including one in Fayetville in April 1989 where she struck and killed Oleta Hardin, a fifty-year old cannery worker, though she never received so much as a ticket.

132 Brown, *"Slick Willie,"* 68.

133 Odom, *Circle of Death,* 127; Leveritt, *All Quiet at Mena,* 296. Skeeter Ward admitted to knowing Bill Clinton socially.

134 Alexander Cockburn, "Beat the Devil: The Secret Life of a Parking Meter Manufacturer," *The Nation,* April 6, 1992, 438, 439; Alexander Cockburn and Jeffrey St. Clair, *Whiteout: The CIA, Drugs and the Press* (London: Verso, 1998), 337.

135 Webb, *One Nation Under Blackmail, Vol. II,* 187. Arkansas Systems founder John Chaimberlain claims to have been the developer of a financial management system for Systematics, a data processing company owned by Jackson Stephens and represented by the Rose Law Firm, which was a primary developer of PROMIS, a CIA software system, for financial intelligence use. Whitney Webb, *A Nation Under Blackmail: Vol. I: Organized Crime that gave rise to Jeffrey Epstein* (Walterville, OR: Trine Day, 2022), 395. Arkansas Systems was located just down the road from Systematics in Little Rock.

136 Evans Pritchard, *The Secret Life of Bill Clinton.*

137 Carpozi Jr., *Clinton Confidential;* Reed, *Compromised,* 169, 170; Leveritt, *All Quiet at Mena,* 301. The effort to get BCCI into the U.S. was started in the 1970s with the assistance of Bert Lance, Jimmy Carter's former budget director. Coral had only recently been established when the loan was issued and took in an amazing amount of money in a short period of time. In its first 14 days of operation, Coral received $474 million of reinsurance premiums from AIG.

138 Carpozi Jr., *Clinton Confidential;* Reed, *Compromised,* 169, 170; Thorn, *Hillary (and Bill): The Drugs Volume,* 211; Odom, *Circle of Death;* Leveritt, *All Quiet at Mena,* 301. Stephens brought BCCI into the U.S. in 1977 by connecting the Bank's founder, Hasen Abedi, with Bert Lance, the Carter administration's budget director. Stephens also helped BCCI take over other American banks.

139 Stone and Morrow, *The Clintons' War on Women,* 69.

140 Stone and Morrow, *The Clintons' War on Women;* Larry Nichols, *Mary Ellen, 28 Years to Nowhere: An Inspirational Tragedy* (Leading Edge, 2017); David M. Bresnahan, *The Larry Nichols Story: Damage Control—How to Get Caught With Your Pants Down and Still Get Elected President* (New Jersey: Camden Court, 1998), 215; Thorn, *Hillary (and Bill): The Drugs Volume,* 215. Million-dollar loans were being given out to Clinton supporters that were never repaid. Reed, *Compromised,* 274. Roy Drew, a financial manager for Stephens Inc., Merrill Lynch and E.F. Hutton, referred to the ADFA as "Clinton's piggy bank."

141 Morris, *Partners in Power,* 229, 231, 233; Carpozi Jr., *Clinton Confidential;* McDougal, *Arkansas Mischief,* 167; Chase, *Bill and Hillary,* 105. During several of the transactions that Hillary had claimed to make, she was actually also presiding over

meetings in Washington as chairman of the Legal Services Corporation. Andersen, *American Evita,* 80. Later it was also found that records had been falsified and manipulated to cover up the fraud.

142 James Stewart, *Blood Sport: The President and His Adversaries* (New York: Touchstone Books, 1996), 415. Part of the purpose for the investment may have been as a tax shelter for Hillary's illicit gains on the cattle market.

143 Carpozi Jr., *Clinton Confidentiial,* 107.

144 Susan McDougal, T*he Woman Who Wouldn't Talk: Why I Refused to Testify Against the Clintons and What I Learned in Jail* (New York: Basic Books, 2003), 96; Carpozi Jr., *Clinton Confidential,* 108. McDougal had run John F. Kennedy's 1960 winning campaign in Arkansas and become head of the Young Democrats in 1965. He fashioned himself a populist banker, holding that tight credit held back poor Arkansans, lent money right and left, and would dispense for his own purposes millions in depositors publicly insured funds. Morris, Partners in Power, 362.

145 Carpozi Jr., *Clinton Confidential,* 108; Morris, *Partners in Power,* 361, 377.

146 Dick Morris, *Rewriting History* (New York: Regan Books, 2004), 145; Thorn, *Hillary (and Bill),* 225. See also Gross, *The Great Whitewater Fiasco.*

147 Carpozi Jr., *Clinton Confidential,* 460, 461; Jeff Gerth, "The 1992 Campaign: Personal Finances; Clinton Joined S & L Operator in an Ozark Real Estate Venture," *The New York Times,* March 8, 1992; James B. Stewart, *Blood Sport: The President and His Adversaries* (New York: Simon & Schuster, 1997), 197; Morris, *Partners in Power,* 362, 371, 377, 386. Carpozi Jr. writes that McDougal and Clinton managed to "hide their huge profits [with Whitewater] in a manner that would have made Al Capone ashamed to call himself a gangster." If a buyer defaulted on a land purchase, it was as if the transaction had never occurred, as it was not reported to the IRS. There was no record of Soapes' transaction, for example. Clinton conveniently appointed all the members of the state real estate commission who backed off any investigation. McDougal said that Basset—an attorney for the law firm Mitchell, Williams, Selig, Jackson and Tucker (named after Jim Guy Tucker, a friend of Clinton's who succeeded him as governor though he was forced to resign after being caught up in the Whitewater scandal)—was his choice to head the Arkansas Securities Commission. As an example of tax fraud, Morris reports that the Clintons sold a choice piece of Whitewater property on the White River for more than $1,000 an acre in 1980 but tax stamps listed the price of the property as only $2,000, some $30,000 less than the actual sale recorded elsewhere, and later confirmed by the buyer. Jim McDougal also told Sheffield Nelson, Clinton's opponent in the 1990 Gubernatorial election, that the Clintons never paid him interest for the Whitewater mortgage though the First Couple had deducted several thousands of dollars in such payment from their taxes. One loan repayment, McDougal claimed, was made by the corporation and thus was "over-reflected on their income taxes." The Clintons claimed not to have known about malfeasance by McDougal but profited over $150,000 in the Whitewater deal.

148 McDougal, *Arkansas Mischief,* 206; Stewart, *Blood Sport,* 433. For a conflicting account of this latter meeting, which took place in March 1986, and suggestion that McDougal never got the permits, see Gene Lyons, *Fools for Scandal: How the Media Invented Whitewater* (New York: Harper's, 1996), 92. Diamond Jim and hot pants Susan both drove Jaguars and Jim also owned a Bentley, which was eventually repossessed. Susan was featured in an ad riding a white horse in tight pants around their property.

149 Morris, *Partners in Power,* 372; Micah Morrison, "Governor's Travels in Whitewater Country," *The Wall Street Journal,* September 26, 1994 in *Whitewater, Volume II: From the Editorial Pages of the Wall Street Journal,* ed. Robert L. Bartley, with Micah Morrison and Melanie Kirkpatrick and editorial page staff (New York: Dow Jones & Company, 1996), 8.

150 Morris, *Partners in Power,* 376. *The Wall Street Journal* editorialized that "like aristocracy in some medieval barony, the Clintons felt entitled to support, and it was the responsibility of subordinates and minions to make sure that money and excuses were always available to keep the Clintons' permanent political campaigns and careers above water." In "What is Whitewater," *The Wall Street Journal,* August 9, 1995, in *Whitewater, Vol. II,* 116.

151 Stewart, *Blood Sport,* 225, 331.

152 Jeff Gerth, with Stephen Engleberg, "U.S. Investigating Clinton's Links to Arkansas S & L," *The New York Times,* November 2, 1993; Stewart, *Blood Sport,* 429; Morris, *Partners in Power,* 380, 381. Hale reported that the loan was going to a "disadvantaged businesswoman." Other money from the loan was used to buy new property and stave off lenders and creditors. Stewart, *Blood Sport,* 137, 138. McDougal and Clinton denied Hale's claims about a meeting involving Clinton. The loan, however, is known to have gone through; it was directed to Susan's advertising company. Jim McDougal said that Susan arranged the loan, not him. The money was found to have been used to benefit Whitewater. Hale felt ultimately that he had done nothing wrong, stating: "I've been involved in politics with these people since I was eighteen years old. They needed help and I helped them."

153 McDougal, *Arkansas Mischief;* Susan Schmidt, "James McDougal Dies While Awaiting Parole," *The Washington Post,* March 9, 1998, A1. Bill Clinton lied, McDougal says, about ever having taken loans from Madison Guaranty.

154 McDougal, *Arkansas Mischief,* 283, 288. McDougal compared Hillary Clinton to Lady McBeth. He died in prison after being confined to solitary confinement for failing to urinate in a drug test when medications he was taking prevented that. Researchers suspect foul play in his death as his autopsy found an unusual level of Prozac in his system and that he was given other drugs, including Lasix, which are dangerous for heart patients.

155 Robert Sherill, *The Drugstore Liberal* (New York: Grossman Publishers, 1968). See also Hunter S. Thompson, *Fear and Loathing on the Campaign Trail, '72* (New York: Grand Central Publishing, 1973).

156 Thompson, *Fear and Loathing on the Campaign Trail, '72,* 187.

157 Quoted in Ann H. Coulter, *High Crimes and Misdemeanors: The Case Against Bill Clinton* (Washington, D.C.: Regnery Publishing, 1998), 249. Despite being described as a "hustler" by one of Clinton's own National Security Council advisers, Chung had been granted a meeting with President Clinton in March 1995, just two days after he handed a $50,000 check to the First Lady's Chief of Staff. Chung was hoping that his company, the China Ocean Shipping Company (COSCO), would obtain a lease for the Long Beach Naval Station. Clinton himself flew to Long Beach to help secure it.

158 Quoted in Bruce E. Levine, "Lesser of Two Evils: Chomsky v. Greenwald… and the Ignored Factor," *Counterpunch,* June 19, 2020, https://www.counterpunch.org/2020/06/19/lesser-of-two-evils-chomsky-vs-greenwald-and-the-ignored-factor/

CHAPTER 2

Bill Clinton and the Crimes of Mena: Made in Arkansas, Made in America

The 2017 Hollywood blockbuster *American Made,* starring Tom Cruise, spotlighted the escapades of Barry Seal, a legendary drug pilot with a CIA background who smuggled guns and drugs into Nicaragua out of Mena, Arkansas, as part of the 1980s Contra War. In one scene that the filmmakers decided to cut, a young Bill Clinton, the Governor of Arkansas, gets a lap dance at a strip club at the moment when Seal hatches a plan to enlist Clinton in the CIA-backed drug and gun running scheme. Left in, however, was a scene in which Clinton helps facilitate Seal's release from jail so he could begin informing on the Drug Enforcement Administration (DEA).

Hollywood may be known for embellishment, but newly declassified documents show that Arkansas state officials were briefed about a joint CIA-Defense Department operation in Mena to assist the Contras, which Governor Clinton had to have known about. Clinton also, according to numerous whistleblower accounts, helped block investigation into the arms- and drug-running schemes—setting an important precedent for his presidency where he covered up for major state crimes. *American Made* director Doug Liman stated of Clinton's involvement in Mena, "we knew that somehow Barry was operating with immunity. The CIA was operating with immunity in Arkansas. So there had to have been some involvement of the governor's office. There is a prosecutor in Arkansas who was told to back off. And so we combined that with the fact that the CIA was for sure operating in Arkansas and Clinton was the governor, to condense it down into one specific moment."[1]

An Asset of the Three Bad Words

Clinton may have been recruited by the CIA while studying at Oxford University in the late 1960s as a Rhodes Scholar, or while an undergraduate at Georgetown University—a huge CIA recruiting center. He allegedly served as an informant on the antiwar movement in England as part of the CIA's Operation Chaos, giving the CIA the names of fellow protesters and the source of the movement's funding. While at Oxford, Clinton had sought assistance in evading the Vietnam War draft from a fellow Oxford student,

Richard Stearns, international vice president of the National Students Association, which received CIA funds. In exchange, Stearns allegedly helped provide funding for Clinton to travel to Moscow and Eastern Europe in March 1969. Later, Stearns helped set Clinton up as a key organizer for George McGovern's political campaign in Texas—where Clinton made key contacts that helped facilitate his rise to power.[2]

During Clinton's trip to Moscow, he was allegedly part of the mission to smuggle out the memoirs of ex-Soviet Premier Nikita Khrushchev, which were subsequently translated into sixteen languages.[3] This was a coup for Washington because of Khrushchev's denunciation of the crimes of his predecessor Joseph Stalin, which could be used to discredit Soviet communism.

Clinton's Oxford roommate Nelson Strowbridge "Strobe" Talbott III was attacked by Moscow newspapers as a "young sapling of the CIA" after he published one of the translations of Khrushchev's memoirs while working for *TIME* magazine. Talbott had come from an upper-class family in Shaker Heights, Ohio, studied Russian and wrote a thesis at Yale—a haven for CIA recruitment where he was part of the Skull & Bones secret society—on Fyodor Tyutchev, a 19th century Russian poet.[4]

Much later, from his perch as head of the Brookings Institute, Talbott played a key role in disseminating the Steele dossier, which spread misinformation helping to trigger nationwide paranoid and hysterical Russophobia and neo-McCarthyism.[5] Talbott's great-uncle, Harold E. Talbott Jr., as Secretary of the Air Force from 1953–1955, had given away the Air Force's authority to the CIA for overhead reconnaissance, and had worked with the CIA to promote development of the famed U-2 spy plane.[6] Talbott's wife, Brooke Shearer, and brother-in-law, Cody Shearer, who also played a role in RussiaGate, later became part of Bill and Hillary Clinton's "secret spy network."[7]

Washington insider Jack Wheeler related in his 1988 essay "How the Clintons Will Undo McCain" how his friend Cord Meyer Jr., the CIA's Assistant Deputy Director of Plans from 1967–1973 and later London station chief, told him about Clinton's past. Wheeler wrote:

> Back in the 1990s, years after he retired, if Cord drank a little too much scotch, he would laugh derisively at those conspiracists who accused Bill Clinton of being connected with the KGB. They all darkly point to Bill's participation in antiwar peace conferences in Stockholm and Oslo and his trip to Leningrad, Moscow, and Prague while he was at Oxford. "Who could have paid for this," they ask "it had to be KGB?" Cord would shake his head. "What

> rot—we paid for it. We recruited Bill the first week he was at Oxford. Bill's been an asset of the Three Bad Words ever since."[8]

This may explain a lot about Clinton's subsequent career, including his role in the Mena coverup.

The 1992 Presidential Election's Dirty Tricks

According to whistleblower Scott Barnes, who served on clandestine CIA missions in Laos in the 1970s and 1980s, the FBI interfered in the 1992 election to help secure Clinton's victory. Clinton's opponents in the election were incumbent George H.W. Bush and Ross Perot, a wealthy Texan and naval veteran who opposed the 1991 Persian Gulf War (supported by Bush and Clinton) and the North American Free Trade Agreement (NAFTA) and had funded efforts to uncover the truth about U.S. POWs allegedly left behind from the Indochina Wars. As a spoiler candidate, Perot was subjected to media smear attacks and FBI surveillance and harassment, forcing him to drop out. Stocks that he traded in were manipulated and a doctored photo was produced of his daughter, Caroline, kissing another woman, making her out to be lesbian.

Barnes says that he and other members of the Intelligence Support Activity (ISA), a secret quasi-paramilitary organization he was part of that was originally run by CIA Director William J. Casey, were contracted by the FBI for an undercover mission. His task was to visit the Dallas office of Jim Oberwetter, a prominent oil industry executive and Texas chairman of the Bush-Quayle campaign, wearing a wire, and to ask him leading questions to get him to say that he had damaging information about Perot. This would make it look like it was the Bush campaign leaking political dirt about Perot and not the FBI or other intelligence agencies—which were the ones actually doing it. The trick made both Bush and Perot look bad—but not Clinton. After the meeting with Oberwetter, Barnes says that he was invited to go on *60 Minutes,* where he was instructed to talk about alleged dirty tricks carried out by the GOP against Perot in the election campaign. Thus, Clinton was made the one to appear clean cut.[9]

According to Bill Hamilton, whose data mining company INSLAW was stolen by rogue officials in the Reagan administration so its software (known as Prosecutors Management Information System—PROMIS) could be used for their own financial gain and by the CIA, Clinton very likely received an unknown sum of off-the-books campaign contributions from U.S. intelligence. The money was obtained through insder trading profits amassed by front companies such as Systematics Inc., which worked closely with the NSA to facilitate intelligence monitoring of banking transactions.[10]

Systematics Inc.'s largest shareholder was Jackson Stephens, owner of Worthen Bank in Little Rock, which bailed Clinton out during the 1992 election campaign when he ran out of money.[11] A close friend of Jimmy Carter who switched from Republican to Democrat abruptly in 1990, Stephens had brought BCCI, which laundered drug money for the CIA, to the U.S. with the legal help of Hillary's Rose Law Firm.[12] Stephens also used his investment house and other banks that he owned to launder money in the Mena drug smuggling operation (discussed below). Stephens emerges thus as a key CIA conduit involved in high finance who helped Company man Clinton gain the highest office in the land.

Smoking Gun of the Whole Iran-Contra Affair

The 1992 election was unique in that both major party candidates were not only intricately tied to the CIA but also caught up in the Iran-Contra scandal. Former CIA Director George H.W. Bush as Vice President under Ronald Reagan had played a key role in the illicit shipment of arms to the Nicaraguan Contras—a counter-revolutionary army funded by the CIA who were seeking to overthrow the leftwing Sandinista government—as declassified government records have revealed.

Bill Clinton might have used this against Bush in the campaign, except that he was also involved in that effort. Bush and Clinton enjoyed a special rapport having been "bound together by the crimes of Iran Contra," as researcher Robert Morrow put it.[13] Arms shipments to the Contras were carried out during Clinton's governorship from the Mena Intermountain regional airport, located in Southwestern Arkansas's Ouachita mountains, "an outlaw's paradise, home to generations of moonshiners and red-dirt marijuana farmers."[14] The airport happened to be in the Congressional district of John Hammerschmidt, George H.W. Bush's former campaign manager (1976 and 1980).

Arkansas had been chosen for the clandestine operation—considered the "smoking gun of the whole Iran-Contra affair" according to army criminal investigator Gene Wheaton—because it was rural, underpopulated, and inland, and had a Governor who was supportive of the Agency and probably an "asset." Further, Mena was located seventy miles south of a large military base at Fort Smith.[15] Mark Swaney, head of the Arkansas Committee, which campaigned to have the Mena scandal investigated, concluded that Clinton at a minimum "knew all along about Mena," and it is "possible and even highly probable, based on a mountain of circumstantial evidence, that he was directly involved."[16] This involvement would have been through the Arkansas Development Finance Authority (ADFA), which according to ADFA marketing director Larry Nichols, helped to launder CIA and drug money from flights out of the Intermountain regional airport in Mena.[17]

Back in the 1970s, the Mena airport had been used to train guerrillas who were being sent on clandestine missions backed by the CIA in Africa. By the early 1980s, Mena had become a hub for a gun running operation to the Contras, Operation Centaur Rose, carried out in violation of the 1984 Boland Amendment. A secret CIA report disclosed the CIA's participation in a Pentagon training exercises at the Mena airport.[18]

Planes from the CIA-linked Evergreen Aviation were found parked at the Mena airport, where one of the hangars was owned by Carben Industries—which was run by CIA pilot Michael Bernard Palmer and whose board of advisers included CIA operatives Oliver North, Richard Secord, and CIA Costa Rican station chief Joe Fernandez; all key players in the Iran-Contra affair.[19] Employees at the airport said they were forced to stay in their offices because airplanes would land and strange faces would be around and people of Spanish origin who had never been seen before.[20] They also said they saw an unusual number of cash transactions in which the cash was left in drawers and people were working at all hours of the night to get planes out.[21]

CIA pilot Richard Brenneke, an expert in handling money transfers for the CIA, told IRS agent Bill Duncan that, starting in 1984, he flew about a dozen missions to Mena in C-130s, some of which involved flying weapons to Panama where they were unloaded by men serving Panamanian leader Manuel Noriega, a key conduit of supplies to the Contras. Brenneke claimed that he sometimes returned to Mena carrying unmarked boxes weighing up to 600 pounds that he later learned contained cocaine.[22]

Barry and the Boys

The plane of Eugene Hasenfus—which exposed the Contra operation when it was shot down over Honduras—had tellingly flown out of Mena; it belonged to Barry Seal, the legendary drug smuggler who worked as both a DEA informant and CIA operative.[23] Seal had been first recruited into the CIA in the mid-1950s as a Trans World Airlines (TWA) pilot when he flew arms first to Fidel Castro to overthrow dictator Fulgencio Batista and then ferried Cuban exiles and explosives into Cuba as part of CIA operations that were designed to overthrow and kill Castro. According to CIA pilot Robert "Tosh" Plumlee, Seal worked for CIA agent Ted Shackley in the 1960s and 1970s and flew covert missions in Vietnam and Laos during the Indochina War.[24]

A corpulent man from Baton Rouge, Louisiana with ties to New Orleans mob boss Carlos Marcello, Seal retrofitted his planes, which were delivered to him by mob-linked companies, at a hangar at the Mena airport, which he used also as a storage and hideout facility. In 1989, journalist John Cummings, in one of the first articles written on Mena, wrote that "Seal had virtually taken over a local aircraft repair and modification operation at the airport, and the good citizens of Mena began to notice some strange goings on: landings at night, tight security around Seal's planes, a hangar converted into a virtual fortress," along with sightings of what appeared to be air drops, the construction of airstrips deep in the woods, and even darker rumors that whatever was happening was sanctioned by the CIA.[25]

William Earle Jr., a Florida drug pilot whose testimony helped convict Seal in Florida in 1984, told Arkansas authorities he flew into Rich Mountain Aviation with Seal on December 13, 1983 and had an illegal auxiliary fuel tank installed on the plane to extend its range. He said later he flew the craft into Colombia and returned with 440 pounds of cocaine.[26] Customs officers surveilling the Mena airport recognized that Seal, who had been kicked out of Louisiana, was smuggling drugs right away because they observed that his plane was dirty—which meant he had been landing in remote areas. The rear seats were out, the edge of the plane's wings were clipped; it had paint chipped off, serial numbers of the plane were altered, fuel tanks were added, and the cargo doors were sealed to enable cocaine bundles to be dropped. And there was an awful lot of money floating around—airport owner Freddie Hampton purchased 109 acres of land in Scott County, Arkansas in 1982 and the following year, $150,000 worth of property near Lake Mena.[27]

Emile Camp, Seal's partner and a fellow Louisianan, died suspiciously in a plane crash in 1985 in the Fourche mountains just North of Mena.[28] Seal told federal and state investigators three months before he was murdered in February 1986 that "a nexus" of front companies—"legitimate" Arkansas companies, banks and airstrips—participated in the shipment of drugs and laundering of drug profits.[29] Seal is estimated to have brought in at least 36 metric tons of cocaine, 104 tons of marijuana and 3 tons of heroin into the U.S. totaling between $3 and $5 billion, dropping much of it off parachutes into the forests surrounding Mena.

A marijuana smuggler named Justin Adams claimed to have information that Seal worked at Mena with Joseph Vernon Haas, a 20-year Customs pilot and CIA agent along with Michael Bernard Palmer, another CIA pilot and drug smuggler, and Oliver North, a principal figure behind the Iran-Contra arms-drug smuggling operation. Another of Seal's associates, Patrick Foley, a veteran of the Flying Tigers (which flew arms to Chaing Kai-Shek during the Chinese civil war) and CIA operative, had recommended a drug smuggling pilot to the State Department for the transportation of "humanitarian supplies" to the Contras. Many of Seal's drug flights were part of the Operation Centaur Rose, though for every drug flight that Seal made for the government, according to an Arkansas police report, he made two for himself.[30]

"Manufacturing Anything in the Way of Weapons"

Clinton, despite his alleged hippie background, was a backer of the Contras, deploying the Arkansas National Guard on a joint military training mission in Honduras on Nicaragua's border. New York Governor Mario Cuomo (D) had boycotted the exercise, calling it a "provocation." Vermont Governor Madeleine Kunin (D) called it a "'backdoor escalation' of the American military presence in Central America."[31]

Arkansas and the area around Mena at this time became a hub for firms producing weapons and weapons parts along with electronic components used in weapons systems. ADFA loans went to military contractors like Missouri Research Labs Inc. (MRL) in the northeast corner of the state, which produced untraceable circuit boards and critical electronic components used in Stinger-missile guidance systems. Iver Johnson's Arms Inc., which was producing sniper rifles, and Brodix Manufacturing (weapons producers) were further given tax breaks by the state and other incentives as part of their reward for supplying Seal's network and providing a cover for clandestine work.[32]

Governor Clinton welcomed and even encouraged—notably at Pine Bluff and Pea Ridge—military arsenals and storage of dangerous materials that other governors of both parties spurned. CIA pilot Chip Tatum, who flew guns and drugs out of Mena to Central America with Barry Seal, alleges that during a clandestine flight to Palmeora Air Force base in Honduras, Clinton's top security man, Raymond "Buddy" Young told Mossad operative Mike Harari that "Arkansas has the capability to manufacture anything in the area of weapons and if we don't have it, we'll get it." When Harari asked about government control, Young replied: "the Governor's on top of it, and if the Feds get nosey, we hear about it and make a call. Then they're called off."[33]

Iran-Contra whistleblower Al Martin alleges that Clinton took a kickback from Arkansas Beltway trucking, which was paid to transport weapons from Ft. Campbell, Kentucky to Mena that were smuggled to the Contras on clandestine flights.[34] In 1991, a C-130 plane linked to Mena crashed in Angola with a mechanic from Arkansas, Chuck Hendricks, on-board. The plane was owned by a company controlled by a shadowy aviation specialist, Deitrich Reinhardt, who was involved in the Iran-Contra affair and the ferrying of arms to the Middle East.[35] The CIA at the time was ferrying arms to Jonas Savimbi and the right-wing National Union for the Total Independence of Angola (UNITA), which was fighting the left-wing Popular Movement for the Liberation of Angola supported by Cuba and the Soviet Union.[36]

Guerrilla Training in Arkansas' Wild West

By allowing the CIA to bring in Contra guerrillas and pilots for training in Western Arkansas, Governor Clinton turned his state in effect into a CIA property. Montgomery County Sherrif James Carmack and Scott County Game Warden Brian McKenzie received reports detailing the presence of contingents of foreigners in camouflage armed with automatic weapons, and caches of weapons secreted in highway culverts (Scott and Montgomery counties border Polk County, where Mena is located). There were also reports of machine gun fire around the Nella airstrip ten miles south of the Mena airport, of wildlife officers being rudely evicted, and sightings of pickup trucks with guns.[37] Car dealer Richie Cunningham and his son believed that they saw CIA agent Oliver North—who became famous during the Iran-Contra hearings—at Mena's Rich airport in 1985 or 1986.[38]

A number of former pilots for Air America (a CIA front company in the Indochina War)—including William Cooper and Wallace "Buzz" Sawyer Jr. who died in the Hasenfus plane crash—worked out of the Mena airport as part of Seal's crew.[39] Bill Holmes, a gun shop owner in Fayetteville, Arkansas, said that in May 1984 two CIA agents, Edward Malone and James Terrell, whose description matched that of CIA agent Jack Terrell, showed him a Mena address when they bought 250 machine guns from him at a price of $100,000, paying $10,000 in advance. The agents said that they had met Seal, who was known as "fat man," and that the guns were for a special operation run out of the Mena airport that had the approval of the White House and Vice President (George H.W. Bush) who was running it. When Eugene Hasenfus' plane was shot down, Malone told Holmes he had to shut down his operation. Holmes never got paid.[40]

Clinton's Direct Involvement

That Governor Clinton had sanctioned the entire operation was evident in his office's issuing of Arkansas Traveler certificates for General John Singlaub, a founding member of the CIA whom journalist Mike Wallace called the "virtual director of the Contra War," and Adolfo and Mario Calero, key commanders of the Contra terrorist army.[41] The ADFA's marketing director, Larry Nichols, who was described as a "romantic jungle fighter type," had served in Vietnam under General Singlaub, and was given authorization to make long distance phone calls to Nicaraguan Contra leaders by ADFA head Wooten Epps.[42]

Larry Douglas (L.D.) Brown, an Arkansas state trooper who worked as Clinton's personal bodyguard, wrote in his memoirs that Clinton helped him to write a paper supporting the U.S. position in Central America to gain employment with the CIA (CIA records confirm Brown's application). Brown then said that he flew missions with Seal, which he later realized were drug running missions. When he reported this to Clinton, Bill asked him "Are you having fun yet? Just do what you're told and don't ask questions." He also stated: "That's Lasater's deal," a reference to his top donor, Dan Lasater, who handled a lot of the money along with Jackson Stephens.[43]

Seal himself, who had an intelligence background, referred to Clinton as "the Guv," indicating a close relationship. Local investigators uncovered that Clinton sent a black assistant, Bob Nash, Hillary Clinton's deputy campaign manager in her 2008 run for the presidency, to allegedly pick up suitcases full of cash from Seal at Mena, which was Clinton's payoff money.[44]

Before he was killed, Barry Seal provided CIA pilot "Chip" Tatum with a list of Iran-Contra "Boss Hogs" who controlled the drug trade, which featured Clinton as well as George H.W. Bush. Tatum recalled being present during a meeting between CIA operatives Oliver North, Felix Rodriguez, Amiram Nir, and General Gustavo Alvarez Martinez from Honduras, which made it clear that Clinton was knee deep in the Mena-Central America cocaine venture.

Tatum said that when he ran cocaine into Mena in coolers, he was greeted by Dan Lasater, by Clinton himself, and by "Buddy" Young, whom he later saw in Honduras posing as a member of the Arkansas National Guard. Young told Harari, according to Tatum, that "we get our ten percent right off the top and that's plenty. GOFUS [pet word for Governor Clinton standing for "Governor of the United States," which is what Clinton thought he was] can make it go a long way."[45]

"An Enticing Climate for Traffickers:" The ADFA and Money Laundering

Founded in the 19th century by one of Arkansas' first Senators (Chester Ashley), the Rose Law Firm, of which Hillary Clinton and Webster Hubbell were senior partners, was an important component of the arms-drug smuggling scheme, allegedly negotiating contracts for the CIA in Mena, and helping to set up numerous fraudulent CIA fronts for cocaine and weapons transit.[46] A lot of his drug money was laundered through the ADFA via Lasater's brokerage house in the First National Bank of Mena and Worthen

Bank, which was owned by two major Clinton donors, Jackson Stephens and Mochtar Riady, and in which the Rose Law Firm held stocks (Rose Law Firm head Joseph Giroir was on its board of directors). The Governor's protection helped these banks evade the Bank Secrecy Act of 1970, which required currency transaction reports to be filed in connection with cash deposits or amounts of $10,000 or more at banking institutions.[47]

The Federal Reserve tellingly reported a 700 percent increase in such transactions between 1985 and 1989. Mary Kathryn Corrigan, the Secretary for Freddie Hampton, along with Kathy Gann and Lucia Gonzalez, two other secretaries at Rich Mountain aviation, all reported that they had deposited more than $10,000 in Union Bank of Mena in one day but in multiple checks to get around IRS regulations.[48] The IRS records were then removed from the state police files so information pertaining to Rich Mountain Aviation's cash transactions at local area banks was unavailable.[49]

The IRS office in Little Rock reported that drug traffickers were "bringing their money to Arkansas from other regions where pressure from authorities is more severe."[50] Under Clinton, Arkansas led the nation in cash surplus gains—a figure considered a reliable reflection of the amount of money being laundered. Cash deposits in Arkansas banks also tripled, suggesting huge amounts of drug money being moved. According to the IRS, a 210 percent increase in Arkansas' cash supply from 1988 to 1989 linked to an unexplained cash influx of $73 million suggested that Arkansas offered an "enticing climate for traffickers seeking to get their money into the legitimate economy."[51]

Three months before he was murdered in February 1986, Seal had testified to federal and state investigators that a "nexus" of front companies, "legitimate Arkansas companies, banks and airstrips participated in the shipment of drugs and laundering of drug profits [in Clinton's Arkansas]." Clinton had been on a first name basis not only with Seal but with a number of other high-profile CIA agents including Donald Gregg (alias Dan Magruder), a top confidante of George H.W. Bush who worked with L.D. Brown, and Felix Rodriguez (alias Max Gomez), the murderer of Che Guevara, who knew his way around the Governor's mansion and used to come in through the back door.[52]

Another Whistleblower Speaks

Terry Reed was a Missouri-born Air Force intelligence officer who in the early 1970s served with Air Force intelligence in Thailand as a member of Task Force Alpha, which controlled the secret air war in Laos and Cambodia. In the 1980s, he opened a machine tool business in Mexico, which served as a front company for moving arms to the Nicaraguan Contras. In his 1995 book, *Compromised: Clinton, Bush and the CIA,* Reed claims that he met with Clinton in July 1984 outside the Cantina Mexican restaurant in Little Rock, where Clinton gave him his blessing to undertake clandestine operations in Mexico with Barry Seal and Oliver North (AKA "Cathey") in support of the Contra operations.

According to Reed, Clinton was glassy eyed and smoked a joint while seated on a captain's chair on the street side of a van whose interior revealed a mobile command post equipped with an array of electronics. He urged Reed to toke on the joint, telling him, "go on, I'm the commander-in-chief here, you won't get busted," and said related to his mission, "that's good, that's good."[53]

Co-owner of an Arkansas-based company that made ultralight aircraft, Reed said that the first day he met Seal, he was "in the company of Dan Lasater and Roger Clinton" (Roger was the driver for Dan Lasater at the time).[54] Subsequently, Reed claimed that he entered into a consulting relationship with Seal, who was then a government intelligence asset. Reed said in a court deposition that Seal helped transport certain items for his aircraft business and wanted to make use of his military background.[55]

In 1983, Reed reported the theft of his twin-engine Piper Arrow airplane from Joplin, Missouri, on which he collected insurance. It was spotted by state policemen at Mena airport—after a gust of wind almost by divine will blew open its hangar door in front of state investigators—three days conveniently before the statute of limitation for federal fraud charges against Reed were set to expire. Just before that, Reed had resigned from the CIA, stating: "stuff our government was doing—they were criminal acts. Things you and I would go to jail for in a New York second."[56]

Reed and his wife Janis were charged with mail fraud but then acquitted. He claimed that "Cathey" had concocted the scheme in which his plane was "stolen" by "The Enterprise" as part of a project called "Donation" that he had been invited by Barry Seal to participate in. This was an operation based out of a Nella, Arkansas airstrip located near Mena called "Jake Bridge" to train Nicaraguan pilots to perform airdrops.[57]

According to Reed, payoff money to Arkansas government officials was flown in at night in what were called "green flights" and dropped in duffle bags on property owned by an associate of Governor Clinton. The money was then picked up and transported to Little Rock, where it was allegedly laundered through the Rose Law Firm and ADFA.[58] Reed also said he had knowledge of drug money being funneled through Dan Lasater, Roger Clinton's boss, with whom Bill enjoyed partying.

The key player in the Rose Law Firm money laundering was allegedly Vince Foster, Hillary Clinton's lover, who became Deputy White House Counsel following Bill's election to the presidency in 1992 and was murdered on July 20, 1993. A former Little Rock mayor and Associate U.S. Attorney General from 1993–1994, then working as a cut-out under Hillary Clinton and Webster Hubbell, Foster worked through Stephens' Systematics Inc., allegedly to wire the transfer of drug payoffs totaling in excess of $50 million to various banks, which then transferred the funds to accounts in the Cayman Islands and Switzerland.[59]

One of the agents who trained Contra paramilitary operatives in Nella was Luis Posada Carilles. He was a right-wing, CIA-linked Cuban terrorist nicknamed "Ramon Medina," who had planted a bomb on a Cuban airliner in October 1976, killing everyone on-board. Reed got chills when he heard Cariilles give a briefing in which he said that key Sandinista leaders would "soon disappear."[60] In Mexico, where he set up a business as a cover for arms and drugs smuggling, Reed said that he worked with North (Cathey), Felix Rodriguez (AKA Max Gomez) and an Israeli arms broker Amiram Nir (AKA Pat Weber) who later died in a plane crash.[61]

Reed's story was in part confirmed by the fact that serial numbers that he gave for planes he said had been used in training missions with the Contras, though stolen, were found by the International Aviation Theft Bureau to have been used in the Contra supply effort, or were found crashed while on illegal drug runs.[62]

Reed claimed that Clinton personally attended a meeting in an army bunker outside Mena whose participants included North, Felix Rodriguez, and one of CIA Director William Casey's top lieutenants, "Robert Johnson," who he thought to be future Attorney General William Barr. The latter threatened to shut down the Mena operation because too much money was being skimmed off the top (the reason Seal was probably killed), and Clinton was giving out too many contracts through the ADFA to Arkansas "good ole boys" who lacked security clearances. The arrest of Clinton's brother, Roger, had also brought unwanted scrutiny.[63]

In the meeting Johnson allegedly significantly referred to Clinton as "Mr. Casey's fair-haired boy" and said that "you and your state have been our greatest asset." He added that "the beauty of this, as you know, is that you're a Democrat, and with our ability to influence both parties, this country can get beyond partisan gridlock. Mr. Casey wanted me to pass on to you that unless you fuck up and do something stupid, you're no. 1 on the short list for a shot at the job you've always wanted."[64]

These comments—if true—would speak volumes about the forces that control American politics and propelled Clinton's political ascendancy from out of nowhere. Larry Nichols told presidential historian Robert Morrow before he died that there was no actual bunker near the Mena airport, so Reed's story may have been embellished—though it could have potentially been culled from a series of private conversations that actually took place.[65]

While Clinton claimed he was unaware of any problems at Mena until 1988, his bodyguard L.D. Brown's daybook records Clinton visiting Mena on May 21, 1984. Many people also reported seeing him at Mena airport, and Clinton's Chief of Staff, Betsy Wright, admitted that the Governor's office had, in the early 1980s, received repeated calls about drug trafficking there [in Mena]."[66]

A CIA secret report, partially declassified in 2020, specifies that "certain Arkansas state and local officials were informed" about CIA activities at Mena, and that unnamed official "personally briefed the supervisor of the Arkansas State Police district" for Mena, "the Mayor of Mena," "the Mena Chief of Police or the county sheriff, and the person responsible for operating Mena Intermountain Airport" about joint-training exercise with the CIA. With Clinton famously wired into everything happening in the state, he would have had to have been briefed.[67]

In September 1998, Desiree A. Ferdinand, the daughter of Colonel Albert V. Carone, a key liaison between the CIA and organized crime who worked closely with Barry Seal at Mena, testified in the U.S. district court of Massachusetts that her father spoke of a meeting off the record between Oliver North, Vice President George H.W. Bush, and Bill Clinton in Mena sometime in the mid 1980s. According to Ferdinand, her father indicated to her that Governor Clinton knew about drug running. He also said that Jackson Stephens "provided the backing of most of the money for half of this stuff [Mena drug smuggling]."[68]

Terry Reed quoted "Robert Johnson" as stating that shortly after ADFA got its initial funding, the CIA agreed to use ADFA to launder the black money it received through arms sales to the "freedom fighters." The deal "cut" with the Clinton administration in 1985 was that the CIA would pay 10% of the funds it received from Operation Centaur Rose to ADFA in exchange for the state's cooperation at all levels. For that percentage of the take, Clinton would ensure that state and local law enforcement agencies wouldn't expose the CIA's operations, prompting Seal to joke that Arkansas was "the only country north of Mexico where drug smugglers could get a police escort."[69] An informant told author George Carpozi Jr. that "Clinton was so much on the take, demanding under the table payments for sanitizing the drug money at the ADFA before it went to pay for the Contra arms, that his angels (the CIA) became disenchanted over his greed."[70]

Military Industrial Landscape and the Murder of a Journalist

The first company to receive ADFA funding, POM, had secret military contracts with the Stormont Labs of Woodland, California and the CIA-linked Wackenhut Corporation, to make weapon parts and guns that were sent to the Contras. It also manufactured chemical and biological weapons, according to Michael Riconosciuto, a CIA computer expert. He said that he supervised high-tech equipment transfers to POM and developed software to help launder the Mena drug money. An army reserve chemical warfare company was conveniently based next to POM's facility, on land previously owned by it. Company owner Seth Ward—a fighter pilot in the Pacific and Korean Wars and associate of James McDougal—had allowed his ranch to be used allegedly as a drop zone for Seal's drug deliveries.[71]

The Rose Law Firm not surprisingly drew up the paperwork for the ADFA's loan to POM. When Mark Swaney visited the POM site, he saw camouflaged trucks with trailers mounted with what looked like generators for creating smoke screens along with military transport trucks. He interviewed soldiers who told him they were part of a "smoke unit." IRS investigator Bill Duncan similarly saw chemical tanker trucks. Both were describing the scene of a military industrial landscape. Riconoscuito had developed computer software to help launder drug money emanating from the Mena operation. He was providing information to investigative reporter Danny Casolaro, who was subsequently murdered. A congressional subcommittee looking into Casolaro's death in September 1992 accused Justice Department officials of criminal misconduct and recommended the appointment of a special prosecutor, a request that was denied by Attorney General William Barr (AKA Robert Johnson).[72]

A Whitewash Like No Other

In September 1991, Arkansas Attorney General Winston Bryant and Congressman Bill Alexander (D) turned over several boxes of evidence to Lawrence Walsh's Office of Independent Council—which investigated the Iran-Contra affair—in the hopes that Walsh would extend his investigation into Mena. Included in the files were depositions, FBI files, and Arkansas state police investigative records. According to Alexander, these documents showed that Mena was "a staging area for the war in Central America." Alexander added: "I have never seen a whitewash job like that what has been executed in this case. There has been a conspiracy of the grandest magnitude that so far has not been prosecuted."[73]

A U.S. Senate subcommittee in 1989 called the available evidence about Mena sufficient for indictments on money laundering charges. However, Bill Clinton ensured that this never happened. Nine state and federal probes—headed by IRS agent Bill Duncan and "Razorback Columbo" Russell Welch, an Arkansas police investigator who had served as an army medic in Vietnam—were halted under higher orders. Welch was subsequently diagnosed with anthrax poisoning after a plot on his life.[74]

Duncan told a House subcommittee in 1991 that he had collected evidence detailing a "bizarre mixture of drug smuggling, money laundering and covert operations" implicating "contract operatives of the U.S. intelligence services" at the Mena Airport, had a 3,000 page file and had prepared 35 indictments for the U.S. attorney but they were never acted upon.[75] He said that the investigations into Mena were interfered with and covered up, and the justice system was subverted."[76]

In 1988, the Arkansas state police had begun shredding its Mena files. The DEA was conspicuously absent in the investigation and Clinton and his aide, Betsey Wright, told former Arkansas Attorney General Winston Bryant in 1990 to back away from the case.[77] State police officers testified that when they submitted a warrant to arrest Seal, they were told by Colonel Tommy Goodwin, head of the Arkansas state police, to leave Seal alone, and to cancel the warrant. Goodwin told them Clinton had ordered them to stand down.[78] (Later, when Seal was killed, the FBI took control of the crime scene and removed boxes from the trunk of Seal's car, which allegedly contained "compelling documents and tapes.")[79]

State trooper Larry Patterson stated that he was in Clinton's presence when Clinton was told about large quantities of cocaine coming into Mena airport and money and guns, and that Clinton did or said nothing. When Charles Black, a prosecutor for Mena-based Polk County, asked for a state probe, Clinton said he would "get a man on it" and furnish him with $25,000, though he never followed up. The $25,000 was such a paltry sum that Black said if it had actually been given, it would have "been tantamount to trying to extinguish a forest fire by spitting on it."[80]

When asked about Mena during the 1992 presidential election campaign, Clinton flat out lied, claiming that he had "authorized the expenditure of state funds in the 1980s to assist with a local investigation into Mena allegations and that 'nothing ever came of that.'"[81] This statement was contradicted by Charles Black, who had "hand-delivered a letter to the governor explaining the situation and asking for some assistance," he said. "I did not hear anything back from him."[82] Authors Roger Stone and Robert Morrow wrote with much accuracy that "Clinton provided the official political protection for the cocaine and drug smuggling [at Mena] while Lasater took care of the nuts and bolts of laundering the hundreds of millions of dirty drug money. And in their spare time it was drugs, parties and corrupting teenage girls."[83]

A Secretive Machine

In 1994, the *Economist* listed "eight unpleasant incidents of suicides and violence" surrounding people connected to the Clinton's and Mena affair.[84] One, Jerry Parks, was murdered in September 1993 driving home from a Mexican restaurant in Little Rock. A friend of Barry Seal, he had worked security for Clinton and allegedly made trips to Mena and would come back with envelopes filled with cash that he gave the Governor. Chip Tatum wrote that Parks assisted Dan Lasater in the pickup from Mena of large white coolers marked medical supplies. Tatum overheard Buddy Young say that if there was a problem [with the Mena operation] "[Jerry]'s the man [to solve it]."[85]

Parks had also kept a file of Clinton's private life, including his extra-marital affairs, with Vince Foster after being hired by Hillary following Bill's loss in the 1980 governor's race. Parks' wife Jane had caught Bill and Roger having drugs-sex parties with underage girls at Roger's up-scale apartment complex in Little Rock which she managed. After Parks' death, representatives of the FBI, Secret Service, IRS, and CIA ransacked Parks' former home and confiscated 130 tapes of phone conversations. Jane Parks said that her contacts in the Arkansas state police told her that Jerry's murder was "a conspiracy hatched in Hot Springs by five men who moved in the social circle of Buddy Young."

Allegedly, after Clinton stiffed Parks on an invoice, Parks had openly threatened to reveal what he and his wife knew about Governor Clinton and the drug trafficking operation out of Mena. Parks' son Gary told British reporter Ambrose Evans-Pritchard that he believed "that Bill Clinton had my father killed to protect his political career. We're dealing with a secretive machine here in Arkansas that can shut anyone up in a moment."[86]

Boys on the Tracks

The Mena cover-up extended to the murder of Kevin Ives and Don Henry, two high school seniors who were killed and then run over by a train on August 23, 1987 in Alexander northwest of Little Rock, after probably witnessing cocaine drops or cash, gold or platinum payments to persons working with U.S. intelligence or the theft of it. The police investigation was so bad that Ives' foot was found on the train tracks days after the murder.

An FBI agent said the State Democratic Party Chairman, Lib Carlisle, had called the state capital to call off the state police investigation of the "train deaths." State medical examiner Fahmy Malak, who had exonerated Clinton's mother after she was accused of helping to kill two patients at a Hot Springs hospital in 1978 and 1981 where she worked as a nurse, advanced the theory that the boys fell asleep on the tracks after smoking twenty marijuana joints and were run over by a train accidentally.

However, smoking twenty marijuana joints would make one euphoric, not incapacitated, and the toxicology lab never even tested for marijuana.[87] All of the engineers on the train reported that the boys were lying motionless beneath a tarp, bodies laid out identically across the tracks with almost military precision. Several witnesses placed two police officers—thought to be Pulaski County narcotics officers Kirk Lane and Jay Campbell, friends of Dan Lasater whose private jet they flew on—beating up two boys at a grocery store near where they found the boys' bodies. Their deaths were eventually determined by an independent investigation to have taken place before the train ran them over; Don Henry was stabbed in the back, and Kevin Ives was struck with a rifle butt in the face.[88]

When Saline County Deputy Prosecutor Jean Duffey, who headed a local drug task force, found witnesses who observed low-flying aircraft and drug pick-ups at the train tracks where Ives and Henry were killed, she was told by her supervisor, Gary Arnold, not to investigate any public officials for drug trafficking. She was then fired on a fraudulent pretext, as the Arkansas police determined, after a woman named Kathy Evans forged checks in her name to make it look like she was embezzling money. She was also smeared in the local media, issued bogus felony warrants, and forced to flee Arkansas and go into hiding out of fear for her safety after discovering that there was a $50,000 bounty out on her.[89]

Duffey felt the criminal conspiracy went up to the Governor's office and CIA, finding it odd that when Oliver North was asked about Mena at the Iran-Contra hearings, his response was given in a closed-door session. In the course of its investigation, Duffey's task force interviewed a CIA pilot living in Amarillo, Texas who went by the pseudonym Joe Evans, who said he dropped drugs over Saline county, and that he took orders from CIA operatives out of Mena. The drug drop the boys stumbled upon was part of Barry Seal's operation, which continued after Seal's assassination—likely by the CIA—in 1986.[90]

Evans' testimony was corroborated by Kevin's father, Larry Ives, who worked as a railroad man and said that Evans described the lights around the drop spot where the boys were killed and other things exactly the way they were.[91] When a Grand Jury was set up by Judge John Cole, key witnesses turned up dead. The victims included bar owner Keith McKaskle who passed on information to Police Deputy Cathy Carty, the only Saline County deputy on the tracks the night the boys died who strongly disagreed that the deaths were an accident, and Greg Collins, 26, who had been with the boys on the night of their death and was subpoenaed in the case.[92]

The Grand Jury investigation was headed by Saline County prosecutor Dan Harmon, a Clinton ally later sentenced to 11 years in prison for drug racketeering, who prevented the jury from ever revealing its findings and made sure that no one was ever charged with the murders. Sharline Wilson, a girl-friend of both Harmon and Roger Clinton who was supposed to make a drug pickup that night but was too high and so waited in the car, stated that Harmon was present when the boys were killed and that they were killed by police, with higher level officials participating in the cover up.[93]

Source: idfiles.com

Consistent with his role as protector of the corrupt Old Boys Network, Clinton refused to meet with Kevin Ives' mother, Linda, and even put her on his presidential enemies list.[94] Clinton stood by Malak's findings and retained him as state medical examiner and even gave him a raise after paying two out-of-state pathologists $20,000 from Clinton's discretionary fund to sanction Malak's work performance when he had botched the Ives-Henry and at least 20 other cases.[95]

Clinton meanwhile blocked the Arkansas state crime lab from conducting tests on the boys clothing, which the crime lab's trace expert wanted. Clinton additionally appointed as his state drug czar Robert Shepherd, a corrupt sherriff and "good ol' boy" from Saline County, who interfered and blocked three separate investigations into the train death, and told the U.S.

attorney Chuck Banks that former deputy prosecutor Jean Duffey, whose witnesses had presented evidence of drug trafficking and public official corruption, was crazy and that there was no corruption in Saline County.[96]

When he became president, Clinton ordered the resignation of all 93 U.S. attorneys, which helped hamstring the Ives-Henry and other investigations. Linda Ives wrote that while Clinton may not have been on the tracks the night Kevin and Don were killed, "make no mistake Bill Clinton's fingerprints are all over my son's murder case and I believe that Clinton pulled the strings from the very beginning and is still pulling them today."[97] Philip Weiss, a freelance magazine journalist, had told Ives at Clinton's victory speech after his last Gubernatorial election victory: "For all Clinton's bright promise and fine beliefs, he long ago made a deal with a benighted political organization that had thugs among its operatives. If you wonder why people hate him, it's because they recognize that training, they sense those crude values, that ruthlessness and lack of moral center. And they want an old-fashioned accounting."[98]

Endnotes

1 Adam B. Vary, "Why Bill Clinton And George W. Bush Are Portrayed In A Tom Cruise Movie About An Infamous Drug Smuggler," *Buzzfeed News,* September 20, 2017, https://www.buzzfeednews.com/article/adambvary/bill-clinton-george-w-bush-american-made

2 "The Real Bill Clinton—Spy, Smuggler, Scoundrel Extraordinaire?" https://monolithik.wordpress.com/2011/08/16/the-real-bill-clinton-cia-agent-drug-smuggler-and-scoundrel-extraordinaire/; Adam Janos, "Nixon and Johnson Pushed the CIA to Spy on U.S. Citizens, Declassified Documents Show," https://www.history.com/news/cia-surveillance-operation-chaos-60s-protest; "Clinton's Long CIA Connection," http://www.oocities.org/capitolhill/8425/CLIN-CIA.HTM; Roger Morris, *Partners in Power: The Clintons and Their America* (Washington, D.C.: Regnery, 1996); Karen Paget, *Patriotic Betrayal: The Inside Story of the CIA's Secret Campaign to Enroll American Students in the Crusade Against Communism* (New Haven: Yale University Press, 2015), 342. Stearns told an interviewer that he was a committed cold warrior. "Fighting communism was something I believed in very strongly." President Clinton appointed Stearns in 1993 to a seat on the United States District Court for the District of Massachusetts. One of the contacts that Clinton made working for McGovern in Texas was Betsey Wright, a future top aide. He said that he could "never have become president" without her. Abby Livingston, "Allies Remember A Driven Hillary Rodham During 1972 Texas Campaign," *The Texas Tribune,* May 16, 2015, https://www.texastribune.org/2015/05/16/clintons-take-texas-1972/. An oddity is that the Clintons spent the entire semester in Texas campaigning for McGovern, took a short vacation in Mexico after the election, and were still able to ace their finals without attending any classes. Either the standard at Yale is very low or somebody powerful was helping them.

3 "The Real Bill Clinton—Spy, Smuggler, Scoundrel Extraordinaire?" https://monolithik.wordpress.com/2011/08/16/the-real-bill-clinton-cia-agent-drug-smuggler-and-scoundrel-extraordinaire/.

4 See Michael Dobbs, "Strobe Talbott and the 'Cursed Questions," *The Washington Post,* June 9, 1996.

5 Tom Couser, "An Open Letter to Strobe Talbott About RussiaGate," *Scheer Post,* November 7, 2021; Paul Sperry, "Meet the Steele Dossier's 'Primary Subsource': Fabulist Russian From Democrat Think Tank Whose Boozy Past the FBI Ignored," *Real Clear Investigations,* July 24, 2020.

6 See Joseph Trevithick, "Before the U-2 Spy Plane, There Was the X-16," *War is Boring,* March 10, 2015, https://medium.com/war-is-boring/before-the-u-2-spy-plane-there-was-the-x-16-536e17d0ae2b; Dino A. Brugoni, *Eyes in the Sky: Eisenhower, the CIA, and Cold War Aerial Espionage* (Annapolis: Naval Institute Press, 2010).

7 Emily Sugarman, "Cody Shearer: Who is the Clinton friend behind 'second Trump-Russia dossier'?" *The Independent,* January 30, 2018; https://en.wikipedia.org/wiki/Terry_Lenzner. Brooke Schearer worked for Investigative Group International (IGI), a private spy agency run by a Clinton political fixer, Terry Lenzner. On the latter's career, see Terry Lenzner, *The Investigator: Fifty Years of Uncovering the Truth* (Blue Rider Press, 2013). The Shearers' father Lloyd wrote a popular column for Parade Magazine and was exposed as a CIA "asset."

8 Roger Stone and Robert Morrow, *The Clintons' War on Women* (New York: Skyhorse Publishing, 2015), 182; Dobbs, "Strobe Talbott and the 'Cursed Questions," *The Washington Post,* June 9, 1996; Morris, *Partners in Power,* 102. A government official who told Morris about Clinton's CIA ties claimed to have seen files long since destroyed. Another CIA retiree recalled Morris going through the archives of Operation Chaos at Langley headquarters and seeing Clinton listed. "He was there in the records," the former agent said, "with a special designation." Still another CIA source contended that part of Clinton's arrangement as an informer had been further insurance against the draft. Hillary Clinton may also have been recruited into the CIA as part of the Operation Chaos to infiltrate the antiwar movement. At Yale allegedly, she used her influence as a student leader to quell antiwar protest. See Victor Thorn, *Hillary (and Bill): The Sex Volume* (Washington: American Free Press, 2008).

9 Jeremy Kuzmarov, interview with Scott Barnes, September 15, 2022; James H. Rubin, "FBI Chief Defends Sting Aimed at Bush Campaign as Fair," *Reuters,* October 29, 1992. FBI Director William Sessions acknowledged mounting an undercover sting operation offering a supposed Ross Perot audio tape to Oberwetter, which Sessions said was "the only way to determine fairly and directly the credibility of the allegations of Republican dirty tricks." But if the sting was set up by the FBI, it was not the Republicans but the FBI that was engaging in dirty tricks while trying to set up Oberwetter. A CIA polygraph test confirmed Barnes had been telling the truth regarding his time in Laos and earlier career.

10 Author interview with Bill Hamilton, May 16, 2023.

11 Author interview with Bill Hamilton, May 16, 2023.

12 Charles R. Kubic, "Did Hillary's Law Firm Help Bring a Terror Bank to America? BCCI Was a Favorite of Terrorists and Money Launderers in the 1980s" *The National Interest,* June 30, 2016, https://nationalinterest.org/feature/did-hillarys-law-firm-help-bring-terror-bank-america-16794. David Bruce, the former President of an aircraft leasing company in Baton Rouge, LA that worked closely with BCCI/

Atlanta, told Bill Hamilton that a former CIA computer systems engineer, working as an independent contractor for Systematics Inc., installed unauthorized, copyright-infringing copies of the IBM mainframe computer version of PROMIS during the late 1970s in BCCI/Atlanta, BCCI/Panama, and BCCI/London.

13 Author Interview with Robert Morrow, January 7, 2023.

14 Micah Morrison, "Mysterious Mena," *The Wall Street Journal,* June 29, 1994, https://www.wsj.com/articles/SB833927551906129500

15 "Guns, Drugs, CIA at Mena, Arkansas: Judicial Watch Demands Answers," *Judicial Watch,* July 22, 2019, https://www.judicialwatch.org/investigative-bulletin/guns-drugs-cia-at-mena-arkansas-judicial-watch-demands-answers/; Deborah Robinson, "Mena, Arkansas: Iran-Contra's Smoking Gun Could Burn State's Democratic Hopeful in '92," University of Arkansas Special Collections, Mullins Library, Arkansas Committee Records, Box 1.

16 "Interview with Mark Swaney: Citizen's Group Investigates Mena Cover-Up," *Executive Intelligence Review 19,* no. 17, April 24, 1992, https://larouchepub.com/eiw/public/1992/eirv19n17-19920424/eirv19n17-19920424_054-mark_swaney.pdf

17 David N. Bresnahan, *The Larry Nichols Story: Damage Control—How to Get Caught with Your Pants Down and Still Get Elected President* (New Jersey: Camden Court, 1998). When the press got wind of the situation, Clinton fired Nichols allegedly for making hundreds of calls to Contra operatives. However, the very fact that he was making those calls breeds suspicion about the function of the ADFA, along with the convenient timing of the alleged discovery of these calls as a basis for firing him.

18 "Mena Uncovered: Judicial Watch Discloses Secret CIA Report," *Judicial Watch,* June 29, 2020, https://www.judicialwatch.org/investigative-bulletin/mena-uncovered-judicial-watch-discloses-secret-cia-report/; Office of the Inspector General Investigations Staff, "Report of Investigation, Unclassified Summary of Investigation Regarding Purported CIA Activities at or around Mena, Arkansas and Related Topics," November 8, 1996, https://www.judicialwatch.org/wp-content/uploads/2020/06/CIA-Mena-Report.pdf; Mara Leveritt, *All Quiet at Mena: A Reporter's Memoir of Buried Investigations* (Little Rock, Ark.: Bird Call Press, 2021), 222.

19 Al Martin, *The Conspirators: Secrets of an Iran-Contra Insider* (National Liberty Press, 2001), 227; Whitney Webb, *One Nation Under Blackmail, Vol. I: The Sordid Union Between Intelligence and Organized Crime That Gave Rise to Jeffrey Epstein* (Walterville, OR: Trine Day, 2022), 401.

20 Terry Reed, *Compromised: Clinton, Bush and the CIA* (New York: SPI Books, 1994), 125.

21 John Crudele, "'American Made' Sheds Light on Shady Arkansas Airfield Deals," *The New York Post,* October 25, 2017, https://nypost.com/2017/10/25/american-made-sheds-light-on-shady-arkansas-airfield-deals/. Local farmers were bought off through government subsidies that did not originate in the agricultural department.

22 Leveritt, *All Quiet at Mena,* 249; Rodney Stich, *Drugging America: A Trojan Horse,* 2nd ed. (Alamo, CA: Silverspeak Publishing, 2007), 54; "Interview with Mark Swaney," https://larouchepub.com/eiw/public/1992/eirv19n17-19920424/eirv19n17-19920424_054-mark_swaney.pdf; Paul Derienzo, Interview with Mark Swaney, WBAI Pacifica Radio, New York, https://totseans.com/totse/en/conspiracy/mena/165618.html; Jack Anderson and Dale Van Atta, "Legacy of a Slain Drug Informer," *The Washington Post,* February 28, 1989; Deborah Robinson, "Speaker: Mena was important Iran-Contra site," University of Arkansas Special Collections,

Mullins Library, Arkansas Committee Records, Box 1. Brenneke claimed that the drugs that he flew in entered the Gambino family distribution system headed by John Gotti, the New York mobster.

23 "Interview with Mark Swaney," https://larouchepub.com/eiw/public/1992/eirv19n17-19920424/eirv19n17-19920424_054-mark_swaney.pdf; Paul Derienzo, Interview with Mark Swaney, WBAI Pacifica Radio New York, https://totseans.com/totse/en/conspiracy/mena/165618.html; Jack Anderson and Dale Van Atta, "Legacy of a Slain Drug Informer," *The Washington Post,* February 28, 1989.

24 "Barry Seal," https://spartacus-educational.com/JFKseal.htm; Michael Haddigan, "'Fat Man' Key to Mystery," *Arkansas Democrat-Gazette,* June 26, 1988. Researcher Ole Dammegard suggests that Seal was recruited at the age of 17 along with Lee Harvey Oswald by CIA agent David Ferrie. Seal's wife Debbie claims that he flew a getaway plane out of Dallas after JFK was killed. Seal was pictured with a group of CIA agents and assassins recruited by David Atlee Philips at a Mexico City nightclub in January 1963. Ole Dammegard, "Operation 40: Origins of CIA's Ultra-Secret Hit Teams," in *JFK: Who, How and Why,* ed. Jim Fetzer and Mike Palecek (Crestview Florida: Moon Rock Books, 2017), 425, 426.

25 Quoted in Webb, *One Nation Under Blackmail,* 340.

26 Rodney Bowers, "Louisiana Heat Drove Seal North," *Arkansas Democrat-Gazette,* University of Arkansas Special Collections, Mullins Library, Arkansas Committee Records, Box 1.

27 Deborah Robinson, "Speaker: Mena was important Iran-Contra site," University of Arkansas Special Collections, Mullins Library, Arkansas Committee Records, Box 1.

28 "Co-pilot held answers sought in investigation, But he died in plane crash in 1985," *The Arkansas Gazette,* June 27, 1988, https://www.whatreallyhappened.com/RANCHO/POLITICS/MENA/witness_dies.html; Leveritt, *All Quiet at Mena,* 324; Deborah Robinson, "Mena, Arkansas: Iran-Contra's Smoking Gun Could Burn State's Democratic Hopeful in '92," University of Arkansas Special Collections, Mullins Library, Arkansas Committee Records, Box 1.

29 Alexander Cockburn and Jeffrey St. Clair, *Whiteout: The CIA, Drugs and the Press* (London: Verso Books, 1998), 328, 331.

30 Reed, *Compromised,* 275; Bresnehan, *The Larry Nichols Story;* Richmond Odom, *Circle of Death: Clinton's Climb to the Presidency* (Huntington House Publishers, 1995), 59–87; Cockburn and St. Clair, *Whiteout,* 327; Justin E. Adams to Mark Swaney, *Arkansas Committee President,* May 4, 1992, University of Arkansas Special Collections, Mullins Library, Arkansas Committee Records, Box 1. Seal was allowed to keep much of the money that he made in smuggling operations that he carried out while he was serving as a DEA informant. Rodney Stitch's CIA sources indicated to him that the profits from drug sales far exceeded what was needed for these [black] operations. They report that most of the profits were hidden in offshore financial institutions, and much of these funds come back in well-disguised forms and corporations, acquiring properties and businesses of all types. Rodney Stich, *Drugging America: A Trojan Horse,* 2nd ed. (Nevada: Silverspeak Enterprises, 2005).

31 Reed, *Compromised,* 383; Clay F. Richards, "The Nation's Governors Disagreed Sharply" UPI Archives, August 26, 1986, https://www.upi.com/Archives/1986/08/26/The-nations-governors-disagreed-sharply-Tuesday-over-the-Pentagons/5836525412800/. Primarily Republican Governors like John Ashcroft of Missouri sent their National Guards to Honduras.

32 Reed, *Compromised,* 63, 168, 169.

33 Gene Tatum, *The Tatum Chronicles: Oliver North, William Barr, Robert J. Mueller, George H. W. Bush. They Have This Dark Secret in Common* (D.G "Chip" Tatum, 1996); 33; https://inthebible.life/cia-whistleblower-clinton-bush-drug-trafficking/

34 Martin, *The Conspirators,* 156.

35 Webb, *One Nation Under Blackmail,* 345; University of Arkansas Special Collections, Mullins Library, Arkansas Committee Records, Box 1.

36 "C-130 Crash in Angola Still a Mystery," *Arkansas Democrat-Gazette,* University of Arkansas Special Collections, Mullins Library, Arkansas Committee Records, Box 1. See William Minter, *Apartheid's Contras: An Inquiry Into the Roots of War in Angola and Mozambique* (London: Zed Books, 1994).

37 Leveritt, *All Quiet at Mena,* 251; Thorn, *Hillary (and Bill),* 131, 132, 133, 134; Morris, *Partners in Power,* 416; Odom, *Circle of Death,* 75, 76; Reed, *Compromised,* 62, 87, 88, 125; "Guns, Drugs, CIA at Mena, Arkansas," *Judicial Watch,* July 22, 2019, https://www.judicialwatch.org/investigative-bulletin/guns-drugs-cia-at-mena-arkansas-judicial-watch-demands-answers/; Deborah Robinson, "Unsolved mysteries in Clinton country," *In These Times,* February 12–18, 1992, University of Arkansas Special Collections, Mullins Library, Arkansas Committee Records, Box 2. An IRS investigator noted "numerous reports of automatic weapons fire, men of Latin American appearance in the area, people in camouflage moving quietly through streams with automatic weapons, aircraft drops, twin-engine airplane traffic." The Ward family ranch was a key drop site for the cash from Mena green flights. Its owner, Seth Ward, was the father-in-law of Webster Hubbell, a partner of Hillary Clinton at the Rose Law Firm and key Clinton crony.

38 Leveritt, *All Quiet at Mena,* 220, 221.

39 Rodney Bowers, "Tale Brings Iran-Contra to Arkansas," *Arkansas Democrat-Gazette,* October 21, 1990, University of Arkansas Special Collections, Mullins Library, Arkansas Committee Records, Box 2.

40 After the 1988 election, thieves broke into Holmes' store and stole thirty guns, and after his shop went bankrupt, he was coerced into making illegal arms sales to make back some of his money. Bill Holmes, "A Kinder, Gentler Government," Unpublished manuscript; "Trial of Gunsmith Begins with Testimony of Agent," *Morning News,* September 8, 1993, 3A; Mark Mintoy, "Gunsmith Says Officials Lured Him to Break Law," *Morning News,* September 9, 1993: Mark Mintoy, "Gunsmith Not Guilty: Entrapment Defense Convinces 11 Jurors," *Morning News,* September 1993, University of Arkansas Special Collections, Mullins Library, Arkansas Committee Records, Box 1. When Holmes' shop went bankrupt, he formed a new firearms company after being approached by another CIA agent named Barr. But again he was put out of business and sought security in old age. Holmes said the whole thing "just ruined me."

41 Levereitt, *All Quiet at Mena,* 242; Deborah Robinson, "Unsolved Mysteries in Clinton Country," *In These Times,* February 12–18, 1992. A summary of Singlaub's centrality to the Contra War is found in Jeremy Kuzmarov, "CIA Bad Boy John Singlaub, Virtual Director of the Contra War, Dies at 100," *CovertAction Magazine,* February 9, 2022, https://covertactionmagazine.com/2022/02/09/cia-bad-boy-john-k-singlaub-virtual-director-of-contra-war-dies-at-100/

42 Webb, *One Nation Under Blackmail,* 362. Nichols was allegedly fired for making these calls though they had been authorized.

43 L.D. Brown, *Crossfire: Witness in the Clinton Investigation* (Black Forest Press, 1999); Office of the Inspector General Investigations Staff, Report of Investigation, Unclassified Summary of Investigation Regarding Purported CIA Activities at or around Mena, Arkansas and Related Topics," November 8, 1996, https://www.judicialwatch.org/wp-content/uploads/2020/06/CIA-Mena-Report.pdf.

44 Author interview with Robert Morrow, August 19, 2022. Morrow told me that Nash, who served as vice-president of the Winthrop Rockefeller Foundation in the early 1980s and then came to head the ADFA under Governor Clinton after serving as his economic adviser, was an alcoholic. In 1993, President Clinton appointed Nash to serve as an Undersecretary in the U.S. Department of Agriculture. In 1995, Nash was named assistant to the president and director of presidential personnel, in which he helped the president select candidates for presidential appointments, and recruited people to work in departments and agencies of presidential staff.

45 Tatum, *The Tatum Chronicles,* 6, 34; David Guyatt, "The Pegasus File," http://www.deepblacklies.co.uk/the_pegasus_file-part1.htm. Tatum was one of the U.S. Air Force's first elite combat controllers during the Vietnam War in Thailand and was captured by the North Vietnamese and held prisoner for 92 days. He was subsequently recruited into the CIA and supported special operations in Central America in the 1980s nicknamed Pegasus under the direction of Oliver North and Felix Rodriguez. When Tatum told North that he had discovered cocaine on his clandestine flights, North allegedly replied that it was one of the trophies of war. Buddy Young was later appointed by President Clinton as director of region 6 of the Federal Emergency Management Authority (FEMA) in Denton, Texas as reward for his service to Clinton and involvement in the Mena operation and its coverup.

46 Stitch, *Drugging America,* 31; Larry Chin, "Political Succession and the Bush-Clinton Nexus: Permanent Criminal State. The Legacy of George Herbert Walker Bush," *The Millenium Report,* December 2, 2018, https://themillenniumreport.com/2018/12/mena-cocaine-connection-when-the-bush-clinton-crime-family-ruled-arkansas/; https://inthebible.life/cia-whistleblower-clinton-bush-drug-trafficking/. Buddy Young allegedly told Mike Harari on a clandestine drug flight to Honduras: "Clinton thinks he's in charge, but he'll only go as far as Casey allows."

47 Thorn, *Hillary (and Bill): The Drugs Volume,* 135, 136. One of the principal stockholders in Stephens' banking consortium was the Director of the board of the Rose Law Firm, Joseph Giroir. An unwitting pawn in the CIA's money laundering schemes, Dennis Patrick, survived three assassination attempts and went into hiding in Florida. Reed, *Compromised,* 171.

48 Criminal Investigation Division, Russel Welch, Interview of Witness, January 7, 1986, University of Arkansas Special Collections, Mullins Library, Arkansas Committee Records, Box 1; Deborah Robinson, "Speaker: Mena was important Iran-Contra site," University of Arkansas Special Collections, Mullins Library, Arkansas Committee Records, Box 1. Lucia Gonzalez, another former Rich Mountain Aviation Secretary, testified before a Grand Jury in October 1985, saying that "on several occasions she had gone to the Union Bank of Mena with more than $30,000 cash and made deposits of less than $10,000 by using different tellers. She said that Freddie Hampton told her to do this to avoid paying taxes," the records said. That allegation was supported by the sworn testimony of Jimmy Dan Neugent, assistant vice president at Union Bank of Mena. Neugent told investigators that there were numerous CTR violations in connection with cash transactions by Rich Mountain Aviation. Rodney Bowers, "Seal Case Observers Cite Government Interference," *Arkansas Democrat-*

Gazette, December 6, 1989, University of Arkansas Special Collections, Mullins Library, Arkansas Committee Records, Box 1.

49 Rodney Bowers, "Seal Case Observers Cite Government Interference," *Arkansas Democrat-Gazette,* December 6, 1989, University of Arkansas Special Collections, Mullins Library, Arkansas Committee Records, Box 1.

50 Leveritt, *All Quiet at Mena,* 241.

51 Leveritt, *All Quiet at Mena,* 242; Stich, *Drugging America,* 69.

52 Stone and Morrow, *The Clintons' War on Women;* R. Emmett Tyrrell Jr., *Boy Clinton: The Political Biography* (Washington, D.C.: Regnery, 1996). Felix Rodriguez was a Cuban exile who fought in the Bay of Pigs and served in black operations in the Vietnam War. He was also a key figure in the Iran-Contra operation working with Oliver North and under George H. W. Bush.

53 Reed, *Compromised,* 320. See also Stone and Morrow, *The Clintons' War on Women;* Tyrrell Jr., *Boy Clinton,* 7, 12, 13, 18; Thorn, *Hillary (and Bill): The Drugs Volume,* 154.

54 Reed, *Compromised.*

55 Deposition of Terry Kent Reed, May 24, 1991, University of Arkansas Special Collections, Mullins Library, Arkansas Committee Records, Box 1. See also David Fallis, "Terry Reed: Covert Operator," *In These Times,* February 6–12, 1991.

56 Fallis, "Terry Reed"; Robinson, "Unsolved Mysteries in Clinton Country."

57 Reed, *Compromised;* Leveritt, *All Quiet at Mena,* 235, 236; Deposition of Terry Kent Reed, May 24, 1991, University of Arkansas Special Collections, Mullins Library, Arkansas Committee Records, Box 1; Rodney Bowers, "Tale Brings Iran-Contra to Arkansas, Arklansas Democrat, October 21, 1990; David Fallis, "Terry Reed: Covert Operator," *In These Times,* February 6–12, 1991, University of Arkansas Special Collections, Mullins Library, Arkansas Committee Records, Box 2. Reed reported that Buddy Young forged documents, used perjured testimony, and falsified evidence seeking to put Reed and his wife in prison. U.S. District Judge Frank Theis blocked their defenses and dismissed evidence showing the sham nature of the charges, claiming the evidence was irrelevant. *Time* also smeared Reed, fitting a pattern of attacks on people exposing government corruption and CIA drug trafficking. Stich, *Drugging America,* 71.

58 Reed, *Compromised;* Craig Roberts, *The Medusa File: Secret Crimes and Coverups of the U.S. Government* (Consolidated Press International, 1997), 325; Stich, *Drugging America,* 69. After Seal was killed, Lasater's bond business suddenly dropped, suggesting that Seal was indeed laundering money through Lasater's business.

59 Roberts, *The Medusa File,* 326–329. According to various sources, the Israeli Mossad learned of Foster's activities and forced him to leak codes and secrets to the Israelis in exchange for their promise not to expose him and his connections with drug running and money laundering for Clinton. However, when the CIA discovered Foster's treachery through use of PROMIS spyware software, Foster made plans to flee the country and may have contacted the Mossad. Subsequently he was murdered with his murder framed as a suicide.

60 Reed, *Compromised,* 113, 114, 177. Reed was charged with fraud.

61 Bowers, "Tale Brings Iran-Contra to Arkansas," University of Arkansas Special Collections, Mullins Library, Arkansas Committee Records, Box 2.

62 Bowers, "Tale Brings Iran-Contra to Arkansas," University of Arkansas Special Collections, Mullins Library, Arkansas Committee Records, Box 2.

63 Reed, *Compromised,* ch. 17; Thorn, *Hillary (and Bill): The Drugs Volume,* 161, 162.

64 Reed, *Compromised,* 277. Johnson continued: "you and guys like you are the fathers of the new government. We are the new covenant."

65 Author interview with Robert Morrow, January 7, 2023. William Barr for his part said that Reed's book was "totally false" and "crackpot.... I have never been in Arkansas. I have never met Clinton. I have never even met Casey, much less had a relationship to represent him in meetings, as the book describes." Dan Lasaater meanwhile told *The Washington Post* that the book "should be labeled fiction." Wally Hall, the sports editor of the *Arkansas Democrat-Gazette* said that Reed was mistaken in claiming that the two had dined together when Reed allegedly met Clinton who was parked outside in a van. Schneider, "Clandestination."

66 Thorn, *Hillary (and Bill): The Drugs Volume*, 157; John Crudele, "'American Made' Sheds Light on Shady Arkansas Airfield Deals," *The New York Post,* October 25, 2017, https://nypost.com/2017/10/25/american-made-sheds-light-on-shady-arkansas-airfield-deals/

67 "Mena Uncovered: Judicial Watch Discloses Secret CIA Report," *Judicial Watch,* June 29, 2020, https://www.judicialwatch.org/investigative-bulletin/mena-uncovered-judicial-watch-discloses-secret-cia-report/; Office of the Inspector General Investigations Staff, "Report of Investigation, Unclassified Summary of Investigation Regarding Purported CIA Activities at or around Mena, Arkansas and Related Topics," November 8, 1996, https://www.judicialwatch.org/wp-content/uploads/2020/06/CIA-Mena-Report.pdf

68 Desiree Ferdinand, testimony in United States District Court for the District of Massachusetts, September 29, 1998, videotaped by Gary Farnsworth of Audio Video Documentation Services, Albuquerque, New Mexico, provided to the author by Peter Osborne.

69 Odom, *Circle of Death,* 197, 198; Thorn, *Hillary (and Bill): The Drugs Volume,* 202.

70 George Carpozzi Jr., *Clinton Confidential: The Climb to Power: The Unauthorized Biography of Bill and Hillary Clinton* (Del Mar, CA: Emery Dalton Books, 1995), 381.

71 Thorn, *Hillary (and Bill): The Drugs Volume,* 206; Sam Smith, "Arkansas Connections," *The Progressive Review,* 1998, http://ontology.buffalo.edu/smith/clinton/arkansas.htm; Odom, *Circle of Death,* 138; Cockburn and St. Clair, *Whiteout,* 334–337; David Stout, "Seth Ward, 79, Businessman Involved in Whitewater Case," *The New York Times,* July 11, 2000. Government investigators concluded that Ward had been a "straw buyer" of parts of Castle Grande to hide the heavy involvement of the McDougals' savings institution in the Whitewater real estate deals. Roger Clinton and Ward's son-in-law, Finis Shellnut, allegedly participated in drug pickups from his ranch.

72 Ibid.; Danny Thomas, *The Octopus: The Secret Government and Death of Danny Casolaro* (Port Townsend, Washington: Feral House, 1996).

73 Deborah Robinson, "Speaker: Mena was important Iran-Contra site," University of Arkansas Special Collections, Mullins Library, Arkansas Committee Records, Box 1.

74 Brown, Crossfire, 226; Micah Morrison, "The Mena Coverup," *The Wall Street Journal,* October 18, 1994 in *Whitewater, Vol. II: From the Editorial Pages of the Wall Street Journal,* ed. Robert L. Bartley et al (New York: Dow Jones & Co.,

1997), 12, 13, and "Mena Coverup? Razorback Columbo to Retire," The Wall Street Journal, May 10, 1995, in *Whitewater, Vol. II,* 73; Thorn, *Hillary (and Bill): The Drugs Volume,* 182; Sam Smith, "Arkansas Connections," *The Progressive Review,* 1998, http://ontology.buffalo.edu/smith/clinton/arkansas.htm; Leveritt, *All Quiet at Mena,* 260.

75 Deborah Robinson, "Unsolved Mysteries in Clinton Country," *In These Times,* February 12–18, 1992.

76 Whitney Webb, "From 'Spook Air' to the 'Lolita Express': The Genesis of the Jeffrey Epstein-Bill Clinton Relationship," *Mint Press,* August 23, 2019, https://www.mintpressnews.com/genesis-jeffrey-epstein-bill-clinton-relationship/261455/

77 Stone and Morrow, *The Clinton's War on Women;* Carpozi Jr., *Clinton Confidential,* 349; Thorn, *Hillary (and Bill): The Drugs Volume,* 139.

78 Bresnehan, *The Larry Nichols Story,* 72; Micah Morrison, "The Mena Coverup," *The Wall Street Journal,* October 18, 1994, in *Whitewater, Vol. II,* 12, 13; Thorn, *Hillary (and Bill),* 218. State Attorney General Winston Bryant and Arkansas Rep. Bill Alexander sent two boxes of Mena files to special prosecutor Lawrence Walsh who never acted on the incriminating information.

79 Webb, *One Nation Under Blackmail,* 344.

80 Cyd Tabyanan, "UA Group charges Clinton did little on Mena inquiry," *Arkansas Democrat-Gazette,* January 30, 1992, 7B, University of Arkansas Special Collections, Mullins Library, Arkansas Committee Records, Box 2.

81 Deborah Robinson, "Speaker: Mena was important Iran-Contra site," University of Arkansas Special Collections, Mullins Library, Arkansas Committee Records, Box 1.

82 Cyd Tabyanan, "UA Group charges Clinton did little on Mena inquiry," *Arkansas Democrat-Gazette,* January 30, 1992, 7B, University of Arkansas Special Collections, Mullins Library, Arkansas Committee Records, Box 2.

83 Stone and Morrow, *The Clintons' War on Women;* Ambrose Evans-Pritchard, *The Secret Life of Bill Clinton: The Unreported Stories* (Washington, D.C.: Regnery, 1996), 236; Leveritt, *All Quiet at Mena.*

84 Tyrrell, *Boy Clinton,* 140, 141. See also Martin L. Gross, *The Great Whitewater Fiasco* (New York: Ballantine Books, 1994), 190–192 for a discussion of the suspicious deaths of others who investigated the Whitewater scandal.

85 Tatum, *The Tatum Chronicles,* 34, 93; Stich, *Drugging America,* 79; "Hillary's Baggage," *The Observer,* May 26, 2006, https://observer.com/2006/05/hillarys-baggage-a-story-from-my-former-life-as-a-clintonhater/. Allegedly Parks was given the nickname "the Archer," which was the code name that Casey and Colby assigned to him.

86 Evans-Pritchard, *The Secret Life of Bill Clinton,* 236, 239, 340; Stone and Morrow, *The Clinton's War on Women,* 33, 376. Author Victor Thorn wrote that Parks was killed because "he had the down and dirty on Mena, including huge payoffs, money laundering, how drug money was diverted into Clinton's campaign coffers, and Vince Foster's direct involvement. He also knew that Foster and Hillary had been lovers—another bombshell." Thorn, *Hillary (and Bill).* Officially, Parks' murder remains unsolved and there is one alternative suspect. https://seekingjusticeforjerryparks.blogspot.com/2016/03/murderer-interviewed-officials-mum-on.html. In April 2013, Gary Parks pleaded guilty to murdering his mother's second husband, marking him as a possible alternative suspect in his father's unsolved murder, according to Robert Morrow. The May 2022 death of Mark Middleton, a

special assistant to President Clinton in the White House, who was found hanging from a tree with a shotgun blast to his chest at a ranch outside Little Rock owned by Heifer International, a non-profit whose funders included Walmart, Blackrock and the Bill & Melinda Gates Foundation, is another suspicious one. Police strangely found little blood at the scene. There was no suicide note and an Arkansas judge sealed all photos, videos and video content related to the alleged suicide. Middleton had been privy to campaign finance irregularities, including donations to Clinton by the head of an Asian criminal syndicate and potentially treasonous action in allowing Chinese intelligence to penetrate the U.S. government in exchange for campaign donations. He had also helped facilitate most of Jeffrey Epstein's 17 White House visits during Clinton's presidency.

87 On Malak's corrupt career, see James Risen and Edward Chen, "Clinton's Ties to Controversial Medical Examiner Questioned," *Los Angeles Times,* May 19, 1992, https://idfiles.com/wp-content/uploads/2022/05/Clintons-Ties-to-Controversial-Medical-Examiner-Questioned.html. It is thought that the boys at most smoked one or two joints.

88 See Mara Leveritt, *The Boys on the Tracks: Death, Denial, and a Mother's Crusade to Bring Her Son's Killers to Justice* (Little Rock: Bird Call Press, 1999); Daniel Hopsicker, "The (Secret) Heartbeat of America: A New Look at the Mena Story," *The Washington Weekly,* May 12, 1997; https://idfiles.com/mena-and-the-cia/. Lane was appointed Arkansas drug czar in 2017 by Governor Asa Hutchinson. The boys' blood was dark and tar-like, indicating they had been dead sometime before they were struck by the train. Forensic pathologist Joseph Burton had determined that they had been beaten to death. Linda Ives told Daniel Hopsicker that "the most amazing thing we learned was that Kevin and Don were killed because of a very large drug smuggling operation that involved public officials and public corruption, even in the murders themselves."

89 Micah Morrison, "The Lonely Crusade of Linda Ives," in *Whitewater II,* ed. Bartley, 328, 329; Author interview, Jean Duffey, Siloam Springs, Arkansas, April 9, 2023.

90 Author interview with Jean Duffey, Siloam Springs Arkansas, April 9, 2023, https://idfiles.com/mena-and-the-cia/. Evans had worked as a mechanic also on Seal's airplanes at Mena airport, having been employed by Louisiana Aircraft.

91 Author interview with Jean Duffey, Siloam Springs Arkansas, April 9, 2023, https://idfiles.com/mena-and-the-cia/. Evans also passed a polygraph. He and some other pilots described mountains near the drop sight and a beacon on top of a building that were only identifiable to someone intimately familiar with the area, and not someone telling tall tales.

92 A full list of those connected to the case who were murdered includes: Keith Coney, who was with Kevin and Don moments before they were murdered; Jordan Ketelson, who was believed to be connected to the McKaskle murder; Boonie Beardon; Mike Samples, a Grand Jury witness allegedly involved in retrieving drugs dropped from airplanes; Richard Winters; and Jeff Rhodes who was murdered after telling his family that he knew too much about the case. See https://idfiles.com/investigations/saline-county-grand-jury/ In most cases there was no proper investigation into the deaths or autopsy performed.

93 Leveritt, *The Boys on the Tracks;* Victor Thorn, *Hillary (and Bill): The Murder Volume* (Washington, D.C.: Sysiphus Press, 2008), 470. Wilson's testimony was corroborated by another witness, subsequently placed in protective custody,

who said that he/she saw Harmon on the railroad tracks the night the boys were killed talking with someone, and that the boys came just after. Wilson herself was subsequently arrested by Harmon and given a draconian 31-year sentence for a minor drug offense. She said that Harmon told her: "Bitch, I told you, if you ever brought my name up, I'll take you down. I'm going to put you in prison and he did." A Democrat who was a gfted courtroom lawyer, Harmon was the one helping to control the media narrative after Duffey had begun to uncover the web of corruption.

94 https://idfiles.com/mena-and-the-cia/.

95 Risen and Chen, "Clinton's Ties to Controversial Medical Examiner Questioned," *Los Angeles Times.* When Linda Ives, mother of Kevin Ives, and others who felt wronged by Malak's decisions formed an organization, Victims of Malak's Incredible Testimony, or VOMIT, Clinton's staff refused to let it present the petitions to the Governor. Then as president, Clinton appointed Jocelyn Elders, the former Arkansas Health Department Director, as Surgeon General as a reward for years of covering up for Malak.

96 https://idfiles.com/mena-and-the-cia/. Duffey's task force significantly had developed information linking Shepherd to drug trafficking.

97 https://idfiles.com/mena-and-the-cia/.

98 Leveritt, *The Boys on the Tracks,* 322; https://idfiles.com/mena-and-the-cia/.

CHAPTER 3

Clinton's Dirty War in the Balkans

"Instead of resolving the humanitarian problem, what has been achieved is a giant humanitarian catastrophe."

—Russian President Boris Yeltsin to Bill Clinton, April 19, 1999[1]

"The war in Bosnia was America's war in every sense of the word. The United States administration helped start it, kept it going, and prevented its early end."

—Sir Alfred Sherman, a Balkan expert and former adviser to British Prime Minister Margaret Thatcher[2]

On August 10, 1995, the U.S. ambassador to the UN, Madeleine Albright put on an astounding performance before the UN Security Council in New York when she showed satellite photos drawn from a U-2 spy plane of areas near the Bosnian town of Srebrenica, the site of an alleged massacre of Muslims by Bosnian Serb forces. One of the satellite photos displayed a large group of Muslim people assembled in a soccer stadium at Nova Kasaba, 14 miles outside Srebrenica around July 13–14, and another a cleared area with freshly dug earth where the ground was supposedly disturbed a few days later, indicating the possibility of a mass grave. Ms. Albright told the Council that 2,000 to 2,700 people may have been killed there and hastily buried, though nothing definitive was proven. Albright repeated the phrase "We must not forget" five times, emphasizing the "magnitude of the suffering" she claimed was caused by the Bosnian Serbs.[3]

The timing of Ms. Albright's presentation was opportune as it helped deflect attention away from Operation Storm, a U.S.-backed Croat offensive in Krajina a mere few days before, which resulted in over 100,000 Serb refugees, the largest act of ethnic cleansing in the entire Balkans War. Albright's satellite photos also significantly did not show any actual killing, dead bodies or the burial or transport of dead bodies of Muslims, and she never actually made them available for public examination.

Like Colin Powell's infamous presentation about Saddam Hussein's alleged WMDs, Albright's presentation served as political theater which helped build momentum for American military intervention in the Balkans, and according to historian David N. Gibbs "made it easier for Clinton to justify a hawkish stance."[4] Albright was convinced that her testimony helped persuade Britain and France—which had long been gun-shy about taking decisive military action in Bosnia—to authorize a broad campaign of illegal NATO bombing later in August.[5] Within months, Clinton launched the Operation Deliberate Force bombing campaign, which was a prelude to the Operation Noble Anvil, the bombing of Kosovo. These operations were supported by liberal luminaries ranging from Samantha Power, Todd Gitlin, Susan Sontag, Vaclav Havel, Elie Wiesel, Bernie Sanders, Paul Wellstone, Maxine Waters, and Christopher Hitchens, to Michael Walzer, Michael Ignatieff, Bernard Kouchner, and Paul Berman.[6]

Vice President Al Gore frequently told the story of how his twenty-one-year-old daughter Karenna, after seeing stories about the Srebrenica atrocities on the news, asked her dad why the U.S. wasn't doing something to stop them.[7] No similar questions were asked, of course, about the Croat atrocities in Operation Storm, which could have been more easily halted by calling off American military and intelligence support.

As addressed earlier, Clinton and others in the "moderate wing" of the antiwar movement significantly had opposed the Vietnam War not because it was imperialistic, as some in the New Left called it, but rather because it was unwinnable. But now, here in the Balkans, they envisaged a war that could redeem the nation's honor tarnished by the earlier lost war, and revitalize the legitimacy of American exercise of its military power—a goal long embraced by the Pentagon—hence ending the "Vietnam syndrome."

Seeking to imply that he felt guilty about dodging the draft in the 1960s, Clinton stated that the war in Kosovo was a "chance [for him] to soothe regrets harbored in [his] conscience." According to a friend, Clinton would lament that "the generation before him was able to serve in a war with a plainly noble purpose, and felt 'almost cheated' that 'when it was his turn he didn't have the chance to be part of a moral cause.'"[8] Now that cause had been found, one which the baby boomers could rally behind. But in truth, it was based on the distorted belief that the Bosnian Muslim forces were striving for a multicultural society, while the Serbs were heirs of the Nazis, and justice had nothing to do with the project. Furthermore, the morally objectionable means adopted to carry out the war—including shady covert operations, illegal arms smuggling, bombing of civilians and media disinformation campaigns—were in actuality a betrayal of the ideals which Clinton and his generation had purported to profess in their youth.

Background to the Conflict and Exposure of Popular Myths

The 1990s NATO conflict in Europe was rooted in the growth of ethno-nationalism and the unraveling of the post-Tito Yugoslavian state, which was encouraged by the U.S. and by Germany, who saw an opportunity to balkanize and weaken Yugoslavia and in turn expand its regional influence. Josef Broz Tito was a communist partisan and leader of the Socialist Federation of Yugoslavia from 1953 until 1980 who promoted multicultural integration and religious tolerance, encouraging the main ethnic-religious groups—Serbs (Orthodox Christian), Croats (Roman Catholic), Bosniaks (Muslim), and Albanians (Muslim)—to work together. A leading country in the non-aligned movement, Yugoslavia's annual GDP growth averaged 6.1 percent during Tito's reign; medical care was free, the literacy rate was about 91 percent and life expectancy was 72 years while the state supported worker self-management.[9] Yugoslav industries ranging from automobiles and pharmaceuticals to household appliances and agricuture were so successful that they were competing with Western brands internationally—a competition which would disappear if the state were destabilized, dismantled and set back developmentally.[10]

Things began to unravel according to Western plans after Tito's death in 1980 when the country fell into debt. By 1990, independence movements arose in the provinces of Slovenia, Croatia, Macedonia, and Bosnia-Herzegovina (hereafter referred to as Bosnia).[11] The economic austerity and privatization imposed by the International Monetary Fund (IMF) enhanced social inequality and led to a collapse in industrial productivity and living standards, creating the conditions which exacerbated ethnic rivalries, and resulted in national disintegration and war.[12]

Joe Biden recounted in his memoirs that when Tito died, Averell Harriman, his political mentor and former U.S. Ambassador to the Soviet Union and Under-Secretary of State for Political Affairs, told him to "get to know Yugoslavia" because it was an "area we could bring into the 21st century as an ally."[13] In 1984, the Reagan administration followed this advice, issuuing a secret memo, NSDD 133, which advocated expanded efforts to promote a "quiet revolution to overthrow Communist governments and parties" while "reintegrating the countries of Eastern Europe into a market-oriented economy."[14] This strategy was continued under the Clinton administration, which supported secessionist movements and imposed sanctions combined with a devastating economic blockade on Yugoslavia—even though the World Court ruled that it was not the aggressor in Bosnia.

Serbia's socialist leader Slobodan Milošević was vilified because of his alleged pursuit of a Greater Serbia—even though the Republic of Serbia had played a central role in trying to preserve a unitary federal state in Yugoslavia, as was mandated under its 1974 constitution, and had supported two diplomatic settlements (the 1992 Lisbon Plan and 1993 Vance Owen Plan), which were rejected if not outright sabotaged by the U.S.[15] The first act of ethnic cleansing in the war was attributed to the Croats and not the Serbs, and the first civilian victim of the war was a Serb, Nikola Gordovic, shot dead by the commander of a Muslim paramilitary unit.[16]

Canadian peacekeeper intelligence files reveal that the Serbs were the most compliant with ceasefire terms while the Bosnian Muslims were the worst violators; that peace talks were impeded by Bosnian Muslim intransigence encouraged by the U.S.; that Bosnian Muslim troops "were going hell for leather" in the early days of the fighting and that most Serb military activity was "defensive or in response to Muslim provocation. "A September 1993 cable noted that in Sarajevo, "Muslim forces continue to infiltrate the Mount Igman area and shell BSA [Bosnian Serb Army] positions around the city daily," the "assessed aim" being to "increase Western sympathy by provoking an incident and blaming the Serbs."[17]

The Balkans war formally started in June 1991 after Slovenia and Croatia announced their independence. The Yugoslav army, dominated by Serbs, tried to put down the secessionist rebellions and occupied Croatia. The fledgling Croat army struck back by driving out two thirds of the Serbs from the capital of Zagreb and torturing and raping Serbs in cities like Vukovar. Croatia's president, Franco Tudjman, revived the traditional Croatian flag and coat of arms last used during the 1941–1945 pro-Nazi Usrasge dictatorship and stripped the Serb minority in Croatia of citizenship, jobs and land ownership.[18]

Valued for "slowly converting Croatia's economy from centralized state management to a market-based and free enterprise system," Tudjman increased his own control over all branches of government and deployed strongarmed tactics against workers involved in labor disputes.[19] According to former British Foreign Secretary David Owen, Tudjman's one purpose in life was to control all the territory he believed belonged to Croatia historically—by any means necessary.[20] Members of his inner circle assassinated a local police chief who tried to deescalate the conflict with the Serbs instead of moving to crush them.[21] In Gospic in September 1991, over 120 Serbs, including prominent professors and judges, were murdered by Croat militias commanded by a member of Tudjman's nationalist party who revived the slogans of the Ustashe.[22]

On October 14, 1991, Muslim and Croat legislators in Bosnia announced their secession from Yugoslavia. Radovan Karadzic, a psychiatrist who considered himself the greatest Serb leader since Karadjordje (AKA "Black George," who had led a Serb uprising against the Ottoman Turks in 1804), subsequently declared an independent Serb Republic of Srpska. American Ambassador Warren Zimmerman wrote that Germany had pushed the European community to support Bosnian independence.[23] The Bosnian army was helped by American Special Forces advisers and wore American military uniforms, supplied by U.S. military contractors.[24]

The new country's head of state, Alija Izetbegovic, managed to suspend an agreed provision that the Bosnian presidency should rotate between Bosnian Croats, Muslims and Serbs due to "extraordinary circumstances."[25] Izetbegovic was a front-man for Turkey who had been imprisoned for counter-revolutionary activity in the early 1980s and from 1946–1949 for his activities in World War II when he allegedly recruited young Muslims for a military unit organized by the SS Gestapo. In 1970, he had written a manifesto for "Islamic renewal," which exalted Pakistan as a model Islamic state, considered Western feminists as a "depraved element of the female sex," and declared: "There can be no peace or coexistence between the Islamic faith and non-Islamic social and political institutions. . . . the state should be an expression of religion and should support its moral concepts."[26]

The Serbs had a history of subjugation by the Ottoman Turks going back to their defeat at the famous Battle of Kosovo in 1389. As such, they had a legitimate reason to fear Izetbegovic and the rise of fundamentalist Islam. One Bosnian Serb asked a reporter why, after fifty years of living in Yugoslavia, should he "become a minority in a Moslem-ruled state?"[27] In 1995, Franjo Tudjman informed American officials that Bosnian-Muslim leaders had told him their plan for the Serbs was to "exterminate them all" and to "drive one and a half million Serbs out of Bosnia."[28]

Yugoslav army soldiers believed they were fighting in Bosnia to prevent an illegal secession and protect Serb minorities from persecution. The Serbs were able to capture 70 percent of Bosnian territory, though at a high human cost. Serb militias led by organized criminals like Zeljko Raznatovic (AKA Arkan) and extreme nationalists like Vojislav Seselj forced the evacuation of Muslim inhabitants from territory that they captured, destroyed Muslim mosques, and committed other crimes.[29]

The Bosnian army committed marked atrocities as well—including murdering three British aid workers, shooting handicapped Serb refugees in front of UN personnel and shelling Serbia's Orthodox church in Sarejevo.[30] In a few cases, Bosnian soldiers cut off a Serb soldier's head and then forced prisoners of war to kiss it or display it on a hook for intimidation.[31] Canadian intelligence files noted that "the Muslims are not above firing on their own people or UN areas and then claiming the Serbs are the guilty party in order to gain further Western sympathy. The Muslims often site their artillery extremely close to UN buildings and sensitive areas such as hospitals in the hope that Serb counter-bombardment fire would hit these sites under the gaze of the international media."[32]

Widespread corruption under Izetbegovic was epitomized by the theft of over $1 billion from public funds and international aid projects and by the indictment of Bosnia's ambassador to the UN, Mohammed Sacirbey, for stealing over $600,000 from Bosnia's UN mission.[33] Equipped with high tech communications equipment supplied by U.S. Special Forces who helped coordinate their offensives, the Muslim fighting regiments were bolstered by an influx of four thousand jihadist fighters from Afghanistan, Algeria and other Islamic countries.[34] They were described by U.S. officials as "pretty good fighters and certainly ruthless," and would videotape themselves committing war crimes against Serbs, including beheadings and torture," according to Lily Lynch, co-founder and editor-in-chief of *Balkanist Magazine.*[35]

Some of the Islamist warriors were recruited through the Al Kiffah Islamic Center in Brooklyn, New York which was managed by Omar Abdel-Rahman, the infamous Blind Sheikh who played a key role in the February 1993 bombing of the World Trade Center.[36] Rodney Hampton El, who was convicted on conspiracy charges in the World Trade Center bombing, said he was summoned to a meeting at the Saudi embassy in Washington D.C. where he was told that wealthy Saudis were sponsoring the holy war in the Balkans and given a budget of $150,000 to recruit and train mujahidin for Bosnia.

The U.S. 9/11 Commission report claims that two of the 19 alleged hijackers—Nawaf al Hazmi and Khalid al Mindhar—fought, along with Khalid Sheikh Mohammed, a mastermind of the 9/11 attacks, in Bosnia and that Osama bin Laden had service offices in Zagreb and Sarajevo. Renate Flottau, a respected journalist with *Der Spiegel,* said that he twice encountered bin Laden—a "tall, striking Arab with piercing eyes, a long, black beard"—in the foyer of the office of President Aliza Izetbegovic.[37]

For a brief period, the Croats and Muslims formed a coalition against the Serbs, though eventually they turned on each other.[38] When a Bosnian Muslim group in the northwest Bihac region led by Fikret Abdic declared its autonomy and established a mini-state allied with the Republic of Srpska after Sarajevo rejected an internationally brokered peace agreement, the Izetbegovic government launched a military attack against it with the assistance of Croatians and six U.S. Generals in violation of a ceasefire and UN declared safe area.[39]

Thousands of Abdic's supporters were killed and Abdic himself was the target of an Iranian trained assassination squad.[40] During the 1990 Bosnian elections, Abdic had gotten more votes than Izetbegovic but was not allowed to take office.[41] Lord David Owen described Abdic as "forthright, confident and different from the Sarajevan Muslims. He was in favor of negotiating and compromising with Croats and Serbs to achieve a settlement, and scathing about those Muslims who wanted to block any such settlement."[42]

The vicious cycle of violence on all sides of the war was captured in an August 1995 *Wall Street Journal* article by reporter Mark Nelson who, when visiting the ethnically cleansed Croat town of Knin, noticed that the only Serbs left were "grandmas and grandpas" who were too old to leave. A German-trained Croat had moved into the empty hospital and a new Croat attendant took over the formerly Serb-run filling station. An army private, Ivan Aulsvic, told Nelson that he had little concern about the Serbs who had departed, since what we did "only mirrors the bombing and burning of Croat houses four years ago [when the war first started]. You may not understand this need for revenge, but I do."[43]

Fake News, Yellow Journalism and Atrocity Fabrication

Each side in the war developed grievances against the other and committed its own share of atrocities, including the Serbs, who were in the beginning most committed to preserving the Yugoslav Union and to supporting diplomatic peace treaties. The mainstream media, however, explicitly advanced the cause of the Bosnian Muslims, who were depicted as the victims of Serb racism and aggression. In his memoir, James Baker, Secretary of State under George H.W. Bush, said that he instructed his press Secretary to help the Bosnian Foreign Minister to utilize the Western media to further the Bosnian Muslim cause, noting that he had her "talk to her contacts at the four television networks, *The Washington Post* and *The New York Times.*"[44]

Many of the most pro-interventionist reporters and intellectuals were liberals with a lineage going back to the 1960s anti-Vietnam War movement. They were looking for a cause and war they could justify on human rights grounds that would reaffirm American exceptionalism. Susan Sontag, author of the 1969 antiwar travelogue, *A Trip to Hanoi,* denounced the United States and the West in an October 1993 essay in *The New York Review of Books* for "giving victory to Serb fascism" and wrote that in the Bosnian capital, she had staged Beckett's *Waiting for Godot,* even though Sarejevans were actually "waiting for Clinton"—to bomb.[45]

Anthony Lewis of *The New York Times,* one of the paper's main critics of the Vietnam War, had written another inflammatory piece a year earlier entitled "Yesterday's Men" in which he described the Serbs jamming Bosnian Muslims into freight cars after seizing a village as the equivalent of Nazis transporting Jews in 1942. Castigating the Bush administration for denouncing then–presidential candidate Bill Clinton's call for meaningful action to stop such Serbian atrocities, he wrote that it "reminded him of Prime Minister Neville Chamberlain explaining in 1938 why Britain should not care about Nazi designs on Czechoslovakia." It was, Chamberlain had said, "'a quarrel in a faraway country among people of whom we know nothing.'"[46]

Roy Gutman of *Newsday* won the Pulitzer Prize for his Bosnia reporting in 1993 jointly with John Burns, pointing to the existence of a Serb run concentration camp, which he likened to a death factory, though his account depended heavily on Croat and Muslim officials and witnesses with suspect credentials and implausible claims which later proved to be false. In a 2003 interview with former French official Bernard Kouchner, President Izetbegovic confessed his exaggeration shortly before his death, stating that the claims were designed to trigger a bombing campaign by western powers.[47]

After the takeover of Srebrenica by the Bosnian Serbs, *The New York Times* ran an inflammatory piece by Stephen Kinzer entitled "Genocide in Bosnia," which had photos of Muslim men hanging from trees and alleged that there had been mass abductions of women and rape. The article was based on second-hand information sources, and acknowledged in fine print that there was no independent verification of the allegations.[48] The style of this and many other articles was reminiscent of the yellow journalism during World War I when the Germans were accused of gruesome atrocities, including mass rapes in Belgium, as part of a propaganda campaign.[49] Slobodan Milošević was depicted as the reincarnation of either Joseph Stalin or Hitler and said to have had the "soul of a mass murderer," as *The New Yorker's* chief Washington correspondent put it.[50]

The Bosnian Muslims and Croats had been savvy in hiring the public relations firms Ruder-Finn and Hill & Knowlton, the latter of which had previously worked for the Kuwaiti government, spreading false stories about Saddam Hussein's atrocities on the eve of the First Persian Gulf War.[51] James Harff, the director of Ruder Finn, emphasized the effectiveness of using words "with high emotional content such as ethnic cleansing, concentration camps, etc." which "evoked images of Nazi Germany and the gas chambers at Auschwitz. No one could go against it [even though he admitted the information was not verified] without being accused of revisionism."[52]

When the UN's chief political officer for Bosnia-Herzegovina Philip Corwin rebuked N*ew York Times* Balkans correspondent Roger Cohen for being a "cheerleader" who practiced "advocacy journalism," Cohen basically agreed, saying, though, that the Serbs were "racists"—an assessment that ignored the fact that the Serbs had experienced 500 years of Turkish occupation and hence had legitimate fears of the Muslims. When Corwin tried to tell Cohen that the Serbs had a reasonable complaint insofar as the international community took away their country and Serbs did not want to live in a Muslim country, Cohen ignored that, retorting that Milošević and Karadzic were war criminals.[53]

Cohen's demonization of the Serbs and adoption of a simplistic good versus evil paradigm was reminiscent of the yellow journalism of the Hearst Papers at the turn of the 20th century when they played up Spanish atrocities in order to rally public opinion to support the Spanish-American War.[54] In the Balkans case, the media aroused liberal opinion against the Serbs and created the perception that the Bosnian Muslims were victims who could only be saved by American military intervention. This dovetailed well with the illusion cultivated by some prominent liberal intellectuals that Izetbegovic's Bosnian Muslim regime was committed to creating a multicultural state.[55]

Bill Clinton was ultimately as responsive to the political climate shaped by the media and intellectual class as William McKinley had been in 1898. According to Dick Morris, the incessant TV coverage of scenes of depravity in Bosnia prompted Clinton to remark, "They keep trying to force me to get America into a war."[56] McKinley no doubt felt the same way in his time, as did Woodrow Wilson during World War I.

Clinton and the Interventionists

While he was astute in recognizing the policy implications of the media coverage, Bill Clinton, as discussed earlier, was a political animal who based every decision on a political calculus rather than morality. He had advanced an imperial agenda going back to the 1980s when he supported the Contra War in Nicaragua. Accordingly, during the 1992 presidential campaign, Clinton issued a policy statement on Bosnia, saying that the U.S. should "take the lead in seeking UN Security Council authorization for air strikes against those who are attacking the relief effort. The U.S. should be prepared to lend appropriate military support to the operation."[57] On August 5, Clinton further challenged the Bush administration's hands-off policy, saying, "We may have to use military force. I would begin with air power against the Serbs to try to restore the basic conditions of humanity."[58]

These latter comments epitomize how Clinton was using Bosnia to show his toughness on foreign policy while at the same time courting Vietnam era doves who wanted the U.S. to promote human rights. The climate for intervention was hastened by the emotions that had been evoked by the opening of the Holocaust museum in Washington, DC and by the visit of

Czech President Vaclav Havel to Washington, who was a strong proponent of military intervention against the Serbs.[59]

In Clinton's rendering, "the renegade regime of Slobodan Milošević" had "sought to expand his power by inciting religious and ethnic hatred," and "unleashed wars in Bosnia and Croatia" which "left two million refugees" and "a quarter of a million people dead."[60] This assessment overestimated the number of deaths by nearly 150,000 and ignored the fact that Milošević's ethnic nationalism was also adopted by his Croat and Muslim counterparts. The wars in Bosnia and Croatia began also when the governments of those regions declared their independence from Yugoslavia, which Milošević and the Serbs opposed.

Clinton's campaign strategists allegedly told him to take up the Bosnian Muslim cause so that Clinton could show that he was supportive of Muslims while still sustaining his support for Israel, which was not involved in the Balkans. He could then in turn exploit a split in the Arab world between the perceived good Arabs who were on America's side—including the Saudis—and bad radical ones led by Saddam Hussein and Muammar Qaddafi of Libya.[61]

Ironically, Clinton had compared Russian President Boris Yeltsin to Abraham Lincoln when he crushed the secessionist movement in Chechnya. The Russians were responsible for 80,000 casualties there from 1994–1996, far more than the number attributed to the Serbs, but Russia was then an American ally and so the Yeltsin regime's atrocities did not inspire a demand for humanitarian intervention like those of the Colombians, Israelis, Indonesians and Turks.[62]

Clinton displayed his political skill in successfully framing the illegal military intervention in Bosnia as having "helped to combat genocide [by the Serbs] in the heart of Europe" and "stop[ing] crimes" and "sav[ing] lives."[63] Clinton's hawkish views—he told French President Jacques Chirac how on different occasions he had "pressed NATO to take tougher action [against the Serbs]"[64]—were shared by his vice president, Al Gore, who had urged Clinton from the beginning to take a strong stand against Milošević and to press for the lifting of the UN arms embargo.[65] Gore had had meetings with Bosnian Muslim representatives even before Clinton's inauguration.[66]

Madeleine Albright, Clinton's appointee as U.S. Ambassador to the UN and later Secretary of State, National Security Council Adviser Anthony Lake, First Lady Hillary Clinton, and Undersecretary of State Richard Holbrooke, also pushed for military intervention against the Serbs. On the other hand, the CIA, Defense Department, and U.S. Army Joint Chiefs of Staff advocated for a more cautious approach compared to the State Department. This reflected a bizarre switch in roles, with a bellicose State Department policy countered by a reticent military.

According to Dutch researcher Cees Wiebes, the CIA under director James Woolsey developed a nuanced view of the conflict that acknowledged Bosnian Muslims and Croat atrocities along with those of the Serbs and repeatedly pointed out that the Muslims had close links with various fundamentalist governments and terrorist movements and were supplied from Iran. The Clinton administration, however, "wanted to hear nothing of this" and inserted that it was possible to establish a multiethnic society in Bosnia. In early 1995, Woolsey resigned from his position. The CIA was thereafter accused of "blatantly distorting intelligence" to support the Muslims' case as the CIA station in Bosnia became among its largest in Eastern Europe.[67]

The UN peacekeeping force was not entirely neutral in the conflict. It subscribed to a predominantly anti-Serb bias, and one State Department cable cited the "right wing sympathies" of the Dutch forces.[68] The Clinton administration's military strategy relied on air power, new drone technology, covert arms supplies and the use of private military contractors. Michael Ignatieff acknowledged in *Virtual War: Kosovo and Beyond* that,

> the American public and its military came away from Vietnam unwilling to shed blood in wars unconnected with essential national interests. The debacle in Vietnam brought the draft to an end and the result widened the gulf between civilian and military culture. Masculinity has slowly emancipated itself from the warrior ideal.... In a society increasingly distant from the culture of war, the rhetoric politicians use to mobilize their populations in support of the military becomes unreal and insincere. The language of patriotism is losing its appeal.[69]

The way to overcome this, according to Ignatieff in a view embraced by the Clinton administration, was by emphasizing the humanitarian imperative underlying the war, enhancing media censorship and distancing the public from the war by ensuring that ordinary citizens had no personal stake in it.

Forging a Third American Empire

A key underlying purpose of the intervention in the Balkans was to justify the existence of the North Atlantic Treaty Alliance (NATO) following the end of the Cold War and to begin facilitation of its expansion into Eastern Europe. Slovenia, Croatia and Montenegro joined NATO in 2004, 2009, and 2017, and Bosnia-Herzegovina joined via a Membership Action Plan, becoming a "NATO aspirant country."[70] Milošević was the last communist leader in Europe, and seen as a relic from a bygone era. In 1999, Clinton began promoting the Southeast European Trade Initiative modeled after the Andean Initiative, which eliminated tariffs on a host of imports from the Balkans, with the exception of Serbia under Milošević, whom the administration was trying to isolate.[71] There had also been talk of setting up a "mini-Marshall Plan" for the Balkans that would foster greater regional economic integration and solidify Western ties to new countries that might be considered for early European Union (EU) or NATO membership.[72]

The secessionist movements in Yugoslavia had originally been supported as part of a strategy of divide and rule adopted by the Austro-Hungarian Empire and Ottoman Turks. Neoconservatives Jacob Heilbrunn and Michael Lind wrote in *The New York Times* in January 1996 that Americans should view the Balkans as the

> western frontier of America's rapidly expanding sphere of influence in the Middle East. . . . The fact that the United States is more enthusiastic than its European allies about a Bosnian Muslim state reflects, among other things, the new American role as the leader of an informal collection of Muslim nations from the Persian Gulf to the Balkans. The regions once ruled by the Ottoman Turks show signs of becoming the heart of a third American empire.[73] [The first two centered on Europe, Latin America, and Southeast Asia.]

The U.S. achieved a giant step towards achieving this goal by expanding its network of overseas military bases with the construction of Camp Bondsteel on 775 expropriated acres of rolling countryside as a spoil of victory in the Kosovo War. The U.S. government was already, at the time of the war, funding feasibility studies for a billion-dollar pipeline to be built by the Albanian, Macedonian and Bulgarian Oil Corporation (AMBO) of Pound Ridge, New York to go from the Black Sea port city of Burgas in Bulgaria to the Albanian Adriatic port of Vlora—the cheapest way to siphon Caspian oil off the European route on the way to the U.S.[74]

In 1999, the Croatian government under Tudjman signed a $600-million road-building contract with Bechtel Corporation of San Francisco, which donated close to $400,000 to the Democratic Party in the Clinton years, and a $175-million contract with the Houston-based Energy company Enron, which gave a $100,000 contribution, for building and operating a power plant and supplying electricity for the next 20 years.[75] In April 1996, Clinton sent Commerce Secretary Ron Brown on a trade mission to Croatia whose purpose was to help U.S. companies such as Boeing get an edge on competition for up to $5 billion in procurement contracts.[76] This was part of the economic stakes of the Balkans war that were largely ignored in the media and by proponents of humanitarian intervention.

A Neocolonial Agreement

Shortly after Clinton's election victory in 1992, his administration blocked a negotiated settlement to the conflict agreed upon by the Serbs, which had been unveiled by Cyrus Vance, Jimmy Carter's Secretary of State now working for the UN, and former British foreign secretary David Owen. The plan called for 43 percent of the land area of Bosnia to be controlled by the Serbs, 32 percent by the Croats and 25 percent the Muslims. Independent observers considered the plan to be most favorable to the Croats.

Milošević and the Serbs, according to former U.S. ambassador to Bosnia, Warren Zimmerman, were willing to sign it.[77] But Clinton administration officials impeded the negotiations. They told Izetbegovic to reject the plan and gave him the impression that U.S. military intervention was imminent after he visited Washington. In the words of Clinton's Secretary of State, Warren Christopher, the Vance-Owen Plan "simply appeased Serb aggression." In fact, however, as historian David Gibbs points out, the Vance-Owen plan was not especially favorable towards the Serbs and did not reward ethnic cleansing as the 43 percent of land that the Serbs were to receive was considerably less than what the Serbs had controlled prior to the onset of the fighting.[78]

With the breakdown of this agreement, the Bosnian war dragged on for another two-and-a-half years with tens of thousands of additional casualties and atrocities against non-combatants. In November 1995, Richard Holbrooke won great fame for bringing the three big leaders together—Milošević, Tudjman and Izetbegovic—to sign the Dayton accords at a U.S. airbase in Ohio. The Accords created the Serb Republic and granted it 49 percent of the total area in Bosnia compared with 51 percent for the Muslim-Croat Federation. The total accorded to the Serbs was greater than that in the Vance Owen Plan, which would have prevented the war if the U.S. hadn't impeded it.[79]

John Hopkins University Dean and Iraq War architect Paul Wolfowitz criticized the Dayton agreement for "pulling Milošević's chestnuts out of the fire."[80] With Yugoslavia now permanently dismembered, peace activists characterized Dayton differently—as a "neocolonial agreement" due to the occupation of Bosnia by 60,000 NATO troops, 20,000 of them American, and the drafting of a new constitution for Bosnia granting full executive powers in all matters to a Swedish official, Carl Bildt, appointed by the UN Security

Council, who could overrule the prime ministers and appointed ministers. The head of the police force was an Irishman appointed also by the UN. The U.S. sustained heavy military training programs and economic policies were controlled by the European Bank of Reconstruction and Development and the IMF, which imposed privatization and austerity measures that served to trap the people in poverty.[81]

In 2003, a European think tank compared Bosnia's relationship with Europe to that of India with Britain during colonial rule, with the creation of the position of high representative akin to that of imperial viceroy.[82] As part of the spoils of this war, NATO had acquired military bases in Zadat and Salvonski Brod, Croatia, while upgrading three military airfields in Bulgaria. A Bosnian Serb, Radoslav Skrba, wondered: "how is it that all those western armies now have bases here? Could it be that was their strategy all along? During the Communist time we were warned that the West wanted to come here and now they are here."[83]

The consequences were hardly positive. In 1998, NATO intervened in municipal elections and threatened to destroy any radio or television station or newspaper that criticized NATO's presence in Bosnia. David Chandler, author of "Bosnia: Faking Democracy After Dayton," wrote in 2004 that "the international powers of the administration, under the Office of the High Representative, have been vastly increased. As far as the engagement of the people of Bosnia or the elected representatives is concerned, little has changed in the ten years since the Dayton agreement was signed. The Bosnian public has been excluded from the transition process."[84]

Phony Pretexts

The Shelling of Sarajevo

From the sinking of the USS *Maine* to the Gulf of Tonkin incident to the mythic WMDs in Iraq, there is a long history of staged incidents in which elements of the U.S. government willfully deceived the American people in order to engender public support for war.[85] Two key incidents in the Balkan War appear to fit this broader historical pattern, serving as the major triggers for American military intervention. The first was the shelling of Sarajevo's Markale Market Square in two separate incidents on February 5, 1994, and August 28, 1995, both of which were attributed to the Serbs. Sixty-eight and thirty-seven civilians were killed in these incidents which provoked great public outrage. Just thirty-nine hours after the latter marketplace explosion, the first wave of U.S. planes started the long-planned-for bombing operations.

Curiously, State Department spokesman Nick Burns was talking about Serb responsibility and airstrikes before the UN investigative report into the atrocity even reached New York. David Binder reported in *The Nation* that four UN Protection Forces (UNPROFOR) specialists (a Russian, a Canadian, and two Americans) had arrived at the incontrovertible conclusion, based on the low trajectory of the shell, that it could not have been the Serbs but was a Bosnian army shell.[86]

The same conclusion was made by Lt. Col John Sray, the former head of the American intelligence section in Sarajevo, and by the British Joint Intelligence committee, the most important British body in the field of intelligence.[87] The intelligence and security services from Canada, the UK, Denmark, Sweden, Norway, Belgium and the Netherlands established independently of each other that the February 5th attack was also carried out by Bosnian forces to show the Serbs in a bad light, or in the words of a British Lt. General, to attract Serb fire "in the hope that the resulting carnage would further tilt international support in their favor."[88]

The Srebrenica Massacre

The Srebrenica massacre of July 13–14, 1995 was another major trigger driving U.S. intervention. In a phone conversation with French Prime Minister Jacques Chirac on July 13th, Clinton indicated that his military advisers had told him that the Muslims could have "made a hell of a fight in Srebrenica and raised the price of the Serbs occupation, but they didn't do it"[89]—suggesting that the Muslims had allowed their own men to be massacred in order to make the Serbs look evil and draw in U.S. military intervention. General Philip Morillon, head of the UN mission, referred to Serb commander General Radko Mladic as having fallen "into a trap" in Srebrenica.[90]

Clinton himself could have prevented any such massacre if he had responded to a hand delivered letter on June 12 written by Radovan Karadzic, the head of the Republic of Srpaska, explaining the Serb fear of Muslim domination and calling for a "Camp David" type peace summit.[91] The proclaimed Srebrenica massacre occurred a month later following a five-day battle for control of the strategic town, which had been occupied by Muslim forces under Naser Oric, the commander of the Bosnian Army's 29th Division who was curiously absent during the peak of the fighting.[92]

Srebrenica's population had swelled as Muslim refugees migrated there with the collapse of Muslim defenses in neighboring regions. It became a "Hobbesian world," according to an official history, "of black marketeers and gun-toting quasi military commanders," with high levels of destitution and disease. Living lavishly from black-market proceeds, Oric cast a romantic figure who was celebrated in Muslim folklore and songs as a symbol of resistance. However, Oric's forces reportedly had killed upwards of 3,000 Serb soldiers and civilians from the Srebrenica area since the war began, including the town Mayor.[93] U.S. Ambassador to Croatia, Peter Galbraith, dismissed these atrocities as being "in the scheme of things, not a big issue,"[94] a callous statement certainly from the point of view of the Serbs whose killings at Srebrenica were carried out in revenge.

During the fighting from July 6th through 11th, four U.S. fighter planes destroyed a Serb tank, though the UN force, consisting of mostly Dutch peacekeepers, failed to intervene decisively or protect Muslim soldiers from Serbian revenge killings. Human Rights Watch referred to the U.S. bombing as a "meager display, too little, too late."[95] Hakija Meholjic, wartime president of the Muslim political party SDA in Srebrenica, claimed that Bosnian Muslim leader Aliza Izetbegovic told them that Bill Clinton had advised him that American intervention would only occur if the Serbs killed at least 5,000 people in one single incident.[96]

Very conveniently, a thirty-five-year-old Muslim refugee purported to present evidence to a UN official, which was passed on to American officials, that the Bosnian Serbs had "massacred many if not all of the 5,000 plus military age men in their custody following the fall of Srebrenica." The refugee said that he and others had been transported to a soccer stadium on trucks and buses that were shot at and then taken to Konjevic Polje where they were made to lie down and machine gunned. Purporting to offer proof that he had been handcuffed, the refugee said he survived only because the bullet grazed his temple, creating a bloody appearance but which did not kill him.[97]

The 5,000 number stands out because it is the precise total that Clinton had said was necessary for U.S. military intervention. Could the report have been exaggerated or made up to satisfy the 5,000 body count figure, which this mysterious refugee could not corroborate were all killed? The numbers and circumstances surrounding the killings at Srebrenica are generally shrouded in mystery. The official version promoted by Western governments and media is that 8,000 Muslim military aged males were executed by Serb forces, after they had been separated from the women, children, and elderly, in the worst war crime or act of genocide in Europe since World War II.

The 2001 International Criminal Tribunal for Yugoslavia (ICTY) judgment of Serb commander Radislav Krstic gave a lower estimate of seven thousand men that were captured by the Serbian forces and concluded that "almost all of them were killed; only very few survived."[98] However, the court's judgment also stated that "few mortal remains" were found near the alleged killing sites because of an attempt to cover up the crimes,[99] though the logistics and ability of the Serbs to do so while fighting a war would have been very difficult.

In July-August 1995, journalists on the scene did not report on any massacres, nor did UN human rights investigator Henry Wieland, who could find no eyewitnesses to atrocities after five days of interviewing 20,000 Srebrenica refugees gathered at the Tuzla airport refugee camp.[100] International Committee of the Red Cross (ICRC) interviews indicated that a total of 3,000 military aged males who were arrested by the Bosnian Serbs in Srebrenica and Potocari and separated from civilians were missing and that one-to-two-thousand of the missing who fled Srebrenica were still unaccounted for as of September 1995.[101]

In a telephone call with President Clinton on July 20, 1995 in which he was urging more "robust air strikes" Bosnia's Muslim President Aliza Izetbegovic cited UNPROFOR estimates that 3,000 people had been "killed" in the "recent tragedy in Srebrenica" though he said he feared that the figure is bigger.[102] Clinton himself in a conversation with French President Jacques Chirac on July 13, 1995, had stated that 3,000 Bosnian troops "left" Srebrenica "under the pressure of shelling.[103]

Two State Department officials reported to National Security Council adviser Anthony Lake on August 4, 1995 that "hundreds and perhaps up to a thousand persons (principally men and boys)" had been executed, which is what he had been told by John Shattuck, the State Department's human rights coordinator who interviewed refugees and had access to the latest intelligence reports.[104] The ICTY later reported that 2,570 bodies had been found in Srebrenica area graves between 1996 and 2001, far less than the official 8,000 figure, in a time-frame extending well beyond the alleged massacre.[105]

The Sarajevo-based International Commission for Missing Persons (ICMP), an adjunct of the ICTY, which matched the DNA from bone samples with family members of persons reported as missing, in 2007 identified a total of 6,930 Srebrenica victims.[106] However, it suspiciously refused to turn over its samples to the defense in the Radovan Karadzic trial and failed to report that some on the list had gone missing or died prior to July 1995. The ICMP study furthermore could not determine the cause of death.[107]

Many of the autopsy reports had referred to bodies where only shell or mortar fragments were found, militating strongly against the thesis that they were executed. Others lacked any bodily injuries or visible injuries derived from firearms, suggesting a death from natural causes or in some other way that rules out execution.[108] An official history refers to the ambush of Muslim soldiers who were retreating from the scene of the battle and seeking to reach Bosnian government-controlled areas. They were killed by mortar and infantry fire, while others died from land mines. Estimates of how many of those killed were armed vary, but 70 percent of victims were part of the Bosnian army, according to military records found by ICTY researchers.[109]

In a 2003 commemorative speech, Clinton condemned the Serb masterminds of the Srebrenica massacre for their "genocidal madness" stating that "bad people who lusted for power killed these good people simply because of who they were," and that Srebrenica had "laid bare for all the world to see the vulnerability of ordinary people to the dark claims of religion and ethnic superiority."[110] Misusing the term genocide, this assessment obscured the context in which the Serb massacres had occurred—if indeed they had—and the motive underlying them. In the weeks and months before, Muslim regiments led by Naser Oric had carried out a reign of terror targeting Serb villages and civilians in which treasured cultural artifacts such as a 14th century Orthodox monastery in the sacked town of Sase were demolished and women and children were taken captive, a practice unknown in modern European warfare.[111] Many of those killed at Srebrenica served in Oric's regiments and were targeted by the Serbs out of revenge.

Oric's brother, Melvuddin, later turned up as one of the main witnesses during the ICTY trial of Serb commanders. Another chief witness, Serbian Drazen Erdemović, was accused by Serb leader Slobodan Milošević of being a mercenary in the pay of a NATO power (France), a charge given some plausibility by the fact that his commander was arrested in Belgrade in 1999 for being part of a mercenary unit which committed atrocities that were blamed on Serbs. Granted a light sentence and new identity in exchange for his testimony, Erdemović claimed that 1,200 people were executed by his unit in a mere five hours which was not substantiated by any forensic evidence (only 138 bodies were found in the area and a small number of cartridges). Another witness claimed that the victims were taken to the killing site at Pilica in seven buses which could seat about 50 people. Seven multiplied by 50 gives a total of 350, far less than the total Erdemović claims.[112]

The full truth about the Srebrenica massacre may never be fully known. Serb forces clearly committed war crimes; however, mainstream depictions obscured the context in which these atrocities occurred while promoting allegations of a massacre which have not been substantiated. The political implications have been considerable as the name Srebrenica continues to sustain the moral credibility of the U.S. military intervention and its alleged humanitarian imperative—and indeed to tarnish that of UN peacekeepers who purportedly stood aside while it took place.

Clinton's Iran-Contra: Smuggling Arms to the Balkans

Bill Clinton, as discussed, was recruited as a CIA intelligence asset at Oxford, and as Governor of Arkansas helped to oversee and cover up an illegal arms, drugs and gun running operation to the Nicaraguan Contras, which was in violation of the 1984 Boland amendment. As President, Clinton again performed a role that he was used to: overseeing a clandestine-arms smuggling operation. This time it was through Iran to Muslim-Croat forces in Bosnia, and was carried out in violation of a UN arms import embargo that had been adopted by the Security Council in September 1991. On April 27, 1994, Clinton approved the plan to deliver arms from Iran despite not only the arms embargo, but also the Clinton administration's own policy of trying to isolate Iran because of its alleged support for international terrorism.[113]

The State Department and U.S. ambassador to Croatia, Peter Galbraith, son of the famous economist John K. Galbraith, were the key drivers behind what Richard Holbrooke termed the "not so secret secret." It was coordinated by the National Security Council without informing Congress or the intelligence community. To make the deliveries—which were packaged as "humanitarian assistance"—U.S. officials cooperated with regional mafias and used cargo aircraft associated with a CIA front company, Southern Air Transport, avoiding use of U.S. Air Force planes. Iran's new embassy quickly became the largest in Sarajevo, with UN personnel forbidden to come near it.[114] Because the secret Iranian flights were landing with such frequency at Zagreb's Pleso airport (three flights per week at its peak), aircraft were diverted to the island of Krk in the Adriatic, where the CIA reportedly operated a base, to deflect awkward questions. The Croats used helicopters to fly the weapons and munitions from Krk after dark to bases in Bosnia for distribution to Muslim forces.[115]

Galbraith and the NSC further coordinated the arms shipments through Saudi Arabia and Turkey, which gave the United States additional plausible deniability. When asked about secretive C-130 cargo flights and night-time air drops on Tuzla delivering arms, a British General responded with great certainty that "they were American arms deliveries. No doubt about that. And American private companies were involved with those deliveries." A British researcher further stated: "who else has the skills and expertise to carry out such a swift, delicate mission covertly? The Saudis, the Turks? The Iranians? Specialized crews and types of aircraft for these night-time operations indeed appeared to point in only one direction: that of the United States."[116]

Operation Storm and the Use of Private Mercenaries

The Clinton administration's reliance on private military contractors (PMCs) was part of the strategy of distancing the public from the war and ensuring plausible deniability. It also reflected the Clintons' embrace of neoliberal ideology and its fetishization of privatization and the market and diminishment of the ideal of public service. A favored company was Military

Professional Resources Inc. (MPRI), whose Virginia headquarters displayed a plaque which read: "War is an ugly thing but not the ugliest of things. The decayed and degraded state of moral and patriotic feeling which thinks that nothing is worth war is much worse." Harry E. Soyster, head of the Defense Intelligence Agency (DIA) when it used private arms dealers to equip the Afghan mujahidin and Nicaraguan Contras, bragged, "we've got more Generals per square foot here than in the Pentagon."[117]

MPRI won the lucrative contract in the Balkans to train and modernize the Croatian army, overseeing the rooting out of "communist dead wood," which set the groundwork for ethnic cleansing by helping to create an ethnically pure Croatian army (many of those purged had served in the Yugoslavian integrated force). The State Department used MPRI to provide a secret conduit of heavy weapons, including artillery batteries used for shelling Serb towns, in violation of the UN arms embargo. An important conduit for these clandestine purchases was Cypress International Inc., a war-materiel supply firm of which MPRI president Vernon Lewis was an eExecutive.[118]

In July 1995, MPRI director Carl Vuono, former Army Chief of Staff, met with General Zvonimir Cervenko at an island retreat to plot strategy for Operation Storm (named after Desert Storm), in which Croat soldiers would kill thousands of Serbs in Krajina, burn their villages and expel over 150,000 in the war's largest act of ethnic cleansing.[119] MPRI helped the Croat army to implement an "air, land and battle doctrine" and provided real time coded and pictorial information from U.S. reconnaissance satellites over Krajina, training units directly implicated in war crimes. Clinton himself gave the green light for the operation through the U.S. military attaché in Zagreb, Colonel Richard Herrick, stating that it had to be "clean and fast," which was then transmitted in real time to the Pentagon.[120] State Department official Robert Frasure wrote to his boss, Richard Holbrooke: "We 'hired' these guys [the Croatian military] to be our junkyard dogs because we were desperate. We need to try to 'control' them. But this is no time to get squeamish about things. This is the first time the Serb wave has been reversed."[121]

Serb victims sued MPRI for complicity in genocide, stating that the company was aware of the pro-Nazi sentiments of Croat leader Franjo Tudjman and his henchmen and that "there could be no doubt of what the training and armaments that MPRI was going to provide." During the contract negotiations, [Defense] Minister [Gojko] Susak told the MPRI representative: "I want to drive the Serbs out of my country.'"[122] This was as strong a blueprint for ethnic cleansing as any other documented in the war. DynCorp International, another company that contributed to the defeat of Serb forces in the Balkans, brought embarrassment when two of its employees were accused of participating in the child-sex slave trade—which flourished during the war years—along with the illegal arms trade.[123] What better embodiment of the moral turpitude of Clinton's foreign policy in Bosnia than that?

Truly Outrageous Human Rights Reports on Croatia

The Clinton Presidential Library in Little Rock, Arkansas includes a collection of human rights reports on Croatia in the aftermath of Operation Storm compiled by the U.S. State Department that were sent to Ivo Daalder, a Director for European Affairs on the National Security Council staff. The reports detailed high incidents of violent assaults, harassment, looting and thefts by Croat soldiers and civilians targeting Croatian Serbs, especially in the town of Knin where the Orthodox Church was blown up along with a monument commemorating World War II. Croat Serbs were subject to discrimination including withholding the distribution of benefits. When refugees returned home after being displaced by Croat military offensives, they frequently found their houses or apartments occupied by Croats and could not rely on the assistance of local authorities in regaining possession of them. When one Croat Serb couple who had worked for 30 years as teachers in the Knin primary school tried to reclaim their home, they were angrily derided by local officials as "chetniks"—a derogatory term for Serbs. Another elderly Serb man was detained by police when he asked for their help after returning to his home in Kakonj, Bosnia only to find it occupied.[124]

Some of the most violent incidents were attributed to persons wearing Croatian military uniforms. One was a "female Croatian army soldier who directed several violent attacks by soldiers in the Knin area." Croat police officers were also alleged to be involved in looting and other crimes."[125] In Northern Bukovica, an elderly couple of mixed Serb-Croat origin were shot dead in their home, which was then set on fire, their corpses thrown into the blaze. Next door, in the village of Berkovac, a 60-year-old woman was beaten and raped before being locked in her closet. In Ocestovo, Serb homes were burned along with the school in the center of the town, while in the Plavna Valley, police and soldiers were involved in the theft of Serb property. When one of the victims who had recorded the license plate of a vehicle used by the looters attempted to report the crime to the police, the police refused to accept the complaint.[126]

The police did little further to investigate arson and physical attacks on NGOs promoting reconciliation with the Serbs or attacks on the president of the Croat Helsinki commission who was beaten in his apartment and had an explosive device thrown into his yard after he expressed criticism of the Croatian government.[127]

In May 1997, a mob of 100–150 Croat refugees beat dozens of elderly Croat Serbs in three villages northwest of Ostarinica and burned their homes. Numerous victims went missing while others were threatened with death if they did not flee to Serbia. UN High Commissioner for Refugees (UNHCR) Pierre Jambour said that two of the UNHCR monitors sent to the scene in order to investigate it had been beaten by the Croatian police. None of this was reported in the government-controlled media, which was fixated at the time with the Franco Tudjman's 75th birthday celebration. According to the U.S. embassy officer, this non-reaction to the events by the Croatian government was "truly outrageous."[128]

Operation Deliberate Force

NATO's Operation Deliberate Force bombing operation was launched from August 30 to September 20, 1995, in response to the alleged Serb shelling of Sarajevo and the Srebrenica massacre as well as general pattern of Serb aggression. The goal of the operation was to destroy Serb strategic facilities—including radio communications centers and weapons storage and ammunition dumps, to protect UN designated "safe areas" (which Srebrenica was supposed to have been), and impede the Bosnian Serb Army's "advantage in conducting successful military operations against the Bosnian army." Though the operation was run by NATO, the United States Air Force flew two-thirds of the 3,535 bombing sorties that dropped over 11,000 bombs, and two-thirds of the aircraft used were American. Gen Rasim Delic, commander of Bosnian forces in Sarajevo, began picking targets—phoning Adm. W. Owens, vice-chairman of the Joint Chiefs of Staff, daily with his wish list of sites. The Pentagon then passed those on to NATO in Naples. As one U.S. officer put it, "We have become the Muslim Air Force."[129]

Operation Deliberate Force provided an important opportunity to showcase new feature weapons that had been developed in the post-Vietnam War revolution in military affairs, including all-weather, sea-launched Tomahawk cruise missiles guided by satellite technology and predator drones which provided eavesdropping and surveillance functions, probed Serb air defense, identified bombing targets, performed battle damage assessment, served as airborne communication relays and jammed Yugoslav communications. A live feed from the drones was set up in the CIA director's 7th floor Langley office, enabling him to monitor events on the ground while communicating through an early form of chat software.[130]

One military analyst called Operation Deliberate Force the "cleanest military operation ever."[131] Slobodan Milošević allegedly told Richard Holbrooke that only 25 Serbs died, though Bosnian Serb media reported that the number was upwards of 200 and included a brother and sister struck in their car and 10 civilians at a hospital in the Sarejevo suburb of Blazuj, which was hit by a missile that overshot its target.[132] Defense Secretary William Perry had described Deliberate Force as a "massive air campaign that stunned the Serbs with its power and effectiveness."[133] Journalist Rick Atkinson said that it was "a coming of age party for a Western alliance that in more than four decades had fired few shots in anger and never fought an extended campaign."[134] Holbrooke said that "never has airpower been so effective in terms of a political result"[135] though bad weather curtailed many missions and the Serbs effectively concealed many of their heavy weapons.[136]

A *New York Times* report quoted Bosnian Serbs who said that missiles in Banja Luka struck water supplies, a communications tower and power plants, resulting in heavy civilian casualties.[137] The firing of over 10,000 rounds of depleted uranium by A-10 warthog planes unleashed toxic chemicals which caused elevated cancer rates, including among UN soldiers.[138] Bosnian Serb Commander Radovan Karadzic, in an open letter to Clinton, Russian Premier Boris Yeltsin and British Prime Minister John Major, called the bombing an "unprovoked and barbaric action."[139]

Military planners admitted that they had "underestimated the Serbs' will to resist."[140] As to the effectiveness of the bombing operation, the Croats and Muslims had already begun to retake the offensive against the Serbs in Eastern Bosnia in the months preceding Deliberate Force. A Brookings Institute study found that the bombing played only a minor support role in the Serbs retreat, as it struck few major targets. More successful was the show of force, epitomized by a strategy of deliberately expending excess bomb cargo on empty bunkers for the television cameras, in what was described as the "CNN target."[141]

Hillary Clinton Comes Under Sniper Fire

The efforts of the Clinton administration to play up their military credentials was displayed by Hillary Clinton in 1996 when she claimed to have come under sniper fire with her daughter, Chelsea, after descending from the airplane in Tuzla, Bosnia, forcing her to run for cover like Special Forces soldiers. Several news outlets, however, showed Clinton walking from the plane, accompanied by her daughter and being greeted by a young girl in a small ceremony on the tarmac with no sign of tension or any danger. Clinton subsequently told reporters that she "had made a mistake" which "happens" and proves that she is "human, which, you know, for some people, is a revelation."[142] The First Lady's "mistake" was very revealing of the political culture in the U.S. which drove her husband to order air strikes in the

Balkans. Clinton revealed to an interviewer in the summer of 1999 that she had urged her husband to bomb Kosovo. "You cannot let this go on at the end of a century that has seen the major holocaust of our time," she said. "What do we have NATO for if not to defend our way of life?"[143]

Another Dirty War Based on Lies

The Clinton administration's bombing of Serb targets in Kosovo and other parts of Yugoslavia from March 24 to June 9, 1999—which killed between 500 and 2,000 civilians—was undertaken without congressional authorization and in violation of the 1974 War Powers Act and UN charter. The goal was to undermine Yugoslav President Slobodan Milošević, whose Serb forces were accused of committing large scale atrocities against the Kosovar Albanian minority. On May 13, 1999, Clinton gave an impassioned speech before the Veterans of Foreign Wars at the National Defense University at Fort McNair, defending the U.S. air strikes on humanitarian grounds, stating that while Milošević's ethnic extermination was not the same as the ethnic extermination of the Holocaust, the two were related as they were both "vicious, premeditated, systematic oppression fueled by religious and ethnic hatred."

Visibly emotional during the speech, Clinton pointed to the existence of mass graves and quoted from Kosovar Albanian refugees who had witnessed Serb atrocities, citing a farmer who was left for dead in a pile of corpses and a pregnant woman who watched Serb forces shoot her brother in the stomach ten times. A refugee in Germany allegedly told Clinton that "nine out of every 10 Kosovar Albanians had been driven from their homes, thousands had been murdered, and at least 100,000 were missing," with over 500 cities, towns and villages torched. All this had been carried out, Clinton averred, "according to a plan carefully designed months earlier in Belgrade." He ended by stating that if "people make decisions to do these kind of things, other people can make decisions to stop them. And if the resources are properly arranged, it can be done. And that is exactly what we intend to do."[144]

It was a masterful performance, the equivalent to Woodrow Wilson's success in selling U.S. intervention in World War I as a humanitarian intervention designed to halt German atrocities, and Barack Obama's success in demonizing Libyan leader Muammar Qaddafi in preparation for launching air strikes under Operation Odyssey Dawn.[145] In a follow-up address to the nation, Clinton demanded rhetorically: "What if someone had listened to Winston Churchill and stood up to Adolph Hitler earlier? How many lives might have been saved?"[146]

But Milošević was not the new Hitler. A UN sponsored investigation turned up only 2,108 bodies in grave sites across Kosovo. None were found at the Trepca mine, the site of an alleged Serb atrocity where bodies were supposed to have been brought for incineration. Some of the victims from the gravesites were thought to be Kosovo Liberation Army (KLA) fighters or people who died ordinary deaths.[147] These findings exposed as false the Clintons' claim that 100,000 had been killed.[148]

The number of refugees generated by the fighting prior to the U.S.-NATO bombing was estimated to be 200,000, not nine tenths of the Albanian Kosovar population or the 900,000 that Clinton claimed. Many of the refugees were Serbs whose villages were emptied by the KLA and who were targeted in violent attacks. The U.S.-NATO air campaign worsened the ethnic cleansing—as was predicted—causing some 850,000 ethnic Albanians or half their population and thousands of Serbs as well as Roma gypsy to flee Kosovo.[149]

Curiously, the U.S. had showed little interest in the Kosovar Albanians' plight when they excluded their delegates from the Dayton negotiation, avoiding discussion of the Kosovo problem at a time when they might have been able to help advance a political solution to the crisis there—were such to be sought.[150] An underlying goal of the war was to separate Kosovo from Serbia—which Washington wanted to isolate—and establish a Greater Albania under U.S., NATO and Turkish influence, which would comprise a chain of Muslim states, possibly including Bosnia-Herzegovinia, with access to the Adriatic.[151]

While the Serbs did commit war crimes, Clinton's accusation of a genocide on the level of the Nazis was hyperbolic; NATO commander Wesley Clark said he knew of no such planning that would make the two comparable. Left out of the White House's narrative was the fact that Yugoslav counterinsurgency efforts were largely responding to terrorist attacks carried out by well-armed and highly trained militants.[152] In World War II, it was the Kosovar Albanians who had collaborated with the Nazis while the Serbs were persecuted by them.[153] A confidential report by NATO's North Atlantic Council stated that the KLA was "the main initiator of violence" in Kosovo and "launched what appears to be a deliberate campaign of provocation," which led to the outbreak of hostilities with Yugoslav government forces.[154]

A British member of parliament compared the KLA to the "Nicaraguan Contras and other groups armed by the CIA." Clinton's special envoy to the Balkans, Robert Gelbard, branded the KLA as a terrorist organization mere months before the war.[155] Their crimes included gunning down Serb children, organized rapes, and blowing up Serb monasteries. British human rights lawyer Geoffrey Robertson reported to the House of Commons that the KLA "were responsible for more deaths than the Yugoslav army [under Milošević's leadership]."[156]

Some of the KLA's leading cadre had served in Albanian communist party leader Enver Hoxha's secret police, and were close to Albanian president Sali Berisha (1992–1997), a darling of the IMF and NATO to whom the U.S. provided over $200 million in aid between 1991 and 1996 and over three million in military aid in 1996.[157] Berisha was a cardiologist by profession, who pursued the re-Islamicization of Albania after decades of communist rule. Characterizing the Serb forces as "barbarians," he admitted to providing arms and ammunition to KLA fighters. After he was driven from power due to involvement in a criminal extortion scheme that robbed Albanians of their life savings, he turned his family farm into a KLA base.[158]

Some KLA fighters were sent for training in terrorist camps in Afghanistan and Pakistan, with Berisha allegedly helping bin Laden set up a network in Albania through Saudi charity fronts.[159] One of Osama bin Laden's senior lieutenants, Muhammed al-Zawahiri, was the commander of an elite KLA unit that operated during the war.[160] Another KLA commander, Agim Ceku, a "top ethnic cleanser in the Balkans" who had led Operation Storm after training by MPRI troops, was charged by Interpol with the illegal deaths of 669 Serbs.[161]

Joe Biden called future Kosovo prime minister, Hashim Thaçi, the "George Washington of Kosovo," though Thaçi was accused of ordering the assassination of over a dozen KLA commanders and political moderates as part of an internal power struggle, and was implicated in a scandal involving the sale of organs extracted from executed Serb prisoners. In June 2020, Thaçi was forced to cancel a trip to Washington after being indicted by a special court in the Netherlands for war crimes and crimes against humanity, including over 100 murders, forced disappearances and torture.[162]

The KLA sought to establish an ethnically pure Albanian state, with Serbs and other minorities like the Roma singled out for persecution if not liquidation. In the early 1990s, the KLA formed to protect Kosovar Albanians against repression by Serbian authorities who ruled Kosovo, according to the Albanians, like a colonial outpost.[163] Kosovo was for the Serbs something like Jerusalem for Israelis because it was the site of the famous 1389 Battle of Kosovo against Turkey and because it is the birthplace of the Serbian orthodox church and many of the great Serbian monuments and monasteries are there.

Tito's 1974 constitution gave the province considerable autonomy within the Serbian republic, which enabled the Albanian population (about 90 percent of the total) to carve out a dominant position. Systemic harassment and ethnic cleansing of the Serb minority in Kosovo—which had experienced historical waves of pogroms including during World War II when the Kosovo Albanians allied with the fascist powers—created a political opening for Milošević, who emerged as the Serbs' champion.[164]

In 1989, as head of the Serb Republic, Milošević stripped Kosovo of its autonomy and began taking measures to re-Serbianize it and crack down on opposition. The Kosovar Albanians subsequently established a secessionist republic, with a shadow government led by Ibrahim Rugova, which they sought to unite with Albania—a goal promoted by the Albanian lobby in the U.S. Congress.[165]

By the late 1990s, military training to the KLA was provided by British and American Special Forces and Military Professional Resources Inc. under Pentagon contract at a secret base in Albania.[166] This was part of a joint endeavor between the CIA and Germany's Bundesnachrichtendienst (BND), which provided weapons and uniforms.[167] Germany's motive was to destabilize the Balkans—previously it had backed secessionists in Croatia and Slovenia—in order to pursue economic dominance in Mitteleuropa.

James Bissett, Canadian ambassador to Yugsolavia for much of the 1990s, noted that the CIA and British SAS trained the KLA to "foment an armed rebellion in Kosovo," with KLA terrorists sent into Kosovo to "assassinate Serb mayors, ambush Serb policemen and do everything to incite murder and chaos" and in turn provoke a NATO intervention.[168] Once that goal was achieved, some MPRI advisers fought alongside the KLA in combat, according to Col. David Hackworth.[169] A senior KLA commander said the U.K. and U.S. soldiers "either wore uniforms that could not be traced to any Allied unit or were disguised in the combat fatigues of the 'Black Hand' Serb paramilitaries"—who were to be blamed for the atrocities they committed.[170]

The Atlantic Brigade consisted of mercenaries recruited mostly from the anticommunist Albanian exile community in the United States, funded by the CIA and through proceeds from the heroin traffic.[171] Public opinion was galvanized following the alleged massacre by the Serbs of forty-five people at Racak, though an independent investigation found traces of gunshot residue on the hands of victims indicating they were soldiers and not civilians.[172] KLA uniforms with military insignia along with a huge amount of weaponry was also found on the spot, which was a location of KLA headquarters. Danica Marinković, the investigative judge in the case at the district court in Pristina, said that on the basis of lies and fraud, Račak was used as a pretext for NATO aggression against the then FRY [Federal Republic of Yugoslavia].[173] The Serbs were made to be the bad guys further because of their rejection of the February 1999 Rambouillet conference accords. However, the U.S. at the last minute had added an annex mandating that UN peacekeepers would occupy not only Kosovo but potentially all of Serbia and what remained of

Yugoslavia, which no Serb leader could support. No less an establishment figure than Henry Kissinger stated that the conference was really "an excuse to start bombing."[174]

The U.S. Air Force conducted 70 percent of the 38,004 sorties over Kosovo, targeting mainly "critical nodes"—arms supply depots, power-plants, bridges and factories and Slobodan Milošević's compound.[175] Predator Unmanned Aerial Vehicles (UAVs), which first flew in 1994 and now had laser designators integrated into them, provided real time imagery for bombing operations through satellite communication that significantly enhanced surveillance capabilities. Another cutting-edge new weapon used was the Joint Direct Attack Munitions (JDAM) system, which could locate a target using satellite data and enabled delivery of powerful 1,000–2,000 pound warheads day and night, in all weather.[176]

Described in media reports as NATO's "eyes and ears" on the ground in Kosovo, the KLA was using satellite telephones to provide NATO with details of Serbian targets, according to reports in the British media. Some of this communications equipment had been secretly handed over to the KLA a week before the air strikes began by U.S. officers acting as "ceasefire monitors" with the Organisation of Security and Cooperation in Europe. These were in reality CIA agents who had provided the KLA with U.S. army field manuals and field advice on fighting the Yugoslav army and police.[177]

Secretary of State William Cohen claimed the Operation Noble Anvil was the "most precise application of air power in history."[178] To the contrary, a passenger train was struck, 480 schools, 33 hospitals, and an open air market in Surdulica. Bombs further hit a crowd gathered for Holy Trinity Day in Varvarin, resulting in the death of the town priest and the mayor's daughter, along with a field in Bulgaria and a column of Albanian refugees on horses. At least fourteen historic monasteries were bombed by U.S.-NATO forces including the Monastery of the Holy Mother and Monastery of St. Nicholas in Kursumlija, both of which were built in the 12th Century. American warplanes also bombed Zastava automobile plant, a prison holding some KLA fighters, a Serb government TV station, and the Chinese embassy in the part housing intelligence operatives, killing four, likely in an effort to intimidate the Chinese from using their veto over the UN Security Council.[179]

Spanish Captain Martin de la Hoz, who lodged protests with NATO chiefs over the selection of nonmilitary targets, concluded that the U.S. and NATO were "destroying the country." They were "bombing it with novel weapons, toxic nerve gases, surface mines dropped with parachute bombs containing uranium, black napalm, sterilization chemicals, sprayings to poison the crops, and weapons of which even we still do not know anything."[180] The adverse health consequences were felt in Serb towns like Pancevo where over

[Source: tripadvisor.com]

100,000 tons of carcinogens were unleashed into the air, water, and soil from bombed out factories. Clouds of noxious gases hovered over the city for days as residents suffered from vomiting, diarrhea and other illnesses when they drank the water or ate local fish.[181]

At the beginning, General Wesley Clark had predicted with characteristic overconfidence that the bombing would be over in three days. However, Serb resistance held out for over 11 weeks, abating only when Russia withdrew its support. The Serbs followed the footsteps of the Vietnamese and Iraqis, whom a Pentagon official referred to as "professional cruise missile recipients," by displaying dummy tanks and planting microwave ovens that emitted decoy signals and evaded ground sensors. They also fabricated anti-aircraft missiles and constructed a phony bridge.[182]

Today, Bill Clinton is celebrated in Pristina, the Kosovar capital, with a boulevard named in his honor and a statue which portrays the former president with his left arm raised while holding documents bearing the date when NATO started its air campaign against Yugoslavia: 24 March 1999.[183] Since the war, many children have been named after Clinton. Over a decade after gaining its independence from Serbia in 2008, Kosovo remains among the most pro-American countries in the world.[184]

Yet, how much did the Kosovars actually benefit? Kosovo experienced significant problems following the U.S.-NATO bombing, including a huge unemployment rate and staggering political corruption which resulted in Kosovo emerging at the center of the international drug trade and prostitution rings in Europe. Many of Kosovo's resources were privatized and sold to Western multinational corporations and thousands of Serbs and ethnic Roma were driven out. The police service trained by the U.S. was "dominated by fear, corruption and incompetence." The country generally had the feeling of being a colony ruled by viceroys appointed by the U.S. and NATO and dominated by a giant U.S. military base, Camp Bondsteel, which housed Kosovo's main prison.[185]

In December 2004, plans went forward for the construction of a $1.2 billion Trans-Balkan pipeline south of Camp Bondsteel financed by the Overseas Private Investment Corporation. U.S. ambassador Christopher Dell also helped Bechtel (whom he would later work for) secure a billion-dollar highway building contract.[186] These projects, along with the granting of exploration rights to a consortium of American, French, and Swedish investors for the lucrative Trepca mining complex, pointed to another hidden motive for the war beyond the promotion of "human rights" which was never in practice achieved.

The ICTY "Stalinist Show Trial"

The ICTY was a key institution set up to help bolster the idea that a humanitarian intervention had taken place, and to provide a firm legal validation for the U.S. military invasion. Declassified documents show that the ICTY started as an American policy initiative. Key heavyweights behind it, such as David Scheffer and Madeleine Albright, were strong supporters of military intervention. Financing came exclusively from NATO countries and also from the Rockefeller Foundation and billionaire investor George Soros, whose international foundation acted in coordination with U.S. agencies.[187] Richard Holbrooke bragged that "we [the Clinton administration] used it [the ICTY] to keep the two most wanted war criminals in Europe—Karadzic and Mladic [Bosnian Serb commanders]—out of the Dayton peace process and we used it to justify everything that followed."[188]

The ICTY fit with the vision of Strobe Talbott and other key Clinton administration officials, who favored the creation of a world state and the disappearance of nations as meaningful political entities. Talbott wrote:

> I'll bet that within the next hundred years nationhood as we know it will be obsolete; all states will recognize a single, global authority.... The internal affairs of a nation used to be off limits to the world community. Now the principle of "humanitarian intervention" is gaining acceptance. A turning point came in April 1991, shortly after Saddam Hussein's withdrawal from Kuwait, when the UN Security Council authorized allied troops to assist starving Kurds in northern Iraq.[189]

Talbott's vision of Supranationalism aimed to bring the behavior of all states under judicial control in the name of universal human rights as defined and adjudicated by the West. The catch lay in the West's selective and politicized enforcement of human rights norms and violation of state sovereignty rights as mandated under the Westphalian system of international law.

The ICTY was indeed very heavily biased against the Serbs. The main prosecutions were carried out against Serb military commanders and leaders who received much longer sentences than Muslim or Croat commanders or leaders for comparable if not worse crimes. In some cases, Serb defendants were found guilty when the evidence presented against them was problematic. The charge of genocide, for example, directed against Bosnian Serb commanders Radko Mladic and Radovan Karadzic relied on witnesses whose testimony was contradicted by other witnesses, who overheard a rumor while drinking in a bar, were suspected of being double agents and were offered generous plea deals. Karadzic, furthermore, was not allowed to present evidence at his trial of crimes committed against the Serbs or that his forces were acting in self-defense, and the trial chamber refused his request to subpoena documents from the United States.[190]

George Kenney, who worked on the State Department's Yugoslavia desk, referred to the Slobodan Milošević trial as "inherently unfair, amounting to little more than a political show trial." James Bassett, Canada's former ambassador to Yugoslavia, said the trial had taken on all the characteristics of a "Stalinist show trial." Its main purpose, according to political analyst Michael Chossudovsky, was to establish Yugoslavia's liability for the war, which could in turn provide a basis for demanding that Serbia pay war reparations, as the Iraqis were forced to do after the first Persian Gulf War.[191] Though Milošević was found guilty, the prosecution did not prove that Milošević had sanctioned genocide or even ethnic cleansing or participated in a criminal plan to permanently remove Bosnian Muslims and Bosnian Croats from Bosnian Serb claimed territory.[192] This latter determination was highly significant in light of the official pretexts for entering the war and Milošević's reputation as the "Butcher of the Balkans."

A team of Canadian team of lawyers led by Michael Mandel aimed to highlight the double standards of the ICTY by charging sixty-seven U.S. and NATO officials with war crimes, including Bill Clinton. The charges included: willful causing of great suffering and serious injuries; extensive damage to property unjustified by military necessity; employment of weapons causing unnecessary suffering; wanton destruction of cities, towns or villages; damage to, or destruction of, religious, charitable and educational institutions; and destruction of historic monuments. Mandel told Alexander Cockburn of *The Nation* that: "They've admitted publicly the essentials of all these crimes. It's a no-brainer."[193]

The Color Revolution Against Milošević

Milošević's arrest and indictment by the ICTY was a culmination of a "color revolution" directed against him by the Clinton administration, which paid over $70 million to Serb opposition groups before the October 2000 Yugoslav elections. Milošević lost these under dubious legal circumstances to Vojislav Kostunica, who pushed a privatization agenda, allowed for

Milošević's arrest, and froze the wages of working people under the instructions of the IMF, which he allowed Yugoslavia to rejoin.[194]

In July 2000, President Clinton had authorized the CIA to commence covert operations against Belgrade to topple Milošević, who since 1996 had served as the president of the Yugoslav federation. For years before, Milošević's opponents had been supported by grants from the NED, which financed trade unions and media networks. The CIA's covert operations coincided with the ratcheting up of economic sanctions, which Madeleine Albright hoped would "lead people to blame Milošević for their suffering."[195]

Following Clinton's decree, the CIA began computer hacking against Milošević's security services and international bank accounts and chief henchmen while doling out cash to his opponents and funding election monitors and a get-out-the-vote campaign. A senior British diplomat noted that there was so much money pouring into the opposition that "Milošević would have been justified in cancelling the election on grounds of outside interference."[196]

The Washington Post reported the "extraordinary U.S. effort to unseat a foreign head of state, not through covert action of the kind the CIA once employed in such places as Iran and Guatemala, but by modern election campaign techniques."[197] In October 1999, Doug Schoen, a Democratic Party campaign consultant who had helped reelect Boris Yeltsin in Russia in 1996, gave a closed-door briefing hosted by the Washington-based National Democratic Institute (NDI) to leaders of Serbia's previously fractious opposition in Budapest's Marriot hotel, summarizing the results of a polling survey conducted by his firm, Penn, Schoen & Berland Associates, which pointed to Milošević's electoral vulnerability. U.S.-funded consultants went on to play a crucial role behind the scenes in virtually every facet of the anti- Milošević drive, running tracking polls, training thousands of opposition activists and helping to organize a vitally important parallel vote count. U.S. taxpayers paid for 5,000 cans of spray paint used by student activists to scrawl anti-Milošević graffiti on walls across Serbia, and 2.5 million stickers funded by USAID with the slogan "He's Finished (*Gotov Je!*)," which became the revolution's catchphrase.[198]

Milošević had been a bank executive and risen through the ranks of Serbia's communist party before refashioning himself as a champion of Serb interests in the late 1980s when he gave a famous speech defending the Serb minority in Kosovo.[199] Though there were authoritarian features to his rule and he was accused of killing political opponents, Milošević also won fair elections, allowed opposition media and had a certain appeal as a "romantic nationalist."[200] For a long time, Milošević was even respected by Western diplomats as a moderate who had a good grasp of economics and spoke good

English. During negotiations in the Bosnian War, he got along well with American officials and was willing to make concessions. After street protests broke out during the U.S.-backed color revolution, Milošević stated exasperatingly: "I gave Clinton Dayton. I gave him Peace. I gave him a second term. Why are they plotting against me and trying to organize this against me?"[201]

The answer had a lot to do with Milošević's socialist leanings and independent streak as head of a country that was of vital geostrategic importance. *The Christian Science Monitor* and *The New York Times* had reported on his "revoking some privatization and free-market measures" and "determination to keep state controls [of industry]" while *The Washington Post* editorialized that Milošević had "failed to understand the message of the fall of the Berlin Wall. . . . while other communist politicians accepted the western model . . . Milošević went the other way."[202]

Providing a template for future regime change operations, the Clinton administration's "color" revolution relied heavily on student dissidents in the Optor movement led by Srda Popovic, which received the bulk of the National Endowment for Democracy's $3 million monthly budget. It was lavished with cell phones, fax machines, radio transmitters and sophisticated communications and printing equipment by CIA-funded NGOs.[203]

Some Optor leaders were paid by the CIA-subsidized International Republican Institute (IRI) to attend a seminar on nonviolent resistance at the Hilton hotel in Budapest, where they received training in such matters as how to organize a strike, how to communicate with symbols, how to overcome fear and how to undermine the authority of a dictatorial regime. The principal lecturer was retired U.S. Army Col. Robert Helvey, a Vietnam veteran who promoted nonviolent resistance methods around the world. Helvey introduced the student activists to the writing of Gene Sharp, "the Clausewitz of the nonviolence movement," who provided a blueprint for how to organize protests designed to bring down authoritarian governments.[204] Back in Serbia, Otpor activists set about undermining Milošević 's authority by the adoption of sophisticated public relations techniques, including polling, leafleting and paid advertising, alongside the coordination of traditional protests which turned violent when Otpor activists burned down the parliament.[205]

The CIA's paid assets ultimately played a crucial role in Milošević's political demise, thus enabling the fulfilment of the U.S.-NATO war aims. With the last socialist removed from power, the U.S. could now exploit the region economically and promote greater capitalist penetration. A May 2002 *Wall Street Journal* article marveled at the role of Serbia's post-Milošević finance minister—who had advised Poland's 1991 privatization program along with Dr. Jeffrey Sachs—in removing government price controls, simplifying the tax code, launching a sweeping privatization program, and "passing a labor law that allows companies to hire and fire."[206]

When the first post-Milošević Prime Minister, Zoran Djindjic signaled that he didn't want to hand over war archives and Generals to the ICTY, wanted to revise the Dayton agreement, and had come to be seen as a threat to American regional designs, he was assassinated under suspicious circumstances.[207] By 2005, the Yugoslav federation had completely dissolved as Serbia and Montenegro became independent nations. In 2009, Croatia also joined NATO. A balkanized region was generally favored over the strong Yugoslav state under Tito which supported the non-aligned movement and continued to strive for economic independence.

Bill Clinton's performance in serving what Noam Chomsky termed the "masters of mankind" had been brilliant in the Balkan conflict. Many liberals who had opposed the Vietnam War were among its staunchest supporters. It didn't hurt, of course, that the Dow Jones average closed above 10,000 points for the first time while Kosovo was being bombed.[208] Clinton had been preparing for the role of commander-in-chief his entire career. Back at Oxford, he had first tried to coopt the antiwar movement by serving as an undercover informant. As Governor of Arkansas, he had perfected the art of public manipulation with Hillary by his side and had gained experience providing a cover for clandestine operations.

Like Ronald Reagan, Clinton was a gifted orator and actor with a magnetic personality who appeared to genuinely empathize with oppressed peoples, unlike Donald J. Trump. Particularly poignant in Clinton's selling the Balkan war was his ability to invoke heart-felt emotion for the plight of the Kosovar Albanians. Clinton invocation of Nazi analogies and hatred for the arch-villain Milošević further resonated. Never before, so it seemed, had a war been so morally justified and never before had the political costs been so low. The end result, however, was less than satisfying for the affected people. And for America, short-term gain would yield long-term pain as the war fractured the relations between the U.S. and Russia that Clinton had cultivated throughout his presidency. The U.S. generally was coming to be seen more widely as a bully for whom might makes right.

Endnotes

1 "Telephone Conversation with Russian President Yeltsin," April 19, 1999, Oval Office, Declassified Materials, William J. Clinton Presidential Library, https://clinton.presidentiallibraries.us/items/show/57569

2 In F. William Engdahl, *Manifest Destiny: Democracy as Cognitive Dissonance* (Wiesbaden: Mine.books, 2018), 94.

3 See Eric Schmitt, "Spy Photos Indicate Mass Grave at Serb-Held Town, U.S. Says," *The New York Times,* August 10, 1995, A1; Barbara Crossette, "From Overrun Enclave New Evidence of Mass Killings," *The New York Times,* August 19, 1995, 4; *Deconstruction of a Virtual Genocide: An Intelligent Person's Guide to Srebrenica,* ed. Stephen Karganovic et al., *NGO Srebrenica Historical Project, The Netherlands* (Belgrade: Den Haag, 2011), 29, 30.

4 David N. Gibbs, *First Do No Harm: Humanitarian Intervention and the Destruction of Yugoslavia* (Nashville: TN: Vanderbilt University Press, 2009), 162.

5 Michael Dobbs, R. Jeffrey Smith, "New Proof Offered of Serb Atrocities," *The Washington Post,* October 29, 1995, https://www.washingtonpost.com/archive/politics/1995/10/29/new-proof-offered-of-serb-atrocities/56a684eb-7b54-4a9f-934d-4129d02d4070/

6 Gibbs, *First Do No Harm,* 2; Paul Gigot, "How Doves Learned to Love the B-2 Bomber," *The Wall Street Journal,* March 26, 1999, A22.

7 Alexander Cockburn and Jeffrey St. Clair, *Al Gore: A User's Manual* (London: Verso, 2000), 220.

8 John F. Harris, "In Handling a Crisis, a Different President; Aides Note Clinton's Calm, Steady Focus," *The Washington Post,* June 8, 1999.

9 James A. Lucas, "Media Disinformation and the War in Yugoslavia," *Global Research,* September 5, 2005, https://www.globalresearch.ca/media-disinformation-on-the-war-in-yugoslavia-the-dayton-peace-accords-revisited/899

10 A.B. Abrams, *Atrocity Fabrication and its Consequences: How Fake News Shapes World Order* (Atlanta: Clarity Press, 2023), 205.

11 See Roger Peace, Jeremy Kuzmarov, and Brian D'Haeselear, "The Post Cold War Era," http://peacehistory-usfp.org/post-cold-war-era/. Regarding theories of why the former Yugoslavia descended into ethnic-political wars in the 1990s, see Randy Hodson, Dusko Sekulic, and Garth Massey, "National Tolerance in the Former Yugoslavia," *American Journal of Sociology 99,* no. 6 (1994): 1534–58.

12 Gibbs, *First Do No Harm,* 46; Michel Chossudovsky, "Dismantling Yugoslavia, Colonizing Bosnia," *CovertAction Quarterly,* Spring 1996.

13 Joe Biden, *Promises to Keep: On Life and Politics* (New York: Random House, 2007), 248.

14 Michel Chossudovsky, "Dismantling Yugoslavia, Colonizing Bosnia," in *NATO in the Balkans,* ed. Sarah Flounders (New York: International Action Center, 1998), 82.

15 Gibbs, *First Do No Harm;* Evangelos Mahairas, "The Breakup of Yugoslavia," in *Hidden Agenda: U.S./NATO Takeover of Yugoslavia,* ed. John Catalinotto and Sara Flounders (New York: International Action Center, 2002), 47–54; *NATO in the Balkans,* ed. Flounders, 48, 49; In November 1990, the U.S. Congress passed the Bush administration's Foreign Operations Appropriations Act which threatened to cut off U.S. financial aid to any part of Yugoslavia failing to declare independence.

16 *The Srebrenica Massacre: Evidence, Context and Politics,* ed. Edward S. Herman (Evergreen Park, Illinois: Alphabet Soup, 2011), 22; Andy Wilcoxson, "Radovan Karadzic—Serb Hero," March 22, 2019, http://www.slobodan-milosevic.org/news/smorg_aw032219.htm#_ftn13.

17 Kit Klarenberg and Tom Secker, "Declassified Intelligence Files Expose Inconvenient Truths of Bosnian War," *The Grayzone Project,* December 30, 2022, https://thegrayzone.com/2022/12/30/declassified-intelligence-files-bosnian-war/. Another cable stated that Bosniak and foreign Mujahadeen (flown in by USA) fighters were "not above firing on their own people or UN areas."

18 Warren Zimmerman, *Origins of a Catastrophe: Yugoslavia and Its Destroyers – America's Last Ambassador Tells What Happened and Why* (New York: Random House, 1996), 75; Gibbs, *First Do No Harm,* 87; *Hidden Agenda,* ed. Catalinotto and Flounders, xx; Gary Wilson, "The Dayton Accords Reshape Europe," in *NATO in the Balkans,* 151. According to a *New York Times* profile, Tudjman came to power helped by financing from anticommunist Croatian émigres in the U.S. and Canada. Many had fascist leanings and were financed by the CIA.

19 American embassy Zagreb to Secretary of State, Washington, D.C., December 1995, Clinton presidential records, NSC Cables, box 2, William J. Clinton Presidential Library, Little Rock, Arkansas. Tudjman's party, the Croatian Democratic Union (HDZ) held the majority of seats in both of Croatia's houses of parliament. In the Tito-era, Tudjman had been jailed twice as an opponent of communism.

20 David Owen, *Balkan Odyssey* (New York: Harcourt Brace & Jovanovich, 1995), 74. In 1989, the year before his election, Tudjman wrote a book with passages like: "A Jew is still a Jew. Even in the camps they retained their bad characteristics: selfishness, perfidy, meanness, slyness and treachery." Quoted in Jack Cashill, *Ron Brown's Body: How One Man's Death Saved the Clinton Presidency and Hillary's Future* (Nashville, TN: WND Books, 2004), 284.

21 Dr. Karl Mueller, "The Demise of Yugoslavia and the Destruction of Bosnia: Strategic Causes, Effects and Responses," in *Deliberate Force: A Case Study in Effective Air Campaigning,* ed. Colonel Robert C. Owen (Maxwell Air Force Base, Alabama: Air University Press, 2000), 11.

22 Tim Judah, *The Serbs: History, Myth and the Destruction of Yugoslavia* (New Haven: Yale University Press, 2010), 1; Diana Johnstone, *Fools Crusade: Yugoslavia, NATO, and Western Delusions* (New York: Month Review Press, 2002), 29.

23 Zimmerman, *Origins of a Catastrophe.*

24 Gary Wilson, "The Dayton Accords Reshape Europe," in *NATO in the Balkans,* ed. Flounders, 147. General John Galvin, a former NATO commander and head of West Point, planned and executed Bosnian army offensives.

25 Engdahl, *Manifest Destiny,* 97.

26 Roger Peace, Jeremy Kuzmarov, and Brian D'Haeselear, "The Post Cold War Era," http://peacehistory-usfp.org/post-cold-war-era/; Philip Corwin, *Dubious Mandate: A Memoir of the UN* (Durham, NC: Duke University Press, 1999), 22; David Binder, "Aliza Izetbegovic, ex-President of Bosnia, Dies at 78," *The New York Times,* October 19, 2003, https://www.nytimes.com/2003/10/19/international/europe/alija-izetbegovic-expresident-of-bosnia-dies-at-78.html; Engdahl, *Manifest Destiny,* 99; Alija Izetbegovic, *The Islamic Declaration* (Sarajevo, 1990). A 1980 follow-up book by Izetbegovic was titled *Islam: Between East and West.*

27 Corwin, *Dubious Mandate,* 22. See also Tim Judah, *The Serbs,* and Steven L. Burg and Paul S. Shoup, *The War in Bosnia-Herzegovinia: Ethnic Conflict and International Intervention* (Armok, NY: M.E. Sharpe, 1998). In the former Yugoslavia, the Serbs were in the minority but had the protection of the larger state.

28 Minutes of the Meeting Held on 16 August 1995 in the North Lounge of the Presidential Palace in Zagreb at 13:50 hours, ICTY ERN #0187-0722-0187-0757-ET, 11.

29 Corwin, *Dubious Mandate;* Judah, *The Serbs.*

30 American embassy Zagreb to Secretary of State, Washington, D.C., December 1995, Clinton presidential records, NSC Cables, box 2, William J. Clinton Presidential Library, Little Rock, Arkansas.

31 Author interview, survivor of Bosnian war, Moscow, Russia, May 9, 2018; Johnstone, *Fools Crusade,* 61; Engdahl, *Manifest Destiny,* 108 citing ICTY court records.

32 Klarenberg and Secker, "Declassified Intelligence Files Expose Inconvenient Truths of Bosnian War."

33 Johnstone, *Fools Crusade,* 63; Burg & Shoup, *The War in Bosnia Herzegovinia,* 67.

34 John R. Schindler, *Unholy Terror: Bosnia, Al Qaida, and the Rise of Global Jihad* (London: Zenith Press, 2007); Richard J. Aldrich, "America Used Islamists to Arm the Bosnian Muslims," *The Guardian,* April 22, 2002); Nafeez Mosaddeq Ahmed, *The War on Truth: 9/11, Disinformation, and the Anatomy of Terrorism* (Northampton, MA: Olive Branch Press, 2005), 34. The Algerians were members of the Algerian Goupe Islamique Armée (GIA) held responsible for massive massacres of Algerian civilians during the Algerian civil war. The Afghan mujahidin had been trained in terrorist methods by the CIA.

35 Schindler, *Unholy Terror;* Lynch quoted in Alexander Rubinstein, "Did the CIA Pressure Yemen to Release Al-Qaeda Propagandist Anwar al-Awlaki," *The Grayzone Project,* March 22, 2021, https://thegrayzone.com/2021/03/22/cia-yemen-al-qaeda-anwar-al-awlaki/

36 Schindler, *Unholy Terror;* John Sray, "Selling the Bosnian Myth," *Foreign Military Studies,* Fort Leavenworth, Kansas, October 1995. The mujahadins' terror arsenal included fragmentation bombs disguised as children's toys. A Congressional report authored by Republicans concluded that the Clinton administration had helped turn Bosnia into a "militant Islamic base." Ahmed, *The War on Truth,* 34.

37 Schindler, *Unholy Terror,* 122, 123; *The 9/11 Commission Report: Final Report of the National Commission on Terrorist Attacks Upon the United States,* Official Government Edition, 55, 146–147, 155, 238–239. Al-Qaeda's second in command, Ayman Al-Zawahiri also allegedly made several trips to Bosnia, and another one of the fighters, Jamal al-Badawi, was involved in the 2000 terrorist attack on the USS. Cole in South Yemen. Lily Lynch, co-founder and editor-in-chief of *Balkanist Magazine,* told journalist Alex Rubinstein. "The Bosnian War drew extremists of all types from all over the world. The El Mujahid, the unit of foreign mujahideen fighters in Bosnia, videotaped themselves committing war crimes against Serbs including beheadings and torture. There are also reports that the mujahideen terrorized the local Bosniak population by making aid contingent upon radical conversion." Alex Rubinstein, "Did the CIA pressure Yemen to release al-Qaeda propagandist Anwar al-Awlaki?" *Substack,* March 22, 2021, https://realalexrubi.substack.com/p/leaked-cia-pressured-yemen-to-release

38 Burg & Shoup, *The War in Bosnia Herzegovina,* 137. On the Croat side, a criminal gangster named Mladen Naletelic-Tuta led special punishment squads, Burg and Shoup report, which burned and pillaged Muslim villages. The Muslims and Serbs had their own special units, often led by criminals as well, which adopted the same practices.

39 Sara Flounders, "Bosnia Tragedy: The Unknown Role of the Pentagon," in *NATO in the Balkans: Voices of Opposition* (New York: International Action Center, 1998), 59; General Charles G. Boyd, "Making Peace with the Guilty: The Truth About Bosnia," *Foreign Affairs,* September/October 1995. A wealthy businessman accused of illegal smuggling, Abdic had favored the preservation of Yugoslavia. Paramilitary units that he operated were implicated in war crimes directed against supporters of

the Bosnian government. Abdic served 10 years in prison after the war after being convicted on war crimes charges, which appear to have been unfair. The Bihac region had a strong tradition of anti-fascist resistance going back to the World War II era.

40 Justin Raimondo, "Free Fikrit Abdic," July 20, 2001, http://www.antiwar.com/justin/j072001.html. Raimondo described the campaign against Abdic's forces by the Bosnian fifth army in Velika Kladusa as a campaign of murder, terror, and rapine that equals any of the more widely touted atrocities, such as the "rape" of Srebrenica, in which the Muslims are always the victims.

41 Karen Dawisha and Bruce Parrot, *Politics, Power and the Struggle for Democracy in Southeast Europe* (New York: Cambridge University Press, 197), 133.

42 Owen, *Balkan Odyssey;* Raimondo, "Free Fikrit Abdic." General Charles Boyd, deputy chief of the U.S. European Command at the height of the Bosnian war, wrote in *Foreign Affairs* magazine that Abdic created "one of the few examples of successful multiethnic cooperation in the Balkans."

43 Mark M. Nelson, "Croatia's Military Drive Spurs New Round of Talks," *The Wall Street Journal,* August 14, 1995, A6.

44 James A. Baker, *The Politics of Diplomacy* (New York: Putnam, 1995), 643–644.

45 Susan Sontag, "Godot Comes to Sarajevo," *The New York Review of Books,* October 21, 1993. Sontag's son, David Rieff, became a leading intellectual champion of the Bosnian cause and war.

46 In Owen, *Balkan Odyssey,* 19.

47 See Gibbs, *First Do No Harm,* 124, 125; Edward S. Herman, "The Politics of the Srebrenica Massacre," *Global Research,* July 07, 2005; *Srebrenica,* ed. Herman; Abrams, *Atrocity Fabrication and its Consequences,* 216. A week after Gutman's piece appeared, *U.S. News & World Report* heightened the historical analogy by describing "locked trains . . . once again carrying human cargoes across Europe," and charging that "the West's response to this new holocaust has been as timid as its reactions to the beginnings of Hitler's genocide."

48 Stephen Kinzer, "Genocide in Bosnia," *The New York Times,* July 14, 1995, https://genocideinbosnia.wordpress.com/tag/fall-of-srebrenica/.

49 See Philip Knightly, *The First Casualty: The War Correspondent as Hero and Myth Maker* (New York: Harcourt, Brace Jovanovich, 1975).

50 Sidney Blumenthal, *The Clinton Wars* (New York: Plume Books, 2003), 630.

51 Gibbs, *First Do No Harm,* 127, Cees Wiebes, *Intelligence and the War in Bosnia 1992–1995* (Hamburg and London: Lit Verlag Munster, 2003), 70.

52 Flounders, "Bosnia Tragedy," 55, 56.

53 Corwin, *Dubious Mandate,* 87. Ironically, in the 1980s, Western journalists and diplomats had defended the Serb viewpoint. *The New York Times* published reports of the plight of Serbs being driven out of Kosovo by Albanian ethnic cleansing. Western governments supported modernizers such as Milošević who saw the need to reduce Kosovo's autonomy in order to enact economic reforms. Johnstone, *Fools Crusade,* 219.

54 See Susan Brewer, *Why America Fights: Patriotism and War Propaganda from the Philippines to Iraq* (New York: Oxford University Press, 2011).

55 See David Rieff, *Slaughterhouse: Bosnia and the Failure of the West* (New York: Simon & Schuster, 1995).

56 Dick Morris, *Behind the Oval Office: Winning the Presidency in the 1990s* (New York: Random House, 1997), 245, 253.

57 Quoted in Owen, *Balkan Odyssey,* 13.

58 Quoted in Samantha Power, *"A Problem from Hell:" America in the Age of Genocide* (New York: Crown, 2003), 271–72, 277, 274. Clinton at the time said he supported lifting a 1991 arms embargo.

59 Burg & Shoup, *The War in Bosnia-Herzegovinia,* 141.

60 "Transcript: Clinton Justifies U.S. Involvement in Kosovo," May 13, 1999, https://www.cnn.com/ALLPOLITICS/stories/1999/05/13/clinton.kosovo/transcript.html

61 Corwin, *Dubious Mandate,* 146, 147.

62 Clinton's remarks on Chechnya and casualty figures cited in "Russia's Road to Corruption: How the Clinton Administration Exported Government Instead of Free Enterprise and Failed the Russian People," March 2000, House of Representatives (Washington, D.C,: G.P.O., 2000), 77, 78, https://fas.org/irp/congress/2000_rpt/russias-road.pdf. See also Noam Chomsky, *A New Generation Draws the Line: Kosovo, East Timor and the Standards of the West* (London: Verso, 2000). Chomsky has great discussions of Kosovo, East Timor, Colombia and Israel but omits discussion of Russia and Chechnya as an example of the double standards of U.S. human rights policy and preaching of the humanitarian interventionist crowd.

63 Transcript, "Clinton Addresses Nation on Yugoslavian Strike," March 24, 1999, http://edition.cnn.com/ALLPOLITICS/stories/1999/03/25/clinton.transcript/

64 David Halberstam, *War in a Time of Peace: Bush, Clinton and the Generals* (New York: Scribner, 2001); Gibbs, *First Do No Harm,* 149; Teleconference With French President Jacques Chirac, July 13, 1995, Oval Office, William J. Clinton Presidential Library, Clinton Presidential Records, Declassified Material, Bosnia, https://clinton.presidentiallibraries.us/items/show/36593.

65 Halberstam, *War in a Time of Peace*, 158, 159.

66 Mark Danner, "Clinton, the UN, and the Bosnia Disaster," *The New York Review of Books,* http://www.markdanner.com/articles/clinton-the-un-and-the-bosnia-disaster

67 Wiebes, *Intelligence and the War in Bosnia 1992–1995,* 65–67; George Jones, "Evidence Builds Up of Muslim Bias at CIA," *The Daily Telegraph,* March 6, 1995; Abrams, *Atrocity Fabrication and its Consequences,* 208.

68 American Embassy The Hague, to Secretary of State, "Dutch Report on Srebrenica to Offer Grist for Defenders or Detractors of Blue Helmet Actions," October 1995, William J. Clinton Presidential Library, Declassified Documents Regarding Yugoslavia, https://clinton.presidentiallibraries.us/items/show/36632. The report also cited the Dutch forces' abuses of women, including within their own units.

69 Michael Ignatieff, *Virtual War: Kosovo and Beyond* (New York: Picador, 2001).

70 For Richard Holbrooke's support for NATO and NATO expansion, see Abrams, *Atrocity Fabrication and Its Consequences,* 241; and George Packer, *Our Man: Richard Holbrooke and the End of the American Century* (New York: Alfred A. Knopf, 2019).

71 Bob Davis, "Clinton to Propose Ending Some Tariffs to Boost Development in the Balkans," *The Wall Street Journal,* July 30, 1999.

72 "Strategy For the Balkans Conflict," from Ambassador Albright to National Security Council Adviser, August 4, 1995, William J. Clinton Presidential Library, Clinton Presidential Records, Declassified Materials, https://clinton.presidentiallibraries.us/items/show/36591; Richard Schifter, Memo for Anthony

Lake, "A Proposal for a Southeastern European Cooperative Development Initiative," September 18, 1995, https://clinton.presidentiallibraries.us/items/show/36593. Named after Secretary of State George Marshall, the original Marshall Plan of 1949 was a massive program of economic aid to Europe to prevent the growth of communism and better integrate European markets.

73 Jacob Heilbrunn and Michael Lind, "The Third American Empire," *The New York Times,* January 2, 1996, https://www.nytimes.com/1996/01/02/opinion/the-third-american-empire.html

74 Johnstone, *Fools Crusade,* 219, 232. On hidden underlying objectives, see also Sean Gervasi, "Why is NATO in Yugoslavia?" in *NATO in the Balkans,* ed. Flounders

75 Cashill, *Ron Brown's Body* (Nashville, TN: WND Books, 2004), 284, 285; Kathryn Krahold, "Enron Agrees to Build, Operate $175 Million Plant in Croatia," *The Wall Street Journal,* March 31, 1999; David North, "The U.S. and Ethnic Cleansing in Croatia – the Case of Croatia," *World Socialist Web Site,* April 15, 1999, https://www.wsws.org/en/articles/1999/04/croa-a15.html; Asif Ismael, Michael Wiesskopf, "Enron's Democrat Pals," *TIME,* August 17, 2002. Commerce Secretary Ron Brown was killed in a plane crash on April 3, 1996 while on a mission to Bosnia and Croatia along with twelve chief executives from major corporations seeking greater investment in the Balkans, including from AT&T and Bechtel.

76 Tracey L. Brown, *The Life and Times of Ron Brown* (New York: William Morrow and Company Inc., 1998), 3, 12. Brown's daughter Tracey writes that "it was my father's intention to disrupt an arrangement between the Croatian government and Airbus Industries, a European plane-manufacturing consortium. His goal was to convince the Croatians to place their eighteen-plane, one billion dollar [contract] with Boeing, an American company."

77 Gibbs, *First Do No Harm,* 143, 144, 146; Owen, *Balkan Odyssey;* Major General Lewis Mackenzie, *Peacekeepers: The Road to Sarajevo* (Toronto: Douglas & McIntyre, 1993), 115. The Vance-Owen Plan mandated the replacement of Yugoslav army troops with UN peacekeepers in UN protected regions.

78 Gibbs, *First Do No Harm,* 143, 144, 146; Owen, *Balkan Odyssey.* Critics viewed the Vance-Owen Plan as an attempt to cantonize Bosnia into ethnic enclaves and cement the breakup of Yugoslavia, which would better enable the exploitation of the region by outside powers.

79 Gibbs, *First Do No Harm,* 169, 170. On Holbrooke's role in the Dayton negotiations, see Packer, *Our Man.*

80 Paul A. Gigot, "The Clinton Way of War Meets Reality," *The Wall Street Journal,* April 2, 1999, A10.

81 Mahairas, "The Breakup of Yugoslavia"; and John Catalinotto, "Washington's NATO Strategy," in *Hidden Agenda,* ed. Catalinotto and Flounders, 49, 50, 158; Michael Chossudovsky, "Dismantling Yugoslavia, Colonizing Bosnia," *CovertAction Quarterly,* Spring 1996; Carol Shaffer, "The West's Charming Lies: How the Dayton accords and privatization have kept Bosnia in tragic limbo," *The Nation,* January 9/16, 2023, 27–31. Chossudovsky wrote that "the neo-colonization of Bosnia is the logical culmination of long Western efforts to undo Yugoslavia's experiment in market socialism and workers' self-management and impose in its place the diktat of the free market."

82 Shaffer, "The West's Charming Lies," 31. The locals used the term ubleba—charming lies to sell snake oil—to describe western intervention in Bosnia.

83 Gregory Elich, "Bringing Democracy to Bosnia-Herzegovinia," *CovertAction Quarterly,* Spring-Summer 2000, 53.

84 Lucas, "Media Disinformation and the War in Yugoslavia."

85 See Peter Dale Scott, *The War Conspiracy* (New York: Bobbs Merrill, 1972) and for a fuller illumination of the pattern, David Ray Griffin, *The American Trajectory: Divine or Demonic?* (Atlanta: Clarity Press, 2018) and *America on the Brink: How U.S. Foreign Policy Led to the War in Ukraine* (Atlanta: Clarity Press, 2023).

86 Wiebe, *Intelligence and the War in Bosnia 1992–1995,* 68; David Binder, "Bosnia's Bombers," *The Nation,* October 2, 1995; Lt. Col. John Sray, "Selling the Bosnian Myth to America: Buyer Beware," Foreign Military Studies Office, Fort Leavenworth, Kansas, October 1995.

87 Wiebe, *Intelligence and the War in Bosnia 1992–1995,* 68; Wiebe, *Intelligence and the War in Bosnia 1992–1995,* 68; Sray, "Selling the Bosnian Myth to America." Bosnian units carried out sniper attacks designed to engender Serb counterattacks or frame the Serbs.

88 Wiebes, *Intelligence and the War in Bosnia 1992–1995,* 68; Gibbs, *First Do No Harm,* 125, 126. See also coverage of Markale massacre, which the ICTY blamed on the Serbs, in Klarenberg and Secker, "Declassified Intelligence Files Expose Inconvenient Truths of Bosnian War." David Owen, a European community negotiator, noted that "UN personnel had long suspected that at least some of the attacks were being undertaken by Muslim units firing on their own people." Such suspicions were confirmed in August 1995 when a French UN team pinpointed some of the sniping to a building which they knew was controlled by Bosnian government forces. Later, several international witnesses testified in the Karadzic trial that the Bosnian Muslims had shelled their own people in order to give NATO a pretext to bomb the Serbs. (Col. Richard Gray, Col. Andrey Demurenko, and even a protected witness from inside the Bosnian government, plus numerous documents from the UN, all attest to this).

89 Teleconference With French President Jacques Chirac, July 13, 1995, Oval Office, William J. Clinton Presidential Library, Clinton Presidential Records, Declassified Material, Bosnia, https://clinton.presidentiallibraries.us/items/show/36593.

90 *The Srebrenica Massacre,* ed. Herman, 22. See also David N. Gibbs, "How the Srebrenica Massacre Redefined U.S. Foreign Policy," *Race, Class and Corporate Power,* 3, 2, 2015; Cees Wiebes, *Intelligence and the War in Bosnia, 1992–1995* (London: Lit Verlag, 2003). Journalist Tim Ripley wrote that "to Western military men in Sarajevo, the Bosnian strategy of using children, old people, and other civilians as 'staked goats' to generate international sympathy was abhorrent." Cees Wiebes' study raises also questions as to whether the U.S., UN or Dutch could have prevented the killings given their monitoring of Srebrenica, a UN designated safe zone.

91 Radovan Karadzic, President Republic of Srpaska, Letter to Bill Clinton, July 24, 1995, William J. Clinton Presidential Library, The Dissolution of Yugoslavia Collection, https://clinton.presidentiallibraries.us/items/show/72146

92 "An Evaluation of the Washington Post article – Would Lifting the Embargo Help Bosnia," DCI Interagency Task Force, August 3, 1995, William J. Clinton Presidential Library, The Dissolution of Yugoslavia collection, https://clinton.presidentiallibraries.us/items/show/72146

93 "The Fall of Srebrenica, July 1995, Bosnia's Darkest Hour: Srebrenica: Background and Battle," William J. Clinton Presidential Library, Yugoslavia

Genocide, Srebrenica, https://clinton.presidentiallibraries.us/items/show/53013. Oric also flouted wealth that he gained through the black market economy, driving a fancy Mercedes Benz. Radko Mladic sent an outraged letter to the UN charging that Muslim forces from within the enclave repeatedly violated the UN safe area and caused the death of more than 100 Serb civilians.

94 Engdahl, *Manifest Destiny,* 107.

95 "Bosnia-Herzegovinia: The Fall of Srebrenica and Failure of UN Peacekeeping," *Human Rights Watch,* 7, 13 (October 1995), https://www.hrw.org/legacy/summaries/s.bosnia9510.html

96 *Deconstruction of a Virtual Genocide,* ed. Karganovic, 20. In 2010, Meholjic added further details, claiming that Izetbegovic wanted the victim's throats slit.

97 Alexander Vershbow to Peter E. Bass et al., "Massacre at Srebrenica," July 25, 1995, William J. Clinton Presidential Library, Clinton Presidential Records, Declassified Material, Bosnia, https://clinton.presidentiallibraries.us/items/show/36593. Vershbow, the National Security Council official who was in contact with the UN official, used the refugee's claims to advocate for immediate military intervention.

98 "Radislav Krstic Becomes the First Person To Be Convicted of Genocide at the ICTY and Is Sentenced to 46 Years Imprisonment," UN, ICTY Press Release, August 4, 2001, https://www.icty.org/x/cases/krstic/tjug/en/010802_Krstic_summary_en.pdf

99 Ibid. A team of ace reporters with the *New York Times* in October 1995. (Stephen Engleberg and Tim Weiner, with Raymond Bonner and James Perlez, "Srebrenica: The Days of Slaughter," *The New York Times,* October 19, 1995) gave a figure of 6,000 Muslims killed, and also cite an intelligence report estimate of between 5,000 and 8,000 killed. The lack of precision with the numbers is highly problematic.

100 *Deconstruction of a Virtual Genocide,* ed. Karganovic; The Srebrenica Massacre, ed. Herman.

101 U.S. Mission Geneva to Secretary of State, Washington, D.C. "Request for Reference to ICRC in Yugoslavia, Peace Agreement, No programs on Srebrenica Missing," September 1995, William J. Clinton Presidential Library, Declassified Documents, Declassified Documents on Yugoslavia, https://clinton.presidentiallibraries.us/items/show/36632 Five thousand had fled before Srebrenica fell, with an estimated three to four thousand of those believed to have safely escaped Bosnian Serb territory. The ICRC demand for access to detainees resulted in visits with only 164 and requested more information as to whether reported mass grave sites near Kasaba actually contained corpses. Later, the ICRC provided a figure of 7,079 Bosnian Muslims killed, executed, died on march or unaccounted for (the latter were not necessarily killed but could have fled and taken up arms against the Serbs behind enemy lines).

102 "President's Telephone Call with Bosnian President Izetbegovic," The White House, July 20, 1995, 1:47 PM-2:02 PM, William J. Clinton Library photocopy, Declassified Materials, Bosnia, https://clinton.presidentiallibraries.us/items/show/36589. UNPROFOR had initially reported on the abduction of 150–300 men aged 16–60 by Serb forces.

103 Teleconference With French President Jacques Chirac, July 13, 1995, Oval Office, William J. Clinton Presidential Library, Clinton Presidential Records, Declassified Material, Bosnia, https://clinton.presidentiallibraries.us/items/show/36593. The top German representative Eitel, in October 1995, referenced the massacre of 6,000 military aged males at Srebrenica, which he says was the worst war crime since World War II.

104 Memo for Anthony Lake, through Morton Halperin, from Rob Malley, "Human Rights Atrocities in Bosnia," August 4, 1995, William J. Clinton Presidential Library, Clinton Presidential Records, Declassified Material, Bosnia, https://clinton.presidentiallibraries.us/items/show/36593.

105 See Edward S. Herman, "The U.S. Media Coverage of Srebrenica," in *Deconstruction of a Virtual Genocide,* ed. Stephen Karganovic et al., 153. Researcher Ljubisa Simic estimated that the actual total was between 1,919 and 1,923. Human Rights Watch, while documenting Bosnian Serb atrocities, only speculates that thousands were executed.

106 https://www.icmp.int/press-releases/over-7000-srebrenica-victims-recovered/; David Rohde, "Denying Genocide in the Face of Science," *The Atlantic,* July 17, 2015.

107 Edward S. Herman and David Peterson, "The 'Srebrenica Massacre' Turns Twenty Years Old," *Dissident Voice,* August 5, 2015, https://dissidentvoice.org/2015/08/the-srebrenica-massacre-turns-20-years-old/. Military service records showed that 140 of the total had been killed in combat, months or years before the fall of Srebrenica. *Deconstruction of a Virtual Genocide,* 186. Some on the Red Cross's missing list also turned up on voter rolls later on and could have been captured or killed in other battles.

108 *Deconstruction of a Virtual Genocide,* 76, 77. Researcher Ljubisa Simic determined that 627 of 1,913 bodies died from combat related injuries and 442 were likely victims of executions. Another study determined that 947 bodies showed signs of execution, a far cry from the 8,000 figure reported in the mainstream. Ninety percent of the bodies were so disfigured that a cause of death could not be determined at all. Combat operations it should be noted were reported to have occurred in areas where mass graves were found.

109 "The Fall of Srebrenica, July 1995, Bosnia's Darkest Hour: Srebrenica: Background and Battle," William J. Clinton Presidential Library, Yugoslavia Genocide, Srebrenica, https://clinton.presidentiallibraries.us/items/show/53013. Some of the survivors appeared dazed and prone to hallucination, leading to speculation that they had been subjected to a chemical weapons attack, but this has not been corroborated.

110 Lizette Alvarez, "At Memorial in Bosnia, Clinton Helps Mourn 7,000," *The New York Times,* September 21, 2003.

111 *Deconstruction of a Virtual Genocide,* ed. Karganovic, 65, 66, 68; Danner, "Clinton, the UN and the Bosnia Disaster." Oric's forces attacked the Serb town of Kravica on orthodox Christmas, killing 30. They rarely made a distinction between civilians and combatants and machine- gunned women and children in Skelani. Oric himself bragged and showed videos of some of his gruesome exploits to Western reporters, though this story was little picked up in the mainstream. Oric was eventually only sentenced to two years in jail by the ICTY.

112 *Deconstruction of a Virtual Genocide,* ed. Karganovic, 20. Erdemović's commander in the Srbrenica execution unit, Milorad Pelemis, worked for French intelligence and had committed atrocities in Bosnia and Kosovo for which the Serbs were blamed. Some of its members were with the French foreign legion. See George Pumphrey, "More Evidence on the Srebrenica 'Numbers Game," *Global Research,* July 28, 2019, https://www.globalresearch.ca/more-evidence-srebrenica-numbers-game/5684686 Another of the ICTY's chief witnesses happened to be Nasser Oric's brother, Melvudin. Lieutenant General Hans Couzy, the commander in chief of Dutch ground forces, said Dutch troops had witnessed no incidents of rape at Srebrenica and were aware of only limited incidents that could be labeled war crimes.

113 James Risen and Doyle McManus, "Clinton Okd Iranian Arms for Bosnia, Officials Say," *Los Angeles Times,* April 5, 1996, https://www.latimes.com/archives/la-xpm-1996-04-05-mn-55275-story.html; Schindler, *Unholy Terror,* 182; Michel Chossudovsky, "Twenty years ago. NATO's War on Yugoslavia: Bill Clinton Worked Hand in Glove with al-Qaeda: 'Helped Turn Bosnia into Militant Islamic Base,'" *Global Research,* March 22, 2019, https://www.globalresearch.ca/bill-clinton-worked-hand-in-glove-with-al-qaeda-helped-turn-bosnia-into-militant-islamic-base/5474094.

114 Schindler, *Unholy Terror,* 182, 183. The arms included automatic weapons, rocket-propelled grenade launchers, anti-armor rockets and TOW missiles. When an Iranian Boeing 747 flying out of Zagreb was inspected, Croatian officials discovered 4,000 guns, more than a million rounds of ammunition and 20 to 40 Iranians huddled in the back. Michael R. Gordon, "Iran Said to Send Arms to Bosnians," *The New York Times,* September 10, 1992.

115 Schindler, *Unholy Terror,* 182, 183; Wiebes, *Intelligence and the War in Bosnia 1992–1995,* 177, 178. The Krk base was also used to operate predator drones. The U.S. relied for the airdrops on the Cengic family which were described by Western intelligence services as "mafia." The head of the family was a personal confidante of Izetbegovic, who also had ties to the Croat Defense Ministry and was described as having radical Islamist views. In Visoko, which was controlled entirely by his militias, he built his own $5 million airfield for arms supplies.

116 Wiebes, *Intelligence and the War in Bosnia 1992–1995,* 194; Gibbs, *First Do No Harm,* 157. A U.S. Senate investigation based on perusal of DoD and Pentagon documents did not find conclusive proof of U.S. coordination, however, there was no extensive Congressional investigation like with the Nicaraguan Iran-Contra affair for partisan political reasons.

117 See Jeremy Kuzmarov, "Distancing Acts: Private Mercenaries and the War on Terror in American Foreign Policy," *The Asia Pacific Journal,* December 21, 2014, https://apjjf.org/2014/12/52/Jeremy-Kuzmarov/4241.html.

118 Deborah Avant, *The Market for Force: The Consequences of Privatizing Security* (New York: Cambridge University Press, 2005), 110; *Genocide Victims of Krajina v. L-3 Communications Corp. and MPRI Inc.,* in the United States District Court Northern District of Illinois, Eastern Division.

119 Leslie Wayne, "America's For Profit Secret Army: Military Contractors Are Hired to Do the Pentagon's Bidding Far From Washington's View," *The New York Times,* October 13, 2002, B1; Peter Singer, *Corporate Warriors: The Rise of the Privatized Military Industry* (Ithaca: Cornell University Press, 2003), 126; Ken Silverstein, *Private Warriors* (London: Verso, 2000), 172; Stephen Armstrong, *War PLC: Rise of the New Corporate Mercenary* (London: Faber & Faber, 2009), 73, 74.

120 Ivo Pukanic, "Thrilled with Operation Flash, President Clinton Gave the Go Ahead for Operation Storm," *Nacional* (Zagreb), May 24, 2005, http://mprofaca.cro.net/operation_storm_2.html. Richard Holbrooke and Ambassador Peter Galbraith also told Tudjman that they supported the offensive because it assisted the U.S. and Croat position at the bargaining table.

121 Gibbs, *First Do No Harm,* 164. Operation Storm was carried out under the supervision of the U.S. ambassador to Croatia, Peter Galbraith.

122 *Genocide Victims of Krajina v. L-3 Communications Corp. and MPRI Inc.,* in the United States District Court Northern District of Illinois, Eastern Division. The judge said that he was not qualified to preside over the case because the crimes occurred

in Bosnia. Croat army units trained by MPRI killed 185 Serb civilians in Mrkonjic in southwestern Bosnia. See also Tony Geraghty, *Soldiers of Fortune* (London: Pegasus Books, 2009), 175. U.S. warplanes provided support to the Operation Storm by bombing a Krajina Serb airfield and destroying radar installations, allowing Croatian planes free rein to bomb and strafe columns of fleeing civilians.

123 Singer, *Corporate Warriors,* 126; Robert Capps, "Outside the Law," *Salon,* June 25, 2002; "Sex Slave Whistle-Blowers Vindicated," *Salon,* August 6, 2002. The whistleblower in the case, Ben Johnson, was himself fired from DynCorp and none of the perpetrators of crimes ever faced prosecution. DynCorp also played a role in training Kosovo's police service following the NATO bombing.

124 Dp:ds-unit.un.org to Ivo H. Daalder, "Further Report on Situation of Human Rights in Croatia Pursuant to Security Council Resolution, 1019 Serbs," January 1995–December 1996, Clinton Presidential Records, National Security Council cables, box 1, William J. Clinton Presidential Library, Little Rock, Arkansas.

125 Dp:ds-unit.un.org to Ivo H. Daalder, "Further Report on Situation of Human Rights in Croatia Pursuant to Security Council Resolution, 1019 Serbs," January 1995–December 1996, Clinton Presidential records, National Security Council cables, box 1, William J. Clinton Presidential Library, Little Rock, Arkansas.

126 Dp:ds-unit.un.org to Ivo H. Daalder, "Further Report on Situation of Human Rights in Croatia Pursuant to Security Council Resolution, 1019 Serbs," January 1995–December 1996, Clinton Presidential records, National Security Council cables, box 1, William J. William J. Clinton Presidential Library, Little Rock, Arkansas.

127 Dp:ds-unit.un.org to Ivo H. Daalder, "Further Report on Situation of Human Rights in Croatia Pursuant to Security Council Resolution, 1019 Serbs," January 1995–December 1996, Clinton Presidential records, National Security Council cables, box 1, William J. Clinton Presidential Library, Little Rock, Arkansas.

128 "1996 Croatian Human Rights Report," American embassy Zagreb, Dp:ds-unit.un.org to Ivo H. Daalder, "Further Report on Situation of Human Rights in Croatia Pursuant to Security Council Resolution, 1019 Serbs," January 1995–December 1996, Clinton presidential records, National Security Council cables, box 3, William J. Clinton Presidential Library, Little Rock, Arkansas.

129 David Binder, "Bosnia's Bombers," *The Nation,* October 2, 1995.

130 Tracey Wilkinson, "U.S. Fires 13 Cruise Missiles at Serbia Targets in Bosnia," *Los Angeles Times,* September 11, 1995; Michael G. Vickers, "Revolution Deferred: Kosovo and the Transformation of War," in *War Over Kosovo: Politics and Strategy in a Global Age,* ed. Andrew Bacevich and Eliot A. Cohen (New York: Columbia University Press, 2001), 195, 196; Eric Schmitt, "In U.S. Peacekeeper Arsenal, Weapons Honed for Bosnia," *The New York Times,* December 5, 1995, A1; Richard Whittle, *Predator: The Secret Origins of the Drone Revolution* (New York: Henry Holt, 2014); Randy Schwartz, "Patrolling the Empire: Mapping, Imagery and National Security," *CovertAction Quarterly,* Winter 1996–1997, 34, 35. The percentage of Precision Guided Munitions (PGMs) used in this conflict was much higher (69%) than in the Persian Gulf War.

131 Conversino, "Executing Deliberate Force, 30 August–14 September 1995," in *Deliberate Force,* ed. Owen, 161.

132 Lt. Col. Mark J. Conversino, "Executing Deliberate Force, 30 August–14 September 1995," in *Deliberate Force,* ed. Owen, 161; Wilkinson, "U.S. Fires 13 Cruise Missiles at Serbian Targets in Bosnia"; David Rhode, "A Reversal of Fortune: Bosnian Serbs as Victims," *The Christian Science Monitor,* September 13, 1995.

133 *Deliberate Force,* ed. Owen.

134 Rick Atkinson, "Put to the Test, NATO Shows Its Mettle," *International Herald Tribune,* November 20, 1995.

135 Lt. Col. Mark J. Conversino, "Executing Deliberate Force, 30 August–14 September 1995," in *Deliberate Force,* ed. Owen, 194.

136 "Bombs Without Boots," Brookings Institute, https://www.brookings.edu/wp-content/uploads/2017/04/9780815732419_ch1.pdf.

137 Eric Schmitt, "NATO Shifts Focus of Its Air Attacks on Bosnian Serbs," *The New York Times,* September 11, 1995.

138 Carlo Pona, "Depleted Uranium," in *Hidden Agenda,* ed. Catalinotto and Flounders, 234, 235; Jonathan Dalhlburg, "Munitions Blamed for 'Balkan Syndrome," *Los Angeles Times,* January 6, 2001, https://www.latimes.com/archives/la-xpm-2001-jan-06-mn-9083-story.html. Six Italian soldiers got leukemia thought to be linked to the DU, prompting the Italian government to demand an investigation. Five Belgians also died.

139 Quoted in Rhode, "A Reversal of Fortune."

140 Burg & Shoup, *The War in Bosnia Herzegovina,* 355.

141 "Bombs Without Boots," Brookings Institute, 32 https://www.brookings.edu/wp-content/uploads/2017/04/9780815732419_ch1.pdf

142 Jeff Mason, "Hillary Clinton Calls Bosnia Sniper Story a Mistake," *Reuters,* March 25, 2008.

143 Quoted in James Bovard, "Kosovo: Moralizing with Cluster Bombs," in *"Feeling Your Pain:" The Explosion and Abuse of Government Power in the Clinton-Gore Years* (New York: St. Martin's Press, 2000), 328.

144 Transcript: Clinton Justifies U.S. Involvement in Kosovo, May 13, 1999, https://www.cnn.com/ALLPOLITICS/stories/1999/05/13/clinton.kosovo/transcript.html. Adding to his own numbers, Clinton went on to claim that 900,000 Albanians had fled to refugee camps while 600,000 were trapped within Kosovo lacking shelter or food.

145 See Jeremy Kuzmarov, *Obama's Unending Wars: Fronting the Foreign Policy of the Permanent Warfare State* (Atlanta: Clarity Press, 2019).

146 Patrick Maney, *Bill Clinton: New Gilded Age President* (Lawrence: University of Kansas Press, 2016), 242.

147 Stephen Erlanger, with Christopher S. Wren, "Early Count Hints at Fewer Kosovo Deaths," *The New York Times,* November 11, 1999.

148 Ibid.; Abrams, *Atrocity Fabrication and Its Consequences,* 241, 242. State Department spokesman James P. Rubin said that "100,000 men were unaccounted for" and that "based on past practice, it is chilling to think where those 100,000 men are."

149 Gibbs, *First Do No Harm,* 193, 198. Ethnic cleansing of Serbs is discussed in Engdahl, *Manifest Destiny,* 113.

150 Noam Chomsky, *Rogue States: The Rule of Force in World Affairs* (Cambridge, MA: South End Press, 2000), 36; James Hooper, "Kosovo: America's Balkans Problem," *Current History,* April 1999.

151 Abrams, Atrocity Fabrication and Its Consequences, 223; Gervasi, "Why is NATO in Yugoslavia," in *NATO in the Balkans,* 30.

152 Abrams, *Atrocity Fabrication and Its Consequences,* 227.

153 Sheldon Drobny, "Kosovo's Nazi Past: Historical Perspective," *The Huffington Post,* May 25, 2011, https://www.huffpost.com/entry/kosovos-nazi-past-histori_b_87845, Drobny quotes from Carl Sovich's essay on Kosovo's Nazi past

which asserts that in World War II and the Holocaust, Kosovar Albanians killed 10,000 Kosovo Serbs and expelled 100,000, taking over their lands and houses. Kosovo Serb women were raped. Kosovo Serb Orthodox priests were arrested, tortured, and murdered. Serbian Orthodox churches and monasteries were attacked and destroyed. Serbian monuments, cemeteries, and gravestones were desecrated and demolished. Kosovar Albanian Nazi SS troops further participated in the roundup of Kosovo Jews, who were later killed at Bergen-Belsen.

154 Abrams, *Atrocity Fabrication and Its Consequences,* 226.

155 Philip Shenon, "U.S. Says it Might Consider Attacking Serbs," *The New York Times,* March 13, 1998; Abrams, *Atrocity Fabrication and Its Consequences,* 226.

156 Noam Chomsky, *A New Generation Draws the Line: Kosovo, East Timor and the Standards of the West* (London: Verso, 2000), 34, 35, 106, 112; Abrams, *Atrocity fabrication and Its Consequences,* 224.

157 Michael Radu, "Don't Arm the KLA," *Foreign Policy,* April 1, 1999, https://www.fpri.org/article/1999/04/dont-arm-the-kla/; Jane Perlez, "Bitter Albanians Facing Anarchy, Arm Themselves," *The New York Times,* March 14, 1997; Bill Clinton letter to Carl Levin, "Situation in Albania," May 4, 1995, William J. Clinton Presidential Library, digital archive, Republic of Albania, https://clinton.presidentiallibraries.us/items/show/99718 ; Eliot Engel to the President, July 29, 1994, William J. Clinton Presidential Library, Digital Archives, Albania, https://clinton.presidentiallibraries.us/items/show/99706; Human Rights Watch Report, 1998 Albania, https://www.refworld.org/docid/3ae6a8a40.html. Berisha opened Albania's economy to Western multinationals and banks and, when he became Prime Minister again in 2009, had Albania join NATO. Bob Dole (R-KS), head of the Congressional Albanian lobby called Berisha one of the "most impressive post-communist leaders." A group of Congressmen that included Eliot Engel (D-NY); Joseph Kennedy II (D-MA) and Ronald Dellums (D-CA) wrote a letter to Clinton referring to Berisha as a "bulwark of peace and stability" in the region. Letter to President Clinton, July 21, 1994, William J. Clinton Presidential Library Digital Archive, https://clinton.presidentiallibraries.us/items/show/99707

158 "Was Albania's Ex-President Sending Arms to Kosovo Liberation Army Terrorists?" *Sputnik News,* June 4, 2017, https://sputniknews.com/europe/201704061052357541-berisha-kla-arms/; Chris Hedges, "Kosovo Rebels and Their New Friend," *The New York Times,* June 9, 1998; https://en.wikipedia.org/wiki/Sali_Berisha. Stevan Djurovic, the chief of Serbian counterintelligence in Kosovo during the war, said that Berisha organized financing for the 15 KLA training centers in Albania and the transfer of terrorists to Kosovo. On Berisha's ties to the Albanian mafia and drug trafficking, see Marko Milivojevic, "The Balkans Medellin," *Jane's Intelligence Review,* February 1, 1995, 7, 2 68, https://balkania.tripod.com/resources/terrorism/kla-drugs.html#a25. In 2021, the State Department barred Berisha, then in his 70s from entering the U.S. due to his corrupt acts. In August 1994, Clinton had received a letter from the President of the Pan-Messenian Federation of the USA and Canada pointing to Berisha's government carrying out a "campaign of terror and intimidation against persons of Greek heritage" in Albania, with six Greeks belonging to a human rights organization having been tortured. Chris Tomaras and Aikis Tsoutsias to William J. Clinton, August 26, 1994, William J. Clinton Presidential Library, Digital Archives, Albania, https://clinton.presidentiallibraries.us/items/show/99712. Human Rights Watch had reported in 1996 that Berisha's secret police, the state-owned media

and the judicial system were used to silence political opponents. "There have been numerous violations of the right to association, peaceful assembly, freedom of speech and freedom of the press directed against the political opposition and other initiatives that express views critical of the state."

159 Peter Dale Scott, *The Road to 9/11: Wealth, Empire, and the Future of America* (Berkeley: University of California Press, 2007), 168; http://historycommons.org/context.jsp?item=complete_911_timeline_2861.

160 Scott, *The Road to 9/11,* 131.

161 Dan Bilefsky and Matthew Brunwasser, "Kosovo Ex-PM Arrested on War Crimes," *The New York Times,* June 24, 2009; "The Democrats and the War Criminal," *Counterfire,* June 25, 2009, https://www.counterfire.org/articles/opinion/254-paramilitary-thug-with-long-history-with-top-us-democrats-arrested-for-war-crimes; Jeremy Scahill, "Washington's Men in Kosovo: A Year After the NATO Occupation, Terror Reigns," *Common Dreams,* July 19, 2000. Ceku had won glory and the rank of General from Tudjman for commanding Croatia's notorious 9th army brigade in scorched earth anti-Serb operations in South Croatia in September 1993. Croatian troops under his command murdered 88 Serb civilians and torched the villages of Divoselo, Citluk and Docitelj in Medak pocket. American Embassy Zagreb, "Belgrade Burba," Clinton Presidential records, National Security Council cables, box 3, William J. Clinton Presidential Library, Little Rock, Arkansas.

162 Paul Lewis, "Report Identifies Hashim Thaçi as Big Fish in Organized Crime," *The Guardian,* June 24, 2011, https://www.theguardian.com/world/2011/jan/24/hashim-thaci-kosovo-organised-crime; Doreen Carvajal and Marlise Simons, "Report Names Kosovo Leader as Crime Boss," *The New York Times,* December 15, 2010; Shawn Walker and Julian Borger, "Kosovo President Hacim Thaçi Indicted on War Crimes Charges," *The Guardian,* June 24, 2020; Dan Bilefsky, "Kosovo's Thaçi Aspires to Statesmanship, But Guerilla Past Haunts Him," *The New York Times,* July 12, 2013; James Bovard, "America's Forgotten Bullshit Bombing of Kosovo," *Counterpunch,* August 20, 2019, https://www.counterpunch.org/2019/08/20/americas-forgotten-bullshit-bombing-of-serbia/. A KLA member referred to the KLA to a relative as a "rogue's gallery of drug dealers, criminals and terrorists."

163 James Pettifer, *The Kosova Liberation Army: Underground War to Balkan Insurgency 1948–2001* (New York: Columbia University Press, 2012); Chris Hedges, "Kosovo Leader Urges Resistance, but to Violence," *The New York Times,* March 13, 1998; Abrams, *Atrocity Fabrication and Its Consequences,* 223.

164 Zimmerman, *Origins of a Catastrophe,* 11, 13, 23; Bovard, "Kosovo"; Dr. Rajen Singh, "The Kosovo Crisis and the Quest for a Diplomatic Solution," *India Quarterly, 56,* 1, 2 (January-June 2000), 1–2; Gibbs, *First Do No Harm,* 176, 177. *The Christian Science Monitor* quoted a resident of Kosovo who stated that many of his fellow Albanians "want to drive the Serbs and Montenegrins from Kosovo. They talk of an 'ethnically clean' Kosovo." A.B. Abrams characterized the KLA as a direct successor to Italian fascist backed militias during World War II.

165 Gibbs, *First Do No Harm,* 177. Rugova promoted a nonviolent approach and was rumored to be supported by the CIA. Senator Bob Dole (R-KS), the Republican Party's 1996 presidential nominee, was a key backer of the Albanian Lobby.

166 Gibbs, *First Do No Harm;* Peter Dale Scott, *American War Machine: Deep Politics, the CIA Global Drugs Connection, and the Road to Afghanistan* (New York: Rowman & Littlefield, 2014); Lewis, "Report IDs Hashim Thaçi as Big Fish in Organized Crime"; Peter Klebnikov, "Heroin Heroes," *Mother Jones,* January/

February 2000; John Laughland, *Travesty: The Trial of Slobodan Milošević and the Corruption of International Justice* (London: Pluto Press, 2007), 21. KLA commander and future prime minister Hashim Thaçi is alleged to have ordered the assassination of over a dozen KLA commanders as part of an internal power struggle.

167 Wayne Madsen, "Mercenaries in Kosovo: The U.S. Connection with the KLA," *The Progressive,* August 1999, https://www.projectcensored.org/22-us-and-germany-trained-and-developed-the-kla/; Michel Chossudovsky, "Kosovo 'Freedom Fighters:' Financed by Organized Crime," *CovertAction Quarterly,* Spring-Summer 1999. The KLA also funded some of its arms purchases through the drug trade.

168 Abrams, *Atrocity Fabrication and Its Consequences,* 226.

169 Peter Dale Scott, "Bosnia, Kosovo, and Now Libya: The Human Costs of Washington's On-Going Collusion with Terrorists," *The Asia-Pacific Journal 9,* issue 31, no 1, August 1, 2011.

170 Mark Curtis, "Blair's Former Allies on Trial for War Crimes," *Consortium News,* April 14, 2023, https://consortiumnews.com/2023/04/14/blairs-former-allies-on-trial-for-war-crimes/

171 Gary Wilson, "The Hidden Hand," in *Hidden Agenda,* ed. Catalinotto and Flounders, 176, 177.

172 Pettifer, *The Kosovo Liberation Army;* Chomsky, *A New Generation Draws the Line,* 105; Doris Pumphrey and George Pumphrey, "The Racak 'Massacre': Causis Belli for NATO," in *Hidden Agenda,* ed. Catalinotto and Flounders, 105–116; Michael Mandel, *How America Gets Away with Murder: Illegal Wars, Collateral Damage, and Crimes Against Humanity* (London: Pluto Press, 2004), 72–80; Mark Cook, "William Walker, Man With a Mission" *CovertAction Quarterly,* Spring-Summer 1999, 15.

173 "Judge Marinković: Walker knew the truth about Racak, she didn't answer to him," *RT News,* January 14, 2023, https://rt.rs/news/15185-istina-o-racku-na-strani-srbije/. Finnish forensic scientist Helena Rante, whose team investigated the Račak case, stated that William Walker, a veteran U.S. diplomat and head of the Organisation for Security and Co-operation in Europe (OSCE) who had covered up the murder of six U.S. nuns by death squads when he was ambassador to El Salvador, threw a pencil at her and pressured her when she was not willing to use language about the Serbs that he considered sufficiently strong. Ari Rusila, "Finnish forensic expert Helena Ranta: Because of report on Racak everyone pressured me," May 12, 2017, *Insider,* https://insajder.net/english/focus/finnish-forensic-expert-helena-ranta-because-of-report-on-racak-everyone-pressured-me

174 Department of Defense, Policy Initiatives of the Clinton Administration, Volume 1, William J. Clinton Presidential Library, Digital Archives, https://clinton.presidentiallibraries.us/files/original/adc7cee6f65dec68c4dccd2707a8b49e.pdf; Gibbs, *First Do No Harm,* 189, 190. A senior administration official thought to be Madeleine Albright stated that "we intentionally set the bar too high for the Serbs to comply. They need some bombing and that's what they are going to get." The accords curiously had a provision to convert Kosovo's economy to a purely free market when most of its mines had previously been state owned ventures. Richard Becker, "The Rambouillet Accord: Declaration of War Disguised as Peace Agreement," in *Hidden Agenda,* ed. Catalinotto and Flounders, 192, 193, 194.

175 Gibbs, *First Do No Harm,* 197–198.

176 Stephen J. Glain, "With Peace on Hold is Either Side a Winner?" *The Wall Street Journal,* July 26, 2000, A18.

177 Curtis, "Blair's Former Allies on Trial for War Crimes."

178 William M. Arkin, "Operation Allied Force: 'The Most Precise Application of Air Power in History,'" in *War Over Kosovo,* ed. Bacevich and Cohen.

179 Gibbs, *First Do No Harm,* 197–198; Robert Fisk, "Serbs Murdered by the Hundred Since 'Liberation,'" *The Independent,* November 24, 1999; Peter Dale Scott, *The War Conspiracy: JFK, 9/11, and the Deep Politics of War* (Delaware: Skyhorse, 2013), 148; Diana Johnstone, *Queen of Chaos: The Misadventures of Hillary Clinton* (Petrolia California: Counterpunch Books, 2015), 64. One Serb woman in the village of Lacarak died from a U.S. air strike when splinters from a shell struck her while she stood in the yard of her house.

180 Michael Parenti, *To Kill a Nation: The Attack on Yugoslavia* (London: Verso, 2000), 122, 123. The U.S.-NATO dropped an estimated 35,000 cluster bombs which shed bomblets the size of a soda can and armor depleted uranium, which left tens of thousands of radioactive waste that poisoned the air, waters and soil of the entire region. *Hidden Agenda,* ed. Catalinotto and Flounders, 135–148. More than 10,000 unexploded bomblets were scattered around the landscape when the bombing ended. The terrible environmental costs of the war were compounded by the bombing of chemical plants, petroleum and natural gas refining, processing and storage facilities and fertilizer plants which resulted in the release of toxic, radioactive and other dangerous substances into the atmosphere, soil, ground water, and food chain.

181 Chris Hedges, "Serbian Town Bombed by NATO Fears Effects of Toxic Chemicals," *The New York Times,* July 14, 1999.

182 Andrew Cockburn, *Kill Chain: The Rise of the High Tech Assassins* (New York: Henry Holt, 2015), 61, 62; John Barry and Evan Thomas, "The Kosovo Cover-Up," *Newsweek,* May 15, 2000, 23; Michael R. Rip and James Hasik, *The Precision Revolution: GPS and the Future of Aerial Warfare* (Annapolis: Naval Institute Press, 2002), 395; Daniel Williams, "19 Killed in NATO Attack on Prison," *The Washington Post,* May 22, 1995, A1; *Hidden Agenda,* ed. Catalinotto and Flounders, 135.

183 "Kosovo Unveils Clinton's Statue," *BBC,* November 1, 2009.

184 Stacey Sullivan, "Kosovo's America Obsession," *TIME,* https://time.com/kosovo-independence-america-obsession/ For eight years after the war, Kosovo had served as a UN protectorate.

185 See Sara Flounders, "Washington Gets a New Colony in the Balkans," *Workers of the World,* February 21, 2008, https://www.workers.org/2008/world/kosovo_0228/; Diana Johnstone, "NATO's Kosovo Colony," *Counterpunch,* February 18, 2008, https://www.counterpunch.org/2008/02/18/nato-s-kosovo-colony/; David Binder, "Kosovo Auf Deutsch," *Balkananalysis.com,* November 18, 2007. Kosovo also became a haven for Islamic fundamentalism and extremism.

186 Peter Dale Scott, *The Road to 9/11: Wealth, Empire and the Future of America* (Berkeley: University of California Press, 2007), 169; Sally Denton, *The Profiteers: Bechtel and the Men Who Built the World* (New York: Simon & Schuster, 2016), 306.

187 Laughland, *Travesty*; Lenora Forestel, "Demonization and the Media Blitz," in *Hidden Agenda,* ed. Catalinotto and Flounders, 89. Even Richard Goldstone, the ICTY's first chief prosecutor, said that international justice was "all about politics."

188 Interview with Richard Holbrooke, "United Nations or Not? The Final Judgement: Searching for International Justice," *BBC Radio,* September 9, 2003, http://www.bbc.co.uk/radio4/news/un/transcripts/transcript_programme3.shtml

189 In Laughland, *Travesty.*

190 Andy Wilcoxson, "Radovan Karadzic: Serbian Hero," March 22, 2019, www.slobodanmilosovic.org

191 Michael Chossudovsky, "Economic Terrorism," in *Hidden Agenda,* ed. Catalinotto and Flounders, 293.

192 Laughland, *Travesty;* Andy Wilcoxson, "The Exoneration of Milošević: The ICTY's Ruling," *Counterpunch,* August 1, 2016, https://www.counterpunch.org/2016/08/01/the-exoneration-of-milosevic-the-ictys-surprise-ruling/

193 "If Slobo, Why Not Bill," *The Nation,* June 3, 1999, https://www.thenation.com/article/archive/if-slobo-why-not-bill/

194 Michael Chossudovsky, "Economic Terrorism," in *Hidden Agenda,* ed. Catalinotto and Flounders, 286. Kostunica also released KLA terrorists from Serb jails.

195 Albright quoted in Gregory Elich, "The CIA's Covert War: How the U.S Achieved the Overthrow of Milošević in Yugoslavia," *CovertAction Quarterly,* April-June 2001, 40. NED grants to Milošević's opponents is discussed in William Blum, "Trojan Horse: The National Endowment for Democracy," https://williamblum.org/chapters/rogue-state/trojan-horse-the-national-endowment-for-democracy; "National Endowment for Democracy Programs," Congressional Record, June 14, 1995, https://www.govinfo.gov/content/pkg/CREC-1995-06-14/html/CREC-1995-06-14-pt1-PgE1240.htm.

196 Richard Sale, *Clinton's Secret Wars: The Evolution of a Commander-in-chief* (New York: Thomas Dunne, 2009), 375, 385, 386, 396. During a run-off the Kosovo vote in the 2000 Yugoslav election was canceled, thus handing the victory to Kostunica. See "Interview with Krsljonin: Serbia as an Occupied Country," October 17, 2010, *Workers World,* https://www.workers.org/2010/world/serbia_1021/ In October 1999, Clinton announced his opposition to allowing emergency heating oil to be supplied to Yugoslavia for the winter months after the war, as part of a strategy of trying to make the population suffer so they would turn against Milošević.

197 Michael Dobbs, "U.S. Advice Guided Milošević Opposition," *The Washington Post,* December 11, 2000.

198 Dobbs, "U.S. Advice Guided Milošević Opposition." See also Engdahl, *Manifest Destiny,* 121–132. A symbol of the clenched fist was adopted by the Harvard University students' protests of 1968/69. Engdahl writes that the Pentagon had become very sophisticated in learning to conceal its coup d'états under the guise of nonviolence.

199 See Adam LeBor, *Milošević: A Biography* (New Haven: Yale University Press, 2002).

200 LeBor, *Milošević,*

201 LeBor, *Milošević,* 267.

202 In Brian Becker, "Pentagon Enforces Globalization," in *Hidden Agenda,* ed. Catalinotto and Flounders, 249.

203 Richard T. Sale, *Clinton's Secret Wars: The Evolution of a Commander in Chief* (New York: Thomas Dunne Books, 2009), 388, 396, 397. The whole covert operation was run out of the office of U.S. ambassador Richard Miles.

204 Dobbs, "U.S. Advice Guided Milošević Opposition."

205 Dobbs, "U.S. Advice Guided Milošević Opposition." The U.S. invested a lot of money in local media. See also Carl Gibson and Steve Horn, "Wikileaks Documents Expose Famed Serbian Activists' Ties to Shadow CIA," *In These Times,* December 2, 2013, https://inthesetimes.com/uprising/entry/15945/wikileaks_docs_

expose_famed_serbian_activists_ties_to_shadow_cia. Otpor tactics were later adopted in Ukraine to try and unseat the pro-Russian leader there. Popovic went on to work for the private intelligence company Stratfor and wrote a blueprint for how to unseat Venezuela's socialist president, Hugo Chavez, in September 2010. For another profile of him, see Jon Henley, "Meet Srda Popovic, the Secret Architect of Global Revolution," *The Guardian,* March 8, 2015.

206 Marc Champion, "How a Team of Whiz Kids is Shaking up Serbia," *The Wall Street Journal,* May 14, 2002, A14. Serbia's Finance Minister was named Bozidar Djelic.

207 https://en.wikipedia.org/wiki/The_Third_Bullet#Background.

208 Andrew Bacevich, *American Empire* (Cambridge, MA: Harvard University Press, 2004), 192. During the second month of the bombing, the Dow surpassed 11,000.

CHAPTER 4

The Failed Crusade to Remake Russia

"We had too much faith in [economic] 'shock therapy,' and not enough concern for its social consequences."

—Anthony Lake, National Security Advisor[1]

"What Russians needed was 'less shock' and more therapy."

—Strobe Talbott, Clinton's Russia hand[2]

"Everything the Communists told us about communism was a complete and utter lie. Unfortunately, everything the Communists told us about capitalism turned out to be true."

—Muscovite aphorism

In March 2000, the Republican-controlled House of Representatives released a damning 286-page indictment of Clinton's Russia policy entitled "Russia's Road to Corruption: How the Clinton Administration Exported Government Instead of Free Enterprise and Failed the Russian People." Written with input from eight congressional committee chairmen, the report highlighted how Clinton's policy was carried out by a troika consisting of a) Vice President Al Gore, b) Treasury Secretary Lawrence Summers, and c) Deputy Secretary of State Strobe Talbott, an old Oxford friend of Clinton's with family connections to the CIA who had enthused in the 1980s that the "United States was turning the tables on Moscow by aiding the mujahidin rebels [in Afghanistan] to the tune of many millions of dollars per year."

Excluding Congress and the Russian legislature from their decision-making, the troika pushed for the transformation of formerly state-owned monopolies through an ill-planned privatization program and subsidized corrupt officials through an elaborate foreign aid program, which propped up a government whose policies were bankrupting the Russian people.[3] The quality of economic advice that the Clinton administration offered was so bad and results so dismal that 81 percent of Russians believed it was "purposely designed to make Russia a second-rate power." When Clinton addressed the Russian Duma in 1999, only a third of the representatives showed up, and Clinton was "jeered and insulted" both "inside and outside the chamber."[4]

A psychological process of groupthink had taken hold within the administration, according to the report, characterized by "wishful thinking, shaky premises and a tendency to deny facts at odds with the cognitive underpinnings of a course of action to which groups were committed." This led to "flawed decision-making and policy" from officials "unable to admit to their own errors," and who became "trapped in a tangled muddle of self-justification, denial and distortion."[5]

The House report was obviously partisan and reflected the GOP's affinity for free markets and deep animus towards the Soviet Union, considered "one of the cruelest, most violent, least humane and viciously ideological regimes in the history of the world."[6] Yet the report was well grounded in many aspects. It included a detailed explanation of the failings of the privatization voucher system, in which vouchers that could enable people to own shares of newly privatized companies were purchased in bulk by unscrupulous oligarchs with political connections or obtained through extortion. State-owned industries were grossly undervalued in auctions, depriving the Russian people of billions of dollars in revenue. Many poorer Russians by contrast had to sell off their vouchers for quick cash on the black market—or they were encouraged to invest in voucher funds that failed to pay dividends or turned out to be pyramid schemes.[7]

The report included further information on the corruption of two key Russian officials with whom Clinton's troika worked: a) Prime Minister Konstantin Chernomyrdin, one of the richest men in the new Russia, who illicitly obtained significant holdings of stock in Gazprom, Russia's gas monopoly during the firm's privatization, and b) Anatoly Chubais, the Deputy Prime Minister for economic and financial policy and privatization chief. He granted ownership over newly privatized companies to banks who gave loans to his Foundation and organized insider auctions of prime national properties, known as loans for shares. When the CIA issued a report to Al Gore about Chernomyrdin's corruption, Gore repudiated the agency's findings and returned it with a barnyard epithet scribbled on it—*bullshit*![8] Fritz Ermath, a veteran CIA-Russia hand and the former chairman of the National Intelligence Council, spoke of American policymakers' disdain for information about the corruption of their Russian partners. He attributed this primarily to the "warping of intelligence analysis to fit political agendas" and to a cynical Washington habit of "preserving the image of a foreign policy success."[9]

The Harvard Boys' Catastrophic Russian Free Market Transformation

The Clinton administration's Russia policy followed that of the George H.W. Bush administration in its attempt to rapidly transform Russia's formerly command economy into a free-market system. The Bush I administration's policy was directed by future Secretary of State Condoleezza Rice and other so-called Vulcans, who later promoted regime change in Iraq (Dick Cheney, Richard Armitage, Stephen Hadley, Richard Perle, Dov Zakheim, Robert Zoellick and Paul Wolfowitz).[10] Non-governmental organizations funded by Congress such as the National Endowment for Democracy (NED) and the National Democratic Institute (NDI) provided financial assistance to Russian anticommunist leaders at this time, and to supposedly pro-democracy movements in the Baltics, Ukraine, Azerbaijan, Armenia and Georgia.[11]

In October 1992, President Bush signed the "Freedom for Russia and the Emerging Eurasian Democracies and Open-Market Support Act," which authorized up to $350 million in aid to be provided and managed by USAID, which already had an advance team working informally in Russia at the government's invitation. The purpose of the aid was to "establish the rule of law, adopt commercial codes, and replace the Soviet regulatory system with regulations hospitable to domestic and foreign investment."[12]

One of the recipients of a USAID grant under the terms of the Bush signed bill was the Harvard Institute for International Development (HIID) a 30-year-old entity based in Cambridge, MA that concentrated on assisting nations that were changing from government-run to market-driven economic systems.[13] Its Russia Project operated out of one of Moscow's fanciest addresses with a marble lobby and twenty-four-hour security. The "Harvard Boys" did not just advise the Yeltsin government (1991–1999), they also wrote numerous laws and regulations. One of HIID's directors, Jeffrey Sachs, was a former economic adviser to the Polish Solidarity movement who six years earlier had developed a similar "shock therapy" plan to swiftly eliminate price controls and subsidies with the goal of cutting hyperinflation in Bolivia. The adoption of harsh economic austerity measures triggered large scale protests there, which were suppressed through violence.[14]

The HIID program ended in disgrace in 1997, a year before Russia's economy completely collapsed. Two Harvard "consultants," Andrei Shleifer, recipient of the prestigious John Bates Clark Medal in economics, and Jonathan Hay, a Rhodes Scholar and recent Harvard Law graduate, were found to have used their management of a U.S. foreign aid program to promote their own personal business investments. USAID was forced to suspend the project after undertaking an internal investigation; and Harvard fired Hay and relieved Shleifer, a tenured professor, of his project duties.[15]

The Russian people were never granted any redress. The HIID's U.S. taxpayer-subsidized privatization scheme resulted in "the largest giveaway of a nation's wealth in history," according to Mortimer Zuckerman, owner of the *U.S. World & Report* (2011), and the "biggest robbery of the century, perhaps of human history," according to Russia's Deputy Prime Minister for Finance, Boris Fyodorov.[16] Russia's gold reserves were looted and its wealth taken by predatory financial interests and mafia-connected oligarchs who were able to purchase state-owned companies for a fraction of their actual cost. Over $150 billion left the country in just six years, much of it to be stored in Western or offshore banks. Russian poverty and inequality rose dramatically during that time, with the decline of the social safety net.

Cuts in the state budget and funding for education reduced the number of Russian scientists by over two million, resulting in an annual net loss of between $500 and $600 billion. Millions lost their life savings after Russia defaulted on its debt and devalued its currency in response to crippling hyperinflation. Life expectancy plummeted by over seven years for men and diphtheria cases in children soared from 2,000 in 1990 to over 50,000 in 1996.[17]

Clinton Promises "New Dawn, " Continues Shock Therapy

The promise of a new dawn in U.S.-Russian relations bred by the end of the Cold War was apparent in a beautiful speech that Clinton gave in Moscow on V-E Day on May 9, 1995, at the dedication ceremony of the Central Museum of the Great Patriotic War. In his speech, Clinton invoked the memory of a now forgotten incident where U.S. and Russian soldiers embraced on the Elbe River to celebrate their victory over the Nazis and pledged a long-term commitment to friendship and cooperation. Extolling the extraordinary courage of the Russian troops, which had been obscured by the Cold War, Clinton said that they had written "some of the greatest chapters in the history of heroism—at Leningrad, in the battle of Moscow, in defense of Stalingrad, and in the assault on Berlin where your country suffered 300,000 casualties in only 14 days."

Clinton noted further that he had come here on this day

> on behalf of the people of the U.S. to express our deep gratitude for all you gave and all that you lost, to defeat the forces of fascism. In victory's afterglow, the dream of peace soon gave way to

the reality of the Cold War, but now Russia has opened itself to new freedoms and we have an opportunity and an obligation to rededicate ourselves today to the promise of that moment 50 years ago, when Europe's guns fell silent. Just as Russia and America fought against the common evil, so today we must fight for the common good.[18]

Unfortunately, this beautiful vision was undermined by the Clinton administration's ideological fanaticism—the advancement of shock therapy that ruined Russia's economy and promotion of NATO expansion in Eastern Europe (to be discussed in the next chapter) in betrayal of a promise made by George H.W. Bush's administration. Clinton also set the groundwork for a new Cold War by bombing Serbia, orchestrating a regime change operation directed against a close Russian ally in the Balkans, and interfering in Eastern European and Central Asia in an attempt to undercut Russian influence and securing access to strategic resources like oil.

Clinton's "Revolutionary" Russian Investment

Clinton's betrayal of Russia fit with a long pattern in his career that Arkansans like J. Bill Becker of the AFL-CIO knew well. It was not surprising, given Clinton's own pedigree as a cold warrior who had supported Cold War clandestine operations as Arkansas Governor and had been involved in a successful mission with Strobe Talbott back in the late 1960s to smuggle Nikita Khruschev's memoirs out of Russia.

During the 1992 presidential campaign, Clinton criticized Bush for being "overly cautious on the issue of aid to Russia." His administration wound up providing an estimated $2.58 billion in aid to Russia during his presidency. Strobe Talbott specified that this aid was "an investment in revolution, an attempt to help Russia complete the destruction of one system and the building, virtually de novo, of a new one."[19]

Joseph Stiglitz, a distinguished economist and member of President Bill Clinton's Council of Economic Advisers, had recommended an evolutionary rather than revolutionary transition toward market operations, prioritizing the building of a legal infrastructure to support economic reforms and maintenance of public ownership of huge extractive industries to prevent exploitation by oligarchs.[20] History might have turned out differently if Stiglitz' recommendations had been followed. They were not because a hidden underlying goal of U.S. policy was to keep Russia weak following the collapse of the Soviet Union.[21]

An Unlikely Influence: Nixon

Clinton's policy towards Russia was influenced by an unlikely source: disgraced former President Richard M. Nixon. Nixon considered Boris Yeltsin to be "the most pro-Western leader of Russia in history" and a "courageous figure who risked his life to face down a gang of card-carrying killers in a Stalinist coup attempt." (Privately, Nixon told Strobe Talbott that though Yeltsin "may be a drunk," he was "the best we're likely to get in the screwed-up country over there.")[22]

In a leaked March 1992 memo entitled "How to Lose the Cold War," Nixon proclaimed Russia to be a key nation in which the "final battle of the Cold War" would be "won or lost. . . . While no longer communist, it is still Russia with a centuries' old tradition of expansionism. . . . If politically, who lost China was a hot button issue in the 1950s, who lost Russia in the 1990s would be an infinitely more devastating issue."[23] So a great investment was needed to keep Russia capitalist and pro-American.

Clinton and Yeltsin, Sitting in a Tree...

In an attempt to fulfill Nixon's advice, Clinton met with Yeltsin a record eighteen times, stating that he was "genuinely committed to freedom and democracy, genuinely committed to reform."[24] Personal correspondence between the two leaders available at the Clinton library show a warm relationship in which Clinton conveyed sincere interest in Yeltsin's background and health and a commitment to helping boost his political fortunes.[25] In a meeting on May 17, 1998 in Birmingham, England, Yeltsin told Bill that: "You and I have an excellent relationship, Bill—more than just a friendship; it's what I would call co-leadership."[26]

Born to a humble peasant family, Yeltsin had risen through the ranks of the communist party during the 1960s and 1970s in Sverdlovsk in the Urals after training as an engineer. In the 1980s, he supported Soviet Premier Mikhail Gorbachev's economic liberalization (perestroika), though he said that the reforms did not go far enough. In 1987, Yeltsin was the first to resign from the communist party's governing Politburo, establishing his popularity as an anti-establishment figure.[27]

This reputation was cemented when he helped rally public opposition to a coup attempt against Gorbachev in August 1991 led by the head of the KGB, Vladimir Kryuchkov, and Vice President Gennady Yanayev. Yeltsin made a memorable speech on the turret of a tank, which many Russians believe was staged. Gorbachev subsequently gave up without a fight, the Soviet Union was dissolved, and Yeltsin became the new president.[28]

Clinton administration officials considered Yeltsin to be a "Russian democratic alternative to the imperial authoritarianism of the traditionalists."[29] However, 80 percent of Russians had opposed the dissolution of the Soviet Union and historians now characterize Yeltsin's political ascendancy as a coup.[30] The CIA had been split between moderate Republicans and liberals who supported Gorbachev's push to transform Russia into a social democracy, and conservatives led by Paul Weyerich, who favored the more right-wing Yeltsin. Back in the 1970s, Weyerich had traveled to Russia, discovered Yeltsin and helped him to run American-style political campaigns making use of effective public relations. These helped Yeltsin to rise in the communist party hierarchy first in Sverdlovsk, and then enabled him to challenge Gorbachev for national power.

George H.W. Bush originally favored Gorbachev, though his administration supplied Yeltsin with portable telephone equipment, which he used to make secure calls to military commanders whom he urged not to back the KGB putsch. President Bush further ordered the National Security Agency (NSA) to make available to Yeltsin real-time reports made by the coup plotters on their special government telephone.[31]

Despite being heralded by Clinton for his commitment to freedom and characterizing him as the "Father of Russian democracy," Yeltsin actually took to calling himself Boris I, as if he was the new czar.[32] Clinton's obliviousness to the catastrophic impact of shock therapy was epitomized by his comments to Yeltsin in a meeting on May 17, 1998 in Birmingham, England, a mere three months before the collapse of stock and bond market, and devaluation of the Russian ruble which caused massive hyperinflation. Clinton said:

> You know Boris, we really are working with the stuff of history here. I'm convinced that twenty years from now when the Russian economy is booming, people will look back and say we were right, we did the right things. I just hope you get all the credit you deserve when you're still around because you've done a terrific job of leading your country during one of the two or three most important moments in Russian history.[33]

These comments were about equivalent to Herbert Hoover hoping to receive acclaim for his economic policies on the eve of America's Great Depression. If Clinton and Yeltsin were indeed working with the stuff of history, it was not at all a positive one.

Yeltsin and the Storming of Russia's Parliament

On September 21, 1993, Yeltsin lived up to his Boris I title as a new czar by disbanding parliament in violation of the Russian Constitution. The Communist Party opposed Yeltsin's mass privatization along with conservative pan-Slavic and Russian nationalist organizations in a left-right coalition Yeltsin referred to as a "red-brown alliance." Parliament responded to Yeltsin's heavy-handedness by declaring his decision null and void, and impeaching Yeltsin, whom they had accused of "impoverishing," "tormenting" and "selling out Russia."

On October 3, the crisis escalated as demonstrators took over the new parliament building—nicknamed Russia's White House because it was a white skyscraper—along with the Moscow mayor's office and the main TV broadcasting center. Participants in the protests detected the presence of government provocateurs. On the same day, Yeltsin, the supposed "father of Russian democracy," ordered the army to storm the parliament when the protestors refused to leave. He claimed that the goal of his opponents was to "turn back history," and "resurrect the communist past which Russia had done with forever."[34]

Between 187 and 2,000 people were killed, including numerous legislators, and nearly a thousand were wounded by the Russian army.[35] The parliament building was burned in the worst day of violence Moscow had seen since the 1917 revolution. According to Iona Andronov, an elected member of parliament who was in the building before and during the attack, many of the bodies in and around the White House and TV station—victims of the attacks and later executions—were secretly removed and "disappeared" during the night.[36]

Vice President Alexandr Rutskoi, who accused Yeltsin of promoting the "economic genocide of the Russian people" and presiding over Russia's descent into a "banana republic," and Parliament Speaker Ruslan Khasbulatov, who condemned Yeltsin's subordination of Russia's economy to "the savage market . . . [and] raw material corporations of international financial and industrial groups," were arrested under false pretexts along with 1700 other people. They were accused of being communist hardliners though in actuality they were centrists who favored the development of national capitalism. Some of the detainees were interned in a sports stadium, recalling the procedures used by dictator Augusto Pinochet after the 1973 coup in Chile backed by the Nixon administration.[37]

After receiving news that Rutskoi and others of Yeltsin's opponents had surrendered, Strobe Talbott went to the State Department briefing room to congratulate Yeltsin on the victory.[38] Secretary of State Warren Christopher told Yeltsin his blatant assault on Russian democracy was a "superb handling" of the situation.[39] Clinton issued a statement expressing his full support for Yeltsin during the crisis after speaking with Yeltsin, and afterwards signed a large foreign aid bill. He publicly averred that Yeltsin had "bent over backwards to avoid violence" and "had no other choice. . . . If such a thing happened in the United States, you would have expected me to take tough action against it."[40]

Yeltsin subsequently banned opposition parties and shut down their newspapers, including *Pravda*, the communist party newspaper. A new constitution was passed that placed enormous powers in the hands of the president. Finance Minister Boris Fyodor proclaimed gleefully that "we can [now] bring in any budget we like." This included an austerity budget widely opposed by the already suffering people. Yeltsin's conduct during the September 1993 crisis and thereafter underscored the fact that rapid privatization and "shock therapy" policies could only be instituted under an authoritarian climate.[41]

Chechnya and Human Rights Double Standards

Clinton had called the promotion of democracy and human rights in Russia a key administration goal. However, the Clinton administration helped finance a war on Chechnya which resulted in human rights atrocities of a scale greater than those carried out by the Serbs in Bosnia and Kosovo that precipitated the U.S.-NATO bombing. At the height of the NATO shelling of Sarajevo in winter 1995, there were thirty-five hundred detonations a day, while in Grozny [capital of Chechnya], Yeltsin's winter bombing reached a rate of four thousand detonations *an hour*.[42] In the Balkans the U.S. supported secessionist movements and slapped sanctions on Yugoslavia for trying to suppress them, but backed Russia when it did the same with greater ferocity.

Chechnya had been annexed by Russia after the Napoleonic wars and had fiercely resisted Russian rule for many years thereafter, including following the Bolshevik takeover in 1917. Prior to 1940, the region provided as much as 45 percent of the Soviet Union's oil supplies. In World War II, over 600,000 Chechens were deported for alleged collaboration with the Nazis. In later years, the Russians considered the Chechens to be Islamic terrorists supported by foreign powers and waged two brutal campaigns against them from 1994–1996, and again from 1999–2009.

The U.S. indeed provided covert aid to Chechen separatists within the framework of what Zbigniew Brzezinski called "the grand chessboard." Chechnya's leaders received training and funds from jihadist groups backed by the CIA in Afghanistan and from Pakistan. CIA asset Anwar al-Awlaki was among those to recruit Muslim youth to fight in Chechnya. According to terrorism expert Yossef Bodansky, the U.S. saw the Chechnyan conflict as a way to "deprive Russia of a viable pipeline route through spiraling violence and terrorism. . . . U.S. assisted escalation and expansion of the war in Chechnya shoud deliver the desired debilitation of Russia." Russian Defense Minister Igor Sergeyev (1997–2001) said similarly that a "permanent smoldering of manageable armed conflicts resulting [in a weakened Russia] will help the U.S. control . . . the Northern Caucuses."[43]

The first Chechen campaign was overwhelmingly opposed by the Russian people as Yeltsin ordered the military assault without even bothering to submit a decree to the Duma as required by his own constitution. The bloody two-year war was in many ways a logical extension of the shelling of the White House and was even led by the same general, Pavel Grachev. A central objective was the retention of control of a pipeline, which Chevron had agreed to help finance, that transported enormous quantities of Caspian Sea oil to the world market.[44]

According to Amnesty International, the 1994–1996 military operation in Chechnya resulted in the death of between twenty to eighty thousand civilians—only slightly lower than those killed in the entire Balkans conflict, with thousands more displaced. Many died as a result of "indiscriminate attacks by Russian Federation federal forces on densely populated, residential areas," especially in Grozny where many homes were burned, and people were driven out.[45] Chechen women were raped at so-called "filtration camps" where prisoners were beaten with hammers and clubs and tortured with electric shocks.[46]

Despite the fact that the city was razed, President Clinton spoke to *Time* magazine about Russia's impending "liberation" of Grozny. The Clinton administration blamed another massacre at Samashki, where over 350 Chechen homes were set ablaze, leaving human corpses burned beyond recognition, on "inadequate military discipline" rather than state policy, and concluded that American relations with Russia could not be "held hostage to one issue [Chechnya]" because of "the stakes involved."[47]

In a letter to Yeltsin in January 1995, Clinton expressed concern for "the growing cost in human life" of the war, while reaffirming the official U.S. position that Chechnya was both an "internal matter" and part of Russia and that America "opposed any effort to change international borders by force," including "by means of armed secession."[48] This did not, of course, reflect the U.S. position with regard to the NATO assault on Yugoslavia.

When Yeltsin asked, at an April 1996 summit, whether the U.S. should have been more critical of Russian policies in Chechnya, Clinton responded: "I would remind you that we once had a civil war in our country in which we lost, on a per capita basis, far more people than we lost in any of the wars of the 20th century over the proposition that Abraham Lincoln gave his life for, that no state has a right to withdraw from our union."[49] *The New York Times* reported that "even Mr. Clinton's aides were appalled by his off-the-cuff remarks." A few days afterwards, the widow of Chechen President Dzokhar Dudayev told CBS News that Clinton's support for Russia's war in Chechnya "in effect signed her husband's death warrant," as a few hours later a Russian war plane had rocketed his car.[50]

Journalist Wayne Madsen suggests that the U.S. was the only country with satellite technology which could have helped the Russian security services pinpoint Dudayev's location and that it was probably not a coincidence that Clinton happened to be in Moscow the day that Dudayev was assassinated (April 21, 1996) by two laser guided missiles while using a satellite phone. British researcher Nafeez Mosaddeq Ahmed wrote that Clinton had reportedly ordered the CIA to supply Moscow with top-secret electronic targeting devices that allowed the Russians to assassinate Dudayev. The main motive would have been to ensure Yeltsin's reelection, as Yeltsin and the army were starting to look impotent as Russian troops suffered their worst setback, with 90 of them killed in Chechen attacks in Yarysh-Mardy in mid-April and in Budenarsk in Russia.[51]

In February 1996, the Clinton administration pressured the IMF to grant $10.2 billion in credits to Russia, which was used to subsidize Yeltsin's reelection campaign along with the Kremlin's military operations in Chechnya. This loan, combined with an early one for $6.4 billion, exceeded most estimates of the total cost of the first Chechen war, leading some observers to argue that the West actually "paid for the Russian invasion."[52] Former National Security adviser Zbigniew Brzezinski, a Russophobe who stridently opposed the war, made reference to the "genocide inflicted on the Chechnyans" by Russia.[53] The choice of words was interesting because the alleged genocide of the Serbs had been a basis for U.S. military intervention in the Balkans but since Russia was a staunch ally, the term did not gain any currency in this case.

Winning the Russian Elections for Yeltsin

When the United States in 2016 accused Russia of meddling in the American election on behalf of Donald Trump, few Americans were conscious of the fact that America had played a decisive role twenty years earlier in tilting the elections in Russia in favor of Boris Yeltsin. Like with the U.S. 2016 elections, the 1996 Russian elections were significant ones, which were set to provide a referendum on the privatization and shock therapy programs advanced by President Boris Yeltsin and the United States.

In a discussion about the election at the White House on April 21, 1996, Yeltsin said that he did not need to run again for the presidency but felt compelled to do so to save the country from the communists who had gained in popularity because of the dire economic crisis afflicting the country. Yeltsin said that the Communist Party leader, Gennady Zyuganov, who was his main opponent, claimed to be a social democrat but he would "cancel reforms and abolish privatization."

According to Yeltsin, "most of the communists were fanatics" who wanted to "take back Crimea and abolish the boundaries between the republics of the former Soviet Union" and would "destroy everything. It would mean civil war." Clinton responded by telling Yeltsin that he didn't have to worry about American support as America was equally committed to ensuring that the communists did not prevail. "We spent fifty years working for that result," Clinton said.[54]

The Clinton administration subsequently lobbied the IMF to give Russia the $10.2 billion loan, some of which Yeltsin distributed to woo voters and boost his popularity, which was in the single digits in February. In return for the loan, Yeltsin said he would exempt the exports to Russia by Arkansas-based Tyson Chicken (a longtime Clinton donor)—then a $700 million annual business—from a threatened 20 percent import tariff increase.[55] Clinton told his point man for Russia, Strobe Talbott: "I want this guy [Yeltsin] to win so bad it hurts."[56]

The National Endowment for Democracy (NED)—which gave nearly $1 million between 1990 and 1992 to support the anticommunist Democratic Russia Movement, which provided Yeltsin with his political base[57]—received USAID grants for providing seminars, conferences, and exchanges on party organization, message development, focus groups, polling methods, and television ads to members of Yeltsin's political machine. Three American political consultants went to work on Yeltsin's reelection bid, including George Gorton, a veteran of the Nixon, Ford and Reagan presidential campaigns, and Richard Dresner, a veteran of the Clinton campaign in Arkansas and associate of Dick Morris, Clinton's top political adviser.

Working through his daughter Tatyana, the consultants promoted dirty tricks and urged Yeltsin to "go negative" by rallying the oligarch-controlled Russian media to whip up "a wild anti-Communist psychosis among the people," as one sympathetic news editor put it. Every week, Dresner would send to the White House the Yeltsin's campaign's internal polling. Dresner also advised Clinton on what to say when he was in Moscow that would lend support to Yeltsin's reelection. Clinton meanwhile often passed on his own advice to Yeltsin and even phoned him to urge him to run a political ad prepared by Dresner which proved to be effective.[58]

Fresh from helping to elect Pete Wilson (R) as Governor of California, the American consulting team acknowledged that they were trying to help an unpopular candidate win. One of their first memos read: "Voters don't approve of the job Yeltsin is doing, don't think things will ever get any better and prefer the Communists' approach. There exists only one very simple strategy for winning: first, becoming the only alternative to the Communists; and second, making the people see that the Communists must be stopped at all costs." The final TV spots were all about the communists' repressive rule. Mikhail Margolev, who coordinated the Yeltsin account at Video International, a Russian TV company trained by the American PR firm Oglivy and Mather, said that "the Americans were vital. They helped teach us Western political advertising techniques."[59]

TIME magazine's now famous report on the American meddling came with the brazen cover lead, "Yanks to the Rescue." Later, it inspired a Showtime film, *Spinning Boris*, about how American political consultants "saved Russia from communism." Correspondent Michael Kramer rationalized the American intervention in pure Machiavellian logic: "Democracy triumphed—and along with it came the tools of modern campaigns, including the trickery and slickery Americans know so well."[60]

Despite his disastrous policies and poor health, Yeltsin won the election by thirteen percent. At an Independence Day rally in Ohio, Clinton proclaimed that in "a free and fair election . . . the Russian people chose democracy."[61] However, the Yeltsin campaign conducted extensive "black operations," including disrupting opposition rallies and press conferences, spreading disinformation and false campaign material attributed to their communist opponent, and denying media access to the opposition. Campaign donations from financial oligarchs exceeded a legal spending cap by an estimated $1.7 billion and were used to pay out bribes and curry favor among political bosses.[62] The American embassy reported on a political scandal involving Yeltsin's deputy, Anatoly Chubais, "whose people [had] handed Yeltsin illegal cash contributions by the boxload."[63]

An independent British election monitoring team found widespread voter fraud. One million people were said to have voted in Chechnya when the population was only 500,000. Yeltsin allegedly received 70 percent of the vote despite the fact that he had ordered the invasion and bombing of Chechnya. Michael Meadowcroft, a British election observer and former member of parliament, stated: "They'd been bombed out of existence and there they were all voting for Yeltsin.... It's like what happens in Cameroon."[64]

The Gore-Chernomyrdin Commission and the "Thirdworldisation" of Russia

The Gore-Chernomyrdin Commission was set up in December 1994 to coordinate cooperative policies between the U.S. and Russia in areas such as customs, taxes, tariffs, intellectual property rights, family planning, the spread of infectious diseases, space, the Arctic, and oil spills and other environmental problems along with energy and U.S. business in Russia. Gore met with Chernomyrdin twice per year and eight special committees were set up that met regularly at a Russian-American petroleum club.[65]

Critics referred to the commission as an "alternative State Department" and Gore as a "proconsul" to the Russian Federation because of his tremendous power to affect policy and the commission's lack of transparency.[66] At a White House press conference, Gore specified that "no aspect of our work together [with Chernomyrdin] is more important than our efforts to create a healthy and open climate for trade and investment in Russia."[67] Gore's function as an economic fixer was evident during the so-called "chicken war" in 1996 when he was able to force the dropping of an import tax after Russian officials raised health concerns about the import of U.S. chicken parts, the largest being Tyson Inc. of Arkansas.[68]

In the hope of promoting disarmament and non-proliferation, Gore oversaw an agreement to buy Soviet weapons grade uranium; an energy department agency took the uranium, diluted it and resold it to power plants, with the agency subsequently privatized under Gore's reinventing government program. However, when the market for uranium collapsed, the newly privatized company, USEC, was stuck with a contract to buy Russian uranium at above market prices and U.S. taxpayers were on the hook for an extra $200 million.[69]

The records of the commission at the Clinton Presidential library reveal a strong push for privatization, the elimination of oil export quotas and regulatory burdens on oil companies, reduction in taxes, licenses and tariffs, tax exemptions for foreign joint ventures and removal of other barriers for foreign investment.[70] American Energy Secretary Hazel O'Leary at one point told Chernomyrdin that American oil executives had "expressed their appreciation for his governments' efforts to alleviate the tax and regulatory burden on U.S. oil companies operating in Russia." Texaco, Exxon and Amoco negotiated to develop the oil fields in the Timan Pechora Basin northeast of Moscow above the Arctic circle, which potentially held 2 billion barrels.[71]

Commerce Secretary Ron Brown praised Chernomyrdin for exempting six joint ventures from the "crippling" oil export tax. He established the U.S.-Russia Business Council, whose board of directors were staffed with

CEOs of clients of Akin Gump—AT & T, Westinghouse, Bechtel, Upjohn Pharmaceuticals and Pfizer.[72] Brown led a trade mission with corporate executives from Westinghouse, Duracell, Tenneco, Raytheon, and other companies which did more than four hundred million dollars in business in the new Russia.[73]

The Gore-Chernomyrdin Commission's health committee championed a $100 million program by USAID that helped privatize Russia's pharmaceutical industry and other programs which supported private U.S. investment in the production of critical pharmaceutical products, along with the upgrading of health information systems, drug distribution, and creation of partnerships between American and Russian hospitals.[74]

By December 1994, the American Overseas Private Investment Corporation (OPC) had approved over $2.5 billion in insurance and loans for dozens of business ventures by U.S. companies in what it termed Russia's "booming markets." The OPC's aggressive approach towards supporting U.S. investment in Russia extended to the telecommunications industry, printing, computers, agribusiness, trucking, as well as ports, manufacturing and infrastructure projects.[75]

The U.S. Trade and Development Agency (TDA) under Director Joseph Grandmaison supported aircraft projects, and Diesel trucks and Caterpillar bulldozer machines.[76] In 1997, Al Gore boasted that American companies had come to account for a third of all foreign investment in Russia—an amount that eclipsed the period before Russia's communist revolution.[77] An unforeseen problem was that of tax evasion; the state tax service estimated its occurrence in August 1998 at a 60 percent rate, amounting to half the size of Russia's official economy. The rate of capital flight was also estimated to be anywhere from $15 billion to $500 billion per year or as high as $20 billion per month.[78]

The Gore-Chernomyrdin Commission produced positive cooperation in the realm of space exploration, environmental cleanup and conservation, nuclear warhead safety, and nonproliferation, exemplified in the the Nunn-Lugar program, which led to the withdrawal of nuclear weapons from Belarus, Kazakhstan, and Ukraine. However, a U.S.-dominated consultancy called the Non-Proliferation Trust also helped to broker a corrupt scheme by which Russia's nuclear agency, Minaton, was offered $10 billion in return for the right to dump an estimated 200 tons a year of high level radioactive material in Russian waste sites in the Urals.[79] This latter deal flew in the face of Gore's vision that the transition to a free market economy in Russia could be "compatible with environmental protection."[80]

Again on the positive side, USAID initiated a project to cut emissions from district heating plants in Novovyatsk, upgraded the city's water treatment facilities and conducted industrial audits to reduce pollution. Elsewhere, feasibility studies were financed for alternative energy sources to fossil fuels and nuclear power plants, grants were provided for creation of an environmental youth corps and protection of endangered species, and the Environmental Protection Agency promoted reforestation. Both countries also agreed to implement the climate convention.[81]

Unfortunately, Gore's environmentalism did not coincide with the promotion of sound economic policies. Political scientist Michel Chossudovsky significantly titled a chapter in his book about Russia in the 1990s: "The Thirdworldisation to the Russian Federation." He compared the economic medicine imposed by the Clinton administration and IMF to that imposed on debtor countries in Latin America and sub-Saharan Africa. An explicit goal of the "economic hitmen"[82] was to enforce debt servicing through the slashing of state expenditures, which resulted in impoverishment for most of the population.

By 1998, 30 percent of the Russian budget was devoted to debt service. New laws were introduced that enabled foreign capital to take over large sectors of the national economy. Marlboro and Phillip Morris, for example, acquired control over state production facilities for sale in the domestic market and British Airways gained access to domestic air rates in a joint venture with Aeroflot.[83] Marc Rich, who bought a pardon from Clinton after his conviction for tax fraud and tax evasion, used his control over an off-shore bank, Nordex, to snap up Russian oil refineries being auctioned off.[84] The jobs lost through public sector cuts were never made up through the private sector, as Clinton and Gore had envisioned, and the massive loss of tax revenues plunged living standards to third world levels as civil service wages, pensions and public services were dramatically cut.

By the late 1990s, Russia's GDP was below its GDP during the Second World War and the death rate reached or eclipsed wartime levels.[85] Alcoholism, drug use, infant mortality and HIV rates all skyrocketed. Organized crime came to control up to 50 percent of the Russian economy and infiltrated the highest levels of the state, looting tons of diamonds, jewels, silver, and gold from the Russian National Treasury.[86] Anatoly Chubais told the *L.A. Times* in September 1998 that "we conned them [the U.S.] out of $20 billion." He was referring to the U.S. and IMF loans which went to foreigners and Russian speculators along with corrupt government officials who stashed the money in offshore banks.[87]

In August 1999, *The New York Times* reported that billions of dollars were laundered from Russia through the Bank of New York, with many of the transfers originating at a Moscow bank chaired by a financial advisor to the Yeltsin family.[88] Chubais granted ownership over newly privatized companies to banks who gave loans to his foundation, and organized insider auctions of prime national properties, known as loans for shares, in which the Harvard Management Company (HMC), which invested the university's endowment, and billionaire speculator George Soros were the main participants. HMC and Soros in turn became significant shareholders in Novolipetsk, Russia's second-largest steel mill, and Sidanko Oil, whose reserves exceed those of Mobil.[89]

In 1997, Soros purchased 24 percent of Sviazinvest, a telecommunications giant, in partnership with Vladimir Potanin. It was later learned that shortly before this purchase, Soros had tided over Yeltsin's government with a backdoor loan of hundreds of millions of dollars. According to *Wall Street Journal* reporter Anne Williamson, the American assistance program in Russia was rife with such conflicts of interest involving HIID advisers and Chubais' allies.[90]

Venyamin Sokolov, the Russian government's chief auditor under Yeltsin, told *Mother Jones Magazine* that "under the guise of establishing a market in Russia, the authorities created an economic monstrosity that has nothing to do with a market system." He went on to describe how because of a lack of money, Russians were forced to resort to a barter system "similar to that which existed in primitive societies in which people exchanged stone axes for mammoth skins." The Yeltsin government was corrupt and immoral, with teachers and medical workers laid off owing to the embezzlement of government funds. Sokolov said that giving more loans to the Yeltsin government was comparable to "giving a drug addict a fresh supply of narcotics." Russian workers were "reduced to serfs like under the tsars."[91] When Yeltsin left office on December 31, 1999, he had an approval rating of two percent.[92] Desensitized from the suffering of his people, he spent much of his second term in a drunken stupor. Clinton, Gore and the others, however, were completely sober.

Endnotes

1 Quoted in Timothy J. Lynch, *In the Shadow of the Cold War: American Foreign Policy from George Bush Sr. to Donald Trump* (New York: Cambridge University Press, 2020), 59.

2 Lynch, *In the Shadow of the Cold War,* 59.

3 Representatives Christopher Cox, Ben Gilman, Porter Goss, et al. "Russia's Road to Corruption: How the Clinton Administration Exported Government Instead of Free Enterprise and Failed the Russian People," Members of the Speaker's Advisory Group on Russia, U.S. House of Representatives, Washington, D.C., September 2000 (286-page report), https://fas.org/irp/congress/2000_rpt/russias-road.pdf, Talbot quote on Afghanistan taken from Andrew Bacevich, *America's Greater War For the Middle East: A Military History* (New York: Random House, 2016), 54.

4 David N. Bossie, *Intelligence Failure: How Clinton's National Security Policy Set the Stage for 9/11* (Nashville, Tennessee, WND Books, 2004), 127. Thousands also participated in anti-American demonstrations in Moscow

5 Representatives Christopher Cox, Ben Gilman, Porter Goss, et al. "Russia's Road to Corruption: How the Clinton Administration Exported Government Instead of Free Enterprise and Failed the Russian People," Members of the Speaker's Advisory Group on Russia, U.S. House of Representatives, Washington, D.C., September 2000 (286 page report), https://fas.org/irp/congress/2000_rpt/russias-road.pdf,

6 Ibid.

7 Ibid.

8 Paul Klebnikov, *Godfather of the Kremlin: Boris Berezovsky and the Looting of Russia* (London: Mariner, 2001), 325; James Risen, "Gore Rejected CIA Evidence of Russian Corruption," *The New York Times*, November 23, 1998; David Ignatius, "Who Robbed Russia? Did Al Gore Know About the Massive Lootings?" *The Washington Post*, April 25, 1999.

9 Fritz Ermath, "Seeing Russia Plain: The Russia Crisis and American Intelligence," *The National Interest*, Spring 1999, 5–14; available at: https://lists.h-net.org/cgi-bin/logbrowse.pl?trx=vx&list=h-diplo&month=9906&week=a&msg=SL740S46TBgGo7IIL%2BCzlQ&user=&pw=

10 See James Mann, *The Rise of the Vulcans: The History of Bush's War Cabinet* (New York: Penguin Press, 2006). Defense Secretary Dick Cheney advocated for the dissolution of the USSR and the breakaway of Ukraine and other former Soviet Republics, which he felt would be geopolitically advantageous to the United States. Brent Scowcroft, a longtime associate of Henry Kissinger and National Security Council advisor under Bush I, argued for a more moderate position within the administration.

11 James M. Goldgeier and Michael McFaul, *Power and Purpose: U.S. Policy Towards Russia after the Cold War* (Washington, D.C.: Brookings Institution Press, 2003), 29, 30.

12 David McClintock, "How Harvard Lost Russia," *Institutional Investor*, January 13, 2006.

13 McClintock, "How Harvard Lost Russia." In Indonesia, HIID helped revise the tax system and liberalize financial markets. It also had been active in Colombia, Kenya, Pakistan, and Zambia. Russia was its biggest and most important project. Other notable professors who worked with Sachs to promote privatization included: Graham Allison of the Harvard Kennedy School, Anders Aslund, David Lipton, and Marshall I. Goldman.

14 Naomi Klein, *The Shock Doctrine: The Rise of Disaster Capitalism* (New York: Metropolitan Books, 2007), ch. 7. Sachs believed in free markets, though backed by debt relief and generous aid. His anticommunist and anti-socialist views may have derived from his wife, Sonia Ehrlich, a pediatrician who fled Communist Czechoslovakia with her family when she was twelve. According to a Spanish newspaper, Sachs personally edited Yeltsin's decrees. Like in Russia, Sachs' economic austerity program in Bolivia was implemented by fiat without popular consent, in this case by Bolivian President Victor Paz Estenssoro, who had ironically overseen the nationalization of Bolivia's tin mines and land redistribution policies after leading Bolivia's 1952 revolution. The protests were violently crushed by Estenssoro's government, with many killed. Many Bolivians were subsequently forced to work as coca growers. Sachs' key counterpart, Gonzalo Sanchez de Losada (Goni) later

became president of the country where he oversaw the renewed massacre of protestors opposing privatization initiatives.

15 Janine R. Wedel, "The Harvard Boys Do Russia," *The Nation Magazine*, May 14, 1998; Steve Liesman and C. Anne Roberts, "Aborted Mission: How an Aid Program Vital to the New Economy of Russia Collapsed," *The Wall Street Journal*, August 13, 1997, A1; McClintock, "How Harvard Lost Russia." In 2000, the U.S. Attorney in Boston filed an 11-count claim against Harvard University, Shleifer, and Hay for defrauding the government by making personal investments in Russia against the terms of their contract. In June 2004, a U.S. District Court Judge upheld the U.S. Attorney's claim in a 100-page decision and forced the defendants to pay $31 million in fines. Harvard University, which was cleared of the fraud allegations but still faced damages for breaching its contract with the USAID, was forced to pay $26.5 million, and Shleifer and Hay, $2 million each. Both men were also barred from working for USAID for two and five years respectively. In 2013, Russian President Vladimir Putin publicly identified Shleifer and Hay as CIA agents. Whether this is true or not is uncertain.

16 F. William Engdahl, *Manifest Destiny: Democracy as Cognitive Dissonance* (Wiesbaden: Mine Books, 2018), 29–69; Christopher Cox et al. "Russia's Road to Corruption: How the Clinton Administration Exported Government Instead of Free Enterprise and Failed the Russian People," U.S. House of Representatives, Washington, D.C., September 2000, 101.

17 Stephen Cohen, *Failed Crusade: America and the Tragedy of Post-Communist Russia* (New York: W.W. Norton, 2001); Ron Ridenour, *The Russian Peace Threat: Pentagon on Alert* (New York: Pinto Press, 2018); I. Marshall Goldman, *The Privatization of Russia: Russian Reform Goes Awry* (New York: Routeledge, 2003); Peter Reddaway and Dmitri Glinski, *The Tragedy of Russia's Reforms: Market Bolshevism Against Democracy* (Washington, D.C.: U.S. Institute of Peace Press, 2001), 2, 3.

18 "Remarks by President Clinton at Dedication Ceremonies of Central Museum of the Great Patriotic War," May 9, 1995, Presidential Trip to Russia and Ukraine, May 8–12, 1995, Clinton Presidential Records, NSC, Russia, Ukraine and Eurasian Affairs, Gore-Chernomyrdin Commission, Moscow, box 2, William J. Clinton Presidential Library, Little Rock, Arkansas. On the 1945 Elbe River meeting, see *Yanks Meet Reds: Recollections of U.S. and Soviet Vets From the Linkup in World War II*, ed. Mark Scott and Semyon Krasilshchik (Mass.: Capra Press, 1988).

19 Goldgeier and McFaul, *Power and Purpose*, 90, 91, 93, 213.

20 Robert Brent Toplin, "The Lost Opportunity to Set Post-Soviet Russia on a Stable Course," *History News Network*, April 3, 2022, https://historynewsnetwork.org/article/182848

21 In an April 1993 meeting with Polish President Lech Walesa Clinton stated almost gleefully "we do not believe that Russia is at present too strong," as if this was a good thing. Memorandum of Conversation, Meeting with President Lech Walesa of Poland, April 21, 1993, William J. Clinton Presidential Library, Declassified Documents Concerning Poland, https://clinton.presidentiallibraries.us/items/show/16198

22 Strobe Talbott, *The Russia Hand: A Memoir of Presidential Diplomacy* (New York: Random House, 2002), 46.

23 Richard M. Nixon, "How to Lose the Cold War," March 1992, reprinted at Richard Nixon Foundation website, https://www.nixonfoundation.org/artifact/how-

to-lose-the-cold-war/ On deep rooted Russophobia—which is evident in Nixon's writings—see Guy Mettan, *Creating Russophobia: From the Great Religious Schism to anti-Putin Hysteria* (Atlanta; Clarity Press Inc., 2017).

24 Masha Gessen, "The Undoing of Bill Clinton and Boris Yeltsin's Friendship and How it Changed Both of Their Countries," *The New Yorker*, September 5, 2018.

25 Eg. Clinton Library, Declassified Documents, "The White House, Luncheon Meeting with Russian President Boris Yeltsin," April 21, 1996, https://clinton.presidentiallibraries.us/items/show/57569

26 Memo of Conversation, The White House, May 17, 1998, Birmingham, England, https://clinton.presidentiallibraries.us/items/show/57569. In a speech at Harvard University's Kennedy School in April 2021, Clinton said that "Yeltsin, I think, was the best leader we could've gotten out of Russia at that time."

27 Leon Aron, *Yeltsin: A Revolutionary Life* (New York: St. Martin's Press, 2000); Timothy J. Colton, *Yeltsin: A Life* (New York: Basic Books, 2008); Steven Otfinoski, *Boris Yeltsin and the Economic Rebirth of Russia* (Brookfield, CT: The Milbrook Press, 1995); David Kotz and Fred Weir, *Russia's Path From Gorbachev to Putin: The Demise of the Soviet System and the New Russia* (New York: Routeledge, 2007), 127, 128.

28 Aron, *Yeltsin*, 453, 454; David Marples, *The Collapse of the Soviet Union, 1985–1991* (New York: Routeledge, 2004), ch. 5, 6; Vladimir Zubok, *A Failed Empire: The Soviet Union in the Cold War from Stalin to Gorbachev* (Chapel Hill: The University of North Carolina Press, 2009), 333.

29 Colton, *Yeltsin*, 191.

30 Roger Keeran and Kenny Thomas, *Socialism Betrayed: Behind the Collapse of the Soviet Union* (iuniverse, 2010).

31 Reddaway and Glinski, *The Tragedy of Russia's Reforms*, 203. There are suggestions in some sources (ie. Engdahl, *Manifest Destiny*) that the CIA paid the coup plotters, and thus helped stage the coup as a means of facilitating the collapse of the USSR. This charge is yet to be verified with declassified documents. Andrei Kozyrev, a top aide to Yeltsin reported that during the crisis, the Western embassies "in effect began to work for us; through them, we received and passed on information." In John Dunlop, *The Rise of Russia and the Fall of the Soviet Empire* (New Jersey: Princeton University Press, 1993), 216.

32 Klein, *The Shock Doctrine*, 226; Amy Knight, *Orders to Kill: The Putin Regime and Political Murder* (New York: Thomas Dunne Books, 2017), 79. The father of Russian democracy reference was in Memorandum of Conversation, Bill Clinton and Boris Yeltsin, September 12, 1998, 11:32 AM-11: 59 AM, Oval Office, https://clinton.presidentiallibraries.us/items/show/57569

33 Memo of Conversation, The White House, May 17, 1998, Birmingham, England, https://clinton.presidentiallibraries.us/items/show/57569

34 Reddaway and Glinski, *The Tragedy of Russia's Reforms*, 370, 424; Aron, *Yeltsin*, 498, 499, 501, 524, 552; Andrew Higgins, "Russian Crisis: Fears of Fascism Grow as 'Red-Brown' Allies Emerges," *The Independent*, October 4, 1993, https://www.independent.co.uk/news/world/europe/russian-crisis-fears-of-fascism-grow-as-redbrown-allies-emerge-1508578.html

35 Ridenour, *The Russian Peace Threat*, 261.

36 Karen Talbott and Ellen Ray, "Roots of Chechnya Wars: Russia's Sovereignty," *CovertAction Quarterly*, Spring-Summer 2000, 19.

37 Klein, *The Shock Doctrine*, 228, 229; Aron, *Yeltsin*, 498, 499, 501, 524, 552; James DeFronzo, *Revolutions and Revolutionary Movements*, 5th ed. (New

York: Routeledge, 2014), 60; Colton, *Yeltsin*, 278, 279; Michel Chossudovsky, "The Thirdworldisation of the Russian Federation," in *The Globalization of Poverty: Impacts of IMF and World Bank Reforms* (London: Zed Books, 1997). Economic genocide quote from Steven Otfinoski, *Boris Yeltsin and the Economic Rebirth of Russia* (Millbrook Press, 1995), 82.

38 Michael Dobbs, "Strobe Talbott and the 'Cursed Questions,'" *The Washington Post*, June 9, 1996, https://www.washingtonpost.com/archive/lifestyle/magazine/1996/06/09/strobe-talbott-and-the-cursed-questions/bd8dbc3c-019d-4884-abac-b6bf91f22955/

39 Svetlana Savranskya and Tom Blanton, "Yeltsin Shelled Russian Parliament 25 Years Ago, U.S. Praised "Superb Handling" National Security Archive, October 4, 2018, https://nsarchive.gwu.edu/briefing-book/russia-programs/2018-10-04/yeltsin-shelled-russian-parliament-25-years-ago-us-praised-superb-handling; Higgins, "Russian Crisis." Few members of the U.S. Congress opposed Yeltsin's actions or urged the Clinton administration to denounce them. Senator Robert Dole (R-KS) was among the few to question on national television whether it was wise for the United States to urge countries like Russia to impose shock therapies. Congressman Bernard Sanders (D-VT) also opposed the shock therapy policies. Reddaway and Glinski, *The Tragedy of Russia's Reforms*, 425.

40 Sean Guillory, "Dermokratyia, USA," *Jacobin*, March 13, 2017; David S. Foglesong, *The American Mission and the "Evil Empire: The Crusade For a "Free Russia" Since 1881* (New York: Cambridge University Press, 2007), 208; Helen Thomas, "Clinton Supports Yeltsin in Crisis," *UPI Archives*, September 21, 1993, https://www.upi.com/Archives/1993/09/21/Clinton-supports-Yeltsin-in-crisis/7235748584000/

41 See Klein, *The Shock Doctrine*. Blaming Strobe Talbott for the fact that U.S. policy had become personalized and identified with Yeltsin, Sergey Rogov, director of the USA Institute in Moscow, stated that the attack on the parliament was "a major blow to the democratic process. After this mini-civil war, the attempt to create a system of checks and balances is over. We in Russia have never suffered from the excessive authority of the legislative branch. Today, there are no checks on the power of the executive branch. In that sense, Yeltsin's decision to dissolve parliament led directly to the Chechen war." Dobbs, "Strobe Talbott and the 'Cursed Questions.'" In 1998 journalist Dmitry Kholodov was murdered after he had investigated and revealed the corruption of Yeltsin's defense minister, Pavel Grachev.

42 "Chechnya, Yeltsin, and Clinton: The Massacre at Samashki in April 1995 and the U.S. Response to Russia's War in Chechnya," National Security Archive Briefing Books, edited by Svetlana Savranskaya and Matthew Evangelista, https://nsarchive.gwu.edu/briefing-book/russia-programs/2020-04-15/massacre-at-samashki-and-us-response-to-russias-war-in-chechnya#_ednref8; David Remnick, *Resurrection: The Struggle for a New Russia* (New York: Random House, 1997), 263, 264.

43 Webster G. Tarpley, *9/11 Synthetic Terror: Made in USA* (Joshua Tree, CA: Progressive Press, 2006), 124; Nafeez Mosaddeq Ahmed, *The War on Truth: 9/11, Disinformation, and the Anatomy of Terrorism* (Northampton, MA: Olive Branch Press, 2005), 64, 65. An American State Department official and ex-Marine, Fred Cuny, who specialized in disaster relief died during the war under mysterious circumstances, raising suspicion that he was involved in a CIA operation in support of the Chechnyans—a theory promoted by fiction writer Tom Clancy in his book, *The Sum of All Fears*. See George Kenney, "Spy or Savior," *The Nation*, July 8, 1999, https://www.thenation.com/article/archive/spy-or-savior/.

44 Robert H. Donaldson and Vidya Nadkarni, *The Foreign Policy of Russia: Changing Systems, Enduring Interests* (New York: Taylor & Francis, 2019), 257; American embassy Almaty to Secretary of State, Washington D.C., December 1994, Declassified Documents Concerning the Gore-Chernomyrdin Commission, William J. Clinton Presidential Library, declassified documents, https://clinton.presidentiallibraries.us/items/show/36597; Talbott and Ray, "Roots of Chechnya Wars," 19. The second Chechen war was more morally ambiguous as it was started when Chechnya invaded the neighboring Russian republic of Dagestan with the aim of controlling its oil and establishing a Muslim state.

45 "Russian Federation: Brief Summary of Concerns About Human Rights Violations in the Chechen Republic," https://www.amnesty.org/download/Documents/168000/eur460201996en.pdf; U.S. Mission Geneva to Secretary of State, April 1995, National Security Archive, George Washington University, https://nsarchive2.gwu.edu//dc.html?doc=6838422-National-Security-Archive-Doc-20-U-S-Mission

46 Ibid.

47 "A Brief Description of the Events in the Village of Samashki"; U.S. Mission Geneva to Secretary of State, April 1995; Secretary of State to CIS Collective, April 1995; American Embassy Moscow to Secretary of State, April 1995, "Russian Forces Attack on Samashki: Differing Views on Atrocities"; "Chechnya, Yeltsin, and Clinton: The Massacre at Samashki in April 1995 and the U.S. Response to Russia's War in Chechnya," National Security Archive Briefing Books, edited by Svetlana Savranskaya and Matthew Evangelista, https://nsarchive.gwu.edu/briefing-book/russia-programs/2020-04-15/massacre-at-samashki-and-us-response-to-russias-war-in-chechnya#_ednref8. Russian troops threw grenades in homes' cellars and set them ablaze using flamethrowers.

48 Letter Bill Clinton to Boris Yeltsin, January 6, 1995, https://nsarchive2.gwu.edu//dc.html?doc=6838408-National-Security-Archive-Doc-06-President

49 Representatives Christopher Cox, Ben Gilman, Porter Goss, et al. "Russia's Road to Corruption: How the Clinton Administration Exported Government Instead of Free Enterprise and Failed the Russian People," Members of the Speaker's Advisory Group on Russia, U.S. House of Representatives, Washington, D.C., September 2000 (286 page report), https://fas.org/irp/congress/2000_rpt/russias-road.pdf.

50 Ibid.

51 Wayne Madsen, "Did NSA Help Russia Target Dudayev?" *CovertAction Quarterly*, Summer 1997, 46–49; Ahmed, *The War on Truth*, 59.

52 "Chechnya, Yeltsin, and Clinton: The Massacre at Samashki in April 1995 and the U.S. Response to Russia's War in Chechnya," National Security Archive Briefing Books, edited by Svetlana Savranskaya and Matthew Evangelista, https://nsarchive.gwu.edu/briefing-book/russia-programs/2020-04-15/massacre-at-samashki-and-us-response-to-russias-war-in-chechnya#_ednref8.

53 Ibid. Brzezinski was not a neutral observer: he was a Russophobe intent on weakening Russia, who may have spearheaded efforts by the U.S. to covertly arm the Chechnyan terrorists, as many Russians believed. See Talbott and Ray, "The Chechnya Wars," 20.

54 Clinton Library, Declassified Documents, "The White House, Luncheon Meeting with Russian President Boris Yeltsin," April 21, 1996, https://clinton.presidentiallibraries.us/items/show/57569

55 Engdahl, *Manifest Destiny*, 63. Germany also loaned Russia $2.7 billion, three quarters of which was given without conditions on its use.

56 Talbott, *The Russia Hand*, 205. Clinton gave directions that the United States had to go all out in helping Yeltsin [to win.]

57 Colin Cavell, *Exporting "Made in America' Democracy: The National Endowment for Democracy & U.S. Foreign Policy* (Lanham, MD: University Press of America, 2002), 110.

58 Peter Beinart, "The U.S. Needs to Face Up to Its Long History of Election Meddling," *The Atlantic*, July 22, 2018; Guillory, "Dermokratyia, USA"; Eleanor Randolph, "Americans Claim Role in Yeltsin Win," *Los Angeles Times*, July 9, 1996; Michael Kramer, "Rescuing Boris: The Secret Story of How Four U.S. Advisers Used Polls, Focus Groups, Negative Ads and All the Other Techniques of American Campaigning to Help Boris Yeltsin Win," *Time* magazine, July 15, 1996; Fred Weir, "Betting on Boris," *CovertAction Quarterly* (Summer 1996): 38, 41; Holly Sklar and Chip Berlet, "NED, CIA and the Orwellian Democracy Project," *CovertAction Quarterly* 39 (Winter 1991–1992); Dick Morris, *Because He Could*, with Eileen McGann (New York: Regan Books, 2004), 171. Joe Shumate was another consultant, along with Steven Moore, who worked in public relations in the United States and Felix Braynin, a Russian ex-patriot. Zyuganov ran on a platform only slightly more radical than the New Deal, calling for increased public investment in transportation, communications, and energy, raising wages and pensions, reducing raw material prices, steering credit away from speculative activities and towards productive uses, reversing illegal privatization and renationalization of key economic sectors, and increasing spending on science, technology, and education.

59 Ibid. The consultants went on to help elect Arnold Schwarzenegger (R) as Governor of California.

60 Kramer, "Rescuing Boris"; Gerald Sussman, "The Myth of 'Democracy Assistance:' U.S. Political Intervention in Post-Soviet Eastern Europe," *Monthly Review*, December 17, 2006.

61 Guillory, "Dermokratyia, USA."

62 Wedel, "Harvard Boys Do Russia"; Klebnikov, *Godfather of the Kremlin*, 220, 221. In keeping with Russian laws at the time, Zyuganov spent less than three million dollars on his campaign. Estimates of Yeltsin's spending, by contrast, range from $700 million to $2.5 billion. This was a clear violation of the law. A portion of the money derived from illicit black-market operations and was paid in the form of a bribe or as a form of payback for the state's selling off privatized industry at pennies to the dollar.

63 From American Embassy, Moscow, to Secretary of State, November 1996, "Chubay's Campaign Corruption Scandal," Clinton Presidential Library, declassified records, Russia, https://clinton.presidentiallibraries.us/items/show/36594

64 Alexander Zaitchik and Mark Ames, "How the West Helped Invent Russia's Election Fraud: OSCE Whistle-Blower Exposes 1996 Whitewash," *The Exile*, November 20, 2007, http://johnhelmer.net/how-the-west-helped-invent-russias-election-fraud-osce-whistleblower-exposes-1996-whitewash/.

65 Gore first traveled to Russia shortly after he was elected to the U.S. Senate in the early 1980s. He had been introduced around Russia by family friend and benefactor Armand Hammer, chairman of Occidental Petroleum and a friend of the Soviet Union.

66 Robert L. Bartley, "Thinking Things Over: How Gore Lost Russia," *The Wall Street Journal*, August 21, 2000, A19; David N. Bossie and Floyd G. Brown, *Prince Albert: The Life and Lies of Al Gore* (Bellevue, Washington: Merril Press, 2000), 118, 119.

67 "Press Conference by Vice-President Al Gore and Prime Minister Chernomyrdin of Russia," January 10, 1996, Clinton Presidential records, NSC, Russia, Ukraine and Eurasian Affairs, Gore-Chernomyrdin Commission, Moscow, box 1, folder 2, William J. Clinton Presidential Library, Little Rock, Arkansas.

68 Bartley, "Thinking Things Over."

69 Bartley, "Thinking Things Over"; Bossie and Brown, *Prince Albert*, 120, 121.

70 Gore-Chyrnomirden Commission, Energy Policy Committee, June 17, 1994, Clinton Presidential records, NSC, Russia, Ukraine and Eurasian Affairs, Gore-Chernomyrdin Commission, Moscow, box 1, folder 2, William J. Clinton Presidential Library, Little Rock, Arkansas; American Embassy Moscow to White House, December 1994; American Embassy Moscow to Washington D.C., "Energy Committee Meeting, Moscow," December 1994; U.S. Russia Business Development Committee Report to the Gore-Chernomyrdin Commission, American embassy Moscow to Secretary of State, December 1994, Declassified Documents Concerning the Gore-Chernomyrdin Commission, William J. Clinton Presidential Library, declassified documents, https://clinton.presidentiallibraries.us/items/show/36597.

71 "Joint U.S-Russian Statement in Support of Timon Pechora Project," September 2, 1994, Clinton Presidential Records, Press Office, Box 15, William J. Clinton Presidential Library, Little Rock, Arkansas; "Texaco Russia Finally Sign Timan-Pechora Oil Deal," *Associated Press*, December 16, 1996. Pratt & Whitney was another winner, which, backed by $250 million in combined Overseas Private Investment Corporation (OPIC) insurance and loan guaranties, set up a joint venture with two Russian aerospace manufacturers to market a new aero-engine in Russia. In the 1990s, Western oil companies invested $5 billion in Russia.

72 American Embassy Moscow to Washington D.C., "Energy Committee Meeting, Moscow," December 1994, U.S. Russia Business Development Committee Report to the Gore-Chernomyrdin Commission, American embassy Moscow to Secretary of State, December 1994, Declassified Documents Concerning the Gore-Chernomyrdin Commission, William J. Clinton Presidential Library, declassified documents, https://clinton.presidentiallibraries.us/items/show/36597; Cockburn and Silverstein, *Washington Babylon,* 121.

73 Tracey L. Brown, *The Life and Times of Ron Brown: A Memoir* (New York: William Morrow and Company Inc., 1998), 265; Alexander Cockburn and Ken Silverstein, *Washington Babylon* (London: Verso, 1996), 121.

74 American Embassy Moscow to Secretary of State, Washington D.C., "GCC Health Committee, Report to VP Gore and PM Chernomyrdin," December 1994, Declassified Documents Concerning the Gore-Chernomyrdin Commission, William J. Clinton Presidential Library, declassified documents, https://clinton.presidentiallibraries.us/items/show/36597

75 U.S. Russia Business Development Committee Report to the Gore-Chernomyrdin Commission, American embassy Moscow to Secretary of State, December 1994, Declassified Documents Concerning the Gore-Chernomyrdin Commission, William J. Clinton Presidential Library, declassified documents, https://clinton.presidentiallibraries.us/items/show/36597

76 U.S. Russia Business Development Committee Report to the Gore-Chernomyrdin Commission; "Press Conference by Vice-President Al Gore and Prime Minister Chernomyrdin of Russia," January 10, 1996, Clinton Presidential records, NSC, Russia, Ukraine and Eurasian Affairs, Gore-Chernomyrdin Commission, Moscow, box 1, folder 2, William J. Clinton Presidential Library, Little Rock, Arkansas.

77 See William Appleman Williams, *American-Russian Relations, 1781–1947* (New York: Rinehart & Co., 1952) for comparison.

78 Representatives Christopher Cox, Ben Gilman, Porter Goss, et al. "Russia's Road to Corruption: How the Clinton Administration Exported Government Instead of Free Enterprise and Failed the Russian People," Members of the Speaker's Advisory Group on Russia, U.S. House of Representatives, Washington, D.C., September 2000 (286 page report), https://fas.org/irp/congress/2000_rpt/russias-road.pdf.

79 Alexander Cockburn and Jeffrey St. Clair, *Al Gore: A User's Manual* (London: Verso, 2000), 227.

80 U.S. Russia Business Development Committee Report to the Gore-Chernomyrdin Commission, American embassy Moscow to Secretary of State, December 1994, Declassified Documents Concerning the Gore-Chernomyrdin Commission, William J. Clinton Presidential Library, declassified documents, https://clinton.presidentiallibraries.us/items/show/36597

81 American Embassy Moscow to Washington D.C., "Energy Committee Meeting, Moscow," December 1994, Declassified Documents Concerning the Gore-Chernomyrdin Commission, William J. Clinton Presidential Library, declassified documents, https://clinton.presidentiallibraries.us/items/show/36597

82 See John Perkins, *Confessions of an Economic Hit Man* (London: Berrett-Koehler, 2004).

83 Chossudovsky, *The Globalisation of Poverty*, ch. 12.

84 Whitney Webb, *One Nation Under Blackmail: Vol. 1: The Sordid Union Between Intelligence and Organized Crime That Gave Rise to Jeffrey Epstein* (Walterville, OR: Trine Day, 2022), 417.

85 Markar Melkonian, "U.S. Meddling in the 1996 Russian Elections in Support of Boris Yeltsin," *Global Research*, November 11, 2017, https://www.globalresearch.ca/us-meddling-in-1996-russian-elections-in-support-of-boris-yeltsin/5568288. See also Cohen, *Failed Crusade* for more details. Russians spoke about the country being plunged back to the 19th century and the pre-modern age.

86 Stephen Handelman, *Comrade Criminal: Russia's New Mafiya* (New Haven: Yale University Press, 1997); David E. Kaplan, Christian Caryl, "The Looting of Russia," *U.S. News & World Report*, August 3, 1998, https://publicintegrity.org/accountability/the-looting-of-russia/; Representatives Christopher Cox, Ben Gilman, Porter Goss, et al. "Russia's Road to Corruption: How the Clinton Administration Exported Government Instead of Free Enterprise and Failed the Russian People," Members of the Speaker's Advisory Group on Russia, U.S. House of Representatives, Washington, D.C., September 2000 (286 page report), https://fas.org/irp/congress/2000_rpt/russias-road.pdf.

87 Representatives Christopher Cox, Ben Gilman, Porter Goss, et al. "Russia's Road to Corruption: How the Clinton Administration Exported Government Instead of Free Enterprise and Failed the Russian People," Members of the Speaker's Advisory Group on Russia, U.S. House of Representatives, Washington, D.C., September 2000 (286 page report), https://fas.org/irp/congress/2000_rpt/russias-road.pdf. No wonder

that the chief IMF economist, Michael Mussa, referred to the Russian government as consisting of a "bunch of criminals."

88 Representatives Christopher Cox, Ben Gilman, Porter Goss, et al. "Russia's Road to Corruption: How the Clinton Administration Exported Government Instead of Free Enterprise and Failed the Russian People," Members of the Speaker's Advisory Group on Russia, U.S. House of Representatives, Washington, D.C., September 2000 (286 page report), https://fas.org/irp/congress/2000_rpt/russias-road.pdf.

89 Liesman and Roberts, "Aborted Mission"; Paul Klebnikov, *Godfather of the Kremlin,* 115, 116. An audit by the Russian Chamber of Accounts revealed serious misappropriations at the Russia Privatization Center, a private nonprofit linked to Chubais and funded by Western aid money. Much of the money was distributed directly to Chubais' cronies and to key political bosses in return for their support for market "reforms."

90 Liesman and Roberts, "Aborted Mission."

91 Anne Williamson, "Russia's Fiscal Whistleblower: Chief Auditor Venyamin Sokolov Says Western Loans Are Hijacked by the Corrupt Yeltsin Government," *Mother Jones*, June 16, 1998.

92 In Sight, CNN transcript, October 7, 2002, http://transcripts.cnn.com/TRANSCRIPTS/0210/07/i_ins.01.html; Melkonian, "U.S. Meddling in the 1996 Russian Elections in Support of Boris Yeltsin."

CHAPTER 5

NATO Expansion: A Strategic Blunder of Epic Proportions

In 2016, as the U.S. and Russia fought in a proxy war over Eastern Ukraine, Clinton's former Defense Secretary William J. Perry gave an interview to the London *Guardian* in which he acknowledged that the U.S. bore a large degree of blame for the conflict. Perry stated:

> Our first action that really set us off in a bad direction was when NATO [North Atlantic Treaty Organization] started to expand, bringing in Eastern European nations, some of them bordering Russia. At that time, we were working closely with Russia and they were beginning to get used to the idea that NATO could be a friend rather than an enemy . . . but they were very uncomfortable about having NATO right up on their border and they made a strong appeal for us not to go ahead with that.[1]

As these comments suggest, the Clinton administration's policy to go ahead with NATO expansion on Russia's border was undoubtedly one of the most disastrous of his presidency. Supported by Madeleine Albright, Warren Christopher, Tony Lake, Strobe Talbott, Sandy Berger and others, it was driven by military lobbies and Eastern European emigrés and leaders with a strongly Russo-phobic outlook. Alfred de Zayas, the first UN Independent Expert on the Promotion of a Democratic and Equitable International Order, said in an interview with *CovertAction Magazine* that

> the one chance to implement conventional disarmament and reorient the world toward development and peace was thrown away by President Bill Clinton when he approved the eastern expansion of NATO, a grave breach of trust, a needless provocation, and a violation of Article 2(4) of the UN Charter, which prohibits not only the use of force but also the threat of the use of force.[2]

In an April 2022 essay in *The Atlantic*, Clinton tried to defend the policy of NATO expansion by claiming that it was designed to bolster Europe's security if Russia returned to "ultranationalism" and past "aspirations to empire like [in the era of] Peter the Great and Catherine the Great."[3] This ipso facto justification is consistent with the pattern of Western leaders exaggerating Russia's purported expansionist designs.[4] It further evades the fact that NATO expansion fit with a larger policy that was designed to capitalize on the collapse of the Soviet Union to advance American regional power, undercut Russian influence in Eastern Europe and Central Asia, and keep Russia weak. This policy bore the imprint of Zbigniew Brzezinski, Jimmy Carter's former National Security Council adviser and Albright's mentor, who saw control over Eurasia as key to global domination and consolidation of the U.S. empire—which was far vaster and more aggressive than any projected Russian one.[5]

An Epic Strategic Blunder

Despite the huge influx of foreign aid during the 1990s, by the end of the decade, American-Russian relations were far worse than they were at the beginning. In the mid-1990s with its Western-centric tilt, Yeltsin's Russia had participated in the international peacekeeping mission in Bosnia, become a member of the G-8, and joined the Council of Europe. Russia also had withdrawn from Afghanistan, cut subsidies and trade to Cuba and other socialist countries causing severe hardship there, and aligned increasingly with U.S. policy around the world. In September 1994, 300 Americans took part in the first ever joint U.S.-Russia military exercise. Clinton, in a toast to Boris Yeltsin, invoked the embrace on the Elbe River at the end of World War II between U.S. and Russian troops.[6]

A major friction resulted from the Kosovo War, however, of which 93 percent of Russians disapproved, and the Clinton administration's support for NATO enlargement, which had become enshrined in the 1994 National Security Strategy Review. The latter was in violation of a promise made by Secretary of State James A. Baker in the spring, summer and fall of 1990 to then-Soviet premier Mikhail Gorbachev that NATO would not be expanded "one inch to the East"—in return for the Russians agreeing to NATO membership for a unified Germany.[7]

By 1998, Clinton had succeeded in expanding NATO into Poland, the Czech Republic and Hungary, where the Clinton administration had spent $100 million to upgrade military infrastructure at the Taszar military base, which served as a staging point for NATO operations into Bosnia.[8] The ambassador who presided over this latter project, Donald Blinken, was head of a famous investment bank in New York (E. M. Warburg Pincus & Company) and father of future Secretary of State Antony Blinken.[9] Also in

1998, Clinton signed a charter of partnership for the Baltic states, Estonia, Latvia, and Lithuania, which lay the groundwork for their joining NATO a few years later—against the wishes of Russia which had urged the Baltic nations to adopt Finland's neutral stand outside NATO.[10]

NATO had been established as a defense alliance against the Soviet Union during the Cold War. The Clinton administration's view was that NATO was "a force for the rule of law both within Europe's new democracies and among them," in the words of Strobe Talbott, and that expanding NATO in the post-Cold War era was "likely to extend the area in which conflicts like the one in the Balkans simply do not happen." Clinton's Secretary of State Madeleine Albright, whose family had been expelled from Czechoslovakia in a 1948 Soviet backed coup, was among the most fervent supporters of NATO expansion, stating she felt the Central European case for admission "in my bones and in my genes." Clinton embraced the argument of Czech President Vaclav Havel and Polish President Lech Walesa at the opening of the Holocaust Museum in Washington, D.C. that if the world wanted to avoid another European catastrophe, Central Europe should be integrated into Western structures.[11]

In a 1997 West Point graduation address, Clinton emphasized that NATO enlargement would "help secure the historic gains of democracy" and erase the "artificial line in Europe that Stalin drew"[12]—though in reality it created a new division which would lead to a new cold war.[13] At the NATO summit in Brussels in January 1994, Clinton declared that with the Soviet Union gone, "our community of interest endures" and it is "now up to us to build a new security for a new future for the Atlantic people in the 21st Century."[14] The "Atlantic" people excluded the Russians, who could not be admitted to NATO according to Secretary General Willy Claes because "all the orthodox countries which emerged from the former Byzantine Empire have not reached the level of our civilization and will not be able to do so."[15]

Given the existence of such attitudes, it is not surprising that the Russians across the political spectrum continued to view NATO in hostile terms—as a relic of the Cold War.[16] Yeltsin had proposed a "mutually beneficial partnership with the U.S. on the basis of equality."[17] He told Clinton at a May 1995 meeting in the Kremlin following the celebration of the 50th anniversary of the end of World War II that NATO expansion would result in "nothing but humiliation for Russia. How do you think it looks to us if one bloc continued to exist when the Warsaw Pact has been abolished? It's a new form of encirclement if the one surviving Cold War bloc expands right up to the borders of Russia."[18]

Clinton's push for NATO expansion was driven in part by domestic political considerations. During the 1996 election, Clinton and Republican presidential candidate Bob Dole competed to woo midwestern Poles and other Eastern Europeans who had a historical enmity towards Soviet communism and the Russians.[19] Former Black Panther Bobby Rush, whose Chicago district had a large Lithuanian population, lobbied the Clinton administration to support NATO expansion in Lithuania.[20] When Jack Matlock, the last U.S. ambassador to the Soviet Union, testified before a congressional committee to explain why NATO expansion was a bad idea, he was told: "Look, Clinton wants to get reelected. He needs Pennsylvania, Michigan, Illinois; they all have a very strong East European...Many of these had become Reagan Democrats on East-West issues. They're insisting that the Ukraine [sic; NATO] expand to include Poland and eventually Ukraine. So, Clinton needs those to get reelected."[21]

Clinton also of course needed the support of oil companies exploring opportunities around the Caspian and Black Sea, as well as the U.S. aerospace industry and the Wall Street banks that assisted it in a series of mega mergers—who were all for NATO expansion.[22] Political scientist Thomas Ferguson suggested that Clinton's primary motive was to attract defense industry dollars after the Republican triumph in the 1994 mid-term elections, after Congressional Democrats alienated Wall Street by sponsoring hearings into hedge funds and after the U.S. dollar was artificially lowered in a scheme to open Japan's markets.[23] According to an analysis prepared for *The New York Times* by the Campaign Study Group, a research company in Springfield, Va., America's six biggest military contractors spent $51 million on lobbying for NATO expansion between 1996 and 1998.[24]

Another study by the Congressional Budget Office (CBI) predicted that Poland, Hungary, the Czech Republic, and Slovakia (another potential NATO member) would spend at least $42 billion for new weapons and other military equipment by 2010. The Clinton administration at one point tried to get NATO membership applicants to commit to order Lockheed Martin's F-16 fighter aircraft. The U.S. Committee to Expand NATO—a lobby group funded by the arms industry—happened to have been cofounded by Lockheed Martin's Vice-President for Strategy and Planning, Bruce Jackson.[25]

Containment doctrine author George F. Kennan warned that NATO expansion would amount to a "strategic blunder of epic proportions" and the "most fateful error of American policy in the entire post-Cold War era," as it would "inflame the nationalistic, anti-Western and militaristic tendencies in Russian opinion, restore the atmosphere of the cold war to East-West relations," and "impel Russian foreign policy in a direction decidedly not to our liking."[26] Kennan's prediction proved to be true but no one in power was listening to this grand old man of foreign policy anymore. *The New York*

Times reported that there was "virtually no organized opposition to NATO expansion," with the public mostly ill-informed.[27]

During a White House luncheon in April 1996, Clinton told Yeltsin that he was "trying to change NATO" by changing the impression that it was something directed against Russia and by freezing equipment levels.[28] However, this was just rhetoric. After the Helsinki summit, Yeltsin said that "the eastward expansion of NATO [was] a mistake and a serious one at that. … Nevertheless, in order to minimize the negative consequences for Russia, we decided to sign an agreement with NATO."[29]

In meetings with Clinton, Yeltsin had spoken about "an avalanche" of "anti-American" and "anti-NATO sentiment," and referred to the huge American aid package prior to the 1996 election as a "bribe" to get Russia to accept NATO enlargement.[30] Communist Party leader Gennady Zyuganov accused Yeltsin of allowing a "Versailles" for Russia, a reference to the 1919 conference in which Germany was humiliated by the Western allies.[31] An advisor to the Foreign Ministry said that Russia was being treated "like a colony" [of the United States].[32] The old Soviet Union in this context did not seem so bad anymore.

Promoting a "Color Revolution" in a Socialist Bastion

With NATO expansion solidified, the Clinton administration helped set the groundwork for "color revolutions" in former Soviet republics that aimed to replace socialist leaders with links to Russia with pro-western capitalist regimes that would support NATO expansion. A key example is Belarus where in April 2000, Clinton appointed Michael Kozak as a new ambassador. Belarus at the time was run by socialist Alexander Lukashenko, who had effectively resisted shock therapy programs and ensured a strong social safety net, free health care and education and near full employment economy. Inequality levels were lower than any other European country.[33]

Kozak had in the past been directly involved in regime change operations in Nicaragua directed against the socialist Sandinistas and served as special presidential envoy during the U.S. invasion of Panama as well as chief of the diplomatic mission to Cuba, which enjoyed close relations with Belarus. Kozak described Belarus as worse than Cuba, hence insulting Lukashenko before he had even arrived. Once he took up his post, Kozak helped oversee the funding of nongovernmental organizations (NGOs) which had links to Lukashenko's political opposition and to others seeking political change.[34]

During Belarus' 2001 presidential election, Kozak worked on a plan with the head of the UN Organization of Security and Cooperation in Europe

(OSCE) permanent mission to Belarus, Hans-Georg Wieck, to field a unified opposition candidate to oppose Lukashenko in order to avoid dividing the votes between various parties. It was a blatant case of external political interference. Kozak subsequently admitted that U.S. methods were similar in Belarus to what he had done in Nicaragua to help unseat the Sandinistas twenty years earlier.

These methods included promoting anti-Lukashenko demonstrations, which were attended by skinheads and far-right, anti-Russian elements. Kozak's actions helped set the groundwork for the 2005 "denim revolution"—a more coordinated and sustained U.S.-financed effort under the Bush administration to unseat Lukashenko, that dovetailed with other "color revolutions" the U.S. supported in Ukraine and Georgia. The latter gave the illusion of being progressive, but their main purpose was to enable NATO expansion by removing pro-Russian leaders.[35] In Belarus' case, a particular double standard was apparent on the issue of human rights in that Lukashenko's government was denounced for crimes that were never verified.[36]

Prepping Ukraine Before the Storm

While spurning Lukashenko because of his socialism, Clinton cultivated warm relations with Ukrainian president Leonid Kravchuk, an acolyte of Boris Yeltsin, and his successor Leonid Kuchma (1994–2005), who instituted a failed privatization voucher system reminiscent of Yeltsin's while moving to integrate Ukraine more deeply with Western Europe and the European Union (EU). A former member of the central committee of the Ukrainian Communist Party, Kuchma further pleased the U.S. by joining with the leaders of Georgia, Azerbaijan, and Moldova to find an energy transportation corridor from the Caspian basin to Europe, bypassing Russia.[37]

At the G-7 summit in Naples in 1994, Clinton promised Kuchma that if he liberalized Ukraine's economy, the G-7, IMF, and World Bank would provide $4 billion in assistance. The U.S. provided Ukraine with $700 million in economic assistance, marking Ukraine as the fourth largest recipient of American assistance anywhere in the world after Israel, Egypt and Russia.[38]

State Department reports praised Kuchma for adopting radical free market reforms resulting in the privatization of 90 percent of small enterprises and 8,000 of the largest firms, and for bringing in young economic reformers into his government who had a lot of exposure to the West.[39] Kuchma's son-in-law, Victor Pinchuck, got access to lucrative privatization deals, then later became one of the largest donors of the Clinton Foundation, giving at least $8.6 million between 2009 and 2013.[40]

Kuchma's authoritarianism was apparent in his a) ordering the arrest and deportation of Crimean president Yuri Meshkov after Crimeans voted for greater autonomy in March 1994, b) resorting to ballot stuffing measures to fend off a communist challenge in 1999 elections, according to the OSCE's observation mission, c) suppressing a report indicating that military stocks worth $32 billion had been stolen and resold by corrupt officials; and d) being caught on tape ordering the kidnapping of investigative journalist Gerogiy Gongadze who was then murdered.[41]

Clinton nevertheless affirmed that the U.S. "stands with Ukraine," and heralded Kuchma when he visited the White House in November 1994 for "leading a Ukrainian renaissance," comparing him to Franklin D. Roosevelt for "creating hope during a period of economic depression."[42] Kuchma's lack of popularity was apparent, however, in his igniting a separatist movement in eastern Ukraine after his government lifted coal subsidies to reduce budget deficits and inflation, resulting in "mounting financial losses and payment arrears across all sectors of the economy." Austerity measures combined with privatization led ultimately to deindustrialization.[43]

Before visiting Washington, Kuchma had signed a nuclear non-proliferation treaty that resulted in the dismantling of the world's third-largest nuclear arsenal that Ukraine had inherited from the Soviet Union—giving the U.S. an overwhelming monopoly on nuclear weapons.[44] Kuchma also had Ukraine join the Partnership for Peace (PFP), whose aim was to move Ukraine and other signatories closer to NATO, which Kuchma considered a "factor of stability in Europe." Ukrainian troops participated in U.S.-led military training exercises with counterparts in Moldova and Georgia; a particularly provocative exercise in 1997 off the coast of Crimea—home of the Russian Black Sea fleet—prompted anti-NATO protests.[45]

In an attempt to shore up the post-Soviet capitalist order, Ukrainian law enforcement agencies under Kuchma received technical assistance through the State Department's International Criminal Investigative Training Assistance Program (ICITAP) which was established by the Clinton administration to professionalize police services in foreign nations. Police aid was also provided through Department of State's International Narcotics and Law Enforcement Bureau (INL), whose budget for Ukraine was over $3 million in 1999.[46]

The Baltic States: Establishing Neocolonial Dependence

Clinton forged another strong alliance with post-Soviet government of Lithuania, which jailed Soviet sympathizers and was accused by the head of the Jewish organization, B'nai Brith, of "excusing or dignifying Lithuania's war-time Nazi collaborationist past as 'anti-Soviet resistance.'"[47] Lithuania received expanded U.S. economic and security assistance under the Warsaw initiative with the other Baltic states and in 1998 hosted a U.S. military training exercise, which sent a belligerent signal to Moscow.[48]

The Clinton administration considered Lithuania an important ally, grooming it for NATO membership like Ukraine. Accordingly, it saw to it that Lithuania removed Russian troops from its soil and embraced neoliberal economic policies that benefited U.S. investors. Under Algirdas Brazauskas (1993–1998), Lithuania signed a tax treaty promoted by Treasury Secretary Robert Rubin that removed significant tax barriers for U.S. firms. Among the beneficiaries was West Telephone Corporation, a subsidiary of AT&T that signed a $200 million telecommunications contract with the Lithuanian government, which between 1991 and 1996 privatized forty percent of state property.[49]

Clinton's State Department supported a particularly controversial deal by which Lithuania sold a major portion of the formerly state-run oil company, Mazeiku Nafta, to the Williams energy company of Tulsa, Oklahoma including a 319,000 barrel per day refinery near the Latvian border. The Russian company Lukoil stopped shipping oil because it had wanted a controlling interest. Romuldo Ozolas, opposition deputy in the Lithuanian parliament had warned that the Williams sale would "bring about neo-colonial dependence," calling the deal a "crime" in which an "American company dictated conditions that were unacceptable to Lithuanians."[50]

The Clinton administration's strategy, supported by Democrats in Congress like Joe Biden (D-DE) and Richard Durbin (D-Ill), was generally to pry the Baltics and other former Soviet satellites away from the Russian orbit and integrate them into trans-Atlantic political, economic and security structures, as Clinton put it. [51] As in elsewhere in Eastern Europe, the administration pushed for economic liberalization, including privatization and the lifting of price controls, with much foreign aid designed to ease any economic dislocations.[52]

A unique public-private initiative was developed with the George Soros Foundation, which supported new NGOs and civil society organizations that were anticommunist. A major land privatization initiative was also advanced in Moldova.[53] The Clinton administration further supported a $50 million American Enterprise Fund in the Baltic states—modeled after similar funds that were established with other Eastern European countries—designed to promote private sector development, privatization, and joint venture initiatives. This was accompanied by the commitment of millions of dollars to transfer U.S. technical expertise and expand financing for equity and loans in support of private enterprise in the Baltics.[54]

To help sustain the post-communist economic order, the Clinton administration devoted significant funds to beef up security assistance. It developed a Baltic peacekeeping battalion, which took part in field exercises with U.S. and NATO units and served alongside NATO forces in Bosnia. The three Baltic states were now invited to take part in the U.S. foreign military sales program and allowed to make commercial purchases of U.S. defense articles.[55]

A favored Baltic leader was Estonian Prime Minister Mart Laar (1992–1994; 1990–2002), who was awarded the Milton Friedman medal for having instituted a low flat tax, eliminated tariffs, and privatized ninety percent of his country's economy while embracing NATO expansion.[56] Laar was the author of a book that idealized the Forest Brothers, CIA-backed partisans who collaborated with the Nazis in World War II, then fought the Soviet occupation of Estonia during the Cold War.[57] The book gives a good indication of Laar's strong anti-communist, anti-Russian perspective, which the Clinton administration valued.

Pimping for the Oil Cartel: The New Great Game in Central Asia

With the breakup of the Soviet Union, American government officials and oil industry executives saw an opportunity to expand American access to Central Asia's rich oil and natural gas resources, triggering a new "great game" of competition with the Russians that would continue through the 21st century. Future Vice President Dick Cheney, then the CEO of Haliburton, a pipeline services vendor based in Texas, enthused in 1998: "I can't think of a time when we've had a region as suddenly to become as strategically significant as the Caspian. It's almost as if the opportunities have arisen overnight. The good Lord didn't see fit to put oil and gas only where there are democratically elected regimes friendly to the United States. Occasionally we have to operate in places where, all things considered, one would normally not choose to go. But we go where the business is."[58]

Sheila Heslin of the U.S. National Security Council acknowledged that the essence of U.S. intervention in Central Asia and the Caucasus in the 1990s was to "break Russia's monopoly of control over the transportation of oil from the region."[59] Even Boris Yeltsin decried "U.S. penetration" [of Central Asia] which he said hurt Russian interests.[60] Hugh Pope observed in *The Wall Street Journal* that "today's great oil game is just as treacherous [as its predecessor]. . . . [In its present form] the struggle typically pits Western interests against Russians fighting a rear-guard action in their old backyard."[61]

In 1997, the U.S. Department of State told Congress that the Caspian Basin held as much as 200 billion barrels of oil—about ten times the amount found in the North Sea, and a third of the Persian Gulf's total reserves.[62] In the next three years, the Clinton administration provided $175 million in arms and military training and over $1 billion in aid to countries in the region, which strategic planners sought to incorporate into a "vast U.S. dependency." Georgia specifically received $302 million to bolster the government of Eduard Shevardnadze, who had come to power in a coup d'état backed by the Western powers which toppled nationalist Zviad Gamsakhurdia, who died under suspicious circumstances a year later.

Clinton approved a CIA program to send Special Forces into Georgia to protect Shevardnaze, who eliminated political opponents and had close ties to mafia warlord, Jaba Ioseliani. Nicknamed the "old fox," Shevardnadze further led the violent suppression of Russian-backed separatist movements in Ossetia and Abkhazia, where according to one observer, Georgian paramilitary units "marched on village after village burning, pillaging, raping and killing."[63]

Shevardnadze's main value to the West was his commitment to protecting the main export oil pipeline that crossed Georgia from Azerbaijan on the way to Turkey in an attempt to bypass Russia. Shevardnaze also opened up Georgia's economy to foreign capital and acquiesced to Georgia's membership in the World Trade Organization (WTO).[64] CIA agent Robert Baer recounted in his memoirs how he had refused a request by the State Department to sell Shevardnadze a Matador air defense system because the CIA had a video of his intelligence service shooting six blindfolded prisoners in the back of the head.[65]

Another prime recipient of U.S. aid in Central Asia, Nursultan Nazarbayev of Kazakhstan, was described as "somewhere between Franco and Chile [Pinochet]."[66] Nazarbayev's mafia-style tactics were apparent when the decapitated carcass of a dog was left outside the office of a newspaper that reported he had stashed over a billion dollars in state oil money in Swiss bank accounts, with a warning that "there won't be a next time."[67] The money had come from the sale of a 20-percent stake in the Tengiz offshore oil fields to Chevron, and from $78 million in bribes given by an American oil industry consultant, James Giffen, the de-facto U.S. ambassador who worked for Nazarbayev and claimed to have had the approval of the CIA in helping to secure Chevron's concession.[68]

Clinton's close personal relationship with Nazarbayev was solidified in 2005 when he enjoyed a decadent midnight feast with the dictator while helping to secure a uranium mining concession for Clinton Foundation donor James Giustra.[69] Clinton had first met with Nazarbayev in the White House on Valentine's Day in 1994, where he announced a tripling of foreign aid and affirmed that he was impressed by Kazakhstan's openness to U.S. business investment, mentioning Chevron, Philip Morris, and Mobil, which signed a deal for offshore drilling in an area previously designated as a nature reserve that housed some of the earth's largest freshwater fish. Strobe Talbott told Clinton before the meeting that "we want Kazakhstan, with its sea of oil, to be securely fixed in international, economic, political and security structures."[70]

These new structures did not benefit the Kazakh people: 100 oil workers died and many more got sick working on the Tengiz oil field between 1996 and 2004, most of them young men who developed blood and liver problems. A local environmental group claims that the tests from 30,000 seals that died in 2003 revealed similar symptoms. A World Bank study in 2002 found 71 percent of the Kazakh population living on less than $2 per day. The country at the time ranked 122nd out of 145 countries in Transparency International's corruption index.[71]

In 1997, Nazarbayev signed a defense cooperation agreement with Defense Secretary William Cohen calling for regular contacts and exchanges between U.S. and Kazakh officers. The Clinton administration subsequently provided Nazarbayev a fast patrol boat, *the Dauntless*, and advanced training to Kazakh military personnel while carrying out joint military exercises like Operation CENTRAZBAT 97, in which 500 paratroopers from the army's 82nd Airborne Division jumped into a battle zone near the Tien Shan Mountains.[72]

Further exercises were carried out with Uzbekistan under the auspices of the NATO Partnership for Peace (PFP) Program in which the U.S. military nurtured "the embryo of a NATO-led military force in Central Asia."[73] The egregious double standard regarding human rights was exemplified by the harsh rule of Islam Karimov, who employed forced labor and was accused by British ambassador Craig Murray of boiling two of his opponents alive in the face of an Islamist rebellion backed by Saudi Arabia.[74]

Robert Baer wrote that "the deeper I got [into the Washington scene], the more Caspian oil money I found sloshing all around Washington."[75] American oil companies had begun obtaining concessions in Central Asia just after the demise of the Soviet Union, and thereafter began lobbying vigorously for a more interventionist foreign policy. *The Washington Post,* in a three-part series entitled "Pipe Dreams—The Struggle for Caspian Oil," spotlighted the lobbying efforts of Don Stacy, Director of Eurasian Operations at Amoco Corporation, who at a political gathering at the White House on August 6, 1996, emphasized the strategic importance of Azerbaijan's oil deposits.

According to *The Post*, one listener at the gathering was riveted—President Bill Clinton—who jumped in to clarify several geopolitical points, then strode to a blackboard and drew a remarkably accurate map of the Caspian region. Before the meeting ended, Amoco—the largest U.S. investor in Azerbaijan's oil boom—had what it wanted: a promise from Clinton to invite the Azerbaijani President, Heydar Aliyev, to Washington. Six months later, the company, which traditionally donated heavily to the Republicans, contributed $50,000 to the Democratic Party.

After signing a bilateral investment treaty, Clinton subsequently received Aliyev at the White House with full honors, witnessed the signing of a new Amoco oil exploration deal and promised to lobby Congress to lift economic sanctions on Azerbaijan, which had been imposed because of its war with Armenia.[76] Clinton said that "by working closely with Azerbaijan to tap the Caspian's resources, we not only help Azerbaijan to prosper, we also help diversify our energy supply and strengthen our energy security."[77]

On the same visit Aliyev met with Defense Secretary William Cohen to discuss stronger U.S.-Azerbaijani defense cooperation and possible American training of the Azerbaijani army. This alarmed Russia and Armenia, whom the Azeris accused of occupying Azerbaijan territory (Nagorno-Karabakh—the UN Security Council in 1993 called on Armenia to withdraw its troops from Azerbaijan). This prompted Alyiev to initiate a more violent phase of the 1992–1994 war that left 30,000 people dead.[78]

In a joint press conference, Clinton praised Aliyev's success in strengthening Azerbaijan, implementing economic reform, including large-scale privatization, and spurring economic growth.[79] On Aliyev's death in 2003, however, *The New York Times* reported that living standards had declined since the end of Soviet rule and that the average Azeri earned just $650 per year.[80] Corruption was endemic and natural gas was barely available outside the capital, Baku, despite the discovery of world-class natural gas fields by BP, Amoco and others offshore in the Caspian Sea.[81] In his remarks Clinton further left out Aliyev's routine torture of political opponents and the fact that Aliyev was a protégé of Soviet leader Leonid Brezhnev, who first gained power in 1969 after a career as a KGB general.[82]

According to Western diplomatic sources, when Aliyev led an armed uprising in 1993 against Azerbaijan's elected president, Abulfez Elchibey, he was assisted by mercenaries in the employ of Mega Oil, which had employed veterans of the secret war in Laos and the Iran-Contra affair, notably Richard Secord and Heinie Aderholt. The mercenaries were based at three Azeri army camps where they conducted a military training program. American diplomats put the total number of American trainers—who were paid about $12 million—at about a dozen, which suggested they were training a bodyguard force.[83]

These soldiers of fortune were accompanied by up to a thousand Afghan mujahidin, who helped push back Armenian invaders, who had been supplied by Russia, along the Azeri-Iranian border. Russian paratroopers were also training supporters of the Azeri Prime Minister Surat Husseinov as a counterweight to the pro-Western Aliyev, who wanted to open up Azerbaijan's oil reserves to exploration by Western companies and even said he'd welcome a NATO base.[84]

CIA National Council on Intelligence's deputy director, Graham E. Fuller, a key architect in the creation of the mujahidin to fight Afghanistan and later the USSR, had stated that "the policy of guiding the evolution of Islam and of helping them against our adversaries worked marvelously well in Afghanistan against the Red Army. The same doctrines can still be used to destabilize what remains of Russian power."[85] The U.S. Congressional Task Force on Terrorism and Unconventional Warfare's director, Yossef Bodansky, detailed the extent of the CIA's strategy to destabilize Central Asia by using "Islamist Jihad in the Caucasus as a way to deprive Russia of a viable pipeline route through spiraling violence and terrorism"—primarily by encouraging Western-aligned Muslim states to continue to provide support for militant groups.[86] So much for the integrity of Clinton's War on Terror.

In September 1994, Aliyev signed what he called the "deal of the century" in which a consortium called the Azerbaijan International Operation Company (AIOC) agreed to spend $7.4 billion to develop three major oil fields in the Caspian Sea: Azeri, Chirag and Guneshli. The Soviets had banned off-shore drilling in the Caspian Sea, which had been designated as a nature reserve and possessed some of the world's largest freshwater fish.[87] U.S. companies—Amoco, McDermott, Unocal, and Pennzoil—collectively took more than 40 percent of the king's ransom, by far the largest share, with Exxon Corp joining AIOC the following year. In a clear conflict of interest, Deputy National Security Adviser Sandy Berger, who headed an interagency committee on Caspian Oil policy, held $90,000 worth of stock in Amoco, while National Security Adviser Anthony Lake owned over $300,000 in Exxon stock.

Prior to Exxon's joining the AIOC, Aliyev had received a call from the State Department's Deputy Undersecretary for Economic Affairs, Joan Spiro, speaking in the name of Warren Christopher, who threatened to cut off aid to Aliyev if he did not give Exxon a favorable deal. Robert Baer, in hearing about this, wrote in his memoirs that he "found it hard to avoid the conclusion that the Clinton administration was pimping for Exxon."[88] And for Amoco.

The Americans seeking to make their fortune in the new "oil dorado" included such luminaries of the national security establishment as Henry Kissinger, James A. Baker, Dick Cheney, Lloyd Bentsen, John Sununu, and Brent Scowcroft, who were all advisers to the newly U.S.-established Azerbaijan Chamber of Commerce, and Zbigniew Brzezinski, Jimmy Carter's national security adviser, who became a paid consultant to Amoco.[89]

Brzezinski had described Azerbaijan as the "vitally important cork in the bottle containing the riches of the Caspian Sea Basin and Central Asia."[90] In September 1995, he was asked to carry a letter from Clinton to Aliyev asking him to give the U.S. preference to two pipelines, which could transport the oil through Turkey while bypassing Russia and Iran. In return, Clinton said he promised to resolve the dispute with Armenia over Nagorno-Karabakh.[91] Clinton nearly botched the agreement when the first two peace mediators that he appointed, according to one of Aliyev's top advisers, "displayed illiteracy and ignorance of the Armenian-Azerbaijan conflict."[92] He subsequently appointed a more seasoned mediator (Cory Cavanaugh) and in 1999, to Russia's chagrin, the Baku Tbilisi-Ceyhan pipeline was approved and built by 2005.[93]

Oil industry fixer Ely Calil noted that "Americans want their gasoline cheap. But it's not possible without cutting a few corners."[94] This cutting of corners had serious implications that included the irrevocable corruption of the American government, empowerment of sordid dictatorships, and destabilization of much of Central Asia, and triggered a dangerous escalation of conflict with Russia that persisted into the first two decades of the 21st century.

Putin and the New Cold War

The history recounted in this chapter provides a crucial backstop to the escalation of a new cold war and rise of Vladimir Putin, a lawyer with a Ph.D. in economics who has become a key political leader in Russia for over twenty years after his election as president in 2000. Putin's worldview dovetailed with that of Alexander Dugin, author of the 1997 book, *The Foundation of Geopolitics: The Geopolitical Future of Russia*, which called for Russia to rebuild its influence in Eurasia to counter Western imperialism, or Atlanticism, and to reinvigorate the Russian orthodox church. According to Steven Hall, the former CIA Station Chief in Russia, Yeltsin's reliance on Clinton and U.S. interference in the 1996 election greatly disturbed Putin, who concluded that "flirting with so-called democracy was nothing more than the U.S. and other Western countries trying to weaken great Russia."[95] Putin said also that the U.S. had "treated Russia like a colony in the 1990s," with "trillions of dollars siphoned out of the country under a variety of schemes."[96]

When Putin first came to office, one of his first measures was to redraw the map to strengthen Moscow's control over Russia's far-flung regions, issuing a decree grouping the nation's 89 provinces into seven new federal districts, each to be overseen by a representative of the Kremlin.[97] In the 1990s, Putin stated that "the support of separatism in Russia from abroad, including the informational, political and financial, through intelligence services, was absolutely obvious. There is no doubt that they [the U.S.] would have loved to see the Yugoslavia scenario of collapse and dismemberment for us with all the tragic consequences it would have for the peoples of Russia."[98]

Putin's considerable popularity in Russia stemmed from the fact that he prevented the latter outcome, stabilized Russia's economy and restored Russia's independence and self-respect. Famed Russian author Alexander Solzhenitsyn stated, in a strong rebuke to Clinton-Gore policies, that "Putin inherited a ransacked and bewildered country. And he started to do with it what was possible—a slow and gradual restoration."[99]

This was in part achieved by strengthening Russia's military defenses, by ordering oligarchs to pay taxes, by regaining national control over oil and gas deposits sold off to Exxon Mobil and other Western oil companies under Yeltsin, and by implementing policies that improved infrastructure, living standards, and led to a decrease in corruption and crime. Inflation, joblessness, and poverty rates subsequently declined while wages improved, and the economy grew tenfold. Putin cut Russia's national debt, stymied the exodus of Russian wealth abroad and put in place a successful pension system.[100]

Tensions between the U.S. and Russia were elevated when Putin first took office by the mysterious sinking of the most powerful Russian nuclear submarine, the Kursk, in the Barents Sea in August 2000, which Russia attributed to a NATO submarine that had been in the area when the Kursk was lost.[101] While initially Putin had positive diplomatic relations with the George W. Bush administration, those relations began to break down after the Kremlin prosecuted pro-American oligarch Mikhail Khodorkovsky and refused to support the illegal U.S. invasion of Iraq in 2003.

This was followed by a more serious rupture in 2008, when Russia backed a separatist movement in Georgia that was put down by the American-backed regime of Mikheil Saakashvili.[102] After a brief "reset" policy, relations deteriorated further when the Obama administration imposed economic sanctions on Russia in December 2012 in response to alleged human rights abuses, then backed a coup d'état in Ukraine in February 2014.[103]

In January 2018, Senator Ben Cardin (D-MD) released a Foreign Relations Committee staff report purporting to detail Putin's "nearly two decades-long assault on democratic institutions, universal values and the rule of law across Europe and his own country." According to the report's analysis, Putin had restored the totalitarian features of the Tsarist and Soviet systems in Russia, combining "military adventurism and aggression abroad with propaganda and political repression at home."[104]

This assessment was greatly misleading. Among other things, it obscured how many of Putin's foreign policies were initiated in response to the expansion of NATO in countries bordering Russia and aggressive U.S. drives in Central Asia, and as a reaction to the economic cataclysm and degradation of Russian society bred by Clinton and Bush I administration policies. Putin's prior service from 1985–1990 as a KGB agent also enhanced his credibility in confronting organized crime, whose growth was another legacy of the Clinton era.

Unfortunately, the American public was not well attuned to the recent history of U.S.-Russian relations and the story of the shock therapy it suffered and its aftermath. If they had, they would not have fallen so easily prey to the demonization of Putin and rhetoric of the New Cold War. Author Alex Krainer stated in an interview that "Russia was supposed to have continued the course initiated by Boris Yeltsin in the 1990s in turning over its industry and resources to key Western interests and joining the New World Order. Putin has done the opposite. He has asserted Russia's sovereignty, blocked the theft of Russia's resources, including oil, and asserted control over the Russian Central Bank."[105]

This helps to explain the demonization of Putin and bipartisan opposition to him in the United States. Americans had been led to believe that capitalism and democracy were working well to remake Russia anew until Putin took charge and restored the old corrupt authoritarian order. This mendacious view whitewashed among other things American contributions to Russia's corruption during the Yeltsin era through the promotion of over-zealous privatization initiatives.

Many of the people promoting a new Cold War with Russia were the same financial elites who profited from its foreign plunder in the 1990s. One of the chief figures lobbying for economic sanctions, William F. Browder, was a billionaire hedge fund manager and grandson of U.S. Communist Party leader Earl Browder. His Hermitage Capital made millions of dollars in the 1990s selling privatization vouchers which Hermitage bought from desperate Russians. A customer of the money laundering company, Mossack Fonseca, Browder fled Russia after being prosecuted by the Russian government for tax evasion. In 2017, he was convicted by a Russian court in absentia. Subsequent to his escape, he claimed to have been robbed of $237 million by the Russian government, though an independent investigation concluded that he was the one to have likely orchestrated the theft.[106]

British writer John Hobson, in his 1902 classic work, *Imperialism: A Study*, provided an enlightened understanding of how the British Empire was driven by financial elites who sought outlets for new investments and unduly influenced government policy. With regard to the United States, Hobson wrote that "it is Messrs. Rockefeller, Pierpont Morgan, Hannah, Schwab, and their associates who need imperialism ... because they desire to use the public resources of their country to find profitable employment for the capital which otherwise would be superfluous."[107]

A review of the history of America's crusade to privatize Russia's economy in the 1990s and U.S. policies in the Baltics and Central Asia, confirms Hobson's maxim. While the architects of U.S. policy may have believed in the ideals they were espousing, their programs were ultimately designed to benefit financial elites, large corporations, and the capitalist classes rather than the population at large. The expansion of investment opportunities had all along been a main goal of U.S. foreign policy—as Clinton administration officials openly admitted. Their crusade to remake a new Russia following the fall of the Soviet Union and dominate Central Asia was perhaps predictable in light of the previous 80 years of history, but no less damaging to the Russian people and prospects for a peaceful post-Cold War order.

Endnotes

1 Quoted in Thomas L. Friedman, "This is Putin's War. But America and NATO Aren't Innocent Bystanders," *The New York Times,* February 21, 2022, https://www.nytimes.com/2022/02/21/opinion/putin-ukraine-nato.html

2 Arnaud Develay, "A UN Expert Weighs on in Self-Determination, Referenda and the Rights of Minorities in Our Troubled World," *CovertAction Magazine*, November 28, 2022, https://covertactionmagazine.com/?p=48822&preview=true

3 Bill Clinton, "I Tried to Put Russia on Another Path," *The Atlantic*, April 7, 2022, https://www.theatlantic.com/ideas/archive/2022/04/bill-clinton-nato-expansion-ukraine/629499/

4 See Guy Mettan, *Creating Russophobia: From the Great Religious Schism to Anti-Putin Hysteria* (Atlanta: Clarity Press, 2017).

5 See Zbigniew Brzezinski, *The Grand Chessboard: American Primacy and its Geostrategic Imperative* (New York: Basic Books, 1998).

6 "President William Jefferson Clinton, Remarks for the Dinner in Honor of Russian President William Jefferson Clinton, Embassy of the Russian Federation, Washington D.C., September 28, 1994," Clinton Digital Library, White House Offices, Antony Blinken speeches, https://clinton.presidentiallibraries.us/items/show/9058

7 Joshua R. Itzkowitz Shifrinson, "Deal or No Deal? The End of the Cold War and the U.S. Offer to Limit NATO Expansion*,"* *International Security*, 40, 4 (Spring 2016), 7–44; James M. Goldgeier and Michael McFaul, *Power and Purpose: U.S. Policy Towards Russia After the Cold War* (Washington, D.C.: Brookings Institute Press, 2003), 184, 185; Strobe Talbott, *The Russia Hand: A.Memoir of Presidential Diplomacy* (New York: Random House, 2003), 93; See Svetlana Sauranskaya and Mary Sarotte, "The Clinton-Yeltsin Relationship in Their Own Words," National Security Archive, https://nsarchive.gwu.edu/briefing-book/russia-programs/2018-10-02/clinton-yeltsin-relationship-their-own-words. Neoconservative writers supportive of NATO expansion such as Mark Kramer, Mary

Elise Sarotte and Anne Applebaum deny that they had made this promise, though it was confirmed by written documents and reported on by government officials.

8 The mayor of the town near the base told *The Washington Post* that "the arrival of the Americans has meant economic salvation in the form of 1,500 new jobs and an infusion of millions of dollars in construction projects." William Drozdiak, "Staging Post for Bosnia Fortifies U.S.-Hungarian Alliance," *The Washington Post*, February 17, 1997, https://www.washingtonpost.com/archive/politics/1997/02/17/staging-post-for-bosnia-fortifies-us-hungarian-alliance/52ad498f-9a20-45b9-a7c7-d0807bfc1316/. Hungary's Prime Minister from 1994–1998, Gyula Horn, had been in the National Guard during the 1956 Hungarian uprising when it fired on protestors in support of the Soviet invasion. His popularity eroded after he enacted a severe austerity regimen, and he lost power to rightist Victor Orbán, who served as prime minister from 1998–2002 and from 2010 to the present. See documents at Clinton library: https://clinton.presidentiallibraries.us/items/show/57614

9 In 1994, Clinton appointed Donald Blinken as ambassador to Hungary, a position in which he served until 1997. Donald wrote a memoir about his escape from communist Hungary. When Donald died in September 2022, Antony told *The New York Times* that his father's achievements [as ambassador] included helping to set up in Taszar, Hungary, "the largest staging base in Europe since World War II." Alex Traub, "Donald Blinken, 96, Diplomat Who Raised Secretary of State," *The New York Times*, September 24, 2022.

10 Steven Erlanger, "Clinton and 3 Baltic Leaders Sign Charter," *The New York Times*, January 17, 1998.

11 In Anglea Stent, *The Limits of Partnership: U.S.-Russian Relations in the 21st Century* (Princeton: Princeton University Press, 2014), 40.; Talbott, *Russia Hand*, 223; Marie Elise Sarotte, *Not One Inch: America, Russia, and the Making of Post-Cold War Stalemate* (New Haven: Yale University Press, 2021). In 2004, Bulgaria, Estonia, Latvia, Lithuania, Romania, and Slovenia joined NATO, and Albania and Croatia joined in 2009, followed by Montenegro in 2017. The U.S. was also trying to expand NATO into Georgia and Ukraine. See Jonathan Marshall, "NATOs Strange Addition of Montenegro," *Consortium News*, February 28, 2017.

12 Quoted in John Dumbrell, *Clinton's Foreign Policy: Between the Bushes, 1992–2000* (New York: Routeledge, 2009), 125.

13 Andrew Cockburn, *The Spoils of War: Power, Profit and the American War Machine* (London: Verso, 2021), 76. Gorbachev would thereafter state that "one cannot depend on American politicians." Vladimir Putin asked in a furious 2007 speech: "What happened to the assurances our Western partners made after the dissolution of the Warsaw Pact? Where are those declarations today? No one remembers them."

14 James D. Boys, *Clinton's Grand Strategy* (New York: Bloomsbury, 2015).

15 In Andreas Zumach, "NATO Moves East," *CovertAction Quarterly*, Summer 1997, 52. Claes was the former foreign minister of Belgium. On Orientalist stereotypes about Russia, see Mettan, *Creating Russophobia*.

16 Robert Donaldson and Vidya Nadkarni, *The Foreign Policy of Russia: Changing Systems, Enduring Interests* (New York: Routledge, 2019), 261; William J. Burns, *The Back Channel: A Memoir of American Diplomacy and the Case for Its Renewal* (New York: Random House, 2019), 108.

17 Boris Yeltsin Letter to Bill Clinton, June 28, 1994, National Security Archive, George Washington University, https://nsarchive.gwu.edu/sites/default/files/documents/r332yo-fksgt/01.pdf

18 "Summary Report on One-on-One Meeting Between Presidents Clinton & Yeltsin, May 10, 1995, 10:10 A.M-1:19 PM, St. Catherine's Hall, the Kremlin," National Security Archive, https://nsarchive2.gwu.edu//dc.html?doc=4950563-Document-04-Summary-report-on-the-one-on-one

19 "Clinton and Dole and the Polish Vote," *The Chicago Tribune*, May 20, 1996, https://www.chicagotribune.com/news/ct-xpm-1996-05-20-9605200029-story.html

20 Graeme Zielinski, "Lithuanian Leader on a NATO Push," *Chicago Tribune*, April 7, 1997, https://www.chicagotribune.com/news/ct-xpm-1997-04-07-9704070109-story.html

21 James W. Carden, "Captured by the Captive Nations Lobby," *The American Conservative*, October 25, 2022, https://www.theamericanconservative.com/captured-by-the-captive-nations-lobby/

22 Kees ven der Pijl, *Flight MH17, Ukraine and the New Cold War: Prism of Disaster* (Manchester: Manchester University Press, 2018), 17.

23 Thomas Ferguson, "Bill's Big Backers," *Mother Jones*, November/December, 1996, https://www.motherjones.com/politics/1996/11/bills-big-backers/.

24 Katharine Q. Seelye, "Arms Contractors Spend to Promote an Expanded NATO," *The New York Times*, March 30, 1998.

25 Zumach, "NATO Moves East," 51; Cockburn, *The Spoils of War*, 80.

26 George F. Kennan, "A Fateful Error," *The New York Times*, February 5, 1997. See also Branco Marcetic, "The Mysteriously Vanished NATO Critique," *Jacobin*, July 16, 2018; Dombrell, *Clinton's Foreign Policy, 1992–2000*, 125. Democratic Senator Patrick Leahy of Vermont warned that with NATO expansion, young Americans could be sent to war to "protect a couple of countries most Americans haven't heard of." Paul Wellstone warned that NATO expansion might "redivide Europe and again poison relations with Russia." Strobe Talbott and William J. Perry worried that the enlargement of NATO would undermine hopes for a more enduring partnership with Russia, undercutting neoliberal reformers who would see it as a vote of no confidence in their efforts, a hedge against the likely failure of reform, a view shared by many in the U.S. embassy in Moscow at the time. In Burns, *The Back Channel*, 107. Jack Matlock, former U.S. ambassador to the Soviet Union echoed Kennan in considering NATO expansion "the most profound strategic blunder made since the end of the Cold War," threatening to "precipitate a buildup of arms and a competition, an armed competition, then. But there was no reason to do it at that time. Russia was not threatening any East European country. Actually, the Soviet Union in its last years was not, because Gorbachev had accepted the democratization of the East European countries. The Soviet Union in its last years was not threatening any East European country." Jack Matlock Jr. "I Was there: NATO and the Origins of the Ukraine Crisis," *Responsible Statecraft*, February 15, 2022, https://responsiblestatecraft.org/2022/02/15/the-origins-of-the-ukraine-crisis-and-how-conflict-can-be-avoided/

27 Seelye, "Arms Contractors Spend to Promote an Expanded NATO." One Senate aide stated: "The only people who care about this [the issue of NATO expansion] are the think-tank folks and the academics—not much of a voting constituency."

28 The White House, "Luncheon Meeting with Russian President Boris Yeltsin, April 12, 1996, William J. Clinton Presidential Library, Declassified documents, https://clinton.presidentiallibraries.us/items/show/57569

29 Thomas W. Lippman, "Clinton, Yeltsin Agree on Arms Cuts and NATO," *The Washington Post*, March 22, 1997, A1. Earlier, Yeltsin had stated that "it would

be an important part of Russia's security to associate with the only military alliance in Europe [ie. NATO]." James M. Goldgeier and Michael McFaul, *Power and Purpose: U.S. Policy Towards Russia After the Cold War* (Washington, D.C.: Brookings Institute Press, 2003), 48, 49.

30 The White House, "Luncheon Meeting with Russian President Boris Yeltsin, April 12, 1996, William J. Clinton Presidential Library, Declassified documents, https://clinton.presidentiallibraries.us/items/show/57569

31 Luis José Rodrigues Leitao Tomé, "Russia and NATO's Enlargement," NATO Research Fellowship Program, 1998–2000, Final Report, June 2000, https://www.nato.int/acad/fellow/98-00/tome.pdf; Lippman, "Clinton, Yeltsin Agree on Arms Cuts and NATO"; Talbott, *The Russia Hand*, 243.

32 In Stent, *The Limits of Partnership*, 25.

33 Stewart Parker, *The Last Soviet Republic: Alexander Lukashenko's Belarus* (London: Trafford, 2007).

34 Parker, *The Last Soviet Republic,* 136, 137, 138.

35 Parker, *The Last Soviet Republic*, 138–157.

36 Parker, *The Last Soviet Republic*.

37 Katya Gorchinskaya, "A Brief History of Corruption in Ukraine: the Kuchma Era," May 20, 2020, https://eurasianet.org/a-brief-history-of-corruption-in-ukraine-the-kuchma-era; Paul D'Anieri, *Ukraine and Russia: From Civilized Divorce to Uncivil War* (New York: Cambridge University Press, 2019), 88, 93; "Memorandum of Conversation: Restricted Meeting with President Leonid Kuchma of Ukraine," June 5, 2000, William J. Clinton Presidential Library, digital files, https://clinton.presidentiallibraries.us/items/show/101662. Kuchma's appointment in 1998 of the strongly pro-European Borys Tarasiuk as foreign minister signified Ukraine's commitment to Western Europe over Russia. He said that "the European idea has become Ukraine's national idea."

38 "Background Briefing by Senior Administration Officials, the UK House, Kiev, Ukraine, May 11, 1995," Clinton Presidential Records, NSC Cables, Emails, Records Management, Gore-Chernomyrdin Commission, box 2, William J. Clinton Presidential Library, Little Rock, Arkansas.

39 "Background Briefing by Senior Administration Officials, the UK House, Kiev, Ukraine, May 11, 1995," Clinton Presidential Records, NSC Cables, Emails, Records Management, Gore-Chernomyrdin Commission, box 2, William J. Clinton Presidential Library, Little Rock, Arkansas.

40 James V. Grinaldi, "Clinton Charity Tapped Foreign Friends," *The Wall Street Journal*, March 19, 2015.

41 Gorchinskaya, "A Brief History of Corruption in Ukraine: the Kuchma Era." Richard Balmforth, "Ukraine Quashes Murder Charge against ex-President," *Reuters*, December 14, 2011, https://www.reuters.com/article/cnews-us-ukraine-kuchma-idCATRE7BD0KP20111214; Serhy Yekelchyk, *The Conflict in Ukraine: What Everyone Needs to Know* (New York: Oxford University Press, 2015); D'Anieri, *Ukraine and Russia*, 104. The murder charge against Kuchma was eventually dropped when secret tapes that incriminated him were ruled inadmissible in court. Kuchma had told his Minister of Internal Affairs to "drive [Gongadze] out, throw [him] out. Give him to the Chechens." Kuchma was also suspected of being behind the poisoning of opposition leader Viktor Yuschenko, whose face was disfigured as a result.

42 "Memorandum of Conversation: Restricted Meeting with President Leonid Kuchma of Ukraine," June 5, 2000, William J. Clinton Presidential Library,

digital files, https://clinton.presidentiallibraries.us/items/show/101662; "Ukrainian President Arrival," November 22, 1994, https://www.c-span.org/video/?61737-1/ukrainian-president-arrival. Journalist Patrick Lawrence in a December 2022 article aptly characterized Kuchma's reign as "a godawful mess of fraud, corruption and media censorship." Patrick Lawrence, "The Autumn of the Oligarchs in Ukraine," *Consortium News*, December 16, 2022.

43 Ambrose Sylvan, "Western Media Has Falsely Presented the Donbas' Drive For Autonomy as Being Instigated By Moscow," *CovertAction Magazine*. The separatist movement gained strength in 2014 after the Maidan coup backed by the Obama administration which resulted in a devastating civil war that drew the Russians in.

44 "Memorandum of Conversation: Restricted Meeting with President Leonid Kuchma of Ukraine," June 5, 2000, William J. Clinton Presidential Library, digital files, https://clinton.presidentiallibraries.us/items/show/101662

45 T.J. Coles, "'Gods of War:' How the U.S. Weaponized Ukraine Against Russia," *The Grayzone Project*, April 1, 2022, https://thegrayzone.com/2022/04/01/war-us-weaponized-ukraine-russia/; Anatol Lieven, *Ukraine and Russia: A Fraternal Rivalry* (Washington, D.C.: U.S. Institute for Peace, 1990), 120; Secretary of the Treasury Robert Rubin and National Security Adviser Anthony Lake, UK House, Kiev, May 11, 1995, Clinton Presidential Records, NSC Cables, Emails, Records Management, Gore-Chernomyrdin Commission, box 2, William J. Clinton Presidential Library, Little Rock, Arkansas.. In 2003, Kuchma sent Ukrainian troops into Iraq.

46 Dennis J. Kenney et al. "Assessing the Fit Between U.S. Sponsored Training and the Needs of Ukrainian Police Agencies," September 2001, Department of Justice, https://www.ojp.gov/pdffiles1/nij/grants/201357.pdf. Other ICITAP programs were set up in post-communist states in Eastern and Central Europe.

47 Galina Sapozhnikova, *The Lithuanian Conspiracy: Investigation into a Political Demolition* (Atlanta: Clarity Press, 2018); Tommy P. Baer, "Letter to President William Jefferson Clinton," June 17, 1997, William J. Clinton Presidential Library, Lithuania, 1997, 1998, https://clinton.presidentiallibraries.us/items/show/58704. Baer pointed to the case of Aleksandras Liletikis, a Nazi war criminal who was living a comfortable life in Lithuania. U.S. Department of State, Country Report on Human Rights Practices 1996 – Lithuania, https://www.refworld.org/docid/3ae6aa2536.html. Lithuanians were jailed who questioned the dominant narrative about the events of January 13, 1991 when Soviet troops were blamed for shooting unarmed demonstrators when the shooting had actually been undertaken by anticommunist snipers and the Soviets had been set up to make them look guilty.

48 "Estonia, Latvia and Lithuania and U.S. Baltic Policy," Hearings Before the Subcommittee on European Affairs, of the Committee on Foreign Relations, U.S. Senate, 105th Congress, 2nd Session, July 15, 1998, https://www.govinfo.gov/content/pkg/CHRG-105shrg50539/html/CHRG-105shrg50539.htm

49 "Bill Clinton, meeting with Lennart Meri of Estonia, Biuntis Ulmans of Latvia and Algirdas Brazauskas of Lithuania," January 16, 1998, William J. Clinton Presidential Library, digital collection, Lithuania, https://clinton.presidentiallibraries.us/items/show/58709; Press Conference by President Clinton, July 6, 1994, Clinton Presidential Records, Presidential Office, Press Releases, GA #8688, William J. Clinton Presidential Library, Little Rock, Arkansas.

50 Colin McMahon, "Letdown in Lithuania for U.S. Energy Firm," *Chicago Tribune*, June 17, 2000.

51 Richard J. Durbin to President William J. Clinton, May 10, 2000, William J. Clinton Presidential Library, digital archive, https://clinton.presidentiallibraries.us/items/show/58647; William J. Clinton to Richard Durbin, May 26, 2000, https://clinton.presidentiallibraries.us/items/show/58648.

52 FRD 36, "U.S Policy Toward Central and Eastern Europe," December 6, 1993, Declassified Documents Concerning Central and Eastern Europe, Clinton Digital Library, https://clinton.presidentiallibraries.us/items/show/16188

53 "Promoting Democracy and Sovereignty in the New Independent States," https://clintonwhitehouse5.archives.gov/WH/EOP/NSC/html/nsc-13.html

54 "Statement by Press Secretary, "Meeting with President Ulmanis, Meri and Brazauskas," July 6, 1994, Clinton Presidential Records, Presidential Office, Press Releases, GA #8688, William J. Clinton Presidential Library, Little Rock, Arkansas. The American Enterprise Fund in the Baltic states was chaired by Rozanne Ridgeway, who was also a co-chair of the anti-Russian Atlantic Council.

55 "Bill Clinton, Meeting with Lennart Meri of Estonia, Guntis Ulmanis of Latvia and Algirdas Brazauskas of Lithuania," January 16, 1998, William J. Clinton Presidential Library, digital collection, Lithuania, https://clinton.presidentiallibraries.us/items/show/58709; "Statement by Press Secretary—Expanded Military and Defense Cooperation with Baltic States," July 6, 1994, Clinton Presidential Records, Presidential Office, Press Releases, GA #8688, William J. Clinton Presidential Library, Little Rock, Arkansas.

56 "Mart Laar Receives Milton Friedman Prize," https://www.cato.org/policy-report/julyaugust-2006/mart-laar-receives-milton-friedman-prize. Friedman was a famous right-wing economist whom Laar had been inspired by.

57 Mart Laar, *War in the Woods; Estonia's Struggle for Survival, 1944–1956* (Howell's House, 1992); Ben Norton, "Flashy NATO Film Honors Baltic Nazi Collaborators Who Murdered Jews in Holocaust," *The Grayzone Project*, July 20, 2017, https://thegrayzone.com/2017/07/20/nato-film-baltic-nazi-collaborators-forest-brothers/. Some of the Forest Brothers had been in the Waffen SS and murdered Jews. Historian Dovid Katz, one of the foremost experts on the Jews in the Baltic states, characterized the Forest Brothers as "pro-Hitler forces." He added that many of the members of the Forest Brothers "were fascists, including some recycled killers from the 1941 genocide phase of the Latvian Holocaust." The group "served to delay the Soviet advance (in alliance with the United States, Great Britain and the Allies) that would liberate the death camps further west." Among the civilians murdered by the Forest Brothers, Katz pointed out, were Lithuanian organizers of collective farms overseen by the Soviets in Lithuania. Since Laar wrote the book, far right groups in Estonia have appropriated the Forest Brothers' anthem, "Let the Bolsheviks Know."

58 Quoted in Tom Turnipseed, "Bush, Enron, Unocal and the Taliban," *Counterpunch*, January 10, 2002.

59 Michael T. Klare, *Resource Wars: The New Landscape of Global Conflict* (New York: Metropolitan Books, 2001), 89.

60 Dan Morgan and David B. Ottaway, "Pipe Dreams – The Struggle for Caspian Oil," *The Washington Post*, October 6, 1998, A1; Stephen Kinzer, "Azerbaijan Has Reason to Swagger: Oil Deposits," *The New York Times*, September 14, 1997, Russian oil executives viewed the Eurasian corridor as an American plot to thwart the trans-Russian pipeline out of Tengiz.

61 Klare, *Resource Wars*, 89.

62 Klare, *Resource Wars*, 84, 85.

63 Klare, *Resource Wars*, 95, 96; Lutz Klevenman, *The New Great Game: Blood and Oil in Central Asia* (New York: Atlantic Monthly Press, 2003), 44; Michael Pullara, *The Spy Who Was Left Behind: Russia, the United States, and the True Story of the Betrayal and Assassination of a CIA Agent* (New York: Scribner, 2018), 17, 18, 19; Robert Donaldson and Vidya Nadkarni, *The Foreign Policy of Russia: Changing Systems, Enduring Interests*, 6th ed. (New York: Routledge, 2019), 204. Shevardnadze's regime employed Chechen mercenaries to carry out some of their dirtiest work in Abkhazia. The Abkhaz militias committed their own significant atrocities under the oversight of Russian troops who did nothing to halt them.

64 "Promoting Democracy and Sovereignty in the New Independent States," https://clintonwhitehouse5.archives.gov/WH/EOP/NSC/html/nsc-13.html

65 Robert Baer, *See No Evil: The True Story of a Grounded Soldier in the CIA's War on Terrorism*, with foreword by Seymour Hersh (Waterville, OR: Thorndike Press, 2002), 500, 501. Baer also blamed Shevardnadze for failing to properly investigate the murder of CIA State Chief Fred Woodruff near Georgia's capital in 1993. See Pallura, *The Spy Who Was Left Behind.*

66 Klare, *Resource Wars*, 1–3, 97; Ian Rutledge, *Addicted to Oil: America's Relentless Drive for Energy Security* (London: I.B. Tauris, 2005); Ken Silverstein, *The Secret World of Oil* (London: Verso, 2014), 21–22.

67 Peter Baker, "As Kazakh Scandal Unfolds, Soviet Style Reprisals Begin," *The Chicago Tribune*, June 11, 2002, https://www.chicagotribune.com/news/ct-xpm-2002–06-11-0206110214-story.html. The dog's severed head was later put on the editor's doorstep.

68 Ibid; Baer, *See No Evil*, 496, 497; Michael Dobbs, David Ottaway, Sharon LaFreniere, "American at Center of Kazakh Oil Probe," *The Washington Post*, September 25, 2000; Ken Silverstein, *The Secret World of Oil* (London: Verso, 2014), 21, 22. Giffen also gave Nazarbayev and his wife gifts, including his-her snowmobiles, and hundreds of thousands of dollars-worth of jewelry. Giffen never denied paying the bribes but said his actions were fully known by the U.S. government. He had made millions in concessions on Kazakhstan oil deals, enabling him to buy an 11-acre estate by the celebrated Winged Foot Golf Course in New York's Westchester County. In late 2010, the Justice Department dropped bribery charges in exchange for a misdemeanor tax plea, and the judge, William Pauley, imposed no jail time, saying Giffen was a Cold War hero and "one of the only Americans with sustained access to high levels of government in the region. These relationships built up over a lifetime were lost the day of his arrest." Oil fixer Friedelhem Eronat stated that "oil fields are a battleground. If Jim (Giffen] had not been involved, other [non-American] firms would have gotten the contracts, and the loser would have been the U.S. government."

69 Jo Becker and Don Van Natta Jr., "After Mining Deal, Financier Donated to Clinton," *The New York Times*, January 31, 2008.

70 "Meeting with Kazakh President Nursultan Nazarbayev," February 14 ,1994, Declassified Documents Concerning President Nazarbayev of Kazakhstan, February 12, 1994, William J. Clinton Presidential Library, https://clinton.presidentiallibraries.us/items/show/101166; Strobe Talbott, memorandum to the President, "Meeting with President Nursultan Nazarbayev of Kazakhstan, November 14, 1997, Ibid.

71 Garry Leech, *Crude Interventions: The U.S., Oil and the New World (Dis) order* (London: Zed Books, 2006), 64, 65.

72 Klare, *Resource Wars*, 1, 97.

73 Nasser Saghafi-Ameri, "The Emerging NATO: Impact on Europe and Asia," in *Europe and Asia: Perspectives on the Emerging International Order*, V.P. Malik and Erhard Crome, eds. (New Delhi: Lancer Publishers & Distributors, 2006), 153, Strobe Talbott and others in the State Department had warned about becoming enmeshed in any "Great Games" in Central Asia.

74 "Boiled Alive," *The Economist*, October 30, 2003, https://www.economist.com/britain/2003/10/30/boiled-alive. See also Leech, *Crude Interventions,* 72, 73; Neil McFarquhar, "Islam Karimov Dies at 78, Ending a Long, Ruthless Rule of Uzbekistan," *The New York Times*, September 2, 2016, https://www.nytimes.com/2016/09/03/world/asia/uzbekistan-islam-karimov-obituary.html. After 9/11, bases in Uzbekistan were used to carry out the invasion of Afghanistan—as they had been for the Soviets in the 1980s.

75 Baer, *See No Evil*, 502.

76 Dan Morgan and David B. Ottaway, "Pipe Dreams – The Struggle for Caspian Oil," *The Washington Post*, October 4, 1998, A1; Galib Bashirov, "U.S. Foreign Policy Towards Azerbaijan, 1991–2015," Ph.D. Thesis, Florida International University, 2017.

77 Peter Dale Scott, *The Road to 9/11: Wealth, Empire and the Future of America* (Berkeley: University of California Press, 2007), 165.

78 Stephen Kinzer, "Azerbaijan Has Reason to Swagger: Oil Deposits," *The New York Times*, September 14, 1997; Dan Brennan, "Heydar Aliev," December 14, 2003, https://www.theguardian.com/news/2003/dec/15/guardianobituaries.

79 "Joint Statement on Azerbaijan-United States Relations," August 1, 1997, Administration of William J. Clinton, Public Papers of the President of the United States, 1997 (Washington, D.C.: U.S. Government Printing Office, 1997), 1038.

80 Paul Lewis, "H.A. Aliyev, KGB Officer and Azeri Leader, 80, Dies," *The New York Times*, December 13, 2003.

81 Hugh Pope, "Corruption Stunts Growth in ex-Soviet States," *The Wall Street Journal*, July 5, 2000, A17. One Azeri told journalist Lutz Kleveman: "For years, they have been talking about the enormous wealth the oil will bestow on all of us—and all we get is 15,000 manat a month for bread [equivalent to $3 American dollars]." Kleveman, *The New Great Game*, 73.

82 Lewis, "H.A. Aliyev, KGB Officer and Azeri Leader, 80, Dies"; Bashirov, "U.S. Foreign Policy Towards Azerbaijan, 1991–2015"; Klevenman *The New Great Game*, 22. Aliyev was succeeded by his son Ilham, a notorious playboy who had been made head of the oil company, SoCal, in 2003.

83 Alexis Rowell, "U.S. Mercenaries Fight in Azerbaijan," *CovertAction Quarterly*, Spring 1994, 23–25.

84 Rowell, "U.S. Mercenaries Fight in Azerbaijan," 25; Bashirov, "U.S. Foreign Policy Towards Azerbaijan, 1991–2015"; Stephen Kinzer, "Azerbaijan Asks the U.S. to Establish a Military Base," *The New York Times*, January 31, 1999; Thomas Goltz, *Azerbaijan Diary: A Rogue Reporter's Adventures in an Oil-Rich, War-Torn, Post-Soviet Republic* (London: M.E. Sharpe, 1998), ch. 16. A Turkish intelligence source reported that major oil companies including Exxon and Mobil were behind the 1993 coup. Scott, *The Road to 9/11*, 165.

85 *Congressional Record*, V. 151, PT. 17, U.S. Congress, October 7 to 26, 2005.

86 "American political scientist: Western Intelligence used Azerbaijan to export terrorism into Russia," *Panorama*, May 30, 2015.

87 Klevenman, *The New Great Game*, 78, 79.

88 Baer, *See No Evil*, 495, 496, 502; Klevenman, *The New Great Game*, 24.

89 Kinzer, "Azerbaijan Has Reason to Swagger."

90 Brzezinski, *The Grand Chessboard*, 46.

91 Dan Morgan and David B. Ottaway, "Pipe Dreams—The Struggle for Caspian Oil," *The Washington Post*, October 4, 1998, A1.

92 Bashirov, "U.S. Foreign Policy Towards Azerbaijan, 1991–2015."

93 Donaldson and Nadkarni, *The Foreign Policy of Russia*, 218.

94 Quoted in Silverstein, *The Secret World of Oil*, 23.

95 David Shimer, *Rigged: America, Russia, and One Hundred Years of Covert Election Interference* (New York: Alfred A. Knopf, 2020), 137; Jane Burbank, "The Grand Theory Driving Putin to War," *The New York Times*, March 22, 2022.

96 "Text of Putin's Speech Blasting Neocolonial West," *Consortium News*, September 30, 2022, https://consortiumnews.com/2022/09/30/text-of-putins-speech-blasting-neo-colonial-west/

97 Jeanne Whalen, "Putin Redesigns Regions to Consolidate Power," *The Wall Street Journal*, May 15, 2000.

98 Vladimir Putin, Presidential Address to the Federal Assembly, President of Russia, Kremlin, December 4, 2014.

99 Ben Judah, *Fragile Empire: How Russia Fell in and Out of Love with Vladimir Putin* (New Haven: Yale University Press, 2013), 57.

100 Anne Garrels, *Putin Country: A Journey Into the Real Russia* (London: Picador, 2017), 11, 12, 19; Chris Miller, *Putinomics: Power and Money in Resurgent Russia* (Chapel Hill: University of North Carolina Press, 2018); Andrey P. Tsygankov, "The Dark Double: The American Media Perception of Russia as a Neo-Soviet Autocracy, 2008–2014," *Politics*, April 2016; Stephen Cohen, *War With Russia: From Putin and Ukraine to Trump and Russia Gate* (New York: Hot Books, 2019), 4. A former IMF director said that Putin's economic team does "not tolerate corruption" and that Russia now ranked 35th out of 190 in the World Bank's Doing Business Ratings. Miller found that Putin "skillfully managed Russia's economic fortunes."

101 Webster G. Tarpley, *9/11 Synthetic Terror: Made in USA* (Joshua Tree, CA: Progressive Press, 2006), 130; John Helmer, "Putin Comes to APEC summit Riding a Wave of Success," November 15, 2000, https://www.russialist.org/archives/4638.html##12; Jeffrey Steinberg, "A Pearl Harbor Effect in Russia," *Executive Intelligence Review*, September 1, 2000, https://larouchepub.com/eiw/public/2000/eirv27n34-20000901/eirv27n34-20000901_022-a_pearl_harbor_effect_in_russia.pdf

102 See Cohen, *War with Russia.*

103 Ibid., and Tony Kevin, "The Devolution of U.S.-Russia Relations," *Consortium News*, September 13, 2019, https://consortiumnews.com/2019/09/13/the-devolution-of-us-russia-relations.

104 United States Senate Committee on Foreign Relations, "U.S. Senator Ben Cardin Releases Report Detailing Two Decades of Putin's Attacks on Democracy, Calling for Policy Changes to Counter Kremlin Threat Ahead of 2018, 2020 Elections," January 10, 2016, https://www.foreign.senate.gov/press/ranking/release/cardin-releases-report-detailing-two-decades-of-putins-attacks-on-democracy. See also, Jeremy Kuzmarov, "Cardin's Senate Report Repeats Russophobic Charges," *The Huffington Post*, January 12, 2018.

105 Personal Interview (Jeremy Kuzmarov), Alex Krainer, November 2017.

106 Andrei Nekrasov and Torstein Grude, *The Magnitsky Act: Behind the Scenes* (Piraya Films, 2016); Alex Krainer, *The Killing of Bill Browder: Deconstructing Bill Browder's Dangerous Deception* (Monaco: Equilibrium, 2017); Luci Komisar, "The Man Behind the Magnitsky Act: Did Bill Browder's Tax Troubles in Russia Color Push for Sanctions," *100 Reporters*, October 20, 2017. Other forceful advocates of economic sanctions were funded by exiled Russian tycoon Mikhail Khodorkovsky, whom Putin had jailed. Amy Knight, *Orders to Kill: The Putin Regime and Political Murder (New York: Thomas Dunne Books, 2017)*, 279.

107 John A. Hobson, *Imperialism: A Study* (London: James Nisbet & Co. Ltd., 1902 reprinted by Cambridge University Press, 2010), 83.

CHAPTER 6

Imperial Oversight: The Clinton Administration and Southeast Asia

Pax Americana Illusions

Standing in for the president at the annual meeting of the Asia Pacific Economic Cooperation (APEC) forum, whose purpose was to advance free trade, Vice President Al Gore in November 1998 rebuked Malaysian Prime Minister Mahathir Mohamed (1981–2003; 2018–2020) who had imposed capital controls in response to the 1997 Asian financial crisis. Furthermore, Mohamed had rejected the International Monetary Fund (IMF)–recommended austerity measures on the ground that he did "not think that he should have to destroy the economy in order that it should [one day] become better." Gore countered that "democracies have done better in coping with economic crises than nations where freedom is suppressed," and called for "democracy and reform, people power, doi moi, and reformasi," the slogans of reform movements in the Philippines, Vietnam and Malaysia.[1]

Gore's remarks did not sit well with Mahathir Mohamed and the Malaysian government, which accused him of interference in the political affairs of their country, inciting lawlessness and encouraging political enemies bent on overthrowing it. These enemies included deputy Prime Minister Anwar Ibrahim, whose supporters had rioted in the streets demanding the ouster of Mahathir.[2] According to the *Japan Times*, if successful, Ibrahim's supporters would have "strengthened and expanded the power of Islamic radicals and exacerbated conflicts with Malaysia's Chinese community, leading to a possible Kosovo type conflict."[3] Malaysia's Foreign Minister Abdullah Ahmed Badawi said that Malays did not "take kindly to sanctimonious sermonizing from any foreign quarter, especially, the U.S., a country which is known to have committed gross violations of human rights."[4]

The Mahathir episode provides a revealing window into the Clinton administration's foreign policy in Southeast Asia. Mahathir was singled out for rebuke because he had criticized Western policies and challenged the Washington Consensus attempt to export neoliberal economic policies emphasizing deregulation, privatization, cutbacks in the public sector, and lowered taxation and tariffs, through his adoption of capital controls in response to financial crisis. Mahathir also began calling on oppressed Arabs to turn away from suicide bombing and to fight the U.S.-UK combine with the far more potent weapon of dumping the U.S. dollar in favor of the Euro.

After the collapse of the Russian and Brazilian economies in 1998, even the IMF—which adhered strictly to the Washington Consensus—argued that Malaysian-type controls were necessary for emerging countries. The American Chamber of Commerce in Malaysia and ASEAN's Business Council also approved Mahathir's measures. Because of them, businesses in Malaysia were protected from wild fluctuations in exchange rates and the risk of volatile outflows of capital. GDP growth in the country reached 2.5 percent after the controls were introduced, compared to -6.7 percent the previous year.[5] While possessing some authoritarian features, Mahathir was a popular figure in Malaysia who oversaw the country's transformation from an underdeveloped postcolonial state to an industrialized upper-middle income country with the highest living standards in Southeast Asia—with the exception of Brunei and Singapore. He won five elections and became the longest standing leader in the country's history.[6]

By its attitude towards and treatment of Mahathir, the Clinton administration exposed itself as being dominated by political ideologues committed to advancing an economic model which widened social inequality and produced a period of spectacular U.S. economic growth followed by financial disaster. America's commitment to an unregulated style of capitalism was backed by 100,000 military troops stationed mostly in South Korea and Japan, where the U.S. had established military bases after proclaiming a dubious victory in the Korean War, which in actuality split the country and had concluded in an armistice and still unresolved tensions with its northern half. Subscribing to the tenets of American exceptionalism, the Clinton administration claimed that the U.S. troop presence was there because it was beneficial to Southeast Asia (rather than, iner alia, preventing Korean unification), freeing up the region's resources to focus on economic development, upholding democratically elected governments, and protecting the sea lanes for trade, including shipments of oil from the Persian Gulf, which sustained unprecedented economic prosperity and growth.

The 1997 Asian financial crisis, however, punctured many of the illusions about Pax Americana in Southeast Asia and the economic system it had brought forward. The U.S. was exposed in the Mahathir affair not only as a bully, but also as a feckless one. Mahathir was able to survive in the end and advance alternative economic policies which were more popular and successful than those of the Washington Consensus. The APEC meeting ended in rancor with Japan taking the lead in scuttling any further market-opening schemes.[7]

The Clinton era generally saw the beginning signs of revolt against the American-dominated order in Southeast Asia, epitomized further by the downfall in Indonesia of the Suharto regime, a longstanding American client, and protests against American military bases after three Marines raped a teenage girl in Okinawa.[8] For all the triumphalism in Washington during the 1990s—epitomized by Francis Fukuyama's declaration of "the end of history"—the unipolar order in Southeast Asia built up in the aftermath of World War II was not sustainable indefinitely and would with time unravel.

Backing Up Globalization with Military Might: The Nye Report

The blueprint for the Clinton administration's policy in Southeast Asia was laid out in a February 1995 report issued by the Pentagon's Office of International and Security Affairs, headed by Harvard University Professor Joseph Nye. This report advocated sustaining the approximately 100,000 military troops, based predominantly in South Korea and Japan, which Nye claimed "preserved the peace and security of the entire Far East region," as they were "well located for rapid deployment to virtually any trouble spot in the region."

In Nye's assessment, the "American record over the past half century was one of consistent strength and leadership." The American security presence had helped "provide the oxygen for East Asian development," in large part by advancing open economic systems, and deterring any aggression by communist powers like China and North Korea. The U.S. was a great beneficiary as in 1993 its trade with the Pacific region totaled over $374 billion, accounting for 2.8 million U.S. jobs. The Asia Pacific region was the most dynamic in the world whose prosperity was in part the result of successful American policies, which had underwritten Asian security and underpinned Asia's economic development.[9]

While some aspects of its assessment were accurate, the Nye report promoted a triumphalist narrative which ignored the violence and inequality underlying American hegemony in Southeast Asia. The U.S. wars of aggression in Korea and Indo-China resulted in millions of deaths alone.[10]

Bill Clinton echoed many of the themes from the Nye report in his public speeches. From the beginning of his governorship in Arkansas, Clinton had been a particularly strong proponent of American business expansion in Southeast Asia, taking the first Arkansas trade mission to the Far East to Taiwan, Japan and Hong Kong.[11] He and members of his administration saw themselves as crusaders intent on remaking Asia's dysfunctional crony capitalism—with its close links between government, corporations and banks and ruling families—into "free-market" democracies styled after the U.S.[12]

In a July 1993 speech in Seoul, Clinton advanced the vision of a "Pacific community" that was to be based on "shared strength, shared prosperity, and shared commitment to democratic values."[13] This vision was given intellectual rationalization by an influential World Bank report, co-authored by Clinton's Treasury Secretary and former Harvard University President, Lawrence Summers, entitled "The East Asian Miracle." It attributed the region's rapid economic growth from 1965–1990 to market friendly policies that encouraged foreign business investment and high rates of international trade along with fiscal discipline (i.e. austerity) and sound macroeconomic management.

The report claimed that the most successful governments were those that "were less vulnerable and less responsive [than other developing world countries] to organized labor's demands to legislate a minimum wage," and that they focused their efforts on "job generation," effectively boosting the demand for workers.[14] This assessment dovetailed very nicely with the interests of multinational corporations which were looking to offshore production to take advantage of weak labor standards, and which generously financed Clinton's political campaigns.

Karen Talbot provided a critical assessment of Clinton's foreign policy in a fall 1999 article in *CovertAction Quarterly* entitled "Backing up Globalization with Military Might." It quoted from a speech by Dr. Joseph Gerson, Director of the New England branch of the American Friends Service Committee, who stated that "in the Asia Pacific region, the U.S. was enforcing its 21st Century Open Door policy by means of the IMF, World Bank, bases and forward deployments, the Seventh Fleet and its nuclear arsenal, as it seeks to simultaneously contain and engage China, to dominate the sea lanes and straits through which the region's trade and supplies of oil must travel."

Talbott wrote that Washington was regaining even greater access to ports and bases in the Philippines under the 1998 Visiting Forces agreement, which allowed U.S. warships to participate in joint military exercises and exempted military personnel from being tried in local courts for criminal offenses. Washington had also recently arranged to use a new naval base in Singapore, and strengthened ties to Indonesia to prevent loss of access to its natural resources and markets and strategically important shipping lanes. It was also stepping up war games conducted in the Republic of Korea, and supporting Gulf of Tonkin style provocations such as the sinking of one North Korean boat and damaging another in a dispute over crab fishing.[15]

Clinton's greatest value to the national security establishment had always been in his ability, along with his wife, to coopt and neuter the 1960s

Left, and to channel activist energies in support of political causes that either dovetailed with American imperial objectives or diverted attention away from them. Many liberal activists in the 1990s embraced the "Free Tibet" movement, which, like the subsequent "Save Darfur" movement conveniently targeted a geopolitical foe of the United States. Far fewer people embraced the cause of the East Timorese or Okinawans battling against the presence of U.S. military bases on their land or challenged the premise underlying the Nye report and Summers' "East Asian miracle" text, which guided U.S. foreign policy through much of the Clinton era.

Arming Taiwan: Deep-sixing Nixon's Cooperative Approach to China

In May 1995, President Clinton set off a firestorm when he succumbed to Congressional pressure and granted Taiwan President Lee Teng Hui (1988–2000) a visa which enabled him to enter the United States and attend Cornell University's alumni reunion. Lee in turn gave an inflammatory speech—beamed around the world—in which he proclaimed the sovereignty of the Republic of Taiwan, to the cheers of supporters waving Nationalist Party flags, the symbol of Chiang Kai-Shek's government in exile.[16]

Chiang was the leader of the Chinese Nationalists (GMD) who had fled to Taiwan in 1949, with U.S. military support, after his defeat by Mao Zedong in the Chinese civil war. Four years earlier, Taiwan had returned to Chinese sovereignty after fifty years of Japanese colonial rule. Nonetheless, Chiang still ruled Taiwan with an iron fist until his death in 1978 and was succeeded by his son, Chiang Chung-Kuo (1978–1988), who extended the island's period of martial law in which around 200,000 people were imprisoned or tortured and 3,000 to 4,000 were executed by the GMD.[17]

In 1955, the U.S. military established the United States Taiwan Defense Command, deploying nuclear weapons to the island and occupying it with thousands of U.S. troops until 1979. The People's Republic of China (PRC) has always considered Taiwan to be part of the Chinese mainland in a position validated by the UN. In August 2022, the spokesperson for the UN Secretary-General Antonio Guterres said: "The policy of the United Nations on this issue is that we are guided by General Assembly Resolution 2758 from 1971 on one-China," which expelled the representatives of Chiang Kai-shek from the UN.[18]

Predictably, the PRC leadership was angered by Taiwan President Lee's Cornell speech, condemning Lee as a separatist who was seeking to "split the motherland." The PRC responded by firing six ballistic missiles into the East China Sea one hundred miles north of Taiwan, causing the Taiwanese stock market to plunge. Beijing further approved a program of military exercises that included mock amphibious assaults, air combat displays and live fire drills which gave off the appearance of an actual attack on Taiwan. Fearing that a confrontation with the PRC could undermine his presidency, Clinton sent a U.S. naval carrier to the Taiwan straits in the "biggest display of American military might in Asia since the Vietnam War," causing China to back down.[19]

A number of Clinton's advisers, including the departing ambassador to Beijing, J. Stapleton Roy, believed that if only Clinton had been paying attention to China policy all along, he could have foreseen the Congressional steamroller resulting from admitting Lee Teng Hui and preempted the crisis through consultation with Beijing and affirming the One China principle which was at the time and remains official U.S. policy.[20] Instead, Clinton had antagonized the Chinese further by expanding arms sales to Taiwan, which came to rank second to Saudi Arabia as the largest recipient of American arms.[21]

In December 1986, Clinton had given a speech in Taiwan challenging the government to reduce trade barriers and invest its cash reserves in America. The Taiwanese were good customers for Arkansas soybeans and manufactured products such as electric motors and parking meters (made by his friend Webb Hubbell's company), which drove Clinton's desire for stronger relations from that time forward.[22]

In January 1994, Taiwan signed a deal that enabled its purchase of F-16 fighter jets, subsequently ordered 54 American helicopters and had plans to buy Patriot missile technology, American surveillance planes, U.S. made frigates, ship-bound guns and missiles as well as older Patton tanks. In 1999, the Clinton administration informed Congress of its intent to sell Taiwan E-2T Hawkeyes advanced early warning radar aircraft, and delivered to Taiwan Aegis destroyers equipped with state of the art surface to air missiles and Tomahawk cruise missiles to boost its naval capabilities in the Taiwan straits.[23]

From 1996 to 1999, the Commander-in-chief of American forces in the Pacific, Admiral Joseph W. Prueker, had undertaken extensive contingency planning for the defense of Taiwan, on the greatest scale since the 1950s when the 7th fleet twice sent warships into Taiwan Straits to prevent a mainland invasion.[24] This was another clear provocation in Chinese eyes, and a violation of an earlier pledge that America would show restraint by only providing limited defensive arms to Taiwan during the transitional era that was to follow the establishment of formal diplomatic relations with Beijing in 1979.[25]

China at this time began pressing its claims in the South China Sea, whose subsea resources included potentially vast untapped oil and natural gas deposits. The U.S. Seventh Fleet based in Yokosuka, Japan conducted regular military maneuvers in these waters. Their importance was magnified by the fact that "a lot of Japanese oil comes through the Straits of Malacca, turns left, and heads through the South China Sea to Japan," as Admiral Timothy J. Keating, the commander of the Seventh Fleet, explained.[26]

Since the Chinese revolution of 1949, America's grand strategy in Asia had been to build up Japan as a bulwark against communist China while running covert operations to destabillize China and coopt its elite.[27] Samuel Huntington's 1996 book, *The Clash of Civilizations,* identified China as a threat to Anglo-American world domination because of its spectacular economic growth in the late Maoist period and under the leadership of Deng Xiaoping (1978–1992).[28] During the 1992 election, most of the Chinese Communist Party (CCP) leadership had preferred George H. W Bush, whom Clinton had criticized for "coddling the butchers of Beijing" following the purported 1989 Tiananmen Square massacre.[29]

The CCP's judgment was sustained by the Clinton administration's actions—including its bombing of the Chinese embassy in Belgrade; and the arrest of U.S. scientist Wen Ho Lee for allegedly spying for China.[30] Beginning in the mid-1990s, the National Endowment for Democracy (NED) began providing $150,000 per year to the China Strategic Institute, a dissident think tank in Washington which put out a pro-democracy newsletter aimed at Chinese intellectuals and CCP members.[31] Clinton further antagonized the CCP by meeting with Tibet's Dalai Lama on four occasions during his presidency.[32]

The Dalai Lama had lived in exile since 1959 following a failed uprising against the PRC backed by the CIA. China viewed the meetings with the Dalai Lama as "serious interference" in China's internal affairs and part of a campaign of destabilization targeting a Chinese province [Tibet] of key strategic importance, which was a great water source and possessed the world's largest uranium and borax deposits, oil, enormous iron deposits, over 80,000 gold mines, and the largest timber reserves at China's disposal.[33]

Opening the China Market While Playing a Double Game

The Clinton administration played a double game by advancing a military containment strategy designed to undercut China's growing threat to American regional hegemony, while also trying to ameliorate personal relations with China's leaders. Deng Xiaoping, for example, was welcomed to Disneyland and in 1997 when Jiang Zemin visited Washington, Clinton spoke of a "constructive strategic partnership."

Two-way trade between the U.S. and China reached $116 billion in the year 2000. Historian Michael Schaller wrote that "the fabled China market seemed to have finally arrived, but in an unanticipated form: the United States that year [2000] sold China goods valued at about $16 billion while importing $100 billion in Chinese products."[34]

The reason for these lopsided figures was that multinational corporations set up factories in China following reforms initiated by Deng Xiaoping, easing restrictions on foreign businesses taking advantage of cheap labor and increasing their purchase of goods from Chinese factories where there was low overhead cost. Special economic zones like in Shenzen offered no taxes on foreign business and transportation costs were reduced as a result of the CCP's huge infrastructural development program.[35]

Influenced also by business lobbies, the Clinton administration promoted the expansion of trade as a means of integrating China into a regional system dominated by the U.S. The Democratic Leadership Council (DLC) demanded that Clinton renew the country's most favored nation status. Some of its leading corporate contributors had close commercial relations with Peking, including at least three firms holding seats on the Council's board: Xerox, which controlled 45 percent of China's desktop copier market; Pepsico, which held over $350 million investments in China; and Merck Frost, whose CEO visited Peking to explore business opportunities.[36]

To the delight of these and other U.S.-based multinational corporations, in the last year of his presidency Clinton signed a major trade bill—opposed by the AFL-CIO—which supported China's entry into the World Trade Organization (WTO).[37] This represented the fulfilment of the dream of U.S. policymakers going back to the late 19th century of opening up the China market.[38] Prior to this time, the U.S. had slapped high import duties or tariffs on Chinese made goods in response to its human rights record.

Congressman Sander Levin (D-MI) described China's WTO accession as potentially "the most important economic event since Marco Polo, the Venetian traveler, ventured to China 700 years ago."[39] It compelled China to relax over 7,000 tariffs, quotas and other trade barriers and further open up various industries, including telecommunications, to foreign corporations and investment. According to Clinton "by joining the WTO, China is not simply agreeing to import more of our products, it is agreeing to import one of democracy's most cherished values, economic freedom."[40]

Among the biggest winners were Clinton's old Arkansas friends, the Walton family, owners of Walmart, which dramatically increased its investment in production in China, opened hundreds of new stores and made billions of dollars. The biggest losers were many of China's farmers who were uprooted owing to WTO-sanctioned imports of soybeans and other products, along with American manufacturers who couldn't compete with cheaper Chinese imports and American workers who never forgave the Clinton's for their betrayal.[41] Although the U.S. realized genuine economic benefits, largely as a result of this policy America's trade deficit increased from $70 billion in 1999 to $162 billion in 2005.[42] From 1999–2011, competition from China cost the United States more than two million factory jobs, which could be attributed in part to China's joining the WTO.[43]

Clinton's top point man for China, Winston Lord, the Assistant Secretary of State for Far Eastern Affairs from 1993–1998, was an associate of Henry Kissinger and former chairman of the NED. He had tried to promote rapid privatization and free market reforms along the model of Russia and had encouraged protests during the late 1980s while U.S. ambassador which had culminated in the events in Tiananmen Square.

The goal of U.S. strategy at that time appears to have been to create political chaos inside China aimed at weakening control of the CCP over China's economic transformation—a strategy that continued under Clinton.[44] The legislation granting China permanent normal trade relations in 2000 explicitly included a promise of additional funds for the NED to help Chinese dissidents and to support destabilization efforts in Tibet and Hong Kong, which was returned to China in 1997 by Great Britain.[45]

As part of Clinton's double game, however, the Clinton administration allowed China to buy forty-six U.S. made supercomputers that matched those used for U.S. national security purposes and allowed the defense contractor McDonnell-Douglas to ship an almost complete intact missile and strategic bomber factory to the PRC, despite opposition from specialists at the Defense Department. Clinton also turned a blind eye to money laundering by Citibank, which used Chinese funds to pay for U.S. high technology that was then diverted to the Chinese military—including technology that helped China modernize its nuclear strike force.[46]

Clinton furthermore reversed Reagan and Bush era restrictions on the export of advanced technologies to China by removing satellite technologies from the State Department's munitions control list—a measure undertaken against the wishes of the Pentagon and State Department—as a favor to the single largest donor to the Democratic Party around this time, Bernard Schwartz, CEO of Loral Space and Communications, who contributed over $1 million in 1997 alone.[47]

The permission for the waiver was granted by Commerce Department Secretary Ron Brown, past chairman of the Democratic National Committee (DNC) and champion of the opening of China's markets, who was killed in a suspicious plane crash in Croatia in April 1996. A beneficiary, China Aerospace, was a state-run Chinese company that employed Liu Chao Ying, a Lieutenant Colonel in the Chinese Army and daughter of a top Chinese government official who funneled $100,000 to the DNC during the 1996 presidential campaign through Democratic Party fund-raiser Johnny Chung, who was later forced to return the money after being convicted of bank fraud, tax evasion and violating election laws.[48]

While using U.S. technology to beef up its military capability, China resented being lectured at about human rights when the U.S. carried out its own human rights violations. When U.S. Secretary of State Warren Christopher at a March 1994 summit asserted that "human rights will be at the top of my agenda," Prime Minister Li Peng responded that China would "never accept the U.S. concept of human rights," and that "you've got racism and human rights problems in the United States too . . . so don't come over here and talk to us about human rights problems."[49]

At the end of its second term, the Clinton administration facilitated closer strategic ties with India, which at the time was ruled by a coalition government headed by the Bharatiya Janatha Party (BJP)—an extreme right-wing formation, which promoted a Hindu chauvinist agenda.[50] The rampant Sinophobia in the United States at the time was exemplified by the March 24 1997 cover of the conservative magazine, *The National Review*, which portrayed Bill and Hillary Clinton and Al Gore in yellow face, and depicted the president as a buck toothed, squinty eyed house boy wearing a straw hat serving tea. The First Lady wore a Red Guard outfit and waved a copy of Mao's Little Red Book, and the hapless Vice President wore Buddhist robes and carried a monk's begging bowl stuffed with cash. The main article repeated the falsehood that China had bought the 1996 U.S. election and owned the president.[51]

"Our Kind of Guy": Clinton, General Suharto, and Indonesia

The double standards of America's human rights policies were again manifested in Indonesia, where Clinton opposed a measure introduced by Senator Russell Feingold (D-WI) which would have restricted arms sales to the government of General Suharto. Clinton also skirted a Congressional ban on training Indonesian troops by allowing Jakarta to pay for its soldiers' military education in the U.S.[52]

Voted by Transparency International as the most corrupt politician in modern history, General Suharto had come to power in a bloody CIA-backed coup d'état in 1965, which wiped out the Indonesian Community Party (PKI) and killed over a million people. The political establishment in Washington was thrilled at the time to have pried Indonesia away from the communist orbit. The country had a great deal of mineral wealth and was located astride key communications lines.[53]

In November 1994, Clinton's State Department helped secure business deals with Suharto for projects worth over $40 billion. Beneficiaries included AT&T, Motorola—which signed a $104 million contract to provide a state-of-the-art radio communications system—Hughes Corp., and Federal Express. California Energy and UNOCAL signed a groundbreaking deal with Indonesia's state oil company, Pertamina, to expand exploration and development of geothermal generating capacity on the island of Java, while Esso, an affiliate of the Exxon Corporation, was given concessions for developing the largest offshore natural gas field in the Pacific to supply liquified natural gas to Asian markets.[54]

Clinton's personal relationship with Suharto was facilitated in part by Indonesian billionaire Mochtar Riady and his son James, head of the Lippo Group business empire. During the 1992 election, Riady was the largest donor to the Clinton-Gore campaign, giving $450,000 and providing another $600,000 to Democratic Party candidates. Between 1992 and 1996, the Riadys gave $840,000 to the Democratic Party, while many of their associates also gave money, down to an Indonesian gardener who worked for them, Arief Winandnata.[55]

Earning his fortune in weapons smuggling, Mochtar, who commanded the Bank of Central Asia, "the third largest private banking firm in Indonesia," had first met Clinton in the early 1980s over cornbread and grits at one of Jack Stephens' regular lunches. Mochtar had been introduced to Stephens by Bert Lance, Director of Office and Management under Jimmy Carter, who was Stephens' classmate at the U.S. Naval Academy. An investor in the infamous Bank of Commerce and Credit International (BCCI) along with Lance, Mochtar had partnered with Stephens Inc. and put his son James in charge of the Worthen Bank in Little Rock, a loan from which rescued Clinton's 1992 presidential campaign. Mochtar also became an owner of the 1st National Bank of Mena during the height of the Contra smuggling operation.[56]

Described as a "God fearing Christian" who operated in the "robber baron tradition of John D. Rockefeller," James Riady attended Clinton's inaugural and visited the White House twenty times during Clinton's first term. The Riadys welcomed disgraced Clinton associates such as Webb Hubbell, who served 21 months in prison after being convicted of wire and tax fraud, and Jim Guy Tucker, Arkansas' Governor from 1992, who was convicted of fraud in the Whitewater affair, to Jakarta to work with the Lippo Group and opened a Walmart in Indonesia. They also set up a corporation with C. Joseph

Giroir Jr., a former partner at the Worthen Bank and Hillary's former boss at the Rose Law Firm, that matched the Riady conglomerate with American companies looking for business in China and Indonesia.[57]

One of the Riadys' main motives in buying Clinton's favor was to gain entrée into the inner circle of General Suharto, who then helped them to become billionaires.[58] Riady had gained access to classified intelligence information through his connection to John Huang, a Democratic Party fundraiser who was granted a security clearance when he worked for the Commerce Department.[59] Suharto had wanted a better relationship with the U.S. president to facilitate the expansion of trade and investment in Indonesia, to purchase F-16 fighters—which he was ultimately allowed to do—and to secure American support on East Timor.[60] Clinton recalled that James Riady successfully persuaded him to meet Suharto at the 1993 Tokyo summit and their relationship grew from there.[61] A senior administration official who dealt with Asian policy said: "he's our kind of guy."[62]

In February 1994, in the midst of a formal government review of whether to permit Indonesia to continue to receive trade benefits, U.S. Trade representative Mickey Kantor abruptly terminated the review process and announced that the Clinton administration was allowing Indonesia to keep its trade privileges, valued at more than $600 million a year to Indonesian companies.[63] *The Wall Street Journal* raised the question as to whether the major campaign contributions from the Riadys was a key factor that led Clinton to overlook major labor rights abuses in Indonesia, including in American corporations like Nike which ran sweatshop factories there.[64]

The average wage in manufacturing in Indonesia was 28 cents per hour.[65] Mining conglomerates like Freeport McMoran of New Orleans, the first foreign investor in the country after the Suharto coup, dumped thousands of tons of mining waste into local rivers every day, destroying local forests along the riverbank while hiring private mercenaries or calling on the army to repress local resistance.[66]

Corporate opposition to the Feingold amendment (barring arms sales) was coordinated by the U.S.-ASEAN Business Council and American League for Exports and Security Assistance, some of whose members included Clinton donors like Lockheed, General Electric and AT & T—which had won a $64.8 contract in Indonesia.[67] The Clinton administration in total provided over $500 million in economic assistance and sold and licensed the sale of hundreds of millions of dollars in weaponry to Jakarta.[68] It also established a police training program, which was in theory designed to combat transnational crime but was also designed to stabilize Suharto's rule and make sure that the radical left did not reemerge.[69]

State Department cables from the late 1990s reveal that thousands of PKI members remained in jail as political prisoners over thirty years after the 1965 CIA-backed coup.[70] The Indonesian military continued to oversee forced labor on U.S. owned rubber plantations and to commit atrocities, crushing separatist movements in Irian Jaya, Aceh, Papua, and East Timor and targeting Islamic forces in Lampung. Suharto's overcrowded jails were filled with political prisoners and captives from these wars.[71]

Clinton nevertheless praised Suharto for "promoting regional stability during the Cold War and since" and for his "able leadership" of APEC.[72] The Clinton administration sustained support for Suharto right up until his downfall in June 1998 when protests emerged because of the Asian financial crisis, which hit Indonesia particularly hard. The value of the rupiah dropped 90 percent at that time. Clinton told Suharto in a phone call on February 13, 1998 from Camp David, three months before he was deposed, "Your personal leadership has produced unprecedented economic growth and prosperity for Indonesia and its people. I am convinced you can get through the present difficulty."[73]

Declassified documents show that the Clinton administration viewed the Indonesian military as a stabilizing force, even though they were well aware of the activities of the Special Forces in spring 1998 in crushing student-led anti-Suharto protests, torturing and disappearing pro-democracy activists and raping women.[74] A May 1998 State Department cable referenced a secret facility used to detain "disappeared" activists south of Jakarta which student sources said was an elite special forces (Kopassus) unit whose former commander, General Prabowo Subianto, ordered the disappearances following an order from President Suharto (Prabowo's father-in-law).[75] Another cable discussed the massacre by Indonesian army officers of six demonstrators at Triskati University, attributed to Subianto. Yet another emphasized that the ammunition used by Indonesian police and Special Forces who killed 17 people in Semaggi came from American M-16 rifles.[76]

By mid-May, the death toll from Jakarta rioting had eclipsed 500, with the discovery of more remains in burned out buildings.[77] Among the targets that rioters had burned was a supermall owned by the Riadys, which housed a Walmart and Ace hardware store.[78] Besides helping to perpetuate the conditions that had led to the upheaval, the Clinton administration sanctioned the training by American military advisers of elite Kopassus units in sniper techniques, demolition and air operations, and psychological warfare. Arms sales were fronted through the Israelis.

Secretary of Defense William Cohen visited Kopassus headquarters where he spent three hours with Prabowo, implying a "green light" for his use of force to maintain the status quo. Cohen stated that "the U.S. is close to and loves the Indonesian army."[79] When Suharto's fate was sealed after three decades of rule, the Clinton administration maneuvered behind the scenes to maintain the military's power and secure U.S. investor rights under the new "democratic" regime of B.J. Habbibie, Suharto's Vice President who generated anger through his gradual approach towards the release of political prisoners.[80]

After the financial crisis hit, the Clinton administration had played a key role in convincing Suharto to sign off on the IMF's structural adjustment program, which many scholars believe was responsible for Suharto's ouster. The cutting of subsidies for fuel and cooking oil pushed prices up and precipitated the rioting that ultimately brought Suharto down. Furthermore, Clinton nixed Suharto's efforts to create a currency board which had the prospect of artificially stabilizing the value of the rupiah rather than letting it float and continue to get pounded on international currency markets.[81]

Steven Hanke, a John Hopkins economics professor who advised Suharto at the time, alleged that Clinton and the IMF deliberately counseled Indonesia to float its currency in order to hasten the fall of Suharto, who had come to be seen as an obstacle to restoring financial market confidence in the country and had become less compliant with the U.S. and West in his old age. Ford and Toyota were upset because Suharto gave heavy subsidies to a car company owned by his son, Tommy (they didn't like having to compete with "Tommy's toys.")[82] Former Secretary of State Lawrence Eagleburger stated that "we were fairly clever in that we supported the IMF as it overthrew Suharto." Ex-Australian Prime Minister Paul Keating noted that "the U.S. Treasury quite deliberately used the economic collapse as a means of bringing about the ouster of Suharto," something the IMF Director Michel Camdessus bragged about.[83]

Supporting Those Who Matter: East Timor

During the 1992 presidential campaign, Clinton had characterized Indonesia's treatment of East Timor as "unconscionable."[84] Nonetheless, Clinton's generous arms sales to Indonesia (totaling over $150 million) and military training programs helped the Indonesian army, in alliance with local militias, to drive an estimated 750,000 East Timorese people from their homes and kill over 10,000 civilians after East Timor voted for its independence in a September 1999 plebiscite.[85] The recipients of U.S. training included Kopassus commandos implicated in the 1991 Dili massacre and scorched earth operation that followed the September 1999 plebiscite. The latter operations destroyed 70 percent of the territory's buildings and caused a severe humanitarian crisis as Kopassus forces not only raped and slaughtered civilians but also "polluted the wells, destroyed the water supply and phone system, and then stole everything else."[86]

While the State Department tried to discourage the East Timor massacres, the Pentagon—as represented by Admiral Dennis Blair, the commander of U.S. forces in the Asia Pacific—did nothing to challenge the Indonesian military and, according to researcher Joseph Nevins, seemed to actually endorse their militia's campaign of terror.[87] Clinton himself appeared to give a "green light" to the invasion by refusing to discuss with Australia and other countries the sending of an international peacekeeping force to protect the people of East Timor after the election referendum. Furthermore, U.S. government licensed sales of armaments to the Indonesian military had increased five-fold in the year before the invasion took place.[88]

U.S. Ambassador Stapleton Roy was frank in explaining U.S. considerations when he told a *Financial Times* reporter: "The dilemma is that Indonesia matters, and East Timor doesn't."[89] The White House predictably in light of this attitude was silent and did nothing to pressure the Habibie government to halt the atrocities, instead asking the UN to reduce the size of its small peacekeeping force.[90] As late as September 9, Clinton said he favored the UN force only "if Indonesia does not end the violence,"—a condition that allowed more time for the Indonesian army to continue its scorched earth operations.[91]

After a public outcry led to domestic pressure, the Clinton administration changed course by threatening to veto loans and to cancel military cooperation, which induced the Indonesian Generals to accept the international presence now bolstered by 5,000 U.S. troops. By 2002, East Timor was granted its independence.[92] The whole episode illustrated the latent power of the U.S. and how Clinton could have prevented the humanitarian crisis in East Timor if he had pressured the Indonesian government earlier.[93] Rather than being guided by any noble humanitarian imperative, Clinton was generally guided by political and economic calculations and real-politick, which resulted in a gross double standards on human rights.

Strengthening the U.S.-Japanese "Security" Alliance

In September 1995, three U.S. Marines were indicted for abducting and raping a young girl in Okinawa, an island off Japan which housed most of the 45,000 American troops stationed there. Eighty-five thousand people subsequently took to the streets to voice their outrage.[94] The U.S. Commander in the Pacific, Admiral Richard C. Macke, added fuel to the fire when he stated his belief that the "rape was absolutely stupid. For the price they paid to rent the car, they could have had a girl."[95] This was a veiled reference to the underground sex economy in Okinawa which exemplified the quasi-colonial and exploitative relationship between the Americans and Okinawans.

In July 2000, Bill Clinton became the first U.S. president to travel to Okinawa since Dwight Eisenhower in 1960. His purpose was to defend the military's presence on the island and try to defuse some of the anger over the 1995 rape and another more recent incident where a Marine had sexually assaulted a fourteen year old girl after breaking into her home.[96] On the eve of his visit, tens of thousands of local demonstrators formed a human chain around Kadema Air Force base to demand a reduction of bases and U.S. servicemen.[97] Clinton tried to defuse the situation by telling Japan's Prime Minister Yoshira Mori that that case of the fourteen year old girl "hurt me in the heart" while promising the Okinawans that the U.S. would "reduce our footprint on the island.[98]

But then he went on to defend the U.S. military presence in a speech before the Japanese Diet, stating: "Many in the U.S. and Japan believe that, with the Cold War over and won, the two nations should pull back from the world and pull back from each other. With all due respect, I believe those views are wrong." The new world, he went on, has brought new dangers that have been dramatized in both countries (referring to home-grown terrorist attacks) and there were new threats arising from conflict between China and Taiwan and on the Korean peninsula. The U.S.- Japan security alliance was the "cornerstone of stability throughout Asia. Both our nations recognize that peace has its price. But true peace is much less than the cost of putting peace at risk."[99]

Takeshi Kosigi, a Liberal Democratic Party (LDP) member of parliament, said that Clinton had spoken with composure and without notes, which Japanese politicians usually used, and left a great impression. Others complained, however, that Clinton didn't say anything concrete and affirmed a commitment to the status quo.[100] These reactions followed a pattern throughout Clinton's career where his charisma and charm won over public opinion at the same time as he betrayed progressive causes.

At the meeting with Mori, Clinton was able to secure a concession that Tokyo would reduce by $30 million the amount it paid to house the bases on its soil. However, Japan still paid five to seven billion dollars annually for the privilege of having the U.S. occupying its land.[101] It was also the leading purchaser of U.S. arms, with *the Wall Street Journal* reporting that it had "loaded up on Grumman and Lockheed surveillance and sub-hunting planes, and bought Patriot missiles and was now seeking the Thaad U.S. missile interceptor system."[102]

Clinton was successful overall in helping to strengthen the U.S.-Japanese security alliance, even amidst some tensions over trade issues and

Japan's resistance to the opening of its markets to American automakers.[103] This was central to the longstanding strategy of containing China. In 1997, the Clinton administration signed expanded guidelines for a U.S.-Japan Defense Cooperation pact, which committed Japan to supporting American troops in a time of emergency with many forms of assistance—including opening up its airports to American military operations and enforcing naval embargoes. The guidelines were written without consultation with the Japanese Diet (Congress) in a reflection of the fundamentally unpopular and undemocratic nature of U.S. policy in the region, contrary to the rhetoric.[104]

Reversing the Outcome of the Vietnam War

On February 4, 1994, President Clinton ordered an end to the trade embargo on Vietnam, casting away a central remnant of one of America's most divisive wars and paving the way for the resumption of diplomatic relations. At a White House ceremony, Clinton said it was "now time to acknowledge the cooperation Vietnam has shown in the search for evidence of the 2,238 Americans still officially listed as missing from that conflict, which ended in 1975." He said opening the door to trade would benefit that still-unfinished search, adding that he was lifting the trade embargo "because I am absolutely convinced it offers us the best way to resolve the fate of those who remain missing and about whom we are not sure."[105]

Vietnam was a politically sensitive issue for Clinton because of his past as an antiwar organizer and draft dodger who had misled an ROTC Sergeant at the University of Arkansas in order to evade the draft. The idea of reaching out to Vietnam had been vigorously opposed by the American Legion and others among the nation's leading veterans' groups, who had attacked Clinton during his presidential campaign for avoiding the draft.[106] However, the momentum for ending the trade embargo and restoring relations was too strong, and driven in part by business lobbies, which saw great opportunity in Vietnam and wanted to compete with the Japanese who had established strong trading ties there.[107]

Vietnam's communist government had enacted liberalizing economic reforms in the mid-1980s known as *Doi Moi* ("renovation") under the leadership of Nguyen Van Linh ("Vietnam's Gorbachev"). These reforms, combined with IMF structural adjustment programs and the harsh U.S. embargo, had a devastating economic effect that helped undermine the country's victory in the war. Health clinics and hospitals were forced to close, public employees were laid off, local level famines erupted as the price of food staples soared with the elimination of cooperatives, subsidies and price controls, and 750,000 children had to drop out of school.[108] By the late 1990s, Vietnam's economy was dominated by foreign businesses taking advantage of cheap labor and "tax holidays," as Vietnam was reintegrated into the Japanese sphere of influence, one of the primary original war aims of the United States.[109]

In 1993, a secret agreement was allegedly reached in Paris—which in many regards was tantamount to forcing Vietnam to compensate Washington for the costs of the Vietnam War—requiring Hanoi to recognize the debts of the defunct Saigon regime of General Nguyen Van Thieu as a condition for granting fresh credit and lifting the U.S. embargo.[110] Never reported in the mainstream media, this agreement exposed Clinton's official rationale for lifting the embargo as a sham—especially in light of the fact that no American POWs had ever been discovered alive in Vietnam after 1979 when American defector Robert Garwood came out of the jungles.

Clinton had embraced the MIA/POW cause as part of a historical revisionism which attempted to demonize Vietnam for allegedly violating the 1973 Paris Peace accords by keeping American POWs in the country. The claim about withholding POWs had first been advanced by Richard M. Nixon as part of a ploy to discredit the antiwar movement and prolong the war. With time, the POW myth played into the revisionism which characterized Hanoi as the war's aggressor and helped justify the reneging on a 1973 promise made by the Nixon administration to provide $3.25 billion in reparations along with the embargo that was part of a revenge policy.[111]

Historian Robert J. McMahon found little difference between Clinton's rhetoric on Vietnam and that of Republicans Gerald Ford, Ronald Reagan and George H. W. Bush, who had all supported the Vietnam War. Each emphasized the heroism of American veterans and need for reconciliation, healing and the binding of old wounds without any effort to acknowledge the fact of U.S. aggression and magnitudes larger suffering and death of the Vietnamese victims.[112] In a Memorial Day speech at the Vietnam Memorial Wall in 1993, Clinton said that American troops had "fought and died there [in Vietnam] for noble motives. They fought for freedom and the independence of the Vietnamese people."[113]

Whatever may have been the personal intent of the troops, this was blatantly untrue of the intentions of successive U.S. administrations if we consider the fradulent pretexts used to wage war, record number of political prisoners in South Vietnam's jails and dependency of the Saigon government on foreign support.[114] In another speech at Hanoi National University in November 2000, Clinton referred to the "shared suffering" of Americans and Vietnamese.[115] This echoed the outrageous claims of Jimmy Carter in 1979 that the "destruction from the war was mutual." In actuality, nearly four million Vietnamese died and 14 million were made refugees, compared to 58,000 Americans killed.[116]

The spread of capitalism and the inability of Vietnam's communist government to challenge American dictates generally raises the question about who really won the Vietnam War. After Vietnam's opening, *Time* magazine featured a cartoon of Ho Chi Minh (Vietnam's wartime revolutionary leader) holding up an order of French fries sporting the likeness of Colonel Sanders, the spokesperson for Kentucky Fried Chicken.[117] Clinton claimed in a speech at Hanoi University that globalization was the "economic equivalent of a force of nature."[118] However, there was nothing natural about workers producing toys for McDonald's "Happy Meals" half a world away making only six cents an hour when company executives made six figures. Nor for the huge rise in inequality and destitution and the loss of economic sovereignty in a country that had sacrificed so many people in a heroic resistance war.

"They Hate That We Are Communists": Election Interference in Cambodia

Washington's revenge policy towards Vietnam extended to Cambodia, where the Clinton administration used the cover of a UN peacekeeping mission to interfere in Cambodia's 1993 election by supporting the royalist party led by Norodom Sihanouk's son, Ranariddh and the Buddhist linked Khmer People's National Liberation Front (KPNLF) against Hun Sen's Cambodian People's Party (CPP). The latter had gained power after Vietnam liberated the country from Pol Pot and the genocidal Khmer Rouge in 1979—a genuinely humanitarian intervention Washington opposed. When the election results were contested, Washington refused to back a power-sharing arrangement proposed by Sihanouk (Cambodia's leader from 1960–1970) because it gave joint power to the CPP. Sihanouk in turn seized power for himself, sparking secessionist movements by CPP supporters under the leadership of then-Deputy Prime Minister Norodom Chakrapong, which put the country on the threshold of civil war.[119]

CPP leader Hun Sen, who regained power in 1998, stated that the U.S. "considers us pro-Vietnamese and they don't like Vietnam. They hate that we are communists and so found every way so [CPP] would not win elections."[120] This "every way" including the use of a $3 million USAID program to support opposition groups and enrich KPNLF and Royalist zones at the expense of CPP controlled areas (80 percent of the country) where USAID projects were never approved. An NGO delegate called this a "crude form of vote buying and control . . . obviously intended to strengthen the hand of the opposition to the CPP."[121]

Clinton's special envoy to Cambodia during the 1993 crisis, Stephen Solarz (D-NY), had worked for a lobbying firm in Washington which participated in a pitch meeting with Ranariddh, Sen's main rival, to represent Cambodia in Washington, and admitted to being "biased in favor of the opposition [against Hun Sen]."[122] In 1997, the NED, an organization established in the 1980s to carry on the work of the CIA, had a $1.24 million program in Cambodia, channeled through the International Republican Institute (IRI) and other NGOs that was designed to continuously undermine the CPP including through propaganda.[123]

Hun Sen nevertheless won the 1998 election, in large part because of the perception that Ranariddh preferred golf to working and surrounded himself with courtiers.[124] Washington afterwards cut off all foreign assistance in a continuation of its longstanding vendetta against the Vietnamese-backed CPP.[125] Sen went on to rule Cambodia for the next 20 years. While he was no model democrat,[126] Washington's opposition to him was self-serving and destructive by provoking divisions and destabilization in an already shattered nation.[127]

"Our Boys Won Big-Time": Election Interference II —Mongolia

Few Americans are aware that the Clinton administration interfered not only in Cambodian elections but also in 1996 elections in Mongolia. In the latter case, it helped bring to power a right-wing government that provided a boon to U.S. corporate interests. Sitting atop some of the world's largest gold and copper reserves and valued as a launching ground for covert operations aimed at China and Russia, Mongolia had been ruled for decades by the communist Mongolian People's Revolutionary Party (MPRP), which adopted a liberalizing economic agenda following the demise of the Soviet Union—though not to the extent the U.S. wanted.[128]

In 1996, the NED provided $158,327 to the IRI, a corporate-backed organization which helped form a right-wing political coalition—the Democratic Union Coalition (DUC)— that won 57 of 70 parliamentary seats in the Mongolian election. USAID, whose budget for Mongolia was $12 million, gave grants in 1995 to both the IRI and the Asia Foundation, a CIA front which pushed for neoliberal reforms and trained political candidates.

An IRI program assistant remarked after the election: "our boys won big time."[129] This was not good, however, for ordinary Mongolians. Advised by IRI operatives the DUC-led parliament dropped price controls, cut pension rolls, halved the number of government ministries, removed tariff protections from domestic products, slashed taxes, kept up the march of privatization, and proposed a 30 percent flat tax and a regressive value-added tax. It also passed a new mining and foreign investment law to attract foreign companies, particularly for mineral resource exploration and development, which was the purpose behind the electoral manipulation.[130]

With a collapse in world copper prices, unemployment ballooned over 20 percent, helped along by the purging of government departments and the decline of domestic industries under DUC rule. One-third of the population was left to live below nutritional starvation levels, as unscrupulous politicians profited handsomely from the stripping of public assets. Even the founding chairman of one of the parties in the DUC admitted that average real incomes had dropped by 30 percent in the year they were in power.[131]

Myanmar: Destabilizing a Chinese-backed Military Regime

The Clinton administration carried on its defacto war against the People's Republic of China in Myanmar (Burma) where it tried to destabilize the Chinese-backed military junta that had ruled the country since 1962. Washington's main desire was to control the coastline off Myanmar, which provides naval access to the Strait of Malacca, the narrow ship passage between Malaysia and Indonesia through which more than 80 percent of all China's oil imports are shipped.[132]

The main agency for promoting regime change was the NED. Asia program officer Louisa Coan testified before the House Sub-committee on Asia and the Pacific on September 17, 1997 that the NED through its direct grants program supported dissidents belonging to the democracy movement of Daw Aung San Suu Kyi—youngest daughter of the nation's founding father, Aung San. Some of the funding was cycled through groups along the borders in Thailand and in India, and used to support twice daily radio programing through the Democratic Voice of Burma (based in Scandinavia), newsletters, underground newspapers, underground labor organizing, and other programs.[133] The dissident factions included Karen insurgents led by Bo Mya operating along the Thai border, who financed their military operations through drug smuggling.[134]

The NED's initiatives bore fruit a decade later in Burma's Saffron revolution, an uprising led by robed monks, which set the groundwork for Kyi's National League for Democracy winning elections in 2015 and becoming Myanmar's first non-military government in 54 years. However, Kyi's saintly façade crumbled with her active complicity in the government-directed butchery of Rohingya Muslims.[135]

Planning Regime Change and Preemptive War: North Korea

With Vietnam brought into the New World Order, North Korea was the main country—besides China and Cambodia to an extent—that remained defiantly "socialist," at least in name, and intent on forging an independent economic path. North Korea's resistant stand did not exactly turn out well for the country's people. The loss of trading partners in the Eastern bloc combined with heavy investment in the military owing to the fear of renewed invasion and heavy rains and flooding in 1995–96, resulted in a period of severe economic hardship known as the "arduous march."[136]

Under normal circumstances, the "international community" would have intervened to assist the North Koreans to cope with the latter natural disaster. The Clinton administration, however, hoped to use the crisis to sow popular disaffection with the North Korean regime and achieve the longstanding goal of regime change. So it sustained economic sanctions and blocked oil coming into the country, which resulted in 70 percent of Democratic People's Republic of Korea (DPRK) factories shutting down.

According to Kim Ryeon Hui, a North Korean citizen who witnessed the effects of the arduous march firsthand, CIA agents operating on the North Korean-Chinese border offered local farmers a bag of rice in exchange for a cow's tail. The purpose was to ruin North Korea's agriculture and induce starvation as a catalyst for regime change at a time that farmers had to use cows to plough their fields because they lacked oil or electricity.[137]

The Clinton administration's thinking about North Korea was shaped by Zbigniew Brzezinski's 1997 book, *The Grand Chessboard*, which frowned on the unification of the two Koreas because it would alter America and Japan's role in the Far East. According to Brzezinski, South Korea was a key "geopolitical pivot" whose close links to the U.S. enabled America to shield Japan and thereby to keep Japan from becoming an independent and major military power without an overbearing American presence within Japan itself. South Korea's increasing economic power also made it a more important "space" in its own right, control over which had become increasingly valuable.[138] Communist North Korea by implication had to be isolated, weakened, and contained, and its regime overthrown as a means of preventing the growth of a stronger Chinese sphere.

In January 1993, the Clinton administration authorized Team Spirit war games, the largest military exercise in the world, which included the introduction into South Korea of backpack nukes controlled by mobile mounts and practice with nuclear cannons.[139] Congresswoman Elizabeth Furse (D-OR) wrote to Clinton that she found the "level of saber-rattling" she saw "going on in our present relationship with North Korea very disturbing." Furse was "extremely concerned that we are sending additional weapons systems, conducting the Team Spirit war games, and considering a naval blockade when we need to bring the tools of conflict resolution and continuing diplomacy to this situation and be working towards developing relations and eventually trading with North Korea."[140]

Unfortunately, Clinton did not heed these words. In June 1994, a month before long-time leader Kim Il-Sung's death, the Clinton administration nearly went to war with North Korea, triggering a crisis in an attempt to halt North Korea's nascent nuclear weapons program. Under the threat of encirclement and renewed U.S. and South Korean military invasion, the North Koreans had first begun developing a nuclear weapons production program with Soviet support in the late 1950s. When the International Atomic Energy Agency (IAEA) requested unexpected and intrusive inspections of North Korean facilities, Kim Il-Sung's government legitimately refused because they felt they were being singled out and that the inspection teams would be infiltrated by intelligence agents.[141]

The Clinton administration responded by slapping sanctions on Pyongyang intended to cripple its economy. Knowing that Pyongyang had repeatedly denounced sanctions as a "declaration of war," President Clinton on June 16 decided to dispatch substantial reinforcements to South Korea. This act was considered as a provocation by the North Koreans who in turn mobilized for war.[142]

Declassified documents available at the National Security Archive show that Defense Secretary William J. Perry had developed plans for a preemptive first strike on North Korea during the crisis, which involved sending cruise missiles and F-117 stealth fighters to hit a small nuclear reactor at Yongbyon in order to prevent North Korea from recovering the raw materials to make nuclear bombs.[143] Perry had told NBC's *Meet the Press* the previous April that the U.S. did not want to provoke a war, but that "if the U.S. sanctions provoke North Korea into unleashing a war, that is a risk we're taking."

Perry and future Defense Secretary Ashton Carter had studied whether preemptive strikes could be carried out on the Yongbyon nuclear facility without starting another Korean War, and concluded that it couldn't. By mid-June, the Clinton administration had nevertheless devised its war plan, which entailed sending 10,000 American troops to South Korea (the Republic of Korea), dispatching Apache attack helicopters and various other aircraft, and moving in more Bradley fighting vehicles.[144] Some years later, Perry told South Korean Premier Kim Dae Jung that during the 1994 crisis, the U.S. had planned for war. He stated: "of course, with the combined forces of the

Republic of Korea and the U.S., we can undoubtedly win, but war involves many casualties."[145]

Luckily, the crisis was defused when former President Jimmy Carter was able to broker an agreement in which North Korea agreed to freeze its nuclear program in return for new nuclear reactors that didn't produce weapons grade plutonium along with oil to help meet its energy needs.[146] Selig S. Harrison, a State Department official who played an important role in the negotiations, later asserted that while North Korea lived up to its end of the bargain, and ceased operating the Yongbyon reactor, the Clinton administration failed to adhere to its own commitments, notably by refusing to remove economic sanctions the North saw as crucial to solving its economic problems, especially its food shortage, and by failing to provide promised oil deliveries or fund light water reactors.[147]

The blatant double standards of American policy was apparent in that the U.S. had long stationed dozens of nuclear weapons in South Korea, including aircraft carriers equipped to deliver nuclear bombs over North Korea and nuclear tomahawk land attack cruise missiles.[148] The development of a nuclear program by North Korea in this context was completely rational, even more so if we consider how the U.S. Air Force had literally bombed North Korea back to the Stone Age during the Korean War—a war which Clinton presented as "the first resolute and effective action to stem the expansion of communism," which he claimed had "heralded the collapse of the Berlin Wall and demise of Communism."[149]

Clinton's condescending attitude towards North Korea and his historical denialism was apparent in an April 2021 speech at Harvard University in which he said that North Korea's "psychological problem is that no one would ever think about them if they didn't cause trouble."[150] When North and South Korea got together in June 2000 for a historic peace summit, the Clinton administration seemed to regard the prospect of change as unwelcome—for reasons spelled out by Brzezinski in *The Grand Chessboard*—and refused to allow for troop reductions in South Korea.[151]

The Pentagon also continuously simulated nuclear attacks on North Korea. In June 1998, F-15 fighter bombers dropped dummy BDU-38 nuclear bombs on concrete emplacements arrayed like the hundreds that protected North Korean underground facilities. Lt. Gen. Raymond Ayres threatened to overthrow the DPRK, stating that "the entire resources of the U.S. Marines would be sent into battle and would abolish North Korea as a state and reorganize it under South Korean control. We'll kill 'em all."[152] This kind of reckless talk reinforced North Koreans' perception of being under siege, which made the prospects for peace more unlikely.

The 1997 Asian Financial Crisis and End of an Illusion

The 1997 Asian financial crisis helped puncture many of the myths underlying American-led globalization and the purported benefits of the Washington consensus or free market dogma, which the Clinton administration had sought to advance. The crisis first erupted in Thailand in July 1997 when it ran out of foreign exchange reserves and was forced to devalue its currency, the baht. The Thai stock market dropped by 75 percent and unemployment rate soared by 23 percent, resulting in a huge growth in poverty and doubling of the suicide rate.

The crisis in Thailand quickly spread to the rest of Asia. After posting some of the most impressive growth rates in the world, the so-called "Tiger economies" saw their stock markets and currencies lose about 70 percent of their value during the crisis. Various analysts attributed it to the hasty liberalization of capital markets, low wages, over-reliance on exports, inflationary pressures and unsound lending practices, shifting investment to China due to low wages, reckless speculation by international financial investors, the lifting of capital controls, and an inability to develop effective regulatory mechanisms in the face of record levels of foreign investment.[153] Jagdish Bhagwati, a former adviser to the director-general of the General Agreement on Tariffs and Trade (GATT), was among those to see the root of the crisis as lying in an "unregulated financial system" which could "with relative ease become divorced from the productive system it is supposed to serve and so be unnaturally predisposed to 'panics' and 'manias.'"[154]

By refusing to comply with the advice of Western institutions and the U.S. Treasury to deregulate its economy, Malaysia under Mahathir's leadership was one country, along with China, that was spared the worst of the crisis—though Mahathir was himself vilified. Mahathir highlighted Western pressure "to turn all Asian economies [into] Anglo-Saxon laissez faire market economies," accusing the World Bank and IMF of being instruments of the Western neo-colonialism, and Western finance and currency traders of artificially devaluing Asian currencies "so the so-called East Asian economic tigers suddenly turn into meowing cats."[155]

In November 1997, a few months into the crisis, Clinton enraged his Southeast Asian counterparts at the Asia Pacific Economic Cooperation Summit when he dismissed the Asian financial crisis—which his administration had done so much to provoke by advancing neoliberal policies—as a "few little glitches in the road."[156] The crisis, however, had caused over 2.4 million people to lose their jobs, 20 million people to fall into poverty and caused a twenty percent increase in child prostitution in the Philippines and Thailand in one year alone.[157] Clinton prescribed the same remedy as for the

1994 Mexico peso crisis. That is, Thailand would get $17 billion in an IMF-led loan package in exchange for promising to impose high interest rates, restrain government spending, close insolvent banks and let its currency fall in order to expand exports and curtail imports.

MIT economics professor Paul Krugman wrote that: "[Since] Mexico worked how could they not try to repeat the Mexican rescue." However, Thailand was different from Mexico. Its neighbors and main trading partners had been weakened by the Asian financial crisis, whereas Mexico shared a border with the U.S.[158] The U.S. Congress, furthermore, was reluctant to provide a robust financial rescue package to Thailand, which according to former Defense Secretary William Cohen, "sent a signal that the U.S. was pulling away," ensuring that the confidence of foreign investors was not restored.[159]

At the annual meetings of the IMF and World Bank in Hong Kong, Japan proposed an Asian Monetary Fund and urged Asian countries—pointedly excluding the U.S.—to chip in as much as $100 billion to cope with the financial crisis. The sum was immense, but Clinton's chief economic advisers, Robert Rubin and Lawrence Summers, feared that the fund would offer big loans with less stringent conditions than the IMF that would threaten U.S. economic supremacy. Accordingly, U.S. Treasury officials worked the corridors of Hong Kong's Convention Center and the city's private dining rooms to slow the Japanese plan's momentum. It was ultimately defeated with help from China and South Korea who were suspicious of Tokyo's ambitions.

A triumphant Summers, who referred to himself as Mr. Dollar, declared that U.S. economic leadership was "crucial to avoid a descent into the kind of regionalism and protectionism that we saw in the periods between the 1st and 2nd world wars."[160] However, critics suggested that the U.S. Treasury Department under Summers had "Americanized" the crisis without sufficient money or congressional support for the strategy while humiliating its Asian junior partner.

The Wall Street Journal intoned that if "Dr. Dollar [Summers] and its allies produced a quick recovery in Asia, there would be little second guessing. But they didn't. It's like less than successful chemotherapy. The side effects are miserable, the cancer is unconquered and the patient is questioning the doctor's competence."[161] Others compared Summer's mistake to that made by Herbert Hoover when he tried to balance the budget in the face of the Great Depression. The costs for the Asian people were severe, including being forced to endure economic austerity, high interest rates, and reduced subsidies—measures which even Robert Rubin conceded were overly harsh. *The Wall Street Journal* wrote that it was like "siphoning gasoline out of a truck already low on fuel."[162]

Former World Bank President and Vietnam War architect Robert S. McNamara amazingly said that the failure to contain the worst financial crisis in half a century reminded him of the Vietnam War. "Events," he said, "were beyond the ability of government officials to shape and control. The parallel is that you have to dig deeply and understand your problems and do it early."[163] Journalist Naomi Klein, in her book *The Shock Doctrine: The Rise of Disaster Capitalism,* suggests that American policy-makers, driven by Wall Street financial interests, did not actually want a successful recovery because they wanted to take advantage of the crisis by imposing radical free-market economic policies that lessened the role of the state, and which would enable greater penetration of U.S.-based multinational corporations.

Klein quoted from a *Wall Street Journal* article entitled "Wall Street Scavenging in Asia Pacific," which reported on Wall Street firms dispatching "armies of bankers to the Asia Pacific region [in the face of the meltdown] to scout for brokerage firms, asset management firms and even banks that they can snap up at bargain prices. The hunt for Asian acquisitions is urgent because many U.S. Security firms led by Merrill Lynch & Co. and Morgan Stanley have made overseas expansion their priority."[164]

In short order, several major sales went through: Merrill Lynch bought Japan's Yamaichi Securities as well as Thailand's largest securities firm; AIG bought Bangkok Investment for a fraction of its worth; JP Morgan bought a stake in Kia Motors, while Travelers Group and Salomon Smith Barney bought one of Korea's largest textile companies and several other companies. Samsung was broken up and sold for parts: Volvo got its heavy industry division; SC Johnson & Son its pharmaceutical arm; General Electric its lightning division; Bechtel got the contract to privatize the water and sewage system in Eastern Manila and one to build an oil refinery in Sulawesi, Indonesia; Motorola got full control over Korea's Appeal telecom and a New York based energy firm, Sithe, got a large stake in Thailand's public gas company. All told, there were 186 major mergers and acquisitions of firms by foreign multinationals in the span of only twenty months. It was dubbed "the world's biggest going out of business sale by *The New York Times* and a "business buying bazaar" by *Business Week.*[165]

Servant of Empire

Bill Clinton, who had first cultivated alliances with Southeast Asian business elites and led trade missions to the region while governor of Arkansas, was an effective front man of U.S. capitalist interests in Southeast Asia who could generate excitement and woo crowds of people, even while his policies were eroding their nation's sovereignty. McNamara's Vietnam analogy provides perhaps the most fitting epitaph on American Southeast Asian policy during Clinton's presidency. America's best and the brightest in the roaring 1990s were imbued with the same ideological and moral fervor that their predecessors had been in fighting communism during the Cold War. Now with their main ideological adversary removed, they faced no opposition in their efforts to export free-market ideals and expand America's empire of military bases. On the political left, human rights considerations were often invoked to challenge Clinton's engagement with China and at times to promote a hardline policy towards North Korea, but rarely to demand the reduction of U.S. military troops and bases, or renounce American support for dictators like General Suharto, or political meddling by the NED, or the ravaging effects of neoliberal economic policies.

At the end of the day, Washington was no different from the earlier colonial powers which had adopted a liberal veneer as a means of rallying public support for their cause. Clinton at times can be compared with his counterparts in the British and French empires whose personal charisma could effectively diffuse crises. Reckless provocations and artificially created crises as in the Taiwan straits in 1996 and the Korean peninsula in 1994, however, nearly led to the outbreak of nuclear war. The Clinton administration's inability to reverse its market fundamentalist policies following the 1997 Asian financial crisis, furthermore, showed an arrogance reminiscent of the Vietnam era, and helped lay bare the illusions upon which the American Century rested.

Endnotes

1 Mark Landler, "Gore, in Malaysia, Says Its Leaders Suppress Freedom," *The New York Times*, November 17, 1998. Mahathir quoted in Naomi Klein, *The Shock Doctrine: The Rise of Disaster Capitalism* (New York: Metropolitan Books, 2007), 268.

2 Richard Lloyd Parry, "Malaysia Fury at Al Gore's Interference," *The Independent*, November 18, 1992.

3 Eichi Furukawa, "How Mahathir Overcame the Asian Crisis," *Japan Times*, July 18, 1999.

4 Parry, "Malaysia Fury at Al Gore's Interference."

5 Eichi Furukawa, "How Mahathir Overcame the Asian Crisis," *Japan Times*, July 18, 1999; Webster G. Tarpley discusses Mahathir's call to dump the U.S. dollar in *9/11 Synthetic Terror: Made in USA* (Joshua Tree, CA: Progressive Press, 2006), 120–121. Mahathir told the Nikkei forum in Japan in 2003 that "the U.S. dollar is not a stable currency at all. We have to think of some other ways of determining exchange rates. We need to rethink whether we can depend on the U.S. dollar or not. Initially, yes, we have to depend on the U.S. dollar, but we should move away from the U.S. dollar."

6 Won Hwang, *Personalized Politics: The Malaysian State Under Mahathir* (Thailand: Silkworm Books, 2003); A.B. Abrams, *Power and Primacy: A History of Western Intervention in the Asia-Pacific* (New York: Peter Lang, 2022), 25, 408, 409. Mahathir said that his generation had been inspired by Japan's Greater Co-Prosperity Sphere which sought to counter Western imperialism. He wrote that the "success of the Japanese invasion [of the Dutch East Indies and other former European colonies] convinced us that there is nothing inherently superior to the Europeans. They could be defeated. They could be reduced to groveling before an Asiatic race."

7 Chalmers Johnson, *Blowback: The Costs and Consequences of the American Empire* (New York: Owl Books, 2000), 209.

8 Johnson, *Blowback.*

9 "U.S. Security Strategy for the East Pacific Region," Department of Defense, Office of International Security Affairs, February 1995, https://nautilus.org/global-problem-solving/us-security-strategy-for-the-east-asia-pacific-region/

10 See https://peacehistory-usfp.org/korean-war/; https://apjjf.org/2012/10/47/Jeremy-Kuzmarov/3855/article.html.

11 Bill Clinton, *My Life* (New York: Alfred A. Knopf, 2004), 270.

12 David Wessel and Bob Davis, "Markets Under Siege – Limits of Power: How Global Crisis Grew Despite Efforts of a Crack U.S. Team," *The Wall Street Journal*, September 24, 1998, 1; Steven Greenhouse, "Clinton Pushes Business with Asia," *The New York Times*, November 11, 1993.

13 Quoted in Donald K. Emmerson, "U.S. Policy Themes in Southeast Asia in the 1990s," *in Southeast Asia in the New World Order: The Political Economy of a Dynamic Region*, ed. Bruce Burton and David Wurfel (New York: Palgrave McMillan, 1996), 103.

14 *The East Asian Miracle: Economic Growth and Public Policy*, ed. Lawrence Summers et al. (New York: Oxford University Press, 1993), 10, 19.

15 Karen Talbot, "Backing Up Globalization with Military Might," *CovertAction Quarterly*, Fall-Winter 1999, 30–36. See also Michael T. Klare, *Resource Wars: The New Landscape of Global Conflict* (New York: Metropolitan Books, 2001), 135.

16 Patrick Tyler, *A Great Wall: Six Presidents and China: An Investigative History* (New York: Public Affairs, 1999), 22; Steven Greenhouse, "Aides to Clinton Say He Will Defy Beijing and Issue Visa to Taiwan's President," *The New York Times*, May 22, 1995.

17 A.B. Abrams, *Power and Primacy: A History of Western Intervention in the Asia-Pacific* (New York: Peter Lang, 2002), 86. Americans present in Taiwan (Formosa) in the late 1940s equated the imposition of GMD rule with having "put all Formosans [Taiwanese] into slavery." Taiwan was used subsequently as a base for CIA clandestine operations that were designed to destabilize China.

18 Only 13 of 193 UN member states recognized the Republic of China (ROC) in Taiwan.

19 John C. Roper, "U.S. Aircraft Carrier in Asia 'Routine," *UPI Archives,* January 26, 1996, https://www.upi.com/Archives/1996/01/26/US-aircraft-carrier-in-Asia-routine/5535822632400/; "Third Taiwan Strait Crisis," https://en.wikipedia.org/wiki/Third_Taiwan_Strait_Crisis

20 Tyler, *A Great Wall,* 28.

21 Tyler, *A Great Wall.*

22 Clinton, *My Life*, 326.

23 Jeff Cole and Sarah Lubman, "Global Arms Market—Bombs Away," *The Wall Street Journal*, January 28, 1994, A1; Steven Lee Myers, "U.S. Seeks to Curb Israeli Arms Sales to China," *The New York Times*, November 11, 1999. MPRI mercenaries also trained Taiwan's armed forces. Louis Wolff, "MPRI: Washington's New Private Army," *CovertAction Quarterly*, Fall-Winter 1999, 49.

24 Tyler, *A Great Wall.*

25 Tyler, *A Great Wall,* 14; Michel Chossudovsky, "United States War Machine: Reviving the Engines of World War III," *CovertAction Quarterly*, Fall 2002, 41.

26 Klare, *Resource Wars*, 112, 133. "It's the uninterrupted flow of commerce through those waters that is of critical importance to the U.S."

27 On the U.S. containment strategy directed against China, See James Peck, *Washington's China* (Amherst, MA: University of Massachusetts Press, 2006).

28 Samuel Huntington, *The Clash of Civilizations and the Remaking of World Order*, rev ed. (New York: Simon & Schuster, 2011).

29 Tyler, *A Great Wall.* A.B. Abrams' book *Atrocity Fabrication and Its Consequences : How Fake News Shapes World Order* (Atlanta: Clarity Press, 2023 presents evidence contradicting the official view about the alleged Tiananmen Square massacre.

30 "The Neocons Antagonize China," in Tarpley, *9/11 Synthetic Terror*, 133.

31 John Berlau, "Asia Minor," *The New Republic*, March 24, 2002, https://newrepublic.com/article/66182/china-national-endowment-for-democracy-dissident

32 "Clinton Meets Dalai Lama; Discusses Rights in China," *The New York Times*, April 28, 1993; "Clinton Backs Offer by the Dalai Lama," *The New York Times,* April 30, 1994; Philip Shenon, "Dalai Lama Tells Clinton of Chinese Balkiness," *The New York Times*, November 11, 1998.

33 William F. Engdahl, *Target China: How Washington and Wall Street Plan to Cage the Asian Dragon* (San Diego, CA: Progressive Press, 2014), 45. The CIA had long supported the Dalai Lama, and may have helped finance the Free Tibet movement which played up China's human rights abuses in Tibet, while ignoring the authoritarian features of the Dalai Lama's rule. No country has recognized the Tibetan government in exile as the legitimate government of Tibet.

34 Michael Schaller, *The United States and China: Into the Twenty-First Century*, 4th ed. (New York: Oxford University Press, 2016), 192.

35 Engdahl, *Target China*, 162, 163.

36 Alexander Cockburn and Ken Silverstein, *Washington Babylon* (London: Verso, 1996), 20. Clinton also received tens of thousands of dollars for his political campaigns from Chinese state agents or businessmen which may have influenced his policy. See Dick Morris, with Eileen McGann, *Because He Could* (New York: Regan Books, 2004), 227, 228.

37 Johnson, *Blowback*, 140; Michael M. Phillips and Helene Cooper, "Clinton to Send China Trade Bill to Congress," *The Wall Street Journal*, March 8, 2000, A2. Various Democrats stood with organized labor and opposed the trade bill, including Richard Gephardt. They had been disappointed by former president Jimmy Carter, who had endorsed it.

38 See Thomas J. McCormack, *China Market: America's Quest for Informal Empire,* 1893–1901 (Chicago: Quadrangle Books, 1967).

39 Levin quoted in Greg Hitt, "Gephardt is Being Pushed Closer to Clinton on China WTO Entry," *The Wall Street Journal*, May 6, 1999.

40 Quoted in A.B. Abrams, *China and America's Tech War from AI to 5G: The Struggle to Shape the Future of World Order* (Lexington Books, 2022), 251.

41 Engdahl, *Target China*, 163, 164; Robert E. Scott, "The Wall Mart Effect," *Economic Policy Institute*, June 25, 2007, https://www.epi.org/publication/ib235/

42 Antonio Juhasz, "What Walmart Wants From the WTO," *Alternet*, December 13, 2005, https://laborrights.org/in-the-news/what-wal-mart-wants-wto. For positive assessments of Clinton's support for China's WTO accession, see Abrams, *China and America's Tech War from AI to 5G*, 252, 253.

43 Edward Wong, Michael Crowley and Ana Swanson, "Biden Journey on China Has a Hard Turn," *The New York Times*, September 7, 2020, A1, A14, A15.

44 Engdahl, *Target China*, 6; F. William Engdahl, *Manifest Destiny: Democracy as Cognitive Dissonance* (Wiesbaden: mine.books, 2018), ch. 5.

45 John Berlau, "Asia Minor," *The New Republic*, March 24, 2002, https://newrepublic.com/article/66182/china-national-endowment-for-democracy-dissident. The NED nevertheless channeled a lot of its funding away from pro-democracy dissidents like Wei Jingsheng, the leader of the Chinese democracy movement to projects aiming to advance reforms that were palatable to the Chinese Communist Party leadership like village election mobilization. This led the *New Republic* to conclude that the NED had gone soft on China.

46 David Bossie, *Intelligence Failure: How Clinton's National Security Policy Set the Stage for 9/11* (Nashville, TN: WND, 2004), 39, 104, 112, 119; Edward Timperlake and William C. Triplett II, *Year of the Rat: How Bill Clinton Compromised U.S. Security for Chinese Cash* (Washington, D.C.: Regnery Publishing, 1998).

47 Victor Thorn, *Hillary (and Bill): The Murder Volume*: Part three of the Clinton trilogy (Washington, D.C.: American Free Press, 2008), 589; Ann H. Coulter, *High Crimes and Misdemeanors: The Case Against Bill Clinton* (Washington, D.C. Regnery, 1998), 253; William Safire, "U.S. Security for Sale," *The New York Times*, May 18, 1998, https://www.nytimes.com/1998/05/18/opinion/essay-us-security-for-sale.html. The removal of Reagan-Bush era restrictions assisted China in developing its ballistic missile program. Schwartz traveled to China under a trade mission led by Commerce Secretary Ron Brown and used his Chinese contacts to obtain satellite transmission rights for a mobile telephone network, a deal worth billions of dollars. Hughes Electronics also lobbied heavily for the easing of restrictions on satellite technology transmission. It was a major donor to the Democratic Party. When a Loral rocket was tested, it crashed, allegedly killing hundreds of Chinese. China went on to sell some of the missile technology to Pakistan and Iran.

48 "Justice May Probe Links Between China Policy, Campaign Cash," CNN, May 17, 1998, https://www.cnn.com/ALLPOLITICS/1998/05/17/satellite.review/; Coulter, *High Crimes and Misdemeanors*, 252; "Johnny Chung," https://en.wikipedia.org/wiki/Johnny_Chung. On Brown's suspicious death, see Jack Cashill, *Ron Brown's Body: How One Man's Death Saved the Clinton Presidency and Hillary's Future* (World net Daily, 2014).

49 Schaller, *The United States and China*, 193. See Peter Symonds, "Clinton Visit to the Indian Subcontinent Sets a New Strategic Orientation," *World Socialist Website*, March 23, 2000, https://www.wsws.org/en/articles/2000/03/ind-m23.html

50 Symonds, "Clinton Visit to the indian Subcontinent Sets a New Strategic Orientation."

51 Schaller, *The United States and China*, 199.

52 Cockburn and Silverstein, *Washington Babylon*, 181.

53 See Gabriel Kolko, *Confronting the Third World* (New York: Pantheon Books, 1990); Abrams, *Power and Primacy,* 164. Suharto is estimated to have stolen between $15 and $35 billion from the Indonesian treasury. In the Vietnam War, Suharto provided the CIA access to radars that helped in the development of electronic warfare countermeasures against Soviet S-75 air defense systems that had been lent to the North Vietnamese, enabling the U.S. to carry out bombing and napalm saturation of North Vietnamese cities.

54 "A Commercial Strategy for American Businesses and American Workers," Clinton administration and Asia," Clinton Presidential Records, White House Office, Office of Press Secretary, November 16, 1994, Box 10, William J. Clinton Presidential Library, Little Rock, Arkansas.

55 For more on Clinton's relationship with the Riady's, see Timperlake and Triplett II, *Year of the Rat*, ch. 2. James Riady was ultimately fined $86 million for breeching federal election laws resulting from his donations to Clinton.

56 L.J. Davis, "Riady or Not?" *Mother Jones*, January/February 1997, https://www.motherjones.com/politics/1997/01/riady-or-not/; Sharon Lafreniere, John Pomfret and Lena H. Sun, "The Riadys: Persistent Pursuit of Influence," *The Washington Post*, May 27, 1997, A1; Robert L. Jackson, "Clinton Donor Riady Pleads Guilty to Conrpiacy Charge," *Los Angeles Times*, January 12, 2021, Thorn, *Hillary (and Bill)*, 591. In a nod to the Waltons, Riady arranged the opening of a Walmart store at a mall he owned in Jakarta.

57 Jeff Gerth, "Clinton and Arkansas Have Long Ties to Indonesian Family," *The New York Times*, October 17, 1996; William Safire, "The Asian Connection," *The New York Times*, October 7, 1996, A2; Bill Clinton letter to Susato Tanukidjaja, March 18, 1986, Bill Clinton Gubernatorial Group, Natural and Cultural Resources, Economic Development Series, Bob Nash, box 7, Butler Center for Arkansas Studies, Bobby L. Roberts Library of Arkansas, Central Arkansas Library System, Little Rock, Arkansas. Entergy Corporation, another Riady owned corporation, got contracts to build power plants in Indonesia. According to Victor Thorn, Riady paid Webb Hubbell $100,000 as a bribe to prevent him from exposing Hillary Clinton after he was indicted for fraudulent activities carried out when he was at the Rose Law Firm. In exchange, the Clintons secured the appointment of one of Riady's associates, John Huang, as assistant Secretary of Commerce, giving him access to classified CIA briefings on China, which he supplied to Riady and allegedly to the Chinese government through Jackson Stephens. Thorn, *Hillary (and Bill), 594, 595.*

58 James Castle, a business consultant in Jakarta stated that "to James [Riady], the political contributions were like buying a diamond ring. He's buying it to impress people here." Peter Waldman, "East Meets West," *The Wall Street Journal*, October 16, 1996, A1.

59 Timperlake and Triplett II, *Year of the Rat*, 18, 23, 25, 29, 43, 50. Huang had worked for the Lippo Bank, directed all political contributions from the Riady's shell companies to the Clinton campaign and DNC, and was known as the "Riady's man in Washington." It is estimated that Huang saw between 370 and 550 CIA produced pieces of American intelligence. This would have included intelligence that could have benefitted their business empire and that they could have supplied to Suharto.

60 Davis, "Riady or Not?" Lafrenière, Pomfret and Sun, "The Riadys," A1; John Hayward, "90s Clinton Scandal Figure Barred From U.S. Still Giving Money to Clintons," *Breitbart News*, November 5, 2016, https://www.breitbart.com/politics/2016/11/05/90s-clinton-scandal-figure-barred-from-u-s-still-giving-money-to-clintons/tion

61 Lafrenière, Pomfret and Sun, "The Riadys," A1; Peter Waldman, "Clinton's Personal Ties With Indonesia's Suharto to Help So Far, But the Future Could Prove Trickier," *The Wall Street Journal*, January 16, 1998, A11.

62 David E. Sanger, "Real Politics: Why Suharto Is In and Castro Is Out," *The New York Times*, October 31, 1995.

63 Coulter, *High Crimes and Misdemeanors*, 246.

64 Helene Cooper, "Clinton is Criticized for Backtracking on Labor Rights Issues in Other Nations," *The Wall Street Journal*, October 18, 1996, A20; Tim Connor, "Still Waiting for Nike to Respect," *Global Policy Forum*, June 28, 2001, https://www.globalpolicy.org/component/content/article/225/32158.html.

65 Cockburn and Silverstein, *Washington Babylon*, 183.

66 Pratap Chatterjee, "Mercenary Armies and Mineral Wealth," *CovertAction Quarterly*, Fall 1997, 32, 33.

67 Cockburn and Silverstein, *Washington Babylon*, 184; "A Commercial Strategy for American Businesses and American Workers," Clinton administration and Asia," Clinton presidential Records, White House Office, Office of Press Secretary, November 16, 1994, Box 10, William J. Clinton Presidential Library, Little Rock, Arkansas.

68 Joseph Nevins, "The Making of Ground Zero in East Timor in 1999: An Analysis of International Complicity in Indonesia's Crimes," *Asian Survey*, 42, 4 (July-August 2002), 623–641.

69 https://www.justice.gov/criminal-icitap/icitap-historical-milestones. On Cold War era police programs and their impact in Indonesia, see Jeremy Kuzmarov, *Modernizing Repression: Police Training and Nation Building in the American Century* (Amherst, MA: University of Massachusetts Press, 2012), ch. 5.

70 American Embassy Jakarta to Secretary of State, Washington D.C., May 1998, Codel Smith Calls on Justice Minister Muladi," National Security Archive, George Washington University, https://nsarchive2.gwu.edu//dc.html?doc=4616957-Document-24-Telegram-002977-from-US-Embassy. Many of these prisoners were now old and infirm.

71 American Embassy Jakarta to Secretary of State, Washington D.C., August 1998, "Human Rights Commission Calls for Review of National Security Doctrine to Deal with Systematic Abuses," https://nsarchive2.gwu.edu//dc.html?doc=4616961-Document-28-Telegram-004329-from-US-Embassy; Gerard Colby, *DuPont Dynasty* (Seacaucus, New Jersey: Lyle Stuart Inc., 1984), 444.

72 "APEC Jakarta Arrival Statement—Jakarta Arrival Statement," November 13, 1994, Clinton digital library, White House Office, Antony Blinken Speeches, https://clinton.presidentiallibraries.us/items/show/9117

73 Krithika Varagur, "Declassified Files Provide Insight into Indonesia's Democratic Transition," *Voice of America News*, July 24, 2018, https://www.voanews.com/east-asia-pacific/declassified-files-provide-insight-indonesias-democratic-transition

74 Krithika Varagur, "Declassified Files Provide Insight into Indonesia's Democratic Transition," *Voice of America News*, July 24, 2018, https://www.voanews.com/east-asia-pacific/declassified-files-provide-insight-indonesias-democratic-transition; Bradley R. Simpson, "U.S. Promoted Close Ties to Indonesian Military as Suharto's Rule Came to an End in Spring 1998," July 24, 2018, National Security Archive, George Washington University, https://nsarchive.gwu.edu/briefing-book/indonesia/2018-07-24/us-promoted-close-ties-indonesian-military-suhartos-rule-came-end-spring-1998

75 American Embassy Jakarta to Secretary of State, Washington, D.C., "Who's Behind Recent Disappearance?" May 1998, National Security Archive, George Washington University, https://nsarchive2.gwu.edu//dc.html?doc=4616943-Document-10-Telegram-002579-from-US-Embassy

76 U.S. Embassy Jakarta to State Department, "Situation Report, May 13, 1998, https://nsarchive2.gwu.edu//dc.html?doc=4616945-Document-12-Telegram-002672-from-US-Embassy; U.S. Embassy Jakarta to State Department, "Connecting Recent Riots, Kidnappings and Student Killings," September 1998, https://nsarchive2.gwu.edu//dc.html?doc=4616963-Document-30-Telegram-005076-from-US-Embassy

77 U.S. Embassy Jakarta to State Department, "Indonesia Situation Report," May 17, 1998, https://nsarchive2.gwu.edu//dc.html?doc=4616950-Document-17-Telegram-002751-from-US-Embassy

78 Jay Solomon, "Old Boys Network: How Two Principals in Clinton Scandals Joined Up to Do Business in Jakarta," *The Wall Street Journal*, June 28, 2000.

79 Allan Nairn, "Indonesia's Killers: U.S. Support of Military Repression in Indonesia," *The Nation*, March 30, 1998.

80 Johnson, *Blowback*, 72–78; American Embassy Jakarta to Secretary of State, Washington D.C., May 1998, "Codel Smith Calls on Justice Minister Muladi," National Security Archive, George Washington University, https://nsarchive2.gwu.edu//dc.html?doc=4616957-Document-24-Telegram-002977-from-US-Embassy. Many Pentagon strategists saw the best possible outcome as the restoration of military rule, which thankfully did not come to pass.

81 Krithika Varagur, "Declassified Files Provide Insight into Indonesia's Democratic Transition," *Voice of America News*, July 24, 2018, https://www.voanews.com/east-asia-pacific/declassified-files-provide-insight-indonesias-democratic-transition; Wessel and Davis, "Markets Under Siege."

82 Ibid.; Naomi Klein, *The Shock Doctrine: The Rise of Disaster Capitalism* (New York: Alfred A. Knopf, 2007), 271. These companies were used to the "market" being rigged for them.

83 Steve Hanke, "20th Anniversary, Asian Financial Crisis: Clinton, the IMF and Wall Street Journal Toppled Suharto," CATO Institute, June 6, 2017, https://www.cato.org/publications/commentary/20th-anniversary-asian-financial-crisis-clinton-imf-wall-street-journal; Wessel and Davis, "Markets Under Siege." *The Wall Street Journal* supported the regime change operation by spreading stories that Hanke had proposed to set the exchange rate at an overvalued level so that Suharto and his cronies could loot Indonesia's central bank, making him look devious.

84 Peter Waldman, "East Meets West," *The Wall Street Journal*, October 16, 1996, A1.

85 Noam Chomsky, *A New Generation Draws the Line: Kosovo, East Timor and the Standards of the West* (London: Verso, 2000), 78. Jimmy Carter's UN ambassador Richard Holbrooke, who played a key role in carrying out U.S. policy in the late 1970s, continuously disregarded a UN General Assembly vote acknowledging East Timor's right to self-determination.

86 Chomsky, *A New Generation Draws the Line*, 54, 69; Nevins, "The Making of 'Ground Zero' in East Timor in 1999," 631; Alan Nairn, "U.S. Complicity in Timor," *The Nation*, September 27, 1999; John Taylor, *East Timor: The Price of Freedom* (London: Zed Books, 1999); Wayne Madsen, *Genocide and Covert Operations in Africa, 1993–1999* (New York: Edwin Mellen, 1999), 84; Ed Vuillamey and Antony Barnett, "U.S. Aided Butchers of Timor," *London Observer*, September 19, 1999.

Financial Times journalist Sander Thoenes was among those killed after he had exposed corruption at the company of General Prabowo.

87 Nevins, "The Making of 'Ground Zero' in East Timor in 1999," 638.

88 Noam Chomsky, *Rogue States: The Rule of Force in World Affairs* (Cambridge, MA: South End Press, 2000), 52, 54; *Bitter Flowers, Sweet Flowers: East Timor, Indonesia and the World Community,* ed. Richard Tanter, Mark Selden, Stephen R. Shalom (New York: Rowman & Littlefield, 2001).

89 Nevins, "The Making of 'Ground Zero' in East Timor in 1999," 640.

90 Ibid.: Chomsky, *A New Generation Draws the Line*, 52.

91 Nevins, "The Making of 'Ground Zero' in East Timor in 1999," 639, 640.

92 Chomsky, *A New Generation Draws the Line*, 49, 50; Andrew Bacevich, *American Empire: The Realities and Consequences of U.S. Diplomacy* (Cambridge, MA: Harvard University Press, 2002), 157. U.S. military assistance to the Indonesian army quietly resumed a few months after the crisis had passed "without fanfare to avoid criticism on Capitol Hill and among human rights groups."

93 Chomsky, *A New Generation Draws the Line*, 49, 50.

94 Andrew Pollack, "Marines Seek Peace with Okinawa in Rape Case," *The New York Times*, October 8, 1995; Johnson, *Blowback*, 34, 35, 42

95 Quoted in Johnson, *Blowback*, 35.

96 Marc Lacey, "Clinton Tries to Ease Anger at U.S. Troops in Okinawa," *The New York Times*, July 21, 2000.

97 Daniel Smith, "Clinton Visits Okinawa Marine Base," *Associated Press*, July 22, 2000.

98 Smith, "Clinton Visits Okinawa Marine Base."

99 John Broder, "Clinton Defends U.S. Military Presence in Asia," *Los Angeles Times*, April 18, 1996.

100 Lacey, "Clinton Tries to Ease Anger at U.S. Troops in Okinawa."; Broder, "Clinton Defends U.S. Military Presence in Asia."

101 Smith, "Clinton Visits Okinawa Marine Base"; Walter LaFeber, *The Clash: U.S.-Japanese Relations throughout History* (New York: W.W. Norton, 1998), 391.

102 Cole and Lubman, "Global Arms Market, Bombs Away." See also Klare, *Resource Wars*, 132; Stephanie Strom, "Japan Beginning to Flex Its Military Muscles," *The New York Times*, April 18, 1999.

103 See William G. Hyland, *Clinton's World: Remaking American Foreign Policy* (Westport, CT: Praeger, 1999), ch. 9.

104 Johnson, *Blowback*, 61.

105 Douglas Jehl, "Opening to Vietnam; Clinton Drops 19-Year Ban on U.S. Trade with Vietnam; Cites Hanoi's Help on M.I.A.s," *The New York Times,* February 4, 1994.

106 Ibid.

107 LaFeber, *The Clash,* 390.

108 Michel Chossudovsky, *The Globalization of Poverty: Impacts of IMF and World Bank Reforms* (London: Zed Books, 1997), 147.

109 John Pilger, "Vietnam: The Final Battle," *CovertAction Quarterly*, Spring 1998, 60; Noam Chomsky, *For Reasons of State* (New York: Pantheon Books, 1973).

110 Chossudovsky, *The Globalization of Poverty*, 147.

111 Edwin A. Martini, *Invisible Enemies: The American War on Vietnam 1975–2000* (Amherst, MA: University of Massachusetts Press, 2007); H. Bruce Franklin, *MIA, or Mythmaking in America* (New Jersey: Rutgers University Press, 1993); Pilger, "Vietnam: The Final Battle."

112 Robert J. McMahon, "Rationalizing Defeat: The Vietnam War in American Presidential Discourse, 1975–1995," *Rhetoric and Public Affairs*, 2, 4 (1999), 529–549.

113 McMahon, "Rationalizing Defeat," 544. In his speech marking the normalization of relations, Clinton said that "whatever we may think about the political decisions of the Vietnam era, the brave Americans who fought and died there had noble motives. They fought for the freedom and independence of the Vietnamese people." President Bill Clinton, "Remarks by the President in Announcing Normalization of Diplomatic Relations with Vietnam," July 11, 1995, Clinton Presidential Records, press office, box 7, William J. Clinton Presidential Library, Little Rock, Arkansas.

114 See Kuzmarov, *Modernizing Repression,* ch. 7.

115 "Full Text of U.S. President Bill Clinton's Speech on Vietnam," http://patrick.guenin2.free.fr/cantho/vnnews/bclint14.htm; Martini, *Invisible Enemies*. Clinton referred to America's intervention in a purported Vietnamese civil war. This ignores the facts about how the war started and that it was a war of national liberation against a U.S.-imposed puppet regime. When meeting with the Secretary General of the communist party, Clinton denied that the U.S. was an imperialist power and was anything like France. Bernard Von Bothmer, *Framing the Sixties: The Use and Abuse of a Decade from Ronald Reagan to George W. Bush* (Amherst: University of Massachusetts Press, 2010), 160.

116 See John Marciano, *Vietnam: Crime or Commemoration?* (New York: Monthly Review Press, 2016); Nick Turse, *"Kill Anything That Moves: The Real American War in Vietnam* (New York: Metropolitan Books, 2013).

117 Martini, *Invisible Enemies*, 196.

118 Martini, *Invisible Enemies*, 235, 236; "Full Text of U.S. President Bill Clinton's Speech on Vietnam," http://patrick.guenin2.free.fr/cantho/vnnews/bclint14.htm

119 David Roberts, "U.S. Intervention in Cambodia: From Bombs to Ballots," *CovertAction Quarterly*, Fall 1997. Hun Sen had fought as a Khmer Rouge guerrilla against the U.S. imposed puppet regime of Lon Nol in the early 1970s.

120 Roberts, "U.S. Intervention in Cambodia."

121 Roberts, "U.S. Intervention in Cambodia."

122 Tina Rosenberg, "Hun Sen Stages an Election," *The New York Times*, August 30, 1998.

123 Roberts, "U.S. Intervention in Cambodia." One of the IRI's consorts in Cambodia was Raul Garcia Prieto, former vice president of El Salvador and a protégé of death squad leader Roberto D'Aubuisson.

124 Rosenberg, "Hun Sen Stages an Election." The election was not without violence and Sen's forces were accused of killing 41 Rannaridh loyalists. Rosenberg suggests that the UN only endorsed the election to validate the $2 billion it had spent trying to advance democracy in Cambodia. See also: "Cambodia 1998: Fair Elections not Possible," *Human Rights Watch*, June 19, 1998, https://www.hrw.org/news/1998/06/19/cambodia-fair-elections-not-possible

125 Rosenberg, "Hun Sen Stages an Election."

126 See "30 years of Hun Sen: Violence, Repression and Corruption in Cambodia," *Human Rights Watch*, January 12, 2015, https://www.hrw.org/report/2015/01/12/30-years-hun-sen/violence-repression-and-corruption-cambodia#

127 In 2007, the Bush administration hypocritically reversed its stance on foreign aid following the discovery of massive extractable resources in the country,

including gold, bauxite and other minerals, plus potentially large reserves of oil and gas. In 1999, Sen signed a bilateral investment treaty to boost exports in the apparel industry, prompting the relocation of many foreign factories which provided miserably low wages to the locals, many of whom decided to work instead as prostitutes. See Ken Silverstein, *The Secret World of Oil* (London: Verso, 2014), ch. 4.

128 Branko Marcetic, "How Washington Hacked Mongolia's Democracy," *Jacobin,* November 29, 2017, https://www.jacobinmag.com/2017/11/mongolia-elections-mccain-international-republican-institute; Richard Bartholomew, *The Deep State in the Heart of Texas* (Say Something Real Press, 2018), 333.

129 Marcetic, "How Washington Hacked Mongolia's Democracy."

130 Marcetic, "How Washington Hacked Mongolia's Democracy."

131 Marcetic, "How Washington Hacked Mongolia's Democracy." In 2000, the MPRP came back to power in a landslide, and has continued to dominate the country's politics ever since.

132 See William Engdahl, *Target China: How Washington and Wall Street Plan to Cage the Asian Dragon* (Progressive Press, 2014). As Engdahl points out, Myanmar was an integral part of what China terms its "string of pearls," its strategic design of establishing military bases in Myanmar, Thailand and Cambodia in order to counter U.S. control over the Strait of Malacca chokepoint. Myanmar had oil and gas, and the junta leaders were opposed to U.S. militarization of the region, including an air base on Bandeh Aceh in Indonesia.

133 "Chinese Anger at National Endowment for Democracy," Chennai Center for China Studies, July 20, 2009, https://www.c3sindia.org/geopolitics-strategy/chinese-anger-against-national-endowment-for-democracy/

134 See Alfred W. McCoy, *The Politics of Heroin: CIA Complicity in the Global Drugs Trade* (New York: Lawrence Hill Books, 2003).

135 Engdahl, *Target China*; Nick Beake, "Myanmar Rohingya: Aung San Suu Kyi Cuts a Haunted Figure in Court," *BBC,* December 14, 2019, https://www.bbc.com/news/world-asia-50770961

136 See Charles K. Armstrong, *Tyranny of the Weak: North Korea and the World, 1950–1992* (Ithaca: Cornell University Press, 2013).

137 A.B. Abrams, *Immovable Object: North Korea's 70 Years at War with American Power* (Atlanta: Clarity Press Inc., 2020), 371, 372.

138 Zbigniew Brzezinski, *The Grand Chessboard: American Primacy and Its Geostrategic Imperatives* (New York: Perseus Publishing, 1997), 47, 48.

139 Bruce Cumings, *North Korea: Another Country* (New York: The New Press, 2004), 65. In yet more war games in March, the U.S. deployed B1-B bombers and B-52s from Guam as well as naval vessels carrying cruise missiles targeting North Korea.

140 Elizabeth Furse, Letter to President Clinton, April 8, 1994, Clinton Digital Libraries, Korea, January-June 1994, https://clinton.presidentiallibraries.us/items/show/72535. Furse noted that "according to recent press reports, South Koreans do not seem to be nearly so concerned about North Korea's intentions as the U.S. Perhaps they are aware that North and South Koreans are the same people and have a greater motivation to normalize relations than go to war with North Korea." Clinton responded to Furse's letter by stating: "we have coordinated with South Korea on a proposal that, if accepted by the North, would permit resumption of U.S.-DPRK dialogue. At the same time, we are continuing prudent upgrades to the defensive capabilities of our military forces in the south."

141 Abrams, *Immovable Object*, 359.

142 Leon V. Sigal, *Disarming Strangers: Nuclear Diplomacy with North Korea* (New Jersey: Princeton University Press, 1997); Clinton, *My Life*, 591.

143 "Engaging North Korea II: Evidence from the Clinton Administration," ed. Robert A. Wampler, December 8, 2017, https://nsarchive.gwu.edu/briefing-book/korea/2017-12-08/engaging-north-korea-ii-evidence-clinton-administration; "Washington Was on the Brink of War with North Korea Five Years Ago: Pentagon Had Predicted Up to 1 Million Deaths," *CNN*, October 4, 1999.

144 Cumings, *North Korea*, 72.

145 "Engaging North Korea II: Evidence from the Clinton Administration," ed. Robert A. Wampler, December 8, 2017, https://nsarchive.gwu.edu/briefing-book/korea/2017-12-08/engaging-north-korea-ii-evidence-clinton-administration

146 "Washington Was on the Brink of War with North Korea Five Years Ago: Pentagon Had Predicted Up to 1 Million Deaths," *CNN*, October 4, 1999.

147 Abrams, *Immovable Object*, 365, 373, 374.

148 Hans M. Kristensen and Robert S. Norris, "A History of U.S. Nuclear Weapons in South Korea," *Bulletin of the Atomic Scientists,* October 2t6, 2017, https://www.tandfonline.com/doi/pdf/10.1080/00963402.2017.1388656

149 See Jeremy Kuzmarov, "Barbarism Unleashed," http://peacehistory-usfp.org/korean-war/; "Remarks by President Clinton and the President of South Korea at the Dedication of the Korean War Veterans Memorial," July 27, 1995, Clinton Presidential Records, President's Office, box 11, William J. Clinton Presidential Library, Little Rock, Arkansas. Towards the end of the Korean War, General Douglas MacArthur developed a plan to drop between 30 to 50 tactical atomic bombs on air bases and other depots strung across the neck of Manchuria from just across the Yalu at Antung (northwest tip of Korea) to the neighborhood of Hunchun (northeast tip of Korea near the border of the USSR).

150 Christina Pazzanese, "Clinton reflects on foreign policy triumphs and challenges," *The Harvard Gazette*, April 8, 2021, https://news.harvard.edu/gazette/story/2021/04/clinton-reflects-on-foreign-policy-triumphs-and-challenges/

151 Jonathan G. Clarke, "A Foreign Policy Report Card on the Clinton-Gore Administration," *CATO Institute*, Policy Analysis, October 3, 2000.

152 Cumings, *North Korea*, 82, 83.

153 See *The Asian Financial Crisis and the Architecture of Global Finance*, ed. Gregory W. Noble and John Ravenhill (New York: Cambridge University Press, 2000); Abrams, *Power and Primacy*, 380. Joseph Stiglitz, a Nobel laureate in economics, determined that rapid market liberalization, primarily the sudden deregulation of capital flows by lifting capital controls, was the primary cause of East Asia's economic crisis—the exact policies the U.S. Treasury and IMF strongly advocated for and pressed Southeast Asian countries to adopt, which left them vulnerable to speculative attacks.

154 Quoted in Johnson, *Blowback*, 206.

155 Abrams, *Power and Primacy*, 382.

156 Abrams, *Power and Primacy*, 382.

157 Abrams, *Power and Primacy*, 388, 389. In a March 1999 visit to Thailand, U.S. Secretary of State Madeleine Albright shamefully expressed "strong support" for the severe austerity policies imposed by IMF, while at the same time scolding the Thai people for turning to prostitution and "dead end drugs." She emphasized how it was "essential that girls not be exploited and abused and exposed to AIDS. It's very

important to fight back," while promoting the very same policies that forced them into such vices. Albright also lobbied hard for multi-billion dollar sales of fighter jets to the crisis-hit country.

158 David Wessel and Bob Davis, "Markets Under Siege – Limits of Power: How Global Crisis Grew Despite Efforts of Crack U.S. Team," *The Wall Street Journal*, September 24, 1998, 1.

159 Wessel and Davis, "Markets Under Siege."

160 Wessel and Davis, "Markets Under Siege."

161 Wessel and Davis, "Markets Under Siege."

162 Wessel and Davis, "Markets Under Siege."

163 Wessel and Davis, "Markets Under Siege."

164 Klein, *The Shock Doctrine*, 274; Anita Raghavan, "Wall Street is Scavenging in Asia-Pacific," *The Wall Street Journal*, February 10, 1998, CI.

165 Klein, *The Shock Doctrine*, 274, 275, 276; Abrams, *Power and Primacy*, 390, 391. Economists Robert Wade and Frank Veneroso predicted that the IMF program would "precipitate the biggest peacetime transfer of assets from domestic to foreign owners in the past fifty years anywhere in the world." Former U.S. Undersecretary of Commerce Jeffrey Garten had predicted that when the IMF was finished with Asia "there is going to be a significantly different Asia, and it will be an Asia in which American firms have achieved much deeper penetration and much greater access."

CHAPTER 7

Clinton's Excessive and Two-Faced War on Drugs

In January 1985, Bill Clinton's kid brother, Roger, was convicted on six counts of drug dealing and conspiracy. Bill helped him secure a light two-year sentence while publicly insisting that he never knew that Roger had tried drugs. But Roger's drug involvement was impossible to miss as he sang in a rock'n roll band entitled "Dealer's Choice." Roger was also caught on a police videotape saying he needed to get some cocaine for Bill, who "had a nose like a vacuum cleaner." The manager of Roger's apartment complex, Jane Parks, said she had seen and overheard Bill and Roger taking drugs together.[1]

Being the political animal that he was, Bill and his handlers sensed an opportunity to spin Roger's arrest in a positive way. During the trial, Bill regularly showed up in court. After Roger's conviction, Bill told the public that drugs were a "curse which has reached epidemic proportions and has plagued the lives of millions of families including many in our state. . . ." and that he hoped "the publicity" would "discourage other young people from involvement with drugs."[2] Clinton had previously claimed that he wanted his brother's case to be "handled exactly as any other similar case would be."[3] However, Travis Bunn, a Hot Springs undercover policeman, who had tape-recorded evidence of Roger selling cocaine, was never called to testify before the Grand Jury despite his familiarity with the case. A state police investigator loyal to Clinton took it over.[4]

The episode with Roger was significant because it reflected the double standards and hypocrisy of Bill Clinton's War on Drugs, which carried over into his presidency. According to Robert "Tosh" Plumlee, a former CIA pilot, when the Clinton administration was briefed in detail by undercover operatives who had been part of a covert mission to infiltrate and gather intelligence on drug cartels in South America, the administration shut the operation down to protect the corrupt officials, putting the lives of the undercover operatives in danger.[5] The people of the region were left to wonder why it took so long for cartel leaders like Pablo Escobar and the Ochoa brothers who terrorized their country to be taken down.

Initially, Clinton's election had heralded hope for a change in U.S. drug policy because he was the first president to have been a product of the 1960s' counterculture. However, Clinton was guided by the fear of being labeled soft on crime, which had ruined fellow Democrat Michael Dukakis in the 1988 election. Branding young people in the 1960s as naïve for believing drugs weren't dangerous, Clinton told school children in 1996 that drugs had nearly "destroyed our generation" and "the United States military [when he was younger]."[6] The latter was a reference to the myth of the addicted army, which exaggerated the negative impact of drugs on soldiers during the Vietnam War.[7]

Clinton's liberal and hip personae shielded him from public rebuke as he escalated the War on Drugs to new heights. In 1995 alone, the Clinton administration spent $13.2 billion on antidrug programs including $1.6 billion on supply side interdiction.[8] Sociologist Timothy Black noted that "Clinton made Reagan's law enforcement budget look like the minor leagues, increasing annual spending to twenty times the amount the War on Drugs guru himself had spent."[9] The consequence could be felt not only in the overcrowded jails but also in the displacement of peasants in Latin America subjected to chemical sprays. The U.S. government under President Clinton meanwhile continued to protect high-level drug traffickers who served as political assets, as Governor Clinton had done in Arkansas. It further enhanced the growth of the global drug trade through policies which contributed to widening social inequality and made smuggling easier by opening up the border with Mexico.

"A Nose Like a Vacuum Cleaner": Slick Willie's Drug Habit

The 1992 and 1996 elections were interesting manifestations of the cultural wars in America, pitting the supposed liberal hippie Clinton against establishment figures representing America's Greatest Generation (George H.W. Bush and Robert Dole). Clinton played the part effectively by admitting to marijuana use, albeit with the absurd caveat that he had never inhaled. Like he had done in Arkansas, he also tried to win over conservative Middle-Americans by evoking his feelings of empathy for families who had suffered from drug addiction, stating in a televised presidential debate with Dole that his family had "suffered from drug abuse. I know what it's like to see somebody you love nearly lose their lives. And I hate drugs, Senator."[10]

These comments were disingenuous in lieu of what is known about Clinton and drugs. Despite claiming he never used them in Arkansas, various associates have stated publicly that Clinton used drugs routinely for pleasure as an adult in Arkansas.[11] A Democratic State Representative, Jack McCoy, said he remembered once entering the Governor's conference room and it reeked of marijuana.[12] Clinton's lover Gennifer Flowers, with whom he had carried on a twelve-year affair, said that he would carry marijuana joints around with him and sometimes smoke them in her presence. Flowers also said he told her about a party where he got "so fucked up on cocaine. He said it made his scalp itch and he felt conspicuous because he was talking with people who were not aware drugs were at the party and all he wanted to do was scratch his head."[13]

Sally Perdue, a Clinton girlfriend from the mid-1980s, similarly told a journalist that Clinton had "all of the [cocaine snorting] equipment laid out, like a real pro." Another Arkansas party-girl, Sharline Wilson, said that she'd serve Clinton drinks at Le Club Bistro and lines of cocaine on a "glass mirror. One night," she said, "Clinton got so stoned [that] he slid into a trash can."[14] State trooper L.D. Brown also saw Governor Clinton do cocaine while on vacation with his family in Boca Raton, Florida.[15] In 1983–1984, Roger Clinton, on a police surveillance film, was quoted as saying: "[G]ot to get some [cocaine] for my brother. He's got a nose like a vacuum cleaner."[16]

Jane Parks was the manager of an upscale Little Rock apartment complex where Clinton's half-brother, Roger, lived. Once, when she opened Roger's door after she had to carry Roger back to his apartment after finding him drugged out by the pool, Mrs. Parks said that she saw Bill Clinton sitting on the couch, staring straight ahead and "looking stoned," as "lines of cocaine" sat next to him on the table. On other occasions, Mrs. Parks, whose office was adjacent to Roger's room and could hear what was going on there, heard Clinton enthuse over the high-quality cocaine he was using along with sounds of sex coming from the sex parties he and Roger hosted with underage girls.[17]

According to Sam Houston, a respected Little Rock doctor, Bill Clinton was admitted to the University of Arkansas Medical Center for emergency treatment for cocaine abuse and overdose following his defeat in the 1980 Gubernatorial election and had to be cared for at the hospital on one or possibly two occasions. "When Mrs. Clinton arrived, she told both of the resident physicians on duty that night that they would never again practice medicine in the U.S. if word leaked out about Clinton's drug problem," journalist Christopher Ruddy said. Reportedly, Hillary pinned one of the doctors up against the wall, both hands pressed against his shoulders, as she gave him a dire warning.

Ruddy's1999 article "Did Bill Clinton Overdose on Cocaine?" claimed that journalist R. Emmet Tyrrell found one of the nurses who was on the job when cocaine-inebriated Bill Clinton was brought in to the hospital, who then would not say anymore out of fear of losing her job. A Dr. Suen worked at the medical center that took care of Clinton for a sinus problem, which is believed to be related to his cocaine use.[18]

In late 1987 or early 1988, when Larry Nichols, then-director of the Arkansas Development Finance Authority (ADFA), was looking for Bill, he was told by Clinton's chief of staff Betsey Wright that Bill had been sent off to a drug rehabilitation clinic to get off cocaine. Nichols believed that this was probably the Betty Ford clinic in Minnesota. Wright told Nichols that Clinton had been sent to drug rehab more than once.[19]

Clinton's Phony War on Drugs in Arkansas

While Governor Clinton was himself regularly using cocaine and other drugs, his administration in Arkansas passed tough drug control legislation that resulted in a 100 percent increase in Arkansas' incarceration rate. Penalties for drug trafficking offenses were strengthened, and Clinton enacted a program with the Arkansas state police in which random stops were made of suspicious vehicles on state highways in an effort to seize drugs.

Clinton further requested and received permission to use the Arkansas National Guard in an effort to wipe out drug use in Arkansas, with Arkansas National Guard helicopters flying thousands of hours of missions to spot marijuana crops and destroy them.[20] During his 1992 presidential campaign, Cliinton bragged that this campaign resulted in the destruction of one million marijuana plants between 1982 and 1991 that were valued at $1 billion.[21]

On the other hand, the IRS reported that Arkansas led the nation in money laundering during Clinton's governorship and "offered an enticing climate for traffickers seeking to get their money into the legitimate economy."[22] CIA pilot Basil "Bo" Abbott described how Arkansas state police protected drug loads by blocking off roads leading to small airstrips when drug flights arrived.[23] Mena was a particular hub for gun and drug running operations to the Nicaraguan Contras, as chapter 2 details. Political operative Roger Stone and Robert Morrow described Arkansas under Clinton's leadership as a "diseased narco-state run by a cocaine addled governor."[24] Journalist Ambrose Evans-Pritchard referred to it as a "major point for the transshipment of drugs" and "a sort of mini-Columbia within the borders of the United States. . . . An epidemic of cocaine, contaminat[ed] the political establishment from top to bottom," with parties [attended by Clinton] "at which cocaine [was] served like hors d'oeuvres and sex was rampant."[25]

The drug parties were at the home of Dan Lasater, Clinton's closest and most important political contributor, who lent him his plane for campaign trips and was a key figure in the Mena drug trafficking operation. Lasater had been investigated for drug trafficking on planes coming in and out of the

Angel Fire Resort in New Mexico, which had a 8,900 foot runway. Former Angel Fire resort employees claimed that the resort was the focal point for "a large controlled substance smuggling operation and large-scale money laundering activity."[26] In 1977, Lasater's private jet turned up in Las Vegas with Jimmy Chagra, a prominent drug trafficker, onboard.[27] Lasater's chauffer, Lee Curtis "Chuck" Berry, was later given a fifty month sentence for carrying cocaine for Lasater.[28]

A 1988 FBI report considered Lasater a major player in the cocaine trafficking network of the Dixie mafia as early as the mid-1970s, with the DEA opening a file on him in 1983. Clinton claimed that he did not know about investigations into Lasater for drug trafficking until 1986—after Lasater & Co. received $750,000 commission from the sale of $30.7 million in bonds from a new state police radio system—but Republican Governor Frank White said that Clinton had to have known as early as 1983.[29]

In the early 1980s, Lasater had bought a horse farm, which smugglers would use to refuel planes for drug mules to Colombia. Arkansas investigator Russell Welch said that Barry Seal used the ranch frequently. Land owned by Lasater's company Oxley Timber in Pine Bluff, was also the site of more drug drops and possible covert training operations for the Contra war. Residents stated that they would "see people in camouflaged uniforms and hear and see planes flying over low at night with their lights off, almost exactly the things going on at Mena."[30]

Lasater and Bill used to party back at Lasater's mansion, where there would be ashtrays filled with cocaine and girls as young as high-school age. One of the girls whom Dan Lasater got hooked on cocaine was sixteen-year old Patty-Anne Smith, who was also sold into prostitution. She told Pritchard that Clinton was "never acting like a governor when I saw him." He was seen using cocaine on two or three occasions including at Lasater's residence. "He was doing a line. It was just there on the table."[31]

Former Arkansas state trooper J.N. "Doc" DeLaughter told a reporter that a 1986 narcotics investigation of Lasater was shut down for political reasons. DeLaughter stated that he and another state police investigator who worked on the case were excluded when then U.S. Attorney General George Proctor and federal agents interviewed Lasater and others, including Roger Clinton. DeLaughter was given the unusual order to make only oral reports on his findings in the Lasater case, and only to Colonel Tommy Goodwin, the head of the Arkansas police, who was close with Clinton. Lt. Larry Gleghorn, DeLaughter's supervisor, corroborated part of DeLaughter's account, stating that "anything anyone ever did in this investigation went to Little Rock, and none of it ever came back to us."[32]

In another irregularity, the officer assigned to investigate Lasater's finances, Mike Mahone, had previously conducted business with Lasater and was under investigation himself by both the FBI and the state police internal affairs unit for alleged obstruction of justice. Not coincidentally, Lasater's finances were barely actually investigated, and he got off with a short prison sentence in a country club type jail (he served six months of a two and a half year sentence) and a fine of $200,000, which amounted to six cents for every dollar that he had robbed from Arkansas taxpayers. In 1990, Lasater was pardoned by Clinton. His secretary and fixer, Patty Thomasson—who had accompanied Lasater on flights to Latin America—became executive director of the Arkansas Democratic Party, and in 1993 was named as special assistant to the president and director of the Office of the Administration in the White House where, incredibly, she was responsible for drug testing![33]

Among other Arkansas high rollers, the DEA had a file on Jackson Stephens, who was referred to as a "cocaine and alcohol abuser." According to former CIA operative Robert Johnson (AKA William Barr), Stephens placed indirect pressure on U.S. Attorney General Edwin Meese to appoint as U.S. Attorney for the western district of Arkansas, J. Michael Fitzhugh, who then effectively stonewalled investigation into the drug trafficking activities taking place in and around Mena.[34] A state police investigation uncovered that Arkansas "Chicken King," Don Tyson, who had provided secret envelopes filled with cash to Clinton, put "cocaine in the rectums of chickens transported on their trucks," and that his planes were used to ferry drugs between Florida and Arkansas. The investigation, however, was shut down by upper echelons in the Arkansas state police.[35]

The DEA office in Oklahoma City in December 1982 cited confidential information that Tyson smuggled cocaine from Colombia inside racehorses to Hot Springs, Arkansas [Clinton's hometown and a notorious mafia hub], and cited the investigative tracking number for Don Tyson, who was given the nickname "chicken man." A second document from DEA offices in Tucson from July 1984 stated that "cooperating individuals had information concerning heroin, cocaine and marijuana trafficking in the state of Arkansas, Texas and Missouri by the Tyson organization," and noted that Tyson used as a stash location "The Barn," which was located between Springdale and Fayetteville, Arkansas and was frequented by Lasater, Roger Clinton, Barry Seal and Bill.[36]

When the TV series *Unsolved Mysteries* investigated the deaths of Kevin Ives and Don Henry—two teens allegedly killed after they witnessed illicit cocaine drops in Mena—host Robert Stack interviewed Saline County prosecutor Richard Garrett, who stated that "Saline County and the Central Arkansas area are overrun at this time with drug trafficking . . . and it's drug trafficking at a high level that extends to other states and other counties."[37] These comments epitomize the deep-rooted corruption in Arkansas during Clinton's governorship, which set the precedent for his presidency. Arkansas drug money is even suspected of helping to finance Clinton's political campaigns with money that had been laundered through the ADFA, assorted area banks, and Lasater's bond companies.

"Policies Causing Health and Human Services Disasters"

At a campaign stop in New Hampshire during the 2016 presidential campaign, Black Lives Matter activist Daunasia Yancey confronted Hillary Clinton about her shared culpability in America's destructive War on Drugs, stating: "You and your family have been personally and politically responsible for policies that have caused health and human services disasters in impoverished communities of color through the domestic and international War on Drugs that you championed [as First Lady and then subsequently as Senator and Secretary of State]."[38]

Bill Clinton had all but acknowledged that Ms. Yancey was correct fourteen years earlier when he told an interviewer that his greatest failing as president towards the black community was

> in the criminal justice area. There is a grossly disproportionate percentage of African-Americans behind bars, particularly young black men. . . . A lot of them are there for nonviolent offenses, many of them related to drugs, and if they stay a long time its going to have an enormous impact on our social fabric.[39]

Law Professor Michelle Alexander called this the "New Jim Crow"—comparable to the era of legalized segregation that had followed the breakdown of Reconstruction after the Civil War. Alexander pointed out that Clinton's War on Drugs resulted in the largest increases in federal and state prison inmates in American history, a disproportionate number of whom were black.[40] In a testament to the problem of racial profiling, a March 2000 government report found that black women were 900 percent more likely to be x-rayed for drugs by customs agents [as potential smugglers] than white women—even though black women were less than half as likely to be caught with contraband.[41]

Not content with just giving minor drug offenders long prison sentences, the Clinton administration passed laws denying federal financial aid to students with drug convictions, introduced guidelines that required public housing authorities to evict anyone who committed a drug crime, and signed legislation imposing a lifetime ban on welfare and food stamps for anyone convicted of a felony drug offense—an exceptionally harsh measure that disproportionately impacted black Americans.[42] In a vivid reminder of the pay-to-play system in the U.S., Clinton meanwhile granted a pardon to Carlos Vignali, who was sentenced to fifteen years for shipping half a ton of cocaine to Minnesota, after his father gave $160,000 to Democrats in the 2000 cycle and paid $200,000 to Hugh Rodham, Hillary's brother.[43]

During the 1992 presidential campaign, Clinton had criticized George H.W. Bush for "locking up addicts instead of treating them or teaching them to resist using them [drugs] in the first place," and promised to "invert the ratio" under which two-thirds of the drug budget went for interdiction and law enforcement and only one-third for education and treatment. Michael Kramer reported in *Time* magazine on the eve of Clinton's 1996 reelection, however, that the ratio had remained the same, and that nothing had changed.[44] The government continued to lock people up under Clinton's presidency for drug related offenses at a rate of about 700,000 per year.[45] According to *Rolling Stone Magazine*, marijuana-related arrests rose 43 percent under Clinton to 600,000 in 1995, and then 700,000 in 1999, double the total from the early 1990s.[46] The total prison population rose by 673,000 people—or by 235,000 more than it had under President Ronald Reagan, according to a study by the Justice Policy Institute.[47]

Much of this increase was attributable to the Violent Crime Control and Law Enforcement Act, which Clinton had signed in September 1994. What Clinton termed the "toughest and smartest crime bill in American history" provided for 100,000 new police officers and $9.7 billion in funding for prisons as well as a grant program that encouraged police officers to engage in more drug-related arrests. The bill further made large-scale drug traffickers eligible for the death penalty while extending money for states that adopted "truth in sentencing" laws requiring inmates to serve out at least 85 percent of their prison sentences without an early release.[48] The 100–1 sentencing disparity between crack and powder cocaine was preserved against the recommendation of a U.S. Sentencing Commission report.[49] Clinton said that "tough penalties for crack trafficking are required because of the effect on individuals and families, related gang activity, turf battles and other violence."[50]

Clinton tried to further burnish his antidrug credentials by expanding the scope of drug testing in federal and state prisons, forcing parolees to take drug tests, and by proposing that teenagers had to take a drug test before getting their driver's license—an idea the legal director of the American Civil Liberties Union called "drug mania gone crazy."[51] In 1996, more than 8,000

U.S. military personnel took part in 754 counter-drug missions on U.S. soil, resulting in over 1,894 arrests. This was a brazen violation of the 1878 Posse Comitatus Act, which prohibits military involvement in domestic searches and seizures.[52]

Playing War

Clinton's first drug czar, former New York Police Commissioner Lee Brown, had been praised by drug-policy reformers for saying that the nation's drug policy should concentrate on hard-core users and addicts, not casual users, and should expand treatment opportunities. Clinton also in 1993 slashed funding for drug interdiction programs in the Andes from $387 to $174 million after a classified review found them to be ineffective. But Clinton's tune quickly changed after the 1994 mid-term elections when he realized that more progressive policies had made him vulnerable to Republican attacks that he was soft on crime.[53] At that time, the Clinton administration rejected a RAND Corporation Study which recommended that $3 billion in drug funds should be switched from law enforcement to drug treatment.[54]

Surgeon General Dr. Joycelyn Elders incurred disfavor from the White House for suggesting that she was open to the idea of legalizing or decriminalizing drug possession; the ostensible final straw that prompted her dismissal was that she talked about promoting masturbation in sex ed classes." Clinton fired her. He then appointed as his drug czar four-star General Barry McCaffrey, former commander in-chief of the U.S. Southern Command, who oversaw a budgetary increase from $266.1 million to $2.4 billion by 2000 and the transfer of an estimated $727 million in military hardware to law enforcement agencies, including bullet-proof helmets, aircraft, grenade launchers and M-16 rifles. Ridiculing claims of marijuana's benefit as "Cheech 'n' Chong medicine," McCaffrey also established a "troops to cops" program, which subsidized police departments for hiring returning veterans, many of whom had "little patience for carrying out the painstaking detective work necessary to make a case," according to sociologist Peter Kraska, but "just like to play war; they get a rush out of search and destroy missions."[55]

In 1993, the Defense Department's Counterdrug Technology Development Program teamed with the army research laboratory and Defense Advanced Research Projects Agency (DARPA) to organize a face recognition technology program (FERET) that tested and led to advances in facial recognition technologies (biometrics) used for identifying drug traffickers and terrorists.[56] The National Institute of Justice also awarded grants to companies like Tracer Detection of Syosset New York, which developed anti-counterfeiting fibers that could be embedded in documents and chemical taggants used to mark vehicles and contraband and were detectable by chemical sensors.[57]

Stun guns that deployed 50,000 volts of electric shock, police choppers equipped with night-vision devices and computer data-basing and algorithms designed to predict outbreaks of violence were additional tools utilized by police forces in the 1990s as record numbers filled America's prisons thanks to the new tough-on-crime bills.[58] After admitting to his own drug use on MTV, a purportedly penitent Clinton championed a $1 billion media antidrug initiative modeled after Ronald Reagan's "Just Say No" campaign that enlisted Hollywood movie stars and encouraged Hollywood producers to adopt antidrug themes in their films.[59] Clinton's Housing and Urban Development Department adopted a "One Strike and You're Out" policy—upping his infamous "Three Strikes" policy that preceded it, and expelling whole families from public housing on the mere suspicion that one family member was using drugs.[60] This kind of policy bore unfortunate resemblance to the kind carried out in totalitarian states, where neighbors inform on one another, and society is guided by suspicion and fear.

How the Global Drug War Was Compromised

Under McCaffrey's direction, the Clinton administration promoted a supply-side strategy that was designed to halt the flow of drugs entering the U.S. The operations Green Clover and Laser Strike deployed hundreds of U.S. military troops to work with Latin American militaries to monitor and shoot down drug flights. McCaffrey claimed that "the multinational, cooperative effort yielded stunning tactical results."[61]

Yet it was acknowledged that these and other drug war operations had "no impact on the availability and price of cocaine in the United States."[62] Between 1998 and 1999, cocaine imports jumped almost 15 percent. In 1998, more Americans died from drug overdoses, more Americans went to hospital emergency rooms for drug related problems than ever before, and more high school students (90 percent) reported that marijuana was "fairly easy" or "very easy" to get than ever before.[63]

One reason for high supply rates was that high-level traffickers who were assets of the U.S. government continued to enjoy immunity from prosecution.[64] Clinton's experience covering up the Mena scandal in Arkansas made him especially well prepared to cover up high level corruption as president. In Russia, the Clinton administration helped empower what the IMF's chief economist Michael Mussa referred to as a "bunch of criminals" who caused a huge growth in the drug trade, which totalled between $4 and $7 billion per year.[65] Clinton provided extensive military aid and also granted a White House visit to Albanian President Sali Berisha (1992–1997), whom *Jane's intelligence Review,* said "tolerated and even directly profited from the drug trafficking in order to finance secessionist political parties," notably the Kosovo Liberation Army (KLA), which relied heavily on funds from the narcotics trade to fund its operations against Yugoslav forces.[66] KLA leader Hashim Thaçi was later identified in a UN report as having exerted violent control over the regional heroin trade and held connections to a mafia cartel which moved drugs from Turkey to Western Europe through the "Balkans Route."[67]

In Afghanistan, the CIA provided $200,000 per month to Northern Alliance warlord Ahmed Shah Massoud, whose men smuggled large amounts of opium and heroin into Europe, according to the CIA's Counter-Narcotics Center.[68] Clinton further failed to impose sanctions on oil-rich Nigeria, which had become a hub for heroin trafficking under Sani Abacha.[69] Clinton received illicit campaign financing from a business associate of Cambodia's most significant narcotics trafficker, Theng Bunma, and backed the Çiller government in Turkey, which employed state-linked gangs, including the CIA-trained paramilitary Grey Wolves, that wrested control of the $20 billion drug trade from Kurdish "businessmen."[70]

South of the border, one of the CIA's chief assets in the fight against drugs, Peruvian Security Director Vladimir Montesinos, diverted CIA monies, amassing a $264 million personal fortune. Gen. Barry McCaffrey had praised Montesinos as an "outstanding and knowledgeable strategist." Later, Montesinos was charged with death squad activities, corruption, arms and drug trafficking, and illegal enrichment. In 1999, the Senate Appropriations Committee noted that it had "repeatedly expressed concern about U.S. support for the Peruvian National Intelligence Service," and requested that it "be consulted prior to any decision to provide assistance to the SIN." The Clinton administration, however, continued to provide Peru with extensive military aid and Bill wrote a personal letter to President Alberto Fujimori praising him for Peru's admirable progress in the War on Drugs."[71]

Following a similar pattern, the Clinton administration helped cover up the corruption of Mexico's President Carlos Salinas and his brother Raul, who were introduced to the drug trade by their father in the 1970s. *The New York Times* reported that American investigators were forced to file away reports that Raul received at least $500 million for trafficking cocaine into the U.S and funneled drug money into his brother's election campaign. Carlos Salinas enjoyed a close friendship with one of the legendary figures of Mexico's north-border drug trade, Juan N. Guerra. His First Attorney General and Education Minister, Manuel Bartlett Diaz, a CIA asset who spied on left-wing groups in Central America, was suspected of involvement in the murder of DEA agent Enrique "Kiki" Camarena in 1985.[72]

The CIA concluded that Salinas' "hands-on governing style" made it "unlikely that he had no knowledge of his brother's affairs or the shady dealings of other close associates."[73] These associates included Mexico's drug-enforcement chief, General Jesus Gutierrez Rebollo, who was arrested on charges of working for cocaine trafficker Carillo Fuentes. Eight days earlier, Rebollo had stood at attention in Washington as the White House drug-policy chief, Gen. Barry R. McCaffrey, described him as "an honest man" a "guy of absolute unquestionable integrity and a no-nonsense field commander."[74]

The farce of the drug war was further epitomized when Clinton hosted a drug summit in February 1999 in Yucatán at the ranch of a wealthy Mexican banker, Roberto Hernández Ramírez, who was publicly accused, with creditable evidence, of running a major cocaine trafficking operation and laundering illicit drug money.[75] In July 1995, *The New York Times* reported that because of "concern for Mexican stability and the fate of the North American Free Trade Agreement (NAFTA—a cornerstone of Clinton's Mexico policy), officials said that the United States often exaggerated the Mexican Government's progress in the fight against drugs, playing down corruption and glossing over failures."

The article, written by Tim Golden, went on to detail how

> major Mexican traffickers were sometimes captured and let go without a public word from American diplomats. . . . Slow movement by the Mexican Government to stop the laundering of drug profits was accepted almost patiently. Rather than push for the prosecution of the drug-related corruption. . . . American officials usually wrote off such episodes as unavoidable bumps in a long, bumpy road.[76]

These latter comments exemplify how the drug war was subordinate to larger political interests, reminiscent of Arkansas during Clinton's governorship. Drug revenues in Mexico had generated more than half of the foreign exchange earnings that were needed to repay U.S. loans, which bailed the country out in 1994 after the collapse of the peso.[77] When a videotape shot by U.S. Customs agents showed that army soldiers who killed seven drug agents in a remote airstrip in the eastern state of Vera Cruz had been protecting drug shipments and autopsy reports showed that the agents had been shot at point blank range, American diplomats bent over backwards to buttress the Mexican government's attempted cover up of the massacre, claiming to be motivated by what one official called "concern for the big picture."[78] Ambassador John Negroponte (1989–1993) called the shootings a "regrettable accident," which clearly they were not.

A Deal Made in Narco-Heaven

One key to the longstanding failure of the War on Drugs was the unwillingness of law enforcement agencies to go after money laundering banks, which enabled the global drug trade to flourish. The Clinton administration made it easier for drug cartels to launder their money by supporting the deregulation of banks and the financial industry. Raul Salinas had gotten special treatment from Citigroup, which happened to be the future employer of Robert Rubin, the head of Clinton's Council of Economic advisers and a top aide, who was unlikely to back any serious investigation.[79]

Clinton donors, the Stephens and Riady families, were connected to the Bank of Commerce and Credit International (BCCI), a major money laundering haven for drug traffickers.[80] Clinton himself had no compunction about accepting donations from figures known to have profited from the drug trade, including Dan Lasater and Don Tyson. Arkansas restaurateur Charlie Trie funneled millions of dollars illegally in foreign funds to the Democratic National Committee (DNC), including a bundle derived from Ng Lap Seng, the owner of a gambling resort in Macau that served as a haven for Chinese triad gangs who controlled the drug trade from the Golden Triangle. Mr. Ng's largesse won him ten visits to the White House between 1994 and 1996, including at least one with Clinton, who overlooked his connection to organized crime.[81] The level of hypocrisy was astounding if we consider the disproportionately long sentences given out to African American petty dealers and users.

NAFTA furthermore was a "deal made in narco-heaven for the godfathers of the drug trade," according to Phil Jordan, one of the Drug Enforcement Administration's (DEA) leading authorities on Mexican drug cartels.[82] Both the DEA and U.S. Customs services had been significantly prohibited from raising the subject of drugs during the NAFTA negotiations.[83] The loosening of trade barriers along with advances in transportation made smuggling across the border far easier.[84]

1994 saw the biggest jump in commercial-vehicle smuggling on record—a 25 percent increase.[85] NAFTA further led Mexican farmers to plant *more* drug crops in response to decreased income from maize farming, left sweatshop workers without means to care for their kids, and helped provide the infrastructure and labor pool to facilitate more smuggling, with widening domestic inequality and anomie ensuring ample demand.[86] The under-funding of public education, outsourcing of manufacturing jobs, and weakening of unions eroded economic prospects for working class youth, driving many into the underground economy.[87]

In a futile attempt to halt the flow of drugs and refugees, the Clinton administration militarized the U.S.-Mexican border, employing robotic drones for the first time for surveillance along with radar-blimps and military aircraft equipped with high-speed thermal imagers. This was in conjunction with night vision and infrared detection devices, Global Positioning System (GPS) receivers and radio links to law enforcement agencies off the Florida coast and an intelligence center in El Paso Texas, which served as a repository of worldwide drug smuggling data.[88]

On May 20, 1997, Esequiel Hernandez Jr. was killed by a U.S. Marine Corps unit engaged in antidrug surveillance along the U.S.-Mexico border. The gentle eighteen-year-old high school student was herding goats near his home town when he was stalked, shot and allowed to bleed to death. Lt. General Carlton W. Fulford, Commander of the 1st Marine Expeditionary Force at Camp Pendleton, admitted, as reported in *The Washington Post*, that "the killing might not have happened had civilian law enforcement agencies patrolled the border."[89]

Between 1995 and 1997, American antidrug aid to Mexico shot up from $10 million to $78 million per year. The Pentagon launched a $28 million program to train over one-thousand Mexican soldiers each year at American bases, shipped 73 Huey helicopters and other high tech military equipment, quadrupled the budget for military surveillance, and created a specialized counter-narcotics units whose officers were implicated in torture and assassination.[90]

A hidden purpose of the drug war was to fund counterinsurgency operations against leftist groups, which were conveniently accused of trafficking in drugs. Eyal Press of *The Progressive Magazine* pointed to a stunning admission tucked in the footnote of a General Accounting Office report on counter-narcotics: "During the 1994 uprising in the Mexican state of Chiapas, several U.S.-provided helicopters were used to transport Mexican military personnel to the conflict [against the left-wing Zapatistas who opposed NAFTA]."[91] This exemplified the ulterior function of the War on Drugs, which was to sustain U.S. military aid to governments which Congress would not ordinarily fund. The result was a growth in human rights atrocities despite all the pretenses about humanitarian intervention.

The Bolivian "Success"

In 1994, Clinton issued a presidential directive advocating a supply side approach targeting Latin America's coca growing regions.[92] Five years later, Clinton bragged that "we have witnessed a decline in cocaine production by 325 metric tons in Bolivia and Peru over the last four years."[93] He didn't mention, however, that much of the production was transferred to Colombia where production doubled between 1996 and 2000.[94] Despite the expansion of coca leaf eradication by some 323 percent, total cocaine production increased in these years by nine percent and opium poppy production by 16 percent.[95]

The U.S. ambassador to Bolivia, Manuel Rocha, stated in 2001 that Bolivia had "done in the past two-three years what no other country has done in the drug war. In Latin America, this is a success story."[96] This success came at a cost to the Bolivian economy of an estimated $500 million per year, accompanied by the growth of civil unrest and decimation of the coca growing region of Cochabamba. The Reverend Ravario Martinelli spoke of a "human tragedy for thousands of poor families with no way to support themselves now."[97] When the Bolivian government provided pineapples to farmers as an alternative to growing coca, they forgot to provide assistance on how to cultivate the plants, which were left to rot. The cash payments offered were ridiculously low.[98] Clearly more attention was paid to the military effort than to addressing economic alternatives for the impoverished population.

Coca, it should be noted, was chewed by locals to dull hunger and pain and curb indigestion, and as a medicine, and in ritual and ceremonial events. The attempt to eradicate trafficking thus included an assault on a people's culture. The U.S. funded, equipped, and trained Bolivian antinarcotics police, which according to a 1995 report by the Bolivian Chamber of Deputies, "acted with unnecessary displays of power, abuse and indiscriminate attacks against the civilian population in Chapare [Cochabamba]." Their interdiction activities were guided by the assumption that "all Chapare residents are drug trafficking suspects."[99] Under Law 1008, Bolivians were imprisoned without the possibility of pretrial release and had to remain in overcrowded prisons, where malnutrition was rampant because of the absence of kitchen facilities, until the trial court's decision was reviewed by the Supreme Court—a process that usually took years.[100]

A number of Bolivians detained on drug trafficking charges alleged torture by Bolivian law enforcement along with DEA complicity in abusive interrogations.[101] Bolivian soldiers carrying out eradication campaigns burned down homes, stole people's possessions and routinely shook people down, soliciting bribes at checkpoints.[102] Coca growers began engaging in acts of civil disobedience and other forms of resistance. Evo Morales, the head of the coca growers union and a congressman in Chapare, who in 2006 was elected as the country's first indigenous president, said that "we are not going to stop growing coca. And we will defend ourselves from this government, which has decided to blindly obey orders of Washington with no thought given to its own citizens."[103] In April 2001, Morales led coca growers from Cochabamba along with trade union organizing against the privatization of water on a "March of Life and Sovereignty" towards La Paz.[104]

Two years earlier, *The New York Times* reported coca growers had formed self-defense committees in Cochabamba, which made a series of hit and run ambushes on army and police units with sticks of dynamite and old rifles, killing three police officers and wounding fifteen. In response, government units killed up to 12 growers along with a baby who was killed inhaling tear gas. Fearing guerrilla insurrection, the government decided to send units of the Anti-Terrorism National Center, a CIA trained and financed agency, into the antidrug fight. These units paid informers in the cocalero movement and captured code books, a list of "terrorist" leaders, and maps that showed where booby traps were laid to protect the coca fields, officials said, enabling them to defeat the mini insurgency.[105]

Plan Colombia

Even more so than Bolivia, Colombia by the end of the 1990s had the makings of another Vietnam, with the presence of military advisers, high tech listening posts, aerial defoliation, river boats, and helicopters linked up to jungle penetration sensors—all justified under Clinton's War on Drugs.[106] Colombian police chief Rosso Jose Serrano referred to the War on Drugs in Colombia as a "Vietnam type operation."[107]

Colombia's strategic significance had increased by fresh discovery of oil deposits there in the 1990s.[108] The drug war in Colombia furthermore provided a pretext to expand the American military base network in Latin America. While losing a major base in Panama, the Pentagon during the 1990s acquired four new military bases, including one in Manta, Ecuador, which hosted up to 475 U.S. military personnel. The agreement signed by Ecuador's short-lived Mahuad government designated "aerial detection, monitoring, tracking, and control of illegal narcotics activity," as the purpose of U.S. control of the air base.[109] The U.S. Southern Command also operated 17 radar facilities mostly in Peru and Colombia, which were key to increased surveillance operations in Washington's Andean drug war.[110]

During Clinton's first year in office, the U.S. military deployed the full panoply of Cold War surveillance technology to hunt Medellin cartel boss Pablo Escobar, including SR-71 reconnaissance planes capable of flying three times the speed of sound, GPS and helicopter drones, though it was intelligence produced by his Cali rivals that ultimately sealed Escobar's fate.[111] In 1996, Clinton expanded counter-narcotics-related military aid to Colombia by $40 million: $30 million to the Army and $10 million to the National Police. Some military assistance was cut in March because of revelations of narco-trafficking by President Ernesto Samper's campaign, though Special Forces deployments to Columbia were exempt from the ban.[112] The same year, which saw coca production in Colombia expand by 32 percent, Clinton's State Department sold 12 Huey Combat helicopters equipped with 24 M60D door-mounted machine guns and 12 Blackhawk helicopters to Colombia as part of a $64-million weapons sales package.[113]

Journalist Mark Cook observed that a remarkable number of veterans of the U.S. dirty war in El Salvador in the 1980s were now running American policy in Colombia in the 1990s. Examples included Under-Secretary of State for Political Affairs Thomas Pickering, who had justified mass killings of civilians as U.S. Ambassador to El Salvador in 1984, and Assistant Secretary of State Peter Romero, who believed like Pickering that the "Salvador solution" could be the model for Colombia.[114]

This "Salvador solution" entailed paramilitary and death-squad activities and state-sanctioned terrorism. Military and police training missions packaged as part of the War on Drugs now assisted the Colombian government's long war against the leftist Fuerzas Armada Revolucionario de Colombia (FARC) guerrillas, who controlled 43,500 square kilometers of Colombian territory (almost half of its land mass). Stan Goff, a former Special Forces officer who worked in Colombia, stated that

> you were told, and the American public was being told, if they were told anything at all, this was counter-narcotics training. The training I conducted was anything but that. It was pretty much updated Vietnam style counterinsurgency doctrine. We were advised that this is what we would do, and we were further advised to refer to it as counter-narcotics training should anyone ask.[115]

The dismal failure of the War on Drugs in Colombia was reflected in the tripling of cocaine production from 1991–1999 (from 3.8 to 12.3 thousand hectares) and an increase by a multiple of 5.8 (from .13 to .75 thousand hectares) of the cultivation of opium poppy.[116] One reason for this outcome was that IMF and World Bank programs demanding the opening of the border to a flood of heavily subsidized agricultural products from the rich countries had undermined local agricultural production and fueled a boom in the production of drug crops for the export market.[117]

Wide-scale government corruption was another factor. In November 1998, a Colombian Air Force plane landed at Fort Lauderdale International airport with a hidden cargo of sixteen hundred pounds of cocaine. Army officers worked intimately with Carlos Castano, Colombia's chief paramilitary leader and a reported CIA asset, who stated that 70 percent of income for his group, the United Self Defense Forces of Colombia, (AUC), a de-facto wing of the Colombian army which carried out 70–80 percent of noncombat killings in the war against FARC, came from drugs. Castano was close to the powerful Henao-Montoya drug trafficking cartel; he was indicted by the U.S. Department of Justice in September 2002 and charged with trafficking over seventeen tons of cocaine since 1997.[118] The AUC had been placed on the State Department's list of terrorist organizations because of its role in the assassination in August 1999 of TV host Jaime Garzon, who advocated for peace with leftist guerrillas.[119]

Despite the army's intimate connection with a narco-terrorist organization, Clinton and Colombian President Andres Pastrana in 1999 launched Plan Colombia, a $1.3 billion antidrug program; 75 percent of the funds were for the military. The plan was an accelerated version of one proposed by Republicans in Congress. When the Office of Management and Budget proposed taking $100 million to be used for treatment of U.S. addicts, Barry McCaffrey made sure it was nixed. Instead, $400 million under the plan was appropriated for the purchase of 30 Black Hawk helicopters, made by United Technologies of Connecticut, and $144 million for training and equipping two new antinarcotics battalions. Clinton repealed a waiver that would have placed human rights criteria on the transfer of military aid. Over 75,000 Colombian military officers were trained at American military academies under the plan and laser guided bombs were provided to go along with real-time intelligence used to locate, bomb, and kill FARC leaders, who were accused of being narco-traffickers.[120]

Referring to Plan Colombia as "antidrug and pro-peace," Clinton claimed that a condition of the aid [to Colombia] was that "we are not going to get into a shooting war, that this is not Vietnam, neither is it Yankee imperialism."[121] Many Colombians would beg to differ. General Barry McCaffrey told *The New York Times* that "the distinction between rebels and drug traffickers had grown irrelevant" and that Colombia's "poorly equipped and inadequately trained armed forces needed immediate help."[122]

This assessment obscured the fact that the main drug cartels hated the left-wing guerrillas because of their promotion of land reform and taxation on the wealthy and were allied with the right-wing government, and that the FARC guerrillas mainly taxed coca that was grown in territory that they controlled. McCaffrey further left out the army's record of brutality—a week before Clinton's visit, it killed six children taking a nature walk who were mistaken for guerrillas.[123]

In the ten years after Clinton left office, the U.S. government spent $10 billion for counter-narcotics under Plan Colombia. Yet in 2016 Colombia remained the "world leader in coca production." The comparatively paltry hundreds of millions of dollars spent on alternative crop projects—everything from airlifting in chickens to distribute to Colombian farmers to building factories—"melted into the jungle without a trace."[124]

Senator Paul Wellstone (D-MN) had promoted an alternative to Plan Colombia that would have switched $225 million from military aid to drug treatment programs at home. He argued that "we've been down this road forever, forever," and that "more soldiers and more guns have not and will not defeat the source of illegal narcotics." Future Vice President Joe Biden rose immediately to the president's defense, stating that Congress would "wreak a whirlwind" if Plan Colombia "failed to strike back at the drug traffickers," and that President Andrs Pastrana was the "real deal."[125]

However, in January 1999, the head of the Colombian government's peace commission, Victor G. Ricardo, gave FARC documents that detailed Pastrana's links with right-wing paramilitary groups and cocaine barons.[126] The country's leading newsweekly, *Semana*, denounced him for "going along, after obvious pressure, with the opportunism and hypocrisy of U.S. officials," and accepting U.S. "aid" which was a "recipe for destruction, indefinite war and indebtedness."[127]

The worst aspect of Plan Colombia was the aerial fumigation program designed to destroy drug growing fields and move villagers away from FARC-controlled areas or make the way for mega-projects benefiting multinational corporations. Glyphosate or Roundup Weed killer, manufactured by Monsanto, was sprayed at one hundred times the concentration that was allowed in the United States. Though the State Department said that it was no more toxic than "common salt, aspirin or caffeine," a 2015 World Health Organization (WHO) study found that glyphosate "probably causes cancer in humans."[128] Entire regions were left "without butterflies or birds," because of its use.[129]

Gonzalo de Francisco, a Colombian national security adviser, likened the fumigation program to "chemotherapy" as sometimes, he said, "you end up killing the patient."[130] Elsa Niva, a Colombian agronomist who works with the Pesticide Action Network, reported that in two months alone 4,289 Colombians suffered skin or gastric disorders from the chemical spraying while 178,377 creatures were killed, including cattle, horses, pigs, dogs, ducks, hens and fish.[131] An unknown number of farmers died from dehydration, fever and other sicknesses and thousands were displaced—an outcome known in advance, as the initial Plan Colombia package included $15 million for "emergency resettlement and employment of persons displaced by the Push into Southern Colombia program."[132]

Journalist Hugh O'Shaughnessy visited the indigenous Kofan community of Santa Rosa de Guamuez, whose pineapples were stunted and shriveled because of the chemical spraying and once green banana plants were no more than blackened sticks. The children were underweight, suffering from respiratory problems and stomach pains.[133] A local health worker in Putumayo, where thousands of villagers were displaced, recalled how the spraying turned "everything yellow; not a green leaf on a tree. Many jungle animals dead, dead monkeys, dead birds, fish farm tanks with thousands of dead fish floating in them."[134]

In a class action lawsuit, a group of farmers alleged that DynCorp of Fall Church, Virginia– which in 1998 was awarded a five-year $170 million contact to carry out fumigation—caused severe health problems (high fever, vomiting, diarrhea, dermatological problems) and the destruction of food crops and livestock of approximately 10,000 residents in the region bordering Ecuador. The toxicity of the fumigant further caused the deaths of four infants.[135]

Energy Secretary Bill Richardson pointed to an underlying motive behind Plan Colombia when he stated, during a visit to Cartagena in 1999: "The United States and its allies will invest millions of dollars in two areas of the Colombian economy, in the areas of mining and energy, and to secure these investments we are tripling military aid to Colombia."[136] Among the biggest beneficiaries were defense contractors like Sikorsky Aircraft Corporation, which got a $234-million contract to deliver 18 new Blackhawks, and Bell Textron, which hired the former Colombian ambassador as a lobbyist.

DynCorp pilots carrying out fumigation—some of whom were involved in other covert operations—reported being shot at by farmers who had no other means of making a living, firing back in kind. FARC responded by launching missiles at American aircraft as U.S. trained and equipped antidrug battalions began killing FARC rebels in counterinsurgency operations financed in part through the drug trade. Tod Robberson of the *Dallas Morning News* wrote that DynCorp's activities "went well beyond the stated U.S. mission of fighting drug traffickers."[137]

From 1997 to 2003, fourteen American contractors were killed, including two employees manning a surveillance flight in Caqueta Province. An army officer commented: "imagine if 20 American troops got killed here. Plan Colombia would be over [as the U.S. public would not tolerate these deaths]."[138] Several DynCorp employees were themselves indicted for smuggling and a DynCorp subcontractor which exported military technology was suspected of being a drug front.

On May 12, 2000, Colombian authorities intercepted a parcel containing liquid heroin which had been sent from DynCorp's Colombian office to its Florida air base. Several years earlier, a DynCorp pilot died of a cocaine overdose; in 1999, the Colombian state prosecutor launched an investigation into amphetamine smuggling. Documents relating to these cases mysteriously disappeared.[139]

These cases exemplify the continued double standards and corruption underlying the War on Drugs. A memo leaked by Justice Department Attorney Thomas Kent in 2004 alleged that DEA agents in Colombia were assisting narco-traffickers and paramilitary forces in an alliance dubbed "The Bogota Connection," which according to *Narco News* reporter Bill Conroy had "the CIA's footprints all over it."[140] Just before he left office, Clinton pardoned Harvey Weinig, a Manhattan lawyer who was serving an 11-year sentence for his part in laundering $19 million for the Cali drug cartel. The pardon was especially egregious in light of the Clinton administration's own severe condemnation of the Colombian government's "surrender policy" toward the Cali cartel in the mid-1990s, which allowed a reduced prison sentence to those drug kingpins who agreed to surrender.[141]

At best, the weakening of the Colombian drug cartels led the Mexican cartels to start taking over, just as a NAFTA-induced trade boom made it easier than ever to get drugs across the border. At his Senate confirmation hearing, Secretary of State John Kerry claimed that Colombia was a "model for the region [Latin America]; an example to the rest of Latin America about what awaits them if we can convince people to make better decisions."[142] Popular author Robert Kaplan echoed Kerry in writing that "Colombia is what Iraq should look like in our best dreams."[143] Both countries, however, ended up as dystopias rooted on the shoals of American power. In 2012, Clinton acknowledged in a documentary that his administration's effort to limit drug trafficking from Colombia "hasn't worked."[144]

Conclusion

The attitude of the American public towards politics has become completely jaded and cynical because of the actions of government leaders like Bill Clinton. Clinton effectively won the vote of the middle-aged baby boomer population in the 1992 and 1996 elections by presenting himself as one of them; a former hippie from the 1960s who experimented with drugs and who was now committed to enacting a more liberal drug policy. However, in practice, he expanded the War on Drugs to unprecedented heights, eclipsing the antidrug guru himself, Ronald Reagan.

Because of the failings of the mass media, few American voters knew the real truth about Clinton—how he was never a hippie but a CIA informant; how he and his half-brother Roger had lived a playboy lifestyle in which they partook in drug/sex orgies; and how Clinton had protected high level drug traffickers and helped cover up for smuggling schemes while governor of Arkansas—and then again as president.

While structural forces were indeed a powerful obstacle to change, Clinton himself had long been part of the political establishment and lacked any moral integrity. He would sanction any atrocity so long as it gained him some political advantage, despite the negative consequences for thousands of people and the War on Drugs was no exception. And he succeeded, because the American masses judge their politicians based on their public personae and media image and not on their actual policies.

Endnotes

1 See Roger Morris, *Partners in Power: The Clintons and Their America* (Washington, D.C.: Regnery, 1996); Roger Stone and Robert Morrow, *The Clinton's War on Women* (New York: Skyhorse Publishing, 2015); George Carpozi Jr. *Clinton Confidential: The Climb to Power: The Unauthorized Biography of Bill and Hillary Clinton* (Del Mar, CA: Emery Dalton Books, 1995); Ambrose Evans Pritchard, *The Secret Life of Bill Clinton: The Unreported Stories* (Washington, D.C.: Regnery, 1996); and R. Emmett Tyrrell Jr., *Boy Clinton: The Political Biography* (Washington, D.C.: Regnery, 1996); Roger Clinton, *Growing Up Clinton: The Lives, Times, and Tragedies of America's Presidential Family* (Summit Publishing Group, 1995) among other works. Roger routinely took women to the Governor's mansion while high to have sex and bragged about engaging in wild cocaine binges at the Governor's mansion. Contemporaries described Roger as a "fuck up." He had association with members of the Gambino crime family, whom he tried to assist with their legal cases, and had several DUI cases against him.

2 Pritchard, *The Secret Life of Bill Clinton*; Robert E. Levin, *Bill Clinton: The Inside Story*, with introduction by David Pryor (New York: S.P.I. Books, 1992), 165–167.

3 Levin, *Bill Clinton*, 165.

4 Mara Leveritt, *The Boys on the Tracks: Death, Denial, and a Mother's Crusade to Bring Her Son's Killers to Justice* (Little Rock: Bird Call Press, 1999), 223.

5 Author Interview with Tosh Plumlee, former CIA pilot, February 1, 2023. For the historical pattern this would have followed, see Alfred W. McCoy, *The Politics of Heroin: CIA Complicity in the Global Drug Trade* (New York: Lawrence Hill Books, 2003); Douglas Valentine, *The Strength of the Wolf* (London: Verso, 2004); Gary Webb, *Dark Alliance: The CIA, the Contras, and the Crack Cocaine Epidemic* (New York: Seven Stories Press, 1998).

6 Bernard Von Bothmer, *Framing the Sixties: The Use and Abuse of a Decade from Ronald Reagan to George W. Bush* (Amherst, MA: University of Massachusetts Press, 2010), 172.

7 Jeremy Kuzmarov, *The Myth of the Addicted Army: Vietnam and the Modern War on Drugs* (Amherst, MA: University of Massachusetts Press, 2009).

8 "International Drug War," https://www.cato.org/sites/cato.org/files/serials/files/cato-handbook-policymakers/1995/9/104-38.pdf In 1997, he asked for a 10 percent increase, resulting in a budget of over $15 billion. David Plotz, "Clinton's Drug War," *Slate*, June 25, 1996, https://slate.com/news-and-politics/1996/06/clinton-s-drug-war.html

9 Timothy Black, *When a Heart Turns Rock Solid: The Lives of Three Puerto Rican Brothers On and Off the Streets* (New York: Pantheon Books, 2009), 217. Clinton requested $16 billion alone for the drug war in 1998.

10 "Just Say So What," *The Wall Street Journal*, October 16, 1996, A20.

11 Levin, *Bill Clinton*, 180.

12 Victor Thorn, *Hillary (and Bill)): The Drugs Volume, Part II of the Clinton Trilogy* (Washington, D.C.: The Free Press, 2008), 193. A *Texas Daily* reporter said he saw Clinton smoking a joint in Austin in 1972 at the headquarters of George McGovern's Texas campaign. According to Barbara Olsen, author of a book on Hillary Clinton, during Clinton's run for Congress in 1976, the scent of marijuana was palpable at his campaign headquarters, and the "campaign symbol might well have been a hand-rolled cigarette." Barbara Olsen, *Hell to Pay* (Washington, D.C.: Regnery Publishing, 1999), 90.

13 Gennifer Flowers, *Passion and Betrayal*, with Jacquelyn Dapper (Del Mar, CA: Emery Dalton Books, 1995), 42.

14 Stone and Morrow, *The Clinton's War on Women*, 132. Sharline and her friends would go back to governor's mansion and party until the early morning hours. "I thought it was the coolest thing in the world that we had a governor who got high," she said.

15 Stone and Morrow, *The Clinton's War on Women*, 139.

16 Tyrrell, Jr. *Boy Clinton*, xix; Morris, *Partners in Power*; Stone and Morrow, *The Clinton's War on Women*.

17 Tyrrell, Jr. *Boy Clinton*, xvi, xvii; Victor Thorn, *Hillary (and Bill): The Murder File* (Washington, D.C. Sisyphus, 2008), 546; Evans-Pritchard, *The Secret Life of Bill Clinton*, 239, 240. When Mrs. Parks later went to clean Roger's apartment, she found drug paraphernalia, barbiturates, sleeping pills and white powder. In September 1993, her husband Jerry, who had kept a file of Clinton's private life after being hired by Hillary, was shot dead in his car in a professional hit. The files he kept were hidden or stolen.

18 Tyrrell, *Boy Clinton*, xix; Stone and Morrow, *The Clintons' War on Women*. Larry Nichols, then a member of the Clintons' notorious "Kitchen Cabinet," was told by Bill's chief of staff Betsey Wright that Bill was put in rehab in 1987 after he dropped out of the presidential race to "get off cocaine."

19 Stone and Morrow, *The Clinton's War on Women*, 77.

20 "Bill Clinton to Mary Lingo, November 14, 1989, Bill Clinton Gubernatorial Group, Natural and Cultural Resources, Economic Development Series, Craig Smith, box 12, Butler Center for Arkansas Studies, Bobby L. Roberts Library of Arkansas, Central Arkansas Library System, Little Rock, Arkansas; "Drug Eradication Operations," In *Arkansas National Guard: Military Department of Arkansas*, Annual

Report, FY 1990, Bill Clinton Gubernatorial Group, Natural and Cultural Resources, Economic Development Series, Craig Smith, box 8, Butler Center for Arkansas Studies, Bobby L. Roberts Library of Arkansas, Central Arkansas Library System, Little Rock, Arkansas

21 "Governor Bill Clinton's Record in Arkansas: Drugs and Crime," Dianne Blair Papers, Mullins Library, University of Arkansas, Fayetteville, Special Collections.

22 Mara Leveritt, *All Quiet at Mena: A Reporter's Memoir of Buried Investigations* (Little Rock: Bird Call Press, 2021), 242.

23 Rodney Stich, *Drugging America: A Trojan Horse*, 2nd ed. (Nevada: Silverspeak Enterprises, 2005), 39. Eric G. Stacey, *Bagman: The Secret Life of Col. Albert V. Carone* (Landfall Productions, 2006), 102, 103. Colonel Albert V. Carone, who partook in secret drug smuggling operations for the CIA, claims that Clinton kept law enforcement at bay and allowed for the importation of cocaine into Mena beginning when he was Arkansas Attorney General in the late 1970s.

24 Stone and Morrow, *The Clinton's War on Women.*

25 Evans-Pritchard, *The Secret Life of Bill Clinton.*

26 Leveritt, *All Quiet at Mena*, 307. Sheriffs at the time were hearing reports from Angel Fire reminiscent of Mena—strange nighttime traffic, sightings of parachute drops, even hikers' accounts of a "big black military-type cargo plane" seeming to come out of nowhere and swooping low and almost silently over a deserted mountain meadow near the remote ski area."

27 Whitney Webb, *One Nation Under Blackmail: The Sordid Union Between Intelligence and Organized Crime That Gave Rise to Jeffrey Epstein*, Vol. 1 (Walterville, OR: Trine Day, 2022), 347. Two years later, Chagra contracted hitman Charles Harrelson—father of famed actor Woody Harrelson—to assassinate Federal Judge John H. Wood Jr. in San Antonio, Texas.

28 "Lasater's Ex-Chauffeur Asks Reduction in Term for Cocaine Conviction," *The Arkansas-Gazette*, May 12, 1987, in Bill Clinton Gubernatorial Group, Natural and Cultural Resources, Economic Development Series, Bob Nash, box 7, Butler Center for Arkansas Studies, Bobby L. Roberts Library of Arkansas, Central Arkansas Library System, Little Rock, Arkansas.

29 Floyd G. Brown, *"Slick Willie:" Why America Cannot Trust Bill Clinton* (Annapolis, Maryland: Annapolis Publishing Co., 1992); Thorn, *Hillary (and Bill)*, 164, 171.

30 Thorn, *Hillary (and Bill): The Drugs Volume*, 177.

31 Stone and Morrow, *The Clinton's War on Women*, 132, 133; Thorn, *Hillary (and Bill),* 165. Clinton appears to have been introduced to Lasater by his mother, Virginia, who leased a box next to his at Oaklawn racetrack (Virginia loved to bet on horses) and was Lasater's friend. When Roger Clinton got in trouble, Bill turned to Lasater to give him a job as his limo driver and Lasater helped Roger pay off an $8,000 drug debt during Roger's 1983–1984 crisis.

32 Leveritt, *The Boys on the Tracks,* 259. Another law enforcement official described the investigation into Lasater's operations as "either a high dive or extremely unprofessional. Take your pick." U.S. attorneys in Arkansas and Louisiana had long suspected Lasater had ties to organized crime. His chauffeur was reputedly a murderer known to deal drugs on the side. When Lasater was later charged with insurance fraud, the case was handled by Hillary's Rose Law Firm. Lasater had been so close with Clinton he was one of the few allowed to enter the Governor's mansion through the back gate, a privilege normally reserved only for family and senior staff.

33 Leveritt, *The Boys on the Tracks;* Thorn, *Hillary (and Bill);* Gary Aldrich, *Unlimited Access: An FBI Agent Inside the Clinton White House* (Washington, D.C.: Regnery Publishing, 1998), xiv. When White House deputy counsel Vince Foster, Hillary's former Rose Law Firm partner and lover who had insider knowledge of the Whitewater scandal, died under suspicious circumstances, Thomassen was the first to enter his office to find the combination of his safe.

34 Thorn, *Hillary (and Bill): The Drugs Volume*, 182; Richmond Odom, *Circle of Death: Clinton's Climb to the Presidency* (Lafayette, LA: Huntington House Publishers, 1995), 132.

35 Carpozi Jr., *Clinton Confidential*, 278–281; Olson, *Hell to Pay*, 143; Thorn, *Hillary (and Bill))*, 16, 217, 218. According to former Saline County Deputy Prosecutor Jean Duffey, head of a drug task force, members of the Walton family were also involved in drug trafficking.

36 Thorn, *Hillary (and Bill))*, 26, 27; Evans Pritchard, *The Secret Life of Bill Clinton*, 277–278; Odom, *Circle of Death*, 134, 135. Two sets of documents refer also to alleged hit men employed by Tyson to kill drug dealers who owed him money; another report alleged that Tyson was using his business plane to smuggle quart jars of methamphetamine.

37 Leveritt, *The Boys on the Tracks*, 211.

38 Quoted in Donna Murch, "The Clinton's War on Drugs: When Black Lives Didn't Matter," *The New Republic*, February 9, 2016, https://newrepublic.com/article/129433/clintons-war-drugs-black-lives-didnt-matter

39 Dewayne Wickham, *Bill Clinton and Black America* (New York: Ballantine Books, 2002), 164.

40 Michelle Alexander, *The New Jim Crow: Mass Incarceration in the Age of Colorblindness* (New York: The New Press, 2012).

41 James Bovard, *"Feeling Your Pain": The Explosion and Abuse of Government Power in the Clinton-Gore Years* (New York: St. Martin's Press, 2000), 111.

42 Alexander, *The New Jim Crow*, 56; Nathan J. Robinson, *Superpredator: Bill Clinton's Use and Abuse of Black America* (Sommerville, MA: PA Press, 2016), 64, 65. Clinton's administration slashed funds for public housing by $17 billion and boosted corrections by $19 billion (an increase of 171 percent), effectively "making the construction of prisons the nation's main housing program for the urban poor."

43 Dick Morris, and Eileen McGann, *Because He Could* (New York: Regan Books, 2004), 234.

44 Michael Kramer, "The Phony Drug War," *Time* magazine, September 2, 1996. In 1998, the percentage appropriated for law enforcement and military interdiction rose to 66 percent, up from 64 percent in 1994.

45 See Jacob Sullum, *Saying Yes: In Defense of Drug Use* (Tarcher Perigee, 2004).

46 Robert Dreyfuss, "Hawks and Doves," *Rolling Stone*, August 7, 1997; Alexander Cockburn and Jeffrey St. Clair, *Al Gore: A User's Manual* (London: Verso, 2000), 5.

47 Jeff Stein, "The Clinton Dynasty's Horrific Legacy: More Drug War, More Prisons," *Alternet*, April 13, 2015, https://www.alternet.org/2015/04/clinton-dynasty-horrific-legacy-more-drug-war-more-prisons/

48 Robinson, *Superpredator*, 45, 46; German Lopez, "The Controversial 1994 Crime Law That Joe Biden Helped Write, Explained," *Vox,* June 20, 2019, https://www.vox.com/policy-and-politics/2019/6/20/18677998/joe-biden-1994-crime-bill-law-mass-incarceration; Clarence Lusane, "Congratulations, It's a Crime, Bill,"

CovertAction Quarterly, No. 50 (Fall 1994), 18, William Jefferson Clinton, "Remarks on Signing the Violent Crime Control and Law Enforcement Act of 1994 September 13, 1994," U.S. Government Printing Office, https://www.govinfo.gov/content/pkg/PPP-1994-book2/pdf/PPP-1994-book2-doc-pg1539.pdf The main progressive features of the bill were an assault weapon ban and some provisions for treatment as well as support for drug courts which could steer drug offenders away from prison into rehabilitation programs.

49 Thomas Frank, "Bill Clinton's Crime Bill Destroyed Lives, and There's No Point Denying It," *The Guardian*, April 15, 2016, https://www.theguardian.com/commentisfree/2016/apr/15/bill-clinton-crime-bill-hillary-black-lives-thomas-frank

50 Nathan J. Robinson, "Kool Aid and Cyanide," *Jacobin*, September 20, 2016, https://www.jacobinmag.com/2016/09/bill-clinton-drug-war-sentencing-crack-cocaine-racism/; Robinson, *Superpredator*, 58. In the face of criticism about racism, Clinton tried to increase the penalties for powder cocaine rather than reducing the penalties for crack!

51 Robinson, "Kool Aid and Cyanide." Bovard, *"Feeling Your Pain,"* 113.

52 Jim McGee, "Military Seeks Balance in Delicate Mission: The Drug War," *The Washington Post*, November 29, 1996; Eyal Press, "Clinton Pushes Military Aid," *The Progressive*, February 1997. In Utah, 125 soldiers worked to translate telephone conversations garnered by DEA eavesdropping, often on Colombian, Mexican or Nigerian suspects.

53 Dreyfuss, "Hawks and Doves"; Russell Crandall, "Explicit Narcotization: U.S. Policy Towards Colombia During the Samper Administration," *Latin American Politics and Society*, 43, 3 (Autumn, 20001), 95–120.

54 Lusane, "Congratulations, It's a Crime Bill," 22.

55 Peter B. Kraska, "Playing War: Masculinity, Militarism and Their Real World Consequences," in *Militarizing the American Justice System: The Changing Role of the Armed Forces and the Police*, ed. Peter Kraska (Evanston, Il: Northwestern University Press, 2001), 143; Radley Balko, *Rise of the Warrior Cop: The Militarization of America's Police Forces* (New York: Public Affairs, 2021), 212; Bovard, *"Feeling Your Pain,"* 87.

56 Kelly A. Gates, *Our Biometric Future: Facial Recognition Technology and the Culture of Surveillance* (New York: New York University Press, 2011), 28, 29, 48–49. Research into machine recognition of faces traced back to the 1960s to a private company called Panoramic Research Inc. in Palo Alto California, which was funded by the Central Intelligence Agency and Pentagon. Co-Founder Woodrow Wilson Bledsoe was a pioneer in artificial intelligence research.

57 Alan Leo, "Fighting Drugs, Fighting Terror," *MIT Technology Review*, May 3, 2002.

58 "From Batons to Body Cameras: The Revolution of Police Technologies," *Orange County Register*, September 22, 2014; Todd R. Clear and Natasha A. Frost, *The Punishment Imperative: The Rise and Failure of Mass Incarceration in America* (New York: New York University Press, 2014), 108.

59 Gary Fields, "War Against Drugs Enlists Hollywood to Bolster Impact," *The Wall Street Journal*, July 12, 2000, B6.

60 Lance Selfa, *The Democrats: A Critical History* (Chicago, Illinois: Haymarket Books, 2008), 80.

61 Peter Zirnite, "Reluctant Recruits: The U.S. Military and the War on Drugs," *Washington Office on Latin America*, August 1997, https://www.tni.org/files/download/Reluctant%20recruits%20report_0.pdf

62 Zirnite, "Reluctant Recruits,"

63 Bovard, *"Feeling Your Pain,"* 106.

64 See Peter Dale Scott, *Drugs, Oil and War* (New York: Rowman & Littlefield, 2003); Alfred W. McCoy, *The Politics of Heroin: CIA Complicity in the Global Drug Trade*, rev ed. (New York: Lawrence Hill Books, 2003).

65 Representatives Christopher Cox, Ben Gilman, Porter Goss, et al. "Russia's Road to Corruption: How the Clinton Administration Exported Government Instead of Free Enterprise and Failed the Russian People," Members of the Speaker's Advisory Group on Russia, U.S. House of Representatives, Washington, D.C., September 2000 (286 page report), https://fas.org/irp/congress/2000_rpt/russias-road.pdf; Mussa, quoted in David Wessel and Bob Davis, "Markets Under Siege," *The Wall Street Journal*, September 24, 1998, A1. Many Russians developed drug habits to cope with the misery of the American-imposed shock therapy programs transitioning Russia to a privatized economy. Russian criminal groups further began selling high tech equipment, including Surface-to-Air Missiles, AK-47s, Rocket Propelled Grenades (RPGs) and submarine helicopters purchased on the black market to the drug cartels in Colombia, and set up offshore banks in the Caribbean that were ideal for drug money laundering (Russia itself in this period was also considered a paradise for drug money launderers. Douglas Farah, "Russian Mob, Cartels Joining Forces," *The Washington Post Foreign Service*, September 29, 1997, A01).

66 Marko Milivujovic, "The Balkans Medellin," *Jane's Intelligence Review*, February 1, 1995, 7, 2 68, https://balkania.tripod.com/resources/terrorism/kla-drugs.html#a25; Warren Christopher to the president, "Sali Berisha's White House Visit," September 8, 1995, William J. Clinton Presidential Library, Digital Archives, Republic of Albania, http://www.modern-albania.com/wp-content/uploads/2015/09/Berisha-Clinton-meeting-Sept-1995.pdf; A.B. Abrams, *Atrocity Fabrication and Its Consequences: How Fake News Shapes World Order* (Atlanta: Clarity Press, 2023), 225. Abrams points out that even the U.S. chief negotiator and architect of the Rambouillet agreement, Christopher Hill, admitted to the KLA's role as one of the leading drug traffickers.

67 Paul Lewis, "Report Identifies Hashim Thaçi as Big Fish in Organized Crime," *The Guardian*, June 24, 2011, https://www.theguardian.com/world/2011/jan/24/hashim-thaci-kosovo-organised-crime; Jerry Seper, "KLA Finances Fight with Heroin Sales: Terror Group is Linked to Crime Network," *The Washington Times*, May 3, 1999; William F. Engdahl, *Manifest Destiny: Democracy as Cognitive Dissonance* (Wiesbaden: Mine.books, 2018), 111, 112. Thaçi's top deputy, Xhavit Haliti, was allegedly a big figure in the Albanian mafia where he was involved in gambling, prostitution, and drug smuggling. Prince Dobrosh, the boss of the Kosovo-Albanian narco-mafia provided weapons to the KLA that were bought from heroin proceeds. "Rugova Meets with Albanian Narco-Boss in Prague," https://balkania.tripod.com/resources/terrorism/kla-drugs.html#a25

68 Steve Coll, *Ghost Wars: The Secret History of the CIA, Afghanistan, and Bin Laden, From the Soviet Invasion to September 10, 2001* (New York: Penguin Books, 2004), 524.

69 Frank Smythe, "A New Game: The Clinton Administration on Africa," *World Policy Journal*, June 1, 1998. In Georgia, the Clinton administration sent Special Forces to protect Eduard Shevardnadze, who was tied in with the Georgian mafia. Michael Pullara, *The Spy Who Was Left Behind* (New York: Scribner, 2018), 17, 18.

70 Ertugrul Kukrcu, "Trapped in a Web of Covert Killers," *CovertAction Quarterly*, Summer 1997, 10; Edward Timperlake and William C. Triplett II, *Year of the Rat: How Bill Clinton Compromised U.S. Security for Chinese Cash* (Washington, D.C. Regnery Publishing, 1998), 4, 102, 103. The business associate, Ted Sioeng, donated at least $400,000 to the DNC.

71 "U.S. Shrugged Off Corruption, Abuse, in Service of Drug War," *International Consortium of Investigative Journalists*, September 26, 2012, https://www.icij.org/investigations/us-aid-latin-america/us-shrugged-corruption-abuse-service-drug-war/; "CIA and Drugs: Our Man in Peru," *CovertAction Quarterly*, Winter 1996–97, 4. Other senior Peruvian officials closely tied to Montesinos, including the former head of Peru's central military command, also stood accused of taking bribes from drug smugglers. More high-level corruption was covered up in Venezuela where in 1997 General Ramon Guillen Davila, chief of a CIA-created antidrug unit, was indicted in Miami for smuggling coke. Because he served as a CIA asset, when he was arrested for plotting to assassinate President Hugo Chavez, his indictment was still sealed. CIA contact Mark McFarlin, whom the DEA also wanted to indict, was never indicted, but merely resigned. Oliver Villar and Drew Cottle, *Cocaine, Death Squads and the War on Terror: U.S. Imperialism and Class Struggle in Colombia* (New York: Monthly Review, 2011); Alexander Cockburn and Jeffrey St. Clair, *Whiteout: The CIA, Drugs and the Press* (London: Verso, 1996); Douglas Valentine, *The Strength of the Pack: The Personalities, Politics and Espionage Intrigues That Shaped the DEA* (Walterville, OR: Trine Day, 2010) 400.

72 Mark Bowden, *Down By the River: Money, Murder and Family* (New York: Simon & Schuster, 2004); Dawn Paley, *Drug War Capitalism* (Oakland, CA: AK Press, 2014), 49; Tim Golden, "Swiss Recount Key Drug Role of Salinas Kin," *The New York Times*, September 19, 1998; Tim Golden, "Mexico and Drugs: Was U.S. Napping," *The New York Times*, July 11, 1997. Raul Salinas spent a decade in prison for murdering a political rival. His father was close to the founder of the Gulf Cartel. U.S. agents did not pursue investigation into Salinas.

73 Tim Golden, "Mexico and Drugs: Was U.S. Napping," *The New York Times*, July 11, 1997.

74 Ibid.; John Sweeney, "Clinton's Latin America Policy: A Legacy of Missed Opportunities," *The Heritage Foundation*, July 6, 1998, https://www.heritage.org/americas/report/clintons-latin-america-policy-legacy-missedopportunities-0. Over forty military officers were arrested in connection with the arrest of Rebollo but few if any were ever actually tried.

75 Al Giordano, "Clinton's Mexican Narco-pals: The untold story behind February's Yucatán summit redefines the enemy in the war on drugs," *Boston Phoenix*, May 13–20, 1999, https://bostonphoenix.com/archive/features/99/05/13/NARCO.html

76 Tim Golden, "To Help Keep Mexico Stable, U.S. Soft Pedaled Drug War," *The New York Times*, July 31, 1995. John Walters, a Bush administration drug official, was further quoted in the piece stating: "People desperately wanted drugs not to become a complicating factor for NAFTA. There was a degree of illicit activity that was just accepted." Law-enforcement agents who worked in and on Mexico while Mr. Salinas was a prized ally of the United States said they were often discouraged by political pressure to keep the drug issue from jeopardizing improvements in the economic relationship between the two countries. Golden, "Mexico and Drugs."

77 Scott, *Drugs, Oil and War*, 89.

78 Golden, "To Help Keep Mexico Stable, U.S. Soft Pedaled Drug War."

79 Cockburn & St. Clair, *Whiteout*, 365.

80 See Peter Truell, *BCCI: The Inside Story of the World's Most Corrupt Financial Empire* (New York: Bloomsbury, 1992).

81 See Micah Morrison, "The Macau Connection," *The Wall Street Journal*, February 26, 1998, A16.

82 Ryan Grim and Matt Ferner, "Bill Clinton Apologizes to Mexico for War on Drugs," *The Huffington Post*, February 13, 2015, https://www.huffpost.com/entry/bill-clinton-apology-drug-war-mexico_n_6680412

83 Cockburn & St. Clair, *Whiteout*, 359.

84 Eric Zabludoff, "Colombian Narcotics Organizations as Business Enterprises"; in Eric Wilson ed. *Government of the Shadows: Parapolitics and Criminal Sovereignty* (London: Pluto Press, 2009).

85 Ryan Grim and Matt Ferner, "Clinton Apologizes to Mexico for War on Drugs," *The Huffington Post*, February 13, 2015, https://www.huffpost.com/entry/bill-clinton-apology-drug-war-mexico_n_6680412

86 Tony Payan, *The Three U.S.-Mexico Border Wars* (Westport, CT: Praeger Security International, 2006); Black, *When a Heart Turns Rock Solid.*

87 See Philippe Bourgeois, *In Search of Respect: Selling Crack in El Barrio* (New York: Cambridge University Press, 1995); Black, *When a Heart Turns Rock Solid*, 209.

88 Ted Galen Carpenter, *Bad Neighbor Policy: Washington Futile War on Drugs in Latin America* (New York: Palgrave McMillan, 2003), 4; Timothy J. Dunn, *The Militarization of the U.S.-Mexico Border, 1978–1992: Low-Intensity Doctrine Comes Home* (University of Texas at Austin, 1995), 132; "Florida's War on Drugs," *Soldiers Magazine*, May 1996, 13–16; Dale E. Brown, "Drugs on the Border: The Role of the Military," *Parameters*, Winter 1991-1992, 51.

89 Peter Zirnite, "Reluctant Recruits: The U.S. Military and the War on Drugs," *Washington Office on Latin America*, August 1997, https://www.tni.org/files/download/Reluctant%20recruits%20report_0.pdf; Bovard, *"Feeling Your Pain,"* 99. According to Rep. Lamar Smith (R-TX) the Justice and Defense Departments undermined the criminal investigation and prevented the truth from coming out about how Hernandez was killed.

90 Cockburn & St. Clair, *Whiteout*, 373, 374, 379.

91 Eyal Press, "Clinton Pushes Military Aid," *The Progressive*, February 1997; Cockburn & St. Clair, *Whiteout*, 380, 381. Celia Rodriguez, a U.S. spokesman for the Zapatistas stated that "under the guise of fighting drug traffickers, the U.S. government has bolstered an antidemocratic and corrupt Mexican government with a laundry list of high-tech military equipment that has been used to violate the basic human rights of the Mexican people."

92 Zirnite, "Reluctant Recruits."

93 Bovard, *"Feeling Your Pain,"* 101.

94 Ibid.

95 David Scott Palmer, *U.S. Relations with Latin America: Opportunities Lost or Squandered?* (Gainesville: University Press of Florida, 2006), 81.

96 Ben Kohl and Linda Forthing, "The Price of Success: Bolivia's War Against Drugs and the Poor," *North American Congress on Latin America* (NACLA), September 25, 2007.

97 Kohl and Forthing, "The Price of Success."

98 Kohl and Forthing, "The Price of Success." Anthony Failo, "In Bolivia Drug War, Success Has Price: Farmers Victimized by Coca Eradication," *The Washington Post*, March 4, 2001.

99 "Bolivia Under Pressure: Human Rights Violation and Coca Eradication," *Human Rights Watch-America*, May 1996, https://www.hrw.org/reports/1996/Bolivia.htm

100 Ibid.; Human Rights Watch, Bolivia – Human Rights Violations and the War on Drugs," 7, 8, July 1995.

101 Human Rights Watch, Bolivia – Human Rights Violations and the War on Drugs," 7, 8, July 1995.

102 Failo, "In Bolivia Drug War, Success Has Price."

103 Failo, "In Bolivia Drug War, Success Has Price."

104 Kohl and Forthing, "The Price of Success."

105 Clifford Krauss, "Drug Battle in Bolivia 'Making History:' Coca is Cut Back and Could Be Eradicated," *The New York Times*, May 9, 1999.

106 Scott, *Drugs, Oil and War*, 99.

107 Vijay Prashad, *Fat Cats & Running Dogs: The Enron Stage of Capitalism* (Monroe, ME: Common Courage Press, 2003), 175.

108 Scott, *Drugs, Oil and War*, 104; Thad Dunning and Leslie Wirpsa, "Oil Rigged: There's Something Slippery About the U.S. Drug War in Colombia," February 2011, https://www.globalpolicy.org/component/content/article/198/40154.html; Prashad, *Fat Cats & Running Dogs,* 169. Oil was the country's largest export.

109 John Lindsay-Poland, "U.S. Military Bases in Latin America and the Caribbean," in *The Bases of Empire: The Global Struggle against U.S. Military Posts*, ed. Catherine Lutz (New York: New York University Press, 2009), 71, 72.

110 Ibid.; John Lindsay-Poland, "U.S. Military Bases in Latin America and the Caribbean," *Foreign Policy in Focus*, October 5, 2005, https://fpif.org/us_military_bases_in_latin_america_and_the_caribbean/

111 Andrew Cockburn, *Kill Chain: The Rise of the High-Tech Assassins* (New York: Henry Holt, 2015), 98, 101; Mark Bowden, *Killing Pablo: The Hunt for the World's Greatest Outlaw* (New York: 2001); Dana Priest and Cristina Rivero, "CovertActions in Colombia: U.S. Intelligence, GPS Bomb Hits Help Latin American Nations Cripple Rebel Forces," *The Washington Post*, December 21, 2013.

112 John Lindsay-Poland, *Plan Colombia: U.S. Ally Atrocities and Community Activism* (Durham, NC: Duke University Press, 2018), 36, 52, 53; Crandall, "Explicit Narcotization."

113 Doug Stokes, *America's Other War: Terrorizing Colombia* (London: Zed Books, 2005), 89; Villar and Cottle, *Cocaine, Death Squads and the War on Terror*.

114 Mark Cook, "The 'Salvador Boys,'" *CovertAction Quarterly*, Fall-Winter 1999, 18, 19.

115 Douglas Stokes, *America's Other War; Terrorizing Colombia* (London: Zed Press, 2006), 90.

116 Scott, *Drugs, Oil and War*, 76 citing 1999 report by the Bureau for International Narcotics and Law Enforcement Affairs, U.S. State Department.

117 Noam Chomsky, *Rogue States: The Rule of Force in World Affairs* (Cambridge, MA: South End Press, 2000), 71.

118 Scott, *Drugs, Oil and War*, 74. Castano's brother, Fidel, with whom he formed his death squad, amassed a fortune as a drug dealer in league with Pablo Escobar. Mark Cook, "U.S. intervention in Colombia and Ecuador," *CovertAction Quarterly*, Spring-Summer 2000, 28.

119 "Who Killed Jaime Garzón? Document Points to Military/Paramilitary Nexus in Murder of Popular Colombian Comedian," September 29, 2011, The National Security Archive, George Washington University, https://nsarchive2.gwu.edu/NSAEBB/NSAEBB360/index.htm

120 Poland, *Plan Colombia*, 89, 93; Scott, *Drugs, Oil and War*, 73; Chomsky, *Rogue States*, 80. Originally, Plan Colombia was meant to complement economic aid from the European Union (EU), but amidst pressure from Colombian human rights groups and NGOs, the EU pulled back because it disapproved of the U.S. military approach.

121 Neil King Jr., "Clinton Makes an Antidrug Whistle-Stop in Colombia—Peaceful Aspects Stressed, But Neighbor Nations Fear Transfer of Traffic," *The Wall Street Journal*, August 31, 2000, A15.

122 Elizabeth Becker, "Clinton to Offer Aid in Colombian Drug War," *The New York Times*, January 11, 2000.

123 Matt Moffett, "Heading into Sunset, Clinton Hits the Road –Guerrillas and Drugs: Harsh Climate Awaits President in Colombia," *The Wall Street Journa*l, August 25, 2000; Javier Giraldo, *Colombia: The Genocidal Democracy*, foreword by Noam Chomsky (Monroe, ME: Common Courage Press, 1996); Winifred Tate, *Drugs, Thugs and Diplomats: U.S. Policymaking in Colombia* (Palo Alto: Stanford University Press, 2015).

124 Tate, "No Peace for Colombia"; Tate, *Drugs, Thugs and Diplomats*. The chickens were unable to weather Putamayo's climate and were left to starve and made into soup. A $2 million animal feed plant was meanwhile sold off as scrap three years after it opened.

125 David Rogers, "Antidrug Plan Passes a Test in the Senate," *The Wall Street Journal*, June 22, 2000, A6. Senator Gorton (R-WA) promoted an amendment to slash the Plan Colombia package from $934 million to $200 million.

126 Prashad, *Fat Cats & Running Dogs*, 176.

127 Mark Cook, "U.S. intervention in Colombia and Ecuador," *CovertAction Quarterly*, Spring-Summer 2000, 28.

128 Cornelius Friesendorf, *U.S. Foreign Policy and the War on Drugs: Displacing the Cocaine and Heroin Industry* (New York: Routeledge, 2007), 132, 134; Stokes, *America's Other War*; Mark Bowden, *Killing Pablo* (New York: 1993); William Neuman, "Colombia May Halt an Antidrug Program," *New York Times*, May 15, 2015; Gary Leach, *Beyond Bogota: Diary of a Drug War Journalist in Colombia* (Boston: Beacon Press, 2009), 78.

129 Four Arrows (AKA Don Trent Jacobs) and James H. Fetzer, *American Assassination: The Strange Death of Senator Paul Wellstone* (Brooklyn, NY: Vox Pop, 2004), 54.

130 Sean Donahue, "Rand Beers and Colombia," in *Dime's Worth of Difference: Beyond the Lesser of Two Evils* (Oakland, CA: AK Press/Counterpunch, 2004), 253, 254.

131 O'Shaughnessy, "Colombia."

132 Poland, *Plan Colombia*, 53.

133 Hugh O'Shaughnessy, "Colombia: Chemical Spraying of Coca Poisoning Villages," *The London Observer*, June 17, 2001.

134 Tate, *Drugs, Thugs and Diplomats*, 198, 199. The chairman of DynCorp, Herbert S. "Pug" Winokur, was a former CIA agent and Barry McCaffrey was on its board.

135 "DynCorp lawsuits (re Colombia & Ecuador)," https://www.business-humanrights.org/en/dyncorp-lawsuit-re-colombia-ecuador-0?page=1

136 Leach, *Beyond Bogota*, 188.

137 Ken Silverstein, *Private Warriors*, with research by Daniel Burton Rose (London: Verso, 2000), 186.

138 Christopher Hobson, "Privatising the War on Drugs," *Third World Quarterly*, 35, 8 (December 2014); Personal interview, DynCorp Pilot, Tulsa Oklahoma, September 2012.

139 Villar and Cottle, *Cocaine, Death Squads and the War on Terror*; *September 24, 2009, from the State Department in Washington to the U.S. Embassy in Bogota,* BLUE LANTERN: VERIFYING BONA FIDES OF REGISTERED BROKER FERNANDO LOPEZ - CASE NO. K-2547 *http://213.251.145.96/cable/2009/09/09STATE99488.html*. One of the jets used in counter-drug operations under Plan Colombia was owned by Clyde O'Connor who had connections to the CIA and owned another plane that crashed with four tons of cocaine onboard. The co-owner had worked a pilot in undercover CIA missions into Colombia. Bill Controy, "Cocaine Plane Trail is Open Challenge For Obama Administration," *The Narco News Bulletin*, January 11, 2009; https://web.archive.org/web/20140325155626/http:/narcosphere.narconews.com/notebook/bill-conroy/2009/01/cocaine-plane-trail-open-challenge-obama-administration; Bill Conroy, "Mexican Narco-Trafficker's Revelation Exposes Drug War's Duplicity," *The Narco News Bulletin*, April 25, 2011, https://web.archive.org/web/20140311012220/http:/narcosphere.narconews.com/notebook/bill-conroy/2011/04/mexican-narco-trafficker-s-revelation-exposes-drug-war-s-duplicity. Colonel James Hiett, the head of the army antidrug program in Colombia, was also arrested with his wife for shipping cocaine into the U.S. through a diplomatic pouch.

140 Thomas Kent to Jodi Avergus, Chief NDDS, "Re-Operation Snowplow," 12/19/2004, https://web.archive.org/web/20140325183326/http://www.narconews.com/docs/ThomasKentMemo.pdf; Bill Conroy, "New Document Provides Further Evidence That Owner of Crashed Cocaine Jet Was a U.S. Government Operative," *The Narco News Bulletin*, December 1, 2007, https://web.archive.org/web/20140325150649/http://www.narconews.com/Issue48/article2919.html.

141 Russell Crandall, "The Americas: In the War on Drugs, Colombians Die, Americans are Pardoned," *Wall Street Journal*, April 20, 2001, A15. The editorial pages in the Colombian press expressed unanimous contempt for the Weinig pardon. An op-ed in El Tiempo, the country's leading daily, was titled "The Morality of the Strongest." Gustavo De Greiff, a former Colombian attorney general, labeled Mr. Clinton's action "monstrous."

142 At his Senate confirmation hearing, Secretary of State John Kerry stated that Colombia was a "model for the region," an example to the rest of Latin America about what awaits them if we can convince people to make better decisions." Tate, *Drugs, Thugs and Diplomats*, 219.

143 Cited in Forrest Hylton, "Plan Colombia: The Measure of Success," *The Brown Journal of World Affairs*, 17, 1 (Fall/Winter 2010), 99.

144 Kevin Cirilli, "Clinton: Drug War Hasn't Worked," *Politico*, December 7, 2012, https://www.politico.com/story/2012/12/clinton-drug-war-hasnt-worked-084784.

CHAPTER 8

The Relay Runner: Bill Clinton in the Middle East

On October 29, 1994, eleven days before the mid-term elections, President Clinton tried to score some political points by giving a speech threatening Iraqi leader Saddam Hussein aboard a platform in Kuwait erected on the back of two M1-A1 Abrams tanks, with an armored personnel carrier and patriot missile launcher in the background. Clinton stated that "the international community will not allow Baghdad to threaten its neighbors, now or in the future. That is not our threat, that is our promise."[1] Clinton's display of foreign policy swagger was designed to eradicate the image of softness conveyed by Democratic Party presidential candidate Michael Dukakis during the 1988 election and divert attention away from his domestic policy failings.

At the time 9,000 American combat soldiers were stationed in Kuwait as a residue of the First Persian Gulf War which as governor Clinton had supported. Clinton's statements displayed a strong continuity with those of his predecessors, who had expanded the U.S. troop presence in the Middle East beginning in the late 1970s in a drive to control the region's oil.[2] In 1983, the U.S. military possessed no military bases anywhere in the Middle East. By the mid-2000s, U.S. Central Command at McDill Air Force base in Tampa, Florida had built up a military footprint of over 125 bases across the region.[3] Journalist Chip Gibbons compared Clinton to a "relay runner" who handed off to George Jr. the hawkish baton passed on to Bush by his father, especially with regards to Iraq.[4] This is an apt analogy for Clinton's foreign policy in the Middle East more broadly, which set the groundwork for the post-9/11 War on Terror.

Promoting Regime Change: Clinton's Iraq Policy

On June 27, 1993, President Clinton ordered the launching of twenty-three cruise missiles on Iraq's intelligence headquarters in downtown Baghdad. Seven missed their target and struck a residential neighborhood nearby in the middle of the night and killed six people, including a man found with his baby son in his arms and one of Iraq's most celebrated painters, Laylah al-Attar, director general of the Saddam Center for Arts. Many locals thought initially that the attack came from Iran. An angry crowd of 10,000 demanded revenge—some shouting "Vengeance, Vengeance Saddam!"—as they joined a funeral procession for the six people who were reported killed. "Clinton, pay attention—we are the people who toppled Bush [Sr. after the 1st Persian Gulf War]," the mostly Sunni demonstrators sang as six coffins were carried from central Baghdad to a site about a mile away.[5]

The pretext for the bombing was to punish Iraq for having allegedly plotted to assassinate George H.W. Bush during a visit to Kuwait. Washington claimed to have proof that Iraqi military intelligence was behind the assassination attempt; later it emerged that the FBI's chief investigator, Fred Whitehurst, had deemed the evidence inconclusive, and the plot appeared to be amateurish, though this was not made public. One of the defendants who was put on trial later retracted his confession. Others put on trial claimed they had been beaten into making a false confession or had crossed the border on a smuggling expedition.[6]

A theory relayed to ace reporter Seymour Hersh was that Kuwait's ruling al-Sabah dynasty had concocted the story of an assassination plot in order to prevent the Clinton administration from establishing better relations with Saddam.[7] Clinton himself said he felt "quite good about what transpired" the next day on his way to church; it was a view shared by liberal congressmen like Barney Frank and Joseph Moakley of Massachusetts who said "we've got to show these people that we're not sitting targets for terrorism."[8]

At the UN Security Council, Secretary of State Madeleine Albright defended the bombing with an appeal to article 51 of the UN charter which authorized the use of force against armed attack—although this article was reserved for cases when its necessity was overwhelming and where there was no moment for deliberation—not for an alleged assassination attempt two months before.[9] *The Bahrain Daily* observed that Arab lands had "become such fair game for America that Clinton did not even bother to search for a reasonably convincing pretext with which to justify the latest aggression," confident of support in the UN Security Council, which had become "little more than an appendage of the U.S. State Department. What is really happening is that America is humiliating the Arab people whenever it has a chance."[10]

Saddam was targeted primarily because he was an heir to the Pan-Arab legacy of Gamal Abdel Nasser, and threatened to become a regional strongman and to cut off America and its allies' access to the region's oil. Iraq itself sat on 112 billion barrels of crude. It was the "linchpin of a strategy to secure and diversify cheap oil supplies while breaking the clout of the Arab dominated oil cartel, OPEC," journalist Lutz Klevenman wrote. "Lest foreign investors in Iraq be burdened by production limits, a new pro U.S. government could go as far as pulling Iraq out of OPEC."[11] *The San Francisco*

Chronicle on February 22, 1998 reported further that if Iraqi oil were allowed on the international petroleum market, "it would devalue British North Sea oil, undermine American oil production and—much more important—it would destroy the huge profits which the United States stands to gain from its massive investment in Caucasian oil production, especially in Azerbaijan."[12]

In October 1998, Clinton signed the "Iraq Liberation Act," championed by Paul Wolfowitz and Richard Perle of the neoconservative Project for the New American Century, which formalized America's demand for regime change. Ninety-seven million was appropriated to fund Iraqi opposition groups, including most notably the Iraqi National Congress (INC), a collection of Shia clerics, Bedouin chiefs, royals, communist apparatchiks, ex-Ba'athist and ex-military officers, and Kurdish chieftains, headed by Ahmed Chalabi, a Ph.D. from MIT who had been convicted in absentia in Jordan for embezzlement.

Chalabi's cousin, Ayad Allawi, was, according to CIA officer Vincent Cannistraro, a "paid Mukhbarat [secret police] agent for the Iraqis involved in dirty stuff"—allegedly including running a "hit team" that sought out and killed Ba'ath Party dissenters throughout Europe in the 1970s. After developing a taste for money and the high life of the West, Allawi became a British MI-6 agent and was attacked by the Mukhbarat in his home as a traitor. When he became interim prime minister following the 2003 U.S. military invasion, Allawi personally executed terrorist suspects by shooting them in the head.[13]

UN Weapons inspector Scott Ritter resigned after declaring that the UN weapons inspection program provided a front for CIA spying to further the regime change efforts of the INC.[14] One INC member, Kanan Makiya, author of the anti-Saddam book, *Republic of Fear: The Politics of Modern Iraq* (Berkeley: University of California Press, 1989) received funding from the National Endowment for Democracy (NED) to create an archive of secret Ba'athists documents seized during the Iraq War. Makiya spread horror stories about Saddam's human rights abuses (some true, some probably fabricated) and other regime change propaganda from his perch as a professor at Harvard University and later Brandeis University.[15] The INC and other anti-Saddam groups received military advice from retired General Wayne Downing, a Special Forces expert and employee of Science Applications Incorporated Corporation (SAIC), and CIA officer Duane "Dewey" Clarridge, a Brown University graduate who had played a central role in Nicaragua's Contra war in the 1980s.[16]

Another CIA-financed group, the Iraqi National Accord (INA), made up mostly of former Iraqi military officers who fed disinformation about Iraq's alleged weapons of mass destruction (WMD), mounted a coup attempt in 1996 from Jordan.[17] The "Silver Bullet Coup," as it was known, was coordinated by the CIA's Amman Station and approved by the Clinton White House. It aimed to use the UN Special Commission (UNSCOM) in Iraq for weapons inspection to trigger a crisis that would create a pretext for a U.S. military attack against Saddam's personal security force, the Republican Guard, which would allow defectors to then take over the government. Iraq's Mukhbarat, however, took control of one of the CIA's secure satellite communications units, learning every detail of the plan. Saddam rounded up more than 800 suspected plotters, most of whom were tortured and executed. Scott Ritter wrote that "the U.S. had witnessed a covert action fiasco of a kind not seen since the Bay of Pigs in 1961."[18]

The Duelfer report, compiled by a special adviser to the CIA on Iraq's alleged possession of WMD in 2004, revealed that, much like with Fidel Castro after the Cuban revolution, Saddam's regime had made diplomatic overtures to the U.S. in the 1990s. As a continuity of its strategy during the 1980s Iran-Iraq War, Saddam even said that Iraq was "willing to be Washington's best friend in the region—bar none."[19] Washington, however, did not reciprocate, allocating tens of millions of dollars to overthrow Saddam.[20] Part of this money went towards recruiting Iraq's Kurds who had been subjected to reprisals after participating in a failed uprising against Saddam during the 1st Persian Gulf War.

In August 1996, Saddam damaged American efforts to forge a united Kurdish opposition to his regime when his army drove the Patriotic Union of Kurdistan (PUK) from a protected zone in Irbil—with a green light, according to PUK leader Jalal Talibani—and helped drive a wedge between it and the Kurdish Democratic Party (KDP). Factional fighting subsequently left hundreds dead. The KDP and PUKs private security apparatuses carried out torture and assassinations. The Clinton administration retaliated against Saddam by expanding its "no fly zone" in northern Iraq to the 33rd parallel and by launching forty-four computer guided cruise missiles from B-52s against Iraqi air defense installations in southern Iraq (Saddam's drive against the Kurds occurred in the north).[21] Five Iraqi civilians were killed in an errant strike and nineteen wounded.

In an appearance at the National Guard Association, Clinton said that the U.S. aimed "to demonstrate once again that reckless acts have consequences," and also later announced that the U.S. would "maintain a strong military presence in the Kurdish area and will remain ready to use it if Saddam moves against the Kurds."[22] The Clinton administration's concern for the Kurds was self-serving, since on the other hand it supported Turkey's brutal repression of its Kurdish population extending into Iraq. Criticizing the air strikes, KDP leader Masoud Barzani said they were "just part of Clinton's election campaign," and that America had provided only empty promises regarding Kurdish autonomy.[23]

Flashback to the Days of Bomb Shelters

Clinton helped to advance Iraqi regime change propaganda/disinformation in a November 1997 speech to a gathering of Democrats in Sacramento where he warned about the deployment of "chemical and biological weapons and maybe small-scale nuclear weapons" by Saddam—which could "do ten times as much damage as the Oklahoma City bomb." The world had to combat "the organized forces of destruction" that would "spread weapons of mass destruction."[24]

The next morning on ABC's *This Week*, Defense Secretary William Cohen placed on the table a five-pound sack of sugar and asked viewers to imagine it contained anthrax, which Iraq was known to have produced during the Gulf War. If spread over a city the size of Washington, Cohen said, it would kill half the population. Cohen next held up a thimble: if it contained VX, a nerve agent also suspected in Iraq's arsenal, one drop will "kill you within a few minutes."[25]

At a Pentagon briefing ten days later, Cohen said that the United Nations believed Saddam may have in his possession "as much as 200 tons of VX, and this would, of course, be theoretically enough to kill every man, woman and child on the face of the earth."

New York Times columnist Maureen Dowd wrote that Cohen's alarmist performance art "was a flashback to the days of bomb shelters and learning to crawl under your desk if the big one hit." She nonetheless seconded his concern, insofar as "we are talking about a world-class monster [Saddam] who strangles people with his bare hands, gasses entire villages, assassinates members of his family and uses babies as shields. Wondering if the Clinton crowd—alumni of make love not war—has the spine for its first big crisis is giving me a bad case of the jits."[26]

The Cold War–like hullabaloo about Saddam and WMDs, laying the groundwork for the Bush administration's 2003 invasion, was disproven by Scott Ritter, who testified that he saw no evidence the country possessed the capability to produce or deploy chemical, biological, or nuclear weapons, which America's ally Israel had in great abundance, or had operational SCUD missiles, and that his boss, Charles Duelfer had issued a report concluding that Iraq had disarmed by the summer of 1991. Ritter also said that any concealment efforts were designed to protect Saddam from assassination and that Iraq was complying with regulations to limit the number of scud missiles to under 100, though these inconvenient facts were suppressed or denied. According to Ritter, the Clinton administration had "manipulated, suppressed, and fatally undermined the weapons inspection process in support of the agenda of regime change."[27]

Operation Desert Fox

In December 1998, Clinton launched a four day bombing operation known as Operation Desert Fox—the nickname of Hitler's General Erwin Rommel—which killed 62 Iraqi soldiers and 82 civilians while flattening an agricultural school, damaging at least a dozen schools and hospitals and knocking out water supplies for 300,000 people in Baghdad.[28] General Ronald Fogleman, the U.S. Air Force Chief of Staff, characterized Operation Desert Fox as "an air occupation of a country."[29]

The pretext was that Saddam had announced the end of cooperation with UNSCOM—though Saddam never actually ordered the inspectors out. In fact, UNSCOM head Richard Butler says he was told by the U.S. Ambassador to the UN Richard Holbrooke that "it would be wise for him to withdraw UNSCOM personnel before planned U.S. and British bombing marked the end of UNSCOM's inspectors."[30] Secretary of State Madeleine Albright subsequently stated that the U.S. would "act multilaterally if we can [in Iraq] and unilaterally if we must because the U.S. considers this area vital to U.S. interests."[31]

Washington Post columnist William Arkin concluded, based on study of the target list, that the real purpose of Operation Desert Fox was to destroy the Iraqi regime. Saddam's palaces and sleeping quarters were struck along with Iraqi intelligence and Ba'ath party headquarters, as well as eavesdropping and jamming units, radio and television transmission stations and army barracks. Only 13 of the targets were facilities associated with chemical and biological weapons and ballistic missiles, while 35 of them played a role in Iraq's air defense system, which the U.S. needed to cripple as an essential first step in any broader air war and regime change operation.[32] The implications of this assessment is that Clinton's policy not only extended Bush I's war but was a vital first step that lay the groundwork for Bush II's 2003 invasion that toppled Saddam.[33]

Howard Zinn, author of A *People's History of the United States* and leader in the anti-Vietnam War movement, wrote:

> We are living in a time of madness, when men in suits and ties, and yes, a woman Secretary of State [Madeleine Albright], can solemnly defend the use in the present of indiscriminate violence—they do not know what they are bombing!—against a

> tyrant who may use violence in the future. The phrase clear and present danger has therefore lost its meaning. The phrase Weapons of Mass Destruction too has lost its meaning when a nation which has more such weapons and has used them more often than any other uses those words to justify the killing of civilians "to send a message."[34]

After writing these words, Zinn received a letter from Dr. Mohammed Al-Obaidi, an Iraqi citizen residing in the UK, who said that a cruise missile hit his parents' house and killed his mother, and sister-in law and her three children. Zinn responded by saying that the letter had conveyed to him with terrible clarity that "Saddam Hussein and the leaders of our government have much in common. They are both visiting death and suffering on the people of Iraq."[35]

Quiet War and Genocidal Sanctions

Operation Desert Fox was the beginning of a year-long "quiet war" costing over $1 billion in which American and British jet fighters dropped more than 1,800 bombs on Iraq and hit more than 450 targets, killing 120 people and injuring 442.[36] The bombing was combined with economic sanctions, which Madeleine Albright conceded on *60 Minutes* resulted in the deaths of a half a million Iraq children, a price she said was "worth it" to contain Saddam. John Mueller and Karl Mueller wrote in *Foreign Affairs* in May-June 1999 that the economic sanctions may well have "caused the deaths of more people in Iraq than have been slain by all so-called weapons of mass destruction throughout history."[37]

The high death toll resulted from the fact that the U.S.-led coalition had destroyed Iraq's infrastructure during the first Persian Gulf War. The sanctions deprived people of food and medicines along with chemicals for water purification and parts from sewage pumps. Raw sewage spilled into rivers from which people got their drinking water, causing many deaths from disease along with the malnutrition.[38] An iconic piece of Iraqi art from the period by sculptor Mohamed Ghani featured a three-meter figure of a woman, her breasts dry of milk, with a child pleading with her for food, the small frail body merged into her legs.[39]

During a lengthy interview on *Democracy Now* in 2000, Bill Clinton denied any responsibility for the human cost of the sanctions, telling Amy Goodman that Saddam had the money to feed children but had elected not to and was trying to blackmail the UN in order to enable his regime to buy nuclear weapons, chemical weapons and biological weapons.[40] Much of the money was derived from oil sales that were sanctioned under a UN oil for food program. Iraq received oil for food revenue only after money was first paid to Kuwait as war reparation and to the UN to cover its daily operation costs in Iraq, which left an inadequate amount to properly feed the people and address the dire humanitarian situation.[41]

Because of the sanctions, Iraq was also forced to sell its oil far cheaper than the international market price. With nearly 40 percent of Iraq's oil exports ending up in U.S. refineries, the biggest beneficiaries were big U.S. oil companies such as Chevron, Exxon-Mobil, Valero, Clark and Marathon Ashland which made billions of dollars profit from the cheaper oil difference every year in what amounted to "one of the biggest oil schemes in history."[42]

Denis Halliday resigned as coordinator of humanitarian relief to Iraq in 1998 after 34 years with the UN (he was then UN Assistant Secretary-General) because, as he wrote:

> the policy of economic sanctions [was] totally bankrupt. We are in the process of destroying an entire society. It is as simple and terrifying as that . . . Five thousand children are dying every month . . . I don't want to administer a programme that results in figures like these.

Halliday Went on to Suggest that the sanctions policy

> satisfied the definition of genocide: a deliberate policy that has effectively killed well over a million individuals, children and adults. We all know that the regime, Saddam Hussein, is not paying the price for economic sanctions; on the contrary, he has been strengthened by them. It is the little people who are losing their children or their parents for lack of untreated water. What is clear is that the Security Council is now out of control, for its actions here undermine its own Charter, and the Declaration of Human Rights and the Geneva Convention. History will slaughter those responsible.[43]

On February 13, 2000, Hans von Sponeck, who had succeeded Halliday as humanitarian coordinator in Iraq, additionally resigned. "How long," he asked, "should the civilian population of Iraq be exposed to such punishment for something they have never done?" Two days later, Jutta Burghardt, head of the World Food Program in Iraq, also resigned, saying privately she, too, could not tolerate what was being done to the Iraqi people.[44] These resignations and commentaries provide a stinging rebuke to the Clinton administration's Iraq policy which set the groundwork for the disastrous 2003 invasion.

Manufacturing Another False WMD Threat

In May 1995, President Clinton signed an executive order imposing sanctions on Iran that restricted United States trade and investment, including purchases by American companies that accounted for more than 20 percent of that country's oil exports. Conoco was forced to cancel a billion-dollar agreement to develop two Iranian off-shore oil fields. In 1996, Clinton signed the Republican-inspired Iran-Libya sanctions act, which imposed more sanctions on foreign firms investing more than $40 million in Iran's oil and gas industry. Previously, the Clinton administration had refused to permit the U.S. airplane manufacturer Boeing to sell passenger aircraft to Iran, and pressured Azerbaijan to drop Iran from an international consortium developing one of Azerbaijan's offshore oil fields.[45]

Speaking at a dinner of the World Jewish Congress in New York in May 1995 after the imposition of sanctions, Clinton characterized Iran as an "inspiration and paymaster to terrorists" and stated that he was "convinced that instituting a trade embargo with Iran is the most effective way our nation can help to curb that nation's drive to acquire devastating weapons and its continued support for terrorism."[46] These remarks exemplify how Clinton served as a relay runner between the two Bushes on Iran, much as he had with Iraq. As part of a dual containment policy, he singled out Iran as a primary U.S. adversary in the Middle East, foreshadowing G. W. Bush's inclusion of Iran as part of the "axis of evil." Like with the false connection between Saddam and WMD, Clinton's rationale—Iran's alleged development of a nuclear weapons and sponsorship of terrorism—were largely manufactured.

Secretary of State Warren Christopher—who referred to Iran as an "international outlaw" and "dangerous country"—had suggested in a May 1995 press briefing just before Clinton's announcement that American intelligence agencies had information about Iran's development of nuclear weapons. Christopher, however, misrepresented the intelligence as the reports merely showed that Iran was intent on acquiring nuclear enrichment technology, which was in compliance with the Nuclear Non-Proliferation Treaty (NPT), to which Iran was a signatory, if it was put to use for non-military purposes.[47]

In 1993, Iran's president Ali Rafsanjani told *Time* magazine that it would be "irrational for Iran to use its limited resources to develop nuclear weapons," adding that they could never be used in the region and would not help redress Iran's imbalance of power with the United States. A decade later, Iran's Supreme leader Ayatollah Ali Khamenei issued a fatwa against nuclear weapons, and the International Atomic Energy Agency (IAEA) found no evidence of Iranian weapons related activity.[48] Iran at this time was also falsely accused of terrorist attacks for which there was no definitive proof—including the 1993 World Trade Center bombing, and bombing of the Israeli embassy in Buenos Aires.[49]

The demonization and alarmism about Iran had more to do with geopolitical considerations than any real national security threat. The 1979 Islamist revolution overthrowing the Shah, who had been installed in a CIA-backed coup 25 years earlier, had dealt a blow to American interests in the Middle East and desire to control the region's oil, which subsequent administrations worked to try to reverse. The Reagan administration thus supported Saddam Hussein's war on Iran and covered up for Saddam's crimes in that period. Clinton continued Reagan and Bush I's policy of containment and went even further. Martin Indyk, Clinton's Senior Director for the Near East and South Asia on the National Security Council (NSC) recalls Clinton saying that "containment was not a tough enough policy, we had to find a way to change their behavior or change their regime."[50]

One of Clinton's key motives was to scare the American public into repudiating the "peace dividend" advocated by Robert S. McNamara. A new threat had been needed to replace that of the now defunct Soviet Union. American policy at the same time was driven largely by Israeli interests.[51] Clinton's rhetoric followed that of Yitzhak Rabin and his successor Benjamin Netanyahu, who raised alarm about the alleged Iranian nuclear weapons program in a manner which contradicted the findings of Israel's own intelligence agencies (Rabin himself admitted privately based on these reports that Iran was seven to fifteen years away from developing the bomb).

Mark Heller, a senior researcher at the Jaffee Center for Strategic Studies, Tel Aviv University, wrote that the purpose of portraying a threat from Iran in alarming terms was to "help the Rabin government with Israelis who harbored doubts about the peace talks with the Palestinians. ... The argument the Rabin government was making was that if you don't make peace with these guys, look who's coming next—Islamic fundamentalists with nuclear arms behind them."[52]

The Israelis also needed a new threat to enable the U.S. to rationalize the maintenance of its close security relationship with Israel and its large scale arms procurements at the end of the Cold War.[53] Benjamin Netanyahu's main motive for playing up the Iran threat was to help "change the channel" from stalled peace talks according to an aide, at a time that his government refused to abide by the Wye agreements that called for thirteen percent Israeli withdrawal from the occupied territories (Netanyahu had pressed for only

9 percent) and halting of the Israeli withdrawal process as he prepared for general elections.[54]

Iran's president Akber Hashemi Rafsanjani (1989–1997) was considered by the CIA to be a pragmatic moderate who along with the Supreme Leader Ali Khamenei sought improved relations with the United States.[55] Rafsanjani's successor, Mohammad Khatami (1998–2005), was a liberal reformer who promoted a "dialogue of civilizations" as a counter to Harvard University professor Samuel Huntington's contention claiming an inevitable clash of civilizations between the West and Islam.[56]

Clinton at that time expressed interest in improving relations, particularly if Iran cooperated in the investigation of the 1996 bombing of a U.S. military housing quarter in the Saudi city of Khobar that killed 19 U.S. soldiers, behind which members of the Iranian revolutionary guard corps were suspected.[57] Khatami reacted angrily, however, to the insinuation of Iranian guilt in the Khobar attack, stating that the allegations were based on "inaccurate and biased information" and "were fabricated"—a view confirmed by investigative reporter Gareth Porter. Khatami also criticized the U.S. for failing to take action against the crew of the *USS Vincennes* for its 1988 attack on an Iran Air passenger plane that killed all 290 passengers and crew on board.[58]

In a major speech on March 17, 2000, Madeleine Albright formally apologized for the CIA's role in the 1953 coup that overthrew Prime Minister Mohammad Mossadegh and restored the monarchy. She also announced the lifting of sanctions on imports of Iranian food and carpets, approved export of spare parts for Iran's aging Boeing aircraft and offered to settle outstanding legal claims on Iranian assets frozen in U.S. bank accounts since the 1979 U.S. Embassy seizure. A few days later, Iranian Supreme Leader Ayatollah Ali Khamenei dismissed Albright's remarks as worthless—in part because the CIA was still arming groups like the Kurds that were plotting the government's overthrow—and the U.S.-Iran relationship went from bad to worse.[59]

Clinton's hostile policy was part of a forty-year covert war on the Iranian revolutionary regime, which paid a high price for its defiance. Although not as devastating as Iraq, the sanctions were harmful to Iran's economy when the country badly needed revenues to repay foreign debts and modernize its oil fields. *The Wall Street Journal* reported in September 1995 that Iran hadn't yet been able to find customers for 200,000 of the 600,000 barrels a day of crude oil that American companies had been purchasing [prior to the imposition of sanctions] and incurred expenses because it was forced to store some unsold oil in leased tankers and in South Africa.[60]

Pacts with Devils

While punishing Iraq and Iran because of their failure to all into line with the New World Order the Clinton administration shored up its alliance with some of the Middle East's worst dictatorships, including most notably Saudi Arabia and Egypt under Hosni Mubarak (1981–2011). The U.S. sold them high tech equipment as part of Washington's dual containment policy targeting Iran and Iraq. Clinton enjoyed particularly close relations with Mubarak, on whom Clinton counted to play a significant role in Middle East peace talks and praised for "making great strides towards reforming and restructuring Egypt's economy"—along neoliberal lines—and for "creating better conditions to attract U.S. investment in Egypt.[61]

Egypt's police force, the Mukhabarat, under Mubarak was infamous for its cruelty and had been frequently cited by the State Department for torture of prisoners. According to a 2002 report, detainees were "stripped and blindfolded; suspended from a ceiling or doorframe with feet just touching the floor; beaten with fists, whips, metal rods, or other objects; subjected to electrical shocks; and doused with cold water [and] sexually assaulted."[62] Under the terms of the 1979 peace accord between Israel and Egypt, the U.S. had allocated around $2 billion in aid to Egypt, roughly divided between military and humanitarian funds, which the Clinton administration sustained despite negative State Department's assessments regarding human rights.[63] In 1996 alone, Egypt bought $1 billion worth of American aircraft, vehicles, naval equipment, missiles and other munitions.[64]

The Clinton administration at the same time was selling the Saudis 1,500 Raytheon AIM-9L missiles (CIA Director John Deutch sat on Raytheon's Board), 700 laser-guided bombs, hundreds of light armored vehicles and machine guns and helped maintain an airborne warning and control system.[65] *The Wall Street Journal* reported in October 1994 that the Saudis were at the time "by far the largest foreign buyer of U.S. military equipment," including of M-1A2 tanks, whose research and development upgrade wouldn't have been possible without Saudi purchases. On an average day, the Pentagon disbursed $10 million in Saudi payments to U.S. defense contractors; "on a good day it goes as high as $50 million," said a Pentagon official.[66] Clinton's State Department even okayed the sale of body-chains used to restrain prisoners, which were banned in most European countries as devices of cruelty.[67]

The Saudi Royal family was among the most oppressive regimes in the world, with thousands of political prisoners. They were also leading sponsors of terrorism through their attempts to export their version of Wahhabism around the Middle East, supporting jihadist groups through the Islamic Relief Organization. Mohammed al-Khalewi, former First Secretary of the Saudi mission to the UN, said that he had documents showing that the Saudi government funded Hamas (Islamic group in Gaza), supported Saddam Hussein's nuclear arms program and wiretapped Jewish groups.[68] Saudi intelligence also backed an Islamist rebellion in Uzbekistan.[69] CIA agent Robert Baer wrote that "the United States had made a pact with the devil. . . . as long as the Sultan kept buying American weapons and Aramco kept banking our oil, no one in Washington cared what was happening in the kingdom."[70]

Clinton himself had a personal connection to the Ibn Saud royal dynasty through Prince Turki bin Faisal, the head of the Saudi intelligence service, who was a classmate at Georgetown. As Governor of Arkansas, Clinton had worked hard to secure a multimillion dollar Saudi donation to the Middle East Studies program at the University of Arkansas, Fayetteville.[71] One of the payoffs was Clinton's effectiveness in lobbying for American corporate deals in Saudi Arabia, including for AT & T and for Boeing, which secured a $3.6 billion order for civilian jets and then gave $65,000 to the Democratic National Committee, four times more than it had donated during the previous three years.[72]

America's alliance with the Saudi Royal family went back to the presidency of Franklin D. Roosevelt and gave the U.S. access to cheap oil along with military bases which were used to wage the war on Iraq. In the early 1970s, the Nixon administration had forged a deal with Saudi Arabia that the country would sell its oil in U.S. dollars in exchange for regime protection via covert U.S. military and police assistance.[73] With the Saudis falling on hard economic times following the first Persian Gulf War, the Clinton administration allowed them to purchase their arms on credit, and helped secure a massive $6.2 billion loan from the Import-Export Bank, the biggest deal in its history.[74] The Clinton administration furthermore expanded covert mechanisms of support to Saudi security forces, especially by hiring more private military contractors which, according to journalist Ken Silverstein, "in effect turned the Saudi security apparatus, infamous for its use of torture, into a private subsidiary of the Pentagon."[75]

At the end of the Clinton era, Vinnell Corporation had over 1,000 employees in Saudi Arabia, many of them Army Special Forces veterans who instructed Saudi troops in using new weapons and offered tactical training to mechanized units. Another active company was the San Diego-based SAIC, which helped to assist the Navy in systems analysis and helped run Saudi air defense operations. O'Gara Protective Services was also hired to protect the Royal family and its property and Booz Allen & Hamilton oversaw the Saudi Marine Corps and ran the Saudi Armed Forces Staff College where they taught senior level military skills including tactical training.[76]

Saudi Arabia was a member state of the Gulf Cooperation Council (GCC) along with Bahrain, Kuwait, Oman, Qatar, and the United Arab Emirates (UAE), to which the Clinton administration provided vast quantities of arms in order to improve their ability to assist American forces in the event of a major conflagration. Between 1990 and 1997, the United States provided these countries with arms and ammunition worth over $42 billion—the largest and most costly transfer of military equipment to any region in the world by any single supplier in recent history, according to political analyst Michael T. Klare.[77] The transfers included 20 Lockheed F-16 aircraft to Bahrain worth $303 million in 1997; 256 Abrams tanks, 16 Apache attack helicopters and 16 Black Hawk helicopters to Kuwait; and 80 upgraded F-16 fighters to the UAE worth an estimated $7 billion in March 2000.[78]

The three latter countries were run by oppressive Sunni ruling families (Kuwait—Al Sabbah; Bahrain—Al Khalifa; UAE—Al Nahyan). All were cited by human rights organizations for banning opposition parties, torturing and disappearing political opponents, violently suppressing uprisings and carrying out ethnic cleansing operations.[79]

The GCC arms transfers epitomize the double standards of the Clinton administration regarding human rights and mass atrocity-prevention. Another good example of this was Jordan. The Clinton administration provided it with a $300 million military aid package in 1996, supported by the Israelis. It resulted in the transfer of 16 F-16 fighters along with 50 M60A3 tanks, 18 UH helicopters, an AC-130 cargo plane, M578 armored recovery vehicles and other military equipment.[80] Jordan was a "soft authoritarian regime" under King Hussein, which had a record of repressing its Palestinian population.

The U.S. embassy in Amman under Ambassador William J. Burns, the future CIA Director, promoted "free-market reforms," including privatization, tariff reduction and cutting public services. The new rules led to a 20% increase in the price of medicines in Jordan. Burns also helped support Jordan's bid to join the World Trade Organization (WTO) in Spring 2000, which he says was an essential first step in negotiating a bilateral free-trade agreement, the first with an Arab country.[81] The advancement of neoliberalism in Jordan had to be backed up by force, and reflected a selective application of the concept human rights, which excluded the rights of people to free quality health services and education and basic living standards.

Pipeline Politics: The Clinton/Taliban Teeter-Totter

Clinton's anti-Iranian policy resulted in support for the Taliban regime in Afghanistan for a period. Backed by the Pakistani intelligence services, the Taliban were Sunni fundamentalists who promoted a strict version of sharia law. Their leaders had mostly grown up in refugee camps in Pakistan and gained primacy in Afghanistan's civil war. The Taliban accused Iran of trying to fragment Afghanistan owing to the fact it was "scared that the Sunnis [in Iran] might revolt against it" in light of Afghanistan's "success as a Sunni Islamic emirate." According to the Taliban, Iran had spent a lot of money in Afghanistan, providing weapons and inciting rebellion in the largely Shiite province of Mazar-e-sharif.[82]

U.S. foreign policy elites recognized the strategic location of Afghanistan at "the crossroads between what Halford Mackinder [British imperial strategist] called the world's heartland and Indian subcontinent," wrote Elie Krakowski, special assistant to the Secretary of Defense for International Security policy from 1982–1988. Afghanistan had great potential for "opening the sea for the landlocked new states of Central Asia," which had "large oil and gas deposits" that the U.S. wanted to pry away from Russian control.[83]

After the Taliban took Kabul on September 27, 1996, the State Department issued a statement saying that it saw "nothing objectionable" about the Taliban—including in its imposition of Islamic law and harboring of Osama bin Laden, who had gone to Afghanistan in June 1996. U.S. Senator Hank Brown (R-CO) noted "the good part of what has happened is that one of the factions [in Afghan's civil war] at least [Taliban] seems capable of developing a government in Afghanistan."[84]

Besides using it as a wedge to contain Iran, the U.S. primary interest in Afghanistan was the building of a pipeline from Turkmenistan through Pakistan by UNOCAL, a company based in southern California. UNOCAL allegedly financed the Taliban through the bin Mahfouz commercial bank in Saudi Arabia, and had hired top lobbyists such as Henry Kissinger and Robert Oakley, the former U.S. ambassador to Pakistan.[85]

The oil pipeline was particularly important in enabling access to Central Asia's oil, whose reserves were estimated to reach more than 60 billion barrels—enough to service Europe's oil needs for 11 years.[86] With Iran out of the picture, Afghanistan was the only possible route of access other then Russia. A U.S. diplomat told journalist Ahmed Rashid: "the Taliban will probably develop like the Saudis did. There will be Aramco, pipelines, an emir, no parliament and lots of Sharia law. We can live with that."[87]

The preliminary feasibility study for the pipeline was performed by Enron, the soon notorious U.S. energy corporation, which received a $750,000 U.S. Agency for Trade and Development grant. U.S. intelligence sources and Enron officials confirmed that Enron covertly gave the Taliban millions of dollars, with the Clinton administration's apparent blessing, in a bid to strike a deal for the pipeline. The State Department was funneling arms to the Taliban at this time along with Pakistan's ISI and the Saudis.[88]

Republican Congressman Dana Rohrbacher (CA), who had been involved with Afghanistan since the early 1980s as special assistant to President Ronald Reagan, was stonewalled when he requested access to documents; criticized the Clinton administration's covert policy of supporting the Taliban, whom he called the "most anti-Western, anti-female, and anti-human rights regime in the world"; and pushed for support for the Northern Alliance.[89] Nonetheless, in April 1998 Clinton dispatched Assistant Secretary of State Rick Inderfurth and Bill Richardson, UN ambassador, to convince anti-Taliban forces in Panjshir not to attack or retake Kabul.[90]

However, relations with the Taliban soured and the CIA began covertly backing the Northern Alliance when the Taliban turned to a competitor of UNOCAL which had the support of the Saudis for the construction of the fossil fuel pipeline—the Argentine company, Bridas. The Union Oil Company of California (UNOCAL) had refused the Taliban's demand for more than $100 million per year in rent for the pipeline route in the form of roads, water supplies, telephone and electricity lines, and a tap on the pipeline to provide oil and gas for Afghanistan. Unlike UNOCAL, Bridas promised that the pipeline would provide energy to the domestic market and not only for exports.[91]

Secretary of State Madeleine Albright then began highlighting the Taliban's repression of freedom and rights, particularly towards women. A deal was struck with Northern Alliance commander Ahmed Shah Massoud in which the U.S. agreed to supply him with arms and ammunition in exchange for Massoud providing intelligence reports about Osama bin Laden.[92] The Clinton administration subsequently seized the Taliban's assets in the U.S., imposed sanctions and bombed Afghanistan under the pretext that the Taliban were harboring bin Laden.[93]

Silent Spectator to a Massacre

In a December 1997 meeting in Washington with Karl F. Indefurth, the Assistant Secretary for South Asian Affairs, three members of the Taliban—Armad Jan, the acting minister of mines and industry; Amir Khan Mottaqi, the acting minister of information and culture; and Din Mohammed, an ethnic Tajik who was acting minister of planning—did not mince words in condemning the double standards of the U.S. towards human rights and the Clinton administration's silence in the face of massacres carried out by Northern Alliance commanders with a rapacious track record against Taliban prisoners in northern Afghanistan.

Defending the Taliban's record on women's rights, which he said was in line with Afghan traditions, Mr. Mottaqi specifically questioned the neutrality of the international community in Afghanistan's civil war when

Russia and Tehran were supporting anti-Taliban Northern Alliance fighters in Mazer-I-Sharif with weapons and training, and when Northern Alliance leader Burhanuddin Rabbani, head of the Tajik-dominated Jamiat-i Islami Party, retained the Afghan seat at the UN General Assembly.

Mottaqi said that the Rabbani regime had cheated and lied to the Taliban. It had overseen the horrific massacre of 1632 Taliban prisoners by Northern Alliance militias in the Lailey desert near the town of Shiborghan in Jozjan province, North Afghanistan. Several hundred men imprisoned in Mazer-I-Sharif and 372 imprisoned in Faryab were also executed. Numerous prisoners had died under torture while others were savagely maimed and had their limbs amputated before they were killed.

At the time of the massacre, Rabbani claimed to be president of Afghanistan, with his government based in Mazer-I-Sharif. A former professor of Islamic theology at Kabul University and leader of the anti-Soviet mujahadin, Rabbani had served as a mentor to both Ahmed Shah Massoud and Gulbuddin Hikmatyar, one of the CIA's top assets in Afghanistan. The general who gave the orders for the Lailey desert massacre, Malik Pahlawan, was the second-in-command of Uzbeki warlord Rashid Dostum, who served as Vice-President of Afghanistan from 2014–2020 during the period of U.S.-NATO occupation and fled afterwards to Iran.

Jan told Inderfurth pointedly that

> when the hair of a person is cut in Kabul, the whole media is talking about it. Now, 3,000 people have been killed by the opposition militia and there is no serious interest. The U.S. advocates human rights throughout the world, but still it has not condemned the tragic human holocaust in the Laily desert. The people of Afghanistan never expected the U.S. government to be a silent spectator when thousands of Afghan men and women from all racial backgrounds are mourning the massacre of their relatives in Afghanistan. We want you to bring the culprits to trial and prosecute them according to international norms and principles.[94]

This prosecution would never take place because the Clinton administration by this time had turned against the Taliban and begun arming the very opposition forces that had carried out the human holocaust in the Lailey desert—under the pretext of waging a War on Terror. Ironically, Jan said that not only did the Taliban want friendly relations with the U.S., but that they had not been the ones to invite Osama bin Laden into Afghanistan. Rather he had come to Nangarhar province as a guest of the previous regime—led by Berhannudin Rabbani. When the Taliban took over, they stopped allowing bin Laden to give public interviews and frustrated Iranian and Iraqi attempts to get in contact with him.[95]

More Victims Not Worth Mentioning: Turkey's Kurds

While spotlighting abuses by Saddam Hussein against the Kurds in Iraq, the Clinton administration provided $800 million in arms annually to Turkey which had a long history of mistreating the Kurds. It approved the sale of 145 attack helicopters, training 976 Turkish military personnel including mountain commandos who massacred Kurdish rebels and destroyed hundreds of villages.[96] Lockheed F-16 jet fighters, Cobra and Black Hawk helicopters, cluster bombs, and M-60 tanks and M-113 armored personnel carriers were U.S. weapons that were used in the deadly counter-insurgency campaigns in the 1990s along with M-16 assault rifles made by Colt Industries. The U.S. also assisted the Turkish armed forces in providing military intelligence.

In 1994, as the atrocities peaked, Turkey became the biggest single importer of American military hardware and thus the world's largest arms purchaser.[97] U.S. sales to Turkey during the Clinton era were more than four times as large as the *entire* value of U.S. arms transfers to Turkey during the 34 years from 1950 to 1983.[98] Turkey's strategic value lay in its vital location on the Bosporus at the nexus of Europe, the Middle East, the Caucasus, and the Caspian. Since the end of World War II, it had served as an important ally of the United States in NATO and sent troops to wars like that in Korea.[99] Furthermore, prior to Erdogan's rise to power in Turkey in 2003, trade between the two countries eclipsed $6 billion in 1999, increasing by 50 percent during Clinton's presidency.[100]

Towards the end of its second term, the Clinton administration was promoting development of a $2.5 billion oil and natural gas pipeline through Turkey from the Caspian Sea basin which would bypass Russia and Iran. The contract had been awarded to PSG Corporation, a consortium of Bechtel Enterprises Inc. and General Electric.[101] Enron had also closed a $1 billion deal to develop two 500 megawatt gas-fired power stations on the Sea of Marmara.[102] Notably, since 1951, Turkey had housed the Incirlik Air Base, which was pivotal to U.S. power projection in the Middle East and provided a launching pad for bombing attacks into Iraq during the Persian Gulf War and in its aftermath.[103]

The presence of the Incirlik air base was undoubtedly a key reason that Turkey was elevated to the role of a "strategic partner" of the United States during President Clinton's visit to Turkey in November 1999."[104] Five years earlier, Clinton had called Turkey "a shining example to the world of the virtues of cultural diversity."[105] These comments were obscene considering the scorched earth operations targeting the Kurds in Southeastern Turkey, Turkey's record imprisonment of journalists, and wide-scale torture, disappearance and killing of Kurdish politicians, businessmen and activists carried out by special counterinsurgency regiments linked to organized crime.[106] Turkish authorities even demanded a three year prison sentence for the deputy manager of the Lufthansa office in Istanbul, Franz Reissig, after he had provided the Istanbul rotary club with an out of date globe with a geographical reference to Kurdistan![107]

Nonetheless, year after year, the Clinton administration blocked moves in the UN to censure Turkey for human rights violations.[108] Turkey instead was praised for "dealing with terrorism in its own borders," as Vice President Gore framed it in a 1994 speech. In 1984, PKK founder Abdullah Öcalan had initiated an armed struggle to create a Greater Kurdistan on Kurdish-populated territories in Turkey, Iraq, Iran, and Syria. Most Kurds felt they had no choice as the alternative to taking up arms was to watch the army raze their homes. Supported allegedly by Syria and Iran, the PKK earned its designation as a foreign terrorist organization based on its history of violence both against the Turkish military and against Kurds accused of collaborating with Turkey's security structures. The PKK's terrorist acts included kidnapping foreign tourists, suicide bombings, assassinating teachers, political figures, and other representatives of the Turkish government, planting mines and attacking Turkish diplomatic offices in Europe.[109]

One of the regions most devastated by the Turkish assault on the PKK was Tunceli, north of the Kurdish capital of Dyirbakir, where one third of the villages were destroyed by the Turkish army and vast tracts were set aflame by U.S.-supplied helicopters and jets. On April 1, 2000, Turkish helicopter gunships supplied by the United States were allowed to cross a no-fly zone in Iraq to attack Kurds, who were supposed to be protected by the U.S. Air Force from Saddam.[110] In March 1995, Clinton had given the green light in a phone conversation with Turkish Prime Minister Tansu Çiller to pursue the Kurds in Iraq.[111] Öcalan himself was kidnapped by Turkish intelligence in 1999 after being doggedly pursued with the support of the CIA and Israeli Mossad, and jailed for the next ten years on an isolated island in the Sea of Marmara.[112]

The most controversial U.S. arms sale to Turkey was the late 1998 decision to grant a license to the Michigan-based AV Technology division of General Dynamics to sell armored vehicles to the Turkish anti-terror and anti-riot police. According to a description by Dana Priest of *The Washington Post*, the deal included "11-ton, armored Patrollers, equipped with water cannons, ramming arms, and front gun ports for urban anti-riot police, and

Dragoons, an armored personnel carrier that would transport anti-terror police" who were implicated in major abuses including torture and rape.[113]

Clinton used his personal charm and "legendary ability to connect with people" to help diffuse criticism against U.S. policy during his November 1999 Turkish trip where he shared tea, lifted up babies in the earthquake shattered town of Izmit and wowed people by remembering the names of diplomats he had encountered years before. While passing a chance to confer with Turkey's military brass, Clinton instead met with human rights advocates and the Greek orthodox patriarch to symbolize his support for the Greek orthodox minority, and in a speech before parliament aligned himself with those demanding greater political liberty. Clinton also said that he hoped it would be possible for the Kurdish citizens of Turkey to reclaim "that most basic of birthrights, a normal life."[114]

Clinton, however, had helped deprive the Kurds of a "normal life" by backing the brutal Turkish countcribsurgency campaign against them. *The New York Times* reported that while Clinton spoke about the need for greater tolerance of free expression, the police were arresting scores of people staging an unapproved protest of his visit.[115] One of the main underlying purposes behind this visit besides public relations was to sign landmark accords for a new oil pipeline from the Caspian Sea with Turkey's President Suleyman Demirel and Turkmenistan dictator Sapurmutat Niyazov, whose rule was so draconian that he banned video games, listening to car radios, and performing operas and ballets, and closed libraries outside the capital of Ashbagat because he was trying to counter Western and Soviet influence.[116]

Clinton's strategic amorality was apparent in his administration's provision of copious arms sales to Turkey's main geopolitical rival, Greece, another NATO member, which helped augment regional tensions. The main beneficiary as per usual was the American war industry. Frigates, destroyers, and Hellfire antitank missiles sold to Greece in the summer of 1998 were matched with a sale of frigates and Harpoon anti-ship missiles to Turkey at the same time. These sales were announced despite the fact that the U.S. was then trying to launch an effort to renew dialogue on the island of Cyprus, which Turkey had invaded.

A report put out by the World Policy Institute and Federation of American Scientists (FAS) concluded that the introduction of each new level of technology "ratcheted up the arms race another notch, fueling expensive purchases on both sides. The Turkish decision to launch a $31 billion-dollar military modernization program over the next 10 years was countered by a Greek decision to reverse its economizing defense cuts and build up its arsenal as well with $24 billion over the next eight years."[117] Once again, vital resources were being siphoned away from badly needed social programs to the benefit of the arms merchants, as the threat of war grew more acute.

Conclusion

The failure of Clinton's Middle East policy was reflected in the rise in terrorist attacks directed against the United States during the 1990s. The callous disregard for Iraqi and Kurdish life, double standards on human rights, stationing military bases in Saudi Arabia, support for dictatorial governments, the vendetta against Iran and favoring of Israel (discussed in the next chapter) were all key factors fueling the militancy giving rise to attacks like the suicide bombing of the U.S.S. *Cole* on October 12, 2000. Steven Meyer of Washington's National Defense University wrote accurately that the administration "can't simply and arrogantly dismiss these attacks as the work of a few vicious malcontents who simply do not understand our good intentions in the Middle East."[118] Rather they should be understood as a form of blowback against America's neocolonialist policies, efforts to dominate the region militarily and incessant arms provision.

Osama bin Laden, the head of the al-Qaeda network which carried out the U.S.S. *Cole* attack, charged that ever since Operation Desert Storm, the United States had been "occupying the lands of Islam in the holiest of places, the Arabian peninsula, plundering its riches, dictating to its rulers, humiliating its people, terrorizing its neighbors, and turning its bases in the Peninsula into a spearhead through which to fight the neighboring Muslim people." To put an end to this intolerable situation, bin Laden now declared it "an individual duty for every Muslim" to kill American soldiers and civilians alike. Evicting foreign armies from "all the lands of Islam" and liberating the Muslim holy sites in Mecca and Jerusalem required and justified violence.[119] These comments provided a stunning rebuke to Clinton's foreign policy approach and that of his predecessors in the Middle East. Their primary legacy was the ignition of a civilizational war by humiliating the Muslim people and trampling on their rights, leaving Americans more vulnerable to terrorism in the process, and putting the nation on a permanent war footing, which would contribute to the decline of its democratic structures.

Endnotes

1 Douglas Jehl, "Clinton Visits U.S. Troops in Kuwait," *The New York Times*, October 29, 1994.

2 See Andrew Bacevich, *America's Greater War for the Middle East: A Military History* (New York: Random House, 2016).

3 See David Vine, *Base Nation: How U.S. Military Bases Abroad Harm America and the World* (New York: Metropolitan Books, 2009).

4 Chip Gibbons, "When Iraq Was Clinton's War," *Jacobin*, May 6, 2016, https://jacobinmag.com/2016/05/war-iraq-bill-clinton-sanctions-desert-fox

5 "Raid on Baghdad: The Iraqi Capital; On Baghdad Streets, Angry Demands for Revenge," *The New York Times*, June 28, 1993.

6 Robert Fisk, *The Great War for Civilization: The Conquest of the Middle East* (New York: Alfred A. Knopf, 2006), 715; Tim Weiner, "Plot by Baghdad to Assassinate Bush is Questioned," *The New York Times*, October 25, 1993; Alexander Cockburn and Jeffrey St. Clair, *Al Gore: A User's Manual* (London: Verso, 2000), 212.

7 Seymour M. Hersh, "A Case Not Closed," *The New Yorker*, November 1, 1993.

8 Noam Chomsky, *World Orders Old and New* (New York: Columbia University Press, 1996), 17. Congress almost unanimously approved the bombing as did most of the mainstream media. *The Washington Post* praised Clinton for "confronting foreign aggression" and relieving the fear that he might be less prone to violence than his predecessors. Clinton's poll numbers increased by eleven percent afterwards.

9 Chomsky, *World Orders Old and New*, 17.

10 Quoted in Chomsky, *World Orders Old and New*, 21. See also Naseer Aruri, "America's War Against Iraq: 1990–2002," in *Iraq Under Siege: The Deadly Impact of Sanctions and War*, ed. Anthony Arnove (Boston: South End Press, 2002), 38.

11 Lutz Klevenman, *The New Great Game: Blood and Oil in Central Asia* (New York: Atlantic Monthly Press, 2003), 262.

12 In Aaron Good, *American Exception: Empire and the Deep State*, foreword by Peter Phillips (New York: Skyhorse Publishing, 2022), 70.

13 Greg Guma, "Allawi's Mean Streak," April 17, 2010, *Counter Currents*, https://countercurrents.org/guma170410.htm; Jon Lee Anderson, "A Man of the Shadows," *The New Yorker,* January 16, 2005; Anthony Shadid, "Iraq's Last Patriot," *The New York Times Magazine*, February 4, 2011. Born to a wealthy Shia family, Allawi was known as an impetuous and authoritarian man who had scared classmates in high school. One recalled: "If he wanted to play handball, everybody would leave the court because they were afraid of him." Only a small portion of the funds intended for the INC were released—against the urging of Vice President Gore, a hawk on Iraq.

14 See Scott Ritter, *Iraq Cofidential: The Untold Story of the Intelligence Conspiracy to Undermine the UN and Overthrow Saddam Hussein* (New York: The Nation Books, 2005). Ritter's accusations were further substantiated in articles published in *The Boston Globe* and *The Washington Post*. Column Lynch, "U.S. Used UN To Spy on Iraq, Aides Say," *Boston Globe*, January 6, 1999, 1; Barton Gellman, "U.S. Spied on Iraqi Military Via UN," *The Washington Post*, March 2, 1999, A1.

15 National Endowment for Democracy, Annual Report, 1995, https://en.calameo.com/read/000366846c0505492d725. This author met Professor Makiya when he taught at Brandeis University in the political science department. At a forum on the eve of the Iraq War, Makiya repeated Dick Cheney's claim that U.S. troops would be welcomed in Baghdad with flowers. I asked him if he ever read Edward Said's book *Orientalism*, and he said "no."

16 Chip Gibbons, "When Iraq Was Clinton's War," *Jacobin*, May 6, 2016, https://jacobinmag.com/2016/05/war-iraq-bill-clinton-sanctions-desert-fox; Ken

Silverstein, *Private Warriors* (London: Verso, 2000), 257; Robert Baer, *See No Evil: The True Story of a Ground Soldier in the CIAs War on Terrorism*, foreword by Seymour Hersh (Walterville, OR: Thorndike Press, 2002), 394, 395. Chalabi was later the Bush administration's choice to succeed Saddam after his overthrow in 2003 but received only one percent of popular support when elections were held.

17 James Risen, "The Nation; the Clinton Administration's See No Evil CIA," *The New York Times*, September 10, 2000.

18 Ritter, *Iraq Confidential*, 163, 164; Scott Ritter, "The Coup That Wasn't," *The Guardian*, September 28, 2005, https://www.theguardian.com/world/2005/sep/28/iraq.military; Stefanie Nanes, "Slouching Towards Baghdad: Clinton's Policy Towards Iraq," in *Foreign Policy in the Clinton Administration*, ed. Rosanna Perotti (New York: Nova Science Publishers, 2019), 168; Tim Weiner, *Legacy of Ashes: The History of the CIA* (New York: Doubleday, 2007), 463. The ringleader was Mohammed Abdullah Shawani, a former commander of Iraqi Special Forces whose sons were executed when the plot was uncovered by Saddam.

19 Jim Lobe, "Politics U.S.: Did Saddam Try and Kill Bush's Dad?" *Interpress Service*, October 18, 2004, http://www.ipsnews.net/2004/10/politics-us-so-did-saddam-hussein-try-to-kill-bushs-dad/

20 Vera Beaudin Saeedpour, "Conflicted Kurdistan," *CovertAction Quarterly*, Fall 1995, 22.

21 Robert O. Freedman, "American Policy Toward the Middle East in Clinton's Second Term," Strategic Studies Institute, U.S. Army War College, 1999; Johanna McGeary, "Slamming Saddam Again," *Time* magazine, September 16, 1996; Michael M. Gunter, "U.S. Foreign Policy Towards the Iraqi Kurds During the Clinton Administration," in *Foreign Policy in the Clinton Administration*, ed. Perotti, 154.

22 Alison Mitchell, "U.S. Launches Further Strike Against Iraq After Clinton Vows He Will 'Extract' Price," *The New York Times*, September 4, 1996; Gunter, "U.S. Foreign Policy Towards the Iraqi Kurds During the Clinton Administration," in *Foreign Policy in the Clinton Administration*, ed. Perotti, 154.

23 Hugh Pope, "U.S. Abandoned Us, Say Kurds," *The Independent*, September 4, 1996, https://www.independent.co.uk/news/us-abandoned-us-say-kurds-1361688.html. High-powered U.S. diplomats dropped by infrequently and left soon afterwards, making little lasting impact. KDP officials said that the only Western diplomat who visited them with any regularity was the much-liked Frank Baker from the British Embassy in Ankara in Turkey.

24 Patrick Maney, *Bill Clinton New Gilded Age President* (Lawrence: University Press of Kansas, 2016), 246.

25 Maney, *Bill Clinton New Gilded Age President*, 246.

26 Maureen Dowd, "Liberties; Anthrax, Shmanthrax," *The New York Times*, November 19, 1997, https://www.nytimes.com/1997/11/19/opinion/liberties-anthrax-shmanthrax.html. Echoing Dowd, Madeleine Albright told an audience at Tennessee State University that no one should doubt the Iraqi leader's capacity for evil; perhaps not since Hitler had the world seen "somebody who is quite as evil as Saddam Hussein." Maney, *Bill Clinton New Gilded Age President,* 246. On U.S. support for Saddam's use of chemical weapons in the Iran-Iraq War, see https://foreignpolicy.com/2013/08/26/exclusive-cia-files-prove-america-helped-saddam-as-he-gassed-iran/.

27 "Myths and Realities Regarding Iraq and Sanctions," In *Iraq Under Siege*, ed. Arnove, 86; Ritter, *Iraq Confidential*, 289; Scott Ritter, "The Case for Iraq's

Qualitative Disarmament," *Arms Control Today*, 30, 5 (June 2000); Scott Ritter, "Powell and Iraq: Regime Change, Not Disarmament, the Fundamental Lie," *Consortium News*, July 19, 2020; Ritter, *Iraq Confidential*; John Steinbach, "Nuke Nation: Israel's Weapons of Mass Destruction," *CovertAction Quarterly*, April-June 2001. Rolf Ekeus, the director of UN disarmament observers in Iraq from 1991 to 1997, told journalist Andrew Cockburn that Clinton tried to prevent Iraq from being certified as free of weapons of mass destruction, which Ekeus believed that they were.

28 Fisk, *The Great War for Civilization*, 721. The Pentagon acknowledged that 11 percent of the bombs missed their targets. Thomas E. Ricks, "Assessing Success of Iraq Bombing May Take Months," *The Wall Street Journal*, December 22, 1998, A20.

29 Quoted in Bacevich, *America's War for the Greater Middle East*, 140.

30 Nanes, "Slouching Towards Baghdad," in *Foreign Policy in the Clinton Administration*, ed. Perotti, 168.

31 Ibid.

32 William Arkin, "The Difference Was in the Details," *The Washington Post*, January 17, 1999, B1.

33 Gibbons, "When Iraq Was Clinton's War."

34 "Iraq Bombing 'Another Lie,' Says Historian Zinn," *Mother Jones*, December 16, 1998.

35 Howard Zinn, "One Iraqi's Story," in *Iraq Under Siege*, ed. Arnove, 133.

36 Jonathan S. Landay, "Who's Winning Quiet War in Iraq?" *The Christian Science Monitor*, March 4, 1999, https://www.csmonitor.com/1999/0304/p1s1.html

37 John Mueller and Karl Mueller, "Sanctions of Mass Destruction," *Foreign Affairs*, May-June 1999, 45–53.

38 George Capaccio, "Sanctions: Killing a Country and a People," in *Iraq Under Siege*, ed. Arnove, 171–181; Dilip Hiro, Iraq: *In the Eye of the Storm*, 2nd ed. (New York: Thunder's Mouth Press, 2002); Roger Normand, "Sanctions Against Iraq: New Weapon of Mass Destruction," *Covert Action Quarterly*, Spring 1998; Fisk, *The Great War For Civilization*, 707. Iraq's education system was also decimated by the sanctions as many kids had to work from a young age to help support their families.

39 John Pilger, "Collateral Damage," in *Iraq Under Siege*, ed. Arnove, 77, 78.

40 Gibbons, "When Iraq Was Clinton's War."

41 George Capaccio, "Sanctions: Killing a Country and a People," in *Iraq Under Siege*, ed. Arnove, 172, 173.

42 Lee Siu Hin, "U.S. Using UN Program to Steal Iraq's Oil," *CovertAction Quarterly*, Spring-Summer 2000, 32, 33.

43 "Squeezed to Death," *The Guardian*, March 3, 2000.

44 "Squeezed to Death," *The Guardian*, March 3, 2000.

45 Robert O. Freedman, "American Policy Towards the Middle East in Clinton's Second Term," Strategic Studies Institute, U.S. Army War College, 1999; Presidential Documents, Executive Order 12959 of May 6, 1995, https://www.treasury.gov/resource-center/sanctions/Documents/12959.pdf. The Clinton administration was also focused on building alternative pipeline routes from the Caspian oil fields which exclude both Iran and Russia.

46 Todd S. Purdum, "Clinton To Order a Trade Embargo Against Iran," *The New York Times*, May 1, 1995.

47 D. Gareth Porter, *Manufactured Crisis: The Untold Story of the Iran Nuclear Scare* (Charlottesville, Virginia: Just World Books, 2014), 106.

48 Porter, *Manufactured Crisis*, 19, 66, 73, 119, 124.

49 Porter *Manufactured Crisis*, 108, 109, 110; Bacevich, *America's War for the Greater Middle East,* 142. James Bernazzani, head of the FBIs Hezbollah office who was sent to Buenos Aires to investigate acknowledged years later that the investigation turned up no real evidence of Iranian involvement.

50 Martin Indyk, *Innocents Abroad: An Intimate Account of American Peace Diplomacy in the Middle East* (New York: Simon & Schuster, 2009), 16, 31; Porter *Manufactured Crisis,* 104.

51 Porter, *Manufactured Crisis*.

52 Clyde Haberman, "Israel Eyes Iran in the Fog of Nuclear Politics," *The New York Times*, January 15, 1995, 4; Porter, *Manufactured Crisis*, 117.

53 Porter, *Manufactured Crisis,* 120.

54 Porter, *Manufactured Crisis*, 127, 129.

55 Porter, *Manufactured Crisis*, 92.

56 Anthony J. Dennis, *Letters to Khatami: A Reply to The Iranian President's Call for A Dialogue Among Civilizations* (Wyndham Hall Press, 2001).

57 John Lancaster and Roberto Suro, "Clinton Reaches Out to Iran," *The Washington Post*, September 29, 1999, A2. After the Khobar bombing attack, the U.S. had a contingency plan to attack Iran, though former Defense Secretary William Perry said that the evidence was not to either his or Clinton's satisfaction. (Perry suspected al-Qaeda was behind it). Perry, "U.S. Eyed Iran Attack After Bombing," *UPI*, June 6,2007, https://www.upi.com/Defense-News/2007/06/06/Perry-US-eyed-Iran-attack-after-bombing/70451181161509/

58 "Message President Clinton, to President Mohammad Khatami, June 1999, National Security Archive, George Washington University, https://nsarchive.gwu.edu/dc.html?doc=6585712-National-Security-Archive-Doc-08-Message; "In the Name of God," Iranian Response," Clinton presidential library, reprinted at https://nsarchive2.gwu.edu/NSAEBB/NSAEBB318/doc03.pdf; Gareth Porter, "Who Bombed Khobar's Towers? Anatomy of a Crooked Terrorism Investigation," *Truthout*, September 1, 2015, https://truthout.org/articles/who-bombed-khobar-towers-anatomy-of-a-crooked-terrorism-investigation/ Osama bin Laden publicly claimed responsibility for the Khobar attacks. Saudi secret police had tortured suspects to gain false confessions that would implicate the Iranians.

59 Bruce Riedel, "The Clinton Administration," The Iran Primer, U.S. Institute for Peace, https://iranprimer.usip.org/resource/clinton-administration

60 Robert S. Greenberger, "Iran Creates Fresh Problems for the White House with Senator D'Amato Adding Pressure of His Own," *The Wall Street Journal*, September 1, 1995, A8.

61 David S. Cloud, "Clinton Stops to Lobby Egyptian Leader – As Arafat's Deadline Nears, U.S. is Hoping Mubarak Can Spur Mideast Talks," *The Wall Street Journal*, August 30, 2000, A21; Bill Clinton meeting with Hosni Mubarak," October 26, 1994; Remarks by the President in Photo Opportunity with President Mubarak," Clinton Presidential Records, White House Press Office, box 7, William J. Clinton Presidential Library, Little Rock, Arkansas.

62 Jane Mayer, "Outsourcing Torture: The Secret History of America's 'Extraordinary Rendition' Program," *The New Yorker*, February 7, 2005, https://www.newyorker.com/magazine/2005/02/14/outsourcing-torture; Jason Brownlee, *Democracy Prevention: The Politics of the U.S.-Egyptian Alliance* (New York: Cambridge University Press, 2012).

63 Stephen J. Glain, "With Peace on Hold, Is Either Side a Winner?" *The Wall Street Journal*, July 26, 2000, A18.

64 *The Middle East Military Balance, 1996*, ed. Mark Heller (New York: Columbia University Press, 1998), 75.

65 Robert Baer, *Sleeping with the Devil: How Washington Sold Its Soul for Saudi Crude* (New York: Three Rivers Press, 2004), 152.

66 Geraldine Brooks, "Roiled Rulers: Saudi Arabia is Facing Debts and Defections That Test U.S. Ties," *The Wall Street Journal*, October 25, 1994, A1.

67 Alexander Cockburn and Ken Silverstein, *Washington Babylon* (London: Verso, 1996), 180.

68 Brooks, "Roiled Rulers."

69 Ahmed Rashid, *Descent Into Chaos: The United States and the Failure of Nation Building in Pakistan, Afghanistan and Central Asia* (New York: Viking, 2009), 68.

70 Baer, *Sleeping with the Devil*, 185.

71 Tim Weiner, "Clinton and his Ties to the Influential Saudis," *The New York Times*, August 23, 1993.

72 Cockburn and Silverstein, *Washington Babylon,* 284.

73 See Medea Benjamin, *Kingdom of the Unjust: Behind the U.S. Saudi Connection* (OR Books, 2016); Victor McFarland, *Oil Powers: A History of the U.S. Saudi Alliance* (New York: Columbia University Press, 2020).

74 Stephen Engleberg, "U.S. Saudi Deals in 90s Shifting Away From Cash Towards Credit," *The New York Times*, August 23, 1993.

75 Ken Silverstein, *Private Warriors*, research by Daniel Burton Rose (London: Verso, 2000), 180.

76 Silverstein, *Private Warriors*, 181; Andrew Thomson, *Outsourced Empire: How Militias, Mercenaries, and Contractors Support U.S. Statecraft* (New York: Pluto Press, 2018), 125.

77 Michael T. Klare, *Resource Wars: The New Landscape of Global Conflict* (New York: Metropolitan Books, 2002), 64, 65.

78 Klare, *Resource Wars*, 65, 66, 67.

79 "Human Rights Watch Report, 1995 – Kuwait," https://www.refworld.org/docid/467fcab623.html; "Bahrain: A Human Rights Crisis, Amnesty International, September 25, 1995, https://www.amnesty.org/en/documents/mde11/016/1995/en/ Adam Curtis, "If You Take My Advice, I'd Repress Them," BBC, May 11, 2012, https://www.bbc.co.uk/blogs/adamcurtis/2012/05/if_you_take_my_advice_-_id_rep.html Fisk, *The Great War for Civilization*;

80 "Jordan Received U.S. Military Aid," *The Spokesman-Review*, December 15, 1996, https://www.spokesman.com/stories/1996/dec/15/jordan-receives-us-military-aid/; "Jordan Gets Military Aid from the U.S.," *Associated Press*, December 25, 1996.

81 William J. Burns, *The Back Channel: A Memoir of American Diplomacy and the Case for Its Renewal* (New York: Random House, 2019), 132.

82 "Taliban Aide on bin Laden," August 21, 1998, Clinton Presidential Records, NSC Cables, January 1995–December 1996, box 1, William J. Clinton Presidential Library, Little Rock, Arkansas.

83 Nafeez Mosaddeq Ahmed, *The War on Truth: 9/11, Disinformation, and the Anatomy of Terrorism* (Northampton, MA: Olive Branch Press, 2005), 15.

84 Vijay Prashad, *Fat Cats & Running Dogs: The Enron Stage of Capitalism* (Monroe, ME: Common Courage Press, 2003), 180. *The New York Times* reported that "the Clinton administration has taken the view that a Taliban victory [in Afghanistan's civil war] would act as a counterweight to Iran and would offer the possibility of new

trade routes that could weaken Russian and Iranian influence in the region." Ahmed, *The War on Truth*, 19.

85 Prashad, *Fat Cats & Running Dogs*, 181.

86 Prashad, *Fat Cats & Running Dogs*, 181.

87 Ahmed Rashid, *Taliban: Militant Islam, Oil and fundamentalism in Central Asia* (New Haven: Yale University Press, 2000), 179.

88 Ahmed, *The War on Truth*, 20, 23.

89 Ahmed, *The War on Truth*, 22. Rohrbacher had traveled to Afghanistan to mingle with mujahadin fighters and participated in the battle of Jalalabad against the Soviets. He testified before the Senate Foreign Relations Committee in April 1999 that the covert U.S. policy of supporting the Taliban was based on the assumption that the Taliban would bring stability to Afghanistan and permit the building of oil pipelines from Central Asia through Afghanistan to Pakistan.

90 David N. Bossie, *Intelligence Failure: How Clinton's National Security Policy Set the Stage for 9/11* (Nashville, TN: WND Books, 2004), 101, 102; Thomas W. Lippman, "U.N. Ambassador Will Deliver Message to Afghan Faction," *The Washington Post*, April 9, 1998.

91 Ahmed, *The War on Truth*, 24.

92 "Decision to Attack Usama's Bases," *Urdu Daily*, July 19, 1999, Clinton Presidential Records, NSC Cables, January 1995–December 1996, box 1, William J. Clinton Presidential Library, Little Rock, Arkansas. Russia, Iran, and India were also supplying the anti-Taliban forces in Afghanistan.

93 Ahmed Rashid, *Descent Into Chaos: The United States and the Failure of Nation Building in Pakistan, Afghanistan and Central Asia* (New York: Viking Books, 2008). 69; Lucas Paschalides, *Capitalism's Crisis, The Theory of Deep State Factions & The New Great Game*,

94 Karl F. Inderfurth, "Afghanistan: Meeting with the Taliban," From Secretary of State Washington, D.C., to American Consul Peshawar, December 1997, Clinton Presidential Records, NSC Cables, January 1995–December 1996, box 5, William J. Clinton Presidential Library, Little Rock, Arkansas. Mottaqi said the Taliban had brought stability to Afghanistan and were working to eliminate the drug trade. Women were not traditionally educated in Afghanistan but the Taliban were open to doing so and that Afghans wanted women to weir the veil. Mottaq in turn invited the international community to come to Afghanistan to see for themselves how women were treated, though he qualified that by reminding Inderfurth that Afghanistan was "not a normal country because of the vast destruction it has suffered [due to the U.S.-provoked Soviet invasion and civil war]."

95 Karl F. Inderfurth, "Afghanistan: Meeting with the Taliban," From Secretary of State Washington, D.C., to American Consul Peshawar, December 1997, Clinton Presidential Records, NSC Cables, January 1995–December 1996, box 5, William J. Clinton Presidential Library, Little Rock, Arkansas.

96 Noam Chomsky, *A New Generation Draws the Line: Kosovo, East Timor and the Standards of the West* (London: Verso, 2001), 11; Tamar Gabelnick, William D. Hartung and Jennifer Washburn, *Arming Repression: U.S. Arms Sales to Turkey During the Clinton Administration* (World Policy Institute, October 1999); John Tirman, *Spoils of War: The Human Cost of America's Arms Trade* (New York: The Free Press, 1997). A 1995 State Department report found that "U.S.-origin equipment, which accounts for most major items of the Turkish military inventory, has been used in operations against the PKK during which human rights abuses have occurred." The

report also found "highly credible" evidence that U.S.-manufactured Sikorsky Black Hawk transport helicopters, Bell-Textron Super Cobra attack helicopters, and FMC Corp. M-113 armored personnel carriers had been used to attack Kurdish villages and violate the human rights of civilians. Citing evidence from 1992 through 1995, during the height of Turkey's campaign to depopulate Kurdish villages, the report notes that "it is highly likely that such equipment was used in the evacuation and/or destruction of villages."

97 Ayse Gul Altmay and Amy Holmes, "Opposition to the U.S. Military Presence in Turkey in the Context of the Iraq War," In *The Bases of Empire: The Global Struggle Against U.S. Military Posts*, ed. Catherine Lutz (New York: New York University Press, 2009), 271–275; William D. Hartung, "Weapons at War," *World Policy Institute,* May 1995, http://www.newschool.edu/wpi/projects/arms/reports/wawrep.html; Chomsky, *A New Generation Draws the Line*, 11.

98 Tamar Gabelnick, William D. Hartung and Jennifer Washburn, *Arming Repression: U.S. Arms Sales to Turkey During the Clinton Administration* (World Policy Institute, October 1999).

99 Altmay and Holmes, "Opposition to the U.S. Military Presence in Turkey in the Context of the Iraq War," in *The Bases of Empire*, ed. Lutz, 276; Bill Clinton, "Remarks to American and Turkish Business Leaders in Istanbul Turkey, November 16, 1999, *Public Papers of the President of the United States, William J. Clinton*, Book 3 (Washington, D.C. G.P.O., 1999).

100 Clinton, "Remarks to American and Turkish Business Leaders in Istanbul, Turkey."

101 Steve Liesman, "Three Oil Giants and Kazakhstan Will Push Plan for Caspian Sea Pipelines to Turkey," *The Wall Street Journal*, December 10, 1998, A4; Robert S. Greenberger and Steve Liesman, "Major Oil Firms Are Conducting Talks With Kazakhstan on Caspian Sea Pipelines," *The Wall Street Journal,* December 9, 1998, A2; Majoud Farivar, "U.S. To Help Settle Dispute Over Caspian Sea," *The Wall Street Journal*, June 1, 1999, B9.

102 Cockburn and Silverstein, *Washington Babylon,* 294.

103 Altmay and Holmes, "Opposition to the U.S. Military Presence in Turkey in the Context of the Iraq War," in *The Bases of Empire*, ed. Lutz, 276.

104 Altmay and Holmes, "Opposition to the U.S. Military Presence in Turkey in the Context of the Iraq War," in *The Bases of Empire*, ed. Lutz, 276.

105 Vera B. Saedpour, "Conflicted Kurdistan," *CovertAction Quarterly,* Fall 1995, http://mediafilter.org/caq/CAQ54contents.html.

106 Gabelnick, Hartung and Washburn, *Arming Repression*; Ertugul Kurkcu, "Trapped in a Web of Covert Killers," *CovertAction Quarterly*, Summer 1997, 6–12.

107 Saeedpour, "Conflicted Kurdistan," 19.

108 Jane Hunter, "Ocalan's Odyssey," *CovertAction Quarterly,* Spring-Summer 1999, 33.

109 Greg Bruno, "Inside the Kurdistan Workers Party," *Council on Foreign Relations*, October 19, 2007, https://www.cfr.org/backgrounder/inside-kurdistan-workers-party-pkk; David Phillips, Kelly Berkel, "The Case for Delisting the PKK as a Foreign Terrorist Organization," Lawfare, February 11, 2016, https://www.lawfareblog.com/case-delisting-pkk-foreign-terrorist-organization; Saeedpour, "Conflicted Kurdistan"; Aliza Marcus, *Blood and Belief: The PKK and the Kurdish Fight for Independence* (New York: NYU Press, 2007).

110 Chomsky, *A New Generation Draws the Line*, 14.

111 William S. Hartung, "Nixon's Children: Bill Clinton and the Permanent Arms Bazaar," *World Policy Journal*, 12, 2 (Summer 1995), 30. Clinton administration officials offered contorted explanations as to why it was okay for Turkey to attack the Kurds but not Saddam.

112 "Prison island trial for Ocalan" *BBC News. 24 March 1999; Hunter, "Ocalan's Odyssey," 31.*

113 Gabelnick, Hartung and Washburn, *Arming Repression;* Dana Priest, "New Human Rights Policy Triggers Policy Debate – Military Aid Restrictions Said to Harm U.S. Interests," *The Washington Post*, December 31, 1998. In 1996, a deal for Bell Textron Cobra helicopters was shelved by the Clinton administration due to concerns about Turkey's use of U.S.-supplied helicopters against Kurdish civilians in its war on the PKK. However, the Clinton administration still maintained a huge flow of weapons to Turkey and under pressure from the arms makers, cleared the way for Boeing and Bell Textron to compete for a $4 billion sale of advanced attack helicopters to Ankara that were sure to be put to repressive use.

114 Stephen Kinzer, "From Babies to Dignitaries, Clinton Charm Was on Display in Turkey," *The New York Times*, November 20, 1999; Stephen Kinzer, "Clinton's Visit in Turkey May Help Speed Up Reform," *The New York Times*, November 21, 1999.

115 Mark Lacey, "On Visit, Clinton Nudges Turkey on Rights," *The New York Times*, November 16, 1999.

116 Kinzer, "From Babies to Dignitaries, Clinton Charm Was on Display in Turkey"; https://en.wikipedia.org/wiki/Human_rights_in_Turkmenistan#:~:text=Former%20Turkmenbashi%20Saparmurat%20Niyazov%20banned,to%20enforce%20conformity%20of%20appearance; Klevenman, *The New Great Game*, 149, 150.

117 Gabelnick, Hartung and Washburn, *Arming Repression.*

118 Hugh Pope, "Islamic Resentment of U.S. Builds, Undercutting Its Mideast Policy," *The Wall Street Journal*, November 15, 2000, A23.

119 Quoted in Bacevich, *America's War for the Greater Middle East*, 202.

CHAPTER 9

Clinton's War on Terror

On September 13, 1995, U.S. agents helped kidnap Talaat Fouad Qassem, one of Egypt's most wanted terrorists, in Croatia. Qassem had fled to Europe after being linked by Egypt to the assassination of former Egyptian president Anwar Sadat (1970–1981), for which he had been sentenced to death in absentia. Croatian police seized Qassem in Zagreb and handed him over to U.S. agents, who interrogated him aboard a ship cruising the Adriatic Sea and then took him back to Egypt, then ruled by Hosni Mubarak (1981–2011), a very close ally of the U.S. Once in Egypt, Qassem disappeared. There is no record that he was ever put on trial. Hossam el-Hamalawy, an Egyptian journalist who covers human rights issues, said, "We believe he was executed."

A more elaborate rendition operation was staged in Tirana, Albania, in the summer of 1998. According to *The Wall Street Journal*, the CIA provided the Albanian intelligence service with equipment to wiretap the phones of suspected Muslim militants. Tapes of the conversations were translated into English, whereupon U.S. agents discovered that they contained lengthy discussions with Ayman al-Zawahiri, bin Laden's deputy. The U.S. pressured Egypt for assistance; in June, Egypt issued an arrest warrant for Shawki Salama Attiya, one of the militants. Over the next few months, according to the *Journal,* Albanian security forces working with U.S. agents killed one suspect and captured Attiya and four others. These men were bound, blindfolded, and taken to an abandoned airbase, then flown by jet to Cairo for interrogation. Attiya later alleged that he suffered electrical shocks to his genitals, was hung from his limbs, and was kept in a cell in filthy water up to his knees. Two other suspects, who had been sentenced to death in absentia, were hanged.[1]

The above operations marked the origins of the "extraordinary rendition" program that became infamous during the Bush administration's War on Terror. Under this latter program, American agents would kidnap terrorist suspects and transport them to allied countries in the Middle East where it was known that they would be tortured or executed. Contrary to criticism of Bill Clinton for being soft on terrorism and the "Neville Chamberlain of his generation" who appeased al-Qaeda and allowed the 9/11 attacks to happen,[2] the Clinton administration raised the FBI's counter-terrorism budget by 283 percent from $78 million in 1993 to $301 million in 1999, increasing the number of agents asigned to counter-terrorism from 550 to 1383, and overall counter-terrorism spending by forty percent in its last four years to $9.3 billion in 2000.[3] The Clinton administration further helped lay the groundwork for Bush era policies through the adoption of rendition, drone surveillance, sanctions directed against alleged state-sponsors of terrorism, bombing attacks targeting terrorist training camps and even assassination.[4]

In December 1996, Richard Barnett wrote in *The Nation Magazine* that Clinton's war on terrorism was "being used not only to unite the country behind a confused foreign policy but to polish the President's image." At the Democratic convention in August, Clinton had "thundered against so-called rogue states that were out to spread panic and destruction in the United States," then subsequently proclaimed "U.S. missile attacks on Iraq to be a courageous blow against terrorism," and called upon members at the UN General Assembly to "isolate states that refuse to play by the rules we have all accepted for civilized behavior," recasting himself as leader of the so-called Civilized World.[5] This all prefigured the rhetoric and strategy of George W. Bush and other post-9/11 leaders, marking Clinton as an important bridge figure between the Reagan-Bush I era and Bush II-Obama-Trump-Biden eras, including in helping to condition the American public to accept heavy handed, unlawful and often dubious foreign policy methods.

"Fighting the Depraved Opponents of Civilization"

As the Cold War reached exhaustion in the 1970s and 1980s, another threat to national security emerged which could be used to rally the American public in support of military spending and interventions: terrorism. The Clinton administration extended the Reagan era's popular first "War on Terrorism" that was used to justify the expansion of U.S. military power in the Middle East, including regime change operations targeting U.S. adversaries like Libya's leader, Muammar Qaddafi.

The cornerstone of Reagan's War on Terror was the Counterterrorism Center (CTC), headed initially by "Dewey" Clarridge of Iran-Contra fame, who recruited 25 of the CIA's most aggressive field officers, including Robert Baer. The CTC had a mandate to intercept and sabotage terrorists' supplies, carry out surveillance, disrupt their finances and mount preemptive and retaliatory strikes. Foreshadowing later abuses, coercive interrogation methods were adopted and there was an executive authorization to kidnap suspects and return them to the United States.[6]

Claire Sterling's 1981 book, *The Terror Network* helped shape public thinking on terrorism, arguing that it occurred mostly in democratic societies and their allies and was perpetrated by Arab terrorists and the Soviet KGB.

The Soviets had financed Palestinian Liberation Organization (PLO) training camps in Czechoslovakia in the late 1960s, though funding was cut thereafter and there was little actual evidence the Soviets officially backed any terrorist operations by the PLO or by left wing groups such as the Baader Meinhof gang and Italian Red Brigades.[7] Several terrorist incidents attributed to left wing groups were later uncovered to have actually been black flag operations orchestrated by Western intelligence services with the goal of discrediting the left. A car bomb in Beirut in 1985 that killed 80 people and wounded 256 was traced by journalist Bob Woodward to a senior Saudi official and CIA director Bill Casey.[8]

Reagan set another dangerous precedent on April 14, 1986, by bombing Libya—which was accused of carrying out a major terrorist attack—without evidence of its guilt. The Pentagon purported to have communications intercepts linking Muammar Qaddafi, considered the "Daddy Warbucks of terrorism," to the bombing of a West Berlin discotheque which killed three American servicemen and wounded 229 others. The chief of the antiterrorism police in Berlin, however, said the police had no "hard evidence let alone proof [of Qaddafi's involvement]." Evidence brought forward at the trial of one of the alleged plotters revealed the existence of a CIA informant who paid the bombers $30,000 to carry out the attack.[9]

Al-Qaeda Declares War on America—With the Complicity of the Clinton Administration

The War on Terror of the 1990s targeted the al-Qaeda network which emerged during the 1980s U.S.-supported holy war against the Soviet Union in Afghanistan. Once the Soviets had been expelled, al-Qaeda focused on countering American colonization of the Middle East, while aiming to re-establish an Islamic empire. Founder Osama Bin Laden, the son of a wealthy Saudi construction magnate and financier of the Afghan mujahidin, was angered by America's stationing of military bases on Muslim holy ground in Saudi Arabia during the first Gulf War, the retention of Saddam Hussein (a secular nationalist) in power in Iraq combined with devastating U.S. bombing and sanctions on that country, and by American support for Israeli violence in its occupied territories and in Lebanon.[10]

In a prelude to the 9/11 terrorist attacks, Bin Laden began launching terrorist attacks against U.S. installations starting with the 1992 bombing of a Yemeni hotel where U.S. troops headed to Somalia were supposed to have been stationed (they were actually staying at a different hotel). A year later, al-Qaeda operatives detonated a bomb in a basement garage in the World Trade Center in New York, killing six people and injuring 1,042 others. The alleged mastermind of the attack, Sheikh Omar Abdel Rahman (AKA the "blind sheik") had been a valued CIA asset in the Afghan war against the Soviets and in recruiting mujahadin for the war in Bosnia and had slipped into the U.S. with CIA protection.[11]

Some of the other terrorists involved in the plot had contacts with Oklahoma City bomber Terry Nichols, a suspected U.S. government agent, and were trained by Ali Mohamed, a onetime CIA asset and double agent inside al-Qaeda who illegally fought against the Soviets in Afghanistan while on active U.S. military duty and was curiously protected from prosecution by the CIA as one of 118 unindicted co-conspirators in the World Trade Center attack.[12] The FBI had infiltrated the terrorist cell that carried out the attack and had a plan to substitute fake powder in the bomb and arrest the perpetrators, but never did. Jack Blum, an investigator of the Senate Foreign Relations Committee, had complained that "one of the big problems here is that many suspects of the World Trade Center bombing were associated with the mujahadin. And there are components of our government that are absolutely disinterested in following that path because it leads back to people we supported in the Afghan war."[13]

In November 1995, al-Qaeda struck a facility in Riyadh where Americans were training the Saudi National Guard. It was also suspected of being behind the June 1996 bombing of an apartment complex in Khobar, Saudi Arabia near the Aramco oil headquarters of Dhahran, which left 19 U.S. Air Force officers dead. Bin Laden said that the explosion [in Khobar] resulted from America's colonization of Saudi Arabia and because of "American behavior against Muslims, its support of Jews in Palestine and of the massacres of Muslims in Palestine and Lebanon—of Sabra and Shatila and Qana—and of the Sharm el-Sheikh conference [conference in Egypt where Bill Clinton condemned the terrorism of Hamas and Hizbollah but not Israel]."[14]

On August 7, 1998, al-Qaeda bombed the U.S. embassies in Nairobi, Kenya and Dar es Salaam, Tanzania, killing 224 people, and injuring 5,000 more. According to National Security Agency (NSA) whistleblower Thomas Drake, the NSA's Chop Chain of senior leaders had failed to disseminate significant intelligence that might have prevented the attacks. The NSA had been monitoring al-Qaeda's Yemen hub for two years and were hence aware of kills made by one of the bombers, Mohamed al-Owhali, but did not alert the FBI or CIA or even the State Department—possibly in order to protect members of the al-Qaeda network who had done covert work for U.S. government agencies.[15]

In his book, *The War on Truth: 9/11, Disinformation, and the Anatomy of Terrorism,* British based researcher Nafeez Mossadeq Ahmed points to the existence of a secret CIA agreement with Bin Laden lieutenant Ayman Al-Zawahiri by which Zawahiri agreed not to attack U.S. forces in the Balkans in exchange for U.S. government acquiescence to al-Qaeda terrorist attacks in the Middle East and North Africa (including the bombing of the Luxor pyramid in Egypt in 1997), and efforts to overthrow the Mubarak government in Egypt.[16]

In October 2000, alleged al-Qaeda operatives struck the U.S.S. *Cole,* a billion-dollar guided missile naval destroyer equipped with computer-linked radar that was refueling in the Yemeni port of Aden. Blowing a hole twenty feet high and forty feet wide in the Cole's hull, the attack killed seventeen U.S. sailors, and injured thirty-nine. The U.S.S. *Cole* was supposed to be impenetrable, with seventy tons of armor shielding its vital spaces, and a hull capable of withstanding an explosion of fifty-one thousand pounds per square inch.[17] Afterwards, CIA Director George Tenet, according to newly uncovered documents, pressured for the release from a Yemeni prison of one of the alleged masterminds of the attack, Anwar Al-Awlaki, who was then a protected CIA asset.[18]

If the bombing of the U.S.S. *Cole* was a false flag incident, its purpose was to create a pretext for wider U.S. military intervention in the Middle East and the suspension of constitutional principles. Al-Qaeda's motive for the attack, on the other hand, appears to have been to lure the U.S. into a destructive military invasion of Afghanistan, the traditional graveyard of empires, where Bin Laden was based after moving from Sudan. Clinton, to his credit, did not take the bait and stood up to military demands to launch air strikes in Afghanistan after the bombing of the U.S.S. *Cole*. Clinton said that he did not think it would be responsible for a president to launch an invasion of another country just based on a "preliminary judgment [that Bin Laden was responsible]."[19]

Providing a New Moral Purpose for U.S. Foreign Policy

Islamic terrorism arrived at the right time, coinciding with the end of the Cold War. It provided a new moral purpose under cover of which the U.S. expanded American military power in the Middle East and Central Asia, where the world's largest untapped oil resources lay.[20] During the 1992 election campaign, Clinton said that he wanted "strong special forces operations forces to deal with the terrorist threats."[21] Treating the 1993 World Trade Center bombing as a criminal matter, Clinton, with time, changed his tune to move along lines suggested by House Speaker Newt Gingrich (R-GA), who said that "every time we have any display of weakness, any display of timidity.... There are people on the planet eager to take advantage of us."[22]

Clinton effectively framed the struggle against terrorism in apocalyptic and morally righteous terms, which helped condition the public to accept a more aggressive, militarized response. In a speech at George Washington University in August 1996, Clinton characterized terrorism as "the enemy of our generation" and said we would prevail if we maintained our confidence and our leadership as the world's "indispensable force for peace and freedom."[23] Seeking to mobilize popular support in the manner of World War II, Clinton subsequently characterized terrorism as "part of an unholy axis" with drug traffickers and organized criminals that threatened "open societies" and went on to state that although fascism and communism are dead or discredited, the forces of hatred and intolerance live on. The challenge of the 1990s, he intoned, was "ethnic violence, religious strife, terrorism" which sought to spread "darkness over light, disintegration over integration, chaos over community."[24]

Clinton said in another address that he believed that threats of the modern era represented a "clash between the forces of the past and the forces of the future, between those who tear down and those who build up, between hope and fear, chaos and community." America, he told the nation in 1998, was a target of terrorism not because its foreign policies had enflamed people in the Arab world but "because we are leaders; because we act to advance peace, democracy, and basic human values; because we're the most open society on Earth; and because, as we have shown yet again, we take an uncompromising stand against terrorism."[25] These comments exemplify Clinton's reaffirmation of American exceptionalism combined with a depoliticization and dehumanization of those resisting it—whom Clinton called "hate filled cowards."[26] All this helped engender public support for a militarized response.

Limiting Personal Freedom: The Oklahoma City Bombing and 1996 Anti-Terrorism Bill

After the 1993 World Trade Center bombing, the CTC established a 24/7 task force to collect intelligence and the NSA ramped up its telephone intercept network.[27] Clinton was quoted in *USA Today* stating that "we can't be so fixated on our desire to preserve the rights of ordinary Americans." Subsequently he stated on MTV that "a lot of people may think there's too much personal freedom. When personal freedom's being abused, you have to move to limit it."[28] In line with this view, Clinton proposed a new Homeland Defense Force that would allow the U.S. military to police its citizens. With the threat of terrorism replacing that of the Soviet Union, the Doomsday Project—designed to give secret powers to the White House for anything considered an emergency—was also preserved.[29]

On April 19, 1995, the Alfred P. Murrah Federal Building in Oklahoma City was bombed in the largest act of domestic terrorism on U.S. soil. 168 people were killed and over 670 injured. Timothy McVeigh, a disgruntled Persian Gulf War veteran, was accused of carrying out the attack to avenge the government's massacre of innocent people in a botched raid at Ruby Ridge and on the Branch Davidian compound in Waco, Texas in 1993.

A year after the Oklahoma City bombing, Clinton signed the Antiterrorism and Effective Death Penalty Act, which provided a $500 million windfall for the FBI and curtailed habeus corpus rights by empowering the Secretary of State with the ability to establish a list of foreign terrorist organizations. The government now had the right to determine the legality of political movements in violation of the first amendment, according to the American Civil Liberties Union (ACLU). Author David Hoffman wrote that the Antiterrorism and Effective Death Penalty Act, which was introduced by then Senator Joe Biden, "gutted the First, Fourth, Sixth and Eighth Amendments to the constitution, [laid] the framework for an entrenched police state, and [gave] the Federal government full power to target anybody deemed a threat to its authority."[30]

Clinton aggressively promoted the Antiterrorism and Effective Death Penalty Act when it was being held up in Congress, arguing that "the tools we need to fight terrorism have been shoved into a dark corner of the House of Representatives by an alliance of extremists on the left and right."[31] First proposed by CIA officer Theodore Shackley, the Act included clauses to deport terrorists, to limit the right to appeal of death row inmates, to allow "no knock" searches and expand the use of wiretaps and illegally seized evidence for use in court. It further permitted federal and local police agencies to trace financial information without obtaining evidence of a crime and for the military to intervene in domestic situations deemed a national security threat, while establishing a new FBI counter-terrorism center with 1,000 new "anti-terrorist" agents and providing a $66 million windfall for the Bureau of Alcohol, Tobacco and Firearms (ATF).[32]

Section 328 amended the Foreign Assistance Act to bolster assistance in the form of arms and ammunition to certain countries for the purpose of fighting terrorism. This led in 1997 to the creation of a secret "Eyes Only" liaison agreement between the CTC and Saudi Arabia, followed by a subsequent CIA agreement in 1999 with Uzbekistan (i.e. two of the most repressive regimes in the world at that time).[33]

In June 2001, McVeigh was executed after being found guilty of masterminding the Oklahoma City bombing along with accomplice Terry Nichols. However, military explosives experts stated that the crudely constructed bomb linked to McVeigh that was detonated in a Ryder truck could only have torn the flooring from a few floors in the Murrah building. Many eyewitnesses heard two explosions, and a former CIA agent on the scene, Joe Harp, said he smelled sulfur, indicating daisy cutter bombs used by the U.S. army in Vietnam. Local news media reported unexploded bombs located in the Murrah Building. The FBI at the time had infiltrated provocateurs into the Elohim ranch outside Oklahoma City, a mecca for radical white nationalists. McVeigh was believed to be one of these infiltrators who may have been set up as a patsy as part of his last army assignment along with Nichols, McVeigh's old army buddy, who met with Islamic terrorist groups that had been infiltrated by U.S. intelligence in the Philippines.[34]

Back to the Bad Old Days?

Following the 1998 embassy bombing in Tanzania, President Clinton signed a secret intelligence finding authorizing the CIA to use covert means to disrupt and preempt Osama bin Laden's operations.[35] The Clinton administration subsequently doubled the counterterrorism budget and tripled the resources allocated to the FBI and CTC while permanently stationing two L.A. class submarines in Middle Eastern waters in preparation to launch missile attacks that could take out bin Laden or other terrorist suspects.[36]

The Foreign Intelligence Surveillance Act (FISA) was utilized to engage in over 5,000 operations during the Clinton administration, entailing an expansion of government surveillance and carrying out of government searches without a warrant (and without ever letting the targets know they have been searched). Critics feared that the FBI had successfully exploited the evolving situation to claw back powers that had been surrendered in the wake of the Church investigation of its COINTELPRO operations. A White House official noted: "if FBI infiltrators were put into every [right-wing] militia, it would be back to the bad old days."[37]

In May 1998, the Clinton administration drafted PDD 62 "Protection Against Unconventional Threats to the Homeland and Americans Overseas," which emphasized the administration's "zero-tolerance" approach to international terrorism and vowed to use multilateral and bilateral initiatives to "eliminate sanctuaries, penalize states that sponsor terrorism, and assist friendly states victimized by terrorism." George Tenet said in 1998, three years before 9/11: "We are at war."[38]

The new war necessitated a new investment in bio-terrorism training and equipment, stockpiling of pharmaceuticals and expanding research into antibiotics and vaccines capable of treating anthrax and the plague, along with other drugs capable of offsetting chemical attacks. $30 million was also invested in a new cybersecurity program, along with $312 million in aviation security.[39]

At this time, a senior director for counterterrorism and national counter-terrorism czar, Richard Clarke, was appointed to head the expanded counter-terrorism infrastructure. A close friend of Israeli officials known as a "bureaucratic pile driver," Clark was a throwback to the CIA's action faction. In his view, the current generation of CIA officers had "over-learned" the lessons of the 1960s and 1980s that covert action is "risky" and "likely to blow up in your face."[40]

With the support of a president with long CIA ties (who took office after a president who had actually formerly been a CIA director), the agency ran a covert operation in Afghanistan to recruit and train tribal elements who had been part of the Northern Alliance to capture or kill bin Laden and fight the Taliban.[41] Military bases were provided as launching points for these efforts by the Tajik government, headed by thc brutal autocrat Emomali Rahmon.[42] In a reflection of the egregious double standards of Clinton's War on Terror, British journalist Robert Fisk referred to the Northern Alliance as a "gang of terrorists"; a loose "confederacy of warlords, patriots, rapists and torturers who control a northern sliver of Afghanistan," and have "done their fair share of massacres on [their] home turf."[43]

Head of Alec Station Richard Blee and fellow CIA agent Cofer Black provided over $200,000 per month and communications equipment to Tajik warlord Ahmed Shah Massoud, "the lion of Panjshir" who had won acclaim for his guerrilla fighting exploits against the Soviets.[44] The State Department distrusted Massoud because he was an enemy of Pakistan, a regional ally whose intelligence services supported the Taliban. Massoud had also signed an agreement with the Argentine rival of the Union Oil Company of California (UNOCAL), which had been pushing for a pipeline project through Afghanistan, with U.S. backing, that would bypass Russia and Iran.[45]

On Christmas eve 1998, Clinton approved a memorandum drafted by National Security Council advisor Sandy Berger and CIA director George Tenet that would allow the killing of bin Laden if the CIA and the locals judged that capture was not feasible—a judgment that, according to the 9/11 commission report, had already been reached. The Clinton administration's position was that under the laws of armed conflict, killing a person who posed an imminent threat to the United States would be an act of self-defense.[46] This measure was significant in setting the groundwork for 21st century foreign policies and the drone war in which assassination became an accepted method for fighting terrorism.

Targeting Alleged State Sponsors of Terrorism While Supporting Terrorist States

Clinton's state-centric approach was evident in the Clinton-era National Security Strategy (NSS) documents, which designated state sponsors of terrorism as rogue states. The Iran and Libya Sanctions Act of 1996 (ILSA) signed by Clinton imposed economic sanctions on firms doing business with Iran and Libya.[47] The goal was to weaken the two countries' economies and cause disaffection with the existing regimes, prompting the people to rise up in rebellion, and to weaken military preparedness by blocking the sale of spare parts needed by their air forces. Speaking at George Washington University on the day ILSA was signed, Clinton said that: "you cannot do business with countries that practice commerce with you by day while funding or protecting the terrorists who kill you and your innocent civilians by night. That is wrong. I hope and expect that before long our allies will come around to accepting this fundamental truth."

Iran's real crime was defiance of the U.S.-led world order. The country's leaders were accused of numerous terrorist attacks where the evidence against them was thin, including the 1996 bombing of Khobar towers in Saudi Arabia, which al-Qaeda appears to have been behind.[48] Libyan ruler Muammar Qaddafi was a longstanding target of U.S. regime change because, after overthrowing the pro-western King Idris in 1969, he had closed a major U.S. air base, nationalized Libya's oil industry and supported African liberation movements and the Palestinian resistance. The Clinton administration emphasized Qaddafi's responsibility for the December 1988 bombing of Pan Am Flight 803 over Lockerbie, Scotland, which had killed all 243 passengers along with 16 crewmembers and 11 Lockerbie residents. However, the case against Libyan intelligence officer Abdelbaset al-Megrahi, who was implicated, relied on forensics evidence that proved to be false and on an unreliable Libyan defector.[49]

The NSA obtained top secret electronic intercepts which demonstrated that Tehran had commissioned a Palestinian guerrilla group, the PFLP, to down the Pan-Am flight in retaliation for the U.S.S. *Vincennes* shooting down an Iranian air bus in July 1988.[50] An alternative theory holds that the bomb that took down the aircraft was introduced by an unwitting drug mule in a CIA-protected suitcase, and was planted to silence three members of the CIA's Beirut station who had key evidence about a drug smuggling operation connected to Iran-Contra.[51]

In its effort to overthrow Qaddafi, the CIA covertly supported Islamic fundamentalists, some of whom were later empowered after the 2011 U.S.-NATO military invasion of Libya under cover of the UN's Responsibility to

Protect initiative. While Clinton's War on Terror publicly denounced terrorism where it served U.S. interests, it nonetheless entered into alliances with brutal regimes whose leaders committed acts of state terrorism, negotiating, for example, a secret intelligence sharing liaison with Uzbekistan, whose president, Islam Karimov, had jailed and executed thousands of political opponents and even boiled some of the latter alive. After surviving an assassination attempt, Karimov's security forces carried out draconian sweeps, which he justified as part of a crackdown on bin Laden's allies.

The CIA subsequently began funding and training a counterterrorism strike force which could carry out snatch operations against bin Laden and his lieutenants. Karimov allowed the CIA and NSA to install monitoring equipment designed to intercept Taliban and al-Qaeda communications, and made air bases available to the CIA for transit and helicopter operations and some drone flights.[52]

A War Crime: Clinton's Sudan Strike

The failure of Clinton's War on Terror was apparent in the bombing of the al-Shifa pharmaceutical plant in Khartoum, Sudan's capital. The plant was alleged to have manufactured chemical weapons for use in possible terror attacks, though actually possessed vital medicines which were needed by the local population. The bombing occurred on August 20, 1998, during Clinton's impeachment trial, and a few weeks after the bombing of the U.S. embassies in Dar-es-Salaam, Tanzania, and Nairobi, Kenya by Bin Laden's al-Qaeda network.

The Sudanese government of Omar al-Bashir had been slapped with U.S. sanctions at the time as a state sponsor of terrorism. However, Sudan had expelled Osama Bin Laden at U.S. urging and offered to provide its extensive intelligence file on him and his terrorist network to the U.S. and to cooperate with U.S. counter-terrorism investigations in Sudan in exchange for the normalization of U.S.-Sudan relations. The offer was sent through a Democratic Party donor, Monsoor Ijaz, though was rebuffed, it is believed, because Clinton was enmeshed in too many scandals and did not want to be seen as currying favors for a party donor—or perhaps for larger geostrategic motives. The U.S. had long supported secessionist rebels in the oil rich south in an attempt to destabilize the country and undermine Bashir's Islamist government.[53]

Treasured by the Sudan government as the "pride of Africa" after its opening in June 1997, the al-Shifa factory had provided over 50 percent of Sudan's medicines, including 90 percent of the most critically needed drugs. Government subsidies enabled free distribution to Sudan's poor. Recently, the factory had received authorization to provide badly needed medicines to Iraq—which may have prompted its bombing.[54] Scattered throughout the wreckage were thousands of packs of antibiotics, empty glass bottles and containers filled with veterinary medicines. Sudan was subsequently left without supplies of chloroquine, the standard treatment for malaria.[55]

Germany's then ambassador to Sudan, Werner Daum, estimated that the destruction of the al-Shifa plant led to thousands of deaths, though reliable data has never been amassed. Jonathan Belke reported in *The Boston Globe* that

> without the lifesaving medicine it produced, Sudan's death toll from the bombing has continued to quietly rise . . . this factory provided affordable medicine for humans and all the locally available veterinary medicine in Sudan . . . and produced 90 percent of Sudan's major pharmaceutical products. Sanctions against Sudan make it impossible to import adequate amounts of medicines required to cover the serious gap left by the plant's destruction. Thus, tens of thousands of people—many of them children—have suffered and died from malaria, tuberculosis, and other treatable diseases.[56]

The CIA claimed, based on analysis of a soil sample found outside it, that al-Shifa manufactured chemicals used in the production of deadly nerve gas had been financed by bin Laden. After the bombing Clinton described the plant as an "imminent threat to our national security." National Security adviser Sandy Berger stated: "let me be very clear about this. . . . This was a plant that was producing chemical warfare-related weapons and we have physical evidence of that fact."[57]

A classified review by the Defense Intelligence Agency, however, concluded that the decision to bomb the factory was based on bad data, poor science and a faulty intelligence process.[58] The CIA tests of the soil sample were never verified by an independent laboratory, and it turned out that the CIA had mistaken Roundup, a common legal herbicide, for EMPTA, a precursor for making VX nerve gas. The CIA informant who gathered the sample was a Tunisian who had links to the Sudanese People's Liberation Army (SPLA), which was trying to overthrow the Sudanese government, and had been caught lying to the CIA in the past. The Clinton administration also never verified previous UN inspection reports.[59] The plant's owner, Salid Idris, said he had never met bin Laden.[60]

An independent fact-finding mission led by former Attorney General Ramsey Clark determined that the plant was solely a medicine factory, whose bombing followed the definition of a war crime. Donald Peterson, the American ambassador to Sudan from 1992 to 1995, said that the bombing of the al-Shifa plant was "a mistake. The [Clinton] administration failed to produce conclusive evidence that chemical weapons were being made at the pharmaceutical factory. The administration had grounds for suspicion, but to commit an act of war, which the missile attack was, the evidence should have been more ironclad."[61] Peterson's successor, Ambassador Tim Carney, further admitted that "the decision to target al-Shifa continues a tradition of operating on inadequate intelligence about Sudan."[62] Afterwards, the Clinton administration characteristically blocked any investigation.

Attack on the Afghan People

The Sudan strike came on the same day, August 20, 1998, as the launching of 79 GPS-guided cruise missiles from U.S. naval vessels in the Red and Arabian Seas aimed at an al-Qaeda training camp in Khost southeast of Kabul. The camp was described by Secretary of Defense William Cohen as a "Terrorist University." The missiles—which cost about $750,000 each—were intended as retaliation for the bombing of the U.S. embassies in Kenya and Tanzania thirteen days earlier and were accompanied by the use of cluster munitions.[63]

Clinton wrote in his memoir that "most of the missiles hit the target but bin Laden was not in the camp, where the CIA thought he would be hit when missiles hit it. Some reports said he had left the camp only a couple of hours earlier, but we never knew for sure. Several people associated with al-Qaeda were killed, as were some Pakistani officers who were reported to be there to train Kashmiri terrorists."[64] Sandy Berger, Clinton's national security adviser, falsely claimed that twenty or thirty al-Qaeda operatives were killed when in fact six were killed: a Saudi, an Egyptian, an Uzbek and three Yemenis, along with 28 others.[65]

According to General Hamid Gul, former head of the Pakistani Intelligence Services (ISI), more than half of the missiles fell in Pakistani territory, killing two Pakistani citizens and prompting the Pakistani government to take violations of its air and space to the UN Security Council.[66] Two military analysts concluded that the number of missiles fired compared to the type of targets selected and the damage wrought was "out of proportion."[67]

Mullah Omar, the Taliban's leader, said that the failed Khost attack ended any chances for dialogue between the Clinton administration and Taliban as the U.S. had

> encroached on Afghan territory without any justification or proof. [The attack] violated the accepted international norms [and] was regarded not just as an attack targeting Usama bin Laden but as an attack on the entire Afghan people. The U.S. has shown the world that it is the leader of terrorism in the world. This was a big mistake the U.S. has made—it will be held responsible for any negative repercussions of this mistake.[68]

These negative repercussions included transforming bin Laden into a celebrated figure of resistance wherever America "with its narcissistic culture and the majestic presence of its military forces" made itself unwelcome, as journalist Lawrence Wright put it. Children even in Kenya and Tanzania were afterwards spotted wearing bin Laden t-shirts.[69]

Extraordinary Rendition: "A New Boom Industry for the CIA"

Historian James D. Boys defined "extraordinary rendition" as the "transfer without formal charges, trial, or court approval of a person suspected of being a terrorist or supporter of a terrorist group to a foreign nation for imprisonment and interrogation on behalf of the transferring nation."[70] Ronald Reagan was the first U.S. president to adopt the practice when he tried to render the Palestinian hijackers of the Achille Lauro in October 1985, and later ensnared Fawaz Yunis, who had led a team of hijackers that took control of Royal Jordanian flight 402 at Beirut International airport.[71]

Bill Clinton expanded rendition under the advice of Al Gore, who dismissed White House Counsel Lloyd Cutler's objection that it violated international law. According to Richard Clarke, Gore told Clinton: "That's a no-brainer. Of course it's a violation of international law, that's why it's a covert action. The guy is a terrorist. Go grab his ass."[72] Providing a "boom industry for the CIA," suspects under the rendition program were arrested and brought to the U.S. to face criminal trial in a process that Sandy Berger claimed took on a "new art form." The most prominent captive was Ramzy Yousef, who was arrested by Pakistani intelligence in Room 16 of the Su-Casa Guest House in Islamabad, handed over to U.S. authorities in February 1995, tried in southern district court of New York and jailed for life for involvement in 1993 World Trade Center bombing.[73]

A 1996 NSS document specified that since Clinton came to office in 1993, "more terrorists [had] been arrested and extradited to the U.S. than during the totality of the previous three administrations."[74] Clinton personally approved every internationally illegal snatch that he was asked to review during his presidency.[75] PDD-39 signed by Clinton in June 1995 put in place a mechanism for covertly expelling suspected terrorists to nations with poor human rights records, including Jordan, Syria, Morocco, and Egypt.[76] CIA officer Michael Scheuer, who helped craft the program, explained that the goal was to get belligerents "off the street" by turning them over to "Arab tyrannies."[77]

The worst of these tyrannies was Egypt's Hosni Mubarak, who kept thousands of Muslim Brotherhood members in "administrative detention" along with other civil society activists as part of a determined war against Islamic jihadists.[78] CIA agent Robert Baer noted half sarcastically that "if you want a serious interrogation send them to Jordan; if you want them to be tortured, send them to Syria; if you want someone to disappear—never to see them again—send them to Egypt."[79]

Soon Egypt became a hub for rendition under Clinton, receiving eleven alleged militants from 1995 through 2000.[80] Edward Walker, the U.S. ambassador to Egypt at the time, said that the Egyptian security authorities gave assurance that the suspects would have a fair trial and wouldn't be tortured, a premise scoffed at by Scheuer who stated "if you accepted an assurance from any of the Arab tyrannies who are our allies that they weren't going to torture someone, I have got a bridge for you to buy."[81]

Political scientist Jason Brownlee observed that extraordinary rendition spawned a generation of militants. Ayman al-Zawahiri, bin Laden's top deputy, conveyed to the Americans that Al-Qaeda had "received the [American] message," and "a reply is currently being written. We hope that they read it well as, God willing, we will write it in the language they understand." Three days later, two truck bombs struck the U.S. embassies in Nairobi and Dar es Salaam.

The Drone—A Secret Weapon in the War on Terror

The Clinton administration was the first to actively incorporate drones into the front lines of U.S. military deployments and to recognize their potential as a reconnaissance platform and later as a delivery mechanism for deadly munitions. Drone technology had been tested in World War I and World War II and was adopted on a limited scale by the U.S. military in the Korean and Vietnam Wars. In the late 1970s and 1980s, the Blue Brothers, who bought over General Atomics, helped pioneer the use of the armed drone, while the technology was further developed by Israeli entrepreneur Abe Karem—the "Moses of modern drones" —whose Leading Systems Corporation became part of a $40 million Pentagon black project to develop its Unmanned Aerial Vehicle (UAV) technology.[82]

When Clinton became president, his CIA Director James Woolsey—wanting to have more eyes in the sky—flew to California to inspect Karem's latest projects and bought five Gnats while offering the CIA's expertise to help General Atomics expedite the development of even more high tech machines.[83] In record time, General Atomics' prototypes were then approved for deployment in the Balkan Wars, flying classified missions from the Gjader airfield in Albania, where the pilot sat with several enlisted payload specialists inside a sealed, unmarked van while video images were relayed to Woolsey, who could communicate with them back in Langley, Virginia.[84]

At the time, a debate broke out between those who favored using the drone for traditional intelligence collections, and others who argued that it would be a powerful weapon if it was integrated into what military officers sometimes called "the kill chain."[85] After the bombing of the U.S. embassies in Nairobi and Dar es Salaam in August 1998, the Pentagon considered placing a giant, hidden telescope on an Afghan mountain in the hope of spotting al-Qaeda's gaunt leader. An alternative solution was found in the Predator, which could not only help find him, but could laser-illuminate his location so Tomahawk cruise missiles could be launched from a submarine in the Gulf.[86]

Richard Clarke was a major enthusiast for these latter operations which he would help command in the flight center, often in the wee hours of the night. Journalist Steve Coll described Clarke and the rest of the flight crew as

> like a secret society of video game junkies, role players in a futuristic scenario . . . well aware of their role in pioneering a kind of technical espionage that Hollywood might promote. They sipped coffee and talked to their pilot: "look at that truck! The truck looks like the one he used! Follow that truck!" One participant remembered: "it was very much the O.J. thing with a helicopter following a car down the freeway."[87]

The first unarmed, remotely piloted aircraft crossed into Afghanistan on September 7, 2000, from two secret drone bases in Uzbekistan in a mission Clinton authorized. Over the next few weeks, the Predator made 10 successful flights into the country, and on September 25, 2000, it apparently found bin Laden. Circling high and unseen above Tarnak Farms near Kandahar, the Predator fed back live pictures of a tall, white-robed man surrounded by a security detail. According to one senior Pentagon official with close knowledge of the operation, in total al-Qaeda's leader was directly observed by the CIA's drones for four hours and 23 minutes over a number of missions.[88]

Showing the bin Laden video to the Secretary and Chief of Staff of the Air Force, the CIA recommended using a Hellfire—a lightweight antitank missile that could be laser-guided onto its target "quick, black and dirty."[89] Even though this strike was called off, the rush was now on to use the Predator not just as for spying but also as an assassination tool.

Double Standards and a Failed Destiny

The double standards of Clinton's War on Terrorism were seen in placed like Baku, Azerbaijan, where Richard Secord, Henie Aderholt and other veterans of the secret war in Laos turned up under the cover of MEGA Oil to set up an airline on the model of Air America to ferry in mujahidin fighters, who provided the muscle for a coup that reoriented the former Soviet province to the West and ensured an 8 billion contract for a consortium of companies led by British Petroleum (BP).[90] Bin Laden subsequently established an NGO in Baku, which became a base for jihadi operations against Dagestan and Chechnya in Russia, and a trans-shipment point for Afghan heroin to the Chechen mafia.[91]

Ex-FBI agent Ali Soufan noted that U.S. foreign policy empowered Muslim jihadists in Bosnia, Afghanistan, Chechnya, Qatar and Pakistan.[92] Much like after the Bay of Pigs in Cuba, the CIA often protected former "assets" linked to criminal actions, including al-Qaeda organizer Ali Abdelsaoud Mohamed, who had trained Afghan mujahidin fighters as part of a CIA effort to establish a pro-Pakistani regime in Kabul. Mohamed came to the U.S. on a visa-waiver program designed to shield "those who have performed valuable services for the country" and was subsequently connected to the 1993 World Trade Center bombing that killed 6 people and injured 1,000. For a time, he was an instructor at the al-Khiffa training center in Brooklyn, which was set up by bin Laden's mentor, Abdullah Azzam, another CIA-connected mujahidin veteran, to train jihadists for conflicts in Bosnia and Yemen.[93]

In 1993, Mohammed was inexplicably released from RCMP custody in Vancouver as a result of the intervention of San Francisco FBI agent John Zent, even though Mohammed had come in order to smuggle another wanted terrorist into the U.S. Five years later, Mohammed was arrested for his role in the Nairobi embassy bombing.[94]

Shedding further light on Clinton's purported War on Terror was the U.S. regional alliance with Gulf monarchies such as the United Arab Emirates (UAE) and Qatar, whose minister of religious endowments, Sheikh Abdullah bin Khalid al-Tahni, was known to harbor Islamists loyal to bin Laden. A plan to capture future 9/11 planner Khalid Sheikh Mohammed was nixed ostensibly due to the White House negotiating an important air force basing agreement with Qatar.[95]

That the Clinton administration was engaged in a War on Terror rather than facilitating terror was further undermined by its extending its alliance with Pakistan, whose intelligence services (ISI) supported Islamic fundamentalists in Uzbekistan[96] along with the Taliban. The latter were valued as a hedge against Pakistan's chief geopolitical rival, India, and for helping them to enhance their trade links with Central Asia.[97] Pakistan had become a haven for Islamic fundamentalism during the regime of Zia al-Huq, who had been supported by Ronald Reagan as a proxy assisting it in carrying out the anti-Soviet War in Afghanistan.[98] The Clinton administration followed suit by easing aid restrictions and went forward with military training programs—in part because Pakistan was the third largest foreign buyer of American wheat.[99]

The reality of Clinton's War on Terror was most illminated by the U.S. alliance with Saudi Arabia. Though bin Laden had been expelled from Saudi Arabia and opposed the decision to allow for U.S. military bases on its soil, the Saudi Royal family continued to support him covertly and was a major donor to al-Qaeda as it spent at least $87 billion over several decades to propagate Wahhabism abroad.[100] Saudi Royal family money was behind the Islamic Relief Organization (IIRO) which supported Sunni terrorists in Southeast Asia, Chechnya, Kenya and Bosnia.[101]

Khalid al-Midhar and Nawafal-Hazmi, alleged 9/11 hijackers, are suspected of being Saudi double agents who penetrated al-Qaeda on behalf of the Royal family.[102] The CIA had known of al-Midhar and Hazmi's participation in meetings where the U.S.S. *Cole* and 9/11 terrorist plots were discussed and had passed the two names and details about al-Midhar's U.S. visa to the FBI, without asking the FBI to follow-up. When al-Midhar and Hazmi traveled to the U.S., they sailed through customs with immigration authorities never alerted that they were on a terrorist watchlist.[103]

Former federal prosecutor John Loftus stated that the Clinton State Department pressured investigators to abandon an examination of Saudi-operated Islamic foundations, institutions, and charities in Virginia with more than a billion dollars in assets. The Saudi charities allegedly had helped finance 9/11 hijacker Mohammed Atta.[104]

This example among others epitomizes the covert dark side of the War on Terror. Its purported rationale was undermined by the U.S. government's entangling geopolitical alliances and support for terrorists in carrying out clandestine operations along with failed coordination among U.S. law enforcement and intelligence agencies. Billions in American taxpayer dollars were ultimately invested in the War on Terror, which Clinton carried forward. This war was destined to fail to quell terrorism—thereby providing a pretext to expand American military power in the Middle East and Central Asia—a boondoggle for military contractors.

Endnotes

1 Jane Mayer, "Outsourcing Torture: The Secret History of America's 'Extraordinary Rendition' Program," *The New Yorker*, February 7, 2005, https://www.newyorker.com/magazine/2005/02/14/outsourcing-torture.

2 Richard Miniter, *Losing Bin Laden: How Bill Clinton's Failure Unleashed Global Terror* (Washington, D.C.: Regnery Publishing, 2003), xix. Chamberlain was the British Prime Minister who signed the 1938 Munich Pact, which was designed to avert war by acquiescing to Nazi Germany's takeover of the Czech Sudetenland.

3 "Annual Report to Congress on Combating Terrorism," Clinton Presidential Records, Naitonal Security Council, Transnational Threats, Box 12, William J. Clinton Presidential Library, Little Rock, Arkansas; Carolyn J. Dollar to Lisa E. Hagerty, November 25, 1999, Clinton Presidential Records, NSC Emails, March 1997–January 2001, box 5, William J. Clinton Presidential Library, Little Rock, Arkansas.

4 James D. Boys, *Clinton's War on Terror: Redefining U.S. Security Strategy, 1993–2001* (London: Lynne Riener, 2018); Chin-Kuei Tsui, *Clinton, New Terrorism and the Origins of the War on Terror* (New York: Routeledge, 2017).

5 Richard J. Barnett, "The Terrorism Trap," *The Nation*, December 2, 1996, reprinted at https://www.thefreelibrary.com/The+terrorism+trap.-a018922060

6 David C. Wills, *The First War on Terrorism. Counter-terrorism Policy During the Reagan Administration* (New York: Rowman & Littlefield, 2003).

7 Clair Sterling, *The Terror Network: The Secret War of International Terrorism* (New York: Henry Holt, 1981); David C. Martin & John Walcott, *Best Laid Plans: The Inside Story of America's War Against Terrorism* (New York: Touchstone Books, 1989), 49, 55. When Ronald Spiers of the State Department sent Secretary of State Alexander Haig a short paper prepared by the Intelligence and Research staff which concluded that terrorist groups essentially operated independently both of Moscow and of each other, Haig sent the paper back to Spiers with a handwritten note in the margin: "if you really believe this hogwash, you've been brainwashed."

8 See Daniele Ganser, *NATOs Secret Armies: Operation Gladio and Terrorism in Western Europe* (New York: Routledge, 2005); Bob Woodward, *Veil: The Secret Wars of the CIA, 1981–1987* (New York: Simon & Schuster, 1987), 453. NSA staffer, Robert "Bud" MacFarlane, acknowledged that the "operatives who carried out the attack may have been trained by the U.S."

9 David Hoffman, *The Oklahoma City Bombing and the Politics of Terror* (Venice, CA: Feral House, 1998), 404, 405. West German officials concluded that the CIA was behind the bombing of the discotheque as part of a black flag operation to provide a pretext for bombing Libya and trying to overthrow Qaddafi. After the fall of the Berlin Wall, prosecutors uncovered Stasi documents that implicated a Lebanese Stasi agent and his German wife and a Libyan agent who worked at the East Berlin embassy. The prosecution was unable to prove though that Colonel Qaddafi was behind the attack.

10 See Peter L. Bergen, *The Osama bin Laden I Know: An Oral History of al-Qaeda's Leader* (New York: Free Press, 2006); Steve Coll, *The Bin Ladens: An Arabian Family in the American Century* (New York: Norton, 2009); Lawrence Wright, *The Looming Tower: Al-Qaeda and the Road to 9/11* (New York: Alfred A. Knopf, 2006). Bin laden dated his hatred for America to 1982 "when America permitted the Israelis to invade Lebanon and the American Sixth Fleet helped them." He recalled the carnage: "blood and severed limbs, women and children sprawled

everywhere. Houses destroyed along with their occupants and high rises demolished over their residents. The situation was like a crocodile meeting a helpless child, powerless except for his screams. As I looked at those demolished towers in Lebanon, it entered my mind that we should punish the oppressor in kind and that we should destroy towers in America in order that they taste some of what we tasted." Wright, *The Looming Tower*, 151.

11 Nafeez Mosaddeq Ahmed, *The War on Truth: 9/11, Disinformation, and the Anatomy of Terrorism* (Northampton, MA: Olive Branch Press, 2005), 34, 35.

12 Peter Dale Scott, "Systemic Destabilization in Recent American History: 9/11, the JFK Assassination and the Oklahoma City Bombing as a Strategy of Tension," *The Asia Pacific Journal*, September 22, 2012, https://apjjf.org/2012/10/39/Peter-Dale-Scott/3835/article.html; David Hoffman, *The Oklahoma City Bombing and the Politics of Terror*; Ahmed, *The War on Truth*, 47, 48.

13 Jon Rappaport, *Oklahoma City Bombing: The Suppressed Truth* (Escondido California: The Book Tree, 1995), 66; Craig Roberts, *The Medusa File: Secret Crimes and Coverups of the U.S. Government* (Bahamas: Consolidated Press International, 1997), ch. 31; Webster Griffin Tarpley, *9/11 Synthetic Terror: Made in USA* (Joshua Tree: Progressive Press, 2005), 159; Ahmed, *The War on Truth*, 37, 38, 39. The FBI even assisted in construction of the bomb that took down part of the World Trade Center. According to one senior investigator, a collection of documents amounting to a "road map" to the World Trade Center bombing sat in an FBI storage locker unexamined and untranslated until after the bombing took place. A key organizer of the bombing, Egyptian intelligence officer, Emad Ali Salem, was a longstanding FBI informant who was paid over $2 million for the infiltration of the Blind Sheik's terrorist cell. The FBI's conduct suggests that it may have deliberately wanted to stage the attacks to enhance public fears about terrorism which would allow for passage of new police state measures and ensure ample funding for the FBI from Congress.

14 Robert Fisk, *The Great War for Civilization: The Conquest of the Middle East* (New York: Alfred A. Knopf, 2006), 20, 21.

15 John Duffy and Ray Nowosielski, *The Watchdogs Didn't Bark: The CIA, NSA, and the Crimes of the War on Terror* (New York, NY: Hot Books, 2018), 25, 26; Kevin Fenton, *Disconnecting the Dots: How CIA and FBI officials helped enable 9/11 and evaded government investigations* (Walterville, OR: Trine Day, 2011), 15.

16 Ahmed, *The War on Truth*, 52–57. For Ahmed this explains the CIA Station Chief's suppression of an investigation into an al-Qaeda terrorist cell and the State Department failure to follow up on credible leads that could have halted the Kenyan embassy bombings.

17 Wright, *The Looming Tower*, 174, 177, 319. In the 1992 attack on a Yemeni hotel, an Australian tourist and Yemeni hotel worker died, and seven other Yemenis were injured. The U.S.S. *Cole* had launched the missiles into Afghanistan in Operation Infinite Reach [discussed below].

18 Alex Rubinstein, "Did the CIA pressure Yemen to release al-Qaeda propagandist Anwar al-Awlaki? More evidence of CIA support for al-Qaeda exposed," *Substack*, March 22, 2021, https://realalexrubi.substack.com/p/leaked-cia-pressured-yemen-to-release. In 2011, Awlaki, his sixteen-year-old son and daughter were killed in drone strikes ordered by Barack Obama. Awlaki had relationships with Saudi intelligence officers and trained with the mujahadin in Afghanistan in the 1980s. In the 1990s, he had recruited students to fight for Chechen Islamic forces against Russia.

19 Glenn Kessler, "Osama Bin Laden and the Missed opportunities to Kill

Osama Bin Laden," *The Washington Post*, February 16, 2016.

20 Peter Dale Scott, *The American Deep State: Wall Street, Big Oil, and the Attack on U.S. Democracy* (New York: Rowman& Littlefield, 2015), 95–96; Michael T. Klare, *Resource Wars: The New Landscape of Global Conflict* (New York: Metropolitan Books, 2005), 95.

21 Steve Coll, *Ghost Wars: The Secret History of the CIA, Afghanistan, and Bin Laden, from the Soviet Invasion to September 10, 2001* (New York: Penguin Books, 2004), 241.

22 Quoted in Miniter, *Losing Bin Laden*, 31.

23 Bill Clinton, *My Life* (New York: Vintage, 2005), 719. On Clinton's success in framing the War on Terror and use of the rising threat of terrorism to his advantage, see Derick L. Hulme Jr., *The Domestic Politics of Terrorism: Lessons From the Clinton Administration* (Lanham, MD: Lexington Books, 2020).

24 Boys, *Clinton's War on Terror*, 174.

25 Boys, *Clinton's War on Terror*, 98.

26 Tsui, *Clinton, New Terrorism, and the Origins of the War on Terror*, 72.

27 Coll, *Ghost Wars*, 251.

28 Hoffman, *The Oklahoma City Bombing and the Politics of Terror*, 378.

29 Scott, "Systemic Destabilization in Recent American History." The Doomsday Project enabled hawkish Republicans like Dick Cheney and Donald Rumsfeld, who were selected for it, to establish a shadow government that provided a blueprint for their advancement of greater executive branch secrecy after 9/11.

30 Boys, *Clinton's War on Terror*, 98; Jeremy Scahill, "1996 Antiterrorism and Effective Death Penalty Act," *Joe Biden: Empire Politician, The Intercept*, April 27, 2021, https://theintercept.com/empire-politician/biden-antiterrorism-and-effective-death-penalty-act/; Hoffman, *The Oklahoma City Bombing and the Politics of Terror*, 378, 386; James Ridgeway, "In Search of John Doe #2," *Mother Jones*, July 2007. Biden's importance in supporting the legislation is detailed in Jeremy Scahill, "1996 Antiterrorism and Effective Death Penalty Act," *The Intercept*, April 27, 2021, https://theintercept.com/empire-politician/biden-antiterrorism-and-effective-death-penalty-act/

31 Hulme Jr., *The Domestic Politics of Terrorism*, 52.

32 Ibid., Rappaport, *Oklahoma City Bombing*, 47.

33 Scott, "Systemic Destabilization in Recent American History." Secret liaison agreements—with Saudi Arabia and Uzbekistan—may have provided the cover for secret CIA withholding of information before 9/11 about the designated 9/11 culprits Nawaf al-Hazmi and Khalid al-Mihdhar.

34 Hoffman, *The Oklahoma City Bombing and the Politics of Terror*; Victor Thorn, *Hillary (and Bill): The Murder Volume*: Part three of the Clinton trilogy (Washington, D.C.: American Free Press, 2008), 551–585; Craig Roberts, *The Medusa File II: The Politics of Terror and the Oklahoma City Bombing* (CreateSpace Independent Publishing Platform, 2017); Ambrose Evans-Pritchard, *The Secret Life of Bill Clinton: The Unreported Stories* (Washington, D.C.: Regnery, 1997), 1–111; Jeremy Kuzmarov, "Oklahoma City Bombing: Was Timothy McVeigh a Patsy in a Sinister Black-Flag Operation?" *CovertAction Magazine*, April 19, 2022, https://covertactionmagazine.com/2022/04/19/oklahoma-city-bombing-was-timothy-mcveigh-a-patsy-in-a-sinister-black-flag-operation/. McVeigh had a background in army intelligence and was seen meeting with ATF agents in the days before the bombing. McVeigh was supplied with explosives by a CIA informant named Roger

Moore and delivered weapons to Cuban exile groups in Florida on Moore's behalf. Suspicion that McVeigh was set up as a patsy is enhanced by his abysmal escape plan—he drove out of Oklahoma City in a car without a license plate, ensuring that he would be stopped by state troopers. He told his cell mates that he was part of an army plot and thought that his superior, "the Major," would rescue him from prison. Though the ATF was supposedly a target of the attack, its agents were tipped off and told not to come into work that day—so none died. Terrence Yeakey, one of the first police officers on the scene who worked tirelessly to save victims, was later found dead after he had expressed doubts about the official story and was carrying out his own investigation. One theory hold that the Murrah building was targeted because it contained incriminating documents related to the Mena affair, which were among those removed from the building—even before the rescue crews had finished rescuing victims of the blast.

35 Thomas E. Ricks and Susan B. Glasser, "U.S. Operated Secret Alliance with Uzbekistan," *The Washington Post*, October 14, 2001, A1.

36 John Miller, Michael Stone, with Chris Mitchell, *Inside the 9/11 Plot, and Why the FBI and CIA Failed to Stop It* (New York: Hyperion, 2002), 217, 218.

37 Boys, *Clinton's War on Terror*, 98, 184; Rappaport, *Oklahoma City Bombing*, 61. On COINTELPRO and its abuses, see Ward Churchill and Jim Vanderwall, *The COINTELPRO Papers: Documents from the FBI's Secret Wars Against Dissent in the U.S.* (Boston: South End Press, 2001).

38 Boys, *Clinton's War on Terror*, 98; John C. Miller et al. *The Cell: Inside the 9/11 Plot, and Why the FBI Failed to Stop It* (New York: Hachette Books, 2002), 218; Coll, *Ghost Wars*, 459.

39 "Annual Report to Congress on Combating Terrorism," Clinton Presidential Records, National Security Council, Transnational Threats, Box 12, William J. Clinton Presidential Library, Little Rock, Arkansas. Whether these programs were misused and provided a cover for the U.S. development of bioweapons is uncertain and suspicious.

40 Coll, *Ghost Wars*, 493. According to Webster G. Tarpley, Clarke had been dropped from the State Department by James Baker III, accused of concealing Israeli exports of U.S. military technology to the People's Republic of China, which is banned under U.S. law, and which the Israelis had agreed in advance not to do. During the First Persian Gulf War, he had worked with Israeli officials to sell Patriot missiles to Israel. Clarke was a protégé of Arnold L. Raphael (killed in the same plane crash with Pakistani General Zia Al-Huq) and worked closely with Morton Abramowitz. Webster G. Tarpley, *9/11 Synthetic Terror: Made in USA* (Joshua Tree, CA: Progressive Press, 2006), 19.

41 Jeffrey St. Clair and Alexander Cockburn, "How Bush Was Offered bin Laden and Blew It," *Counterpunch*, November 1, 2004. According to Kabir Mohabhat, an Afghan businessman who served as a State Department envoy to the Taliban, by the end of 1999, U.S. sanctions and political ostracism were costing the Taliban dearly and they had come to see Osama bin Laden and his training camps as "just a damn liability."

42 "Decision to Attack Usama's Bases," *Urdu Daily*, July 19, 1999, Clinton Presidential Records, NSC Cables, January 1995–December 1996, box 1, William J. Clinton Presidential Library, Little Rock, Arkansas. Rahmon has remained in power for the last twenty-nine years, since 1994.

43 Ahmed, *The War on Truth*, 13.

44 Coll, *Ghost Wars*; Paul Fitzgerald and Elizabeth Gould, *The Valediction: Three Nights of Desmond* (Walterville, OR: Trine Day, 2021), 142. Overlooked was Massoud's association with heroin trafficking, the massacre of Taliban forces, and history of throwing acid in the faces of women who refused to wear the veil.

45 Coll, *Ghost Wars*, 329.

46 Thomas H. Kean and Lee Hamilton, *The 9/11 Report: The National Commission on Terrorist Attacks Upon the United States*, with reporting and analysis by *The New York Times* (New York: St. Martin's Paperbacks, 2004), 192, 193.

47 "Iraq and Libya Sanctions Act," https://en.wikipedia.org/wiki/Iran_and_Libya_Sanctions_Act#:~:text=The%20Iran%20and%20Libya%20Sanctions,business%20with%20Iran%20and%20Libya.&text=The%20Act%20empowers%20the%20President,to%20renewal%20every%20six%20months; Tsui, *Clinton, New Terrorism and the Origins of the War on Terror*, 106. ILSA was approved in the House of Representatives by a 415–0 vote, exemplifying the wide support for Clinton's approach towards the Middle East at this time.

48 Miniter, *Losing Bin Laden*, xxii; Gareth Porter, *Manufactured Crisis: The Untold Story of the Iran Nuclear Scare* (Charlottesville, Virginia: Just World Books, 2014),

49 The prosecution failed to identify Megrahi as the buyer of clothing in Malta that showed up at the Lockerbie site. The diaries of the Scottish police investigator referenced payoffs by witnesses and the U.S. Department of Justice which have never been explained. Scottish law professor Robert Black called Megrahi's trial the "most disgraceful miscarriage of justice in Scotland for a hundred years," and UN observer Hans Kochler called the decision [to convict Megrahi] "totally incomprehensible and a spectacular miscarriage of justice." Edward S. Herman, "Lockerbie and the Propaganda System: Release of Al-Megrahi Evokes Selective History," *Fairness and Accuracy in Reporting*, October 1, 2009; John Ashton, *Megrahi: The Lockerbie Evidence* (Birlinn, 2012); http://www.lockerbietruth.com/. In 1989, British Prime Minister Margaret Thatcher had been urged by representatives of the American government not to enquire into the attack.

50 John R. Schindler, "The Truth Behind This Bomb That Took Down Pan Am 103 Over Lockerbie Remains a Thirty-Year Mystery," *London Observer*, December 21, 2018. The PFLP was allegedly paid $10 million and had used a similar bomb which brought down Pan Am flight 803 in another jetliner attack. A veteran NSA analyst told Schindler that his counter-terrorism team had "no doubt of Iranian culpability" while renegade CIA agent Robert Baer said that the CIA had reached the same conclusion.

51 Allan Francovitch, "The Maltese Double Cross—Lockerbie" 1994, https://www.youtube.com/watch?v=0B5hv6scbBo; Kenn Thomas and Jim Keith, *The Octoopus: Secret Government and the Death of Danny Casolaro* (LA: Feral House, 2004), 93.

52 Coll, *Ghost Wars*, 439; Ahmed Rashid, *Descent into Chaos: The United States and the Failure of Nation Building in Pakistan, Afghanistan and Central Asia* (New York: Viking, 2008), 68, 69. Karimov also sent Uzbek Special Forces into Afghanistan to assist the anti-bin Laden unit there.

53 Miniter, *Losing Bin Laden,* 127–149; Richard Becker, Sara Flounders, and John Parker, "Sudan: Diversionary Bombing," *CovertAction Quarterly*, Winter 1999, 16; Tarpley, *9/11 Synthetic Terror*, 141, 142; Ahmed, *The War on Truth*, 87–89. A senior Sudanese officer made a similar offer to the FBI a year and a half later, which the FBI rejected.

54 Becker, Flounders, and Parker, "Sudan," 12, 13.

55 Becker, Flounders, and Parker, "Sudan," 15. The damage from the bombing was estimated at $100 million. A month after the attack, thousands of people marched in Khartoum to denounce the U.S. bombing.

56 Nathan J. Robinson, *Super Predator: Bill Clinton's Use and Abuse of Black America* (Demilune Press, 2016), 170; Jonathan Belke, "Years Later, U.S. Attack on Factory Still hurts Sudan," *The Boston Globe*, August 22, 1999.

57 Quoted in Seymour Hersh, "The Missiles of August," *The New Yorker*, October 12, 1998, 34.

58 Wayne Madsen, *Genocide and Covert Operations in Africa*, 1993–1999 (New York: Edwin Mellen, 1999), 472; Michael Rip and James Hasik, *The Precision Revolution: GPS and the Future of Aerial Warfare* (Annapolis: Naval Institute Press, 2002), 367–369; Timothy Naftali, *Blind Spot: The Secret History of American Counterterrorism* (New York: Perseus Books, 200 5), 266; Marc Lacey, "Look at the Place! Sudan Says 'Say Sorry,' but U.S. Won't," *The New York Times*, October 20, 2005; Seymour Hersh, "The Missiles of August," *The New Yorker*, October 12, 1998, 34–41.

59 Miniter, *Losing Bin Laden*, 185.

60 Becker, Flounders, and Parker, "Sudan," 12, 13. Bashir had also cooperated in the hunt for leftist terrorist Carlos the Jackal, ensuring his arrest and extradition to France.

61 Tim Weiner, *Legacy of Ashes: The History of the CIA* (New York: Doubleday, 2007), 470.

62 Weiner, *Legacy of Ashes*, 470.

63 Andrew Bacevich, *America's War for the Greater Middle East: A Military History* (New York: Random House, 2016), 207; Coll, *Ghost Wars*, 411.

64 Bill Clinton, *My Life* (New York: 2004), 803; Miniter, *Losing Bin Laden*, 182; Glenn Kessler, "Osama Bin Laden and the Missed opportunities to Kill Osama Bin Laden," *The Washington Post*, February 16, 2016. Journalist Richard Miniter in *Losing Bin Laden* emphasizes that bin Laden escaped because Clinton had decided to surrender the element of surprise, fearing that the missiles crossing its airspace could have been misinterpreted as an attack from India, and had reported the impending strikes to the Pakistani government, whose intelligence services had spies in Bin Laden's network. In December, Clinton rejected another proposed strike in Kandahar because Clinton said it would have destroyed the town and killed 300 innocent women and children.

65 Wright, *The Looming Tower*, 287.

66 Wright, *The Looming Tower*, Bacevich, *America's War for the Greater Middle East*, 207.

67 Rip and Hasik, *The Precision Revolution*, 371; Bacevich, *America's War for the Greater Middle East*, 207. According to Russian intelligence sources, bin Laden sold unexploded tomahawk missiles that had failed to detonate to China for more than $10 million. Wright, *The Looming Tower;* Miniter, *Losing Bin Laden*, 186. Senator Dan Coats (R-IN) accused Clinton of "lies and deceit and manipulation and deceptions."

68 FBI, Reston Virginia to AINS, Davis Mathas, August 21, 1998, "Taleban Envoy in Islamabad Interviewed on U.S. Strikes," Clinton Presidential Records, NSC Cables, January 1995–December 1996, box 1, William J. Clinton Presidential Library, Little Rock, Arkansas.

69 Wright, *The Looming Tower*, 287. Mullah Omar afterwards placed a secret call to the U.S. State Department in which he said that strikes would only arouse anti-American sentiment in the Islamic world and provoke more acts of terrorism. The Clinton administration subsequently applied sanctions to the Taliban which came to see bin Laden as a liability, placed him on house arrest and agreed to further missile strikes to take him out, however, an offer extended to the Clinton administration was rejected after the Bush administration took over. Jeffrey St. Clair and Alexander Cockburn, "How Bush Was Offered Bin Laden and Blew It," *Counterpunch*, November 1, 2004.

70 Boys, *Clinton's War on Terror*.

71 Boys, *Clinton's War on Terror*.

72 Patrick Maney, *Bill Clinton New Gilded Age President* (Lawrence: University of Kansas Press, 2016), 249; Boys, *Clinton's War on Terror*, 217.

73 Boys, *Clinton's War on Terror*.

74 Boys, *Clinton's War on Terror*.

75 Boys, *Clinton's War on Terror*, 218.

76 Boys, *Clinton's War on Terror*, 218.

77 Jason Brownlee, *Democracy Prevention: The Politics of the U.S.-Egyptian Alliance* (New York: Cambridge University Press, 2012), 63.

78 Brownlee, *Democracy Prevention*, 63.

79 "Extraordinary Rendition: A Back Story," *The Guardian*, August 31, 2011, https://www.theguardian.com/world/2011/aug/31/extraordinary-rendition-backstory

80 Brownlee, *Democracy Prevention*, 63, 65.

81 Brownlee, *Democracy Prevention*, 63.

82 See Richard Whittle, *Predator: The Secret Origins of the Drone Revolution* (London: Picador, 2015).

83 Chris Woods, "The Story of America's First Drone Strike," *The Atlantic*, May 30, 2015, https://www.theatlantic.com/international/archive/2015/05/america-first-drone-strike-afghanistan/394463/

84 Woods, "The Story of America's First Drone Strike"; Coll, *Ghost Wars*, 529.

85 Coll, *Ghost Wars*, 530.

86 Woods, "The Story of America's First Drone Strike."

87 Coll, *Ghost Wars*, 532.

88 Woods, "The Story of America's First Drone Strike." See also Miniter, *Losing Bin Laden*, 204.

89 Woods, "The Story of America's First Drone Strike."

90 Peter Dale Scott, *The Road to 9/11: Wealth, Empire and the Future of America* (Berkeley: University of California Press, 2007); Scott, *The American Deep State*, 54–56, 69. Coup leader Heidar Aliyev was an ex-KGB agent who presided over a brutal regime that facilitated the construction of a vast pipeline that could transport oil to the West without going through Russia or Iran.

91 Scott, *The Road to 9/11*, 164.

92 Scott, *The American Deep State*, 61.

93 Mohamed had served in the Praetorian Guard of Egyptian President Anwar el Sadat, fought the U.S. Marines in Somalia and directly trained al-Qaeda operatives in terrorist methods including airplane hijacking using box-cutters.

94 Scott, *The American Deep State*, 47.

95 Coll, *Ghost Wars*, 326, 327.

96 Rashid, *Descent into Chaos*, 68. The chief idealogue of the Islamist forces in Uzbekistan, Tahir Yuldashev, spent several years as a guest of the ISI in Peshawar.

97 See Rashid, *Descent into Chaos*; Pakistani Support for the Taliban, https://www.hrw.org/reports/2001/afghan2/Afghan0701-02.htm#P366_99599

98 See Mahmood Mamdani, *Good Muslim, Bad Muslim: America, the Cold War, and the Roots of Terror* (New York: Penguin, 2004).

99 Colin Cookman and Bill French, "The Pakistan Aid Dilemma," *Center for American Progress*, December 16, 2011, https://www.americanprogress.org/issues/security/reports/2011/12/16/10823/the-pakistan-aid-dilemma/

100 Scott Shane, "Moussaoui Calls Saudi Princes Patrons of al-Qaeda," *The New York Times*, February 3, 2015. The two hijackers may have received money indirectly from the Saudi embassy in Washington.

101 Scott, *The American Deep State*, 75; Kevin Fenton, *Disconnecting the Dots: How 9/11 Was Allowed to Happen* (Walterville, OR: Trine Day, 2011). According to former CIA officer Robert Baer, the IIRO was run "with an iron hand" by Prince Salman ibn Abdul-Aziz al Saud, the brother of Saudi King Abdullah, who "personally approved all important appointments and spending." Saudi intelligence also backed the Islamist rebellion in Uzbekistan, which Islam Karimov brutally suppressed.

102 Scott, *The American Deep State*, 75.

103 Miller et al. *The Cell*, 271, 272; Fenton, *Disconnecting the Dots*. Fenton provides evidence to indicate that Alec Station was compromised by the CIA's association with Saudi Arabia and al-Qaeda in various covert operations.

104 Bossie, *Intelligence Failure*, 94.

CHAPTER 10

Clinton: The Most Pro-Israeli President Since Truman

Perhaps the hallmark moment of Clinton's presidency was the famous image in September 1993 of Israeli Prime Minister Yitzhak Rabin, flanked by Clinton, shaking hands with Palestinian Liberation Organization (PLO) leader and former fedayeen guerrilla, Yasser Arafat, after the signing of the Oslo peace accords. *New York Times* foreign affairs correspondent Thomas L. Friedman wrote that it was the Middle East equivalent of the "fall of the Berlin Wall."[1]

Under the terms of the peace agreement, Israel transferred control of the occupied territories to the Palestinian Authority (PA) and agreed to withdraw troops from Gaza and Jericho in return for Arafat's commitment to recognition of Israel's right to exist and to renounce the use of terrorism and violence. Only three weeks before, Rabin, IDF commander during the 1967 Six-Day war, had referred to the PLO as a terrorist organization, but now he expressed optimism that decades of bloodshed between Arabs and Israelis could be brought to an end.[2]

Unfortunately, the promise of that crisp fall day did not last very long. Rabin was assassinated allegedly by a right-wing Jewish settler, Yigal Amir, on November 4, 1995, Palestinian suicide bombing attacks resumed as Israeli occupation of the West Bank and Gaza continued and Palestinians continued to be treated as second class citizens, and subsequent peace talks broke down following the election of Benjamin "Bibi" Netanyahu, who headed the right-wing Likud party. In 2000, Israeli Prime Minister Ariel Sharon ignited the second Palestinian Intifada after he visited the Temple Mount in Jerusalem, a Palestinian holy site, and Israeli snipers opened fire on Palestinian demonstrators. A bloody round of violence followed, putting an end to the hopes that had been raised at Oslo.[3]

Many Palestinians did not consider Oslo to offer anything positive in the first place. Palestinian literary scholar Edward Said termed it "an instrument of Palestinian surrender" and the "Palestinian Versailles" because Arafat had abandoned Palestinian demands for their own state and accepted the marginalization of Palestinian enclaves surrounded by more prosperous

Jewish settlements around the West Bank. Arafat also did not press for the 1948 refugees' right of return or freeing of Palestinian political prisoners.[4]

Said compared Clinton's performance to a "20th Century Roman emperor shepherding two vassal kings through rituals of reconciliation and obeisance, all these only temporarily obscuring the truly astonishing proportion of the Palestinian capitulation."[5] Rabin himself referred to a "new form of occupation from outside," made possible by new drone and other surveillance technologies. Israel deployed these to keep watch on the Palestinians and to signal when to redeploy troops, as they did in September 1996 in Ramallah to quell a Palestinian uprising sparked by Israeli tunneling near the Al-Aqsa mosque.[6]

The Jewish settler population in the West Bank tellingly increased from 250,000 to 380,000 in the aftermath of Oslo and came to incorporate nearly half the land surface of the West Bank. Between the signing of the Oslo Accords in 1993 and March 1998, 629 Palestinian homes were destroyed by Israeli bulldozers, 535 in the West Bank and 94 in Jerusalem, more than a third under the Israeli Labor government and the rest under Likud.[7]

The Rabin government imposed onerous constraints on exports of Gaza oranges, its main cash crop, causing much of it to rot, along with new requirements that all produce be purchased by Israeli agents for sale in Israel or export through Israeli enterprises. The goal, according to researcher Sarah Roy, was to "turn parts of Gaza into a branch plant economy designed to serve Israeli interests . . . primarily, with Israel retaining control over land, zoning, water and any development that may take place in the areas released to local self-administration."[8]

One of the most controversial aspects of the Oslo agreements was the creation of a Palestinian Authority (PA) police force, which enforced the Israeli occupation of the West Bank and Gaza and also evolved into a personal instrument of Yasser Arafat.[9] Political analyst Norman Finkelstein wrote that: "now the PLO was doing the torturing, doing the murdering, doing the jailing."[10] British journalist Patrick Cockburn reported on the case of Youssef Baba, who was the twelfth Palestinian to be tortured to death at the hands of the PA police force following the Oslo Accords. Baba had been taken into custody following a dispute over a land deal during which he offended someone in military intelligence.[11] Israeli journalist Gideon Levy wrote in *Haaretz* in June 1996 that the interrogation dungeons of the Shin Bet [Israeli secret police] had provided an excellent school for the Palestinian torturers. "It is no coincidence that the Palestinians tortured by the PA police describe methods that are amazingly similar to the Shin Bet interrogation methods.[12]

The Clinton administration played an important role in helping to finance, train and oversee the new PA police force through a secret CIA program sanctioned by Israeli Prime Minister Benjamin Netanyahu, who nonetheless never trusted the Palestinian police.[13] Clinton's CIA director George Tenet sustained a very close relationship with Arafat. The Islamist group Hamas in turn claimed that they were "up against the world's largest intelligence organization." Americans helped strengthen the PA police intelligence in key areas such as the ability to infiltrate terrorist groups, improve clandestine communication and interrogation methods, enhance computer technology related to intelligence and intelligence processing, and in improved intelligence gathering techniques. The CIA even played a role in monitoring the interrogation of suspects, which bred complaints among Palestinians that it was tacitly supporting the PA's use of torture, prolonged detention without trial and other human rights abuses.[14]

While presenting himself as a southern law and order man, President Clinton was never much bothered about human rights abuses, except when they could be played up for political advantage. At a private dinner at the White House with junior members of the Jordanian Royal family, Clinton announced to his guests that he was "the most pro-Israeli president since Truman."[15] As a savvy politician, Clinton recognized the power of the American Israeli Public Affair Committee (AIPAC) lobby, before which Clinton had first spoken as Arkansas governor in 1984. During his 1992 presidential campaign, Clinton's General Counsel, David Ishfin, was an adviser to AIPAC.[16] Pro-Israeli PACs distributed over $4 million to political candidates in that cycle, most of them Democrats.[17]

Clinton's inner-circle mostly had hawkish views regarding Israel. They included: a) Vice President Al Gore, who was a protégé of *New Republic* founder Martin Peretz, who in 1982 had tossed flowers at Israeli pilots returning from bombing Lebanese refugee camps, b) Secretary of State Madeleine Albright, who hailed from a Jewish family that fled the Nazis in Czechoslovakia, c) National Security adviser Sandy Berger, a former lobbyist for Caterpillar, whose armed bulldozers were used extensively by Israel in attacks on Gaza, d) Defense Secretary William Cohen, who grew up going to Hebrew school, and e) Rahm Emanuel, a senior adviser whose father was in the Irgun, a Zionist terrorist organization that bombed the King David Hotel in 1946, and who first traveled to Israel during the 1967 Six-Day War.[18]

Clinton's strong emotional connection to Israel stemmed in part from his upbringing in the heart of the Bible belt. After his defeat in the 1980 Arkansas gubernatorial election, Clinton and his wife went on a religious pilgrimage to Israel with a group organized by Reverend Worley Oscar Vaught, the pastor of Immanuel Baptist Church in Little Rock. Their tour included the old city of Jerusalem, the Western Wall, Masada, and the Galilee.[19]

Clinton's biographer Robert Levin wrote that "the trip reinforced Clinton's support for the people of Israel. Bill and Hillary understood the profound effect that Israel has on American Jews and around the world," said Sarah Ehrman, a friend from the McGovern campaign "and share a feeling for the security and stability of the state of Israel." According to Levin, Reverend Vaught greatly influenced the Clintons' attitudes towards Israel. "I have believed in supporting Israel as long as I have known anything about the issue," Clinton said later. "It may have something to do with my religious upbringing. For the last several years until he [Vaught] died, I was very much under the influence of my pastor . . . He was a close friend of Israel and began visiting even before the state of Israel was created. And when he was on his deathbed, he said to me that he hoped someday I would have a chance to run for president, but that if I ever let Israel down, God would forgive me . . . I will never let Israel down."[20]

Clinton ultimately followed his pastor's advice, never letting Israel down. When he became president, his administration provided over $15 billion in military aid to Israel, including a then record $3.120 billion in 2000, and over $32 billion in foreign aid.[21] Israel was allowed to purchase $700 million of the latest U.S. military equipment, including advanced jet fighters (F-15s and F-16s), advanced attack helicopters (Huey Cobras and Black Hawks), hellfire, Sidewinder and Stinger missiles, and the Joint Direct Attack Munitions System along with CS gas cartridges used to suppress Palestinian demonstrations and fuses that were used in tank rounds.[22]

Israel further benefited from offsets, or incentives that American weapons manufacturers offered to convince Israel to sign deals, including co-production of weapons, transfers of technology, and non-military related investment, which reached record levels in 1999. Lockheed Martin promised to spend $900 million in Israel to secure a $2.5 billion F-16 sale; other offsets included a $750 million counter-trade investment from Boeing for the sale of F-15 fighters and Black Hawk helicopters.[23]

A Pentagon official tellingly told *The New York Times* in November 1999 that given the amount of weaponry that the United States shared with Israel, it was difficult to separate American military technology from Israel's own.[24] In March 1996, Clinton asked Congress for the first installment of a $100 million request to purchase advanced bomb detection scanners and sniffers, x-ray systems, robotics for handling suspect packages and advanced thermal trader sensors." Clinton said that the two countries were "determined to use every tool at their disposal to fight against extremist violence."[25]

A year earlier, Clinton told an AIPAC conference Israel's military edge was "greater than ever" because the U.S. had "kept its word," supplying Israel with fighter aircraft, attack helicopters, supercomputers, and the Arrow missile system while delivering the "most advanced multiple launch rocket system in the world." Highlighting deepening intelligence cooperation and staging of the largest ever joint military exercises, Clinton presented himself in his speech as Israel's political savior from "back-door isolationists on the left and right," who "under the cover of budget cutting, want to cut the legs off our relationships in the Middle East and around the world," and "deny the U.S. the resources we need to supply our allies who take risks for peace."[26]

One theory holds that Clinton's fealty to Israel was the result of his having been blackmailed by Israeli intelligence, which had obtained compromising information about his sexual escapades from the Jeffrey-Epstein-Ghislaine Maxwell child-sex spy ring. Between 1993 and 1995, Epstein visited the White House at least 17 times and Epstein and Clinton were reportedly as close as brothers.[27]

Clinton's chief negotiator on the Israel-Palestine conflict, Dennis Ross, and ambassador to Israel Martin Indyk, were both AIPAC members and hostile to the UN.[28] Just after Oslo, the Clinton team sought to restrict or terminate UN activities with regard to Israel-Palestine, claiming that past resolutions were "obsolete and anachronistic" in light of the recent Israel-PLO agreement. The Clinton administration also called for abolishing the UN's special committee on Palestinian rights, which it termed "biased, superfluous and unnecessary," and refused to condemn Israel's settlement activity because it is "unproductive to debate the legalities of the issue." In 1995, Clinton vetoed a UN Security Council resolution condemning the Israeli confiscation of Palestinian land in East Jerusalem. Clinton also reversed long standing U.S. support for UN resolution 194 of December 11, 1948—a direct application of the Universal Declaration of Human Rights, which affirmed the rights of Palestinian refugees who had fled or had been expelled during the fighting to return to their homes. For the first time, the U.S. joined Israel in opposing the resolution, which was reaffirmed by a vote of 192–2 (abstentions included the Russian Federation).[29]

In another significant development, Clinton administration officials ceased referring to the West Bank and Gaza as "occupied territories," now calling them "disputed territories." Later, it announced that all options would be left open including demand even for full annexation of the territories under Israeli sovereignty, which was a demand of the extreme Israeli right wing. Noam Chomsky points out that Clinton's increased support for Israel was a consequence of the end of the Cold War and disappearance of the Soviet Union as an ally of the Arab states and was combined with a dual containment policy aimed at both Iran and Iraq who threatened joint American-Israeli regional hegemony.[30]

In July 1994, Clinton helped broker a peace treaty between Israel and Jordan, in which the two countries agreed to intelligence sharing and Jordan agreed to keep Palestinian activism in check.[31] Clinton further gave diplomatic support to Israel and weapons as it invaded Southern Lebanon in July 1993 and then again in April 1996 under Operation Grapes of Wrath. The Israelis boasted that a U.S.-built targeting system, TQP-37 Firefinder, could pinpoint enemy positions with surgical precision; nonetheless, hundreds of civilians were killed in these operations which were carried out under the pretext of defending Israel from Katyusha rocket attacks launched by Hizbollah guerrilla fighters (Hizbollah had been founded as a resistance organization following Israel's 1982 invasion of Lebanon).[32]

American-built F-16 fighter jets with laser-guided bombs were used in the Israeli attacks. Even the Israeli massacre of over 100 refugees sheltering at a UN base at Qana was justified by President Clinton as a "tragic misfiring by Israel in its legitimate exercise of its right to self-defense" in response to a "deliberate tactic of Hizbollah" to position rockets near civilians.[33] Clinton's claim about self-defense ignored the fact of the Israeli occupation of Lebanon, carried out in violation of UN resolution 425 of March 1978, which had generated Hizbollah's resistance, and the brutality of the South Lebanon Army, an Israeli proxy force founded by Saad Haddad, which was known for brutalizing the local population.[34]

The Clinton administration claimed credit for brokering cease fire agreements in Lebanon, but these agreements ensured that the Israeli occupation would be enduring. In May of 2000, Israel attacked Southern Lebanon's electrical grids using U.S.-supplied F-16s and attack helicopters, which fired hellfire and other air to ground missiles that had been delivered in the previous years. The attacks violated the 1996 ceasefire and international humanitarian law since the electrical stations had played no part in Hizbollah's military campaign. They were criticized by the U.S. State Department, which made no mention of U.S. weapons sales to Israel.[35] The State Department had previously criticized the IDF for killing Palestinian demonstrators, without mentioning U.S. sales of weapons that could be used in the commission of such abuses, including $3.5 million worth of anti-personnel riot control chemicals authorized in FY1998, plus 28,539,400 rounds of ammunition, 12,768 military guns, and 32 grenade launchers delivered or authorized for export during FY 1996–98.[36]

Clinton personally favored Israel's Labor Party over the right-wing Likud, which was less open to negotiation with the Palestinians, and admitted to trying to help Labor leader Shimon Peres (architect of the Operation Grapes of Wrath) defeat Benjamin Netanyahu in Israel's 1996 elections.[37] Labor party leader Ehud Barak hired Clinton's famous team of consultants—Stanley

Greenberg, James Carville and Bob Shrum—to help defeat Netanyahu in the 1996 elections.[38]

In May 1995, when Clinton became the first active U.S. president to speak before AIPAC, he used his platform to defend Israel's actions in Operation Grapes of Wrath.[39] Clinton's pardon of Marc Rich—a commodities trader convicted of violating the U.S. oil embargo on Iran, tax evasion, wire fraud and several other crimes—was enacted as another favor to Israel, after extensive lobbying by Israeli Prime Minister Ehud Barak. Rich had performed many services for the Mossad and was a main source addressing Israel's oil and energy needs during the Arab oil embargo following the 1973 Yom Kippur War.[40]

In 1998, Clinton helped preside over a summit between his nemesis Netanyahu and Arafat along with Jordan, which resulted in the Wye River agreement in which Israel agreed to undertake a series of gradual withdrawals from the occupied territories and to turn over a small area of the northern West Bank to Palestinian control. Clinton subsequently became the first U.S. president to visit Palestinian controlled territory when he went to Gaza.[41] This important gesture was typical of his political style, which at the end of the day was hollow, given his unwillingness to try to pressure Israel to make any major concessions to the Palestinians.

At the Camp David summit in July 2000, Ehud Barak's offer—which had the sanction of the Clinton administration—left Israel in control of thirteen percent of the West Bank while his final offer reduced it to twelve percent. However, the proposal separated the southern and central Palestinian cantons from the northern one and from Gaza and effectively cut off the major Palestinian towns (Bethlehem, Ramallah, Nablus) from one another. The Palestinian fragments were also separated from East Jerusalem, the center of Palestinian commercial, cultural, religious and political life and institutions.[42] Furthermore, under this deal Israel retained control of most of Jerusalem and most of the water aquifers of the West Bank and its most fertile lands, and control over the Jordan Valley, while refusing to recognize the right of return of Palestinian refugees. The Clinton administration blamed Arafat for rejecting the deal, which no self-respecting Palestinian leader could have in fact supported.[43]

In December 2000, during negotiations at Bolling Air Force base, Clinton made a more generous offer to the Palestinians, recommending 94 to 96 percent of the West Bank for the Palestinians with a land swap from Israel of 1 to 3 percent, and an understanding that the land kept by Israel would include 80 percent of the settlers in blocs. Israeli forces would withdraw over a three-year period and be replaced by an international force. The new state of Palestine would be non-militarized but have a strong security force and sovereignty over air space, and the Palestinians would be granted sovereignty over the Temple Mount and the Israelis sovereignty over the Western Wall.[44]

Finally, some progress appeared to be forthcoming at the meetings in Taba, Egypt in January 2001, where Israel accepted Clinton's plan, which called for a return to pre-1967 borders.[45] Some issues continued to be contested and still had to be worked out and Arafat was reluctant to give up the Palestinian right of return, though each side believed a viable deal would be struck after future talks. This all changed, however, with the election of Ariel Sharon of the Likud Party later in the year and Sharon's visit to the Temple Mount, which triggered the second Intifada.

At the end of his term and unencumbered by the pressure of another election, Clinton had displayed greater sympathy for the Palestinian position and helped advance some fleeting hope during the Taba talks. Clinton's ultimate legacy, nonetheless, was to help to institutionalize Israel's occupation at Oslo. To his shame, Clinton sanctioned Israel's illegal incursions into Southern Lebanon, its settlement expansion, and its disregard for UN resolutions, and supplied Israel with billions of dollars in arms and high-tech weapons systems that were used against the Palestinian and Lebanese peoples. Clinton saw himself as a friend of Israel, but at the end of the day he did a disservice both to the country and to the Jewish people by giving Israeli leaders a false sense of invincibility by virtue of their unlimited backing by the United States. The result was the development of a certain arrogance among Israeli leaders and unwillingness, with the exception of the fleeting moment at Taba, to offer the concessions that were needed for a durable peace capable of ensuring both the short and long-term security of Israel's citizens.

Endnotes

1 Quoted in Noam Chomsky, *World Orders Old and New* (New York: Columbia University Press, 1996), 248.

2 Avi Shlaim, "The Oslo Accord," *Journal of Palestine Studies*, 23, 3 (Spring 1994), 24–40.

3 Avi Shlaim, "It's Now Clear: The Oslo Peace Accords Were Wrecked by Netanyahu's Bad Faith," *The Guardian*, September 12, 2013; Robert Fisk, *The Great War for Civilisation: The Conquest of the Middle East* (New York: Alfred A. Knopf, 2006), 440.

4 Shlaim, "It's Now Clear," Edward Said, "The Morning After," *London Review of Books*, October, 21, 1993, https://www.lrb.co.uk/the-paper/v15/n20/edward-said/the-morning-after.

5 Said, "The Morning After." See also Norman G. Finkelstein, *Image and Reality of the Israel-Palestine Conflict*, 2nd ed. (London: Verso, 2003), xix. Finkelstein wrote

that the real meaning of the Oslo Accords was to create a "Palestinian Bantustan by dangling before Arafat and the PLO the perquisites of power and privilege, much like how the British controlled Palestine during the Mandate years through the mufti of Jerusalem, Amin al-Husayni, and the Supreme Muslim Council." The occupation continued after Oslo "albeit by remote control and with the consent of the Palestinian people, represented by their sole representative, the PLO."

6 Randy Schwartz, "Patrolling the Empire: Mapping, Imagery and national Security," *CovertAction Quarterly*, Winter 1996–1997, 34.

7 Finkelstein, *Image and Reality of the Israel-Palestine Conflict*, xx; Robert Fisk, *The Great War for Civilisation: The Conquest of the Middle East* (New York: Alfred A. Knopf, 2005), 428.

8 Chomsky, *World Orders Old and New*, 254.

9 Alaa Tartir, "The Evolution and Reform of Palestinian Security Forces ,1993–2013," *International Journal of Security and Development*, 4, 1 (2015). The main impact of the Oslo agreement, according to political scientist Rex Brynen, was not just to reaffirm the Israeli occupation by proxy, but also to institutionalize a new Palestinian elite that ruled based on a neo-patrimonial style of governance.

10 John Dirlik, "Scholar Norman Finkelstein Calls Oslo Agreement a 'Sordid Detour' on Path to a Just and Lasting Peace," *Washington Report on Middle East Affairs*, January-February 1997.

11 Patrick Cockburn, "Torture Deaths That Shame Palestine," *The Independent*, February 21, 1997; Brynjar Lia, *Building Arafat's Police: The Politics of International Police Assistance in the Palestinian Territories After the Oslo Agreements* (New York: Ithaca Press, 2007).

12 Gideon Levy, "The Legacy of Occupation," *Haaretz*, June 23, 1996; Human Rights Watch, Torture and Physical Abuse by the Security Forces, https://www.hrw.org/reports/1997/palestina/Israel.htm

13 Lia, Building *Arafat's Police*; Dean Klovens, "The CIAs Role in the Peace Process," *Middle East Intelligence Bulletin*, 3, 1 (January 2001).

14 Klovens, "The CIAs Role in the Peace Process."

15 Fisk, *The Great War for Civilisation,* 436.

16 Jill Abramson, "Democrats, Outsiders on the Campaign Trail, Turn to Beltway Insiders for Fundraising Help," *The Wall Street Journal*, November 26, 1999, A16. Clinton mentions speaking before AIPIAC in 1984 in Remarks by President Clinton to AIPAC Policy Conference, Sheraton, Washington, D.C., May 7, 1995, Clinton Presidential Record, Press Office, box 15, William J. Clinton Presidential Library, Little Rock, Arkansas.

17 Alexander Cockburn and Ken Silverstein, *Washington Babylon* (London: Verso, 1996), 132.

18 Avinoam Bar Yosef, "The Jews Who Run Clinton's Court," *Maariv*, February 9, 1994. On Gore, Peretz and Israel, see Alexander Cockburn and Jeffrey St. Clair, *Al Gore: A User's Manual* (London: Verso, 2000); Cockburn and Silverstein, *Washington Babylon,* 6; https://www.jewishvirtuallibrary.org/rahm-emanuel. Berger's ties to Caterpillar are detailed in Sam Smith, *Shadows of Hope: A Freethinker's Guide to Politics in the Time of Clinton* (Bloomington: Indiana University Press, 1994), 123. Clinton gave the cold shoulder to his former boss, J. William Fulbright, after Fulbright took on the Israeli lobby, stating on national TV that Israel controlled the U.S. Senate and that "we should be more concerned about American than Israeli interests."

19 Bill Clinton, *My Life* (New York: Alfred A. Knopf, 2004), 294.

20 Robert E. Levin, *Bill Clinton: The Inside Story*, with introduction by David Pryor (New York: S.P.I. Books, 1992), 147; also Clinton, *My Life*, 353.

21 https://www.jewishvirtuallibrary.org/total-u-s-foreign-aid-to-israel-1949-present

22 Fisk, *The Great War for Civilization*, 762; https://en.wikipedia.org/wiki/Israel%E2%80%93United_States_military_relations#:~:text=Under%20the%20Bill%20Clinton%20administration,Joint%20Direct%20Attack%20Munition%20system.

23 https://fas.org/asmp/profiles/israel.htm.

24 Steven Lee Myers, "U.S. Seeks to Curb Israeli Arms Sales to China," *The New York Times*, November 11, 1999.

25 Michael K. Frisby, "Clinton is Seeking Money for Israel To Fight Terrorists," *The Wall Street Journal*, March 15, 1996, A7.

26 Remarks by President Clinton to AIPAC Policy Conference, Sheraton, Washington, D.C., May 7, 1995, Clinton Presidential Record, Press Office, box 15, William J. Clinton Presidential Library, Little Rock, Arkansas. Clinton also emphasized in the speech the Pentagon's purchase of $3 billion in high quality products from israeli companies.

27 Jeremy Kuzmarov, "While Guilty for Sex Trafficking, Ghislaine Maxwell Takes Fall for Alleged Sexual Blackmail Operation Run by Western Intelligence Agencies," *CovertAction Magazine*, July 14, 2022, https://covertactionmagazine.com/2022/07/14/while-guilty-for-sex-trafficking-ghislaine-maxwell-takes-fall-for-alleged-sexual-blackmail-operation-run-by-western-intelligence-agencies/

28 Chomsky, *World Orders Old and New*, 236, 237; Fisk, *The Great War for Civilisation*, 438.

29 Chomsky, *World Orders Old and New*, 219; Stephen Zunes, "U.S. Policy Towards Jerusalem: Clinton's Shift to the Right," *International Policy Studies*, July 1, 2000.

30 Chomsky, *World Orders Old and New*, 220, 236.

31 "Israel-Jordan Relations: Overview of Peace Negotiations," *Jewish Virtual Library*, https://www.jewishvirtuallibrary.org/overview-of-israel-jordan-peace-negotiations

32 "Crossfire," *Newsweek*, April 28, 1996.

33 Noam Chomsky, *Fateful Triangle: The United States, Israel and the Palestinians*, updated edition (Boston: South End Press, 1999), 529.

34 See Julian Abi Ramia, "Life and Death of the South Lebanon Army (SLA)," *L'Orient le Jour*, September 19, 2019, https://www.lorientlejour.com/article/1187230/life-and-death-of-the-south-lebanon-army-sla.html

35 "No Additional U.S. Air to Ground Missiles to Israel," *Human Rights Watch*, May 23, 2000, https://www.hrw.org/news/2000/05/22/no-additional-us-air-ground-missiles-israel

36 https://fas.org/asmp/profiles/israel.htm

37 "Bill Clinton Admits He Tried to Help Peres Beat Netanyahu in 1996 Elections," *The Times of Israel*, June 10, 2020, https://www.timesofisrael.com/bill-clinton-admits-he-tried-to-help-peres-beat-netanyahu-in-1996-elections/

38 "Clintonism in Israel," *The Wall Street Journal*, February 2, 2000, A26.

39 Nathan Jones, "Clinton, Peres, Open AIPAC 1996 Convention," *Washington Report on Middle East Affairs*, May-June 1996, 41–44, https://www.wrmea.org/1996-may-june/jews-and-israel-clinton-peres-open-aipac-1996-convention.html

40 Whitney Webb, "From 'Spook Air' to the 'Lolita Express': The Genesis and Evolution of the Jeffrey Epstein-Bill Clinton Relationship," *Mint Press*, August 23, 2019, https://www.mintpressnews.com/genesis-jeffrey-epstein-bill-clinton-relationship/261455/. Rich had also donated over $1 million to Democratic Party candidates in the 1990s.

41 William B. Qaundt, "Clinton and the Arab-Israeli Conflict: The Limits of Incrementalism," *Journal of Palestine Studies*, 30, 2 (Winter 2001, 26–40.

42 Noam Chomsky, *Failed States: The Abuse of Power and Assault on Democracy* (New York: Metropolitan Books, 2007), 180, 181; Noam Chomsky, *Hegemony or Survival: America's Quest for Global Dominance* (New York: Metropolitan Books, 2003), 170; Ron Pundak and Shaul Arieli, "From Oslo to Taba: What Went Wrong?" *Survival*, Autumn, 2001.

43 See Jeremy Pressman, "What Happened at Camp David and Taba?" *International Security*, 28, 2 (Fall 2003), 5–43; Jerome Slater, "The Irresponsibility of Thomas Friedman," *Tikkun*, January 25, 2009.

44 Clinton, *My Life*, 936, 937.

45 The "Moratinos Report" on the Israeli-Palestinian Talks at Taba January 27, 2001, United States Institute of Peace, https://ccf.org.il/media_items/966; Pressman, "What Happened at Camp David and Taba?"

CHAPTER 11

Clinton and Africa: Black African Lives Didn't Really Matter

In March 1998, Bill Clinton was greeted like a rock star on a trip to Africa—the most comprehensive by any American president. On his trip, Clinton visited Robben Island with Nelson Mandela, where Mandela had been jailed and gave an eloquent speech at the Door of No Return in Gorée Island, Senegal, the point where Africans were taken to slavery in North America.[1] Political scientist Brian J. Hesse wrote in the *Journal of Contemporary African Studies* that Clinton's visit to Senegal "looked as much like a superstar event as a presidential visit. At one point in Senegal's capital, Dakar, Clinton waded into a cheering crowd surging forward to see and greet him."[2]

From the outset of his presidency, Clinton had set out to establish a more progressive policy towards Africa than his predecessors, emphasizing the promotion of democracy, human rights, and trade. In 2001, the administration provided a record $935 million in aid to the continent while earlier instituting a $120 million initiative to increase the quality of, and technology for, education.[3] Clinton's first national security advisor, Anthony Lake, was well-known as an Africanist and intentionally chose Africa as the subject of his first speech.[4] In Clinton's second term, the civil rights icon Jesse Jackson was named as a special envoy for democracy promotion and the State Department cooperated with NGOs to assist in the technical preparation for elections and election monitoring.[5]

But Clinton was ultimately no real friend of Africa. According to Human Rights Watch, his administration adopted a "selective approach to human rights" and turned a "blind eye in African countries considered to be strategically or economically important."[6] The Pentagon at the same time began planning a network of military installations across the continent from Somalia to Senegal, which began to be built after 9/11.[7]

On his March 1998 trip, Clinton heralded Paul Kagame of Rwanda, Meles Zenawi of Ethiopia, and Yoweri Museveni of Uganda as "part of a new generation" of African leaders committed to democracy, though all three leaders stayed in power for many years owing to rigged elections, muzzled dissent and terrorized political opponents.[8] Kagame even established an open air crematorium to dispose of the bodies from massacres committed during the Rwandan civil war and genocide and is considered by some to be an "African Hitler."[9] In 1998, Museveni and Kagame, the two "great democrats" invaded and plundered the Democratic Republic of Congo with U.S. backing, causing what Glenn Ford characterized as "the worst genocide since World War II."[10]

Absolving whites for coloniizing and enslaving Africans while appointing Britons to run many of his ministries, Museveni was a "darling of U.S. diplomats" as a result of his promotion of "fiscal discipline and free-market economics," according to *The New York Times*.[11] The Clinton administration was trying to remold America's role in Africa "to replace costly and paternalistic aid programs with more trade and investment."[12] While in theory this might sound good, in practice these efforts paved the way for a new kind of neocolonialism by reinforcing foreign ownership and control over African resources and nascent industry.

The Clinton administration did special harm in pushing structural adjustment programs through the World Bank and International Monetary Fund (IMF), which cut back on social services, lowered trade barriers and tax revenues, enabled greater capital flight and stifled efforts to empower labor unions and adopt land reform initiatives that held the potential for creating greater social equality.

"Not Inflicting Enough Pain on These Fuckers"

Clinton's failings towards Africa were apparent in his handling of the famous Black Hawk Down incident in Somalia. On October 3, 1993, following a raid by American Special Forces in what they termed "Indian country," Mogadishu militia fighters loyal to Mohammed Farah Aideed—whom the U.S. initially supported but then turned against when he spurned U.S. oil interests—shot down two Black Hawk helicopters using rocket propelled grenades. Mobs then hacked the fallen pilots to death with machetes and dragged their mutilated bodies through the streets as trophies. The images of the dead were pasted across the front cover of Western newspapers, reinforcing stereotypes of Somalis as barbarians.

That the perpetrators' homes had been attacked and family members killed by U.S. forces was never reported, nor that some were ex-Afghan mujahidin trained by CIA intermediaries in shooting down helicopters. In their rescue operations of U.S. Special Forces, American helicopter gunners and Special Forces had fired into crowds, killing and wounding hundreds of Somalis, a third of them women and children, compared to eighteen American dead and 84 wounded in the course of the conflict.[13]

After being briefed about the events, Bill Clinton exploded into one of his rages, shouting to aide George Stephanopoulos: "We're not inflicting enough pain on the fuckers. When people kill us, they should be killed in greater numbers."[14] These comments speak volumes about Clinton's lack of regard for black African lives—particularly when they held a different world view from his own—and his vindictive spirit. Clinton had previously told Anthony Lake that he couldn't believe that "we're being pushed around by those two-bit pricks."[15]

After the killing of U.S. troops, Congress had demanded an immediate withdrawal from Somalia. Clinton disagreed, opting for a six-month transition while dispatching ex-CIA officer Robert Oakley to secure the release of captured pilot Mike Durant. In his memoirs, Clinton wrote that he was "haunted by the Battle of Mogadishu" which he compared to President Kennedy and the Bay of Pigs, where U.S. trained forces were routed by Cuban communists loyal to Fidel Castro.[16] The effect moved his and subsequent administrations to lend support towards a more covert strategy of military intervention.

Sudan—Safeguarding American Interests

The Clinton administration applied harsh sanctions on Sudan and provided military training and financing to the Sudan People's Liberation Army (SPLA), a Christian guerrilla group headed by John Garang in the oil-rich south, which was criticized by Amnesty International for deliberately shooting down civilian airliners, indiscriminately using land mines, recruiting child soldiers, and kidnapping and murdering relief workers.[17] Sudanese General Mohammed Oweida, head of the Security and Defense Committee in Sudan's parliament, stated that the CIA was funding an Israeli intelligence center in Eritrea and that the "U.S. is going to use Africa armies, especially those hostile to Sudan, to achieve its ambition of safeguarding American interests in the region."[18] These interests were largely economic; South Sudan sat atop mounds of oil, ranking third in oil reserves in Sub-Saharan Africa, which were mostly untapped.[19]

Since 1989, Sudan had been led by Omar al-Bashir, a Muslim who had opposed the First Persian Gulf War and allied with China. This made him a target of regime change. On November 10, 1996, *The Washington Post* reported that the U.S. sent $20 million in military equipment to Ethiopia, Eritrea and Uganda when these three countries were all supporting the SPLA and in Uganda's case, directly invaded South Sudan, in support of it.[20] Small contingents of U.S. troops were reported to be fighting with the SPLA as well.[21] In December 1998, Secretary of State Madeleine Albright met with Garang, who rejected the Khartoum peace agreement signed by the Bashir government, which had accepted a referendum for self-determination for the South and offered amnesty to rebel groups.

The August 1998 bombing of the al-Shifa pharmaceutical plant in Khartoum—under the pretext that it manufactured chemical weapons used by al-Qaeda (see chapter 9, Clinton's War on Terror)—coincided with the collapse in peace talks between the SPLA and Khartoum, and after it had become apparent Sudan was backing Laurent Kabila's forces in Congo against the U.S.-backed alliance of Uganda, Rwanda, and Tutsi-led Congolese rebels. The Bashir government had also recently taken steps to access a $300 million barrel reservoir of crude oil in the south.[22] If we consider the larger geopolitical context, the al-Shifa attack was probably not a mistake but an act of intimidation, exemplifying how the War on Terror was used as a pretext for military operations that were designed to further U.S. strategic designs in Africa and advance the U.S. pursuit of its New World Order.

Nigeria: A Base for Enforcing Foreign Interests

Clinton's alleged concern for black African lives was compromised in Nigeria by his administration's support for dictator Sani Abacha (1993–1998), who had seized power in a coup d'état, ousting the democratically elected Moshood Abiola and upholding U.S. interests in Nigeria. Abacha allowed U.S.-based and other multinational corporations access to Nigeria's oil and sustained the special relationship whereby Nigeria served as a base for training Africans to carry out clandestine operations across the continent on behalf of outside interests.[23]

Despite international pressure, Clinton refused to enact an economic embargo on Nigeria in an attempt to undermine Abacha's government, despite the fact that the latter was linked to thousands of fraudulent scams while killing hundreds of political opponents and imprisoning thousands more, including members of the Yoruba tribe, which wanted to secede in the oil-rich South. Supported by Shell Oil Co., which drilled on Ogoni land and made direct payments to the Nigerian security forces, Abacha sanctioned ruthless military operations against the Ogoni people.[24] In November 1995, Abacha ordered the execution by hanging of eight activists with the Movement for the Survival of the Ogoni People (MOSOP) in Southeastern Nigeria, including Ken Saro-Wiwa, who accused the government of destroying their homeland.[25]

On the eve of his execution, Saro-Wiwa wrote that

> whether I live or die is immaterial. It is enough to know that there are people who commit time, money and energy to fight this one

> evil among so many others predominating worldwide. If they do not succeed today, they will succeed tomorrow. We must keep on striving to make the world a better place for all of mankind—each one contributing his bit, in his or her own way.[26]

Though the Clinton administration recalled its ambassador, Walter C. Carrington, after Saro-Wiwa's death, Clinton's true orientation became apparent when he suggested that he would welcome Abacha running for election as a civilian. On a trip to Nigeria in 1994, Clinton had touted the tenfold increase in U.S. assistance to $108 million and the arrival of American troops to train and equip five Nigerian battalions, ostensibly for peacekeeping duties in Sierra Leone.[27]

This support was contingent on the fact that U.S. exports to Nigeria in 1997 totaled $814 million—second only to those to South Africa. Nigeria surpassed all African countries as a source of U.S. imports, and further exported oil and gas and other commodities worth $3 billion to the U.S., making it the 5th largest foreign supplier of oil to the U.S., with Mobil and Chevron being the main U.S. buyers.[28] Clinton had brought along 100 corporate executives on his 1994 trip to Nigeria, including an agro-industrial group from Baton Rouge, Louisiana, F.C. Schaffer & Associates Inc. which thereafter began to build a $200 million sugar cane growing and refining operation in Nigeria.[29]

When civil rights icon Jesse Jackson visited Nigeria in July 1994 as Clinton's special envoy, he was booed and pelted with rotten tomatoes at Lagos airport by locals because of U.S. support for Abacha. Jackson's mission was to convince Abacha to release Moshood Abiola, a Yoruba elder and presidential contender, from prison.[30] Abacha had gained the support of some black congressmen and leaders through a heavily funded public relations campaign in Washington. Abacha also benefited from financial donations to the Democratic National Committee made through a supposedly non-profit voting registration group by businessman Gilbert Chagoury, a Lebanese national who built up a business empire in Nigeria through his close connection to Abacha.

On December 21, 1995, Chagoury had been invited to a special White House dinner for financial donors to the Democratic Party, even though foreign nationals were prevented from doing this under U.S. law.[31] Chagoury's influence brings attention to the role played by such lobbyists and wealthy special interests in influencing U.S. government policy in the Clinton era rather than any actual administration commitment to democratization or human rights.

Liberia and Sierra Leone: "Humanitarian Intervention"

Liberia was an important showcase for the new doctrine of humanitarian intervention in the 1990s. The Clinton administration supported a peacekeeping force led by Nigerians and Ghanaians, which provided an African veneer for a proxy U.S. force in Liberia's civil war that paved the way for the reinvigoration of American influence in Liberia afterwards.

In the 1980s, the Reagan administration had provided over $500 million in aid and sent Green Berets on training missions to assist the regime of Samuel K. Doe, an ethnic Krahn with only a fourth-grade education who seized power in a bloody coup during which his forces murdered left-leaning president, William Tolbert (1971–1980) and most of his Cabinet. Afterwards, Doe pleased the U.S. by privatizing state owned enterprises and cutting relations with Libya and the Soviet Union.[32]

The primary U.S. interest in Liberia was to protect those of Firestone Rubber, which had set up vast rubber plantations in Liberia beginning in 1926, when it had leased a million acres for 99 years at 6 cents an acre.[33] The U.S. furthermore wanted to sustain access to three "national security" facilities near Monrovia for which it was paying a ridiculously low rent. These included a large diplomatic-intelligence community relay station, a Voice of America (VOA) broadcast center, and a Coast Guard navigation station. The U.S. also enjoyed unlimited access to the Roberts field airport, which was used to send military equipment to anti-communist rebels in Angola.[34]

The CIA had used Liberia's communications facilities in covert operations in support of Chad's leader, Hissene Habré. Liberia was also a key operational area to carry out covert operations against Libyan ruler Muammar Qaddafi, who had nationalized Libya's oil and removed U.S. military bases from Libya.[35]

In the late 1980s, the Reagan administration began to sour on Doe and began covertly supporting the opposition led by Charles Taylor.[36] Educated at Bentley College outside of Boston, Taylor was a former chief of government procurement who fled to the U.S. after he was accused of stealing $900,000 from the state treasury. In November 1985, the CIA allegedly assisted Taylor's escape from a Plymouth, Massachusetts prison days before Taylor's friend, Thomas Quiwonkpa, launched a coup against Doe, which was financed and backed by the CIA.[37]

Taylor afterwards returned home to lead an armed insurgency, the National Patriotic Front of Liberia (NPFL) with backing from Libya, Ivory Coast and Burkino Faso. On the surface, the U.S. government appeared to be wary of Taylor because of his support from Muammar Qaddafi,[38] though an investigation by an Italian filmmaker determined that Taylor had been sent by the CIA to infiltrate African liberation movements in Libya as part of the quid pro quo.[39]

In September 1990, Doe was tortured and then killed by rebels associated with a breakaway faction of the NPFL—the Independent National Patriotic Front—led by Prince Yormie Johnson, a defector from Doe's regime. According to Alexander Yearsley, an investigator in West Africa with the NGO Global Witness, Taylor was "advised [by the U.S.] on how to carry out the conflict [in Liberia]," though eventually the U.S. government distanced itself from him when he helped ruin the country and U.S. strategic facilities were closed down.[40]

Officially, the Clinton administration briefly supported Prince Johnson, and then, realizing that he was not strong enough to take over the country, supported a Western African-nation-led peacekeeping force known as ECOMOG (Economic Community of West African States Monitoring Group), whose aim was to solidify an interim government under Amos Sawyer, a Pan-Africanist intellectual accused of being a CIA "asset" and plotting a coup against Doe in the 1980s.

ECOMOG allied with the Armed Forces of Liberia (AFL) and United Liberation Movement for Democracy in Liberia (ULIMO), which consisted mostly of Doe loyalists from his ethnic Khran and Mandingo ethnic groups. Taylor's forces (NPFL) by contrast included ethnic Gio and Americo-Liberians. Horrific atrocities were committed on all sides of the conflict, including by ECOMOG, which bombed and strafed villages. It was accused of providing a cover for Doe supporters and installing a Nigerian occupation of Liberia, as Taylor alleged.[41]

The Clinton administration provided ECOMOG with over $85 million between 1993 and 1998, with $35.6 million provided in 1996.[42] Further covert support was provided with the deployment of mobile training teams to regional countries that staffed ECOMOG such as Nigeria and Senegal along with provision of military equipment from Pentagon stocks and $230 million in humanitarian assistance.[43] Prince Johnson stated that it was "written all over that ECOMOG was made in America."[44]

In April 1996, Clinton launched Operation Assured Responses, in which he activated U.S. military helicopters from Freetown, initiated aircraft from Senegal, and deployed a U.S. amphibious force off the coast of Monrovia along with 2,000 Marines. The official purpose was to evacuate U.S. citizens, though only 49 were actually evacuated. The NPFL considered the operation as a support mission for ULIMO, which was enhanced by the private military contractor, Pacific Architects & Engineers (PAE), who delivered arms to ULIMO.[45] Around this time, a high-level U.S. diplomatic delegation headed by Deputy Assistant Secretary of State William Twadell promised

$30 million in U.S. assistance to the contending factions as an incentive to end the war. Elections followed in July 1997 that were won by Taylor and his National Patriotic Party (NPP) with 75 percent of the vote.[46]

The Clinton administration at this time recognized Taylor—even though Twadell testified before Congress that Taylor had illegally trafficked in so-called blood diamonds.[47] In a futile attempt to ensure good relations with Washington and secure access to Clinton and other policymakers, Taylor spent about $630,000 between September 1997 to April 1999 on the firm of a powerful Washington, D.C. lawyer, Lester Hyman.[48]

Clinton's key point man on Africa, Jesse Jackson, had been friendly to Taylor, believing that he was the key to resolving the conflict in Liberia. In March 1998, Clinton rewarded Taylor with a thirty-minute call from Air Force One, which he made at Jackson's request. Jackson subsequently hosted a $400,000 reconciliation conference at the PUSH headquarters in Chicago which was considered by the exile-Liberian community as a "slick scheme to promote Taylor and his repressive government."

Jackson also supported Foday Sankoh, Libyan trained commander of the Sierra Leone's Revolutionary United Forces (RUF) and an ally of Taylor, whom Jackson persuaded the State Department to supply with communications equipment. The equipment helped him to coordinate RUF operations directed against the government led by Ahmed Tejaz Kabbah along with UN peacekeeping forces.[49]

A former U.S. intelligence officer told researcher Kenneth Timmerman that the U.S. sent "clearly more than just two-way radios." Jackson had compared Sankoh to Nelson Mandela and went on to play an important role in brokering the July 1999 Lomé accords, which led to Sankoh's release from jail and appointment as a vice-president and chairman of the commission for the management of strategic mineral resources, a prize that he and Taylor had long been seeking.[50]

Mary McGrory described the Lomé Accords in *The Washington Post* as "insane" because it included blanket amnesty to warlords and the handing over of the country's greatest treasure, its diamonds, to those same warlords."[51] However, better these "warlords" who were native to their country and would use the profits to fund local development, than foreign interests or proxies. When the RUF took 500 UN peacekeepers meant to supervise the implementation of the accords hostage, the Clinton administration tried to distance itself from the accords, though U.S. officials had drafted entire sections of it.[52] The Clinton administration in turn began training and equipping military units from Nigeria, Ghana and Senegal with the assistance of private military contractors to help restore "stability" in the country as the scramble for West Africa's diamond wealth continued.[53]

The Clinton administration's intervention under the guise of peacekeeping operations ultimately paid dividends when the Bush administration intensified efforts to undermine Taylor, who angered the U.S. government by refusing an exploitative agreement with Halliburton for oil exploration, stating that "Liberia is not for sale." The U.S. secured de facto control over Liberia under Taylor's successor, Ellen Johnson Sirleaf, a former World Bank employee, who offered Liberian territory for the headquarters of the U.S. Africa Command (AFRICOM). The CIA re-established a major presence operating within the confines of the American embassy further under Sirleaf's corrupt rule, the Pentagon rebuilt Liberia's armed forces and Sirleaf awarded exploration rights for offshore oil deposits to Exxon-Mobil and Chevron and signed a generous agreement with Firestone, enabling it to expand its operations in Liberia.[54]

Recolonization: AGOA and the Advancement of Corporate Power

On May 17, 2000, President Clinton signed the Africa Growth and Opportunity Act (AGOA) after unveiling a $150 million "modern Africa investment fund" in which the U.S. government insured U.S. private sector investment.[55] Clinton declared that the legislation—originally sponsored in Congress by Jim McDermott (D-WA)—would inaugurate "a dynamic new Africa ... making dramatic strides toward democracy and prosperity." Vernon Jordan, the president's advisor and frequent envoy to Africa, said that as a result of Clinton's plan, the world would witness the birth of "African economic lions"—comparable to "Asian tigers."[56]

The tigers were to be created by lowering tariffs for African goods and eliminating import quotas for African textiles—with the exception of Asian yarn woven into African sweaters.[57] Clothing made in Africa from African fabric was allowed to rise from 1.5 percent of U.S. Imports to 3.5 percent over eight years, boosting African exports of these products from about $250 million a year to as much as $4.2 billion.[58]

With America exporting around $18 billion worth of goods per year to Africa by the mid-1990s, the Clinton administration said that it would no longer concede the African market to the old colonial powers.[59] AGOA added 1835 more products from 34 eligible African countries to be exempted from duty under U.S. Generalized System of Preferences (GSP).[60] AGOA further provided loans for small and medium sized African businesses and funds for infrastructural projects—for nations that privatized industries, liberalized trade and investment rules, and met certain human rights and labor standards.[61]

The Wall Street Journal characterized Senator Russel Feingold as a "trade Cro-Magnon" for suggesting that AGOA would simply be an "act of political theater" if "the U.S. did not forgive African debts."[62] Clinton indeed asked Congress to write off $35 million in debt to those countries which made economic reforms, though the *Journal* conceded that this amount was a pittance compared to Africa's total debt burden of $130 billion, of which at least $5 billion was owed to the U.S. government.[63]

Randall Robinson of Trans Africa characterized AGOA as an "African Recolonization Act" because it was designed to encourage American and European businesses to "grab the assets of Africa."[64] Jesse Jackson wrote that the bill was designed to force African economies into a straitjacket of economic austerity and deepening poverty in order to benefit transnational and financial institutions, wealthy investors and large corporations." There were no provisions to protect workers' rights or the environment; AGOA in fact provided a disincentive to adopt policies favoring substantial public investment in education, health care and infrastructure."[65]

Zambia: Selling the Family Silver

In a 1994 speech to the U.S.-Zambia Business Council, National Security Council adviser Anthony Lake stated that Zambia provided a

> fine example of the trend away from post-independence patterns of state ownership and centralization towards privatization, free markets and local control, President [Frederic] Chiluba's government deserves credit for its efforts to liberalize trade, remove subsidies, lift controls on foreign exchange, reduce budget deficits and bring down inflation from 187% to an estimated 30% this year. His continued attempts to privatize state-owned industries and return land ownership to individuals are also noteworthy, as Zambia [and Zimbabwe] show signs that "structural adjustment" does yield economic growth.[66]

In Zambia today, however, Chiluba is regarded as a crook who was found in court to have laundered around $50 million from his impoverished people for his personal benefit, while structural adjustment is viewed as an unmitigated disaster.[67] According to South African analyst Khadija Sharif, the latter resulted in "systematic exploitation by multi-national corporations, national assets sold for a 'song' and persistent tax dodging."[68]

Under the terms of the deal that was struck, the foreign multinationals had to pay only a paltry 0.6% royalty tax, below the still low continental average of 3%. British Prime Minister Harold Macmillan once likened the privatization process to "selling the family silver"—which accurately reflects the Zambian experience. USAID paid the salary of five Wall Street bankers who staffed Zambia's privatization agency. Among the beneficiaries was the Arizona-based company Phelps Dodge, which gained majority control of Metal Fabricators of Zambia, which produces wire, cable, and copper rods.[69]

Like in Russia, tens of thousands of Zambians lost their jobs under Chiluba's liberalization policies as labor and environmental standards worsened. Public services were slashed in the midst of the unfolding HIV-AIDS pandemic and Zambia became a dumping ground for cheap imports. Leo Mulenga, a Copperbelt resident, said in 2015: "We used to grow cabbages, potatoes, tomatoes and bananas but now, there's no future here—only poverty and suffering for everyone because this land is damaged and spoiled."[70] When the copper mines (Zambia's main industry) were under national control, miners enjoyed subsidized health care, housing, and education but the Copper Belt's schools and hospitals were sold along with the mines.[71]

The CIA had first given Chiluba its seal of approval back in 1981 as a replacement for socialist Kenneth Kaunda (Zambian president from 1964–1991) whom the CIA had plotted a coup against. Appointees of Chiluba's government awarded bids to companies they were allowed to acquire stakes in.[72] The most profitable copper mines were taken over by Glencore Corporation, a Swiss based company founded by commodities trader Marc Rich, whose lavish donations to the Democratic Party would earn him a pardon by Clinton for crimes for which he had received a 325-year prison sentence.[73] Another winner of the privatization process was Barrick Gold, a Canadian mining company that appointed Clinton's top adviser, Vernon Jordan, to its board. Yet another was First Quantum Minerals of Vancouver Canada, whose major shareholders included J.P. Morgan Chase & Co., L.A. based Capital Group, and Blackrock Inc, one of the world's largest asset management firms which also owned shares in Glencore and was a top shareholder of another big-time Clinton supporter, Walmart.[74]

More Crude Interventions

The subsidization of U.S. business by the Clinton administration through "foreign aid" programs was exemplified by a $64 million loan provided by the Export-Import Bank in 1999 to the Angolan state oil company Sonangol for the purchase of equipment and services from more than twenty U.S. energy companies, including Dick Cheney's Haliburton. An earlier loan was designed to help develop oil wells in Cabinda in partnership with foreign oil companies. The loans were no risk, even though it was known that the

Angolan government was corrupt, meaning that the U.S. taxpayers ultimately had to foot the bill.[75]

In 1996, the State Department reported that 21 percent of U.S. crude oil imports came from Africa, a total that was anticipated to increase considerably over the coming decade.[76] The close ties between the Clinton administration and energy industry was exemplified by the administration's threats to withhold development funds from Mozambique—the majority of whose budget was financed by foreign aid, including at least $40 million from USAID—if its government didn't sign a deal with Enron to develop the Pande natural gas fields in the south and to build a 900 kilometer pipeline to carry the gas to an iron steel plant in South Africa.

John Kachamila, Mozambique's minister of Natural Resources, told the *Houston Chronicle* that U.S. diplomats, notably Mike McKinley, deputy chief of the U.S. embassy, pressured him to sign a deal that was not good for Mozambique." Kachamila went on to suggest that McKinley was "not a neutral diplomat. It was as if he was working for Enron. We got calls from American senators threatening us with this and that if we didn't sign. Anthony Lake even called to tell us to sign."[77]

In 1995, when the deal was in trouble, Lake directly wrote to President Joaquim Chissano that the U.S. would not release $13.5 million in aid funds unless Mozambique accepted the Enron bid. According to Vijay Prashad, Lake's efforts "reveal the real meaning of 'free trade:' government bullying to force weaker countries to favor global corporations."[78] In 2000, the U.S. Overseas Investment Company (OPIC) provided $373 million in loan guarantees for the construction of a methanol plant in Equatorial Guinea partly owned by two U.S. companies—Noble Affiliates and Marathon Oil, which later contributed to Hillary Clinton's 2016 presidential campaign.[79]

This methanol plant deal was part of the warming of relations with the regime of Teodoro Obiang Ngeuma, a caricature of African dictators, who accepted million-dollar bribes by U.S. oil companies after off-shore oil deposits were discovered in the mid-1990s, and Equatorial Guinea emerged as an oil producer.

A State Department human rights report said that Obiang's security forces "committed numerous abuses, including torture, beating and other physical abuse of prisoners suspects, which at times resulted in deaths." Another State Department report pointed to Obiang's repeated rigging of elections.[80] Human rights considerations and support for democracy were subordinated to the quest for money and access to oil in this case and many others.

A soft spot for the political right was apparent in the Clinton administration's refusal to enforce UN sanctions against the diamond trading which enriched Jonas Savimbi, a CIA backed warlord who had destabilized Angola since the 1970s and still controlled parts of the country. Clinton's State Department promoted an equal role for Savimbi in an ongoing reconciliation process, failing to label him what he was—a terrorist.[81]

African Crisis Response Initiative: An Instrument of Neocolonialism

Neoliberal and neo-colonial economic policies were accompanied, as elsewhere, by expanded military assistance programs which paved the way for AFRICOM in the early 21st Century. U.S. military support went to 49 out of Africa's 53 countries in the 1990s, and Washington shipped about $400 million in military hardware to the continent between 1991 and 1995.[82] An African Center for Strategic Studies was launched by the Pentagon in 1999 to impart Pentagon doctrines to African military officers and help develop their loyalties to the U.S.[83]

In 1996, President Clinton launched the African Crisis Response Initiative (ACRI), a $15 to $20 million per year training program that was accompanied by the provision of military equipment, including communications gear. Thousands of African troops were trained officially as peacekeepers under ACRI, though the instruction was also "appropriate for quelling internal insurgencies."[84]

The Pentagon framed the ACRI as a mechanism of "conflict resolution" whose purpose was to enable "Africans to take the lead in resolving conflicts and in peacekeeping efforts in the region."[85] Many Africans, however, viewed it as a patronizing attempt by outsiders to define Africa's problems and dictate solutions.[86] It fit the model for neocolonial intervention outlined by Ghanaian President Kwame Nkrumah in which the foreign powers "supply the money, aircraft, military equipment of all kinds, and the strategic and tactical command from a General Staff down to officer 'advisers,' while the troops of the puppet government bear the brunt of the fighting."[87]

Nigerian scholar Adekeye Adebajo wrote that under ACRI, "Africans would do most of the dying, while the U.S. would do some of the spending to avoid being drawn into politically risky interventions."[88] Presidents Julius Nyerere of Tanzania and Nelson Mandela of South Africa rejected the notion of such a force on the basis that Africans had not been consulted about the proposal. President Muammar Gaddafi of Libya saw the writing on the wall, presciently anticipating what would eventually become AFRICOM. At a 1999 summit of the Organization of African Unity (OAU—the predecessor of the African Union), Gaddafi instead proposed the creation of a continental army that would explicitly serve the purpose of protecting Africa from the meddling of external neocolonial powers, though alas it was not to be, and Gaddafi would be overthrown in 2011 at the behest of Hillary Clinton, who was gleeful after Qaddafi had been lynched.[89]

Political scientist Paul Omach explained in *African Affairs* that governments participating in ACRI "[did] so with the primary motive of enhancing the capacities of their military forces for anti-insurgency operations" as well as for military intervention in regional conflicts that were often for control over natural resources.[90] Uganda's army was one of the early recipients of ACRI training in 1997. The country was not democratic; 1996 elections were rigged in favor of Yoweri Museveni (1986–present), who was valued by the Clinton administration for privatizing state companies and liberalizing trade restrictions, and for his commitment to creating an environment that would assist in "bringing confidence to American corporations," as Ugandan Ambassador to the U.S., Edith Sempala, put it.[91]

In 1999, Human Rights Watch criticized the Ugandan military for its "serious abuses against civilians in areas of conflict, for which individual soldiers were rarely held to account."[92] Horrendous atrocities were carried out in the Democratic Republic of Congo, and in Northern Uganda targeting the Acholi people, who had supported Museveni's predecessor, socialist Milton Obote. Even the U.S. State Department expressed alarm at the "repeated incidents of human rights abuses by Ugandan security forces operating in Northern Uganda," which it found to be both "objectionable and counter-productive to the goal of internal reconciliation."[93] The Ugandan forces burned huts and villages, carried out routine torture and even deliberately spread HIV-AIDS, "behaving worse towards the Acholi than Idi Amin [the notoriously brutal leader in 1970s]," according to one Bishop.[94]

In 1998, the Clinton administration initiated a partnership with Ethiopian forces under ACRI. Like the Ugandans, the Ethiopians were no choirboys—in the 1998–2000 Eritrean-Ethiopian War, they were responsible for large-scale destruction and looting of civilian property, harassment of civilians," and "a high incidence of rape." The Clinton administration halted its ACRI training to save face but continued sending money to the Ethiopian army via the International Military Education and Training (IMET) program.[95]

Protecting Big Pharma: Clinton and HIV-AIDS

At a rally on June 28, 1999, in Philadelphia, some 3000 members of the coalition AIDS Drugs for Africa tried to disrupt an Al Gore rally by chanting "Al Gore Kills For Greed." The protestors demanded that Gore stop blocking access to affordable drugs to combat the spread of HIV-AIDS in South Africa.[96] South Africa was deeply impacted by the HIV-AIDS scourge in the

1990s. With an average income of $2,600 per year, few South Africans could afford anti-retroviral drug treatment, which cost up to $10,000 annually.

In 1997, Nelson Mandela's African-National Congress (ANC)-led government introduced a measure that would allow for the importation or local production of generic drugs, which involved paying a fixed fee to patent holders, leading to the reduction of the local cost of the drug by up to 90%. However, an alliance of the largest American drug companies claimed that their intellectual property rights had been violated. Labeling South Africa's action piracy, they challenged the law in South African courts and using the Podesta Group lobbying agency, began campaigning against it in Washington.[97]

John Podesta was then Bill Clinton's chief of staff. Clinton by consequence worked to pressure South Africa to honor the patent rights of American companies, insisting wrongly that South Africa had violated WTO rules on patents. As a penalty, the U.S. trade representative rescinded South Africa's trade benefits, refusing to grant tariff breaks on exports, and the Clinton administration placed South Africa on a major trade watch list.[98] Gore, who was appointed to lead negotiations with Deputy President Thabo Mbeki, stood firmly by the drug companies' position, refusing to grant South Africa concessions.

The New York Times editorialized that the Clinton administration's policy had been dominated by the "desire to protect American pharmaceutical patents," and sensibly insisted that "Washington should stop pressuring South Africa to change the law." Ralph Nader, who challenged Al Gore's presidential candidacy on a third-party ticket in 2000, was even more pointed, writing with James Lowe a letter to the Vice President in April 1999 accusing the Clinton administration of

> deploying an astonishing assault on South African sovereignty and critical health public responsibilities and literally asking South Africa to abandon the lives of millions of infected citizens. Why should President Mandela, Deputy President Mbeki and Health Minister Nkosazana Auma permit their populations to be defenseless simply because Glaxo Welcome and Bristol Myers Squibh (pharmaceutical companies) want the power to set prices for U.S. taxpayer-funded and government developed HIV-AIDS drugs in Africa?[99]

Eventually, well into the final year of his presidency, Clinton relented and began promising South Africa new anti-AIDS initiatives, and later helped raise tens of millions of dollars to fight HIV-AIDS in Africa and elsewhere through the Clinton Foundation.[100] However, many lives had been lost in the interim. When Clinton gave a speech at the National Africa summit, he had the audacity to blame cultural factors for causing a spike in HIV-AIDS cases and said that we had to change attitudes, presumably about sex, though Clinton himself was a sex addict and serial philanderer and probably rapist who allegedly bit the lips of his victims.[101]

The Last Stage of Imperialism

Ghanian President Kwame Nkrumah's 1965 book, *Neo-Colonialism: The Last Stage of Imperialism*, provided a sophisticated framework for understanding how Western capitalist interests were intent on penetrating and exploiting the African continent even after the European countries had relinquished their formal colonies.[102] Had he still been alive in the 1990s, Nkrumah would have recognized the Clinton administration's policies as a perfect embodiment of what he had warned against. Clinton carried out classic neocolonial policies by aggressively trying to open up Africa to foreign economic exploitation while ramping up U.S. military intervention under the cover of peacekeeping operations that utilized primarily African proxy forces. Clinton's policies ultimately helped pave the way for Bush, Obama, Trump and Biden administration policies that resulted in a major expansion of the U.S. military footprint in Africa. Under Clinton, the promised new era of enlightenment and African renaissance never came to pass, as wars backed by the West festered, new dictators rose, and African economies remained underdeveloped and vulnerable to exploitation. The continent at this time lacked visionary leaders like Nkrumah who could uphold the Pan-African tradition and could not mount effective enough resistance. One leader who stood his ground, Zimbabwe's Robert Mugabe, was taken care of through a draconian sanctions bill promoted by Senator Hillary Clinton carrying on her husband's legacy. The Zimbabwean Democracy and Economic Recovery Act (ZDERA) of 2001 destroyed the economic progress Zimbabwe had made since it obtained independence in 1980 and precipitated a major economic crisis designed to send a message to countries that wanted to go the socialist route.[103]

Endnotes

1 Roger Simon, "Clinton Ends Visit by Touring Slave Port," *Chicago Tribune*, April 3, 1998, https://www.chicagotribune.com/news/ct-xpm-1998-04-03-9804030153-story.html; Bill Clinton, *My Life* (New York: Alfred A. Knopf, 2004), 783. In his speech there, Clinton stated that "those who survived the murderous 'middle passage' emerged from a dark hold to find themselves, yes, American. But it would be a long time before the descendants enjoyed the full meaning of that word."

2 Brian J. Hesse, "Celebrate or Hold Suspect? Bill Clinton and George W. Bush in Africa," *Journal of Contemporary African Studies*, 23, 3 (September 2005), 327–344. In Accra, half a million people turned out to hear Clinton speak.

3 "History of Department of State, Africa, XV Africa Regional and Bilateral Issues, William J. Clinton Presidential Library, Digital Records, https://clinton.presidentiallibraries.us/files/original/ce5f02f4774954a8c2ec50ec14e5bddb.pdf

4 "USA: Clinton Administration Policy and Human Rights in Africa," Human Rights Watch, March 1, 1998, https://www.refworld.org/docid/3ae6a8504.html

5 John F. Clark, "The Clinton Administration and Africa: White House Involvement and the Foreign Affairs bureaucracies," *Issue: A Journal of Opinion*, 26, 2, 1998, 8–13.

6 Frank Smythe, "A New Game: The Clinton Administration on Africa," *World Policy Journal*, June 1, 1998.

7 Helen C. Epstein, *Another Fine Mess: America, Uganda, and the War on Terror* (New York: Columbia Global Reports, 2017).

8 Marian Tupy, "Bill Clinton's 'New Generation' of African Leaders Mostly Still Around in 2016," *Reason Magazine*, February 2, 2016, https://reason.com/2016/02/02/bill-clintons-new-generation-of-african/. On Zenawi's reign of terror, see Melakou Tegegn, "Meles Zenawi's Legacy of Terror," *The Ethiopian Review*, September 28, 2012; and on Museveni and Kagame's, see Epstein, *Another Fine Mess*. According to Tegegn, Meles' army (the Tigrayan People's Liberation Front-TPLF, which was integrated into the Ethiopian army) committed massacres in Gambela, ostensibly to crush a resistance by the Anuak; in the Ogaden on the excuse of crushing the Ogaden National Liberation Front (ONLF); and in the streets of Addis Ababa and other towns under the guise of putting down protests against the stealing of the election results in 2005. In his earlier days in power, Meles' regime was also involved in three little known massacres targeting Amhara communities in Wollega.

9 Judi Rever, *In Praise of Blood: The Crimes of the Rwandan Patriotic Front* (Toronto: Random House Canada, 2018); Yaa Lengi M. Ngemi, *"Joseph Kabila," Identity Thief, Impostor, and Rwandan Trojan Horse in Congo: Hyppolite Kanambe a.k.a. Joseph Kabila: Rwandan Tutsi and Hitler Paul Kagame's Agent in DRC* (Create Space Independent Publishing, 2017).

10 Glen Ford, "16 Years of U.S. Genocide in Congo," *Black Agenda Report*, December 12, 2012, https://blackagendareport.com/content/16-years-us-genocide-congo?page=12

11 James C. McKinley Jr., "Clinton in Africa: The Region; A New Model in Africa; Good Leaders Above All," *The New York Times*, March 25, 1998, https://www.nytimes.com/1998/03/25/world/clinton-in-africa-the-region-a-new-model-for-africa-good-leaders-above-all.html; Bill Berkeley, "An African Success Story? Uganda, of all Places, is enjoying a Period of Peace, but the Price of Stability Has Been High," *The Atlantic*, September 1994, https://www.theatlantic.com/magazine/archive/1994/09/an-african-success-story/670697/

12 McKinley Jr., "Clinton in Africa."

13 Mark Bowden, *Black Hawk Down: A Story of Modern War* (New York: Atlantic Monthly Press, 1999), 10; Scott Peterson, *Me Against My Brother: At War in Somalia, Sudan and Rwanda—A Journalist Reports from the Battlefields of Africa*(New York: Routledge, 2000), 141; Rick Atkinson, "The Raid That Went Wrong: How an Elite U.S. Force Failed in Somalia," *The Washington Post*, January 30, 1994, A1. One Marine, when asked how many Somalis he had killed, told a reporter: "I can't keep fucking count anymore." A UN report estimated that between 625 and 1500 Somalis were killed, half of them women and children.

14 Quoted in Richard Miniter, *Losing Bin Laden: How Bill Clinton's Failure Unleashed Global Terror* (Washington, D.C.: Regnery Publishing, 2003), 67.

15 Nigel Hamilton, *Bill Clinton: Mastering the Presidency* (New York: Public Affairs, 2007), 196.

16 Clinton, *My Life*, 552.

17 Richard Becker, Sara Flounders, and John Parker, "Sudan: Diversionary Bombing," *CovertAction Quarterly*, Winter 1999, 12, 17, 18.

18 "Sudanese General Points to CIA Base," *The Washington Times*, October 9, 1997, A15; Clark, "The Clinton Administration and Africa."

19 Manyang David Mayar, "South Sudan's Oil Industry Remains Dependent on Foreign Help," *Voice of America,* July 6, 2021, https://www.voanews.com/a/africa_south-sudan-focus_south-sudans-oil-industry-remains-dependent-foreign-help/6207908.html

20 Becker, Flounders, and Parker, "Sudan," 17.

21 David Michael Smith, *Endless Holocausts: Mass Death in the History of the United States Empire* (New York: Monthly Review Press, 2023), 228, 229.

22 Wayne Madsen, *Genocide and Covert Operation in Africa 1993–1999* (New York: Edwin Mellen, 1999); Becker, Flounders and Parker, "Sudan: Diversionary Bombing," 16.

23 Nigeria's special role as a base for subversion operations across Africa is discussed in Sadie L. DeShield and Leonard T. DeShield, *Beneath the Cold War: The Death of a Nation* (Chapel Hill, NC: Professional Press, 1999), 59, 60.

24 Garry Leech, *Crude Interventions: The U.S., Oil and the New World (Dis) Order* (London: Zed Books, 2016), 96, 97, 98, 99. The attack on the Ogoni was followed up by attacks on the Ijaw after they demanded that Chevron hire more local workers and clean up oil pollution in the Niger Delta. Chevron pilots transported the Nigerian forces to the Ijaw villages, which they assaulted.

25 Smythe, "A New Game."

26 Leech, *Crude Interventions*, 98.

27 James Bovard, "The Latest Salvo in Clinton's Textile Trade War," *The Wall Street Journal*, July 5, 1994, A12. "Virginia-based Military Professional Resources, Inc. (MPRI) provided training to the Nigerian army in tactics designed to combat secessionists." *Wayne Madsen Report,* April 8, 2014, http://www.intrepidreport.com/archives/12659

28 Smythe, "A New Game," Cassandra Rachel Veney, "U.S.-Africa Relations With the Big Three: Ethiopia, Nigeria, and South Africa," in *U.S.-Africa Relations: From Clinton to Obama*, ed. Cassandra Rachel Veney (New York: Lexington Books, 2014), 104.

29 James Bovard, "The Latest Salvo in Clinton's Textile Trade War," *The Wall Street Journal*, July 5, 1994, A12.

30 Kenneth R. Timmerman, *Shakedown: Exposing the Real Jesse Jackson* (Washington, D.C. Regnery Publishing, 2004).

31 Timmerman, *Shakedown.* Chagoury was known as "Abacha's bagman."

32 DeShield and DeShield, *Beneath the Cold War*; Niels Hahn, "U.S. Covert and Overt Operations in Liberia, 1970s to 2003," *ASPJ Africa & Francophonie*—3rd Quarter 2014 , https://www.airuniversity.af.edu/Portals/10/ASPJ_French/journals_E/Volume-05_Issue-3/Hahn_e.pdf. The CIA had tried to undermine Tolbert by supporting the Progressive Alliance for Liberians (PAL) headed by Backus Matthews and then by backing the coup that brought Doe to power in 1980. In 1985, the U.S. failed to object to stolen elections as Doe was a valued ally at the time.

33 Blaine Harden, "Who Killed Liberia? We Did," *The Washington Post*, May 26, 1996; Arthur L. Hayman and Harold Preece, *Lighting Up Liberia* (Creative Age Press, 1943).

34 Herman J. Cohen, *Intervening in Africa: Superpower Peacemaking in a Troubled Continent* (New York: St. Martin's Press, 2000), 128. Cohen notes that the U.S. had paid a ridiculously low rent of $10.

35 Lester S. Hyman, *United States Policy Towards Liberia 1822–2003: Unintended Consequences?* (Cherry Hill, New Jersey: Africana Homestead Legacy Publishers, 2003), 41. According to *Washington Post* journalist Bob Woodward, CIA Director William Casey had selected Samuel Doe as one of twelve heads of state from around the world to receive U.S. support from a special security assistance program. Through this program, the CIA wound up training his personal security forces.

36 S. Byron Tarr, "Extra-Africa Interests in the Liberian Conflict," in *Peacekeeping in Africa*, ed. Magyar and Conteh-Morgan, 155; George Klay Kieh Jr. *The First Liberian Civil War* (New York: Peter Lang, 2008).

37 Tracey Gurd, "Taylor Alleges U.S. Government Helped Him Escape From Prison," July 15, 2009, https://www.ijmonitor.org/2009/07/taylor-alleges-us-govt-helped-him-escape-from-us-prison/; "Charles Taylor Worked For CIA in Liberia," *BBC*, January 19, 2012; Marlise Simons, "Ex-Leader of Liberia Cites CIA in Jail Break," *The New York Times*, July 17, 2009; Chris Arsenault, "Accused War Criminal Taylor 'Worked with CIA,'" *Al Jazeera*, January 20, 2012, https://www.aljazeera.com/indepth/features/2012/01/201212019424323526.html. In 2009, during testimony at his war crimes trial, Taylor said a jail guard opened his cell door and allowed him to sneak out a window. He then claimed a "government car" drove him to New York, before he made his way to Mexico and eventually back to Liberia. Lester Hyman in *United States Policy Towards Liberia 1822–2003* questions whether Taylor actually stole the money.

38 Hyman, *United States Policy Towards Liberia 1822–2003*, 42, 44, 45.

39 https://www.thomassankara.net/assassination-of-thomas-sankara-evidence-of-a-documentary-by-rai-3-involve-france-cia-and-blaise-compaore/?lang=en

40 Arsenault, "Accused War Criminal Taylor 'Worked with CIA'"; Niels Hahn, "U.S. Covert and Overt Operations in Liberia, 1970s to 2003," *ASPJ Africa & Francophonie*—3rd Quarter 2014 , https://www.airuniversity.af.edu/Portals/10/ASPJ_French/journals_E/Volume-05_Issue-3/Hahn_e.pdf. The U.S. made alternative arrangements for these facilities to move them to other parts of Africa with the destruction in Liberia caused by the civil war. See also Cohen, *Intervening in Africa*, chapter 5. Cohen is largely favorable towards Taylor and says the U.S. should have supported him more extensively at the outset. However, by the late 1990s, the Clinton administration was supporting an armed insurgency against him led by rival Prince

Johnson, who had been behind the death of Samuel K. Doe. In 2003, Taylor was forced into exile in Nigeria and subsequently placed on trial at the International Criminal Court (ICC).

41 *Liberia: Waging War to Keep the Peace: The ECOMOG Intervention and Human Rights*, June 1993, https://www.hrw.org/reports/1993/liberia/; Cohen, *Intervening in Africa*, 157. One report had ECOMOG using cluster bombs on NPFL positions at Harbel. Karl P. Magyar, "ECOMOG's Operations: Lessons for Peacekeeping," in *Peacekeeping in Africa: ECOMOG in Liberia*, ed. Karl P. Magyar and Earl Conteh-Morgan (New York: St. Martin's Press, 1998), 69. In June 2021, ULIMO commander Alieu Kosiah pled guilty to the murder of civilians along with rape, cruel treatment of civilians and using child soldiers. The court in his trial heard gruesome stories of summary executions and the torture of civilians. Another former ULIMO commander at the time was being tried in France for murder, torture, rape, and other atrocities. Nick Cumming, "Ex-Warlord Sent to Prison for Atrocities in Liberia," *The New York Times*, June 20, 2021. Yet another ULIMO commander, Mohammed "Jungle" Jabateh, was convicted in the U.S. of defrauding immigration authorities. He was accused also of war crimes and cannibalism.

42 Hahn, "U.S. Covert and Overt Operations in Liberia, 1970s to 2003."

43 Hahn, "U.S. Covert and Overt Operations in Liberia, 1970s to 2003," note 76; Cohen, *Intervening in Africa*, 158.

44 Hahn, "U.S. Covert and Overt Operations in Liberia, 1970s to 2003." The U.S. supported Prince Johnson when he broke from Taylor and the NPFL but switched to supporting ECOMOG when they realized that Johnson's group was not strong enough to gain power.

45 Niels Hahn, *Two Centuries of U.S. Military Operations in Liberia: Challenges of Resistance and Compliance* (Maxwell Air Force Base, Alabama: Air University Press, 2020), 155.

46 Cohen, *Intervening in Africa*, 160. Jimmy Carter monitored the elections and considered them to be free and fair. Many Liberians felt that by voting for Taylor they were voting for an end to the war. A popular slogan at the time was: "he killed my Pa; he killed my Ma; I'll vote for him." Hyman, *United States Policy Towards Liberia 1822–2003*, 43.

47 Mungo Soggot and Phillip Van Niekirk, "The Adventure Capitalist: While Africa's Wars Have Brought Untold Misery to Millions, Some Have Seen Conflict in the Region as a Business Opportunity," *International Consortium of Investigative Journalists*, November 11, 2002, https://www.icij.org/investigations/makingkilling/adventure-capitalist/. Supermodel Naomi Campbell testified at Taylor's war crimes trial that he gave her uncut "blood diamonds" as a gift.

48 Colum Lynch, "Charles Taylor Says He Paid D.C. Firm for Access to Clinton," *Foreign Policy*, February 8, 2010, https://foreignpolicy.com/2010/02/08/charles-taylor-says-he-paid-d-c-firm-for-access-to-clinton-administration/ Hyman later wrote a book whitewashing Taylor's crimes. He was a Kennedy protégé and former chairman of the Democratic Party in Massachusetts.

49 Timmerman, *Shakedown*.

50 Timmerman, *Shakedown*; "The Racist Implications of Clinton's Africa Policy," https://www.theperspective.org/racistpolicy.html; Norimitsu Onishu with Jane Perlez, "How U.S. Left Sierra Leone Tangled in a Curious Web," *The New York Times*, June 4, 2000. Three high ranking State Department officials objected to giving

Sankoh any role in the Sierra Leone government under the Lomé accords. They included Harold Koh, the assistant Secretary of State for Human Rights.

51 Hyman, *United States Policy Towards Liberia 1822 to 2003*, 82.

52 Ryan Lizza, "Where Angels Fear to Tread: Sierra Leone, The Last Clinton Betrayal," *The New Republic,* July 23, 2000. Jackson was attacked in Freetown as an RUF collaborator.

53 See for example James Rupert, "Diamond Hunters Fuel Africa's Brutal Wars," *The Washington Post,* October 16, 1999, A1.

54 Hahn, *Two Centuries of U.S. Military Operations in Liberia*, 164; Jeremy Kuzmarov, "How the CIA Helped Ruin Liberia," *CovertAction Magazine*, July 30, 2021, https://covertactionmagazine.com/2021/07/30/how-the-cia-helped-ruin-liberia/#post-21745-footnote-50; "Government of Liberia and Firestone Sign Agreement," February 25, 2008, https://www.tirereview.com/government-of-liberia-and-firestone-sign-agreement/; Peter Green, "Liberia Braces For Next National Crisis: A Crude Oil Boom," *The Street*, May 10, 2014, https://www.thestreet.com/markets/emerging-markets/liberia-braces-for-next-national-crisis-a-crude-oil-boom-12947459. Despite the wide veneration of her in the mainstream media, Johnson Sirleaf's administration had a high tolerance for corruption. One son, along with the chairman of Ms. Johnson Sirleaf's Unity Party, was on a long list of Liberian officials linked to a bribery scandal run on behalf of a British mining company. Dayo Olopade, "Stop Treating Liberia's President Like a Hero: She's Human," *The New York Times*, April 12, 2017. The U.S. Geological Survey estimated the West African Transform Margin, the offshore oil region that stretches from Guinea through Sierra Leone, Liberia and the edge of Nigeria, holds 7 billion barrels of crude oil, some 60 trillion cubic feet of gas and 1.8 billion barrels of natural gas liquids.

55 Helene Cooper, "Senate Approves Clinton's Proposal on African Trade," *The Wall Street Journal*, November 4, 1999, A8; Robert Block and Michael K. Frisby, "Clinton Tour Aims to Sell New Image of Africa," *The Wall Street Journal*, March 20, 1998, A13. Senator Don Nickles (R-OK) said that the bill's approval showed that the GOP controlled Senate was "not isolationist" or "protectionist."

56 Bill Vann, "A Bid to Make Africa Profitable for U.S. Capital," *World Socialist Web Site*, March 26, 1998, https://www.wsws.org/en/articles/1998/03/bcaf-m26.html. Chitmansing Jesseramslng, the ambassador to the U.S. from Mauritius characteristically said. "You are putting people to work and it's been proved that the magic of the marketplace can do wonders."

57 "Africa Gets a Break," *The Wall Street Journal*, May 16, 2000, A26. As part of the bill, the U.S. agreed to send $600 million in assistance to South Africa over the next three years.

58 Jim Abrams, "Major Africa Trade Bill Clears Congress," *Associated Press*, May 12, 2000, William J. Clinton Presidential Library, Digital Archives, https://clinton.presidentiallibraries.us/files/original/9ef4264faac614b0527e58d47632e05d.pdf

59 "Review of Clinton Administration's Performance in Africa," Hearings Before the Subcommittee on Africa of the Committee on international Relations, House of Representatives, 104th Congress, 2nd Session, September 26, 1996, 14.

60 History of Department of State, Africa, XV Africa Regional and Bilateral Issues, William J. Clinton Presidential Library, Digital Records, https://clinton.presidentiallibraries.us/files/original/ce5f02f4774954a8c2ec50ec14e5bddb.pdf

61 Hesse, "Celebrate or Hold Suspect?"

62 "Africa Gets a Break," *The Wall Street Journal*, May 16, 2000, A26.

63 Block and Frisby, "Clinton Tour Aims to Sell New Image of Africa."

64 George Melloan, "Feeling Africa's Pain is Not a Policy," *The Wall Street Journal*, March 31, 1998, A23.

65 Melloan, "Feeling Africa's Pain is Not a Policy." See also Bill Vann, "A Bid to Make Africa Profitable for U.S. Capital," *World Socialist Web Site*, March 26, 1998, https://www.wsws.org/en/articles/1998/03/bcaf-m26.html. Many in Congress' Black caucus supported Clinton's Africa policy, it should be noted, among them Charles Rangel (D-NY) who said after the passage of AGOA that "at last, like other ethnic groups in America, African Americans will be able to point to a special partnership that connects the United States to our ancestral homes." Robin Hayes (R-NC) was among those to worry about the loss of U.S. manufacturing jobs.

66 Anthony Lake, "Prospects for South Africa: Remarks of Anthony Lake to U.S.-Zambia Business Council," Lusaka, Zambia, December 19, 1994, William J. Clinton Presidential Library, digital archives.

67 David Smith, "Former Zambian President Faces Jail in Unprecedented Corruption Trial," *The Guardian*, August 13, 2009, https://www.theguardian.com/world/2009/aug/13/zambia-frederick-chiluba-corruption-trial

68 Donald G. McNeil Jr., "For Sale: Zambia's Rich Copper Mines; All of Them," *The New York Times*, August 11, 1996, https://www.nytimes.com/1996/08/11/world/for-sale-zambia-s-rich-copper-mines-all-of-them.html; Jeremy Kuzmarov, "Black Africa Lives Matter Too, But Not For Clinton," *The Huffington Post*, April 22, 2016, https://www.huffpost.com/entry/black-african-lives-matte_b_9763346.

69 "Phelps Dodge Boosts Zambian Investment," *UPI Arvchives*, August 27, 1996, https://www.upi.com/Archives/1996/08/27/Phelps-Dodge-boosts-Zambian-investment/8082841118400/. Phelps Dodge had an abhorrent record in its treatment of workers going back to an incident during the Woodrow Wilson administration when it deported striking miners in Bisbee Arizona to the desert. The company's CEO at the time, Cleveland Dodge was one of Woodrow Wilson's biggest donors and a former Princeton classmate.

70 Jeremy Kuzmarov, "Mostly Unnoticed August 12 Zambian Election Could Be Turning Point in Supercharging World's Transition to Clean Energy—But May Well Destroy the Zambian People," *CovertAction Magazine*, August 27, 2021, https://covertactionmagazine.com/2021/08/27/mostly-unnoticed-august-12-zambian-election-could-be-turning-point-in-supercharging-worlds-transition-to-clean-energy-but-may-well-destroy-the-zambian-people/

71 Martin Kapende, "Along the Trail of Destitution in Zambia," https://library.fes.de/pdf-files/iez/global/50040.pdf; Lynne Duke, "Zambia Stakes Its economy on Privatizing Copper Mines," *The Washington Post*, August 11, 1996, https://www.washingtonpost.com/archive/politics/1996/08/11/zambia-stakes-its-economy-on-privatizing-copper-mines/fa9c91d9-47b8-4c4c-afbf-33f14eca8ef0/

72 "Zambia Expels 2 U.S. Diplomats," *The New York Times*, June 23, 1981, https://www.nytimes.com/1981/06/23/world/zambia-expels-2-us-diplomats.html; Chris Phiri, "Authentic Extracts on the Sale of ZCCM Show Why Mr. Hichilema Has Failed to Explain His Source of Wealth—A Case of Entrusting a Barley Field with a Goat for a Second Time," *Zambia Reports,* May 20, 2010, https://zambiareports.com/2020/05/20/authentic-extracts-sale-zccm-show-mr-hichilema-failed-explain-source-wealth-case-entrusting-barley-field-goat-second-time/.

73 "Zambia: Good Copper, Bad Copper," https://www.youtube.com/watch?v=uamzirLswjk

74 See Kuzmarov, "Mostly Unnoticed August 12 Zambian Election Could Be Turning Point in Supercharging World's Transition to Clean Energy—But May Well Destroy the Zambian People."

75 Leech, *Crude Interventions*, 116.

76 *African Crisis Response Initiative—the New U.S. Africa Policy,* ed. Werner Biermann (Hamburg, GE: LIT Verlag, 1999), 96.

77 Vijay Prashad, *Fat Cats & Running Dogs: The Enron Stage of Capitalism* (Monroe, ME: Common Courage Press, 2003), 37.

78 Prashad, *Fat Cats & Running Dogs*, 38.

79 Leech, *Crude Interventions,* 117; https://www.opensecrets.org/orgs/summary?cycle=2016&id=D000000244

80 Leech, *Crude Interventions,* 116, 117, 118; Ken Silverstein, "Oil Firms' Rich Concessions to Tainted African Ruler Probed," *Los Angeles Times*, December 18, 2004, https://www.latimes.com/archives/la-xpm-2004-dec-18-fg-guinea18-story.html

81 See also George Wright, "The Clinton Administration's Policy Towards Angola: An Assessment," *Review of African Political Economy*, 28, 90 (December 2001), 563–576. On Savimbi's historic crimes, see William Minter, *Apartheid's Contras: An Inquiry into the Roots of War in Angola and Mozambique* (South Africa: Whitewatersand University Press, 1994).

82 Bill Vann, "A Bid to Make Africa Profitable for U.S. Capital," *World Socialist Web Site*, March 26, 1998, https://www.wsws.org/en/articles/1998/03/bcaf-m26.html

83 History of Department of State, Africa, XV Africa Regional and Bilateral Issues, William J. Clinton Presidential Library, Digital Records, https://clinton.presidentiallibraries.us/files/original/ce5f02f4774954a8c2ec50ec14e5bddb.pdf

84 Emmanuel K. Aning, "African Crisis Response initiative and the New African Security (Dis)order," *African Journal of Political Science* 6, no. 1 (2001) 43–67, https://citeseerx.ist.psu.edu/viewdoc/download?doi=10.1.1.521.7569&rep=rep1&type=pdf; James Rupert, "U.S. Troops Teach Peacekeeping to Africans," *The Washington Post*, September 26, 1997, https://www.washingtonpost.com/archive/politics/1997/09/26/us-troops-teach-peacekeeping-to-africans/dcb12861-66d1-4248-9937-1e2b1c757919/

85 Dan Henk and Steven Metz, *The United States and the Transformation of African Security: The African Crisis Response Initiative and Beyond* (Carlisle Barracks, PA: 1997), 22, https://studylib.net/doc/11035726/the-united-states-and-the-transformation-of-african-secur.

86 Henk and Metz, *The United States and the Transformation of African Security*, 25.

87 Nkrumah quoted in Hahn, *Two Centuries of U.S. Military Operations in Liberia,* 131: Kwame Nkrumah, *Neocolonialism: The Last Stage of Imperialism* (New York: International Publishers, 1966).

88 Samar Al-Bulushi, "Empire By invitation," *The Intercept*, January 19, 2023, https://theintercept.com/2023/01/19/us-africa-leaders-summit-counterterrorism/

89 Al-Bulushi, "Empire By invitation."

90 Paul Omach, "The African Crisis Response Initiative: Domestic Politics and Convergence of National Interests," *African Affairs* 99, no. 394 (Jan. 2000): 73–95,

https://www.jstor.org/stable/pdf/723548; The White House. Office of the Press Secretary, "Fact Sheet: African Crisis Response Initiative (ACRI)," April 1, 1998, https://clintonwhitehouse4.archives.gov/Africa/19980401-20179.html

91 Alison Mitchell, "Clinton Proposes Incentives for Free Market in Africa," *The New York Times*, June 18, 1997; Joshua Hammer and Marcus Mabry, "Don't Forget the Past: Museveni Wins After Evoking the Ghosts of His Country's History. How Will He Use His Mandate?" *Newsweek*, May 20, 1996, 28, Clinton Presidential Records, National Security Council, African Affairs, Box 1, William J. Clinton Presidential Library, Little Rock, Arkansas. One Western diplomat said that "the rules of the [1996] election were not acceptable in a full-fledged democratic state." Museveni forbade his opponents from forming their own parties and subjected them to harassment while paying off district leaders to bring out the pro-Museveni vote. Museveni also ran political ads linking his opponent, Paul Ssemogerero, unfairly to massacres in Uganda's civil war in which Museveni's National Resistance Movement (NRM) had triumphed.

92 Human Rights Watch World Report 2000 - Uganda, December 1, 1999, https://www.refworld.org/docid/3ae6a8c924.html.

93 "Background on Uganda," Clinton Presidential Records, National Security Council, African Affairs, Box 1, William J. Clinton Presidential Library, Little Rock, Arkansas.

94 Adam Branch, *Displacing Human Rights: War and Intervention in Northern Uganda* (New York: Oxford University Press, 2013)..

95 White House. "Fact Sheet: African Crisis Response Initiative (ACRI)"; "World Report 2001 - Ethiopia," Human Rights Watch, December 1, 2000, https://www.refworld.org/docid/3ae6a8ddc.html; Human Rights Watch World Report, Ethiopia—2001, https://www.refworld.org/docid/3ae6a8ddc.html

96 Lyndon Larouche, *The Pure Evil of Al Gore* (Leesburg, VA: The New Federalist, 1999).

97 Nathan J. Robinson, *Super Predator: Bill Clinton's Use and Abuse o Black America* (New York: Current Affairs, 2016), 162.

98 Robinson, *Super Predator*, 162.

99 Reprinted in Larouche, *The Pure Evil of Al Gore.*

100 History of Department of State, Africa, XV Africa Regional and Bilateral Issues, William J. Clinton Presidential Library, Digital Records, https://clinton.presidentiallibraries.us/files/original/ce5f02f4774954a8c2ec50ec14e5bddb.pdf; Robinson, *Super Predator*, 162.

101 Robinson, *Super Predator*, 162. Roger Stone and William Morrow, *The Clintons' War on Women* (New York: Skyhorse, 2016).

102 Nkrumah, *Neo-Colonialism.*

103 Jeremy Kuzmarov, "U.S. Sanctions Against Zimbabwe Condemned as 'Crime Against Humanity,'" *CovertAction Magazine*, February 16, 2023, https://covertactionmagazine.com/2023/02/16/u-s-sanctions-against-zimbabwe-condemned-as-crime-against-humanity/.

CHAPTER 12

The U.S. Assault on the African Heartland

U.S. Collusion in the Rwandan Genocide and Congo Wars

In March 1998, on a visit to Kigali, Bill Clinton gave a speech whose purpose, he said, was to "pay respect to the victims" who had "suffered and perished in the Rwandan genocide" of April 1994. Clinton used the speech to apologize to the Rwandan people, stating:

> We did not act quickly enough after the killing began. We should not have allowed the refugee camps to become safe haven for the killers. We did not immediately call these crimes by their rightful name: genocide. We cannot change the past. But we can and must do everything in our power to help you build a future without fear, and full of hope. We owe to those who died and to those who survived who loved them, our every effort to increase our vigilance and strengthen our stand against those who would commit such atrocities in the future here or elsewhere.[1]

The theme from Clinton's speech was later echoed by Samantha Power, a Harvard professor appointed as a member of President Barack Obama's National Security Council, in her 2002 Pulitzer Prize winning book, *"A Problem From Hell": America in the Age of Genocide.*[2] She used Rwanda as a cry for action in the future to stop human rights crimes and genocide and inspired the UN"s Responsibility to Protect Doctrine (R2P), which trampled on traditional notions of state sovereignty in international law by supporting the right of foreign powers to intervene in nations around the world to stop human rights crimes and genocide.

But what if Clinton and Power had Rwanda wrong? What if the U.S. was not a "Bystander to Genocide?"[3]—the title of an influential Power article in *The Atlantic*, echoing that same theme put forward in her book? But what if the U.S. had indeed intervened to support one faction in Rwanda's civil war, one which had killed at least as many as the other, and then armed that faction as it invaded and plundered Rwanda's mineral-rich neighbor, the Congo? Would the R2P doctrine hold any legitimacy? Or would it have been abandoned before the U.S. military interventions undertaken in its name in Libya and Syria where the moral stakes of conflicts were hardly as black and white as they appeared in Rwanda, as the U.S. government presented them?

The Official Narrative Is False

The backdrop of the Black Hawk Down incident was supposedly the critical factor dissuading the Clinton administration from intervening to stop the Rwandan genocide in April 1994 where around 800,000 people were slaughtered in a short period. In his memoir, *My Life*, Clinton wrote that his failure to stop the Rwandan tragedy was one of the greatest regrets of his presidency. Clinton recounts his decision to evacuate all Americans from the country and decision to remove UN troops, and writes that:

> We were so preoccupied with Bosnia, with the memory of Somalia just six months old, and with opposition in Congress to military deployments in faraway places not vital to our national interests that neither I nor anyone on my foreign policy team adequately focused on sending troops to stop the slaughter. With a few thousand troops and help from our allies, even making allowances for the time it would have taken to deploy them, we could have saved lives.[4]

Clinton's view of events assumes that the Hutu were the main perpetrators of the genocide and Tutsis the main victims, and that U.S. intervention would have helped save Tutsi victims. However, a wealth of new evidence has emerged that casts doubt on the official narrative of events as described by Clinton and other opinion shapers like Samantha Power and Philip Gourevitch, author of the 1998 book, *We Wish to inform you that tomorrow we will be killed with our families: Stories from Rwanda*.[5]

A major problem with the official narrative that the Hutu did all the killing is the fact that the 1991 census in Rwanda listed 596,000 Tutsi living in the country, with 300,000 estimated to have survived. That would mean that 296,000 Tutsi were killed by Hutu and that the rest of the dead, over 500,000, were Hutu.[6] Researchers Allan Stam and Christian Davenport found that both Hutu and Tutsi were attackers as well as victims, and that the theatres where the killing was greatest correlated with spikes in military operations carried out by the Tutsi-led Rwandan Patriotic Front (RPF).[7]

On February 6, 2008, a Spanish judge, Fernando Andreu Merelles, issued a 182-page report which found the RPF responsible for the deaths of 320,000 civilians in the war—ten times more than had been claimed by Human Rights Watch researcher Allison Des Forges, whose 590 page book, *Leave None to Tell The Story*, devoted only 12 pages to RPF crimes.[8] These killings continued in the months after the war, where Stephen Smith, an Africa specialist for the French Magazine *Liberation*, estimated that between 17,000 and 25,000 Hutu were killed in the Gitarama district alone. Survivors told Smith that petrol and firewood was brought in by trucks with Ugandan license plates to assist the RPF in burning and burying the bodies of Hutu that had been executed.[9]

Notably, Timothy Wirth, the Undersecretary for Global Affairs in the Clinton administration, was given instructions to suppress a human rights investigation by Robert Gersony, an American consultant to the UN, detailing that the RPF in three prefectures (Kigali, Nutare, Kibungo) had committed "systematic and sustained killings and persecution of their civilian Hutu population," killing at least 30,000. One of their methods was to call Hutu residents to a meeting, and then massacre them all with grenades or manual instruments like machetes and nail-studded clubs.[10] The U.S. and UN also ignored a letter to the UN Commission of Inquiry by ex-RPF military officer Christophe Hakizimana, which claimed that the RPF was responsible for killing as many as two million Hutu in Rwanda and the Democratic Republic of Congo, and that by indicting Hutus, the International Criminal Tribunal for Rwanda (ICTR) was focusing on the wrong side in the conflict.[11]

The ICTR in fact could not provide enough evidence to convict Hutu suspects of any planned genocide. They found evidence of arms transfers from the Rwandan army to Hutu militias known as the Interhamwe and that the Interahamwe had drawn up lists of suspected opponents of the Habyarimana regime, but such lists were "not focused exclusively on ethnicity." An alleged "genocide fax" sent in January 1994 by General Romeo Dallaire, commander of UN peacekeeping forces, to another Canadian General, Paul Baril, warning of a premeditated plot by Hutu extremists, has all the markings of a fabrication.[12] The fax did not surface until November 1995 when it was mysteriously sent to UN headquarters bearing the address of the British military academy at Sandhurst.

The informant upon whom Dallaire based his information, Jean Pierre Turatsinze, was an Interhamwe defector married to a Tutsi who had been suspected of selling arms illegally to Burundi. Turantsinze had ties to opposition parties and is believed to have been an RPF double agent tasked with penetrating the Interhamwe and spreading disinformation as part of a psychological warfare operation, something Kagame had studied at Ft. Leavenworth,

KS. Dallaire claimed that Turatsinze afterwards went back to the Interhamwe because he was disillusioned with Western inaction, but in fact he joined or rejoined the RPF in Tanzania and then was conveniently killed in battle.[13]

"What Better Way for Kagame To Become a Hero?"

The triggering event for the Rwanda genocide was the shooting down of the Hutu President Juvenal Habyarimana's airplane when he was returning from peace talks in Arusha, Tanzania. A power sharing agreement had been worked out at the talks and blueprint established for fair elections in Rwanda, which Kagame and the RPF knew they would lose.

The Clinton administration and media placed blame for the shooting down of Habyarimana's plane on Hutu extremists, led by Théoneste Bagasora. However, an eight-year investigation by French magistrate Jean-Louise Bruguière, along with other independent investigations, including one by a UN-appointed team, found that the RPF shot down Habyarimana's plane, and had launched a planned and coordinated assault on the Rwandan government afterwards.[14]

The Rwandan army was found to have had radio signal intercepts recording an RPF commander stating that "target is hit" after the crash. In October 2011, RPF commander Paul Kagame's former aide, Théogene Rudasingwa, stated that Kagame told him "with characteristic callousness and much glee" that he had ordered Habyarimana's plane shot down.[15] Kagame's former military chief of staff, Faustin Nyamwasa, and six other high-ranking RPF officers, have also testified that Kagame ordered the shoot down of Habyarimana's plane.[16]

Among them is former RPF Captain Frank Tega, who claims that he was with Kagame and others at Kanombe in late July 1994 when they were having drinks and boasting about the RPF's killing of Habyarimana. Kagame's former bodyguard, James Munyandinda, who had been charged with guarding the missiles, said that two RPF commandos, Eric Hakizimana and Frank Nziza, admitted to him in July 1994 that they had brought the missiles to Masaka and fired them at Habyarimana's jet.[17]

In 2007, an RPF defector writing in the *Uganda Free Press* claimed that members of the RPF team that shot down President Habyarimana's plane were all killed in order to erase evidence of the crime. Two members of the crew—Private Joseph Nyamtale and Bosco Rumenera—were hacked to death at a roadblock immediately after fleeing from the scene. The defector said that he survived based on luck after escaping from detention because of a careless guard, and had fled to Uganda. Journalist Judi Rever reported on the killing of Christophe Kayitare, who was allegedly stationed at the airport control tower to signal the arrival of Habyarimana's plane and communicated with the missile team in Masaka, and Eric Leandre Ndayire, whose sister's home was used to hide the missiles used in the attack.[18]

FBI Special agent Jim Lyons said that RPF informants told him during his investigation that a network of agents put together by Kagame had plotted to shoot down the presidential aircraft, and that there was no evidence that the Hutu government was behind it. According to Lyons, "what better way for Kagame to become a hero than to start the genocide himself by shooting down the plane and then marching into Kigali with his army and saving everybody."[19]

The missiles recovered shortly after the crash were Russian-made SAM 16s, which the RPF, not the Rwandan army, was known to possess.[20] Belgian historian Filip Reyntjens found that the serial number was identical to a missile that had been fired by the RPF in May 1991 but had failed to explode. About three weeks after the crash, local farmers found two SAM 16 single launchers in a valley near Masaka Hill within range of the airport that was accessible to the RPF. According to the Russian military prosecutor's office, the launchers had been sold to Uganda by the USSR in 1987.[21]

French army Captain Paul Barril, who served as an adviser to Habyarimana, claimed alternatively that the SAMs had Iraqi numerical markings and that after Operation Desert Storm, the CIA transferred the missiles to the RPF from seized Iraqi arms caches. The warehouse where they were stored and then re-assembled in Kigali was rented by a Swiss front company tied to the CIA, according to a whistleblower's report published on the website intabaza.com. French Foreign Minister Alain Juppé and Defense Minister François Leotard also claimed that members of the RPF received specialized missile training near Phoenix, Arizona, which would indicate a direct American complicity.[22]

Christopher Black, the lawyer for Augustin Ndindiliyimana, chief of staff of the Gendarmerie under Habyarimana who was acquitted of war crimes charges, alleged that Canadian General Romeo Dallaire, Commander of the United Nations Assistance Mission for Rwanda (UNAMIR), arranged for one axis of the runway at the airport to be closed at the request of the RPF, making it easier to shoot down the plane as it tried to land.[23]

Dallaire had earlier turned a blind eye to the infiltration into Kigali of possibly 13,000 RPF combatants when they were permitted only 600 under the Arusha Peace Accords signed in October 1993, and was seen regularly in the company of RPF soldiers in his office. Dallaire's boss, Jacques Booh-Booh, concluded that Dallaire "abandoned his role as head of the military to play a political role. He violated the neutrality principle of UNAMIR by becoming an objective ally of one of the parties in the conflict."[24]

According to J.E. Murphy, a former RPF intelligence officer writing under a pseudonym, the assassination [of Habyarimana] bore the signature of Bill Clinton, the U.S. President.

> Clinton wanted Habyarimana killed for Kagame to take over the country [Rwanda] no matter what cost. Important for Clinton was to get Mobutu out of Congo using Kagame and Museveni to carry out their mission. Several American corporations were interested in Congolese minerals, and the president had to enable them to get their piece of pie, and the only obstacle to that business was Mobutu, the dictator in Kinshasa who once was the cherished boy of [the] United States.[25]

After the plane crash, Kagame's RPF forces significantly circled around Kigali rather than heading south, where most of the Interhamwe killings were taking place.[26] According to Luc Marchal of UNAMIR, the RPF's military maneuvers had to have been pre-planned over weeks or months and could not simply have been in reaction to the first massacre of Tutsis, as the RPF claimed.[27]

That the RPF did not halt the genocide, as it is often credited for, is further evidenced by the fact that Kagame refused the Rwandan government forces' repeated requests for a ceasefire to allow civilian protection measures. An ICTR witness recounted specific examples of General Kagame ordering his troops not to intervene to save civilians and of officers being removed from their command for attempting to do so. The greater the massacres, the better their justification for seizing power—a goal the U.S. and UK government shared.[28]

Rwanda: A Central Theater in the New Great Game

In October 1990, the Bush administration had supported the RPF's illegal invasion of Rwanda from Uganda, against the wishes of the U.S. ambassador to Uganda Robert Flaten who had wanted to impose sanctions.[29] This invasion triggered the three-and-a-half-year civil war which culminated with the April 1994 bloodletting and RPF's takeover of power.

Harald Marwitz, USAID desk officer in East Africa from 1987–1991, reported that between 1989 and 1992, the Bush administration had provided almost $183 million in economic aid to Uganda—a higher amount than in the 27 years combined—enabling Uganda to channel increasing domestic resources into the war with Rwanda.[30]

During Bush's last year in office, the White House asked Congress for a 33 percent increase in the International Military Education and Training (IMET) budget of $200,000 to train Ugandan President Museveni's officers, who were primarily Rwandan Tutsis.[31] In September 1992, a personal assistant to Museveni was apprehended by U.S. Customs trying to procure 400 U.S. TOW missiles and 34 launchers for the RPF in violation of a UN arms embargo. The Justice Department later dropped the case after being pressured by Clinton's State Department, suggesting the operation was overseen by the Pentagon or CIA.[32]

The Hutu-Tutsi conflict had developed during the colonial era, when the Belgians helped to elevate the Tutsi to a privileged societal position. When the country achieved independence, Hutu intellectuals led by Grégoire Kayibanda, an ex-seminarian, spearheaded a movement to supplant the old Tutsi aristocracy, forcing many Tutsis, including a young Paul Kagame, into exile. From the squalor of refugee camps in Uganda, Burundi and Tanzania, Tutsi exiles organized guerilla forces in the hopes of recapturing their former privileged positions, and were often subjected to brutal reprisal killings in the late 1960s when the Hutu government was supported by the CIA.[33]

Kagame and his circle had played a key role in supporting Ugandan President Yoweri Museveni as he fought a guerilla war against socialist Milton Obote under the banner of the National Resistance Army (NRA). They then took up armed struggle against the Habyarimana regime after they had been cast off from the Ugandan army. Many of the techniques that they would apply in Rwanda and the later Congo wars were learned during the Ugandan bush war—including the adoption of torture tactics and importance of carrying out political assassinations. A key turning point in Museveni's victory was his shooting down of the helicopter of one of Obote's top military commanders, David Oyite-Ojok.[34]

In October 1990, a dispute had erupted between Paul Kagame, who had earned the nickname Plato for his ruthlessness among NRA guerrillas, and RPF commander Fred Rwigyema, who wanted to proceed with the invasion of Rwanda cautiously—to first politicize the peasantry and get their rural masses on the RPF side. According to researcher Justin Podur, Rwigyema was a "brilliant man whose combination of royal legitimacy and revolutionary charisma made him a probable future national leader." Unfortunately, Rwigyema was shot and killed by one of Kagame's confidantes. Abdul Ruzibiza, an RPF veteran stated that "Kagame [now] found himself at the head of an army that did not accept him. He maintained his rule through terror, assassination, imprisonment and executions."[35]

In the parts of Rwanda that RPF rebels controlled in 1992–1993, massacres of Hutu civilians were widely known but little reported in major Western media. According to Major Furuma Alphonse, from the time of the Arusha peace agreement up until around 1996, Kagame carried out a deliberate policy of using all means possible to reduce the Hutu population in the Umutura, Kibongo and Bugesera regions—a policy of ethnic cleansing.[36]

During the Cold War, the U.S. had supported the Hutu governments of Rwanda because the Tutsi had supported pro-Lumumba forces in the Congo and were considered leftists with close ties to the Chinese. However, by the late 1980s, France had begun to support the Habyarimana regime, which the State Department criticized for its "elephantine bureaucratic procedure" and a "go-slow bureaucratic mentality" which hindered private enterprise.[37]

Rwanda by the early 1990s had become the central theatre of a reinvigorated Great Game pitting the U.S. and UK against France in the struggle for control of Central Africa's mineral wealth. The Democratic Republic of Congo, whose aged leader Joseph Mobutu was on the way out, was the ultimate prize. Kagame was considered "America's Man in the Great Lakes" and the "fair haired boy of British intelligence and the CIA," according to FBI agent Jim Lyons.[38] After receiving training in psychological warfare operations at Ft. Leavenworth, he allegedly planned the October 1990 invasion of Rwanda in Uganda with Roger Winter, executive director of the U.S. Committee for Refugees and an alleged CIA agent, along with British SIS officers and David Kimche of the Israeli Mossad.[39]

Notably, Roger Winter was decorated by Kagame at the July 4, 2012, celebration of the 18th anniversary of the RPF's victory in Rwanda. In the early 1980s, he had supported the National Resistance Movement (NRM) in Uganda led by Yoweri Museveni, Uganda's current leader, as well as Kagame and the Hemi Tutsi elite, who fought against Uganda's then-president Milton Obote. For the remainder of the decade, Winter worked to advance the militant plans of the Rwandan Tutsi elite, which had been expelled from Rwanda when the Hutu took over in the 1960s.

Winter helped establish U.S. Committee for Refugees funding for RPF propaganda tracts and the RPF's journal, *Impuruza,* running from 1982 to 1994, which dehumanized the Hutu people, and organized a major conference of Tutsi exiles in Washington, D.C., in 1988, where a military solution to the Tutsi problem was decided. In 1992, Winter put Kagame in touch with high-ranking bureaucrats in the U.S. State Department and allegedly briefed Clinton administration officials on the RPF's military achievements when he was on the war's front lines.[40]

According to Bernard Lugan, a French historian and editor of the online journal *L'Afrique Réelle*, Winter was present at Kagame's headquarters at Mulundi [in Rwanda] on the night of April 6, 1994, when the plane crash occurred. According to Ugandan dignitary Remigius Kintu: "Roger Winter was the chief logistics boss for [RPF] Tutsis until their victory in 1994." Winter allegedly told a South Sudanese exile at the time [1994]: "I have now stabilized Rwanda and will turn my full attention to Sudan."[41]

Enabling Genocide

During the heart of the genocide in April 1994, political analyst Wayne Madsen noted that the United States could have easily brought the RPF to a ceasefire and leveraged France, Zaire and Kenya to do the same with their Hutu allies.[42] America's main priority, however, was not a negotiated settlement but getting its "man in the Great Lakes" in power. Commerce Secretary Ron Brown said openly in May 1995 that the United States would "no longer concede African markets to traditional colonial powers [ie. France]."[43]

The narrative that the U.S. was a bystander to genocide is false. The Pentagon admitted that it had provided military training to the RPF beginning in January 1994, three months before the mass killings, partly in response to France's military assistance to the Hutu Gendarme.[44] In April 1994, 330 U.S. Marines and seven aircraft landed at Burundi's Bujumbura airport. Their mission was to evacuate Americans from Rwanda although U.S. Navy Captain Gordon Peterson said there were "no reports of specific threats against U.S. citizens."[45] In Mombassa harbor, four U.S. military ships off-loaded material said to be humanitarian aid but rumored to be weapons for overland transport to Rwanda.[46]

In June 1994, over 200 American soldiers were deployed to rebuild and control Kigali's airport and provided military training, satellite surveillance and arms to the RPF.[47] The total of American troops was later increased to 800. A U.S. soldier from Texas said that "we are not supposed to let our families know that we were sent to Rwanda." Another soldier from Connecticut allegedly said, "human rights and democracy are none of our concerns. We are concerned with making sure that Kagame's regime is well planted and can survive."[48]

By the end of July 1994 Washington had awarded diplomatic recognition to the RPF and begun dispatching large-scale aid.[49] National Security Council Advisor Anthony Lake visited Rwanda to assure support.[50] A sophisticated communications system was shipped from a U.S. military support facility at Uganda's Entebbe airport under the cover of a humanitarian relief operation to the U.S. embassy in Kigali, which French intelligence sources claimed housed a listening post run by the Defense Intelligence Agency (DIA). The humanitarian relief operation achieved very little, leading many to believe that it gave priority to military, intelligence, and psychological warfare operations.[51]

In 1995, American aid to Rwanda totaled over $140 million. Among other things, it went to paying off World Bank and IMF arrears so that their hundred-million-dollar programs could resume, reequipping eleven ministries, caring for unaccompanied children, funding demining, restructuring the Ministry of Justice, combating HIV/AIDS, promoting women's economic development in the rural areas, and expanding police training.[52]

On August 7, 1995, Defense Secretary William J. Perry wrote a letter to Paul Kagame stating: "I am pleased with the progress you have made" and "I am especially happy that the U.S. has been able to play a role in that reconstruction." Perry continued:

> When we met in August and again when you visited me last December, I said that I would do what I can to help. You asked me to assist you win support within my government for lifting the arms embargo. I have done so. I said that I understand and strongly support your request for training to help professionalize and downsize your country's army. Our training of your soldiers at Newport and soon in Kigali regarding the role of militaries in civil societies is an important first step. I fully agree with Ambassador David Rawson's request for training in such areas as intelligence, counterinsurgency, leadership development, logistic, management and administration. I intend to advocate initiating such training as soon as possible. The next logical step to this training would be a series of combined exercises and I will pursue that with General Joulwan at the appropriate time.[53]

On November 6, 1995, Mr. Perry sent another letter to Mr. Kagame saying:

> Over the past several months, we have worked very hard with our colleagues both in the Executive Branch and in Congress on the resumption of a formal IMET [International Military Education and Training] program this coming year. I am confident that Rwandese officers and soldiers will enjoy the fruits of formal training alongside American soldiers at U.S. military schools next year. We have also arranged for our European Command to offer you a Joint Combined Exercise for Training (JCET) for next year in Rwanda.[54]

No concern was shown in Perry's letters about how this military aid and counterinsurgency training might be used. Nor with the plight of tens of thousands of displaced Hutu refugees who were mercilessly hunted down and killed by the RPF in the forests of Congo under the pretext that they were all *génocidaires* plotting the reinvasion of Rwanda.[55]

The Clinton administration was actively supporting the RPF at a time that it was implicated in these systemic massacres. Kagame deployed assassination teams against rivals, killed witnesses prepared to give evidence about the Habyarimana assassination or other crimes, and oversaw a massive penal complex where Hutu suspects died like flies in overcrowded cells. Kagame and the RPF further developed open air crematorium to more efficiently dispose of the bodies of all the Hutu that they had killed.[56]

Despite a glistening capital built with stolen Congolese loot and high ranking on the World Bank's "ease for doing business index," Rwanda was the second poorest country in East Africa with a per capita income of $697.3. Its per capita GDP ranked 197th out of 213 countries, below Zimbabwe under Robert Mugabe. Youth unemployment or underemployment topped 40 percent, imports quadrupled exports, and forty-four percent of children under five had stunted growth.[57] But still for Bill Clinton, Kagame was "one of the greatest leaders of our time."[58]

Deploying Post-Genocide Rwanda Against the Democratic Republic of Congo

The U.S. and Great Britain were key sponsors of the Rwandan-Ugandan invasion of Congo, which resulted in the death of an estimated five million Congolese and rape and wounding of tens of thousands more. Emma Bonino, European Commissioner for Humanitarian aid, spoke of "incomprehensible carnage" and accused Kagame's army and its proxies of having transformed the entire region into a "slaughterhouse." The spoils from coltan alone in 2000 was estimated to be between $80 and $100 million, the total of Rwanda's entire defense budget. The UN estimated that up to 70 percent of coltan exported from Congo was mined under the direct surveillance of the RPF.[59]

The original goal of the invasion—considered by locals as part of "an international plot to weaken a major African country"—was to overthrow the regime of Joseph Mobutu, a long-time U.S. client who supported the Hutu and increasingly came to favor French, Belgian and South African companies over American and Canadian ones.[60] When Clinton took office, the U.S. was looking for a "Zairean untainted by Mobutu," as a State Department official put it.[61] They found him in Laurent Kabila, an ex-Marxist rebel turned diamond smuggler who once fought with Che Guevara as part of the Simba rebellion. Mobutu crushed the latter rebellion with the aid of the CIA. Now, however, the U.S. used Rwanda and Uganda to replace Mobutu with

Kabila after they invaded Congo in October 1996. During Kabila's march on Kinshasa, he was in regular contact with Peter Whaley of the U.S. embassy in Kigali; their meetings in the field were so frequent that the conflict became known as "Whaley's War" in some diplomatic circles.[62]

In a July 1997 interview, Paul Kagame said that he informed the State Department in August 1996 that Rwanda was ready to dismantle Hutu refugee camps in Eastern Congo if the international community failed to remove them, and said the Clinton administration "took the decision to let it happen."[63] The Clinton administration further contributed over $100 million in military and other assistance to Kabila, importing $282 million worth of oil, minerals, and other goods from Congo at that time. Business deals were arranged with Kabila's finance commissioner, Mwana Nanga Mawanpanga, who was educated in Kentucky and had business contacts in the U.S.[64]

In time, however, Kabila proved to be too independent, rediscovering his revolutionary spirit by reviving some of Patrice Lumumba's old policies. *The Wall Street Journal* reported that Kabila's nationalizations "sent a worrying signal . . . to foreign companies that are eager to do business in this mineral-rich country."[65] These companies were also upset by concessions that Kabila offered to the Chinese with whom he had a long relationship with. Subsequently, Kabila was murdered by his adopted son, Joseph (real name Hyppolite Kanambe), a Rwandan quisling who had close ties to RPF commanders such as James Kaberebe.[66] Maurice Carney, Director of the NGO Friends of the Congo, said that "Kabila [Kanambe] served as a toll-gate for Western corporate interests, sell[ing] off Congo's riches for pennies on the dollar."[67]

The Pentagon and CIA provided over $10 million in arms to post-genocide Rwanda and Uganda, including through a CIA-run airline, Mountain, which helped evacuate wounded soldiers, and installed a command and communications center in Kigali and in the coastal areas of Uganda to help support their invasion and plunder of the Congo. The National Security Agency (NSA) supplied Kagame with a portable encrypted Motorola satellite phone from which he could receive advice and intelligence from the U.S. government and the CIA provided satellite imagery of refugee movements, some of it free of charge through the defense contractor Bechtel.[68] In February 1997, 160,000 Hutu refugees were spotted through this technology and subsequently attacked in a swampy area known as Tingi Tingi.[69]

Another private firm, Ronco, consisting largely of former U.S. Special Forces, provided explosives, armored vehicles and transport trucks in contravention of a UN arms embargo. Ronco's vehicles assisted in moving RPF troops from Uganda into Rwanda and later from Rwanda into Zaire. The

Americans covered their tracks by insisting that the contract was for the removal of land mines.[70]

American Special Forces and private contractors such as Military Professional Resources Inc. (MPRI) provided counterinsurgency training to RPF and Ugandan fighters guilty of atrocities against unarmed civilians. The training was carried out at a U.S. military base near Cyangugu, Rwanda on the Congolese border, constructed partly by the politically connected U.S. firm of Kellogg, Brown & Root, a subsidiary of Haliburton.[71] A senior U.S. embassy official in Kigali described the Special Forces training program as "killers . . . training killers." One of the recipients, Fred Ibingira, had overseen the massacre of civilians at Byumba soccer stadium and at Kibeho in southwest Rwanda, where between four and eight thousand civilians were killed in April 1995.

The Ugandan fighters were issued American-made uniforms and night vision goggles, as Pentagon officials and old CIA hands were spotted in Kigali and Kampala. A few Americans also reportedly made incursions into Zaire, and some, according to French intelligence sources, participated in massacres of Hutu refugees. Two Green Berets were reportedly killed. French intelligence claimed that American C-130 gunships machine-gunned refugee camps, though this is hard to corroborate.[72]

Journalist Wayne Madsen reported on a 1998 visit that he "could hardly avoid encountering uniformed and non-uniformed U.S. military personnel in the . . . hotels in Kampala and Kigali." An Israeli agent working with U.S. intelligence to assist Kabila's forces was also reportedly killed. The International Rescue Committee may have helped provide a cover for CIA operations in support of Joseph Kabila's rebels. Kabila himself was advised by Robert Stewart, a Bechtel executive.[73]

One of the top war profiteers, American Mineral Fields (AMF), was headquartered in Hope, Arkansas, Clinton's hometown. *The Washington Post* reported that it planned to explore southern Zaire's copper and cobalt deposits, create the world's largest zinc smelter, and build a plant to produce acid for refining with Kabila's cooperation.[74]

The first foreign firm to sign a contract with Kabila's forces was American Diamond Buyers, a subsidiary of AMF, which did hundreds of thousands of dollars in business immediately thereafter.[75] AMF's CEO Jean-Rymond Boulle had been a guest at Clinton's first White House inauguration; he had promoted a venture digging for diamonds in Arkansas in the 1980s when then-Governor Clinton approved Boulle's drilling in the Arkansas state park. The CEO of Boulle's main investor, Robertson Stephens Investment Management Company, Sanford Robertson, gave hundreds of thousands of dollars to Democratic Party causes and hosted fundraisers for Clinton.[76]

Another company that received mining concessions was Barrick Gold, which appointed Clinton's chief of staff, Vernon Jordan, to its international advisory board.[77] During Clinton's March 1998 visit to the Great Lakes, he was accompanied by Maurice Templesman, a diamond merchant married for a period to Jackie Kennedy Onassis, who had lucrative investments in the Congo and had employed former CIA station chief Larry Devlin, who was behind the ascendancy of Joseph Mobutu in the 1960s.[78]

The nightmare for Congolese continued in the 1990s when Kanambe's U.S.-backed army was blamed for at least 134 mass killings targeting Mai Mai and other resistance forces in the occupied North Kivu Province. Kanambe poisoned and killed many of his rivals, among them trade union and human rights activists and priests, and even killed his own sister.[79] In the gold and diamond rich Ituri province, Ugandan militias killed some 50,000 locals between 1998–2003 and displaced half a million as they "looted property, committed murders, and grabbed land," in the words of journalist Helen C. Epstein, and as "villagers were raped, herded into churches and burned alive."[80] Similar abuses were carried out by Rwandan militias headed by such notorious figures as Laurent Nkunda and Bocoe Ntganda (AKA "The Terminator"), who were accused of recruiting child soldiers as young as twelve.[81]

The Clinton administration was complicit in these crimes. It had helped bring to power and supported the post-genocide Rwandan and Ugandan governments, and sponsored their invasion of Congo, which it had helped mastermind.

Endnotes

1 "Text of Clinton's Rwanda Speech," March 29, 1998, https://www.cbsnews.com/news/text-of-clintons-rwanda-speech/

2 Samantha Power, *"A Problem From Hell": America in the Age of Genocide* (New York: Basic Books, 2002).

3 Samantha Power, "Bystanders to Genocide," *The Atlantic*, September 2001, https://www.theatlantic.com/magazine/archive/2001/09/bystanders-to-genocide/304571/

4 Bill Clinton, *My Life* (New York: Alfred A. Knopf, 2004), 593. Clinton went on to state that in his second term and after he left office, he did what he could to "help the Rwandans put their country and their lives back together. Today, at the invitation of President Paul Kagame, Rwanda is one of the countries in which my foundation is working to stem the tide of AIDS."

5 Philip Gourevitch, *We Wish to Inform You That Tomorrow We Will be Killed with Our Families: Stories from Rwanda* (New York: Picador, 1998); Power, *"A Problem from Hell."* Both books provide poor historical context and are ridden with oversimplifications.

6 Marijka Verpooten, "Rwanda: Why Claim That 200,000 Tutsi Died in the Genocide is Wrong," *Africa Arguments*, October 27, 2014.

7 Christian Davenport and Allan Stam, "What Really Happened in Rwanda?" *Miller-McCune*, October 6, 2009, http://faculty.virginia.edu/visc/Stam-VISC.pdf; Christian Davenport and Allan Stam, *Rwandan Political Violence in Space and Time*, http://www.cdavenport.com; Edward S. Herman and David Peterson, *The Politics of Genocide* (New York: Monthly Review Press, 2010), 58, 132, 133. Davenport and Stamm suggest only 200,000 Tutsi were killed based on the belief that there were 506,000 Tutsis in Rwanda in 1996, though other researchers like Marijke Verpooten suggest that the 506,000 figure was too low and that there around 596,000 Tutsi in Rwanda. However, even if accepting her figure, the official total of Tutsi dead would be far less than the version promoted by Clinton, Gourevitch, Power and others.

8 Barrie Collins, *Rwanda 1994: The Myth of the Akazu Genocide Conspiracy and Its Consequences* (New York: Palgrave Macmillan, 2014); Allison Des Forges, *Leave None to Tell the Story: Genocide in Rwanda (*Human Rights Watch, 1999).

9 American embassy Paris to USIA and other American embassies throughout Africa, "Africa in the French Press: February 24 to March 1, 1996," March 1996, Clinton Digital Library, Rwanda, Rwandan Patriotic Front, https://clinton.presidentiallibraries.us/items/show/99009

10 Judi Rever, *In Praise of Blood: The Crimes of the Rwandan Patriotic Front* (Toronto: Random House Canada, 2018), 96, 97; J.E. Murphy, *U.S. Made* (Meadville, PA: Christian Faith Publishing, 2015), 135, 136; Collins, *Rwanda 1994*, 35.

11 Herman and Peterson, *The Politics of Genocide*, 132.

12 Hazel Cameron, *Britain's Hidden Role in the Rwandan Genocide: The Cat's Paw* (London: Routeledge, 2013), 126; Christopher Black, "The Dallaire Genocide Fax: A Fabrication," December 7, 2005, www.sandersresearch.com.

13 Michael Dobbs, "The Shroud Over Rwanda's Nightmare," *The New York Times*, January 9, 2014; Michael Dobbs, "The Rwandan Genocide Fax: What We Now Know," National Security Archive, January 9, 2014, https://nsarchive2.gwu.edu/NSAEBB/NSAEBB452/

14 Herman and Peterson, *The Politics of Genocide*, 56, 60; Carla de Ponte, *Madame Prosecutor: Confrontations with Humanity's Worst Criminals and the Culture of Impunity* (NY: The Other Press, 2009); John Conroy, *Rwanda's Untold Story* (BBC, 2014). The Chief Prosecutor for the Rwanda tribunal, Canadian judge Louise Arbour, ordered the UN investigation closed on the shoot down of the plane, blocking legal action against Kagame. Carla del Ponte, who had pushed for the investigation, was fired.

15 Michael Deibert, *The Democratic Republic of Congo: Between Hope and Despair* (London: Zed Books, 2013), 213; Collins, *Rwanda 1994*, 25.

16 Conroy, *Rwanda's Untold Story*; Murphy, *U.S. Made*, 51; Peter Erlinder, *The Accidental Genocide* (International Humanitarian Law Institute, 2013), 25.

17 Collins, *Rwanda* 1994, 25.

18 Walter Melon, with narration by Timothy Kalyegira "Paul Kagame Ordered the Assassination of Habyarimana," *The Uganda Free Press,* January 17, 25 and 28, 2007, https://freeuganda.wordpress.com/2010/02/05/paul-kagame-ordered-the-assasination-of-habyarimana/; Jeremy Kuzmarov, "Still Unsolved: The Great Crime That Triggered the 1994 Rwandan Genocide," *CovertAction Magazine*, April 6, 2021, https://covertactionmagazine.com/2021/04/06/still-unsolved-the-great-crime-that-triggered-the-1994-rwandan-genocide/; Rever, *In Praise of Blood*, 178.

19 Rever, *In Praise of Blood*, 178.

20 Helen Epstein, *Another Fine Mess: America, Uganda and the War on Terror* (New York: Columbia Global Reports, 2017), 112; Collins, *Rwanda 1994*, 25. Since the RPF had no aircraft, the Rwandan army had no need for anti-aircraft weapons.

21 Epstein, *Another Fine Mess*, 111, 112.

22 Wayne Madsen, *Genocide and Covert Operations in Africa, 1993–1999* (Lewiston, NY: Edwin Mellen, 1999), 113, 125; Collins, *Rwanda 1994*, 67; "Who Killed Habyarimana Juvenal and Uwringiyimana Agathe? The Death of a President and Prime Minister," http://intabaza.com/?p=1394&lang=en; Kuzmarov, "Still Unsolved,"

23 Christopher Black, "Top Secret: Rwanda War Crimes Cover-Up," *New Eastern Outlook*, October 22, 2018, https://l-hora.org/?p=9374&lang=en. Black noted that Dallaire sided with the RPF during his mandate, gave continuous military intelligence to the RPF about government army positions, let the RPF get arms and allowed UN forces to train them, according to Gilbert Ngjo, political assistant to the civilian commander of UNAMIR. Dallaire took his orders from the American and Belgian ambassadors and lied to his boss, Jacques Roger Booh-Booh, about his knowledge of a build-up for a final Ugandan Army-RPF offensive.

24 Yves Engler, *Left, Right: Marching to the Beat of Imperial Canada* (Montreal: Black Rose Books, 2019), 166, 167.

25 Murphy, *U.S. Made*, 52, 53.

26 Epstein, *Another Fine Mess*; Collins, *Rwanda 1994*.

27 Marc De Miramon, "Brutal From the Beginning: The Truth About Everyone's Favorite Strongman" *Harper's Magazine*, July 2019, https://harpers.org/archive/2019/08/brutal-from-the-beginning-paul-kagame-rwanda/

28 Collins, *Rwanda 1994*, 17; Rever, *In Praise of Blood*; Murphy, *U.S. Made*.

29 Helen C. Epstein, "America's Secret Role in the Rwandan Genocide," *The Guardian*, September 12, 2017, https://www.theguardian.com/news/2017/sep/12/americas-secret-role-in-the-rwandan-genocide

30 Harald Marwitz, "Another Side of Rwanda's Bloodbath," *Washington Times*, August 11, 1994, A12; Barry Crawford, "From Arusha to Goma: How the West Started the War in Rwanda," *Africa Direct*, February 17, 1995; Remegius Kintu, "The Truth Behind the Rwandan Tragedy," Presented to UN Tribunal on Rwanda, Arusha, Tanzania, March 20, 2005, file:///C:/Users/jeremykuzmarov/AppData/Local/Packages/Microsoft.MicrosoftEdge_8wekyb3d8bbwe/TempState/Downloads/3588%20(1).pdf. Epstein (*Another Fine Mess*, 106) reports that following the RPF's invasion of Rwanda in October 1990, Western donors had doubled aid to Ugandan strongman Yoweri Museveni who backed the RPF's invasion.

31 Madsen, *Genocide and Covert Operations in Africa 1993–1999*, 42, 105. U.S. military advisers had encouraged the Ugandan army to organize separate RPF battalions for future actions inside Rwanda. The Tutsi cadres of exiles also received military training from British forces at a base in Jinja, Uganda. In addition, Museveni solicited military aid for the RPF from Eritrea, and from the Somali warlord faction of Mohammad Farah Aideed, India, and ironically North Korea, which was on the same side as the U.S. in this conflict. U.S. Ambassador Herman Cohen said that the U.S. silently acquiesced in the RPF's invasion of Rwanda, which is an understatement.

32 Marwitz, "Another Side of Rwanda's Bloodbath"; Madsen, *Genocide and Covert Operations in Africa 1993–1999*, 41, 42. The missiles and launchers had been disguised as construction and refrigeration equipment. Madsen suggests that they

were being smuggled as part of a Pentagon-CIA operation and that a Florida Judge was also pressured to throw out the charges.

33 See Mahmood Mamdani, *When Victims Become Killers: Colonialism, Nativism, and Genocide in Rwanda* (New Jersey: Princeton University Press, 2001); Stephen Kinzer, *A Thousand Hills: Rwanda's Rebirth and the Man Who Dreamed It* (New York: Wiley, 2008). On CIA support for the Hutu government, see Jeremy Kuzmarov, *Modernizing Repression: Police Training and Nation Building in the American Century* (Amherst, MA: University of Massachusetts Press, 2012), chapter 8.

34 Justin Podur, *America's Wars on Democracy in Rwanda and the Democratic Republic of Congo* (New York: Palgrave McMillan, 2020); "Paul Kagame is a Very Bad Man," June 22, 2015, https://paulkagame.info/paul-kagame-is-a-very-bad-man/. Kagame had been a Ugandan police officer in the 1970s and worked as a spy for Museveni's Front for the National Salvation (FRONASA—precursor to the NRA), many of whose men were integrated into dictator Idi Amin's national intelligence agency. In the NRA, Kagame oversaw the execution of captured soldiers loyal to Milton Obote, Museveni's rival, and NRA operatives suspected of being double agents. He also handled the hijacking of a Ugandan airlines F-27 aircraft, and asphyxiation of Obote soldiers who were locked into a trailer which Kagame ordered shut for days (when it was opened finally the decomposed bodies of the men spilled out). An NRA intelligence officer recounted an incident years later where Kagame, as head of administration in Ugandan military intelligence, released a guerrilla who had printed bank notes after he was paid a bribe.

35 Podur, *America's Wars on Democracy in Rwanda and the Democratic Republic of Congo*; "Paul Kagame is a Very Bad Man." There is a rumor that in October 1990, Kagame killed another rival for power in the RPF, Lt. Col. Adam Wasswa, who died in a car accident at Lyantonde in central Uganda when he and Kagame were in the same Toyota Land Rover together travelling to an RPF high command meeting inside Rwanda. Wasswa was a Rwandan Tutsi royal supported by the ousted Rwandan King, Kigeli V. Kagame was from the Abega ethnic Tutsi group and Wasswa the Abanyiginya, who consider themselves the true kings of Rwanda.

36 "Paul Kagame is a Very Bad Man." Kagame appointed Rubulika Kayongo and a Colonel Twahirwa Dodo to coordinate killings carried out with hoes because of their ruthlessness.

37 Ambassador Herman Cohen for National Security Council, "How Habyarimana Runs Rwanda"; American ambassador (Herman Cohen) to Secretary of State, "Rwanda's Private Sector: Battling the Bureaucrats," April 1988; "Rwanda: Even a Worse Future Ahead," December 11, 1987, Ronald Reagan Presidential Library, Simi Valley California, African Affairs, Box 1, Folder Rwanda.

38 Gourevitch, *We wish to inform you that tomorrow we will be killed with our families*, 212.

39 " Keith Harmon Snow, "Exposing U.S. Agents of Low Intensity Warfare in Africa," August 8, 2012, https://www.wrongkindofgreen.org/2012/08/16/special-report-exposing-u-s-agents-of-low-intensity-warfare-in-africa/

40 Snow, "Exposing U.S. Agents of Low Intensity Warfare in Africa"; Kuzmarov, "Still Unsolved."

41 Snow, "Exposing U.S. Agents of Low Intensity Warfare in Africa"; Kuzmarov, "Still Unsolved."

42 Madsen, *Genocide and Covert Operations in Africa 1993–1999*, 147.

43 Madsen, *Genocide and Covert Operations in Africa 1993–1999*, 236.

44 Madsen, *Covert Operations and Genocide in Africa, 1993–1999*, 125, 126. The military training, as outlined by a U.S. diplomat to Amnesty International, included short courses in basic infantry for about 30 RPF soldiers and was designed to "professionalize what started as a guerrilla army and to expose their officers to management of a multiethnic force."

45 Madsen, *Genocide and Covert Operations in Africa 1993–1999*, 156. From 1962–1992, the United States had given $131.4 million in economic and military aid to the Tutsi government of Burundi which slaughtered over 450,000 Hutu. Marwitz, "Another Side of Rwanda's Bloodbath." In 1996, a Tutsi leader, Pierre Buyoya overthrew Hutu president Sylvestre Ntibantunganya, and supported ethnic cleansing operations which left 6,000 Hutu dead. The Clinton administration covertly gave $145,000 to Buyoya through USAID, money that was used to lobby against any peacekeeping mission. Madsen, *Covert Operations in Genocide in Africa 1993–1999*, 225–227.

46 Madsen, *Genocide and Covert Operations in Africa 1993–1999*, 194 citing Agence France press reports.

47 Madsen, *Genocide and Covert Operations in Congo 1993–1999*, 148; David Himbara, *Kagame's Economic Mirage* (South Carolina: Create Space Independent Publishing, 2016), 85; Michael Wines, "U.S. Sending Force of 200 to Reopen Rwandan Airport," *The New York Times*, July 30, 1994; Remigius Kintu, "The Truth Behind the Rwandan Tragedy," March 20, 2005, https://hungryoftruth.blogspot.com/2009/01/truth-behind-rwandan-tragedy.html. The number of U.S. Special commandos in Rwanda may have exceeded 800.

48 Kintu, "The Truth Behind the Rwandan Tragedy."

49 Herman and Peterson, *The Politics of Genocide*, 56; Robert E. Gribbin, *In the Aftermath of Genocide: The U.S. Role in Rwanda* (New York: IUniverse, 2005), 168, 170.

50 Lt. Col. Thomas P. Odom, "Guerillas from the Mist: A Defense Attache Watches the RPF Transform From Insurgent to Counterinsurgent," *Small Wars Journal*, 5 (July 2006). Ambassador David Rawson, a former oil executive who had funneled arms to dictator Siad Barre in Somalia, and Lt. Col. Richard Orth, a military attaché who arrived in Kigali on April 7, 1994, were staunchly pro-RPF and advised Kagame after he consolidated power.

51 Madsen, *Genocide and Covert Operations in Africa 1993–1999*, 156. Judging by the number of antennas on the roof, researcher Wayne Madsen believes the facility was run by the NSA. Kigali, he says, was an excellent choice for a listening post because it was located above sea level in the heart of Central Africa.

52 Gribbin, *In the Aftermath of Genocide*, 168, 170.

53 Kintu, "The Truth Behind the Rwandan Tragedy."

54 Kintu, "The Truth Behind the Rwandan Tragedy."

55 On the counterinsurgency campaigns targeting Hutu refugees and their brutality, see Marie Beatrice Umutesi, *Surviving the Slaughter: The Ordeal of a Rwandan Refugee in Zaire*, translated by Julia Emerson (Madison, WI: University of Wisconsin Press, 2004).

56 See Erlinder, *The Accidental Genocide*; Murphy, *U.S. Made*; Rever, *In Praise of Blood*; John Conroy, Rwanda's Untold Story (BBC 2014), https://vimeo.com/107867605. The most prominent of Kagame's rivals killed in exile by RPF death squads are: Théoniste Lizinde (1996) and Seth Sendashonga (1998) in Kenya; Théogène Turatsinze (2012) in Mozambique; and Patrick Karageya (2013) in South

Africa. A State Department report emphasized that some people were killed in jail after being beaten to death by corrupt prison officials. It also conceded to extrajudicial killings in the DRC by the Rwandan army. American embassy Kigali to Secretary of State, Washington, D.C., "Rwanda 2000 Human Rights Report," October 2000, Clinton Digital Library, Rwandan Patriotic Front, https://clinton.presidentiallibraries.us/items/show/99012.

57 Himbara, *Kagame's Economic Mirage*.

58 Anjam Sundaram, "Rwanda: The Darling Tyrant," *Politico,* March/April 2014, https://www.politico.com/magazine/story/2014/02/rwanda-paul-kagame-americas-darling-tyrant-103963/

59 See Wayne Madsen, *Jaded Tasks: Brass Plates, Black Ops, & Big Oil* (Walterville, OR: Trine Day, 2006); Rever, *In Praise of Blood*, 47. Coltan is used in the manufacture of electronic devices. Glen Ford reported that in the late 1990s, Uganda became a significant diamond exporter, even though it had previously produced no diamonds at all. Ugandan gold exports also increased fifty-fold between 1994 and 2000, while Rwanda increased its gold production ten to seventeen times between 1995 and 2000. Glen Ford, *The Black Agenda Report*, with a new preface by Margaret Kimberley (New York: OR Books, 2022), 264.

60 Madsen, *Genocide and Covert Operations in Africa 1993–1999*, 94; de Miramon, "Brutal from the Beginning"; Robert Block, "Ailing Zaire: Searching for a Scapegoat – Was Revolt Mobutu's Fault or International Conspiracy," *The Wall Street Journal*, November 21, 1996, A19. On Mobutu's long ties to the CIA, see Sean Kelley, *America's Tyrant* (University Press of the Americas, 1989).

61 Podur, *America's War on Democracy in Rwanda and the Democratic Republic of Congo*, 123.

62 Epstein, *Another Fine Mess,* 130.

63 Clinton Administration Policy and Human Rights in Africa, March 1998, https://www.hrw.org/legacy/reports98/africa/africlin.htm

64 Cindy Shiner, "U.S. Firms Stake Claims In Zaire's War," *The Washington Post*, April 17, 1997, https://www.washingtonpost.com/wp-srv/inatl/africa/april/17/usstake.htm; Frank Smythe, "A New Game: The Clinton Administration on Africa," *World Policy Journal*, June 1, 1998.

65 T.J. Coles, "Backed by AFRICOM, Corporations Plunder DR Congo For 'Climate Friendly Materials' and Blame China," *The Grayzone Project*, November 30, 2021, https://thegrayzone.com/2021/11/30/africom-corporations-dr-congo-climate-china/

66 Filip Reyntjens, *The Great African War: Congo and Regional Geopolitics, 1996–2006* (New York: Cambridge University Press, 2009); *The African Stakes in the Congo War*, ed. J.F. Clark (New York: McMillan, 2002); Gérard Prunier, *From Genocide to Continental War: The Congolese Conflict and the Crisis of Contemporary Africa* (London: Hurst & Co., 2009); Yaa-Lengi M. Ngemi, *"Joseph Kabila," Identity Thief, Imposter, and Rwandan Trojan Horse in Congo: Hyppolite Kanambe a.k.a. Joseph Kabila: Rwandan Tutsi and Hitler Paul Kagame's Agent in DRC* [The Evidence] (New York City, 2017) which includes discussion of Kanambe's reign of terror. Ché wrote in his diary that Kabila had "not set foot on the front since time immemorial and was too addicted to drink and women" to be of any value to the world revolution. After making his fortune smuggling diamonds, Joseph Kabila ran a personal fief in which he allegedly enslaved female concubines and at one time kidnapped three Americans working with Jane Goodall for ransom. He came out of

retirement when the CIA proposed that he lead a rebellion against his old nemesis, Mobutu.

67 Quoted in Jeremy Kuzmarov, "Congo's Imposter President and the Moral Depravity of the West," *Counterpunch*, July 6, 2018, https://www.counterpunch.org/2018/07/06/congos-imposter-president-and-the-moral-depravity-of-the-west/. Kanambe's first move upon assuming the presidency was to fly to the United States to give back mining concessions to the companies that had had them revoked by the father who had unwisely adopted him.

68 Murphy, *U.S. Made*, 135; Madsen, *Genocide and Covert Operations in Congo, 1993–1999*, 157.

69 Madsen, *Genocide and Covert Operations in Africa, 1993–1999,* Prepared Testimony and Statement of Wayne Madsen, May 17, 2001, http://www.hartford-hwp.com/archives/27e/791.html

70 Madsen, *Genocide and Covert Operations in Congo, 1993–1999*, 157.

71 Madsen, *Genocide and Covert Operations in Africa, 1993–1999,* Prepared Testimony and Statement of Wayne Madsen, May 17, 2001, http://www.hartford-hwp.com/archives/27e/791.html. Kellog, Brown and Root was a huge war profiteer in the Balkans, which helped build Camp Bondsteel and also provided logistical support to U.S. troops in the 1990s in Somalia and Haiti. The company was infamous because of its association with Lyndon B. Johnson and wealth derived from base building projects in Vietnam and subsequently Iraq.

72 Reyntjiens, *The Great African War*, 67–73; William Hartung and Bridget Moix, *Deadly Legacy: U.S. Arms to Africa and the Congo War* (Washington, D.C.: World Policy Institute, 1994); Lynne Duke, "U.S. Military Role in Rwanda Greater Than Disclosed," *The Washington Post*, August 16, 1997, A1; Madsen, *Genocide and Covert Operations in Africa, 1993–1999*, 197, 200, 205, 212, 439; Murphy, *U.S. Made*, 133–135; Epstein, *Another Fine Mess,* 131.

73 Madsen, *Genocide and Covert Operations in Africa, 1993–1999*, 197, 200, 205, 212, 439.

74 Dena Montague, Frieda Berrigan "The Business of War in the Democratic Republic of Congo: Who benefits?" *Dollars and Sense*, July/August 2001, http://www.projectcensored.org/top-stories/articles/19-american-companies-exploit-the-congo/; Keith Harmon Snow and David Barouski, "Behind the Numbers: Untold Suffering in the Congo," *Third World Traveler*, http://www.thirdworldtraveler.com/Africa/Congo_BehindNumbers.html; Madsen, *Genocide and Covert Operations in Africa 1993–1999*, 69–74; Peter Eichstadt, *Consuming the Congo: War and Conflict Minerals in the World's Deadliest Place* (New York: Lawrence Hill Books, 2011). AMF would control 51 percent of the venture, and Kabila's Alliance of Democratic Forces for the Liberation of Congo-Zaire 49 percent. Cindy Shiner, "U.S. Firms Stake Claims In Zaire's War," *The Washington Post*, April 17, 1997, A1.

75 Shiner, "U.S. Firms Stake Claims In Zaire's War."

76 "Friends in High Places," *Forbes Magazine*, August 10, 1998, https://www.forbes.com/global/1998/0810/0109038a.html?sh=20b4a2503aac; Boulle was also heavily involved in diamond mining in Angola. Paul Beaver, a consultant to the reputable *Jane's* defense publications which specializes in mercenaries, says the Clinton administration forced the Angolan government to ditch mercenaries it had been employing and replace them with groups of Washington-approved mercenaries. One such security company to emerge was a Brussels-based outfit called IDAS Belgium S.A. (International Defense & Security). The Angolan government granted a

Netherlands Antilles IDAS subsidiary 50% of the diamond rights in more than 36,000 square kilometers of rebel-controlled bush. The quid pro quo was that they cleared out the rebels in return for a share of the diamonds. Starting in May 1996, Boulle's AMF began buying the IDAS affiliate holding the diamond rights, paying $2.3 million in cash and shares, plus a back-end share of profits capped at $84 million.

77 "Barrick's International Advisory Board Issues Statement on Vernon Jordan, https://www.barrick.com/English/news/news-details/2021/vernon-jordan/default.aspx; Podur, *America's War on Democracy in Rwanda and the Democratic Republic of Congo.* Phelps Dodge Corporation, a copper giant, secured ownership of the cobalt producing Temke-Fungunume mine with the help of the U.S. embassy. The Washington-based New Millenium Investment Ltd. opened the first bank in the rebel stronghold of Goma and signed a contract to "revitalize Goma's telecommunications." Comsat, based in Bethesda, further signed an agreement to sell satellite telephone equipment in Goma. Citibank also expressed interest in Congo.

78 "Friends in High Places"; David Gibbs, *The Political Economy of Third World Intervention: Mines, Money, and U.S. Policy in the Congo Crisis* (Chicago: University of Chicago Press, 1991).

79 Ngemi, *Joseph Kabila, Identity Thief, Imposter and Rwandan Trojan Horse in Congo.* See also Kuzmarov, "Congo's Imposter President and the Moral Depravity of the West."

80 Epstein, *Another Fine Mess*, 128.

81 "D.R. Congo Arrest Laurent Nkunda for War Crimes," *Human Rights Watch*, https://www.hrw.org/news/2006/02/01/dr-congo-arrest-laurent-nkunda-war-crimes

CHAPTER 13

The Third Conquest of Latin America

In October 1997, Bill Clinton made his first trip to Latin America as president, making Venezuela his first stop. The country had recently become the largest exporter of oil to the United States, surpassing Saudi Arabia, after privatizing its petroleum sector (reversing the nationalization policy of the 1970s). Venezuela's president, Rafael Caldera, was a Christian Democrat who acquiesced to an IMF-supported austerity and privatization program that was designed to curb inflation and ease the deficit. Accompanied by his special Latin American envoy, Thomas F. "Mack" McLarty III,[1] a former Arkansas Natural Gas Executive and boyhood chum, Clinton was there to promote a bilateral investment plan that would privilege U.S. corporate interests, while doubling Venezuela's oil production, which concerned environmentalists.[2]

From Caracas, Clinton went on to visit with the presidents of Brazil and Argentina (Fernando Henrique Cardoso and Carlos Menem), who both promoted the so-called Washington Consensus, or conservative economic policies which privileged free-trade and foreign investment, along with deregulatory measures and privatization. A long-term goal was the establishment of a new free-trade zone for all of the Americas, the Free-Trade Agreement of the Americas (FTAA), which was christened in 2005.[3]

The French *Le Figaro* editorialized that Clinton appeared to have adopted Calvin Coolidge's old doctrine that "The business of America is business."[4] When Clinton came back from his trip, the House of Representatives launched an investigation into his association with a right-wing Venezuelan banker, Orlando Castro Llanes, who had contributed $50,000 to Clinton's 1992 election campaign and $100,000 to Clinton and other Democrats through his U.S. adviser, Attorney Charles Intriago. In 1994, when the Venezuelan banking system collapsed, Castro-Llanes was forced to flee Venezuela to avoid charges of bank fraud.[5]

Clinton packaged himself publicly as the first U.S. president in two generations who was "free of the virus of a U.S. obsession with communism that has poisoned hemispheric relations for half a century," as a leading Latin American analyst termed it.[6] An Italian correspondent called Clinton's 1997 South American trip, coming forty years after the protests against then vice-president Richard Nixon, a public relations masterpiece.[7] Clinton had tried to burnish his progressive image by laying a wreath on the tomb of

Simon Bolivar, the great Latin American liberator, during the trip and later offered some acknowledgment of past misdeeds, such as the CIA's 1954 coup in Guatemala.[8] But Clinton was not greeted favorably everywhere he went. In Brazil, for example, where the country's assets were put up for sale by President Cardoso under a large-scale privatization initiative, Clinton's limousine was pelted by protesters with manure.[9]

The era of the Monroe Doctrine had not generally ended. Latin America became a crucial showpiece for a new dollar diplomacy in the 1990s and received loads of high-tech weaponry that was used to repress social movements.[10] In August 1997, Clinton ended a twenty year policy of restricting transfers of advanced weapons such as combat aircraft to Latin America—a decision welcomed by U.S. military contractors.[11] Lockheed Martin at the time was vying for a $500 million Chilean contract for 20 combat aircraft in competition with French Mirage 2000s and Russian MIG-29s. A U.S. government official stated that the Chilean deadline was "a driving force in the timing of the decision." Massachusetts Representative Nita Lowery (D-NY) who had introduced legislation prohibiting the sale of aircraft in the region, stated that the U.S. "must not allow McDonnell Douglas and Lockheed Martin to dictate our foreign policy"[12]—which under Clinton, to a large extent, it did.

According to historian Greg Grandin, Clinton carried forward the legacy of Ronald Reagan in presiding over the "third conquest" of Latin America, resulting from large scale privatization programs beginning in the 1980s that led to the selling off of Latin American state assets to private capitalists and intensified looting of its resources by multinational corporations and foreigners.[13] U.S. cultural penetration intensified with the popularity of the Back Street Boys and Jennifer Lopez, and the spread of American chains like Walmart and McDonald's in Latin America.[14]

Total U.S. private direct investment on the continent significantly increased by 237% in the 1990s, from $71 billion to $239 billion, while the number of Latin Americans living in poverty increased by almost 7%, from 200 million to almost 214 million. Unemployment rates nearly doubled from 4.6% in 1990 to 8.6% in 1999 and forested areas were depleted at a rate two times greater than in the rest of the world.[15]

These statistics epitomize the failings of the Clinton administration's foreign policy in Latin America and Washington Consensus, which enriched certain segments of the population while fueling greater social inequality and environmental despoliation. This notably fueled the regeneration of the political left, reflecting popular disaffection with the neoliberal economic program advanced by Clinton.

Devastating Haiti

During the 2016 election campaign, Republican contender Donald Trump referenced the hatred for the Clintons in Haiti he had encountered among Haitians he met in Florida. While Trump is known for blowing hot air and himself cared little about the Haitian people, he was right about the antipathy towards the Clintons. In March 2010, Bill Clinton publicly apologized for forcing Haiti to drop tariffs on imported subsidized U.S. rice during his time in office, which wiped out Haitian rice farming and seriously damaged Haiti's ability to be self-sufficient. "It may have been good for some of my farmers in Arkansas, but it has not worked. It was a mistake," Clinton said. "I have to live every day with the consequences of the lost capacity to produce a rice crop in Haiti to feed those people, because of what I did."[16] The two largest beneficiaries were Rice Mill and Riceland Foods, one of the largest rice exporters in the world headquartered in Stuttgart, Arkansas. The CEOs of both companies were donors to Clinton's presidential campaigns.[17]

The liberalized trade policy had been adopted in 1995 by Haitian President Jean-Bertrand Aristide who had been restored to power a year earlier with the support of the U.S. military. Aristide was a populist priest with a strong base among Haiti's poor. After acceding to power in 1990 following years of misrule under the Duvaliers, Aristide was ousted in a coup d'état, which the Bush I administration had supported covertly.

Raoul Cédras replaced Aristide as the head of state. During the interim years, CIA "assets" in the army and police carried out a reign of terror, targeting supporters of Aristide's Lavalas party in the urban slums.[18] According to CIA Director James Woolsey (1993–1995), the CIA had a big problem with Aristide. It considered him a "mentally disturbed guy and murderer . . . you don't know what he could do if he goes off his medication."[19]

In September 1994, with support from the Congressional Black Caucus, Clinton authorized the deployment of some 20,000 Marines to Haiti to remove what he called "the most brutal, the most violent regime anywhere in our hemisphere," a "regime guilty of executing children, raping women, killing priests and of slaying orphans." Eleven months earlier, the Clinton administration had been humiliated when the U.S.S. *Harlan* had sailed into Port-au-Prince and was forced to turn around when it was greeted by a mob of Cédras supporters waving machetes and pitchforks who chanted 'Somalia! Somalia!"[20]

The supposed humanitarian imperative of the September 1994 invasion—whose goal was the removal of the bastard Cédras regime—won over liberal opinion-shapers who had opposed the Vietnam War. An example was *New York Times* columnist Anthony Lewis, who characterized the intervention as an "amazing success."[21] Michael Tomasky, the editor of the *New Republic* and a contributor to the *New York Review of Books*, said that it "set a precedent that the U.S. was capable of a quick and successful humanitarian intervention."[22]

Operation Uphold Democracy, however, was carried out in violation of international law and the U.S. War Powers Act, which required Congressional authorization, and helped undermine Haiti's economic sovereignty.[23] On the day of the invasion, the UN's Haiti negotiator Dante Caputo resigned, denouncing the "unilateral action" of the U.S. as part of a "scenario" planned long before, and saying the U.S. treatment of the Haitian military regime with honor and as "heroes of the film" was "scandalous."[24]

This concerned the reference to the ruling military junta as "honorable partners" by U.S. special envoys Jimmy Carter and Colin Powell—who had been sent by Clinton to negotiate the surrender of the military junta prior to the Marine landing. An outrageously generous asylum package was arranged which enabled them to live comfortably in the U.S.[25] U.S. troops in Haiti cooperated closely with leading pro-coup families in the business elite like the Mevs and the Boulos, and went out of their way to protect right-wing paramilitary groups who were never formally disarmed while spying on Aristide and his supporters.

Journalist Allan Nairn concluded that the main aim of the occupation, rather than restoring Aristide's power and functioning democracy, was

> to prevent the Haitian population from taking politics into its own hands and to forestall the danger of radical mass mobilization. . . . The United States intends to contain Haiti's popular movement by force if necessary. . . . The objective, in the words of one U.S. Army psychological operations official, is to see to it that Haitians don't get the idea that they can do whatever they want.[26]

Like in the first U.S. Marine invasion of Haiti under President Woodrow Wilson in 1917, U.S. military advisors were given a desk in most of the country's ministries (Interior, Education, Justice, Foreign Affairs, Finance, Tourism and Information). A Pennsylvania banker inside the Finance Ministry who worked previously in Panama and Kuwait helped open up the Central Bank.[27] The Clinton administration pushed for the institution of a structural adjustment program that included the sale of public utilities and publicly owned businesses and reduced the already pitifully inadequate public services.[28]

Funding was poured into the private sector through a program directed by Ira Lowenthal, an American anthropologist with connections in the Haitian business community whom a former Aristide aide likened to the "new governor of Haiti." Scores of labor unions and neighborhood groups were coopted, shifting from demanding higher wages and denouncing U.S. imperialism to thanking Bill Clinton for intervening in Haiti. Clinton's Deputy Secretary of State, and old Oxford pal, Strobe Talbot, explained in 1995 that: "Even after our [military] exit in February 1996, we will remain in charge by means of the USAID and the private sector."[29]

When Aristide tried to raise the minimum wage from $1 a day, the Clinton administration blocked him; a USAID official stated that Haiti "wasn't ready to consider an increase in the minimum wage."[30] The Clinton administration further thwarted every effort by Aristide to prosecute crimes committed during the coup regime of Raoul Cédras and worked to limit the power of the national commission for truth and justice, which Aristide established in March 1995 to investigate human rights abuses under the coup regime.

With Aristide's abolishment of the Haitian army, the Clinton administration replicated an old Cold War strategy of ramping up funding for the national police, which was then equipped with military style weapons and mobilized against Aristide.[31] The training was headed by Raymond Kelly, a Vietnam combat veteran who had promoted high-tech surveillance and stop and frisk policies as New York City Police Commissioner (1992–1994; 2002–2013) that led to an expansion of racial profiling.[32]

Guy Phillippe, a key commander in the Haitian police with whom Kelly worked, was known for his links to the drug trade and involvement in human rights violations in the post-1991 coup period. Retired U.S. Sergeant Stan Goff, who led a Special Forces team in Haiti in autumn 1994, confirmed that the CIA was recruiting sympathetic members of the former military into the new civilian police force throughout 1994 and 1995. More than 50 percent of the top police commissioners were recycled Haitian army personnel, while a group of reformist army officers who had refused to support the 1991 coup were purged.[33]

In September 1996, *The New York Times* reported that while most U.S. troops had left Haiti, the U.S. continued to be deeply involved in the day-to-day management of this country—and relied on the unilateral application of force to achieve its objectives. The U.S. seemed to be mounting a parallel security and support system, with Haiti's reluctant compliance, in order to turn Haiti into what one diplomat described as an "American protectorate."[34]

Jane Regan wrote in *CovertAction Quarterly* about a "permanent irreversible invasion" run by USAID, the World Bank and National Endowment for Democracy (NED), whose troops were technicians and experts, furthered by weapons development projects and lots of money, which was spent with the goal of "bringing Haiti into the 'new world order' appendaged to the U.S. as a source for markets and cheap labor."[35]

USAID's Haiti programs tellingly focused on agribusiness and U.S. investment rather than peasant farming, thereby undermining food security. The agency held up an allotment of aid until Haiti's cement and flour mills were sold, and hired a public-relations firm to sell the virtues of privatization to the Haitian public.[36]

In 1996, Aristide was succeeded by René Préval, who advanced privatization initiatives that sold off public assets to wealthy investors. Countering such policies, Aristide co-authored *Eyes of the Heart: Seeking a Path for the Poor in the Age of Globalization* (2000), which accused the IMF and World Bank of working on behalf of wealthy nations rather than the poor. He called for "a culture of global solidarity" to eliminate poverty and as an alternative to "neoliberal" economic policies championed by the U.S.[37] After having returned to power, Aristide was once again removed and exiled to South Africa in a 2004 coup backed by the Bush administration. These events were a culmination of the decade and a half U.S. campaign of intervention against him and his left-wing ideals.

Clinton's lack of regard for human rights was apparent in his administration's treatment of Haitian refugees trying to come to the United States. During the 1992 presidential campaign, Clinton had condemned the Bush administration's use of the U.S. Coast Guard to return Haitian refugees escaping the vicious post-coup government and poverty on the island as "cruel." However, in June 1993, once again he broke a promise by announcing his continuation of Bush's policy.[38] It wasn't as if he didn't recognize, at the time, what was cruel.

Clinton went further than Bush by instituting mandatory HIV testing and then segregating those who tested positive. He then created the world's first HIV detention camp at Guantanamo Bay, where conditions were horrible. As political analyst Nathan J. Robinson described it, the facility was a "leaky barracks with poor sanitation, surrounded by razor wire and guard towers," and was overrun with snakes, lizards and scorpions.

Refugees that were gravely ill were deprived life-saving medical care, resulting in a huge number "unnecessary early deaths." When the detainees mounted a hunger strike, the ringleader was put in solitary confinement. One refugee recalled that

> we had been asking them to remove the barbed wire; the children were playing near it, they were falling and injured themselves. The food they were serving us, including canned chicken, had maggots in it. And yet they insisted we eat it. . . . And it was for these reasons that we started holding demonstrations. In response they began to beat us.[39]

Clinton has never apologized for all this, despite the fact that a judge called the treatment of the refugees "outrageous, callous and reprehensible" while criticizing Clinton for imposing on refugees "the kind of indefinite detention usually reserved for spies and murderers. . . . The Haitians' plight is a tragedy of immense proportion and their continued detainment is totally unacceptable to this court."[40]

Given the foregoing, it is not surprising that during the 2016 election Donald Trump would state that the Clinton name was not well received in Haiti. Clinton compounded his poor reputation there during the 2010 earthquake when he used his position as head of the Interim Haiti Recovery Commission (IHRC) team to help secure government contracts for donors to the Clinton Foundation and other cronies like Hillary's brother Hugh Rodham. This was a part of a "reconstruction gold rush," as a cable from the U.S. ambassador at the time, Kenneth Merten, described it, which enriched foreign companies and investors, often at the expense of the local population.[41]

In 2011, *The Nation* reported that makeshift trailers provided by the Clinton Foundation, which were to be used as temporary classrooms and hurricane-proof shelters, had been badly built and contained dangerous levels of formaldehyde. The company that built them, Clayton Homes, had been sued by the U.S. government after Hurricane Katrina in New Orleans for providing similarly defective trailers. Clayton Homes was owned by Berkshire Hathaway, the holding company owned by Warren Buffet, one of the notable private sector members of the Clinton Global Initiative, and a prominent Clinton dynasty supporter and fundraiser.[42] This incident epitomizes the consequences of a pay to play political system, where corrupt players use their political connections to gain wealth, and the people of impoverished countries like Haiti are left to suffer.

Hammering Fidel: Clinton and Cuba

With Cuba's economy devastated by the collapse of the Soviet Union, a triumphalist spirit prevailed in Washington as the Clinton administration saw an opportunity to achieve the long-held U.S. goal of regime change. Shortly after Clinton took office, Secretary of State Warren Christopher gave voice to the administration's perspective when he said that "Cuba's failure was everywhere and for all to see" with the "desperate flight of Cuban refugees crossing treacherous seas in flimsy rafts." According to Christopher, Cubans were "seeing their economy collapse, suffocated by the state's centralized control over all aspects of life and squandering of their resources on a bloated military machine. Now without the $6 billion in in annual Soviet aid that once kept Cuba's economy afloat, Cuba is in dramatic free-fall. The regime has lost its allies, its subsidies, its lifeline "as Castro continues to rule through oppression and repression." But Cubans should "not be left behind while their neighbors all prosper."[43]

Clinton himself had a history of hostility to the Cuban revolution and refugee population (see chapter 1), which continued during his presidency. He endorsed a bill by Senator Robert Torricelli (D-NJ) pushing for an expanded embargo on Cuba that would block other countries from trading with it. Torricelli claimed that the law would "cause Castro to fall within weeks" because Cuba's economy had already been severely debilitated by the collapse of the Soviet Union.[44]

In a 1993 interview, an anonymous Clinton staffer told researchers Peter Kornbluh and Philip Brenner that Clinton's Cuba policy was made by the political staff and not foreign policy specialists. During the 1992 presidential campaign, Clinton allegedly had been propositioned by Jorge Mas Canosa, head of the powerful Cuban American National Foundation (CANF), that if he endorsed Torricelli's bill, Canosa would provide entry for him into Little Havana's wealthy political world. Clinton subsequently spoke at a fundraiser in Miami on April 23 which netted him over $100,000. He said that he liked the Torricelli bill and that the Bush administration had "missed a big opportunity to put the hammer down on Fidel Castro."[45]

In the election, Clinton won twenty percent of the Cuban American vote, an increase from the 5% won by Michael Dukakis in 1988.[46] Canosa later vetoed Clinton's nomination of Mario Baeza as Assistant Secretary of State for Inter-American Affairs because he was allegedly soft on Castro. At a 1994 Miami fundraiser, the Democratic National Committee got over $500,000 from Cuban Americans, whose votes were crucial to Clinton's 1996 re-election campaign in Florida.[47]

Clinton returned the favor by not only expanding the embargo on Cuba but also adopting measures to heighten travel restrictions and reduce remittances. The CIA continued to provide weapons and explosives to paramilitary groups in Florida, which launched at least one terrorist attack on Cuba in October 1994, ending in the death of a fisherman and capture of the attackers by Cuban authorities.[48] On December 26, 1996, Cuba accused the U.S. of staging a biological attack by using a crop duster to spread insects over the island.[49] When 30,000 refugees tried to flee the island because of its economic collapse, Clinton agreed to increase the number of legal Cuban immigrants allowed into the U.S. annually while permitting the U.S. Coast Guard to halt those who attempted to enter illegally (i.e.. by raft). Those interdicted at sea were sent either to another country or to the U.S. naval base at Guantanamo Bay.

On March 12, 1996, Clinton signed the Helms-Burton bill into law, tightening the U.S. embargo against Cuba further and permitting Cubans who had become U.S. citizens to sue in U.S. courts anyone who had purchased property once belonging to them in Cuba but was then confiscated by the Castro regime after the revolution. Fidel Castro characterized Helms-Burton as a "shameful act" paving the way for "economic genocide." It increased support for Cuban exile groups, barred trade with Cuba by any U.S. company regardless of where it was based, and made it official U.S. policy to support regime change in Cuba. NED, AID, and the CIA consequently intensified their coordinated programs targeting Cuban civil society.[50]

Clinton initially opposed Helms-Burton but changed his mind after the Cuban Air Force shot down two civilian aircraft attempting to shower the island with anti-Castro leaflets, which Cuba claimed had violated Cuban air space.[51] The Helms–Burton Act was opposed by the National Association of Manufacturers (NAM) and European-American Chamber of Commerce, which saw it as a threat to U.S. export markets and investment, and felt it would clog the courts and be costly for U.S. taxpayers.[52] The Council of Europe, the European Union, Britain, Canada, Mexico, Brazil, Argentina and other U.S. allies believed that it ran counter to the spirit of international law and sovereignty.[53]

Syndicated columnist Mike Royko wrote an alternative speech in which Clinton acknowledged that the aircraft that were shot down after trying to shower the island with anti-Castro leaflets had no right to violate Cuban air space and admitted that the Miami Cubans wanted to return to the pre-Castro order during which they and their elders had "prospered as part of the wealthy class that supported dictator Fulgencio Batista."

Royko wrote that

> with Batista—with his graft, corruption gambling, prostitution, and police death squads—there was something for everyone from the American mafia to the big sugar companies to the elite class of Cubans. Something for everyone but the peasant class and the students who challenged the evil they saw. Ah, the good old days.[54]

Of course, Clinton would never have given this speech, because the Miami Cubans would have then called him an enemy of freedom if he had, pulled their support, and Clinton would have lost the forthcoming election.

Covering Up for Atrocities in Central America—and Supporting Yet More

Bill Clinton clearly would have been implicated in the Iran-Contra scandal if a full-investigation into his activities as Governor of Arkansas had ever been carried out. It was not surprising, then, that during his presidency, Clinton's administration would undertake "damage control" and seek to whitewash U.S. government crimes during the 1980s in Central America. Iran-Contra whistleblower Al Martin points out that Clinton retained the unusually high number of 1,100 Reagan and Bush era officials, over two thirds of whom had been alleged, during a congressional hearing or some lawsuit, to have been involved in the Iran-Contra coverup, the destruction of documents, or manipulation of witnesses.[55]

While apologizing for U.S. support for military dictatorships over three decades in Guatemala, Clinton administration officials repeatedly denied information to U.S. lawyer Jennifer Harbury regarding the fate of her husband, a Guatemalan guerrilla commander who had been tortured and killed by an army colonel and former paid agent of the CIA during Guatemala's dirty wars in the 1980s.[56] The Pentagon at the same continued to finance Guatemala's army and intelligence services, which dominated the civilian administration, under the pretext of antidrug operations.[57]

In July 1993, Secretary of State Warren Christopher commissioned a report on U.S. policy in El Salvador in the 1980s which a number of prominent Democratic Congressmen explicitly called a "whitewash." Though criticizing the State Department's handling of the El Mozote massacre, in which 900 civilians were killed by a U.S.-trained El Salvadoran army unit, the report accepted as legitimate U.S. policy objectives and rejected accusations that U.S. diplomatic officials regularly lied to Congress about human rights violations in order to maintain the flow of military aid, and even complimented Washington for promoting human rights in El Salvador.[58]

George S. Vest, who directed the report, stated that

> in principle, in my heart, I'm with the people who wanted human rights to be our sole priority but in the real world, you don't have the luxury of having an absolute choice. The essential test is: to what extent did the policy succeed? This policy hasn't succeeded

> totally but it's made some progress. El Salvador is a much better place to live in than it was when all this started.[59]

Vermont Senator Patrick J. Leahy stated that the report "glosse[d] over the lies, half-truths and evasion that we came to expect from the State Department during that period"—an assessment that was corroborated by a UN Truth Commission finding that U.S. backed Salvadoran armed forces and allied paramilitary groups were responsible for most of the 13,562 reported murders and disappearances during El Salvador's civil war.[60]

When Joe Moakley (D-MA) requested the declassification of Justice Department documents related to subjects explored in the Truth Commission, including U.S. support for Salvadoran death squads, and an FBI investigation of the right-wing National Republican Alliance (ARENA) party's fundraising in the U.S., the Clinton administration stonewalled him. Alexander Watson, the Assistant Secretary of State for Inter-American Affairs, at the same time cast aspersions on the credibility of the diplomatic cables that the Clinton administration did release, which showed that a 1981 kidnapping plot targeting the head of Salvador's football federation had been hatched in the home of Salvadoran president Armando Calderón Sol (1994–1999) of the ARENA Party.[61]

A wealthy lawyer who had been part of a seven-man neofascist group under the direction of Roberto D'Aubuisson that carried out death squad activities and acts of terrorism in the 1980s, Sol was favored by Clinton over Ruben Zamora, his left-wing Farabundo Marti National Liberation Front (FMLN) rival in Salvador's 1994 elections, because of Sol's promise to extend the market liberalization policies of his predecessor, Alfredo Cristiani (1989–1994). The latter came to include: a) privatization of El Salvador's banking, telecommunications and electrical sectors along with public hospitals and pension funds, b) expansion of intellectual property rights to the benefit of foreign investors; c) reduction of tariffs, d) initiation of plans for the institution of the Central American Free Trade Agreement (CAFTA) by 2005 as the Clinton administration wanted, and e) the removal of protection for local agriculture, which forced farmers to seek employment in low-wage maquiladoras set up for the benefit of multinational corporations.[62]

These policies combined with the slashing of public services caused a spike in inequality, the growth of criminal gangs, and a flood of migration to the U.S. that Clinton dealt with harshly.[63] Clinton enjoyed close relations with Sol's successor, Francisco Flores Pérez of the ARENA party, who adopted the U.S. dollar as El Salvador's currency and allowed the U.S. Southern Command beginning in August 2000 to fly aircraft out of the Comalapa air base near San Salvador under the pretext of the War on Drugs.[64]

Throughout the 1990s, Clinton extended over $50 million in police aid to El Salvador through the State Department's International Criminal Investigative Training Assistance Program (ICITAP). He did this even though the ARENA government under Cristiani (a former Monsanto employee who was forced to flee to Italy after an arrest warrant was issued to him for his involvement in the murder of six Jesuit priests) had violated 1992 peace agreements by allowing former members of the Treasury Police and National Guard linked to human rights abuses and death squads in the 1980s to join a revamped national police force, which was supposed to have been demilitarized and depoliticized. Human Rights Watch subsequently documented a rise in political murders of FMLN leaders and U.S. funding for a specialized investigative police and anti-narcotics unit that had a history of human rights abuses.[65]

Trying to Undo the Sandinista Revolution

In the case of Nicaragua, rather than encouraging a process of national reconciliation between the left-wing Sandinistas and right-wing Contras who had fought in the 1980s war, Clinton's State Department, under the pressure of Congress, withheld aid in a manner that exacerbated divisions and made resolution of problems like those related to the redistribution of property more difficult. President Rafael Angel Calderon of Costa Rica said U.S. policy "only helped worsen the situation in Nicaragua," while his foreign minister said the policy made the region "feel punished."[66]

In Nicaragua's 1996 election, the Clinton administration predictably sided against former Sandinista revolutionary leader Daniel Ortega, Ronald Reagan's old nemesis, whom *The Wall Street Journal* described as a "fire-breathing Yanqui hater and sworn enemy of oligarchs."[67] State Department spokesman Nicholas Burns chided Ortega for "not being a democrat," stating that while "we do believe in redemption," we also "remember the past."[68] Nicaraguans remembered the past too; and many considered Ortega a hero for leading the 1979 revoution against Somoza tyranny.[69] To counter Ortega, the Clinton administration supported conservative Arnoldo Alemán, a darling of the anti-Castro Cuban lobby and right-wing Nicaraguan exile community, who would be sentenced to a 20-year prison term in 2003 for money laundering, embezzlement and corruption.[70]

A coffee grower and lawyer, Alemán had been arrested in 1980 for counter-revolutionary activities and claimed to have been interrogated and psychologically tortured by Sandinista interior minister Tomas Borge. He also claimed that while he was imprisoned in 1989, his family's farm was expropriated by the Sandinista government. After his election as mayor of Managua in 1990, Alemán was unremitting in his opposition to the Sandinistas. One of his first acts was to wash off revolutionary Sandinista murals of workers and peasants. He also turned off the gas to the eternal flame on the grave of Carlos Fonseca, a Sandinista martyr, causing Sandinistas to retaliate by destroying the mayor's office.[71]

President Alemán continued his mission of undoing the legacy of the Sandinistas by pushing for the privatization of state-run industries, and reduction of social services and tariffs like his counterparts in El Salvador while restoring property rights, courting foreign investors and solidifying good relations with the U.S.[72] The Clinton administration supported these latter objectives, which reversed social improvements during the period of Sandinista rule when public expenditures on health care and education increased dramatically.[73]

The American embassy in Managua acknowledged, ironically, that while liberalizing economic reforms had helped stabilize Nicaragua's currency and brought inflation under control, the "anticipated economic growth [under Alemán] had failed to materialize."[74] Three out of four Nicaraguans at the time lived in poverty and not one in two had steady work.[75] Failing to reverse these numbers, U.S. aid programs in Nicaragua and the rest of Central America were primarily designed like in the Cold War to undercut the left, build markets for U.S. exports and to support privatization initiatives designed to open up new opportunities for U.S. corporations.[76] By the late 1990s, 51% of Central American exports to the U.S. were concentrated in maquiladora production (entailing sweat shop wages and poor working conditions), mainly clothing, while 37 percent consisted of agricultural production.[77]

The Clinton administration did adopt some progressive initiatives in Central America, such as a program to provide land and vocational and academic training to ex-FMLN combatants in El Salvador whose purpose was in part to strengthen the peace process.[78] Clinton also earned plaudits in Nicaragua when he met with the victims of Hurricane Mitch, giving a speech pledging $120 million to build temporary shelters, medical care and remove land mines uprooted by torrential rains beneath a volcano that was still scarred by a hurricane induced mudslide that buried two villages.[79] However, overall not that much had changed from the Cold War; money designated to election monitoring, for example, tended to be directed towards right-wing political parties and for programs designed to monitor human rights violations committed by left-wing groups.[80]

Countering Peru's Shining Path: CIA "Superman" to the Rescue

From 1993–1998, the highest total of U.S. aid to Latin America went to Peru. Its President Alberto Fujimori inaugurated large scale privatization and tax reduction policies in the mining sector where U.S. corporations such as Phelps Dodge had billions in investments. Providing telephoto cameras, listening devices, night-vision goggles and a video camera that could be concealed in a briefcase, the CIA directed a Phoenix style operation led by an agent nicknamed "Superman" against the Maoist Sendero Luminoso, resulting in the disappearance of thousands.[81]

"Superman" headed the training, equipping, and financing of the police counterinsurgency unit that captured Sendero leader Abimael Guzman Reynoso. CIA agents allegedly went through the trash of a local grocery store, which aided them in locating Guzman's whereabouts. Benedicto Jimenez, another one of the heads of the police counterinsurgency unit that hunted Reynoso, told *The Washington Post* that "they [the CIA agents] were very close to us.... Without that support, it would have been a bit difficult to get where we got."[82]

Sendero was known among Latin American leftist organizations for its violent attacks against civilians that ultimately discredited its cause, though the army and police bear considerable blame for instigating the vicious cycle of violence and often outdoing Sendero in their brutality. A lot of the military aid in the counterinsurgency campaign was packaged as part of the War on Drugs. The Clinton administration provided fixed wing aircraft and high-altitude surveillance and satellite imagery of coca cultivation areas through a radar station at Iquitos. American intelligence also monitored movement of planes and then gave orders to Peruvians to shoot them down. Investigation into the killing of an American family in one incident revealed that airspace surveillance had been contracted to a private firm located at Maxwell Air Force base, prompting *the Guardian* to characterize the antinarcotics campaign as a "war of mercenaries."[83]

Colombia: Another Dirty War

The Clinton administration supported another dirty war against the leftist Fuerzas Armada Revolucionario de Colombia (FARC), providing over $1 billion in military assistance, including eavesdropping equipment and satellite intelligence used to track down rebel commanders deep in the jungle along with GPS guidance kits and smart bombs ("Puff the Magic Dragon"), which were launched from Vietnam vintage AC-47 gunships.[84]

When Clinton traveled to Colombia, he was accompanied by Gary Drummond, an Alabama coal baron who faced lawsuits for paying right-wing paramilitary fighters to terrorize the population along the 120-mile rail line from Drummond's two mines—valued at $7.5 billion—to their port on the Caribbean. The paramilitaries tortured and killed innocent people to keep them from giving haven to left-wing FARC rebels who had bombed the railway leading to Drummond's mines in response to their displacement of locals and poisoning of the local environment. A Drummond employee was convicted of arranging for the paramilitaries to kill two Drummond Co. union leaders, Valmore Locarno and Victor Orcasita.[85]

In October 1999, the Colombian president presiding over the dirty war, Andrés Pastrana, traveled to Houston, Texas to meet with oil, gas and electricity industry executives and asked for their assistance to defeat FARC in return for generous concessions in Colombia.[86] President Clinton, for his part, warned Pastrana not to make a deal with FARC as a precondition for the aid package. When Pastrana revealed that his government would allow FARC to control a demilitarized zone as part of its peace talks, a U.S. State Department official noted that "the peace process has frightened the heck out of people [in Washington]."[87] This was because, as a congressional aide put it, "every pirate, bandit—everyone who wants to make money on [the] war—they're in Colombia."[88]

The pirates included the Houston-based energy giant Enron, which owned Centragas, a 357-mile natural gas distribution system in northern Colombia, and Los Angeles-based Occidental Oil—which held controlling interests in the Cano-Limon Convenas oil field and pipeline running from the Venezuelan border. Occidental employed security contractors who participated in counterinsurgency operations against the leftist National Liberation Army (ELN) and FARC and made payments to the Colombian army. Vice President Al Gore, who supported Plan Colombia, happened to have over $500,000 worth of family stocks in Occidental, which contributed at least $250,000 to the Clinton-Gore ticket.[89] The company's founder, Armand Hammer, had been a key benefactor of Gore's political career, along with that of his father, Senator, Al Gore Sr.[90]

In June 2001, a Colombian court heard how an American security firm working for Occidental had played a fatal role in an ill-starred army raid against FARC, "directing helicopter gunships that mistakenly killed eighteen civilians."[91] This was a notable example of the nexus between large corporations, the Colombian government and army, and Clinton administration officials who were complicit in egregious human rights crimes.

Neoliberalism, Authoritarianism and Corruption

In the last four years of his presidency, Clinton's administration increased military and police aid to Bolivia, Colombia, Mexico, and Peru collectively from $161 million (1996) to $977 million (2000).[92] These totals reflected the growing militarization of U.S. foreign policy and the fact that, even with the destruction of the Left during the Cold War, neoliberal economic policies could be continuously sustained only by force and repression.[93]

In April 1995, Brazilian president Fernando Enrique Cardoso, a close Clinton ally who dismantled the state sector and liberalized Brazil's oil industry, tellingly signed a $1.4 billion contract with a consortium of firms led by Raytheon to build a technologically sophisticated Amazon surveillance system (SIVAM), which Clinton said underscored the growing partnership between the U.S. and Brazil.[94] SIVAM was put to use in an offensive against the rural landless movement (MST) that had 150 of its members killed during Cardoso's presidency.[95]

Besides Cardoso, one of Clinton's most stalwart regional allies was Bolivian president Gonzalo Sanchez de Lozada (1993–1997), a multimillionaire mining executive and protégé of Chicago School economist Milton Friedman. He caused thousands to lose their jobs through ill-conceived privatization and austerity measures and was later indicted for repressing popular protests in which 68 people were killed and over 400 injured, mostly from the indigenous Aymara community.[96] As if back in the days of William H. Taft's dollar diplomacy, "Goni" allowed U.S. companies to purchase Bolivia's electric company and major portions of the oil company, with Enron and Shell financing a gas pipeline project.[97]

Another Clinton favorite was Argentine President Carlos Menem (1989–1999), who privatized Yacimientos Petrolíferos Fiscales (YPF), the oldest nationalized oil company outside the Soviet Union. A flamboyant playboy who married a Miss Universe thirty-five years his junior, Menem was sentenced to seven years in prison for illegally smuggling more than 6,000 tons of military weapons to Croatia—which was then under an arms embargo. A staunch anticommunist and proponent of the Washington Consensus, Menem further pardoned leaders of Argentina's military dictatorship (1976–1983) that kidnapped, tortured, and "disappeared" left-wing activists and aligned Argentina's foreign policy almost completely with the U.S., leaving the non-aligned movement and supporting the U.S.-NATO bombing of Kosovo.[98]

When U.S. Secretary of State Warren Christopher called Menem's economic minister, Domingo Cavallo—who imposed a "made in Wall Street" plan for the economy that included the removal of tariffs and subsidies and privatization of 90 percent of formerly state-owned firms—a "hero," Raul Alfonsín, the leader of the opposition Radical Civic Union (UCR) said that Christopher's statements provided "the best acknowledgment that the adjustment plan furthered by the Menem administration is tailor made for U.S. interests." According to Alfonsín, the adjustment policy was a disaster for Argentines; it had "plunged [them] into hunger and unemployment, whereas in the U.S. thousands of new jobs have been created, so no wonder Cavallo is dubbed a hero!"[99]

In Venezuela, when socialist Hugo Chavez won elections in 1998, the NED began heavily funding members of the opposition to subvert Chavez' rule and support a referendum to unseat him.[100] Chavez' predecessor, Rafael Caldera (1969–1974; 1993–1998), had earned plaudits for opening Venezuela's petroleum sector to foreign investment and enacting a sweeping privatization initiative—including in the banking and insurance sectors—that created tremendous trade and investment opportunities for U.S. companies. Chavez sought to limit these in the interests of the Venezuelan people.[101]

Speaking at the tomb of Simon Bolivar—before a plaza that was two-thirds empty—Clinton praised Caldera for playing a "key role" in Latin America's unfolding "quiet revolution" that had "left Cuba the only dictatorship in the hemisphere."[102] No matter that *The Washington Post* had earlier reported on Caldera's suspension of basic constitutional rights after he introduced wrenching austerity measures that triggered street protests.[103] The U.S. State Department further reported "serious human rights problems," including extrajudicial killings and torture by Venezuelan police and military forces, which received around $11.5 million per year from the Clinton administration under the War on Drugs. Many of the abuses were committed while combating Colombian guerrillas along with narcotraffickers in operations, which Chavez' government halted.[104]

Triggering the Pink Tide

As Clinton's first term was taking shape, then-National Security Advisor Anthony Lake wrote that the aim of U.S. policy in the Americas would be the "enlargement" of the area within which free markets and free elections held sway. It was understood by all the relevant players, of course, that what was really being enlarged was the scope of U.S. influence.

The North American Congress on Latin America (NACLA) concluded that "free markets" have not meant the free circulation of goods and services as much as the opening of Western Hemisphere economies to (mostly U.S.-based) transnational investment, bringing low-cost, tax-free production and the easy movement of goods and capital—but not workers—across national borders. According to NACLA, "'Free elections'—important as they are after years of brutal dictatorships in much of the hemisphere—have not allowed sovereign peoples to choose among alternate futures, as much as they have given voters the ability to choose among alternate managers of a U.S.-dominated hemispheric system."[105]

Bill Clinton indeed may have put a more liberal and progressive gloss on U.S. foreign policy in Latin America, but what he instituted were policies that were designed to secure U.S. hemispheric dominance and facilitate the "Third conquest" of the continent by multinational corporations. Venezuela's *El Nacional* aptly editorialized that "the devastating effects in Latin America of the push for open markets and liberalization force the poor either to emigrate to the U.S. or resort to harvesting the coca leaf, poppies or marijuana."[106]

By the dawn of the 21st Century, left-wing forces that had been crushed by U.S.-backed state terror in the 1960s, 1970s and 1980s were reascending. Hugo Chavez's election victory in 1998 helped ignite a left-wing tide that saw election of such progressives as Evo Morales (Bolivia 2005), Lula (Brazil, 2003), Nestor Kirchner (Argentina, 2003), Rafael Correa (Ecuador, 2007), Danel Ortega (Nicaragua, 2007), Fernando Lugo (Paraguay, 2008) and other leaders who attempted to establish greater political-economic autonomy for their people.

Endnotes

1 McLarty, who admitted that he had not mastered Spanish, had been CEO in the 1980s of the Arkansas-Louisiana Gas Company (Arkla) whose executives were accused of taking illicit bribes and overcharging Oklahoma residents for heating, costing them between $35 and $65 million. McLarty later went to work for Kissinger Associates. "Oklahoma Natural Gas Charges Tied to Clinton White House," https://www.oklahomaconstitution.com/ns.php?nid=113

2 "Clinton's First South American Stop: Venezuela," *CNN*, October 13, 1997; Bill Clinton letter to Ike Shelton, November 6, 1997, William J. Clinton Presidential Library, digital collection, Clinton South American Trips. James Brooke, "Venezuela Proposes Opening Oil Industry to Private Investment," *The New York Times*, April 28, 1994; Steve Ellner, "Venezuela: The Politics of Privatization," *NACLA*, September 25, 2007, https://nacla.org/article/venezuela-politics-privatization. The austerity program and law loosening restrictions on foreign investment was written by Teodoro Petkoff, a former leftist guerrilla who was targeted by USAID's Office of Public Safety in the early 1970s.

3 https://clinton.presidentiallibraries.us/items/show/94005

4 "Bill Clinton's Marketing Approach," Clinton Presidential Library, digital collection, Clinton South American Trips, https://clinton.presidentiallibraries.us/items/show/94005

5 Micah Morrison, "Drugs, Money and Justice," *The Wall Street Journal*, September 17, 1998.

6 "Clinton in South America: Some Good Will and Gains on Trade," Clinton Presidential Library, digital collection, Clinton South American Trips, https://clinton.presidentiallibraries.us/items/show/94005

7 "Clinton's Tango Won't Conquer Latin America," Clinton Presidential Library, digital collection, Clinton South American Trips, https://clinton.presidentiallibraries.us/items/show/94005

8 Stephen Schlesinger, "Ghosts of Guatemala's Past," *The New York Times*, June 3, 2011.

9 James Bennet, "U.S. Respects Brazil, Clinton Assures Latin Giant," *The New York Times*, October 15, 1997, https://www.nytimes.com/1997/10/15/world/us-respects-brazil-clinton-assures-latin-giant.html; James Petras and Harry Veltemeyer, *Cardoso's Brazil: A Land For Sale* (New York: Rowman & Littlefield, 2003).

10 See David Sheinin, "The New Dollar Diplomacy in Latin America," *American Studies International*, 37, 3 (October 1999), 81–99.

11 Wade Boese, "Clinton Ends Twenty Year Ban on High-Tech Arms to Latin America," https://www.armscontrol.org/act/1997-08/press-releases/clinton-ends-20-year-ban-high-tech-arms-latin-america

12 Boese, "Clinton Ends Twenty Year Ban on High-Tech Arms to Latin America."

13 Greg Grandin, *Empire's Workshop: The U.S., Latin America, and the Rise of the New Imperialism* (New York: Metropolitan Books, 2005), 188.

14 Sheinin, "The New Dollar Diplomacy in Latin America."

15 David Scott Palmer, *U.S. Relations with Latin America During the Clinton Years: Opportunities Lost or Opportunities Squandered?* (Gainesville: University Press of Florida, 2006), 86. Trade volume increased by some 243% between 1990 and 1998 from $110 billion to $367 billion.

16 "Bill Clinton's Trade Policies Destroyed Haitian Rice Farming," *Democracy Now*, October 11, 2016, https://www.democracynow.org/2016/10/11/bill_clinton_s_trade_policies_destroyed

17 Nathan J. Robinson, *Super Predator: Bill Clinton's Use & Abuse of Black America* (Sommerville, MA: Current Affairs Press, 2016), 188, 189, 190; Maura R. O'Connor, "Subsidizing Starvation: How American Tax Dollars are Keeping Arkansas Rice Growers Fat on the Farm and Starving Millions of Haitians," *Foreign Policy* (January 11, 2013), https://foreignpolicy.com/2013/01/11/subsidizing-starvation/

18 See Peter Hallward, *Damming the Flood: Haiti and the Politics of Containment* (London: Verso, 2007).

19 Quoted in David N. Bossie, *Intelligence Failure: How Clinton's National Security Policy Set the Stage for 9/11* (Nashville, TN: WND Books, 2004), 23.

20 Timothy J. Lynch, *In the Shadow of the Cold War: American Foreign Policy from George Bush Sr. to Donald Trump* (New York: Cambridge University Press, 2020), 63.

21 Anthony Lewis, "We Did it Right: Why all the Carping About the Haiti Mission," *The New York Times*, September 30, 1994.

22 Michael Tomasky, *Bill Clinton* (New York: Times Books, 2017), 45.

23 See e.g. Jack Reed (D-RI) to President William J. Clinton, May 19, 1994, William J. Clinton Presidential Library, digital Collection, U.S. intervention in Haiti, https://clinton.presidentiallibraries.us/items/show/67854; Byron Dorgan to President William J. Clinton, August 16, 1994, William J. Clinton Presidential Library,

digital collection, U.S. intervention in Haiti, https://clinton.presidentiallibraries.us/items/show/67857; Anthony Lake and Susan Brophy, memo to the President, "Congressional Letters Opposing Haiti Intervention," October 13, 1994, https://clinton.presidentiallibraries.us/items/show/67859. Many in Congress had opposed the intervention out of fear it would result in a quagmire like Somalia. Senator Jack Reed (D-RI) felt that Haiti's military regime could be undermined effectively through economic sanctions. The AFL-CIO supported the intervention after raising concern about the killing of trade union activists by Haiti's military junta.

24 Jane Regan, "Aftermath of Invasion: A.I.D.ing U.S. Interests in Haiti," *CovertAction Quarterly*, 51 (Winter 1994–1995), 10.

25 "Report: U.S. Helped Start Violent Anti-Aristide Groups, Lisa Hamm, AP News writer," White House Situation Room, William J. Clinton Presidential Library, U.S. Intervention in Haiti, https://clinton.presidentiallibraries.us/items/show/67885; Allan Nairn, "Our Man in FRAPH: Behind Haiti's Paramilitaries," *The Nation Magazine*, October 24, 1994.

26 Hallward, *Damming the Flood.*

27 Jane Regan, "The Occupation's Best Kept Secret," *CovertAction Quarterly,* 51 (winter 1994–1995), 13.

28 Hallward, *Damming the Flood*, 61; Regan, "A.I.D.ing U.S. Interests in Haiti," 12.

29 Hallward, *Damning the Flood,* 61; Regan, "A.I.D.ing U.S. Interests in Haiti," 56.

30 Hallward, *Damming the Flood*, 61.

31 Hallward, *Damning the Flood,* 67. For continuity with the Cold War, see Jeremy Kuzmarov, *Modernizing Repression: Police Training and Nation Building in the American Century* (Amherst, MA: University of Massachusetts Press, 2012).

32 Lieberman quoted in Chris Francescani, "NYPD's Ray Kelly Oversaw Transformative Era in NY Policing," *Reuters*, December 28, 2013, reuters.com/articles/us-usa-newyork-kelly/nypds-ray-kelly-oversaw-transofmrative-era-in-ny-policing. The executive director of the American Civil Liberties Union in New York criticized Kelly for invoking national security as a pretext for "unbridled policing operations" that threatened to "make the fears of George Orwell seem quaint."

33 Hallward, *Damming the Flood*, 67.

34 Larry Rohter, "U.S. is Recruiting American Police to Join UN Force in Haiti," *The New York Times,* October 2, 1996, letter from Michelle Karshan, January 29, 2007.

35 Regan, "A.I.D.ing U.S. Interests in Haiti," 12.

36 Lisa Haugaard, "Development Aid: Some Smal Steps Forward," *NACLA,* September 25, 2007, https://nacla.org/article/development-aid-some-small-steps-forward

37 Jean-Bertrand Aristide and Laura Flynn, *Eyes of the Heart: Seeking a Path for the Poor in the Age of Globalization* (Monroe, ME: Common Courage Press, 2000).

38 Robert A. Pastor, "The Clinton Administration and the Americas: The Postwar Rhythm and Blues," *Journal of Inter-American Studies and World Affairs*, 38, 4 (Winter 1996), 99–128.

39 Robinson, *Super Predator*, 188, 189, 190.

40 Robinson, *Super Predator*, 190.

41 See Antony Loewenstein, *Disaster Capitalism: Making a Killing Out of*

Catastrophe (London: Verso, 2015), 107, 108, 115, 116; Peter Schweizer, *Clinton Cash: The Untold Story of How and Why Foreign Governments and Businesses Helped Make Bill and Hillary Rich* (New York: Harper, 2016).

42 Loewenstein, *Disaster Capitalism*, 118; Isabel McDonald and Isabeau Doucet, "The Shelters That Clinton Built," *The Nation Magazine*, August 1, 2011.

43 Clintonpresidentiallibrary.us/items/show/10049

44 Robert Pastor, "The Clinton Administration and the Americas: The Postwar Rhythm and Blues," *Journal of Inter-American Studies and World Affairs*, 38, 4 (Winter 1996), 99–128.

45 Philip Brenner and Peter Kornbluh, "Clinton's Cuba Calculus," *North American Congress on Latin America*, September 25, 2007.

46 David Scott Palmer, *U.S. Relations with Latin America During the Clinton Years: Opportunities Lost or Opportunities Squandered?* (Gainesville: University Press of Florida, 2006), 62.

47 Brenner and Kornbluh, "Clinton's Cuba Calculus." See also Jonathan C. Smith, "Foreign Policy For Sale? Interest Group Influence on President Clinton's Cuba Policy, August 1994," *Presidential Studies Quarterly*, 28, 1 (Winter 1988): 207–220. Smith details a $300,000 donation that Canosa gave Clinton after he endorsed Torricelli's bill.

48 Boltzmann Booty, "The CIA Asset Who Funded the OKC Bombing," *Garrison: The Journal of History and Deep Politics*, January 2023, 20. According to Booty's research, Oklahoma City bomber Timothy McVeigh delivered rocket launchers, smoke and CS grenades, flairs and exotic ammunition on behalf of Roger Moore, a CIA informant associated in some way with the Oklahoma City bombing, to a Cuban exile group in the Florida Everglades training for a coup against Fidel Castro.

49 "Cuban Accusations of U.S. Insect Raid on Island to be Studied," *The New York Times*, August 28, 1997, https://www.nytimes.com/1997/08/28/world/cuban-accusations-of-us-insect-raid-on-island-to-be-studied.html. The State Department claimed they had merely released warming smoke meant to ensure visual contact with a nearby aircraft.

50 Pastor, "The Clinton Administration and the Americas"; Philip Agee, "Terrorism and Civil Society as Instruments of U.S. Policy in Cuba," *Counterpunch*, August 3, 2003, https://www.counterpunch.org/2003/08/08/terrorism-and-civil-society-as-instruments-of-us-policy-in-cuba/; https://sanctionstribunal.org/2023/06/08/saturday-and-sunday-june-10-and-11-hearing-on-cuba/.

51 Pastor, "The Clinton Administration and the Americas."

52 Letter to Bill Clinton, National Association of Manufacturers, June 28, 1996, William J. Clinton Presidential Library, digital collections, relations with Cuba, https://clinton.presidentiallibraries.us/items/show/73264; William M. Berry, President of European-American Chamber of Commerce, letter to Bill Clinton, June 21, 1996, William J. Clinton Presidential Library, digital collections, relations with Cuba, https://clinton.presidentiallibraries.us/items/show/73262.

53 https://en.wikipedia.org/wiki/Helms%E2%80%93Burton_Act#; https://www.youtube.com/watch?v=O4H5AWubKHo

54 Mike Royko, "What Clinton Should Say About the Cubans," *The Sacramento Bee*, 1996, Clinton Library photocopy, https://clinton.presidentiallibraries.us/items/show/73254.

55 Al Martin, *The Conspirators: Secrets of an Iran-Contra Insider* (National Liberty Press, 2001), 159, 160, 232. Martin points out that Clinton also did not take

any measures to extradite 17 senior members of government who were wanted in various foreign countries for violating their laws regarding Iran-Contra activities.

56 Pastor, "The Clinton Administration and the Americas." The Clinton administration convened an Intelligence Oversight Board at the end of 1995 whose report was a whitewash, concluding that "no evidence has been found that any employee of the CIA in any way directed, participated in or condoned the murder [of her husband Afrain Bamaca and Michael Devine—a U.S. citizen]" though the killer, Colonel Julio Roberto Aliprez, had in fact been on the CIA's payroll for years

57 Susan Jonas, "Dangerous Liaisons: The U.S. in Guatemala," *Foreign Policy*, Summer 1996, 154.

58 Clifford Krauss, "Testimony in '82 on Salvador Criticized," *The New York Times,* July 16, 1993. The report suggested that some in the State Department and foreign service had performed creditably and on occasion with personal bravery.

59 Doyle McManus, 'State Department Panel Defends Reports on Salvadoran Abuses: Latin America: Democrats in Congress, Human Rights Activists, Call the Study a Whitewash by the Department," *Los Angeles Times*, July 16, 1993.

60 McManus, 'State Department Panel Defends Reports on Salvadoran Abuses."

61 Human Rights Watch Report, Cynthia Arnson, "El Salvador: Darkening Horizons: Human Rights on the Eve of the March 1994 Elections," https://www.hrw.org/report/1994/03/01/darkening-horizons/human-rights-eve-march-1994-elections; Craig Pyes, "Death Squad Democracy," *The Washington Post*, April 17, 1994, https://www.washingtonpost.com/archive/opinions/1994/04/17/death-squad-democracy/f670de04-de21-423b-8f85-6e4fea5be5eb/ Sol had served as personal secretary to D'Aubuisson, the godfather of El Salvador's death squads, and participated in a plot to blow up El Salvador's Agricultural Ministry. The terrorist cell that he was part of expressed admiration for Adolf Hitler because of his war against communism and in 1979 tried to overthrow El Salvador's government because it attempted a moderate land reform program.

62 "The President's Trip to Central America: El Salvador," https://clintonwhitehouse4.archives.gov/WH/New/centralam/elsalvador.html; https://en.wikipedia.org/wiki/Armando_Calder%C3%B3n_Sol; Pyes, "Death Squad Democracy."

63 Neil Hardt, "Ex-President Francisco Flores and the Decimation of El Salvador," *World Socialist Website*, March 28, 2016, https://www.wsws.org/en/articles/2016/03/28/salv-m28.html; Christine J. Wade, *Captured Peace: Elites and Peacebuilding in El Salvador* (Athens: Ohio University Press, 2015).

64 "Comalapa Air Base, El Salvador," https://www.globalsecurity.org/military/facility/comalapa.htm; Gary Maceoin, "U.S. Troops to El Salvador," National Catholic Reporter, http://natcath.org/NCR_Online/archives2/2000d/101300/101300e.htm; Hardt, "Ex-President Francisco Flores and the Decimation of El Salvador." FMLN leader Schafik Hándal characterized the allowance of U.S. troops in El Salvador as a violation of the Salvadoran constitution and 1992 peace agreements. An economist who studies at the University of Massachusetts at Amherst and Harvard, Flores sparked nationwide strikes when he tried to privatize El Salvador's public health facilities. He was accused in May 2014 of pocketing $15 million donated by Taiwan, intended for survivors of the January and February 2001 El Salvador earthquakes, which occurred during his presidency. He was the first former Salvadoran president to be indicted and tried on corruption charges. He was placed under house arrest, but died before he could stand trial.

65 Arnson, "El Salvador: Darkening Horizons," https://www.hrw.org/report/1994/03/01/darkening-horizons/human-rights-eve-march-1994-elections; GAO, Foreign Assistance: U.S. Rule of Law Assistance to Five Latin American Countries, Vol. 6, 1999, https://www.gao.gov/products/nsiad-99–195.

66 Pastor, "The Clinton Administration and the Americas."

67 Jose de Cordoba, "Apparent New President Wants to Undo the Legacy of the Sandinistas," *The Wall Street Journal*, October 23, 1996, A17.

68 Jose de Cordoba, "Change That Tune: Why Daniel Ortega Croons `Ode to Joy'—Yanqui Bashing Is Out, Contras Are In as Old Sandinista Seeks Nicaragua Presidency," *The Wall Street Journal*, October 9, 1996, A1.

69 See Dan Kovalik, *Nicaragua: A History of U.S. Intervention & Resistance* (Atlanta: Clarity Press, 2023).

70 Lisa Haugaard, "Nicaragua," Institute for Policy Studies, May 1, 1997, https://ips-dc.org/nicaragua/; https://en.wikipedia.org/wiki/Arnoldo_Alem%C3%A1n. Alemán received foreign financing—as much as 10 percent of his campaign costs—from the Cuban American Foundation illegally; in exchange he allowed them to set up an anti-Castro radio station in Managua. Mark Caster, "The Return of Somocismo? The Rise of Arnoldo Alemán," *NACLA*, September 25, 2007, https://nacla.org/article/return-somocismo-rise-arnoldo-alem%C3%A1n. Numbers of Aleman's supporters were backers of the Somoza dynasty, which had ruled Nicaragua as a personal fief since the U.S. Marine occupation of the late 1920s.

71 de Cordoba, "Apparent New President Wants to Undo the Legacy of the Sandinistas."

72 de Cordoba, "Apparent New President Wants to Undo the Legacy of the Sandinistas."

73 Holy Sklar, *Washington's War on Nicaragua* (Boston: South End Press, 1998), 64; Kovalik, *Nicaragua*, 140–166.

74 American Embassy Managua to Secretary of State, "1994 Trade Report in Nicaragua" November 1994, Clinton Presidential Records, Press Office, Box 16, William J. Clinton Presidential Library, Little Rock, Arkansas.

75 de Cordoba, "Apparent New President Wants to Undo the Legacy of the Sandinistas." See also Kovalik, *Nicaragua*, 140–166.

76 Lisa Haugaard, "Development Aid: Some Small Steps Forward," *NACLA*, September 25, 2007, https://nacla.org/article/development-aid-some-small-steps-forward; Kovalik, *Nicaragua*, 162. Kovalik highlights that USAID funded the replacement fo Sandinista era schoolbooks with U.S. ones.

77 Ronald Cox, "Transnational Capital, the U.S. and Latin American Trade Agreements," *Third World Quarterly*, 29, 8 (2008), 1527–1544.

78 Haugaard, "Development Aid."

79 John M. Broder, "Clinton Moved by Devastated Nicaragua," *The New York Times*, March 9, 1999.

80 Haugaard, "Development Aid."

81 Charles Lane, "Superman Meets Shining Path: Story of a CIA Success; with Agency Aid, Peru Captured Chief Rebel," *The Washington Post*, December 7, 2000, A1; Timothy Naftali, *Blind Spot: The Secret History of American Counterterrorism* (New York: Basic Books, 2006), 226; Abderrahman Beggar, "The Path of State Terror in Peru" in *When States Kill: Latin America, the U.S. and Technologies of Terror*, ed. Cecilia Menjivar and Nestor Rodriguez (Austin: University of Texas Press. 2005), 266, 267.

82 Lane, "Superman Meets Shining Path," A1; Naftali, *Blind Spot*, 226; Beggar, "The Path of State Terror in Peru" in *When States Kill,* ed. Menjivar and Rodriguez, 266, 267. The former head of Fujimori's Joint Chiefs, SOA graduate Nicholas Hernandez Rios, pleaded guilty to taking $14 million in illegal profits from arms deals and faced charges of "taking protection money from the drug lords the United States was paying Peru to fight."

83 Beggar, "The Path of State Terror in Peru" in *When States Kill,* ed. Menjivar and Rodriguez, 25; Ted Galen Carpenter, *Bad Neighbor Policy: America's Futile War on Drugs in Latin America* (New York: Palgrave McMillan, 2003), 54. Between thirty to fifty planes were shot down from 1994 to 2001, including one carrying American missionaries.

84 Dana Priest and Cristina Rivero, "Covert Action in Colombia: U.S. Intelligence, GPS Bombs Kits Help Latin American Nations Cripple Rebel Forces," *Washington Post*, December 21, 2013; Douglas Stokes, *America's Other War; Terrorizing Colombia* (London: Zed Press, 2006).

85 Anthony Effinger and Matthew Bristow, "Alabama Coal Baron Faces Lawsuits in Colombia Killings," *The Washington Post,* August 2, 2013, https://www.washingtonpost.com/business/alabama-coal-baron-faces-lawsuits-in-colombia-killings/2013/08/01/59cfd3f4-f30e-11e2-bdae-0d1f78989e8a_story.html

86 Vijay Prashad, *Fat Cats & Running Dogs: The Enron Stage of Capitalism* (Monroe, ME: Common Courage Press, 2003), 171.

87 Prashad, *Fat Cats & Running Dogs*, 164.

88 Pedro Ruz Gutierrez and E.A. Torriero, "Military Contractors Line Up For U.S. Drug War in Colombia," *The Chicago Tribune*, September 24, 2000, https://www.chicagotribune.com/news/ct-xpm-2000-09-24-0009240025-story.html

89 John Lindsay-Poland, *Plan Colombia: U.S. Ally Atrocities and Community Activism* (Durham, NC: Duke University Press, 2018), 58, 59; Tony Koran, "Gore's Big Oil Connection: An 'Occident' of Birth?" *Time* magazine, September 25, 2000. Occidental CEO Ray Irani spent two nights in the Lincoln bedroom after giving a $100,000 donation. Occidental expected a payoff from the granting of exploration to a newly discovered oil field called Boqueron, which was expected to yield over 300 million barrels. Enron had given a huge amount of money to the Democratic Party additionally.

90 See Steve Weinberg, *Armand Hammer: The Untold Story* (New York: Random House, 1990); Alexander Cockburn and Jeffrey St. Clair, *Al Gore: A User's Manual* (London: Verso, 2000); Lyndon Larouche, *The Pure Evil of Al Gore* (Leesburg, VA: The New Federalist, 1999).

91 Oliver Villar and Drew Cottle, *Cocaine, Death Squads and the War on Terror: U.S. Imperialism and Class Struggle in Colombia* (New York: Monthly Review Press, 2011), 11.

92 David Scott Palmer, *U.S. Relations with Latin America: Opportunities Lost or Squandered?* (Gainesville: University Press of Florida, 2006), 62.

93 "Venezuela President Assumes Decree Powers," *The Washington Post*, July 24, 1994, https://www.washingtonpost.com/archive/politics/1994/07/24/venezuelan-president-assumes-decree-powers/ea54e70e-03f7-4d7c-945e-6cfe458beff1/.

94 Remarks by President Clinton and President Cardoso of Brazil, April 20, 1995, Clinton Presidential Records, Presidential Office, Press Releases, GA #8688, William J. Clinton Presidential Library, Little Rock, Arkansas; "The Price of Freedom," *The Economist*, May 16, 2022; "Meeting with Brazil Foreign Minister Lamppreia,"

March 2000, Clinton Digital Library, https://clinton.presidentiallibraries.us/items/show/48149; Petras and Veltemeyer, *Cardoso's Brazil*. Cardoso's government opened its oil market in 1999 by inviting foreign firms to drill for oil. It completed the process by abolishing price controls and removed the monopoly of Petrobras (the state oil company) on importing oil products. Purportedly generating 20,000 U.S. jobs, SIVAM adopted remote satellite sensing and imaging and a ground-based sensor system—all coordinated from regional and national centers—and enabled the Brazilian government to better monitor its borders, air space and supposedly protect the environment. The U.S. Export-Import Bank provided the $1.4 billion in financial support.

95 Petras and Veltemeyer, *Cardoso's Brazil*, 16. A sociologist and specialist in political economy and author of 23 books who taught for a period at the University of California, Berkeley, Cardoso had opposed Brazil's military dictatorship and had long ties to the Ford Foundation and other U.S. corporate foundations. Benefitting from a huge U.S. and IMF aid package, Cardoso was credited with bringing down inflation. However, growth stagnated during his presidency, unemployment skyrocketed, and inflation came back as Brazil remained the most unequal country in the world. U.S. direct investment in Brazil doubled between 1994 and 1998, reaching $38 billion, and bilateral trade climbed 48% in the same period, rising from $17.5 billion to $25.8 billion. Cardoso's unpopularity was reflected in his resounding defeat by Lula and the Brazilian Workers Party in 2002 elections. James Petras and Harry Veltmeyer described Brazil under Cardoso as a "regressive stagnant foreign owned subsidiary of overseas credit holders and investors dependent on the largesse of international financial institutions." They said he was the best Brazilian president for "Euro-American transnational corporations and banks."

96 Naomi Klein, *The Shock Doctrine: The Rise of Disaster Capitalism* (New York: Metropolitan Books, 2007), 148–150; Glenn Greenwald, "America's Refusal to Extradite Bolivia's ex-President to Face Genocide Charges," *The Guardian*, September 9, 2012. When Goni had tried to return to power in 2003, his political campaign was run by Democratic Party operatives James Carville, Stanley Greenberg, and Bob Shrum along with Mark Feierstein, who became President Barack Obama's senior director for Western Hemisphere Affairs at the National Security Council. Their strategy was to destroy the reputations of Goni's opponents so as to depress the enthusiasm of Bolivia's poor for both of them, and then mobilize Goni's base of elites to ensure he would win by a tiny margin (he won with a patlry 22.5% of the popular vote).

97 U.S. Bolivian Bilateral Relations, United States Department of State, April 27, 1997, Bill Clinton Presidential Libraries, Declassified Documents Concerning Bolivian Presidents Gonzalo Sanchez de Lozada and Hugo Banzer Suarez, https://clinton.presidentiallibraries.us/items/show/57654.

98 https://en.wikipedia.org/wiki/Carlos_Menem; Rafael Azul, "Argentina: The Death of ex-President Carlos Saúl Menem," *World Socialist Website*, March 1, 2021, https://www.wsws.org/en/articles/2021/03/02/mene-m02.html. Menem's fealty to U.S. interests earned Argentina status as a non-NATO military ally.

99 FBI to American embassy Buenos Aires, "Christopher Praise of Cavallo Said 'Controversial,'" Clinton Presidential Records, NSC Cables, January 1995–December 1996, box 1, William J. Clinton Presidential Library, Little Rock, Arkansas; Azul, "Argentina." By the end of Menem's presidency, 13 million Argentines, out of a total population of 27 million, were classified as poor by the government's own standards,

while one study showed that the profits of the 500 most important firms in Argentina increased by 69 percent between 1993 and 1997.

100 William Blum, "Trojan Horse: The National Endowment for Democracy," https://williamblum.org/chapters/rogue-state/trojan-horse-the-national-endowment-for-democracy

101 U.S. Department of State, Background Notes, Venezuela, September 1997, Clinton Presidential Records, WHORM, Subject File, 1st Lady's Office, Trip of First Lady to Venezuela, box 1, William J. Clinton Presidential Library, Little Rock, Arkansas. Venezuela at the time was the top foreign supplier of oil to the U.S, which in 1996 posted $4.7 billion in exports to Venezuela while purchasing $9 billion in imports from the country.

102 "Clinton Offers Help, Praises Venezuela," *San Antonio Express News*, October 14, 1997, Clinton Presidential Records, WHORM, Subject File, 1st Lady's Office, Trip of First Lady to Venezuela, box 1, William J. Clinton Presidential Library, Little Rock, Arkansas.

103 "Venezuela President Assumes Decree Powers," *The Washington Post*, July 24, 1994, https://www.washingtonpost.com/archive/politics/1994/07/24/venezuelan-president-assumes-decree-powers/ea54e70e-03f7-4d7c-945e-6cfe458beff1/.

104 U.S. Department of State, Background Notes, Venezuela, September 1997, Clinton Presidential Records, WHORM, Subject File, 1st Lady's Office, Trip of First Lady to Venezuela, box 1, William J. Clinton Presidential Library, Little Rock, Arkansas. In his first stint as president from 1969–1974, Caldera favored greater state control over the economy.

105 "Getting Our Way: Clinton's Latin American Policy," *North American Congress on Latin America* (NACLA), September 25, 2007, https://nacla.org/article/getting-our-way-clinton%27s-latin-america-policy

106 Special Report, United States Information Agency, October 20, 1997," Clinton Presidential Records, WHORM, Subject File, 1st Lady's Office, Trip of First Lady to Venezuela, box 1, William J. Clinton Presidential Library, Little Rock, Arkansas.

CONCLUSION

Laying the Groundwork for the U.S. Foreign Policy Disasters That Followed

Historians looking back at America in the 1990s will recognize those years as an era of great prosperity, hubris and overreach. Clinton himself as a man embodied the country's excesses. He strode onto the political scene like a giant and lived the life of a rock star. His decadence epitomized that of America during its moment in the sun before the storm set in, and the country thrust itself on the road to ruin through its over-reaction to the 9/11 terrorist attacks and ill-fated invasions of Iraq and Afghanistan.

Clinton's task, as a longstanding "deep state" operative recognized early for his political talent, had been to help reverse the movement towards isolationism following the Vietnam War, and to sell American wars abroad as "humanitarian interventions" and fights against terrorism and drugs, or other supposedly noble causes. Clinton could pull it off because he had an engaging personality and could win over the aging hippie set by casting himself as a former flower child, when he was in reality always very much part of the political establishment and hungry for power "from the time he was in third grade," as a friend put it.

Like past U.S. leaders, Clinton repeatedly lied and deceived the American public, as he had done to the people of Arkansas when he was governor. In Bosnia, Clinton claimed that the Serbs were Nazis and Milošević was the new Hitler, yet Milošević and the Serbs had tried to keep the Yugoslav federation together. Instead, America allied with Muslim fundamentalists who were in league with Al-Qaeda and Croat militias who committed the largest act of ethnic cleansing in the war.

Clinton told more lies when he bombed Iraq and said that Saddam Hussein had Weapons of Mass Destruction (WMD) and when he sanctioned Iran because it had allegedly sponsored acts of terrorism and was building a nuclear bomb. Clinton also claimed to stand up for human rights but sold massive quantities of weapons to some of the worst human rights violators in the world, including to Turkey, Israel, Indonesia under Suharto, Colombia, and Egypt, and refused to sign on to UN treaties banning land mines and child soldiers. Clinton further helped ruin Russia's economy and rig its 1996 election, blocked efforts to get cheap HIV/AIDS drugs in Africa out of fealty to pharmaceutical companies and helped support Rwanda and Uganda as they invaded and plundered the Congo and massacred hundreds of thousands of people.

In so many ways, Clinton's malign foreign policies set the groundwork for the disasters that were to follow under Bush II, Obama, Trump, and Biden. Although most people associate the "War on Terror" with the presidency of Bush II, who popularized the term, it was Reagan who first launched the concept and Clinton most significantly, who after the 1993 attack on the World Trade Towers, seized upon Reagan's talking points and inflated them into a massive and aggressive program to fight what he called "the new terrorism."

Virtually by fiat, Clinton assumed new and unprecedented presidential powers, including the right to intrude on personal privacy, restrict civil liberties, and send American troops to fight in foreign military conflicts without the consent of Congress. He accomplished these unconstitutional infringements of executive power by panicking the public (and Congress) with threats of bomb-planting terrorists, foreign terrorists, homegrown terrorists, cyberterrorists, rogue-state terrorists, and terrorists for which names hadn't even been invented.

Foreshadowing the next four administrations, Clinton's War on Terror was itself terrorist in nature, ridden with double standards that adopted terror tactics such as extraordinary rendition, targeted assassinations, and the bombing of non-combatant civilians with both piloted aircraft and drones.

Yet even as he terrorized civilian populations in violation of the United Nations Charter of Human Rights, Clinton hypocritically pointed to human rights violations allegedly being committed by others to justify his own illegal military interventions, which were supposedly needed to protect beleaguered people from genocide.

Clinton's administration pressed for regime change in Iraq by deceitfully raising public alarm about mythical WMDs. This enabled him to reward his corporate donors with billion-dollar contracts for exotic new weapons systems, which were then deployed by private mercenaries who didn't show up on the U.S. Army payroll, thereby limiting dissent by keeping his shady military interventions out of sight.

Learning from the master, many Clintonite disciples—including Leon Panetta, Rahm Emmanuel, Susan Rice, less known figures like Ivo Daalder, Harold "Killer" Koh, Wendy Sherman, and Tom Donilon, and of course Hillary Clinton—would go on to help run U.S. foreign policy in the Obama and Biden administrations, which extended Clinton's policies in so many ways.[1] Cloaked in a liberal veneer, these legacy policies of Clinton ratcheted up further provocations towards Russia and China, used Ukraine as a battering ram directed against Russia, invaded Libya under the pretext of a humanitarian intervention, waged a covert war by arming Islamic fundamentalists in Syria, and ramped up the militarized War on Drugs (in Plan Mérida, for example, which was modeled after Plan Colombia).[2]

His administration laid the groundwork for subsequent administrations' further promotion of free trade agreements designed to expand U.S. corporate power and the increasing use of sanctions to ruin the economies of regimes they didn't like, and subsidizing opposition media and political parties in countries that promoted an independent foreign policy. Obama and Biden administration officials were very skilled in fabricating atrocity stories or exaggerating the human rights abuses of U.S. government enemies to win public support for military interventions that killed thousands of civilians and destroyed entire countries.[3] They amplified Clinton's tactic of using smears to destroy political opponents, even manufacturing a fake political scandal called Russia-Gate to accuse a Republican president of treason and ratchet up public support for a war with Russia.

According to a 2016 profile by Mark Landler in *The New York Times Magazine*, entitled "How Hillary Became a Hawk," Hillary carried on Bill's legacy as one of the most hawkish Secretaries of State on record. Called "the "liberal Nixon" by Barbara Olson, chief counsel for the House Oversight Committee that investigated an assortment of Clinton scandals, Hillary tried to pressure President Barack Obama to a) increase U.S. troops presence in Afghanistan beyond the numbers projected under his "surge policy"; b) sustain a U.S. troop presence in Iraq; c) funnel more arms to anti-government rebels in Syria; d) dispatch a U.S. aircraft carrier in waters between North Korea and China as a show of U.S. force; and e) reject the appearance of any public concessions to Russia, even if they be merely symbolic gestures of goodwill, despite supposedly being engaged in a good faith effort to reset the previously antagonistic relationship between the U.S. and Russia.

Hillary also forcefully pressured Obama into attacking Libya, going so far as to promote slanderous and salacious disinformation about Muammar Qaddafi to generate public support for the U.S. military intervention, while invoking the myth of U.S. government inaction during the Rwanda genocide. The pretext for the war that Qaddafi was going to massacre his civilian population was false. The U.S.'s true intent was a) to stop Qaddafi from creating a pan-African currency to replace the dollar, b) seize control of his oil, c) seize control of the even more valuable freshwater reservoir beneath Libya, d) and steal the gold from Libya's treasury, which mysteriously disappeared after the invasion and has never been found.[4] Defense Secretary Robert Gates told *The New York Times* that Hillary Clinton's backing of military intervention in Libya was decisive. Obama had told him privately in the Oval Office that the Libya decision was "51–49," and Gates said: "I've always thought that Hillary's support for the broader mission in Libya put the president on the 51 side of the line for a more aggressive approach."

An aide said that Hillary's foreign-policy instincts were grounded in cold realism about human nature and "a textbook view of American exceptionalism." Mark Landler wrote in his *New York Times Magazine* profile that, "For all their bluster about bombing the Islamic State into oblivion, neither Donald J. Trump nor Senator Ted Cruz of Texas has demonstrated anywhere near the appetite for military engagement abroad that [Hillary] Clinton has."[5] Which was true of Bill Clinton as well.

Clinton was a political animal who almost never acted out of principle. Many of his supporters worshipped him like a cult leader going back to his early career in Arkansas, while others invoked the trope about the "lesser evil" and saw Clinton as a bulwark against the radical right. But in many ways, he was a "greater evil" than either Bush or Dole because Clinton successfully cloaked his neoliberal and neo-imperial policies under a progressive veneer, which enabled him—like Barack Obama, later on—to successfully diffuse antiwar and other populist protest movements.

Bob Dole once said that the relationship between money and politics in this country is "not conducive to good government."[6] This is as true of foreign as it is of domestic policy. Clinton was elected due to the funding and support of his corporate sponsors, so it is no surprise that they drove his policy agenda. He used the military time and again to protect and expand U.S. corporate profits even if it weakened the American economy as a whole, seeking to satisfy the military-industrial-intelligence complex that had helped to make him president, regardless of human cost.

A key part of Clinton's legacy is the slippery slope he created that inexorably led to the later foreign policy excesses of the Bush, Obama and Trump administrations, which now are continued by the Biden administration. Thanks to Clinton's legacy, the U.S. has sacrificed millions of lives and trillions of dollars fighting unjustifiable and unwinnable wars in Iraq, Afghanistan, Libya, Syria—and now in Ukraine, which could very easily turn nuclear.

Rather than being one of the best presidents in American history, Clinton should rank near the bottom with others of this generation. Clinton's charisma and charm may have won over the voters of his day, but historians and contemporary commentators should not be blind to the fact that his deleterious policies set in motion the beginning of America's imperial decline.

Endnotes

1 On the connection between the foreign policy teams in the Clinton and Obama White Houses, see Jeremy Scahill, "20 Hawks, Clintonites and Neocons to Watch For in Obama's White House," *Los Angeles Indymedia*, November 21, 2008, https://la.indymedia.org/news/2008/11/222404.php

2 See Jeremy Kuzmarov, *Obama's Unending Wars: Fronting the Foreign Policy of the Permanent Warfare State* (Atlanta: Clarity Press, 2019).

3 See A.B. Abrams, *Atrocity Fabrication and Its Consequences: How Fake News Shapes World Order* (Atlanta: Clarity Press, 2023), 230.

4 See *The Illegal War on Libya*, ed. Cynthia McKinney (Atlanta: Clarity Press, 2012).

5 Mark Landler, "How Hillary Clinton Became a Hawk," *The New York Times Magazine*, April 21, 2016, https://www.nytimes.com/2016/04/24/magazine/how-hillary-clinton-became-a-hawk.html. After Qaddafi, was lynched following the U.S.-NATO bombing campaign—which she oversaw—Hillary jubilantly and now infamously told a reporter, *"We came, we saw, he died,"* a twisted play on the words of Julius Caesar following his victory over the King of Bosporus at the Battle of Zela around 47 B.C.

6 Alexander Cockburn and Ken Silverstein, *Washington Babylon* (London: Verso, 1996), 64.

Acknowledgments

The author would like to sincerely thank: Diana Collier, Stephen Brown, Robert Morrow, Jean Duffey, Louis Wolf, John Marciano, and the staff at the University of Arkansas at Fayetville Special Collections and Clinton Presidential Library, as well as the interlibrary loan department staff at Tulsa Community College.

Index

B

I

J

K

L

N

O

P

Q

R

V

W